"Gregg Allison's book distances itself from both complementarianism and egalitarianism, choosing a third option designated complementarity (and thus not to be confused with complementarianism). Almost a quarter of the book surveys the dominant strands of the last 2500 years. This part of Allison's work does not aim to break new ground, but ably summarizes the enormously detailed and careful three-volume work by Prudence Allen. The rest of Allison's book surveys the relevant biblical, theological, and pastoral stances of the last few decades, in defense of 'complementarity.' As few writers carefully distinguish between complementarity and complementarianism—and to profit maximally from Allison's work—it is essential to follow his careful definitional distinctives. Complementarianism conjures up a 'normal' stance (usually male-ness) which may be 'complemented' by something further (usually female-ness), thereby destroying the reciprocity by the initial assumptions. Whether or not you become convinced by all of Allison's arguments, it is refreshing to think through the work of an author who operates with fewer shibboleths than most who contribute to the field."

—**D. A. Carson**, emeritus professor of New Testament,
Trinity Evangelical Divinity School

"Gregg Allison, one of the premier Christian thinkers of this generation, has provided thoughtful Christ-followers with a splendid resource that aptly defines a Christian understanding of complementarity, while clearly articulating the equal dignity of men and women as well as their distinctive differences and interdependence. Recognizing that an understanding of complementarity precedes an articulation of questions regarding complementarianism or egalitarianism, Allison is clear that an understanding of complementarity is not intended as a kind of third way. Rather, this encyclopedic treatment provides readers with a depth and breadth of understanding regarding these vitally important matters from a thoroughly informed biblical, historical, philosophical, and theological perspective, doing so with the goal of encouraging relational, familial, vocational, and ecclesial flourishing. It is a genuine privilege to heartily recommend this well researched, carefully organized, and insightful volume."

—**David S. Dockery**, president,
International Alliance for Christian Education

"I recall that in the 1990s, some of us younger egalitarian scholars were discussing with one another how 'complementarity' actually described our own understanding; certainly no egalitarians we knew supported gender uniformity. There is more common ground between most evangelical complementarians and egalitarians than is often recognized, and a gradation of positions exists between the poles. In this carefully organized and developed work, Gregg Allison helpfully highlights our common ground, modeling a humility and respect that invites complementarians and egalitarians past the frequent current impasse and into more productive dialogue and cooperation on values we share."

—**Craig S. Keener**, F. M. and Ada Thompson Professor of Biblical Studies, Asbury Theological Seminary

"Allison is to be commended for his wide-ranging discussion of God's design for males and females in the family, church, workplace, and in relationship with one another. He defines complementarity as how males and females 'fill out and mutually support one another for their individual and corporate flourishing.' Allison states that complementarity is neither complementarianism nor egalitarianism, but neither is it a third way. Rather, he highlights commonalities and differences between the two schools of thought and focuses on the dignity, difference, and interdependence of males and females. While some might desire more specifics on how this affects roles, Allison turns more toward ontology as the foundation on which we build a theology of the sexes."

—**Patrick Schreiner**, Gene and Jo Downing Chair of Biblical Studies, Midwestern Baptist Theological Seminary

"Blessed are the peacemakers, in particular, those who make groundbreaking discoveries that can serve as the basis for peace talks among Christians divided over doctrine. This is precisely Allison's important contribution: a coherent and comprehensive biblical, historical, and theological argument for the principle of complementarity, which posits the equal dignity, significant difference, and relational interdependence of men and women. *Complementarity* beats the swords used in the conflict between egalitarians and complementarians—the evangelical version of the battle of the sexes—into plowshares, effectively showing there is more that unites than divides us. Allison may not win a Nobel Prize, as the physicist Niels Bohr did for his work on another principle of complementarity, but his reward will be great in heaven."

—**Kevin J. Vanhoozer**, research professor of systematic theology, Trinity Evangelical Divinity School

COMPLEMENTARITY

COMPLEMENTARITY

Dignity,
Difference,
and
Interdependence

GREGG R. ALLISON

ACADEMIC®
BRENTWOOD, TENNESSEE

Complementarity: Dignity, Difference, and Interdependence

Published by B&H Academic®
Brentwood, Tennessee

ISBN: 978-1-0877-7386-5

Dewey Decimal Classification: 305.3
Subject Heading: MEN--SOCIAL CONDITIONS \ WOMEN--SOCIAL CONDITIONS \ MAN-WOMAN RELATIONSHIP

The web addresses referenced in this book were live and correct at the time of the book's publication but may be subject to change.

Cover design by Darren Welch Design. Cover image: "The Fall of Man" by Lucas Cranach the Elder. Image sourced from Wikimedia; public domain.

Printed in China
30 29 28 27 26 25 RRD 1 2 3 4 5 6 7 8 9 10

for Nora
with whom I live complementarity
from whom I'm learning complementarity
and because of whom this book on complementarity now exists

CONTENTS

Acknowledgments xi
Introduction xiii
Overview xv

Part One: Definitions, Proposals, and Foundations 1

Chapter 1: My Proposal and Definition of Complementarity 5
Chapter 2: An Initial Biblical Foundation of Complementarity 13
Chapter 3: Definitions of Complementarianism and Egalitarianism and Their Relationship to Complementarity 21

Part Two: Historical Development 27

Chapter 4: Greco-Roman Philosophical Views of Men and Women 29
Chapter 5: Early Church Views of Men and Women 43
Chapter 6: Early Medieval Views of Men and Women (600–1250) 57
Chapter 7: Late Medieval and Reformation Views of Men and Women (1250–1550) 81
Chapter 8: Early Modern to Postmodern Views of Men and Women (1550–Present) 101
Chapter 9: Summary and Implications for the Church, and My Thesis 121

Part Three: Contemporary Context 127

Chapter 10: Modern Feminist Movements 129
Chapter 11: The Rise of Contemporary Complementarianism 143

Chapter 12: Contemporary Patriarchalism 153
Chapter 13: The Rise of Contemporary Egalitarianism 159

Part Four: Biblical Considerations **169**
Chapter 14: Framework and Setting 171
Chapter 15: Old Testament Considerations 223
Chapter 16: New Testament Considerations: Gospels 267
Chapter 17: New Testament Considerations: Acts 313
Chapter 18: New Testament Considerations: Pauline Instructions 337
Chapter 19: Other New Testament Considerations 435
Chapter 20: Conclusion from Biblical Considerations 457

Part Five: Theological Considerations **459**
Chapter 21: Men and Women as Male and Female Image Bearers 461
Chapter 22: Images/Metaphors of the Church 467
Chapter 23: The Offices of Prophet, Priest, and King in the New Covenant 479
Chapter 24: Conclusion from Theological Considerations 499

Part Six: Arenas of Application **501**

Conclusion 509
General Index 511
Scripture Index 525

ACKNOWLEDGMENTS

I express my sincerest thanks to family, friends, and students who have played an important role in conceptualizing, researching, and constructively criticizing early versions of this book.

At a gathering of the Theological Advisory Council of Harbor Network, as we were discussing men and women engaged in church planting, I jotted down an initial definition of the word *complementarity*. My thanks to those friends who were brainstorming as the idea for this topic came to light.

A representative from B&H Academic was present at that gathering and initiated a conversation with me about writing about complementarity. My thanks to Audrey Greeson for being my original acquisitions editor for this book. She was later joined by another acquisitions editor who continued to promote this project. My thanks to Kristen Padilla for shepherding this book through to the end. A big part of the project was overseen by my content editor, who thoroughly checked out the various stages of the manuscript's development: my thanks to Michael McEwen for reading and rereading this book many times. These friends are part of the team at B&H Academic that published this book. My thanks to Ben Mandrell and Madison Trammel for their overall leadership.

Being a professor of systematic theology at The Southern Baptist Theological Seminary has given me the privilege of working with thousands of students and colleagues over the last two plus decades. Some of them have been with me in courses—theology of human embodiment, theological anthropology—that have led to the origin and development of this book. My thanks to Laura-Lee Alford, Sam Cheng, Heidi Dean, Hannah Downing, Scott Gregory, Gracilynn Hanson, Timothy Harper, Thomas Hearne, Randy Johnson, Ruby Khan, Grace YoungEun Kim, Ali Mati, Peter Martin, Jacob Percy, Marshall Perry, Hannah Portwood, John Ree, Thomas Spivey, and Brian Wagers for reading and commenting on the original manuscript. Thanks also to my son Luke, my friend Nancy Guthrie, and my wife, Nora, for their many suggestions for improving it.

INTRODUCTION

Complementarity is God's design for his male and female image bearers to fill out and mutually support one another relationally, familially, vocationally, and ecclesially for their individual and corporate flourishing. Complementarity affirms three principles: equal dignity, significant differentiation, and flourishing interdependence.[1] First, complementarity highlights the equal dignity that both male and female image bearers enjoy before God and before one another. Second, complementarity underscores that God has designed and created women and men to be significantly different in their being, consciousness (or self-awareness), relationships with one another, and relationship with him. Third, complementarity emphasizes that equal dignity and significant differentiation compel men and women to fill out and mutually support one another relationally, familially, vocationally, and ecclesially. Additionally, when women and men embrace and live out that dynamic interdependence, a God-honoring synergy operates for human flourishing.

[1] Prudence Allen, *The Concept of Woman: A Synthesis in One Volume* (Grand Rapids: Eerdmans, 2024).

OVERVIEW

Part One: Definitions, Proposals, and Foundations

Part One sets forth my proposal for this book and expands on the above definition of complementarity (Ch. 1), followed by an initial biblical foundation for it (Ch. 2). As complementarity intersects often with complementarianism and egalitarianism (though it is neither position), I offer brief definitions and descriptions of those positions within the ongoing debate (Ch. 3). I have chosen complementarianism and egalitarianism as my conversation partners because they are both related to as well as developments from complementarity. Though they primarily treat roles of men and women in the church and in the home, and thus are more limited in their scope than is complementarity, they are of deep concern for most of my readers and thus worthy interlocutors.[1]

Part Two: Historical Development

Part Two offers an abbreviated rehearsal of key philosophical, theological, and ecclesiastical developments in five periods. Beginning with the

[1] Though I interact significantly with these two positions, I do not adjudicate between their interpretations of Scripture, their theological foundations, and their applications. Such assessment is beyond the purpose and scope of this book.

Greco-Roman world (Ch. 4), I outline, following Prudence Allen's work, four questions: the metaphysical question of opposites, the natural philosophy question of generation, the epistemological question of wisdom, and the question of moral philosophy or virtue. I also introduce Allen's five-fold categorization of sex identity: sex unity, sex neutrality, traditional sex polarity, reverse sex polarity, and sex complementarity. As for the early church age (Ch. 5), attention is on Augustine, with an excursus on archaeological and ethnographic studies that challenge this historical paradigm. Turning to the early medieval period (600–1250) (Ch. 6), I cover John Scotus Eriugena, Albert the Great, Thomas Aquinas, and Hildegard of Bingen. Topics in the late medieval and Reformation era (1250–1550) include *inter alia* humanism, Christine de Pizan, Nicholas of Cusa, Laura Cereta, and Reformation contributions (Ch. 7). The final period is the early modern to postmodern epoch (1550–present) covering *inter alia* Teresa of Ávila, advances in theories of reproduction, René Descartes, access to education and equal citizenship for women, Immanuel Kant, Sigmund Freud, and integral sex complementarity (Ch. 8). Part Two concludes with a summary of the historical study together with implications for the church, and a thesis regarding our current state of affairs (Ch. 9).

Part Three: Contemporary Context

Part Three completes the historical survey by focusing on several key developments over the course of the last century. Modern feminist movements are numbered as first wave feminism, second wave feminism and Simone de Beauvoir, third wave feminism and Judith Butler, and (perhaps?) fourth wave feminism, with a brief treatment of Christian feminism (Ch. 10). The two major positions—complementarianism and egalitarianism—follow next. The rise of contemporary complementarianism starts with a definition of complementarianism, presents the development of complementarianism in the 1980s, outlines the concept of complementarianism according to *Recovering Biblical Manhood and Womanhood*, and concludes with the spectrum of applications of complementarianism (Ch. 11). Contemporary patriarchalism is briefly treated (Ch. 12). Like its counterpart, the rise of contemporary egalitarianism starts with a definition of egalitarianism, presents the development of egalitarianism in the 1980s, outlines the concept of egalitarianism according to Christians for Biblical Equality, and concludes with the spectrum of applications of egalitarianism (Ch. 13).

Part Four: Biblical Considerations

Part Four explores at length the biblical considerations for complementarity. Before treating Scripture itself, however, I address the framework and setting for those biblical discussions, treating three important topics: hermeneutics, the canonical and covenantal framework of Scripture, and Genesis 1–3 as setting the stage for what follows (Ch. 14). Hermeneutical discussions include the regulative vs. normative principle, descriptive vs. prescriptive biblical language, consideration of eschatology in the interpretation and application of Scripture, and more. As for the canonical and covenantal framework of Scripture, the issue is how the Bible presents itself in terms of its form—the canon of Scripture, that is, the writings that properly belong in Scripture—and its matter—the progressive development of God's relationship with his people according to six covenants. Setting the stage engages with the opening chapters of Genesis as they narrate many foundational elements for complementarity: the creation of divine image bearers as male and female, the formation of the first man and the first woman, and the fall of Adam and Eve and its consequences. Additionally, complementarianism and egalitarianism differ significantly on their interpretation of the key passages—e.g., Gen 1:26–28; 2:7–8, 18–25; 3:16—that address men and women and their relationships.

Old Testament considerations (Ch. 15) begin with nineteen narratives that feature major male and female characters, followed by a discussion of the woman of noble character in Prov 31:10–31. The discussion of New Testament considerations consists of four sections. The Gospels cover over twenty passages that narrate Jesus's interaction with men and women (Ch. 16). Acts treats numerous narratives that portray women and men in the early church community and the expansion of the gospel (Ch. 17). The section on Pauline instructions wrestles with controversial passages regarding men and women in the church and husbands and wives in marriage (Ch. 18). Part Four concludes with two other New Testament considerations—1 Pet 3:1–7 and Paul's list of greetings at the end of Romans (Ch. 19)—followed by conclusions drawn from both Old Testament and New Testament considerations (Ch. 20).

Part Five: Theological Considerations

Complementarity is supported by both Scripture and sound theology, and Part Five explores three theological areas. As complementarity is defined in terms of God's design for his male and female image bearers, discussion about the nature and complementarity of these two sexed/gendered beings inaugurates these theological considerations (Ch. 21). Specifically, two questions are raised and answered—What is a Man? and What is a Woman? Next, biblical images/metaphors of the church highlight the people of God, the body of Christ, the temple of the Holy Spirit, and the family of God and seek implications for complementarity within the church (Ch. 22). Similar exploration is carried out regarding the offices of prophet, priest, and king in the new covenant (Ch. 23), and conclusions about complementarity are drawn from all these theological considerations (Ch. 24).

Part Six: Arenas of Application

Complementarity: Dignity, Difference, and Interdependence concludes with applications in four arenas: complementarity for relational flourishing, complementarity for familial flourishing, complementarity for vocational flourishing, and complementarity for ecclesial flourishing.

PART ONE

Definitions, Proposals, and Foundations

Complementarity is God's design for his male and female image bearers to fill out and mutually support one another relationally, familially, vocationally, and ecclesially for their individual and corporate flourishing. It is essential for the following reasons.

The biblical vision of and call for love, harmony, peace, and unity among disciples of Jesus is both captivating and convicting: Love is "the mark of the Christian" that flourishes along with faith and hope:[1]

> Love is patient, love is kind. Love does not envy, is not boastful, is not arrogant, is not rude, is not self-seeking, is not irritable, and does not keep a record of wrongs. Love finds no joy in unrighteousness

[1] As detailed by Francis A. Schaeffer, *The Mark of the Christian*, 2nd ed. (Downers Grove: IVP, 2006).

> but rejoices in the truth. It bears all things, believes all things, hopes all things, endures all things. (1 Cor 13:4–7)

Unity is both the gift of the Holy Spirit and that for which the church is to earnestly contend, surrounded by seven commonalities that tie its members together:

> [Make] every effort to keep the unity of the Spirit through the bond of peace. There is one body and one Spirit—just as you were called to one hope at your calling—one Lord, one faith, one baptism, one God and Father of all, who is above all and through all and in all. (Eph 4:3–6)

Single-mindedness and unison of declaration is the church's desire, as it prays that it "may glorify the God and Father of our Lord Jesus Christ with one mind and one voice" (Rom 15:6).

The oneness of the church as the body of Christ is vividly portrayed and fostered as it celebrates the Lord's Supper:

> The cup of blessing that we bless, is it not a sharing in the blood of Christ? The bread that we break, is it not a sharing in the body of Christ? Because there is one bread, we who are many are one body, since all of us share the one bread. (1 Cor 10:16–17)

The nature of God's royal work in the world demands that the church works to promote peace and mutual edification:

> The kingdom of God is not eating and drinking, but righteousness, peace, and joy in the Holy Spirit. . . . So then, let us pursue what promotes peace and what builds up one another. (Rom 14:17, 19)

> Become mature, be encouraged, be of the same mind, be at peace, and the God of love and peace will be with you. (2 Cor 13:11)

Steadfastness, holiness, and peace are closely aligned and expressed together:

> Based on his promise, we wait for new heavens and a new earth, where righteousness dwells. Therefore, dear friends, while you wait for these things, make every effort to be found without spot or blemish in his sight, at peace. (2 Pet 3:13–14; cf. 1 Pet 3:10–11)

> Pursue peace with everyone, and holiness—without it no one will see the Lord. (Heb 12:14)

God's eternal purpose for the church features its full attainment to "unity in the faith and in the knowledge of God's Son, growing into maturity with a stature measured by Christ's fullness" (Eph 4:13).

This biblical vision of and call for love, harmony, peace, and unity alerts us to several matters.

First, it provides an ideal at which to aim for the advancement of the church. The church should embrace and work hard to actualize this vision and call. Second, it rebukes the church and calls it to repentance for its past and present failures. The church, mindful of all it is and does to distort this vision and neglect this call, should be prompt in confessing its many sins and exhibiting the fruit of repentance. Third, it sets before the church a crucial *telos* that will one day be an actuality. The church should orient itself toward this end so as to be prepared to take its place in the divine "plan for the fullness of time, to unite all things in him, things in heaven and things on earth" (Eph 1:10 ESV). Fourth, it means that divisiveness, factionalism, discord, strife, conflict, infighting, dissonance, and the like should not find a foothold in—let alone characterize—the church of Jesus Christ.

This biblical vision and call intersect with complementarity and its emphasis on women and men filling out and mutually supporting one another.

CHAPTER 1

My Proposal and Definition of Complementarity

For evangelicalism, racked as it is by many divisions, is it possible to actualize this vision of and call to complementarity so as to arrive at some kind of consensus about male image bearers and female image bearers in relationship to one another, such that both women and men may flourish individually and their churches may flourish corporately?[1] If the answer to this question is negative, this book is an exercise in futility. If the answer is

[1] These descriptions of men and women underscore several aspects of my theological anthropology: (1) The fundamental identity of human beings is that of divine image bearers (Gen 1:26–28); (2) Unlike angels, which are (metaphysically) immaterial or spiritual beings, human beings are (metaphysically) material or physical beings, embodied according to divine design; (3) As embodied creatures, human beings are either male image bearers or female image bearers; (4) The fundamental identity of human creatures is not found in their status (e.g., married, single, widowed) or role (e.g., mother, CEO, pastor, data analyst, retiree). Rather, according to Scripture, God created humanity as male and female image bearers. One kind—humankind—of two types: male and female. From this metaphysical identity flows human functions. For further discussion see Gregg R. Allison, *Embodied: Living as Whole People in a Fractured World* (Grand Rapids: Baker, 2021), chs. 1–2.

positive, the following undertaking is a scholarly attempt by an evangelical systematic theologian to point a possible way to such an actualization.

My proposal focuses on *complementarity*, which I define as God's design for his male and female image bearers to fill out and mutually support one another relationally, familially, vocationally, and ecclesially for their individual and corporate flourishing.[2] Moreover, complementarity embraces

---

[2] With a nod to Henri Blocher and his (rightful) concern about the word *complementarian*, my use and definition of the word *complementarity* does not imply in any way that such mutuality and interdependence flows (primarily or exclusively) from men to women such that women are complementary to men but not that men are complementary to women. Rather, complementarity is equally shared and reciprocated: men and women alike, or women and men alike (and the word order should not be misconstrued to indicate priority), constitute complementarity. Henri Blocher, "Women, Ministry, and the Gospel: Hints for a New Paradigm," in *Women, Ministry, and the Church: Exploring New Paradigms*, ed. Mark Husbands and Timothy Larsen (Downers Grove: IVP Academic, 2007), 240. Moreover, my use and definition of the word is not an attempt to couch the "traditional view . . . in the euphemistic language of 'complementarity.'" Ronald W. Pierce, "Contemporary Evangelicals for Gender Equality," in *Discovering Biblical Equality: Complementarity Without Hierarchy*, ed. Ronald W. Pierce and Rebecca Merrill Groothuis (Downers Grove: IVP Academic, 2004), 67. Furthermore, my use of the word *complementarity* differs from its use in, for example, John Piper's heading "The Biblical Vision of Complementarity"—which in actuality is a biblical vision of *complementarianism*. John Piper, "A Vision of Biblical Complementarity," in John Piper and Wayne Grudem, eds., *Recovering Biblical Manhood and Womanhood: A Response to Evangelical Feminism* (Wheaton: Crossway, 1991, 2006), 31, 52–54. Similarly, Kevin DeYoung uses the term *complementarity* to refer to the vision that is embraced by *complementarianism*. I do not use these terms interchangeably. Kevin DeYoung, "Death to the Patriarchy? Complementarity and the Scandal of 'Father Rule,'" Desiring God online (July 19, 2022), https://www.desiringgod.org/articles/death-to-the-patriarchy.

Celina Durgin and Dru Johnson offer, "Gender discussions of late often concern what women should be or do with respect to men. Ironically, in these discussions, gender is sometimes treated as a 'woman's issue.' . . . In Scripture, men are not the default to which women are 'the other.' Of course, gender is not a 'woman's issue': it is a human issue. Whatever the image of God is, it's at least 'male and female' (Gen 1:27)." Celina Durgin and Dru Johnson, eds., "Introduction," in *The Biblical World of Gender: The Daily Lives of Ancient Women and Men* (Eugene, OR:

three principles: equal dignity, significant differentiation, and flourishing interdependence.[3] First, complementarity affirms that both male image bearers and female image bearers are the highest beings that God created and are divinely accorded dignity before him and before one another (even if this latter aspect is not actualized or actualized poorly in a fallen world). Second, complementarity affirms that, by divine design, women and men are significantly different in their gendered being, gendered consciousness (or self-awareness), gendered relationships with one another, and gendered relationship with God.[4] Third, complementarity affirms that equal dignity and significant differentiation propel/compel men and women to fill out and mutually support one another in the four arenas noted above. By "fill out" one another, I do not mean that women and men complete one

---

Cascade, 2022), xv. Complementarity is not per se a discussion of gender, though gender obviously plays an important role, even in my definition. Throughout my presentation I show that complementarity is a human issue for male image bearers and female image bearers who fill out and mutually support one another. Furthermore, complementarity is not a "woman's issue" with the biblical default mode being male.

[3] Prudence Allen, *The Concept of Woman, Volume 2: The Early Humanist Reformation, 1250–1500* (Grand Rapids: Eerdmans, 2006), 8. She explains the first two principles in more detail: "Each theory of gender identity maintains a position about two things: (1) whether or not men and women have an equal dignity and (2) whether or not differences between women and men are philosophically significant." In her discussion, then, "'equal dignity' serves as a fundamental category of the identity of the man or woman as a human being. . . . [T]he phrase 'significant differentiation' refers to gender-related characteristics that were always or usually associated with either a woman or a man in special ways characteristic of his or her engendered identity" (16). I add the third principle because I believe that the first two principles are divinely designed to propel men and women to live and flourish in relationships of interdependence. This third principle approaches Allen's specific subcategory of complementarity—integral sex complementarity—to be discussed later.

[4] While keenly aware of the contemporary separation of "sex" from "gender," I do not make that distinction in this context. It is beyond the scope of my discussion to address issues such as the biology of sex, the perception of gender, gender dysphoria, transgenderism, intersex, and the like.

another in the sense of adding something that is missing in each person to achieve individual wholeness. On the contrary, each woman and each man is a complete image bearer of God; this status applies to individual human beings as divinely created. In Gen 1:27, the statement "male and female he created them" refers to each image bearer as a created, gendered, individual human being. Rather, by "fill out" one another, I mean that when image bearers collaborate relationally, familially, vocationally, and ecclesially, a synergy occurs that fosters maturation, expansion, fruitfulness, productivity, ministry, and the like. In this sense, the image of God is also expressed corporately. In Gen 1:27, the statements "God created man in his image, in the image of God he created him" refer to the human race corporately as the image of God. When women and men develop a dynamic interdependence, a God-honoring synergy operates for human flourishing.[5]

Acknowledging the separation among evangelicals on this issue and lamenting the apparent impasse that has settled disconcertingly over evangelical adherents and their churches, complementarity claims that there is more that unites us than divides us. It becomes, then, an invitation to listen to and respect one another on this matter, even when there may be fierce and seemingly insurmountable rifts.[6] A hoped-for outcome of this book is to appropriately extend a bridge across the chasm separating evangelical Christian from evangelical Christian and evangelical churches from evangelical churches.[7]

---

[5] For further discussion see Allison, *Embodied*, ch. 2.

[6] Much of the contemporary context derives and is known from popular books, articles, blogs, and podcasts. An example is Andrew Wilson's "Beautiful Difference: The (Whole Bible) Complementarity of Male and Female," TGC (May 20, 2021), https://www.thegospelcoalition.org/article/beautiful-complementarity-male-female/. While some of these productions may be academically sound, I intend to address complementarity from a scholarly perspective; thus, I will interact primarily with academic works on the subject.

[7] My hope is to offer a proposal that might bridge the divide in some measure, acknowledging that the two sides will remain significantly apart even if my ideas are accepted. Moreover, I am well acquainted with the intensity of words and fervency of emotions that this debate brings forth. Some of the aggressiveness is wrong;

More importantly, however, unity among us for the sake of Jesus Christ and his mission is the ultimate goal, in accordance with Jesus's prayer for his disciples, "May they all be one, as you, Father, are in me and I am in you. May they also be in us, so that the world may believe you sent me. I have given them the glory you have given me, so that they may be one as we are one. I am in them and you are in me, so that they may be made completely one, that the world may know you have sent me and have loved them as you have loved me" (John 17:21–23). This Trinity-established and Jesus-desired unity for his followers would include, it seems, their understanding and practice of some type of complementarity, in which female believers and male believers fill out and mutually support one another as divinely-adopted siblings in Christ (relationally); as mothers, fathers, sons, daughters, sisters, and brothers (familially); as colleagues laboring together at their jobs (vocationally); and as fellow citizens of the kingdom, ministers of the shared priesthood, pastors/elders, deacons and deaconesses, and members of their church (ecclesially).[8] This goal includes an appreciation for and

---

when it sustains a violence and quarrelsomeness that is not befitting a leader in the church (1 Tim 3:3), it crosses the line of propriety and devolves into sin. Some of the passion is right; earnestness of conviction is appropriate in civil disputes. My hope is that my proposal may foster such appropriateness in the ongoing debate. Accordingly, a purpose for this book is to fulfill the hope articulated by Ronald Pierce decades ago as he addressed complementarianism and egalitarianism, noting that "the polarity of the two sides presents an ongoing challenge for evangelicals. The need to get beyond this impasse in order to demonstrate unity with diversity in the body of Christ is greater than ever." Pierce, "Contemporary Evangelicals for Gender Equality," 74.

[8] Again, with a nod to Blocher's concern about the word *complementarity*, I approach the discussion differently. Blocher maintains that "the emphasis of the biblical text is not on complementarity but on similarity and commonality: man and woman are both created in God's image, and Calvin rightly drew the consequence: 'it follows that whatever is said in the creation of man also belongs to the female sex,' and one should speak of *equality*. . . . Dorothy Sayers strikes the true biblical note: 'But the fundamental thing is that women are more like men than anything else in the world. They are human beings.' In the light of such data, complementarity should not become the key concept in any doctrine of the man-woman relationship." Blocher, "Women, Ministry, and the Gospel:

valuing of each sex by the other and godly cooperation for the advancement of the kingdom of God.

If a personal note may be permitted, I write this book with an awareness of the many limitations that I bring to this topic.[9] One of these is the blindness due to my sex identity: a man writing about men and women. As Virginia Woolf explained, "For there is a spot the size of a shilling at the back of the head which one can never see for oneself. It is one of the good offices that sex can discharge for sex—to describe that spot the size of a shilling at the back of the head."[10] As a man, I hope to fairly represent women and their contribution to complementarity, and as a particular man to fairly represent men in general and their corresponding contribution to complementarity.

Hints for a New Paradigm," 242. His citations are John Calvin, [Speaking of the creation of man], "Unde sequitur, quod in creatione viri dictum fuit, ad sexum muliebrem pertinere;" *Commentarii in Quinque Libros Mosis: Commentarius in Genesin*, in *Calvini Opera* 23.46; and Dorothy Sayers, *Are Women Human?* (Grand Rapids: Eerdmans, 1992), 37. As my definition underscores, complementarity is indeed about male image bearers and female image bearers, with image bearing being the fundamental identity of human beings created by God. Moreover, complementarity is an important, though not the only, aspect of human relationships, and it is legitimate for my book to focus on that particular aspect. Furthermore, as I will present, Prudence Allen provides an important corrective to Blocher's point: as much as the emphasis should be on similarity and commonality, complementarity embraces that emphasis (for Allen, "equal dignity") as well as the emphasis on diversity (for Allen, "significant differentiation"). Allen, *The Concept of Woman, Volume 2*, 8. As for the broader discussion at which Blocher hints, David Dockery and I are under contract with Crossway to write the final volume in the Foundations of Evangelical Theology series. Our work will treat theological anthropology, which is the doctrinal locus that calls for us to address the many other aspects of humanity, male-female relationships, and much more.

[9] Some of this section reflects the discussion of Prudence Allen, *The Concept of Woman, Volume 3: The Search for Communion of Persons, 1500–2015* (Grand Rapids: Eerdmans, 2016), 2–3.

[10] Virginia Woolf, *A Room of One's Own* (New York: Harcourt, Brace and Co., 1957; reprint, New York: Fall River, 2007), 99.

Another limitation is the bias that besets me, a bias that, as I will show, has over 2,500 years of reprehensible influence in championing and defending the superiority of men and the inferiority of women. I do not pretend to have overcome that entrenched prejudice, but I can say that as I have delved into the history of the relationship between men and women, I have felt deep disgust at how far we have missed and even trampled upon what I consider to be God's design for the two sexes he creates: complementarity.

There are many more personal limitations that will certainly rear their ugly heads. My hope is that such limitations are not so debilitating that they completely sink my project.

CHAPTER 2

An Initial Biblical Foundation of Complementarity

Much of this volume is devoted to significant interaction with over fifty biblical passages in both the Old and New Testaments that are relevant for my notion of complementarity. As an initial biblical foundation for that proposal, I summarize Susan Mathew's account of "Pauline love-mutualism" developed in Romans 12–15.[1] She defines mutualism as "relationships of reciprocity (i.e., where each has something to contribute to the other) whose purpose is mutual promotion (i.e., where the task of each is to serve the interests of the other)."[2] This book focuses specifically on the reciprocal relationships of women and men.

---

[1] Susan Mathew, *Women in the Greetings of Romans 16:1–16: A Study of Mutuality and Women's Ministry in the Letter to the Romans* (London and New York: Bloomsbury, 2013). While I present her theme of "love-mutualism" here, I will return later to her discussion of Paul's greetings in Romans 16. Theologically, I ground complementarity in sociality, which I define as "the universal human condition of desiring, expressing, and receiving human relationships." God has created human beings to orient themselves toward others, which is part and parcel of complementarity. For further discussion see Gregg R. Allison, *Embodied: Living as Whole People in a Fractured World* (Grand Rapids: Baker, 2021),, ch. 4.

[2] Mathew, *Women in the Greetings of Romans 16:1–16*, 15.

Mathew addresses the metaphor of the body of Christ in Romans 12–13, underscoring that the Greco-Roman concept of the body politic emphasized not only unity, but unity that was commonly achieved by the maintenance of traditional hierarchical structures. She notes that "conservative ideology in the Greco-Roman world may be referred to as a benevolent patriarchalism which 'maintained the social hierarchy by urging the lower class to submit to those in authority and the higher class to rule benevolently and gently'. In other words, the upper class continues to exercise its rule without any reversal of position."[3] For Mathew, this traditional structure is the opposite of "Pauline love-mutualism" that calls for love, honor, respect, humility, deference, hospitality, and the like on the part of Christian communities.

Key aspects of the Pauline metaphor of the body in Romans 12–13 include sober-mindedness ("I tell everyone among you not to think of himself more highly than he should think"; 12:3), that is, a mindset that eschews an elevated sense of oneself.[4] By way of contrast, each individual should "think sensibly" by embracing a realistic evaluation of oneself and one's gifting, an assessment that is forged with consideration for the "measure of faith" divinely distributed to each member of the body (12:3). The reason for this soberness and sensibleness is the body metaphor: "Now [γάρ, *gar* = "for" or "because"] as we have many parts in one body, and all the parts do not have the same function, in the same way we who are many are one body in Christ and individually members of one another" (12:4–5). The church consists of many members with great diversity among them, yet they constitute only one body. Only when its diverse members are sober-minded and level-headed will the church experience the divinely designed unity, which is expressed by the phrase "members of one another": "in being the members of one another (not just of something else they all contribute to),

---

[3] Mathew, *Women in the Greetings of Romans 16:1–16*, 117; cf. 121. She cites D. B. Martin, *The Corinthian Body* (New Haven: Yale University Press, 1995), 42.

[4] Mathew, *Women in the Greetings of Romans 16:1–16*, 119–21.

their very identity as a body is composed of the contribution of others."[5] Correlating to the diversity of functions of the human body is the diversity of spiritual gifts in the body of Christ, which are given by grace and consist of prophecy, service, teaching, exhortation, generous giving, diligent leading, and cheerfully showing mercy (12:6–8).[6] Two points of note: these gifts are equally distributed among both men and women and are not confined to church officers.[7]

Paul continues his directives about "love-mutualism." Highlights include the following: (1) "Let love be without hypocrisy" (12:9); mutual love must be authentic and without façade.[8] Moreover, (2) it must be a reciprocating love as Christians are to "love one another deeply as brothers and sisters" (12:10), with φιλαδελφία εἰς ἀλλήλους φιλόστοργοι (*philadelphia eis allēlous philostorgoi*) underscoring the affection of siblings that binds believers in Christ together in familial relationships.[9] (3) Such reciprocity carries over into another directive: "Take the lead in honoring one another" (12:10). In an honor-shame culture such as Paul's, esteeming others was a key mark of the relationships between equal-status citizens: one high-status person showed honor to another high-status person, with equal reciprocity of honor being a desired goal. Additionally, lower-status people like

---

[5] Mathew, *Women in the Greetings of Romans 16:1–16*, 123.

[6] Mathew, *Women in the Greetings of Romans 16:1–16*, 123.

[7] The distinction between spiritual gifts—endowments that are distributed to all church members by the Holy Spirit and that he empowers for the maturation and multiplication of the church—and church officers—believers who are called by God and publicly recognized by their church as its leaders, teachers, and shepherds for its maturation and multiplication—seems to be a key point of debate between complementarians and egalitarians.

[8] Mathew, *Women in the Greetings of Romans 16:1–16*, 124–26. The verse is without a verb in Greek: Ἡ ἀγάπη ἀνυπόκριτος (*hē agapē anupokritos*). Thus, Moo renders it literally "sincere love" and avers that "these words are the heading for what follows, as Paul proceeds in a series of participial clauses to explain just what sincere love really is." Douglas J. Moo, *Romans*, The New International Commentary on the New Testament (Grand Rapids: Eerdmans, 1996), 774.

[9] Mathew, *Women in the Greetings of Romans 16:1–16*, 126–27.

slaves were expected to esteem persons of higher status, but the reverse was never practiced.[10] Yet, such reversal is exactly what Paul's directive demands: whatever their status may be—higher, equal, or lower—Christians are to take the initiative to honor fellow Christians. If Paul's exhortation includes his additional idea of "in humility consider others as more important than yourselves" (Phil 2:3), the enhanced portrait of love-mutualism is Christians of all cultural ranks and diverse social worth "competing" to take the lead in honoring one another more highly than themselves.[11]

These biblical directives promote complementarity.

Furthermore, (4) love-mutualism manifests itself in sharing and hospitality: "Share with the saints in their needs; pursue hospitality" (12:13). As to the first directive, Paul calls upon Christians to offer financial and other types of assistance to those in need of such resources. When that need is a place to stay, Christians are to open their homes to strangers.[12] (5) Returning to the theme of reciprocity in relationships, Paul includes both a dissimilar and a similar exhortation: "Bless those who persecute you; bless and do not curse. Rejoice with those who rejoice; weep with those who weep" (12:14–15). In the dissimilar case, evil is not to be reciprocated for evil; rather, a blessing is to be offered in place of a curse that was inflicted. As for the similar case, Paul calls for solidarity: joy is to be reciprocated for joy and sorrow is to be reciprocated for sorrow. This reciprocity stands at the heart of love-mutualism.[13]

(6) The common goal of harmonious living through the proper mindset is part and parcel of love-mutualism. "Live in harmony with one another. Do not be proud; instead, associate with the humble. Do not be wise in

---

[10] This highly developed, reciprocal system of "benefits" was, according to the first century Stoic philosopher Seneca, "the chief bond of human society." Specifically, "the bestowal of a benefit is an act of companionship—it wins some man's friendship and lays some man under an obligation." Seneca, *On Benefits*, 1.4.2; 5.11.5

[11] Mathew, *Women in the Greetings of Romans 16:1–16*, 127–28.

[12] Mathew, *Women in the Greetings of Romans 16:1–16*, 129–30.

[13] Mathew, *Women in the Greetings of Romans 16:1–16*, 130.

your own estimation" (12:16). Paul's emphasis—φρονέω (*phroneō*, to think) twice and φρόνιμος (*phronimos*, wise) once—is on rightful thinking in three matters. First, Christians are to think the same with regard to one another, not in the sense of identical thinking in strict uniformity, but in terms of diverse views—appropriate ones, within the bounds of orthodoxy and orthopraxy—that Christians correlate for harmonious dwelling together. It is a similar idea to Paul's exhortation "that all of you agree in what you say, that there be no divisions among you, and that you be united with the same understanding and the same conviction" (1 Cor 1:10). Unity in affirmation, mind/thinking, and knowledge/judgment, with diversity but not division, is the goal. Second, Christians are not to think lofty things about themselves. "Do not be proud" (12:16) repeats Paul's call "not to think of [yourselves] more highly than [you] should think" (12:3). This time, however, his antidote is not to "think sensibly" (12:3) but to "associate with the humble" (12:16). Pride is dealt a deathblow through relationships with other believers (who are to be humbly esteemed as more important than oneself), especially with the lowly in cultural status and social worth. Third, Paul exhorts, "Do not be wise in your own estimation" (12:16). Haughtiness replaces humility when Christians assess themselves according to their own (self-centered) criteria, leading to the destruction of harmony between Christians. Harmonious living is the goal as sisters and brothers engage in love-mutualism.[14]

These biblical instructions support complementarity.

(7) Following Mathew's treatment of Romans 12–13, I conclude with her summary of "obligatory love" in 13:8–10 (with emphasis added on the theme of *love*):

> Do not owe anyone anything, except to *love* one another, for the one who *loves* another has fulfilled the law. The commandments, Do not commit adultery; do not murder; do not steal; do not covet; and any other commandment, are summed up by this commandment:

[14] Mathew, *Women in the Greetings of Romans 16:1–16*, 130–32.

> *Love* your neighbor as yourself. *Love* does no wrong to a neighbor. *Love*, therefore, is the fulfillment of the law (13:8–10).

As before, Paul underscores the reciprocal nature of love: Christians are to love one another (τὸ ἀλλήλους, *to allēlous*), love another (τὸν ἕτερον, *ton heteron*), and love their neighbor (τὸν πλησίον, *ton plēsion*); love-mutualism is all-encompassing, without exception. Specifically, love never does harm to another person, and the only thing that is owed is love for one another. Such inclusive love in action is the fulfillment of the law; indeed, "the whole law is fulfilled in one word: 'You shall love your neighbor as yourself'" (Gal 5:14). Love-mutualism is exhibited as obligatory love of Christians for one another.[15]

Though Mathew continues her development of "Pauline love-mutualism" in Romans 14–15, her point has been adequately established—and initial biblical support for complementarity has been provided—such that a summary of her treatment of these two chapters will suffice.

Paul continues his theme of "one another" in Romans 14–15: (1) In relationship to the errors of despising others (the error of the strong toward the weak) and judging others (the error of the weak toward the strong), Christians are to "no longer *judge one another*" (14:13). Looking down upon and judging others brings great harm to fellow Christians; thus, Paul urges, "Instead decide never to put a stumbling block or pitfall in the way of your brother or sister" (14:13).[16] (2) Not only is tearing down one another denounced; Paul positively adds "let us pursue what promotes peace and what *builds up one another*" (14:19). Mutual edification fosters the growth of the church. In this task, "we who are strong have an obligation to bear the weaknesses of those without strength, and not to please ourselves. Each one of us is to please his neighbor for his good, to build him up. For even Christ did not please himself" (15:1–3). Adding to his earlier exhortations for Christians to love, honor, support, show hospitality toward, and live

---

[15] Mathew, *Women in the Greetings of Romans 16:1–16*, 132–33.

[16] Mathew, *Women in the Greetings of Romans 16:1–16*, 149.

harmoniously with one another, Paul directs them to pursue peace and nurture one another toward increasing conformity to Christ, whose image also serves as the model for the church.[17]

(3) Paul returns to his earlier directives regarding agreeable living in two senses. First is agreement in relationships, as he again urges Christians "to live in *harmony with one another*, according to Christ Jesus" (15:5). The second is agreement in mindset, as he echoes: "so that you may glorify the God and Father of our Lord Jesus Christ *with one mind and one voice*" (15:6). Living in peace and being united in thinking and proclamation leads to the ultimate purpose of the church: the glory of God.[18] Thus, Paul offers (4) a final exhortation: "Therefore *welcome one another*, just as Christ also welcomed you, to the glory of God" (15:7). Again, with Christ being the model of an all-inclusive welcome and with the glory of God being the highest aim, Christians are to receive one another.[19] Paul's immediate application is to the Jew-Gentile divide (15:8–12), but for our purposes, an extension of that application may be made to the male-female division: In Christ and as modeled by him, men and women followers of Christ should receive one another to the glory of God.

To summarize, Susan Mathew's discussion of and case for "Pauline love-mutualism" approximates my idea of complementarity and offers some initial biblical support for it. Examining Paul's exhortations in Romans 12–15, we find a clear and oft repeated emphasis on (1) Christians loving one another/others/one's neighbors; (2) outdoing one another in showing honor to one another, no matter the cultural rank or social worth—higher, equal, or lower—of those to be esteemed; (3) supporting others through providing financial and other resources and showing hospitality toward strangers; (4) living harmoniously with one another while promoting and expressing the same mindset and proclamation; (5) pursuing peace with and nurturing one another; (6) and welcoming one another whatever one's particularities

[17] Mathew, *Women in the Greetings of Romans 16:1–16*, 150–52.

[18] Mathew, *Women in the Greetings of Romans 16:1–16*, 153.

[19] Mathew, *Women in the Greetings of Romans 16:1–16*, 144–45.

may be. Such love-mutualism is the appropriate posture and expression for all Christian men toward all Christian women and all Christian women toward all Christian men. In other words, complementarity is all-inclusive and never exclusive. It is at the heart of the Pauline ethic and vision for the church, and its fruit is the glory of God and the flourishing of his female image bearers and male image bearers.

Complementarity is God's design for his male and female image bearers to fill out and mutually support one another relationally, familially, vocationally, and ecclesially. Pauline "love mutualism" offers an initial biblical foundation for it. Before entering discussions and debates surrounding men and women and their roles, I have offered a biblically grounded vision for love, mutuality, reciprocity, respect, honor, and relationality between them.

CHAPTER 3

Definitions of Complementarianism and Egalitarianism and Their Relationship to Complementarity

Having defined complementarity, I turn to a brief discussion of two biblical-theological positions that, while (probably) agreeing on the idea of complementarity, stand opposed to one another on specific matters. These two views are complementarianism and egalitarianism, with whom I engage as conversation partners for reasons already discussed.[1] They are defined in the following two points.

[1] As noted earlier, I do not adjudicate between these two positions in terms of their interpretations of Scripture, their theological foundations, and their applications. Such assessment is beyond the purpose and scope of this book.

Definition of Complementarianism

Complementarianism is the view that men and women are complementary or correspond to one another, being equal to one another in essence and different from one another in certain relationships and roles. Men and women are equal in three principal ways: being created in the image of God, enjoying access to salvation through Jesus Christ, in whose body they are incorporated, and receiving the gifts of the Holy Spirit. At the same time, men and women are different in relationships and roles. Such distinctions may appear in several realms. With respect to the home, husbands lead, and their wives submit to them. In the church, elder/pastor responsibilities are reserved for qualified and called men.[2] Women, while participating in many ministries, may not hold the office of elder/pastor. While many complementarians do not hold to differences in roles in the societal realm, some maintain that men should lead governments and companies and women should serve in positions of lower authority. Women, while working as sales representatives and accountants in a company, may not lead as its CEO. These distinctions come in various combinations.[3] By contrast, egalitarianism denies some or all distinctions.[4]

As we will see, this position is expressed in several ways across a spectrum of minimum, moderate, and maximum complementarianism.

---

[2] Churches and denominations differ significantly as to the terminology and structure of their leadership groups: *pastor, elder, overseer, bishop, priest, minister, deacon, deaconess, trustee,* and more. For simplicity's sake I will use the term *pastor* and *elder* as interchangeable words for the highest level of ecclesial authority and responsibility. I invite readers to adapt my terminology for their own churches and denominations.

[3] Most complementarians agree with differences in roles in the home and the church but do not hold to differences in roles in the societal realm.

[4] This definition is modified from Gregg R. Allison, *The Church: An Introduction* (Wheaton: Crossway, 2022), 132–33.

Definition of Egalitarianism

Egalitarianism is the position that men and women are equal to one another in essence, relationships, and roles. In agreement with complementarianism, this view embraces the great equalities of men and women alike bearing the divine image, being redeemed through Christ and incorporated into his body, and receiving the full range of spiritual gifts. In contrast to complementarianism, egalitarianism affirms equalities in other realms. With respect to the home, husbands and wives share equal authority (or responsibility) and submit (or defer) to each other. In the church, qualified men and qualified women may hold the office of elder/pastor. In society, men and women alike lead governments and companies. Moreover, these equalities come in various combinations. Egalitarianism stands in contrast to complementarianism, which believes men and women to be equal in essence yet distinct in relationships and roles.[5]

As we will see, this position is expressed in several ways across a spectrum of minimum, mixed, and maximum egalitarianism.

Complementarity, Complementarianism, and Egalitarianism

Importantly, complementarity is neither complementarianism nor egalitarianism. In a sense, it embraces the three great equalities agreed on by both positions: Men and women alike bear the divine image. Men and women alike may be rescued from sin by Christ and, united together, be incorporated into his body. And men and women alike receive the full range of spiritual gifts; that is, there are no gender-specific gifts.[6] But complementarity goes

[5] This definition is modified from Allison, *The Church*, 132–33.

[6] Thomas Aquinas offers one reason why this is the case. Referring to the prophetess Deborah, Aquinas explained that "her learning came through the spirit of prophecy, and the grace of the Holy Spirit does not distinguish between man

beyond those commonalities to express and encourage the interdependence and reciprocity of men and women, who fill out and mutually support one another in terms of their relationships, family dynamics, collaborative work, and church ministries. Thus, in another sense, complementarity is a broader framework than both complementarianism and egalitarianism, grounding those two positions that, depending on several factors (e.g., the interpretation and application of certain biblical passages; the understanding of the implications of creation order, manner, and purpose), eventually separate and distinguish themselves from one another. Diagrammatically,

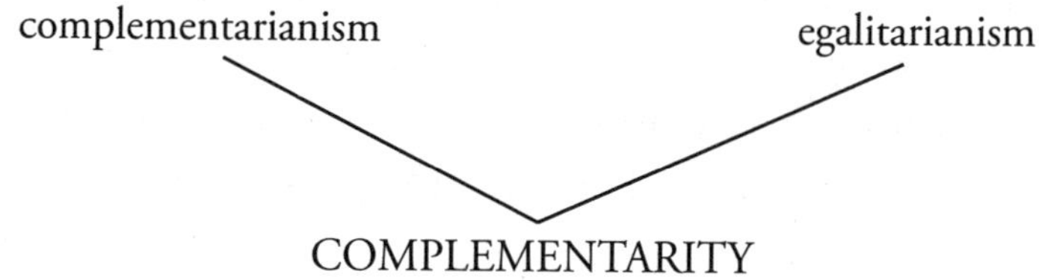

As just noted, a key area of separation between complementarianism and egalitarianism is the roles of men and women in the church and the home (for some, society also). Complementarity makes several points in this regard. First, complementarity does not deny or negate the existence and importance of roles. Both complementarianism and egalitarianism, built on complementarity, envision roles for women and men; therefore, complementarity does not negate the reality and function of roles. Complementarianism details roles in this general way: (1) in the church, qualified and called men exercise the role of pastor/elder, which role is closed to women; and (2) in the home, husbands exercise the role of head/leader and women exercise the role of follower. Egalitarianism details roles

---

and woman." St. Thomas Aquinas, *Commentary on the Letters of Saint Paul to the Philippians, Colossians, Thessalonians, Timothy, Titus, and Philemon*, in *Biblical Commentaries*, vol. 40 of *Latin/English Edition of the Works of St. Thomas Aquinas*, ed. J. Mortensen and E. Alarcón, trans. F. R. Larcher (Lander, WY: The Aquinas Institute for the Study of Sacred Doctrine, 2012), 272.

in this general way: (1) in the church, qualified men and qualified women exercise the role of pastor/elder; and (2) in the home, husbands and wives exercise the role of head/leader and the role of follower interchangeably, with variation due to circumstances, seasons of life, and competencies. Accordingly, complementarity does not deny or negate the existence and importance of roles.

Second, complementarity has to do with the filling out and mutual support of one another relationally, familially, vocationally, and ecclesially for individual and corporate flourishing. Both complementarianism and egalitarianism, built on complementarity, affirm its importance. While complementarianism, generally speaking, affirms role differentiation in the familial and ecclesial areas, it may deny role differentiation in the relational realm (i.e., non-marital relationships between men and women) and vocational realm (i.e., non-ecclesial offices). For example, complementarianism may promote other-gender friendships that are non-hierarchical, with neither the man nor the woman exercising the roles of head/leader and follower, and it may promote both female and male leaders of government and CEOs of companies.[7] Additionally, egalitarianism may affirm undifferentiated or interchangeable roles in all four areas while also insisting on the existence of roles—an almost inescapable part of human existence, production, and society—that may be held equally by men and women.

To avoid misunderstanding or any misplaced hope, my proposal of complementarity is not an attempt to offer a third- or middle-way position between these two views. Such an undertaking might be desirable, but it is probably not possible. Rather, my proposal will describe and apply the unique contributions of complementarity. It will highlight commonalities and honestly address differences between complementarianism and egalitarianism. It will also place the support for and criticism of the two

[7] Some versions of complementarianism would disagree, promoting "roled" approaches in all relationships between men and women and insisting on male leadership in all vocations.

positions near each other so as to compare and contrast them.[8] My proposal will encourage believers and churches on both sides of this issue to renounce obstacles to, and embrace steps toward, the fulfillment of the biblical vision set forth at the beginning of this section.

---

[8] Again, I do not adjudicate between these two positions. As worthy an endeavor as that might be, it is beyond the purpose and scope of this book.

PART TWO

Historical Development

To understand my proposal of complementarity (or, in the vast majority of cases, to grasp the lack of equal dignity, significant differentiation, and flourishing interdependence), it is necessary to comprehend the complex history of the relationship between women and men over the course of the last twenty-five hundred years. Accordingly, Part Two offers an abbreviated rehearsal of key philosophical, theological, and ecclesiastical developments in the (pre-Christian) Greco-Roman world, the early church age, the early medieval period (600–1250), the late medieval and Reformation era (1250–1550), and the early modern to postmodern epoch (1550–present). Part Three, then, treats the contemporary context in which our current discussion of complementarity occurs.[1]

I note three limitations to this historical sketch: First, its brevity runs the risk that the account will be oversimplistic and thus misleading. While

[1] If readers want to skip my detailed discussion of this complex history, they may turn to my summary of it in Chapter 9.

this danger is real and regrettable, space limitations prevent a full-orbed treatment. Second, such an account has already been written and provides the basis for my narrative. Sister Prudence Allen's lifelong work, the three-volume *The Concept of Woman*, is a tour de force that focuses on the (predominantly male) view of women over the course of the centuries.[2] As she notes, "Philosophy, from its beginnings, sought to make distinctions, to develop explanations, and to promote theories about the respective identities of women and men. From this discovery we can conclude that sex identity was a central area for reflection from the beginning of western philosophy."[3] Third, Allen's last phrase mentions a final limitation: this section traces the historical development of the *Western tradition*'s views of the relationship between women and men. It remains for others to trace, for example, Islamic, Eastern, or African traditions.

---

[2] Prudence Allen, *The Concept of Woman: The Aristotelian Revolution, 750 B.C.—A.D. 1250* (Grand Rapids: Eerdmans, 1985); *The Concept of Woman, Volume 2: The Early Humanist Reformation, 1250–1500* (Grand Rapids: Eerdmans, 2006); *The Concept of Woman, Volume 3: The Search for Communion of Persons, 1500–2015* (Grand Rapids: Eerdmans, 2016). Because the first volume was titled as noted above without any indication of a volume number (i.e., *The Concept of Woman: Volume 1*), I will retain the abbreviated form Allen, *The Concept of Woman* in all references to her first volume. The abbreviated forms Allen, *The Concept of Woman: Volume 2*, and Allen, *The Concept of Woman: Volume 3*, will note that they are the two subsequent volumes. A recent publication has been released: Sister Prudence Allen, *The Concept of Woman: A Synthesis in One Volume* (Grand Rapids: Eerdmans, 2024). While some people may question my use of Allen's work, I adopt her framework because of her impeccable scholarship, the breadth of her interaction with hundreds of key persons and movements, the ease of tracking her citations of primary sources, and the persuasiveness of her presentation.

[3] Allen, *The Concept of Woman*, 8. Her focus on philosophy should not be misunderstood to mean that her treatment only covers the philosophical traditions of male and female relationships. As she demonstrates in her books, this tradition deeply influenced theology and the church; thus, my account rehearses the key philosophical, theological, and ecclesiological developments over two and half millennia.

CHAPTER 4

Greco-Roman Philosophical Views of Men and Women

To provide a framework for discussion, Allen presents four categories of questions: *opposites* (i.e., what are the differences between men and women?), *generation* (i.e., what are the contributions of women and men to the mothering and fathering of children?), *wisdom* (i.e., what is the relationship of men and women to wisdom/rationality?), and *virtue* (i.e., are women and men characterized by the same or different virtues?).[1]

1. *The metaphysical question of* **opposites**: *in what ways are male and female opposites?*

Greco-Roman philosophy raised this key issue: Are women and men equal in dignity and worth? Are there any philosophically significant differences

[1] Allen herself presents the diversity in this Greco-Roman perspective. Plato, for one, differs significantly at many points from it. Aristotle is highlighted because of his influence on Thomas Aquinas and, through him, Roman Catholic theology. Allen traces the widespread acceptance of Aristotelian sex polarity in later medieval Christianity (*The Concept of Woman*, 361–407).

between women and men? Allen summarizes this philosophical tradition in terms of five basic theories of sex identity.

One answer is *sex unity*: women and men are equal, and they are not significantly different.[2] This view is often accompanied by a devaluation of the materiality/embodiment of human beings. According to Plato, for example, human beings are souls, which both men and women possess; therefore, they are equal in nature. Additionally, in the future, human beings will reunite with the eternal Forms; therefore, men and women, as disembodied sexless/agendered souls, will be equal in nature forever.[3]

A second answer, which is a derivative of sex unity, is *sex neutrality*: women and men are equal and not significantly different. As an example from the early modern period, René Descartes' substance dualism insisted that a human being is characterized as a "thinking thing" with no reference to sex differentiation. This theory ignores differences between the sexes rather than arguing directly for the equality of women and men, as does the first theory.

A third answer is *traditional sex polarity*: women and men are significantly different, and men are superior to women.[4] Aristotle believed that male and female are opposites as contraries; furthermore, as a pair of contraries, the female must be the privation of the male. Specifically, the female is inferior to the male and is identified with matter (rather than form), passivity, and the lowest elements of human nature. Oppositely, the male is superior to the female and is identified with form (rather than matter), activity, and with the higher elements of human nature.[5]

Furthermore, according to Aristotle, one aspect of human materiality—the ability to produce seed (sperm)—is key to all valuation of sex identity and is the fundamental philosophical basis for the evaluation of men as

[2] This view bears some resemblance to contemporary unisex theories.

[3] He develops these ideas in Plato, *The Republic* and *The Dialogues*.

[4] Though Allen names this category *sex polarity*, I will at times refer to it as *traditional sex polarity* to distinguish it more clearly from the fourth category, *reverse sex polarity*.

[5] Allen, *The Concept of Woman*, 89.

superior to women. This view is often accompanied by an over-evaluation of one particular aspect—sperm production and the ability to impregnate—of the materiality of human beings.[6] Regretfully, for the most part, humankind has been characterized by this position of sex polarity for over 2,500 years.

A fourth answer is *reverse sex polarity*: women and men are significantly different, and women are superior to men. Some have advanced reverse sex polarity by arguing that first, in terms of virtues, those of women are better than those of men, and second, in terms of vices, those of men are worse than those of women. In contemporary expressions of this position, one aspect of human materiality—the capacity for giving birth—is key to all valuation of sex identity and is the fundamental philosophical basis for the evaluation of women as superior to men. This view is often accompanied by an over-evaluation of one particular aspect—the production of ova and the capacity of pregnancy—of the materiality of human beings.

A fifth answer is *sex complementarity*: women and men are significantly different, and they are equal. Historically, this view was often accompanied by the realization that both the mother and the father contribute one-half of the seed/reproductive material that is needed for the production of the fetus; that is, through the union of differentiated, equal, and necessary male sperm and female ovum, a child is generated.[7] While this physiological fact of human reproduction is taken for granted today and its absence seems almost unbelievable, it was not known for several millennia, thus contributing to a distorted view of male and female contributions to the production of children.

---

[6] Allen, *The Concept of Woman*, 4.

[7] Contrast this understanding with that of Plato, who tended to associate the man/fathering with form and the woman/mothering with matter. Accordingly, in the act of sexual intercourse/generation, a woman is a passive receptacle with no identity of its own and that awaits a form from the man; indeed, human identity comes from the (sexless/agendered) mind/soul and not at all from the body: "a woman's or a man's nature flows directly from the character of her or his soul . . . which is neither male nor female." Allen, *The Concept of Woman*, 61.

Though two versions of sex complementarity did not develop until very late in history, I mention them early on as an introduction with more discussion to come: (1) *Fractional sex complementarity*: as with complementarity in general, women and men are significantly different, and they are equal. Additionally, this subgroup "ascribes specific masculine and feminine characteristics to the two sexes, dividing them so that a woman may have one, a man the other," and through their complementarity they as fractional (i.e., incomplete, partial) beings constitute one being.[8] (2) *Integral sex complementarity*: in addition to the principles of complementarity in general, this subgroup considers a woman and a man "as two separate and complete human individuals who are equal in dignity and worth and who have philosophically significant differences. They are not fractional beings who together make up one being. Instead, they are two whole beings who, together, synergetically generate more than just the sum of themselves" through interdependence.[9]

As this position of sex complementarity, specifically the second variety, is the one championed in this book, I will draw particular attention to its development. However, as the following discussion demonstrates, the prevailing position in the Greco-Roman tradition was that of sex polarity.

2. *The natural philosophy question of* generation*: what are the respective functions of mothering and fathering in reproduction or the generation of children?*

As noted above, a significant reason for the rejection of sex complementarity was a pervasive and persistent misunderstanding of human anatomy and physiology, especially when it comes to sperm, ova, menstruation, and the way reproduction occurs. For much of the history of the Western tradition, such error has led to the conclusion that a woman is an inferior, or deformed, man.

[8] Prudence Allen, *The Concept of Woman, Volume 2: The Early Humanist Reformation, 1250–1500* (Grand Rapids: Eerdmans, 2006), 18.

[9] Allen, *The Concept of Woman*, vol. 2, 18.

Aristotle rejected the correct double seed theory—that both male seed (sperm) and female seed (ovum) are necessary for reproduction—and affirmed instead sex polarity based on his incorrect view that the woman provides no seed in generation because she is by nature colder than the man.[10] As the privation of the male, the female is cold; the male, being superior, is hot.[11] Accordingly, in the process of reproduction, the mother provides only matter for generation while the father provides form; that is, the mother provides the material (blood, that is, menstrual fluid) upon which the heat and fertility of the male seed acts to form a child. Clearly, then, the mother does not provide any seed (i.e., ovum) for the reproductive process. Specifically, the soul, or form, of the child is present in the semen of the father, but it does not begin to work until it meets with the proper material (the menstrual blood) of the mother. Viewed negatively, the father contributes nothing material to the child (he provides only the soul) while the mother contributes nothing immaterial to the child (she provides only the body).

In even greater details, Aristotle pictured sexual intercourse as a battle between two contraries in which the two attempt to destroy one another. In this pitched battle, when the seed of the male meets the material of the female, five results may occur:

---

[10] Aristotle's binarity of hot and cold accords with his metaphysical position that male and female are opposites as contraries: the man is associated with hot, the woman with cold, and the hotness of the man accords him superiority to the woman who is characterized by coldness.

[11] "Aristotle, in the *Metaphysics*, further argued that whenever there is a pair of contraries, that one is to be considered the privation of the other. Privation, then, determined the characteristics of the two contraries; indeed, since privation was complete non-being, with no identity of its own, it could not be found in something that had a nature. Therefore, matter was interpreted as the privation of form, and the female as the privation of the male. . . . Matter, privation, and the female, then, were integrated into the foundation of Aristotle's metaphysics of sex polarity." Allen, *The Concept of Woman*, 91.

1. The heated seed meets heated material, and the seed perfectly conquers the menstrual fluid: the result is a boy resembling his father.
2. The heated seed meets heated material, and the menstrual fluid resists the seed: the result is a boy resembling his mother.
3. The heated seed meets cold material, and the menstrual fluid partially resists the seed: the result is a girl resembling her father.
4. The heated seed meets cold material, and the menstrual fluid more fully resists the seed: the result is a girl resembling her mother.
5. The heated seed meets cold material, and the menstrual fluid totally resists the seed: the result is no conception.

While our understanding of the reproductive process, including the genetics of XX and XY chromosomes in the determination of a child's sex, prompt us to laugh at Aristotle's categorization, it should be recalled that such a misunderstanding of human procreation dominated the Western tradition's view of men and women for millennia—with its demise not starting until the seventeenth century!—and led to tragic consequences.[12] To summarize this traditional sex polarity: in comparison with the hotness of a man, the greater coldness of a woman renders her inferior to a man.[13] A woman is an imperfect, inferior, or deformed man: "Because females are weaker and colder in nature . . . we should look upon the female state as being as it were a deformity, though one which occurs in the ordinary course of nature [i.e., is simply and universally the way it is]."[14]

This prevalent and long-enduring misunderstanding of human reproduction contributed to the position of sex polarity.

---

[12] Allen notes that the philosopher Empedocles (c. 450 BC) "was one of the few [philosophers of medicine] before the seventeenth century to have proposed the correct theory of reproduction, namely, that the mother and the father each provide one-half of the seed needed for the production of the fetus." Allen, *The Concept of Woman*, 33.

[13] Allen, *The Concept of Woman*, 97.

[14] Allen, *The Concept of Woman*, 98. The quote is from Aristotle, *Generation of Animals*, trans. A. L. Peck (Cambridge, MA: Harvard University Press and William Heinemann Ltd, 1943), 775a12–16.

3. *The epistemological question of* wisdom*: do women and men relate to wisdom in the same way?*

The Western philosophical tradition has associated the higher capacities of rationality, reason, judgment, and the like with men, and the lower functions of passion, bodily desire, appetite, and the like with women. Wisdom, then, has been traditionally viewed as more the domain of men.

For example, Democritus (c. 460–370 BC) maintained that women, while possessing higher capacities (e.g., rationality, cognition) like men do, should not develop their aptitudes of thought and argumentation, which were crucial for philosophical engagement.[15] As a corollary, "an adornment for a woman is a lack of garrulity [much conversation, which is a trademark of philosophers]" either because speech is inappropriate for women or "because their speech might reveal a less virtuous kind of thought."[16] With public address being closed off to them, women need to develop their capacity for wisdom in ways different from those of men.

For Aristotle, sex polarity was not only grounded on differences in relation to generation; it was also due to divergences in the rational capacities of women and men. He viewed both sexes as characterized by higher faculties or powers—the rational part of human nature (that is, the mind, reason, and cognition), and lower faculties or powers—the irrational part of human nature (that is, emotions, bodily appetites, and passions). In men, whose identity is linked to the higher/rational part, their higher powers have authority to rule over their lower powers. As for women, though they possess the same kind of reason as do men, their higher/rational part lacks authority to rule over her lower faculties; thus, women have an inferior reasoning capacity than men. The outcome of this difference is that women may hold

---

[15] Allen, *The Concept of Woman*, 36. Democritus was the originator of the atomistic theory of creation: the universe and everything in it is the product of the random collision of small particles. He applied this philosophy to human reproduction, which he viewed as the collision of the seed of the father and the seed of the mother. Which seed prevails determines the sex of the resulting offspring.

[16] Allen, *The Concept of Woman*, 36.

and express true opinion but are incapable of true knowledge; they cannot be wise in the same way as men. As such, women cannot be philosophers nor can they participate in public life.[17]

This perspective on the epistemological superiority of men and the epistemological inferiority of women contributed to the position of traditional sex polarity.

4. *The question of moral philosophy or* virtue*: do women and men have the same or different virtues?*

Largely because of the third point, Western tradition has held that men and women have or are capable of different virtues. For men, these were the active virtues of reason, wisdom, speech, public activity, and ruling. Women possessed the passive virtues of opinion, silence/listening, private (home) management, and obedience/submission.

Democritus emphasized the virtue of ruling, maintaining that the male is a superior kind of human being who ought not be dominated by the female: "To be ruled by a woman is the ultimate outrage for a man."[18] He viewed sexual intercourse as a battle for control between a man, who should dominate, and a woman, who should surrender. Democritus considered the sexual act itself to be a case of apoplexy (a man bleeds into a seminal man). Furthermore, he decried having children, insisting on the adoption of children who are selected for eugenic purposes because of the possibility of having a female offspring through sexual intercourse.[19]

In his dialogue *Meno*, Plato presented a dialogue between Socrates and Meno, with the latter advocating for different virtues for men and women based on their different roles or functions in society. Because men are

[17] Allen, *The Concept of Woman*, 109.

[18] Allen, *The Concept of Woman*, 37.

[19] Allen, *The Concept of Woman*, 37.

responsible for managing a city's affairs, a manly virtue is ruling, and because women are responsible for managing their household's affairs, a womanly virtue is obedience. This arrangement—which may be by convention, as the Sophists maintained, or according to nature, as Aristotle maintained[20]—led to a framework of superiority and inferiority. As managing a city was (historically considered to be) superior to managing a household, so ruling was (historically considered to be) superior to obedience.[21] The male function of managing the *polis* corresponded to the male virtue of ruling, rendering men superior to women. The female function of managing the household corresponded to the female virtue of obedience, rendering women inferior to men.

Ultimately (and uniquely), Plato disagreed with Meno, arguing against (1) the view that men and women have different functions and thus have different virtues; (2) the universal assignment of the virtue of ruling to men and obeying to women; and (3) different spheres of activity for the two sexes.[22] By minimizing the human body and emphasizing the three parts of the human soul as that which directs human activity, Plato believed that four virtues—wisdom (the virtue of reason), courage (the virtue of the will), temperance (the virtue of the desires), and justice (the virtue of harmony between these three parts of the soul)—are needed by both men and women. Accordingly, he rejected the idea of separate spheres of activity for men and women.[23]

At the same time, Plato believed in sex polarity at the metaphysical level of form and matter. He identified men with forms (souls, which are active rather than passive, prefer male bodies, and give rise to wisdom), and women with matter (bodies, which are passive rather than active, are

[20] Allen, *The Concept of Woman*, 43.
[21] Allen, *The Concept of Woman*, 41.
[22] Allen, *The Concept of Woman*, 71.
[23] Allen, *The Concept of Woman*, 71.

inhabited by evil, and give rise to ignorance). As a result, men are stronger and women are weaker at birth, men find it easier to learn and women find it more difficult, and male strength provides an advantage in becoming wise and virtuous while female weakness is an obstacle to obtaining them.[24]

Still, Plato contributed significantly to the sex unity position: women and men are equal and they are not significantly different. He identified human beings with their souls (his devaluation of the body is evident), and as both men and women possess souls, they are equal in nature.[25] Furthermore, his view that human destiny is reunification with the eternal Forms (which entails escape from embodied existence and the material world) meant that men and women will eventually become disembodied sexless/agendered souls, equal in nature forever.[26] Clearly, Plato championed the sex unity position by means of a radical devaluation of the materiality/embodiment of human beings.

By contrast, and as noted in point three, Aristotle viewed ethics as involving a capacity to reason and engage in philosophical argumentation; therefore, because women are characterized by inferior rational capacities, they are not capable of virtuous activity in this realm. To be virtuous, women must obediently submit to virtuous men and express their virtues in the context of their household and of their friendships.[27]

Specifically, in terms of the six different categories of character—(1) godliness; (2) virtue; (3) self-restraint; (4) vice; (5) unrestraint; and (6) bestiality (i.e., on the level of an animal)—only the last two categories pertain to women. In both cases, women suffer a natural inability to be virtuous, being either so debilitatingly weak (so as to be unrestrained) or heinously brutish (e.g., engaging in cannibalism) that they are incapable

---

[24] Allen, *The Concept of Woman*, 78.

[25] Plato's view of radical body-soul dualism signified that human identity is entirely about the soul and has nothing to do with the body. Allen, *The Concept of Woman*, 80–81.

[26] Allen, *The Concept of Woman*, 80.

[27] Allen, *The Concept of Woman*, 111.

of ethical judgment and moral activity. Accordingly, because of their naturally passive nature, women cannot be held to the same ethical standards as men; that is, the categories of virtue, self-restraint, and vice cannot pertain to women. At most, women can be godly, not because they are capable of godliness through deliberation but because they may be naturally good.[28]

Positively, the female virtue is obedience, while the male virtue is rulership. Aristotle specifically linked this disparity to the fact that, though men and women alike are characterized by higher and lower faculties, the higher/rational faculty lacks authority in women and thus is incapable of controlling the lower/irrational faculty. Consequently, women as naturally inferior to men can only become virtuous by submitting to the rulership of naturally superior men.[29]

Flowing from his analysis of the animal kingdom, and building upon his definition of human beings as rational animals, Aristotle developed a descriptive (not prescriptive) list of general characteristics of women and men:

> Woman is more compassionate than man, more easily moved to tears, at the same time is more jealous, more querulous [complaining, whining], more apt to scold and to strike. She is, furthermore, more prone to despondency and less hopeful than the man, more void of shame or self-respect, more false of speech, more deceptive, and of more retentive memory. She is also more wakeful, more shrinking [cowardly], more difficult to rouse to action, and requires a smaller quantity of nutriment.[30]

---

[28] Allen, *The Concept of Woman*, 112. Lest Aristotle's final category of godliness because of natural goodness be understood in a positive way, he also considered bestial persons to be naturally brutish.

[29] Allen, *The Concept of Woman*, 112–14.

[30] Aristotle, *History of Animals*, in *The Basic Works of Aristotle* (Cambridge, MA: Harvard University Press, 1943), 608 a 35–608 b 5.

As Aristotle offered this list by way of contrast with the general characteristics of the complete and perfect nature of men, none of these female features is a positive virtue. Rather, they are all manifestations of the incomplete and imperfect female nature, which is essentially passive, expressive of lower/irrational faculty, and inferior to male nature. A woman is a defective man.

This view of the ethical inferiority of women contributed to the position of traditional sex polarity.

In summary, Prudence Allen frames her discussion of the relationship between women and men in four areas: opposites, generation, wisdom, and virtue. In terms of the first category (opposites), she presents five overarching theories of sex identity: (1) *sex unity*: women and men are equal and not significantly different; (2) *sex neutrality*: women and men are equal and not significantly different, without an explanation of the differences; (3) *traditional sex polarity*: women and men are significantly different, with men being superior to women; *reverse sex polarity*: women and men are significantly different, with women being superior to men; and (5) *sex complementarity*: women and men are significantly different and they are equal. Eventually, this category will include two varieties: *fractional sex complementarity* and *integral sex complementarity*. The predominant view arising from Greco-Roman philosophy is sex polarity.[31]

As for the second category (generation), because of a pervasive and enduring misunderstanding (stemming from Aristotle's rejection of the

[31] Concentrating on the contributions of the key philosophers Plato and Aristotle, Allen concludes that the two are correct in one element of their position regarding women's identity and incorrect in another element, yet in contrasting ways: Aristotle correctly affirmed a body-soul unity but incorrectly considered women to be inferior to men, while Plato incorrectly considered the identity of a woman as a body-soul duality but correctly affirmed women to be equal to men. Allen, *The Concept of Woman*, vol. 2, 10.

double-seed theory of procreation) of human anatomy and the process of reproduction, the Western tradition concluded that a woman is an imperfect, inferior, or deformed man. This position is clearly sex polarity.

For the third category (wisdom), the metaphysical division of human nature into higher order faculties associated with reason and lower order faculties associated with desires and appetites resulted in the Western tradition's epistemological position that wisdom (associated with the higher powers) is the domain of men. Women, who are characterized by their lower powers dominating their higher powers, are incapable of reason and deliberation and thus unable to be wise like men. This view is, again, sex polarity.

The fourth category (virtue) embraced both sex unity and sex polarity. As for the former, Plato identified men and women with their souls. As both sexes have souls, they are equal. Such equality was also seen with regard to the future of human existence: when men and women are ultimately reunited with the Forms, they will become disembodied, sexless souls, eternally equal in nature. In terms of the latter, traditional sex polarity was defended in several ways: (1) The identification of men with form and women with matter (and form is superior to matter). Thus, men are accorded an advantage over women in the pursuit of virtue. (2) The grounding of different virtues for men and women on their different societal functions. Thus, because men manage a city (a relatively superior role), their manly virtue is ruling (a relatively superior virtue), and because women manage their household (a relatively inferior role), their womanly virtue is obedience (a relatively inferior virtue). (3) The grounding of different virtues for men and women on their different rational capacities. Thus, because women are characterized by relatively inferior rational capacities, they are not capable of virtue in public, deliberative tasks. Rather, they must submit obediently to virtuous men and live out their virtues at home and in their friendship. Once again, sex polarity was the dominant view.

Tragically, this framework has exerted (and continues to exert) a widespread influence, particularly in Western societies, for well over two millennia. One appalling consequence is the dishonoring and demeaning of women.[32]

I turn now to the early church and its development of sex identity.

---

[32] Some may object to this evaluation, appealing to the fact that at least in some areas, Scripture (e.g., 1 Cor 11:3–12; Eph 5:22–33; Col 3:18–19; 1 Tim 2:12–15; 3:1–7; 5:14; Titus 2:3–5) prescribes the role and posture of men to be public/family rulership with authority and the role and posture of women to be private household management with submission. Confirmation of this view of the relationship between men and women in the early church might come from Clement of Rome's letter to the Corinthians (c. AD 96), whom he praises: "You instructed your wives to do all things with a blameless, becoming, and pure conscience, loving their husbands as in duty bound; and you taught them that, living in the rule of obedience, they should manage their household affairs becomingly, and be in every respect marked by discretion." Clement of Rome, *The First Epistle of Clement to the Corinthians*, chapter 1 in *Ante-Nicene Fathers*, ed. Alexander Roberts, James Donaldson, Philip Schaff, and Henry Wace, 10 vols. (Peabody, MA: Hendrickson, 1994), 1.5. The similarities of role and posture are striking, but this family resemblance stops at the level of action and attitude. Assuming Clement represents an overall biblical worldview as he writes, one hopes that the perspective from which he commends the church is a far cry from, and categorically opposed to, the sex polarity position as articulated and justified by the Greco-Roman philosophical tradition.

CHAPTER 5

Early Church Views of Men and Women

Due to Augustine's stature as a leading theologian and architect of the doctrine and practice of the church, this section focuses on the influence of prevailing Greco-Roman philosophies on his theological and ecclesiastical contributions in this area. Augustine held to an eclectic view of sex identity, embracing sex unity, sex polarity, and sex complementarity as different elements of his view. Again, Prudence Allen's four categories—opposites, generation, wisdom, and virtue—shape this presentation.

1. *The metaphysical question of* **opposites**: *in what ways are male and female opposites?*

All three views of sex identity can be identified in Augustine's wrestling with this category. First, his biblically grounded belief in the resurrection of the body was the basis for his embrace of sex complementarity. As he avers, "The saints [i.e., Christians] will possess at resurrection the very bodies in which they toiled in this life."[1] Furthermore—and representing a rejection of both (historically earlier versions of) sex polarity and sex unity—Augustine believed that both women's bodies and men's bodies are perfect and as such will be retained in the resurrection. According to traditional sex polarity, (1) men are naturally superior to women; (2) there will be no imperfections in heaven; therefore, (3) at the resurrection, women will be changed so as to become perfect, that is, men. Augustine decried this idea: "In the resurrection, the blemishes [imperfections] of the body will be gone, but the nature of the body will remain. And, certainly, a woman's sex is her nature and no blemish [imperfection]."[2] Therefore, women—who are women by nature and not by accident—will not be transformed from imperfect beings to perfect beings, that is, from women to men. Rather, women will be resurrected in their female bodies and men will be resurrected in their male bodies. Both alike will be eternally glorified. This is sex complementarity.

Moreover, Augustine rejected the idea at the heart of sex unity that human identity has nothing to do with the body but concerns only a sexless soul. While this Platonic notion grounded the sex unity position that men and women are equal and not significantly different, Augustine embraced sex complementarity, that is, after the resurrection, men and women are equal and significantly different.[3]

At the same time, Augustine held to a sex unity view when it comes to higher human faculties, specifically the human mind's contemplation of God. In this endeavor, whether one is a woman or a man makes no difference. He references two biblical passages in support: women and men are "co-heirs" of divine grace (1 Pet. 3:7) and, because of their oneness in

---

[1] Allen, *The Concept of Woman*, 219. The citation is Augustine, *The City of God*, 13.19.

[2] Allen, *The Concept of Woman*, 219. The citation is Augustine, *The City of God*, 12.17.

[3] Allen, *The Concept of Woman*, 220.

Christ, "there is no . . . male and female" (Gal 3:28).[4] This unity is specifically true with reference to their mind: men are made in the image of God, "where there is no sex," and women are renewed in the image of God, "where there is no sex," with the divine image located in the mind.[5] Accordingly, when male and female minds are oriented toward God and spiritual reality, women and men are equal and not different.

Of course, men and women fall short in their contemplation of God. When their minds are focused on temporal matters, they cease being in the divine image. As a consequence, and in accordance with traditional sex polarity, men are superior to women. Augustine took two steps to embrace this position. First, he affirmed what was just discussed: "As we said of the nature of the human mind, that if as a whole contemplates the truth, it is in the image of God; and when its functions are divided and something of it is diverted to the handling of temporal things, nevertheless that part which consults the truth is the image of God, but the other part, which is directed to the handling of inferior things, is not the image of God."[6] So, both men and women, when contemplating God, are in the image of God. It would seem, then, both men and women, when focused on temporal matters, would not be in the divine image.

However, with his second step, Augustine moved away from this logical implication. He used the (concept of) woman to symbolize the wrongful focus on temporal matters and the (concept of) man to symbolize the rightful focus on spiritual matters, drawing this conclusion (from 1 Cor 11:7):

---

[4] "You created man male and female, but in your spiritual grace, they are as one. Your grace no more discriminates between them according to their sex than it draws distinction between Jew and Greek or slave and freeman." Augustine, *Confessions*, 12.23.

[5] Allen, *The Concept of Woman*, 220. The citation is Augustine, *The Trinity*, 12.7 and 12.12. The citation is Augustine, *The Trinity*, 12.7.10. The citation is Augustine, *The Trinity*, 12.7.

[6] Allen, *The Concept of Woman*, 221. The citation is Augustine, *The Trinity*, 12.7 and 12.12. The citation is Augustine, *The Trinity*, 12.7.10. The citation is Augustine, *The Trinity*, 12.7.

"man only is the image and the glory of God."[7] Additionally, he appealed to the woman being created as a helper for the man (from Gen 2:18): "The woman with her husband is the image of God, so that the whole substance is one image. But when she is assigned as a helpmate, a function which pertains to her alone, then she is not the image of God, just as fully and completely as when he and the woman are joined together in one."[8] Augustine's articulation of sex polarity, based on his assignment of different symbols for men (spiritual orientation) and women (temporal orientation), underscored male superiority and female inferiority in the earthly realm apart from contemplation of God.

Allen (with my additional comments) summarizes this Augustinian complexity: "We find Augustine caught between three conflicting theories of sex identity: sex complementarity in heaven [in terms of the resurrection of male and female bodies, which are equally perfect in glorification], sex unity in the highest functions of the mind on earth [when male and female image bearers equally engage in the contemplation of God], and sex polarity in the lower functions of the mind in relation to the body on earth [as symbolized by women, who are inferior to men in terms of both image bearing and functioning as helpers for men]."[9]

2. *The natural philosophy question of* generation*: what are the respective functions of mothering and fathering in reproduction or the generation of children?*

Augustine's doctrine of generation began with God's creation of the universe and everything in it. As a corollary, and in opposition to the prevailing Greco-Roman tradition that mothers or fathers determine the sex of their

---

[7] Allen, *The Concept of Woman*, 222. The citation is Augustine, *The Literal Sense of Genesis*, 11, 42, 58.

[8] Allen, *The Concept of Woman*, 222. The citation is Augustine, *The Trinity*, 12.7 and 12.12. The citation is Augustine, *The Trinity*, 12.7.10. The citation is Augustine, *The Trinity*, 12.7.

[9] Allen, *The Concept of Woman*, 222.

child, Augustine's position affirmed God's direct work in the determination of the sex of children.[10]

Augustine's view of divine creation featured two phases with regard to the origination of human beings. The first phase in the process, based on the biblical affirmation in Genesis 1—"So God created man in his own image; he created him in the image of God; he created them male and female" (Gen 1:27)—supported sex complementarity: as divine image bearers, the man and the woman are equal yet different. This act was a generation of potentiality. The second phase, based on the narrative of Genesis 2—the man Adam is created first (Gen 2:7) and the woman Eve is created second and taken from Adam's side (Gen 2:18–24)—supported traditional sex polarity: the man and the woman are different and not equal. This act was a generation of actuality. Uniting the two passages (Genesis 1 and 2), Augustine believed that the first act of potentiality resulted in humankind as male and female, while the second act produced two actual human beings: the man Adam and the woman Eve.[11] Importantly, the creation of Eve second and from Adam's side meant that woman, as to her identity, is incomplete on her own, and she is not in the divine image of God by herself, without man, who is complete on his own, and fully in the divine image.[12] Furthermore, Augustine interpreted the woman's formation from the man's side as a reference to her primary role: to be a helper for the man in the production of other human beings. Surprisingly, Augustine limited this helpful function to procreation—"be fruitful and multiply and fill the earth" (Gen 1:28 ESV)—and denied a woman's role in vocation—"and subdue it, and have dominion" over the rest of the created order (Gen 1:28 ESV)—as well as her part in close friendship with men:

> If it is not to generate children that the woman was given to the man as a helpmate [procreation], in what could she be a help for

[10] Allen, *The Concept of Woman*, 223, 227.

[11] Allen, *The Concept of Woman*, 224–25.

[12] Allen, *The Concept of Woman*, 225.

> him? Is it to work the earth with him [vocation]? But there was no work yet that needed the help of somebody else, and if the need were there, the help of another man would have been preferable. We can say the same of the good of the presence of another person is solitude weighted on him. To live and to talk to each other [friendship], how predictable [preferable] is the companionship of two [male friends] than that of a man and a woman! . . . I do not see for what goal woman would have been given to man as a helpmate if not for generating children.[13]

Augustine affirmed sex polarity with biblical support and, apparently, did not ground it with physiological and reproductive data as was the case in the Greco-Roman tradition.[14]

3. *The epistemological question of* wisdom*: do women and men relate to wisdom in the same way?*

Augustine affirmed the equality of men and women when it comes to the possession and expression of wisdom. He grounded his sex unity position on the belief that when women fervently pursue wisdom through the exercise of their highest reason, they lose their sex identity. Indeed, in the presence of wise women, men forget that these others are women and think of them instead as men. In this realm, Augustine embraced sex unity.

At the same time, he held to sex polarity with regard to the higher and lower faculties of human nature. In this case, men symbolize the higher faculties of mind/soul and women symbolize the lower faculties. This strict dichotomy is expressed in his *Confessions*:

---

[13] Allen, *The Concept of Woman*, 225. The citation is Augustine, *The Literal Sense of Genesis*, 9, 5, 9 (cf. 9, 9, 15; and *The City of God*, 14.22).

[14] For further discussion of marriage and sexuality in the early church, see Peter Brown, *The Body and Society: Men, Women, and Sexual Renunciation in Early Christianity* (New York: Columbia University Press, 2008).

> Just as in man's soul there are two forces—one which is dominant because it deliberates [i.e., rational intelligence/reasoning power of the mind] and one which obeys because it is subject to such guidance [i.e., natural impulses such as physical appetites and bodily desires]—in the same way, in the physical sense, woman has been made for man. In her mind and in her rational intelligence, she has a nature the equal of that of a man, but in sex [i.e., as a woman] she is physically subject to him in the same way as our natural impulses need to be subjected to the reasoning power of the mind.[15]

As to the mind (separated from the body), when it is oriented toward the contemplation of God through the exercise of reason, women and men are equal with respect to wisdom. However, as to the lower realm of human nature (which is linked to the body), when it is oriented toward temporal matters, women are inferior to men and must be subject to them as lower faculties should be subject to higher faculties. Augustine held to sex polarity in this area.[16]

4. *The question of moral philosophy or* virtue*: do women and men have the same or different virtues?*

In a complicated amalgamation of positions, Augustine embraced sex complementarity, sex unity, and sex polarity in the realm of male and female virtues. First, in terms of sex complementarity, Augustine underscored that virtuous believers, whether female or male, are called saints. For example, martyrs (those who had died for the Christian faith) and confessors (those who had kept, i.e., "confessed," the faith through persecution but had not been killed) included both women and men; they were venerated for their virtuous lives and, in the first case, deaths.[17] Moreover, Augustine cham-

[15] Augustine, *Confessions*, 13.32.
[16] Allen, *The Concept of Woman*, 230.
[17] Allen, *The Concept of Woman*, 231.

pioned the four classical virtues—wisdom, courage, temperance, and justice—and the three theological virtues—faith, hope, and love—for men and women alike. Neither sex was favored in the pursuit of these honored qualities, and their attainment was crowned by the resurrection of the body that, as we have seen, maintains its sex as male or female.[18] Furthermore, Augustine held that in the pre-fall state, Adam and Eve experienced sex complementarity in which there was no superiority and inferiority and no ruling and submission. As he averred, "It is not the nature, but the fault of the woman, which brought her to get a master of her husband."[19] These positions indicate that Augustine held to sex complementarity for Adam and Eve before the fall, for the saints who achieve perfect virtue during their temporal existence, and for all resurrected Christians.

Second, and as we have discussed, Augustine also expressed sex unity for men and women during their earthly, temporal life. When women and men have their minds oriented toward God, when through reason they contemplate spiritual matters, they are in the image of God. This is the case without sexual differentiation, and thus human beings without distinction are virtuous. In further support of sex unity was Augustine's insistence that women and men alike, by the correct exercise of the freedom of their will, may be virtuous. For example, in a sharp rebuke to nuns who were dissatisfied with the leadership of their (woman) prioress, Augustine offered several regulations to rectify the situation, concluding with this prayer: "The Lord grant that you may yield loving submission to all these rules, . . . not as bondwomen under the law, but as established in freedom under grace."[20] In a repugnant example, Augustine broke with the tradition of his day that considered women who had been raped as dirty, insisting instead that "in the case of violent rape and of an unshakable intention not to yield unchaste

---

[18] Allen, *The Concept of Woman*, 231.

[19] Allen, *The Concept of Woman*, 231. The citation is Augustine, *The Literal Sense of Genesis*, 11, 37.

[20] Allen, *The Concept of Woman*, 232. The citation is Augustine, *Letter* 211 (423), 16. https://www.newadvent.org/fathers/1102211.htm.

consent, the crime is attributable only to the rapist and not at all to the one who was raped. [Against any who reject this view]. . . . I maintain the truth that not only the souls of Christian women, but also their bodies, remain holy."[21] A rape survivor who, by the right exercise of her free will, refused to acquiesce to the heinous attack, remains virtuous.

Third, as also discussed, sex polarity continued to express itself in Augustine's conception of struggles during this earthly, temporal existence. Wrestling with a theology of human embodiment, he defaulted to the view that the human body is an enemy to defeat, an obstacle to sanctification, and a source of sin. As part of this theory, Augustine considered a woman to symbolize the temptation to lure a man's mind away from its proper orientation (as a man's highest faculty) upward toward God and downward toward physical/temporal matters instead. He voiced his opinion about marriage: "There is nothing I should avoid so much as marriage. I know nothing which brings a manly mind down from the heights more than a woman's caresses and joining of bodies [i.e., sexual intercourse] without which one cannot have a wife."[22] As to the specific reason for women as the source of temptation, Augustine denied it comes as a result of their sinful intention or deceitful cunning and blamed it on "the beauty of their bodies."[23] To hinder such provocation of temptation, women should get married and subject themselves to their husbands or, if they pursue the religious life, they may forego marriage, consecrate themselves and cover their bodies, and submit to their female superiors rather than to men.[24]

Moreover, and again as we have seen, Augustine used the (concept of) woman to symbolize the lower faculties of human beings and the (concept

---

[21] Allen, *The Concept of Woman*, 232. The citation is Augustine, *The City of God*, 2.19.

[22] Allen, *The Concept of Woman*, 233. The citation is Augustine, *The Soliloquies of St. Augustine*, trans. Thomas F. Gilligan (New York: Cosmopolitan Science and Art Service, 1943), I, X, 417, p. 41.

[23] Allen, *The Concept of Woman*, 232. The citation is Augustine, *The Freedom of the Will*, 3.10.

[24] Allen, *The Concept of Woman*, 234.

of) man to symbolize the higher faculties. Applied to marriage, this means the lower faculties must be subject to the higher faculties; that is, wives must submit to their husbands. Commenting on Paul's instructions to husbands to love their wives as they love their "flesh" (Eph 5:28–29), Augustine explained:

> Flesh, then, is put for woman, in the same manner that spirit is sometimes put for husband. Wherefore? Because the one rules, the other is ruled; the one ought to command, the other to serve. For where the flesh commands and the spirit serves, the house is turned the wrong way. What can be worse than a house where the woman has the mastery over the man? But that house is rightly ordered where the man commands and the woman obeys. In like manner that man is rightly ordered where the spirit commands and the flesh serves.[25]

Just as virtue arises when the lower powers of human nature are controlled by the higher powers, so women may be virtuous in marriage when they are ruled by their husbands. Diagrammatically:

human nature	*image bearers*	*female virtue in marriage*	*male virtue in marriage*
higher faculties (mind, reason)	should rule	X	ruling, commanding
lower faculties (desires, body)	should submit	obedience, serving	X

Augustine's sex polarity is not that of Aristotle, who rooted such diverse virtues in the differences between the inferior and superior natures of women

[25] Allen, *The Concept of Woman*, 234. The citation is Augustine, *Homilies on the Gospel of John*, in *Nicene and Post-Nicene Fathers*, ed. Alexander Roberts, James Donaldson, Philip Schaff, and Henry Wace, 1st ser., 14 vols. (Peabody, MA: Hendrickson, 1994), 7:23.

and men. Rather, sex polarity for Augustine is due to the fall, the consequent disturbance in the hierarchy of the higher and lower faculties, and the need to reestablish the correct order of those faculties (the lower submitting to the higher). Women, therefore, are to obey their husbands, who are to rule over them. When this order is maintained, women may be virtuous.

While summarizing Augustine's embrace of sex polarity (our third point), it is to be recalled that he also held to (our first point) sex complementarity before the fall, for perfectly virtuous saints after the fall, and for all resurrected Christians. Moreover, he held to (our second point) sex unity when women and men orient their minds toward God as his image bearers should, and when they exercise the freedom of their will to engage in virtuous acts. Accordingly, Augustine, as a dominant force in the development of the early church's view of women and men, embraced and developed sex complementarity, sex unity, and traditional sex polarity.

Excursus: Archaeological and Ethnographic Studies Challenging This Historical Paradigm

Exactly how Allen's portrait of the seemingly ubiquitous demeaning view of women in the early church comports with archaeological and ethnographic evidence of significant female involvement in many spheres of Greco-Roman society and Jewish culture is the subject of a brief excursus.[26] Some examples of the latter, contrasting view of women follow.

---

[26] Since the time of Allen's writing of her three-volume work, scholars have directed significant attention to archaeological and ethnographic studies of women in the early centuries of the church. Some of these contributions are Celina Durgin and Dru Johnson, eds., *The Biblical World of Gender: The Daily Lives of Ancient Women and Men* (Eugene, OR: Cascade, 2022); Susan E. Hylen, *Finding Phoebe: What New Testament Women were Really Like* (Grand Rapids: Eerdmans, 2023); Susan Mathew, *Women in the Greetings of Romans 16:1–16: A Study of Mutuality and Women's Ministry in the Letter to the Romans* (London: Bloomsbury, 2013); Cynthia Long Westfall, *Paul and Gender: Reclaiming the Apostle's Vision for Men and Women in Christ* (Grand Rapids: Baker Academic, 2021); Bruce W. Winter, *Roman Wives, Roman Widows: The Appearance of New Women and the Pauline Communities*

According to Susan Mathew, at the time of Jesus and the founding of his church, "women were evidently engaged in *politeia* (πολιτεία). This is contrary to the common perceptions that wives in the first century were a 'monochrome group' who were 'confined to domestic dwellings in order to fulfil the role of dutiful wife engaged primarily in childbearing and managing the household. This attitude was assumed of women in the early Christian communities," but research demonstrates the need "to deconstruct the common perception that women were kept away from the public and played the role of the stereotypical housewife."[27] Indeed, according to Bruce Winter, "it is very unlikely that one could epitomize all first-century marriages by a single stereotype of restriction to the home and reproductive activity in the vast Roman Empire."[28]

Mathew presents various arenas in which women were active in the Greco-Roman world: (1) law courts, in which women were legal advisors in both prosecutorial and defense cases; (2) politics, through their support of candidates for office; (3) civic life, in which women held the office of magistrate and engaged in the patronage of festivals, building projects, clubs, and professional guilds; and (4) the priesthood, exemplified in their service of both male and female deities, the upkeep of religious sites, performing ritual purifications, offering sacrifices to the gods and goddesses, and supporting religious festivals.[29] Mathew also discusses the possible inclusion of women in the Jewish faith, including their participation as head of the synagogue,

---

(Grand Rapids: Eerdmans, 2003); Ross S. Kraemer, "The Other as Woman: An Aspect of Polemic among Pagans, Jews and Christians in the Greco-Roman World," in *The Other in Jewish Thought and History: Constructions of Jewish Culture and Identity*, ed. Laurence J. Silberstein and Robert L. Cohn (New York: NYU Press, 1994); Sandra L. Glahn, *Nobody's Mother: Artemis of the Ephesians in Antiquity and the New Testament* (Downers Grove: IVP Academic, 2023). Because of the emergence of these important studies, interaction with them in relationship to Allen's work is appropriate.

[27] Mathew, *Women in the Greetings of Romans 16:1–16*, 46.

[28] Mathew, *Women in the Greetings of Romans 16:1–16*, 46. She cites Winter, *Roman Wives, Roman Widows*, 6.

[29] Mathew, *Women in the Greetings of Romans 16:1–16*, 46–54.

leader in community events, elder, mother of the synagogue (perhaps a designation for an administrative functionary), and priestess (perhaps a designation for the wife or daughter of a priest but not an indication that women themselves could be priest).[30]

Celina Durgin and Dru Johnson add to this portrait of significant public female involvement in the ancient world. Women actively engaged in (1) protecting their family property by taking up legal matters in the courts and with government officials; (2) managing their household and its many undertakings such as doing business deals with clients and overseeing servants and farms; (3) extending hospitality to influential societal and political people; (4) attending banquets to engage with well-positioned citizens; (5) working as shopkeepers and business owners; (6) attending religious festivals; (7) managing large estates and fortunes; (8) benefiting the city and their clients through being patrons of leading officials' families and interests; and more.[31] Susan Hylen adds to this list of female occupations outside of typical household responsibilities: "They were mosaic workers and jewelers, musicians, singers, and actors. Many women sold produce, meat, and other products in the markets. Some women owned and ran restaurants. . . . [W]hile we may expect women to be midwives, they were also doctors and healers."[32]

How do we reconcile these two realities: the philosophical and theological portrait of women according to traditional sex polarity, and the actual participation of those women in a wide variety of significant vocational and social roles? According to Cynthia Long Westfall, "during the first century there was social ferment and some fluidity for the actual behavior of

---

[30] Mathew, *Women in the Greetings of Romans 16:1–16*, 54–64. When it comes to detailing women's roles in the Jewish faith, the difficulties include understanding the nature of synagogue head, leader of the community, elder, mother of the synagogue, and priestess, as well as the precise dating of inscriptional evidence for these designations (for example, evidence for the use of the title "elder" for women is in Greek inscriptions from the fourth or fifth century CE).

[31] Durgin and Johnson, eds., *The Biblical World of Gender*, 32–35.

[32] Hylen, *Finding Phoebe*, 44–45.

women, but very traditional concepts of gender roles were alive and well for both men and women. . . . [S]ome of the lines between the public and domestic spheres were blurred in that women were entering the public sphere in various capacities. . . . However, regardless of inconsistency with the actual behavior of women in the Hellenistic and Greco-Roman period, traditional values were still in place."[33] According to Hylen, "Though the culture deemed women to be inferior to men, nonetheless women participated in community life, including in leadership roles. People at that time did not see this as contradictory, and indeed the tension was part of the social fabric."[34] As it was then, so I will consider it: these two contrasting and seemingly irreconcilable perspectives existed in tension and, rather than trying to resolve that tension, I will accept them as functioning together.[35] For our purposes, then, even when traditional sex polarity was firmly entrenched and vastly exhibited, this framework did not necessarily so straightjacket women that what may be considered the common understanding of women and their roles was the actual case in point.

[33] Westfall, *Paul and Gender*, 17, 24. Westfall also contributes to the discussion about women's household and public roles in the early church (263–68).

[34] Hylen, *Finding Phoebe*, 3.

[35] It may be the case that a key reason for this tension is located in the fact that influential theologians and leading ecclesiastical figures expressed their frameworks for men and women in their teachings and their writings, yet "common" men and women lived out their relationships, families, vocations, and ministries on a practical level, which may or may not have corresponded to the "official" frameworks.

CHAPTER 6

Early Medieval Views of Men and Women (600–1250)

Though this section will largely focus on Thomas Aquinas, I begin with John Scotus Eriugena (800–875) because of his rejection of Augustinian sex complementarity and his neoplatonic proposal of a sex unity and sex polarity combination. Next, I briefly treat Albert the Great (1193–1280), who was Thomas's mentor. After the discussion of Aquinas, I conclude with Hildegard of Bingen (1098–1179) because of her articulation and defense of complementarity in the midst of a strong emphasis on sex polarity.

As he traced the redemptive-historical arc, John Scotus Eriugena (abbreviated JSE) affirmed sex unity before the fall, traditional sex polarity after the fall, and a return to sex unity for the redeemed after the resurrection.[1] He admitted that his proposal was based on reason rather than revelation.

In terms of the original creation of Adam and Eve, JSE opined, "According to divine intention, there would be simply man [i.e., an

[1] Allen, *The Concept of Woman*, 240.

undivided (= sexless) human being], not to be divided by the names of male and female."[2] JSE's "divine intention" was not informed by Scripture but closely resembled the neo-Platonist Plotinus's notion of an original unity/oneness and subsequent multiplicity/fragmentation.[3] In this original state of oneness, undivided human beings would expand the human race by means of angelic reproduction—some type of intellectual act—rather than the bodily act of copulation. Tragically, the fall resulted in the division into men and women who would reproduce through sexual intercourse.[4] The reversal of this sex polarity begins with conversion and advances to the resurrection: "This division has taken the beginning of its unification in Christ Jesus, who truly showed in Himself an example of the restoration of human nature, and exhibited a likeness of the resurrection that is to come."[5] Thus, after the resurrection, sex unity will once again characterize humankind with no division into male and female. Whatever one may say of JSE's

---

[2] Allen, *The Concept of Woman*, 240. The citation is John Scotus Erigena, *Periphyseon (The Division of Nature)*, trans. I. P. Sheldon-Williams, rev. John J. O'Meara (Washington, DC: Dumbarton Oaks, 1987), Book 2, 532C, p. 132.

[3] Allen, *The Concept of Woman*, 241. "For, as our reason teaches us, this world would not have burst forth into a variety of [both] sensible species and the diverse multiplicities of their parts if God had not foreseen the fall and ruin of the first man when he abandoned the unity of his nature; so that at least, after his fall from spiritual to corporeal things, from eternal to temporal, from incorruptible to perishable, from the heights to the depths, from the spiritual man to the psychical man, from a simple nature to the division of the sexes . . . [man] would plead his return to the first state of his honor." John Scotus Erigena, *Periphyseon*, Book 2, 540A, p. 140.

[4] "[Such was] the intention of the divine plan for the creation of man had He not foreknown that he would sin. For he would be 'simply man' created in the simplicity of his nature, multiplied in intelligible numbers, as the holy angels are multiplied. But oppressed by the guilt of his disobedience, he suffered the division of his nature into male and female, and since he was unwilling to keep to the divine mode of multiplying himself [i.e., angelic reproduction], he was degraded by a just decree to the bestial [irrational, animalistic sexual intercourse] and to the corruptible proliferation out of male and female." John Scotus Erigena, *Periphyseon*, Book 2, 532D–533A, p. 132.

[5] John Scotus Erigena, *Periphyseon*, Book 2, 533A, pp. 132–33.

articulation of sex unity, his work defending his view was condemned at the Council of Paris in 1225.

Albert the Great (1193–1280), though best known as mentor to Thomas Aquinas, developed Aristotle's position as his star pupil would monumentally do later. In terms of the category of opposites, Albert's specific points included sex polarity's devaluation of women as contrary to men, cold rather than hot like men, inferior to men in intellect, predominantly emotional rather than rational, submissive and silent rather than ruling and speaking, matter rather than form, passive rather than active—in short, "the female is a misbegotten male."[6] Albert also made advances on some of Aristotle's ideas of generation, claiming some role for women in procreation, some role for men in contributing materially to their offspring's bodily aspect, and the primary role for God—rather than the man—in supplying a soul to conception.[7] Still, he repeated Aristotle's view that a female is conceived as a result of some defect in the male seed/sperm, a weakness that prevents the seed from producing a male, as is its intention. Thus, the female provides the passive principle in procreation, while the male provides the active principle (soul power).[8]

As for the category of wisdom, Albert affirmed that a woman's rationality lacks authority to govern her irrational soul; thus, her intellect and will are weaker than those in a man, her passions and bodily appetites are stronger than in a man, and she is unable to plan properly. Women, therefore, are wise only in terms of true opinion but not practical wisdom like men. They should be silent in public; and they should teach only individuals or small groups of people, not a universal audience (as men may do). In terms of virtues, a woman is virtuous by obeying a man who governs her, a directive aid that is needed due to her weaker rationality that results in her making poor choices. Whatever virtues a woman may have, she should express them

---

[6] Allen, *Concept of Woman*, vol. 2, 117–18. This is Allen's summary of Albert's position from his *Quaestiones super de animalibus*, *Summa de creaturis*, and *Commentary on Aristotle's Metaphysics*.

[7] Allen, *Concept of Woman*, vol. 2, 120–21.

[8] Allen, *Concept of Woman*, vol. 2, 175.

in her private household rather than in public. Susceptible to the influence of her emotions, a woman may lack understanding, continence, and confidence. Worse yet, she may be moved to evil.[9] Albert opined: "It is said commonly, proverbially, and vulgarly, that women are more false and frail, diffident, shameless, and deceitfully persuasive, and that briefly a woman is nothing other than a devil fashioned in human appearance. . . . [T]he female is less suitable for moral [laws] than the male."[10]

Because of Thomas Aquinas's stature as a leading theologian and architect of the doctrine and practice of the Roman Catholic Church, the next section provides a robust discussion of his theological and ecclesiastical contributions while highlighting the influence of Aristotelian philosophy on them.

In general, while Thomas Aquinas made strides to affirm the complementarity of the two sexes and the equality of men and women in terms of infused wisdom and the theological virtues (faith, hope, and love), he echoed Aristotle in the following: (1) men are more perfect reflections of the image of God and women are less perfect reflections; (2) men/fathers as the active sex provide the soul and women as the passive sex provide the matter in reproduction; (3) men, who are characterized by reason, are more capable of the classical/cardinal virtues (wisdom, courage, temperance, and judgment/justice), natural wisdom, and speech, while women, who are weak in reason, are less capable of the classical/cardinal virtues and are (to be) silent; and (4) men rule, being strong in the cardinal virtues and engaging in the public sphere of activity, while women obey, being weak in the cardinal virtues and engaging in the private sphere of activity.

Aquinas's specific development of the four categories of questions—namely, opposites, generation, wisdom, and virtue—is as follows.

---

[9] Allen, *Concept of Woman*, vol. 2, 176–79.

[10] Allen, *Concept of Woman*, vol. 2, 123. Her citation is Albert the Great, *Quaestiones super de animalibus*, XV, q 11.

1. *The metaphysical question of* opposites*: in what ways are male and female opposites?*

Aquinas articulated and defended both traditional sex polarity and sex complementarity in numerous areas. He expressed these two positions in terms of bearing the divine image, degrees of perfection and presence, the resurrection of embodied believers, contributions in reproduction, reason, and wisdom (whether acquired or infused).

Aquinas viewed divine image bearing as pertaining equally to men and women (sex complementarity) while also maintaining that women reflect that image less perfectly than men (sex polarity). He did not ground his view of equality on the idea that one's sex—male or female—was irrelevant to the definition of the image of God. On the contrary, Aquinas believed that personal identity was holistic, consisting of both the immaterial aspect (soul/form/mind/reason/intellect) and the material aspect (body/matter). He appealed to the account of divine creation (Gen 1:27): "Genesis says: God created man after his own image, after the image of God he created them. But the distinction of male and female refers to the body. So, God's image in man refers to the body as well as to the mind."[11] Being created as holistic beings, both women and men are divine image bearers. Additionally (yet without contradiction to this last point), Aquinas believed that the divine image is mostly associated with the higher faculties (mind, reason, intellect), and these higher powers are not related to the body: "The image of God is common to both sexes, being in the mind, which has no distinction of sex."[12] Accordingly, Aquinas concluded, "God's image is found equally in both man and woman as regards that point in which the idea of 'image' is principally realized, namely, an intelligent nature."[13] This is sex complementarity.

[11] Allen, *The Concept of Woman*, 388. Aquinas, ST I a, q. 93, a. 6.
[12] Allen, *The Concept of Woman*, 388. Aquinas, ST I a, q. 93, a. 6.
[13] Allen, *The Concept of Woman*, 388. Aquinas, ST I a, q. 93, a. 4.

At the same time, Aquinas embraced sex polarity on the basis of degrees of perfection.[14] He differentiated male image bearers and female image bearers on the basis of a difference in reflection of the divine image: relatively speaking, men reflect the divine image more perfectly, while women, who are indeed created in the divine image, reflect that image less perfectly. He did not justify this difference by appealing to Augustine's position, noted above, that when it comes to the higher faculties of human nature, when women and men orient themselves toward God and contemplate spiritual matters, they are equal in bearing the divine image. However, when women—who are characterized by the lower faculties, symbolize the wrongful focus on temporal matters, and have been assigned the role of helpmate to men—orient themselves toward temporal existence and marital function, they do not rightly reflect God's image.

Rather than an Augustinian grounding for sex polarity, Aquinas proposed a difference between male image bearers and female image bearers on the basis of degrees of presence, with men containing the image more perfectly than women. This degree of perfection was due to God's creation of Adam (and, consequently, of all men) immediately and directly, a creative act that was not repeated in the case of Eve (and, consequently, of all women), who was derived from Adam (and, consequently, for all women from men). Aquinas developed his idea from the narrative of Genesis (2:7, 18–25) as well as appealing to a Pauline statement (1 Cor 11:7–9):

> God's image is found in man in a way in which it is not found in woman; for man is the beginning and the end of woman, just as God is the beginning and end of all creation. Thus, after saying that

[14] Aquinas maintained that being itself, as well as transcendental excellencies such as truth, beauty, and goodness, are patient of degrees of perfection. For example, God himself is the most perfect being, with all creatures (e.g., angels, humans) being less perfect beings. Also, there is more goodness and less goodness. See Thomas Aquinas's five proofs for the existence of God, the fourth of which is an argument from degrees of perfection. ST, 1 a, q. 2, art. 3.

> "the man is the image and glory of God, while the woman is the glory of man," the apostle goes on to show why he says it, and adds, "for the man was not from the woman, but the woman from the man; and the man was not created for the woman, but the woman for man."[15]

Ultimately, Aquinas grounded this distinction in degrees of perfection by analogy with God's creation of the world: "As God is the principle of the whole universe, so the first man, in likeness of God, was the principle of the whole human race."[16] Aquinas extended this analogy to the distinction in degrees of perfection between all men and all women: "The male among humans has more of the principles of source with respect to the woman. . . . For this reason, it was more fitting that the female human being be taken from the male."[17] Possessing more "source principles" than do women, men reflect the divine image more perfectly. As Allen diagrams Aquinas's position:[18]

first principle of the world	God the Father	pure actuality
first principle of humanity	Adam	direct image of God
first principle of a child	man, the more perfect image of God	woman, the less perfect image of God

To be noticed is the attribution of "pure actuality" (with no mixture of potentiality, which is linked to materiality) to God, a Thomistic/Aristotelian perfection of the divine being. As applied to the scale of perfection, God is

---

[15] Allen, *The Concept of Woman*, 388. Aquinas, ST I a, q. 93, a. 4.

[16] Allen, *The Concept of Woman*, 388. Aquinas, ST I a, q. 92, a. 1–2.

[17] Allen, *The Concept of Woman*, 387. Aquinas, *Commentary on the Four Books of Sentences of Peter Lombard*, Book 2, Dist. 18, Question 1.

[18] Allen, *The Concept of Woman*, 387.

the most perfect being, followed by angels (pure immaterial beings with no materiality), then human beings (both immaterial and material), next animals, and finally plants.[19] Within the category of humanity, Aquinas also located a degree of perfection: because men are (1) closer to the pure actuality of God, (2) created directly in the divine image, and (3) the principle of their children, they are superior to women.[20] With these views, Aquinas clearly embraced sex polarity.

With his last point about relative perfection of men and women, Aquinas returned to sex complementarity. In accordance with Aristotle, Aquinas maintained that though men and women are significantly different (sex polarity), their differences do not render them distinct species/kinds of human beings (sex complementarity).[21] Thus, while their differences mean that an individual man is superior to an individual woman, their equality-with-variety as one species/kind (humanity) undergirds the perfection of humanity: "Just as a variety in the grading of things contributes to the perfection of the universe, so the variety of sex makes for perfection of human nature."[22] The difference between men and women is a matter of degree of perfection and not an absolute difference in kind (humanity).[23]

A question arises: when believers are perfected in the future—which means they will be perfected bodily, as the resurrection is a physical restoration—will their glorified bodies be the same sex as their earthly bodies? Aquinas rejected the well-established earlier answer based on two ideas: the natural superiority of men to women and the removal of imperfections in the heavenly state, and the implication that women will be

[19] Allen, *The Concept of Woman*, 389.

[20] Allen, *The Concept of Woman*, 389.

[21] Allen, *The Concept of Woman*, 389–90.

[22] Allen, *The Concept of Woman*, 389. Aquinas, *Summa Contra Gentiles*, II, 62, 7. See also Aquinas, ST I a, q. 99, a. 2.

[23] Allen, *The Concept of Woman*, 390.

perfected by being resurrected as men.[24] As already discussed, Augustine had denounced this answer, arguing that one's sex is one's nature and not an imperfection; therefore, men will be resurrected as perfected men and women will be resurrected as perfected women.[25] Aquinas also decried this answer but in the way just discussed: he proposed that the variety of sex is more perfect than one sex and will lead to the perfection of humanity; indeed, this "diversity is becoming [appropriate to] the perfection of the species. . . . Therefore, just as men [redeemed human beings, not males] will rise again of various stature, so will they rise again of different sex. . . . It is in the intention of universal nature, which requires both sexes for the perfection of the human species."[26]

Combining two seemingly disparate views, Aquinas embraced two positions: First, the position that, by nature/God's intention in general, an individual man is more perfect than an individual woman, for two reasons. First, the man is directly created in the divine image and more fully reflects it. He is closer to the pure actuality of God, and possesses the principle of procreation; thus, an individual woman is by nature/God's intention imperfect. Second, the position that, by nature/God's intention generally, "the two sexes were better than one, and the 'imperfection' of the generation of an individual woman was balanced by the 'perfection' of women's generation in

---

[24] Allen, *The Concept of Woman*, 391. As Aquinas framed the (wrong) answer: "That which is produced incidentally and beside the intention of nature will not rise again, since all error will be removed at the resurrection. Now the female sex is produced beside the intention of nature, through a fault of the power of the seed [i.e., sperm] which is unable to bring the matter of the fetus to the male form: therefore, the Philosopher [i.e., Aristotle] says [*De Animal.* xvi, i.e., *De Generat. Animal,* ii] that the female is a misbegotten male. Therefore, the female sex will not rise again." Aquinas, ST, Suppl. IIIae, q. 81, art. 3.

[25] Allen, *The Concept of Woman*, 219. Her citation is Augustine, *The City of God*, 12.17.

[26] Allen, *The Concept of Woman*, 391. Her citation is Aquinas, ST, Suppl. IIIae, q. 81, art. 3.

general."[27] In this roundabout way, Aquinas embraced sex complementarity in the midst of sex polarity.

2. *The natural philosophy question of* generation*: what are the respective functions of mothering and fathering in reproduction or the generation of children?*

Following Aristotle, Aquinas held that the birth of a woman is a mistake of nature: "The active principle in the male seed [sperm] always tends towards the generation of a male offspring, which is more perfect than the female. From this it follows that conception of a female offspring is something of an accident in the order of nature."[28] Aquinas offered several ideas for how this error of nature takes place: some debilitation of the active power of the sperm, which then fails to produce a man like itself; the unsuitability of the matter contributed by the woman; and/or some alteration introduced by an outside influence like the damp south wind.[29]

As before, this difference of perfection or imperfection of nature/God's intention on an individual basis must be tempered by Aquinas's insistence that, according to nature/God's intention in general, the reality of two sexes leads to the perfection—here, understood as the multiplication—of humanity: "Only as regards nature in the individual is female something defective and 'manque' [i.e., missing the mark]. . . . But with reference to nature in the species as a whole, the female is not something 'manque,' but is according to the tendency of nature, and is directed to the work of creation."[30] In other words, the sperm's "hitting the mark" in the individual process of procreation appropriately results in a male child half the time, and the sperm's "missing the mark" in the individual process of procreation

[27] Allen, *The Concept of Woman*, 392.

[28] Allen, *The Concept of Woman*, 392. Thomas Aquinas, *Truth* (Chicago: Henry Regnery, 1952), art. 9, p. 245.

[29] Allen, *The Concept of Woman*, 392. Aquinas, ST I a, q. 75, a. 4.

[30] Allen, *The Concept of Woman*, 393. Aquinas, ST I a, q. 75, a. 4.

mistakenly results in a female child half the time. Still, despite this seemingly error-filled process, God intends it for the expansion of the human race. Against John Scotus Eriugena's view that the fall introduced the division of humanity into male and female, Aquinas underscored that God by his creative act of human beings willed both sexes: "When God established a [human] nature, he brought into being not only male but the female too."[31]

To summarize, Aquinas held to (1) sex polarity in the case of the individual procreation of a man or woman and (2) sex complementarity in the case of the human race as a whole.

As for the respective functions of mothering and fathering in reproduction or the generation of children, Aquinas followed Aristotle in underscoring that "the active power resides in the male's sperm . . . while the material of the fetus is supplied by the female."[32] Simply put, the father provides the child's form while the mother provides the child's matter. At the same time, Aquinas did not believe that the sperm contains the soul. Rather, he held that it supplies "soul power" that "acts by disposing matter [provided by the mother] and forming it for the reception of the soul" resulting in a child.[33] Accordingly, the father is the first principle/active source of a child, supplying its form, while the mother is the passive receptacle (for the active principle) of a child, supplying its matter.[34]

This strong sense of sex polarity in the procreative functions led clearly to the superiority of men as the active sex and the inferiority of women as the passive sex. Again, this disparity is true on the level of individual men, individual women, and the individual children they generate. But sex complementarity is true with regard to the human race as a whole: by divine design, the difference between men and women leads to the multiplication of humanity and its eventual perfection in the age to come.

---

[31] Allen, *The Concept of Woman*, 392. Aquinas, ST I a, q. 99, a. 1.

[32] Allen, *The Concept of Woman*, 393. Aquinas, ST I a, q. 118, a. 1.

[33] Allen, *The Concept of Woman*, 394. Thomas Aquinas, *On the Power of God* (Westminster, MD: Newman, 1952), Quest. 3, art. 9, p. 158.

[34] Allen, *The Concept of Woman*, 395.

3. *The epistemological question of* wisdom*: do women and men relate to wisdom in the same way?*

In his discussion of wisdom, Aquinas presented it as a human virtue as well as a divine gift:

> It belongs to the wisdom that is an intellectual virtue to pronounce right judgment about divine things after reason has made its inquiry, but it belongs to wisdom as a gift of the Spirit to judge aright about them on account of connaturality with them. . . . Now this sympathy or connaturality for divine things is the result of charity, which unites us to God, according to 1 Corinthians 6:17: "He who is joined to the Lord, is one spirit." Consequently wisdom, which is a gift, has its cause in the will, which cause is charity, but it has its essence in the intellect, whose act is to judge aright.[35]

For Aquinas, in the case of wisdom as a virtue, men are superior to women because of their higher faculties of intellect and reason, but in the case of wisdom as a divine gift, men and women are alike because the infusion of grace is the same for both sexes.

In the first case of wisdom as a virtue, Aquinas mirrored Aristotle's position that the female's natural faculty of reason is weaker than that of a man's faculty. Specifically, "the female, since she is free, has the power of deliberating, although her deliberation is weak. And the reason for this is that her reason, because of the tenderness of her nature, weakly adheres to decisions and is quickly drawn away from them because of particular emotions (e.g., desire, anger, fear, or such like)."[36] Accordingly, a woman's weaker intellectual abilities, due to the inconstancy of her nature being subject to certain (debilitating) emotions, results in greater difficulty at arriving

---

[35] Allen, *The Concept of Woman*, 399. Her citation is Aquinas, ST IIae, Q. 45, a. 2.

[36] Allen, *The Concept of Woman*, 399. Her citation is Thomas Aquinas, *Commentary on Aristotle's* Politics, trans. Richard J. Regan (Indianapolis: Hacket, 2007), Book 1, Chap. 10, Comment 7 (p. 72).

at a correct judgment through rational investigation. In other words, female wisdom is problematic.

Moreover, according to Aquinas, "to govern and judge belong to the wise person;"[37] thus, because of their deficit of wisdom, women should not rule but be submissive instead. Addressing submission in the civil realm—a subjection that existed for the welfare of human beings even before their fall into sin—Aquinas pronounced, "Good order would have been wanting [lacking] in the human family if some were not governed by others wiser than themselves. So, by such a kind of subjection, woman is naturally subject to man, because in man the discretion of reason predominates."[38] In this view, Aquinas followed Aristotle who, as we have seen, claimed that the higher/rational faculty of female nature lacks authority to rule over its lower faculties; thus, women cannot be wise in the same way as men and, therefore, should not rule but be in submission. They should not participate in public life.

Consequently, for Aquinas, a particular female virtue is silence: "It belongs to the character and worthiness of women to be silent, since it proceeds from the modesty due them. But silence does not belong to the character of men. Rather, it belongs to their character that they speak when it is fitting. And so also St. Paul in 1 Cor. 14:34–35 warns women to be silent in the churches and ask their husbands at home if they wish to learn anything."[39]

Aquinas embraced sex polarity when it comes to wisdom as an intellectual virtue.

In the second case of wisdom as a divine gift, Aquinas explained how it is distinguished from the intellectual virtue: "The wisdom which is called a gift of the Holy Spirit differs from that which is an acquired

[37] Allen, *The Concept of Woman*, 393. Her citation is Aquinas, ST I a, q. 1, a. 6.

[38] Allen, *The Concept of Woman*, 388. Her citation is Aquinas, ST I a, q. 92, a. 1.

[39] Aquinas, *Commentary on Aristotle's* Politics, Book 1, Chap. 10, Comment 8 (p. 73).

intellectual virtue, for the latter is attained by human effort, whereas the former is 'descending from above' (James 3:15)."[40] Though Aquinas did not pronounce a judgment on whether women can obtain such infused wisdom in the same way that men can, it seems that it would be the case because a divine gift is not extended nor received on the basis of human nature, sex, intellectual capacity, role of ruling or submitting, and more. Apparently, then, Aquinas held to sex complementarity in regard to the divine gift of wisdom.

4. *The question of moral philosophy or* virtue*: do women and men have the same or different virtues?*

Aquinas made a distinction between the classical/cardinal virtues (wisdom, courage, temperance, and judgment/justice) and the theological virtues (faith, hope, and love). Extending the last discussion of two types of wisdom, he distinguished the former virtues as being acquired by human effort and the latter virtues as coming from God as infused graces: "Some moral and intellectual virtues can indeed be caused in us by our actions: but such are not proportionate to the theological virtues. Therefore, it was necessary for us to receive, from God immediately [directly, and not by acquisition through human effort], others that are proportionate to these [theological] virtues."[41] Building on what he presented above, Aquinas maintained that women are less capable than are men as to the development of the cardinal virtues of wisdom, courage, temperance, and justice; but women and men are equally capable of receiving the infused virtues of faith, hope, and love.

In the first case, Aquinas rehearsed what has been discussed previously: because of certain female weaknesses, they are less capable of

[40] Allen, *The Concept of Woman*, 400. Her citation is Aquinas, ST IIae, Q. 45, a. 1.

[41] Allen, *The Concept of Woman*, 402. Her citation is Aquinas, ST Ia–IIae, Q. 63, a. 3.

ordering themselves for the acquisition of the cardinal virtues than are men. Consequently, they are not to rule as the ability to rule is closely linked to the capacity for reason, which is inferior in women.

> We should likewise consider the matter regarding moral [cardinal] virtues, since all human beings partake of them, but not in the same way. Rather, each one partakes of them as much as necessary for one's own task. And, so, the one who rules, whether over the political community, slaves, wife, or sons, needs to have complete moral virtue, since his task is absolutely the work of a master builder (i.e., a chief craftsman). For, as the chief craftsman directs and commands his assistants who do manual work, so the ruler directs his subjects. And, so, he has the duty of reason, which is related as the chief craftsman to the inferior parts of the soul. And, so, the ruler needs to have complete reason, but each of the others who are subjects has as much reason and virtue as the ruler conveys to them (i.e., they need to have as much as suffices to follow the direction of the ruler by fulfilling his commands).[42]

Aquinas concluded:

> And, so, it is clear that some moral [cardinal] virtue, namely, for example, moderation, courage, and justice, belongs to all of the aforementioned subjects. But the same virtue does not belong to men and women and other subjects, as Socrates thought. Rather, the courage of men is to command, namely, that no fear cause them to fail to order what should be done, but women and any subjects need to have subservient courage, namely, that they do not fail to do their duty out of fear. So, also, courage in the commander of the army and that of soldiers are different. And we should say the same about all the other virtues that concern

[42] Aquinas, *Commentary on Aristotle's* Politics, Book 1, Chap. 10, Comment 7 (pp. 72–73).

> ruling in the ruler and serving in subjects. And this makes clear that these virtues do not differ by more or less but in some respect by reason.[43]

This is sex polarity in relation to the cardinal virtues.

In summary, both men and women participate in (i.e., can acquire) all the cardinal virtues—wisdom, courage, temperance, and justice—but not in the same manner as men do. It depends on one's reason and station in life and society. Men, in whom the higher/rational faculties exercise authority over their lower/irrational faculties, are to rule over women using well-developed reason and the cardinal virtues. Such is the case because women, whose higher/rational faculties lack authority over their lower/irrational faculties, receive the appropriate reason and sufficient virtue to submit to those in authority over them. Thus, in the example of courage, men possess it for courageous ruling, while women possess the virtue for courageous obedience.[44]

---

[43] Thomas Aquinas, *Commentary on Aristotle's* Politics, trans. Richard J. Regan (Indianapolis: Hacket, 2007), Book 1, Chap. 10, Comment 7 (pp. 72–73).

[44] Aquinas specifies three reasons for this taxis/ordering. The first, as just seen, has to do with women's relatively weaker reasoning capacity: "The female needs the male, not merely for the sake of generation . . . but also for the sake of government [i.e., ruling], since the male is both more perfect in his reasoning and stronger in his [higher/rational] powers." Allen, *The Concept of Woman*, 403. Her citation is Aquinas, *Summa Contra Gentiles*, III, II, 123, 3. The second finds its basis in the manner of creation: Eve was taken from the side of Adam. Working with both Aristotle (in his *Ethics* 8.12) and the Genesis (2:18–25) narrative, Aquinas offered: "The human male and female are united, not only for generation [procreation], as with other animals, but also for the purpose of domestic life, in which each has his or her particular duty, and in which the man is the head of the woman. Therefore, it was suitable for the woman to be made out of man, as out of her principle." Allen, *The Concept of Woman*, 403. Her citation is Aquinas, ST I a, q. 92, a. 2. The third reason for this ordering echoes Aquinas's earlier notion of degrees of perfection among men and women: "Woman is by nature of lower capacity and quality than man; for the active cause [the man] is always more honorable than the passive [the woman]." Allen, *The Concept of Woman*, 403. Her citation is Aquinas, ST I a, q. 92, a. 1.

While embracing sex polarity in relation to the cardinal virtues, Aquinas held to sex complementarity in the case of theological virtues. As presented in the discussion of wisdom as a divine gift, it makes sense that Aquinas would consider the development of faith, hope, and love as infused virtues to be equal in both women and men.

Additionally, Aquinas denied that male ruling and female submission continue after the resurrection; thus, he championed sex complementarity in the realm of virtues in the age to come: "Woman is subject to man on account of the frailty of nature, as regards both vigor of soul and strength of body. After the resurrection, however, the difference in those points will be not on account of the difference of sex, but by reason of the difference of merits."[45] Extrapolating from Aquinas's point about female submission disappearing after the resurrection, it seems right to conclude that he believed that there will be no difference between men and women in terms of virtues in the future.

To conclude, Aquinas embraced both sex polarity and sex complementarity in the four areas of metaphysics, natural science, epistemology, and virtue. As for sex polarity, four points stand out: (1) In this earthly existence, men more perfectly reflect the divine image than do women; thus, in terms of a hierarchy of being, men are superior to women. (2) Men, reflecting God as Father of the world, are the first/active principle in human reproduction, while women are the passive sex. (3) Men, due to their higher/rational faculties being able to rule over their lower/irrational faculties, are more capable of obtaining wisdom and consequently are (to be) characterized by speech; oppositely, women, because their higher/rational faculties are without authority over their lower/irrational faculties, are less capable of obtaining wisdom, and consequently are (to be) characterized by silence. (4) Men, because they are capable of acquiring the cardinal virtues, (are to) rule and engage in the public sphere, while women, because of their lesser

---

[45] Allen, *The Concept of Woman*, 403–4. Aquinas, ST Suppl., IIIae, q. 81, art. 3, reply to objection 2.

capability of acquiring the cardinal virtues, (are to) obediently submit and engage in the private sphere.

As for sex complementarity, Aquinas again offered four points: (1) In this earthly existence, even though men are in the divine image more than women are, the reality of the two sexes is more perfect than if there were only one sex; moreover, in the age to come after the resurrection, men and women will alike perfectly reflect the image of God. (2) By God's will and the intention of nature, there are men and women. (3) Women and men alike are capable of receiving the gift of wisdom through the Holy Spirit. (4) Women and men alike are able to possess the theological virtues because faith, hope, and love are infused graces.[46]

---

[46] While representing Scripture and theology, Aquinas's views also exhibited the strong influence of Aristotle, and they have many implications, represented by three specific applications in the areas of image bearing, procreation, and virtue. The first is the limitation of the conferring of the Roman Catholic Church's Sacrament of Holy Orders upon qualified men. Allen, *The Concept of Woman*, 404. As Aquinas phrased it, the issue is "Whether the female sex is an impediment to receiving Orders," and he affirmed, "Since it is not possible in the female sex to signify eminence of degree, for a woman is in the state of subjection, it follows that she cannot receive the sacrament of Order." Allen, *The Concept of Woman*, 404. Her citation is Aquinas, ST Suppl., IIIae, q. 39, art. 1. Because women reflect the divine image less fully than do men, and because priests must reflect the image of Christ in their very being (even their bodily reality) and in their ruling, women are precluded from becoming priest. The priesthood, conferred by the Sacrament of Holy Orders, is reserved for men alone.

The second application is found in Aquinas's reply to the question, "Whether a man ought to love his mother more than his father?" Allen, *The Concept of Woman*, 405. His response flowed from his view of the man as the chief principle of children in reproduction: "Strictly speaking, the father should be loved more than the mother. For the father and mother are loved as principles of our natural origin. Now the father is principle in a more excellent way than the mother, because he is the active principle, while the mother is a passive and material principle." Allen, *The Concept of Woman*, 405. Her citation is Aquinas, *Commentary on the Four Books of Sentences of Peter Lombard*, II, II, Q. 26, Art. 10. 1. Traditional sex polarity has an important implication for the disparity of love for one's parents.

Over the course of the last one thousand years, theology in general, and Roman Catholic theology in particular, has embraced, modified, corrected, and supplemented Thomistic theology and philosophy. At the same time, it should be recalled that in his papal encyclical *Aeterni Patris* (August 4, 1879), Pope Leo XIII proclaimed Aquinas's writings to be the theological/philosophical framework for the Roman Catholic Church. Indeed, the pope urged the Church "in all earnestness to restore the golden wisdom of St. Thomas, and to spread it far and wide for the defense and beauty of the Catholic faith, for the good of society, and for the advantage of all the sciences."[47] While I affirm that some of Aquinas' positions make good contributions in the area of complementarity, I also plead that sober caution be exercised when it comes to some of his (clearly mistaken) views.

I conclude this section on early medieval church views with a brief treatment of Hildegard of Bingen (1098–1179) because of her articulation and defense of complementarity in the midst of a strong emphasis on traditional sex polarity.[48] As before, her answer to the four questions provides the framework for discussion.

The third application concerns the virtue of friendship. Allen, *The Concept of Woman*, 405–6. Specifically, Aquinas insisted that friendships are egalitarian in nature: "Friendship consists in equality." Allen, *The Concept of Woman*, 406. Her citation is Aquinas, *Summa Contra Gentiles*, III, II, 124–25. While Aristotle maintained that women are inferior to men in this virtue, Aquinas disagreed, pointing to the extensive and intensive relationship between a husband and wife: "The greater the friendship is, the more solid and long lasting it will be. Now, there seems to be the greatest friendship between husband and wife," not only because of sexual intercourse, "but also in partnership of the whole range of domestic activity." Allen, *The Concept of Woman*, 405. Her citation is Aquinas, *Summa Contra Gentiles*, III, II, 123, 6. Consequently, men and women are equally virtuous in the realm of friendship.

[47] Pope Leo XIII, *Aeterni Patris: On the Restoration of Christian Philosophy* (August 4, 1879). https://www.vatican.va/content/leo-xiii/en/encyclicals/documents/hf_l-xiii_enc_04081879_aeterni-patris.html

[48] Prudence Allen admiringly calls Hildegard "the foundress of the sex complementarity position." Allen, *The Concept of Woman*, 292.

1. *The metaphysical question of* opposites*: in what ways are male and female opposites?*

Using the Aristotelian theory of the elements—with fire and air being the two higher elements and water and earth being the two lower elements—Hildegard maintained that man is more like fire, the highest element, and earth, the lowest element, while woman is more like air and water, the middle elements. With this identification, she averred that the two sexes balance out each other, with neither sex superior nor inferior to the other. Theologically, Hildegard underscored man's association with earth: Adam was created from the dust of the ground. As for woman, she is not associated with earth—Eve was taken from Adam's body—and thus possesses "an airy character, a very artistic talent and a previous virality, for the burden of the earth did not press upon her."[49]

Hildegard also emphasized that both men and women are created in the image of God. Because God has both masculine and feminine aspects, Hildegard maintained that both male and female image bearers reflect this duality in their sexual identity and nature. Thus, within the souls of both men and women, there exist both masculine qualities (strength, courage, and justice) and feminine qualities (mercy, penance, and grace). Hildegard insisted that the two sexes, which are equally important, develop both feminine and masculine qualities. Accordingly, though Hildegard embraced (what we call) gender essentialism (men possess certain characteristics and women possess other characteristics) she did not hold that such characteristics are completely unique to one or the other sex but should be fully developed in both sexes.[50] This view is sex complementarity.

---

[49] Hildegard of Bingen, *Heilkunde: das Buch von den Grund und Wesen und der Heilung der Krankheiten (Causas et Curae)*, trans. Jasmin el Kordi-Schmitt (Salzburg: O. Müller Verlag, 1972), 103. Allen, *Concept of Woman*, 297.

[50] Allen, *Concept of Woman*, 297–98.

2. *The natural philosophy question of* generation*: what are the respective functions of mothering and fathering in reproduction or the generation of children?*

For Hildegard, the generation of children was different before and after the fall. Before the fall, reproduction did not involve sexual intercourse: a woman generated children by herself. After the fall, which occasioned the descent of testicles and the presence of generative seed (sperm) in man, reproduction began to occur through sexual intercourse. Hildegard followed a modified Aristotelian view of reproduction, with the man contributing a cold seed/sperm that was subsequently heated up and strengthened by the woman's blood and enlivened by God's work of implanting a soul. She also insisted that human existence is a holistic integration of body and soul, an integration that means that in the resurrection, maleness and femaleness will persist and not be destroyed (against John Scotus Eriugena's sex unity view). Hildegard's perspective, while incorrect from a reproductive perspective but correct from a resurrection perspective, made an advance toward sex complementarity.[51]

3. *The epistemological question of* wisdom*: do women and men relate to wisdom in the same way?*

Hildegard set forth four types of men and four types of women.[52] She called for both sexes to develop a self-knowledge of the type of person they are, a self-awareness that requires wisdom to "learn about one's own basic material constitution and how this kind of personality might affect other people."[53] This pursuit of self-knowledge through wisdom is the same for both women and men, which is sex complementarity.

---

[51] Allen, *Concept of Woman*, 298–302.

[52] Allen, *Concept of Woman*, 303–9.

[53] Allen, *Concept of Woman*, 305.

4. *The question of moral philosophy or* virtue*: do women and men have the same or different virtues?*

As noted above, Hildegard maintained that male image bearers with their masculine virtues of strength, courage, and justice should develop feminine virtues of mercy, penance, and grace to be fully human. Similarly, female image bearers with their feminine virtues of mercy, penance, and grace should develop masculine virtues of strength, courage, and justice to be fully human. Accordingly, though men have masculine virtues for their starting point, and though women have feminine virtues for their starting point, both sexes are expected to develop the "opposite" virtues, which then become commonly shared and expressed by both men and women.

As for the traditional view that men naturally rule and women naturally submit, Hildegard agreed with this lead/obey structure. However, she did not ground it in Aristotle's idea that women lack control over their emotions. On the contrary, in a grand reversal, she held that precisely because women are more in control of their emotions than men, women submit out of their "greater position of quiescence." Thus, obedience on the part of women—a nun, for example, or a wife—flows out of self-control and strengthens self-control rather than being due to female weakness.[54] At the same time, and demonstrating the ongoing influence of traditional sex polarity, Hildegard objected to the ordination of women to the priesthood "because they are an infirm and weak habitation, appointed to bear children and diligently nurture them."[55]

---

[54] Allen, *Concept of Woman*, 311. Allen underscores the fact that "Hildegard is writing about subjection in the context of a Benedictine monastic tradition in which obedience is understood as a valuable method for learning to overcome the limitations of selfishness, egotism, and personal will. In this context, obedience towards the Abbot or Abbess of the monastery, as the representative of Christ, constituted an important element in the development of virtue. Here is made little difference whether one obeyed a woman or a man" (313).

[55] Hildegard of Bingen, *Scivias* (1151/1152), Book 2, Vision 6, 78. My thanks to Gracilynn Hanson for this reference.

Hildegard also challenged the traditional division of men being vocal (i.e., in the public sphere) and women being silent (i.e., in the private sphere). She pointed to biblical examples of prophetesses (e.g., Huldah, Deborah), illustrations that overturn the traditional female virtue of silence and require women to speak. Moreover, taking her own extensive travel and public speaking engagements as examples, Hildegard upset the traditional female role of being restricted to the private sphere.[56]

In summary, Hildegard of Bingen articulated and defended sex complementarity in the midst of a strong emphasis on traditional sex polarity. As the next discussion demonstrates, that latter position will gain ascendancy after Hildegard's contribution to sex complementarity and will remain in force for centuries to come.

To conclude, Chapter 6 has traced the development of early medieval views of men and women from 600 to 1250. John Scotus Eriugena proposed a sex unity and a sex polarity combination while rejecting sex complementarity. Albert the Great paved the way for Thomas Aquinas and his limited embrace of sex complementarity and his prioritization of sex polarity. This traditional view was deeply influenced by Aristotelian philosophy and would continue to exert a dominant influence for centuries to come. In the midst of these developments, Hildegard of Bingen championed sex complementarity.

[56] Allen, *Concept of Woman*, 312–13.

CHAPTER 7

Late Medieval and Reformation Views of Men and Women (1250–1550)

Prudence Allen summarizes the situation regarding the concept of woman up to the middle of the thirteenth century, underscoring that at that juncture, the philosophical foundations for Aristotle's sex polarity were well established. She notes two specific factors that contributed to this development: the replacement of Benedictine monasteries (in which both women and men were trained) with urban universities (which denied women access to academic learning) as the center for education,[1] and the translation of Aristotle's works (which championed sex polarity) into Latin

[1] This was the educational culture in which Hildegard of Bingen lived and wrote. As Gracilynn Hanson (personal correspondence, April 2024) explains, "Though scholars have long appreciated the formal contributions of Benedictine monasticism to scholarship, the educational standards for women in the Middle Ages uniquely reflect the prevalence of ascetic and monastic ideals in medieval theology. The intellectual accomplishments of Hildegard demonstrate that the same monasticism which expanded and formalized scholarship also initiated the isolation and limitation of the education of women according to the definition of biblical womanhood of Benedictine theology. The same movement which preserved

and their dissemination throughout the universities.[2] She explains, "the Aristotelian Revolution had a strong double effect on moving the concept of woman away from either sex complementarity or sex unity. . . . In spite of his sex polarity claims, Aristotle's premise of the conjoined rationality and materiality in the human being as a soul-body unity provided the foundation for a concept of woman in the line of sex complementarity."[3]

Recalling the earlier discussion of five theories of sex identity, to this point in history, attention has been focused on three of the five because of their prevalence:[4] *sex unity*: women and men are equal, and they are not significantly different (with arguments offered for the lack of difference); *traditional sex polarity*: women and men are significantly different, and men are superior to women; and *sex complementarity*: women and men are significantly different, and they are equal. As the discussion moves on, two other sex identity theories are advanced and thus come to our attention: *sex neutrality*: women and men are equal and not significantly different (with sexual differences considered unimportant and thus not patient of arguments for the lack of difference); and *reverse sex polarity*: women and men are significantly different, and women are superior to men. Additionally, following Allen, sex complementarity will be divided into the two subgroups of *fractional sex complementarity* and *integral sex*

---

intellectualism in monasticism produced an environment in which the education of women became isolated and personally costly."

[2] Allen, *Concept of Woman*, vol. 2, 9.

[3] Allen, *Concept of Woman*, vol. 2, 10–11.

[4] When she comes to the second volume in her three-volume work, Allen switches from using the word "sex" to the word "gender." She explains: "When I use the term 'gender,' I am using it to include also the biological foundations of a woman's or man's identity. . . . My use of 'gender' to include sex runs counter to common practice of many scholars in the social sciences and in philosophy who prefer to separate the two terms and use 'sex' only for biological aspects and 'gender' only for psycho-social aspects." Allen rejects this separation but seeks to incorporate the word "gender" in light of contemporary usage. Allen, *Concept of Woman*, vol. 2, 15. I will continue to use "sex" rather than "gender" unless when quoting Allen and her switch to "gender."

complementarity. In the following discussion I will discuss key figures in the concept of woman from 1250 to 1550 and how they developed these theories of sex identity.

With the domination of Aristotelian philosophy in European universities, which excluded women from their student bodies, academic discussions of women were pursued without their participation in them. The questions that male students debated reveal a strong tendency toward the sex polarity position. For example, "Whether nature intends a woman?" and "Whether woman's nature is as intelligent as man's?"[5] At the same time, due to the inclusion of logic as part of the educational curriculum, sex neutrality made advances as logic seemed to dispense with sexual identity altogether.[6] Despite appearances, sex neutrality in logic hid other sex theories such as sex polarity. For example, in his (theoretically sex neutral) logical discussion of "substance"—both primary substance and secondary substance—Aristotle never employed "woman" as an example of either type.[7] Moreover, in his presentation of substance and accidents, Aristotle considered sex as "accidental" (and, thus, not essential) and, as reflective of his sex polarity position, he classified woman as "a male who had an accident" or as "an accidental male."[8] At the same time, the scholar Robert Grosseteste (1175–1253), by integrating physics, mathematics, and inductive experiments, developed a

---

[5] Allen, *Concept of Woman*, vol. 2, 72.

[6] Allen, *Concept of Woman*, vol. 2, 75.

[7] Allen, *Concept of Woman*, vol. 2, 76.

[8] Allen, *Concept of Woman*, vol. 2, 78. Aristotle developed two important ideas: (1) a *substance* is a thing that exists in itself and not in something else, and that has attributes of two types: (1a) *essential attributes* at the core of a thing and that cannot be lost without losing the thing itself, and (1b) *accidental attributes* not at the core and that can be lost without losing the thing itself. Some of these accidental attributes, or (2) *accidents*—appearance, taste, smell, texture, and sound—can be empirically detected through the senses. By considering sex as accidental, Aristotle relegated it to the category of non-essential and, by describing woman as "an accidental male," he relegated women to an inferior position in relation to men. This Aristotelian framework of substance and accidents contributed significantly to traditional sex polarity.

demonstrative scientific knowledge that excluded all consideration of sex identity. This position was sex neutrality.[9]

With the advent of humanism—rooted in Christianity, Neo-Platonism, and Stoicism—a new age in the history of the concept of woman dawned. Women benefitted especially by an expanding sex complementarity position.[10] As for the latter two roots of humanism, Neo-Platonism and Stoicism tended "toward a gender unity, which emphasizes the equality of women and men because of the centrality of the soul and the devaluation of the body."[11] As for the Christian influence on humanism, Dante Alighieri portrayed wise and virtuous women in his writings. Two female characters—Beatrice and Lady Philosophy—display nobility, the power of reason, intellectual acumen, beauty, joy, friendship, courtesy, goodness, social greatness, wisdom, love, contemplation, self-governance, and more. Contra Aristotle, Dante depicted female characters fully engaged in public dialogue and who are the superior partner in friendships with men.[12] Dante broke from the common Aristotelian sex polarity that demeaned women.

As another example, Petrarch portrayed the character Laura as possessing "an army of virtues such as honor, modesty, prudence, moderation, benignity, courtesy, purity, and mature thoughtfulness. . . . The variety of Laura's virtues . . . is significant, for they do not limit her to the traditional female virtues of the gender polarity tradition."[13] A final example is Giovanni Boccaccio (1313–1375), whose female characters exhibit virtue, a passion ruled by reason, knowledge of philosophy and other disciplines, wisdom, courage, intelligence, strength of will, conscientiousness, forethought, self-governance, constancy, beneficence, and more.[14] Through their literary portraits of female characters, these humanists offered counterexamples to the dominant Aristotelian position of sex polarity and its devaluation of

---

[9] Allen, *Concept of Woman*, vol. 2, 82–83.

[10] Allen, *Concept of Woman*, vol. 2, 226.

[11] Allen, *Concept of Woman*, vol. 2, 231.

[12] Allen, *Concept of Woman*, vol. 2, 240–59.

[13] Allen, *Concept of Woman*, vol. 2, 265.

[14] Allen, *Concept of Woman*, vol. 2, 276–314.

women. Their contributions promoted a position of sex complementarity: women are equal in dignity to, yet significantly different from, men.

Despite these advances fueled by humanism, dismal views and treatment of women persisted. Allen focuses on satirical writings of the fifteenth and sixteenth centuries, noting four characteristics of women that emerged from these satires:

> (1) an increase in the claim that women always tend to deceive men; (2) an increase in the claim that women intentionally choose to harm men; (3) an increase in the claim that women's cooperation with supernatural evil becomes a direct or indirect danger for men; and (4) an increase in the intermingling of satirical texts with religious texts. These new developments were seen to have serious consequences for individual women who were arrested and tried for the heresy of witchcraft.[15]

The common litany of female defects continued to be sounded: women are deceptive, foolish, dangerous to men, lustful, spiteful, overly emotional, feeble minded, weak in nature, undisciplined, and more. To a greater or lesser degree, the foundation of these anti-women satirical writings was sex polarity.

Such dismal evaluations of women were countered by a growing number of concerned people. A stellar example is Christine de Pizan (ca. 1344–1430). While borrowing from and interacting with the work of scholars and poets from her time, she succeeded in philosophically challenging and overhauling the anti-women sex polarity tradition. For example, she underscored the senselessness of the satirical view of women that was based on their alleged weakness of nature, requiring men to rescue them by elaborate strategies:

> But now, if women are such easy marks,
> If they're the fickle, foolish, faithless lot

[15] Allen, *Concept of Woman*, vol. 2, 532.

> That certain clerks [an order of clerics] maintain they are, then why
> Must men pursuing them resort to schemes,
> To clever subterfuge and trickery?
> And why don't women yield more readily,
> Without the need for guile to capture them? . . .
> I can't imagine or make sense of it,
> Such force applied against so frail a place,
> Such ingenuity and subtlety.
> Then necessarily it must be thus:
> Since craft is needed, cleverness and toil,
> To gull [trick] a peasant or a noble born,
> Then women mustn't have such fickle wills
> As some declare, nor waver in their deeds.[16]

By assuming the portrait of women as weak, Christine used irony against it and underscored the error of male views of women.

Christine carried over this ironical strategy into her theological discussions. Against the common theological view that women are of an inferior nature, she countered that, because Eve was not taken from mud, as was Adam, but from his side, women possess a more noble nature than that of men. Against the common theological position that Eve deceived Adam into eating the forbidden fruit, Christine maintained that Eve's motive was not one of fraud but a sincere desire, born out of innocence, to truthfully inform Adam about the serpent's words. Against the common theological position that female virtues are inferior to those of men, and female vices are worse than those of men, she appealed to a sense of justice: in actuality, women do not engage in the heinous actions—murder, treason, arson, stealing, war—that are typical of men.[17] Christine concluded,

[16] Allen, *Concept of Woman*, vol. 2, 569–70. Her citation is Christine de Pizan, *Poems of Cupid, God of Love*, 1.379–406, 53. Her ironical attack targeted the famous medieval poem *Le Roman de la rose*.

[17] Allen, *Concept of Woman*, vol. 2, 571–74.

So through these just, veracious arguments
I demonstrate that reasonable men
Should value women, love and cherish them;
Nor should they have a mind to deprecate
The female sex, from whom each man is born.[18]

Christine's strategy to counter Aristotelian devaluation of women sought to underscore its error as she defied the common view that (1) women are passive, by pointing to many examples of active women; (2) women are by nature weaker than men, by marshalling multiple examples of strong women; (3) women are virtuous by being silent, by demonstrating the wisdom of women expressed in both oral and written form; (4) women have no control over their emotions, by underscoring examples of the female virtue of self-governance; (5) women are defectively created by God as prone to vice, by offering a counterargument that if such is indeed the case, then God would not be good; and more.[19]

One may evaluate Christine de Pisan's contribution as favoring reverse sex polarity—women and men are significantly different, and women are superior to men—but it may be more likely that she employed her strategy to overcome the extensiveness and intensiveness of the traditional sex polarity position, which so heavily favored men and demeaned women, to swing the proverbial pendulum a bit toward the center of sex complementarity. Moreover, she stood out as an equal to men and a stellar example of female wisdom and virtue, while also clearly differentiating herself from men and appreciating the many contributions of humanist men. These two principles—equal dignity and significant differentiation—are at the heart of complementarity.

The latter part of the Middle Ages also witnessed the development of educational centers that included both male and female students. For example,

---

[18] Allen, *Concept of Woman*, vol. 2, 574. Her citation is Christine de Pizan, *Poems of Cupid, God of Love*, 1.711–24, 69.

[19] Allen, *Concept of Woman*, vol. 2, 656.

Vittorino da Feltre (1378–1446) opened a humanist school in Mantua that encouraged women to read, write philosophy, educate their children, and become proficient orators. Similarly, Guarino of Verona (1370–1460) launched humanist schools in Venice and Verona that encouraged women to read, write, and educate their children.[20] Humanist scholars authored books on the education and identity of women. For example, Leonardo Bruni d'Arezzo (1369–1444), Chancellor of Firenze, wrote *On the Study of Literature* (1424), a treatise addressed to a woman and that encouraged moral philosophy, history, poetry, and oration for women. Francesco Barbaro (1390–1454) combined Neo-Platonism and Aristotelian views of gender identity while highlighting the biological and intellectual roles of women in their children's formation, the restriction of women's speech to the private sector of their households, and women's self-governance and virtues.[21] These educational developments, which promoted dialogue among men and women, contributed to a progressive understanding of sex identity that eschewed the devaluation of women and promoted mutual interaction and appreciation.

The pathway to progress took many twists and turns. At times, humanist scholars combined several views of sex identity. For example, Nicholas of Cusa (1401–1464) incorporated certain aspects of Neo-Platonism, Scholasticism, humanism, and Christianity into his theory of sex identity.[22] Specifically, drawing upon Albert the Great and Thomas Aquinas, Cusanus embraced a traditional sex polarity position grounded on Aristotelianism. Thus, the male is actuality, the female potentiality; the male is like the whole, the female like the part; the male is closer to light, the female is closer to dark; the male is unity in nature, the female is otherness in unity.[23] He also appropriated the Platonic and Neo-Platonic tradition's emphasis on both sex unity and sex neutrality.[24]

---

[20] Allen, *Concept of Woman*, vol. 2, 756–57.

[21] Allen, *Concept of Woman*, vol. 2, 759.

[22] Allen, *Concept of Woman*, vol. 2, 762–63.

[23] Allen, *Concept of Woman*, vol. 2, 778–79.

[24] Allen, *Concept of Woman*, vol. 2, 765.

At the same time, Cusanus wrestled freshly with the traditional notion that male and female are opposites as he sought to establish some kind of correspondence among them.[25] Though they are opposites—and, according to the traditional sex polarity position, the male is superior to the female—Cusanus believed that from a divine perspective, such opposites are equal, with neither superior to nor inferior to the other. He concluded that "the opposites, masculine and feminine, are reconciled and harmonized in infinity."[26] With this in mind, he specifically critiqued Aristotle's theory of opposites as contraries, with the woman as the privation of the male. According to Cusanus, "If Aristotle had understood the principle, which he named *privation*, so that this privation is the principle which establishes coincidence of opposites and is thus deprived of contrariety, because it precedes the duality which is necessary in opposites, then he would have seen correctly."[27] In other words, while the framework of opposition is correct—male and female are indeed opposites—and while the sex polarity position is right to consider the female to be the privation of the male, Aristotle failed to see that privation is necessary in relationship to primary substance for there even to be a duality, which is in turn necessary for the coincidence of opposites—not the contrariety of opposites. While clearly presenting a problem for sex polarity, Cusanus paved the way for its demise and its replacement by another sex identity position.

Sex neutrality grew in popularity as another sex identity position, though it had been traditionally favored (as we have seen) in the area of logic (i.e., logical arguments such as syllogisms are completely without reference to maleness or femaleness). An example in the fifteenth century was the humanist Giovanni Pico Della Mirandola (1463–1494), who "adopted

[25] Allen, *Concept of Woman*, vol. 2, 766–67.

[26] Allen, *Concept of Woman*, vol. 2, 768.

[27] Allen, *Concept of Woman*, vol. 2, 785. Her citation is Nicolas of Cusa, "On Beryllus," in *Towards a New Council of Florence: "On the Peace of Faith" and Other Works by Nicolaus of Cusa,* trans. William F. Wertz, Jr. (Washington, DC: Schiller Institute, 1993), XXV, 322 (italics added).

a stance of intentional non-advertence to sex and gender differentiation for a new foundation for gender neutrality."[28] Surprisingly, Pico attempted to wed the Aristotelian (sex polarity) and Platonic (sex unity) ideas of women. He did so by locating the two positions on different levels: Aristotle's concept on the level of nature, and Plato's concept on the level of the supernatural. Though touching on these two concepts of sex identity, for the most part Pico paid no attention to such matters, adopting instead a sex neutrality position.[29] Avoiding such topics, and writing an essay "On the Oration and Dignity of Man," Pico focused on what is truly important—the human dignity of self-determination according to God's design—by which he meant not the dignity of male human beings, nor of female human beings, but "man" in a neutral sense, that is, humanity or humankind: all men and all women.[30]

Reverse sex polarity also inserted itself into the arena of sex identity in the fifteenth century. Several writings that promoted the superiority of women over men were Martin Le Franc's *Le Champion des Dames* (*The Champion of Ladies*; 1442, 1485), Antonio Cornazzano's *De Mulieribus Admirandis* (*On Admirable Women*; 1467), Vespasiano de Bisticci's *Il Libro delle Lode e Commendazione delle Donne* (*The Book of Praise and Commendation of Women*; c. 1480), Giovanni Sabadino degli Arienti's *Gynevera de le Clare Donne* (1483), Bartolomeo Gogio's *De Laudibus Mulierum* (*On the Merits of Women*; 1487), and Cornelius Agrippa von Nettesheim's *De Nobilitate et Praecellentia Foeminei Sexus* (*On the Nobility and Superiority of the Female Sex*; 1509).[31]

---

[28] Allen, *Concept of Woman*, vol. 2, 904.

[29] Allen, *Concept of Woman*, vol. 2, 912.

[30] Allen, *Concept of Woman*, vol. 2, 921. Allen points out that Pico's idea of gender neutrality emerged from his rejection of human embodiment and materiality in general and his appreciation for angelic (i.e., immaterial) nature (929–30). She also notes that his philosophy did not include relationships between human beings on earth, thereby preventing him from embracing and defending an integral sex complementarity position (931).

[31] Allen, *Concept of Woman*, vol. 2, 1037–38.

Challenging this reverse sex polarity position while also refusing to accept the traditional sex polarity position (not to mention the sex unity position) was Laura Cereta (1469–1499). She affirmed the natural equality of both sexes; that is, not only men, but also women, possess capabilities to learn, to progress in self-governance, and to contribute to the common good of humanity. Accordingly, she rejected traditional sex polarity—male superiority—without falling into the other extreme of reverse sex polarity of female superiority. In addition to embracing the equal dignity and capacities of men and women, she affirmed the significant differences between the sexes, thus avoiding sex unity. As for female uniqueness, Cereta indicated "women's history, women's experience of being female in a particular culture, women's domestic service expanded from the home into society, and most interestingly, particular attention to the development of the human person in all situations."[32] In all these areas, women make their own choices as to the kind of women they become, as

> nature imparts one freedom to all human beings equally—to learn. But the question of my exceptionality [i.e., how I differ from other women] remains. And here choice alone, since it is the arbiter of character, is the distinguishing factor. . . . May we women, then, not be endowed by God the grantor with any giftedness or rare talent through the sanctity of our own. Nature has granted to all enough of her bounty, she opens to all the gates of choice, and through these gates, reason sends legates to the will, for it is through reason that these legates can transmit their desires.[33]

Cereta clearly affirmed the equality of men and women in terms of the freedom of choice to become what they will to become through learning, hard work, knowledge, and more.

---

[32] Allen, *Concept of Woman*, vol. 2, 1038.

[33] Allen, *Concept of Woman*, vol. 2, 1040. Her citation is a letter of Laura Cereta dated January 13, 1448, in Diana Robin, ed., *Laura Cereta: Collective Letters of a Renaissance Feminist* (Chicago: University of Chicago Press, 1997), 78–79.

But men and women are mixed beings, with both positive and negative characteristics. Cereta listed superior male qualities—authority, strength, and security—and inferior male qualities—rage, anger, and fear. Her corresponding list detailed superior female characteristics—natural ability, contentment, practical judgment, and restraint when an enemy flees—and inferior female characteristics—cunning, suspiciousness, and apathetic contentment. This is sex complementarity, underscoring both the equality of the sexes as to both their positive and negative characteristics, and their significant differences. More specifically, "Laura Cereta's theory of complementarity is 'integral' rather than 'fractional' because she emphasized the development of the whole person."[34]

A major disruption in Europe occurred through the protestations of key church leaders during the sixteenth century, resulting in a division between Roman Catholicism and what came to be known as Protestantism. The Reformation challenged some of the long-held concepts of men and women, their virtues and duties, and their spheres of activity, but also reinforced many traditional notions. As Kirsi Stjerna summarizes, "With the rejection of the monastic life and convents in pro-Reformation cities, women lost significant opportunities for spiritual formation and vocations."[35] That is, capable women who were leaders of convents and religious orders no longer had those avenues available to them for personal and sisterhood development.[36]

---

[34] Allen, *Concept of Woman*, vol. 2, 1043.

[35] Kirsi Stjerna, *Women and the Reformation* (Malden, MA: Blackwell, 2009), 33.

[36] Martin Luther rejected the monastic system of the Roman Catholic Church, a system of which he had been part and from which he rescued his eventual wife, Katherina von Bora. In his rejection of clerical celibacy, Luther was joined by other Protestant leaders, who denounced this vow as contradicting the biblical doctrine of justification by grace alone through faith alone in Christ alone. As salvation from sin is a free gift, the practice of clerical celibacy was nothing more than a wrong-headed attempt to add good works so as to merit salvation; thus, it accomplished nothing and should be abandoned. Additionally, the Reformers critiqued celibacy for being against God's design for his image bearers to "be fruitful and multiply and fill the earth" (Gen 1:28).

At the same time, women were no longer under the illusion that celibacy and the call to religious vocation were the highest virtue and station in the divine purpose and kingdom. "Reformation principles of the priesthood of all believers and 'Scripture alone' as the clear and available authority for Christians blew wide open what it meant to have a spiritual calling, and at least in theory condoned all vocations as being equal. The sanctification of marriage and the spousal role was enormously important for women, who were traditionally expected to devote their lives to wifehood and motherhood any way."[37]

Specifically, the Reformers' elevation of marriage over celibacy led to them giving much attention to that institution. In *The Christian State of Matrimony* (1540), Heinrich Bullinger listed three reasons for the divine creation of marriage. These reasons were subsequently incorporated in the first edition (1549) of *The Book of Common Prayer*, which explained "the causes for the whiche matrimonie was ordained:" first, "the procreacion of children;" second, "for a remedie agaynst sinne, and to avoide fornicacion;" and third, "for the mutuall societie, helpe, and coumfort, that the one oughte to have of the other, both in prosperitie and adversitie."[38] As for their comportment in the marriage, a husband must love his wife,

Addressing *The Estate of Marriage* (1522), Martin Luther urged, "For this word which God speaks, 'Be fruitful and multiply [Gen 1:28],' is not a command. It is more than a command, namely, a divine ordinance which it is not our prerogative to hinder or ignore." Martin Luther, *The Estate of Marriage*, in *Luther's Works*, ed. Jaroslav Pelikan, Hilton C. Oswald, and Helmut T. Lehmann, 55 vols. (St. Louis: Concordia, 1955–1986), 45:18. Some of the above discussion is adapted from Kathleen Crowther, "Sexual Difference," in *The Oxford Handbook of the Protestant Reformations* (rep. ed.), ed. Ulinka Rublack (Oxford: Oxford University Press, 2019), 667–87; and Sasja Emilie Mathiasen Stopa, "Women as wives and rulers in Martin Luther's theology," *Dialog: A Journal of Theology* (April 26, 2023), https://doi.org/10.1111/dial.12788.

[37] Stjerna, *Women and the Reformation*, 214.

[38] *The booke of the common prayer and administracion of the Sacramentes, and other rites and ceremonies of the Churche: after the use of the Churche of England* (London: Edouardi Whitchurche, 1549).

and a wife must "treat her husband as her superior and show obedience, give in to him, be humble and let him be right, unless it is against God."[39] As Prudence Allen demonstrates, the marriage vow of the wife to obey, serve, love, honor, and care for her husband was incorporated not only into Protestant wedding ceremonies but also into the Roman Catholic sacrament of marriage.[40]

The Reformation largely left intact the traditional, patriarchal concept of the family. Justus Menius, a German pastor, articulated it: "A husband has two functions: first, he should rule over his wife, children, and servants and be head and master of the entire house; second, he should work and produce enough to support and feed his household."[41] Nuancing this portrait of patriarchy through the writings of Protestant pastors, Scott Hendrix summarizes, "A family ruled by the husband and father was by no means a family that lacked affection or was incapable of emotional exchanges. Spouses could be tender toward each other, and parents could cherish their children even if the housefather was in charge. . . . Women who obeyed their husbands in the home could simultaneously be partners in the family business, work alongside their spouses at hard jobs, or contribute income from their own labor."[42] Rather than typecasting married men "as strict, insensitive, withdrawn, or unyielding, . . . these Protestant preachers viewed men neither as supermen nor as weaklings. Their patriarchs were vulnerable

---

[39] Martin Luther, *On Good Works,* WA 6:264.10ff.

[40] Prudence Allen, *The Concept of Woman,* Volume 3*: The Search for Communion of Persons, 1500–2015* (Grand Rapids: Eerdmans, 2016), 43–53. Regretfully, Allen's treatment of sixteenth century Protestantism and post-Reformation Protestantism is very underdeveloped, one of the few marks against her otherwise brilliant three-volume work.

[41] Justus Menius, *Erynnerung was denen so sich ynn Ehestand begeben zu bedencken sey* (Wittenberg, 1528). Cited in Scott H. Hendrix, "Masculinity and Patriarchy in Reformation Germany," in *Masculinity in the Reformation Era*, ed. Scott H. Hendrix and Susan C. Karant-Nunn, Sixteenth Century Essays and Studies 83 (Kirksville, MO: Trueman State University Press, 2008), 71.

[42] Hendrix, "Masculinity and Patriarchy in Reformation Germany," 72.

instead of vulgar, needing structure for their sexual fulfillment, and requiring care from their spouses. When they misbehaved in relationships, men received less sympathy and consideration than did women, because men were held to high standards of public responsibility and quickly blamed when they violated those standards."[43]

While John Calvin and the city-church government of Geneva functioned within a traditional patriarchal culture, the pastor-theologian's emphasis on the devastating impact of sin (i.e., total depravity and total inability) on all people—along with their corresponding absolute need for divine grace through the gospel—leveled the playing field, so to speak, by underscoring the common characteristics of men and women.

> Both were weak, sinful, and unable to accomplish any good without the grace of God. Both were responsible for taking care of their spouses. Although husbands and wives had different specific tasks within a marriage, both were expected to love their spouses and to strive to live a life of godly discipline. And both were expected to provide for the material and spiritual care of their children . . . and to raise them to be faithful members of the Reformed community.[44]

Still, husbands/fathers were primarily responsible for such spiritual formation. "The father, the ancient and revered *paterfamilias*, assumed a sacerdotal role at the very heart of the family. Much as he directed other aspects of family life, the father became its spiritual and ethical guide. Ideally, he conducted himself with firm benevolence."[45] Men were leaders not only in their families and households but also in civic government and the church, where ministerial authority and responsibility were restricted to qualified

---

[43] Hendrix, "Masculinity and Patriarchy in Reformation Germany," 87–88.

[44] Karen E. Spierling, "Father, Son, and Pious Christian: Concepts of Masculinity in Reformation Geneva," in *Masculinity in the Reformation Era*, 116.

[45] Raymond A. Mentzer, "Masculinity in the Reformed Tradition in France," in *Masculinity in the Reformation Era*, 125.

men as pastors, doctors, elders, and deacons.[46] Specific ecclesial and liturgical elements that were the sole domain of men were, for example, church discipline and the administration of the Lord's Supper.

While the Reformation functioned within such traditional structures, that is only part of its legacy. The gospel, justification by faith, the priesthood of all believers, the sanctity of marriage, the dignity of human vocations other than religious professions, and other earth-shattering Protestant doctrines and practices provided for (at least theoretically) sex complementarity in some arenas.

Specifically, Martin Luther articulated and defended the priesthood of all believers—both men and women. As will be discussed more fully later, Luther insisted that the divine, salvific work of justification—the material principle of Protestantism—necessarily results in Christians being constituted a priesthood. He also denounced the centuries-old Roman Catholic division of human reality into a "spiritual estate" (the realm of the church's priestly caste) and a "temporal estate" (the realm of everyone else as the laity). This move toppled the entrenched concept of human beings as divided into two categories according to different natures: men and women, and priests. As the first two now constitute a priesthood, both men and women alike can carry out priestly duties; Luther listed seven functions: (1) teach and preach the Word of God; (2) administer baptism; (3) administer the Lord's Supper; (4) exercise the keys by binding and loosing sins; (5) pray for others; (6) sacrifice in terms of spiritual offerings, such as praise and thanksgiving; and (7) judge doctrine by testing false teachers and discerning false teaching.[47] This inclusion of women along with men as priests was a radical departure from Roman Catholicism and a major expression of complementarity between

[46] Apparently, John Calvin believed there are two kinds of deacons, one engaged in giving financial support to the poor, the other providing actual physical care to the poor and the sick. For Calvin, women could do the latter work; thus, he personally favored women deacons in the second sense. However, the *Ecclesiastical Ordinances* of the Genevan Consistory limited the diaconate to men.

[47] This discussion is adapted from Uche Anizor, *Kings and Priests: Scripture's Theological Account of Its Readers* (Eugene, OR: Pickwick, 2014), 154–58.

the sexes. At the same time, Luther retained the office of ministry with traditional male leadership roles.

From the formal principle of Protestantism—*sola Scriptura*—arose a significant advancement in complementarity. "As Church tradition and ecclesial authority were challenged with the enforced principle of Scripture being the sole authority in matters of salvation, people were invited to read the Scriptures for themselves and in their own languages. Luther himself was interested in ensuring that all people, including women, learned to read and love the Bible."[48]

Advances were also made in terms of the equal dignity of men and women. Mary Potter summarizes John Calvin's perspective on gender equality and gender hierarchy: "Calvin's entire theology is an uncompromising view of women as equal to men. Whether discussing the doctrine of creation, fall, or redemption, Calvin explicitly argues for the equality of male and female human beings."[49] Specifically, Calvin maintained that both women and men alike are created in the divine image, both are sinful and responsible for evil, and both enjoy equal access to salvation through Jesus Christ. This is a Protestant affirmation of sex complementarity.

At the same time, "Also permeating Calvin's entire theology is the uncompromising view that women are innately inferior to men."[50] Though affirming that both men and women are created equally in the divine image, he believed that women are so created to a lesser/inferior degree; thus, "men are preferred to females in the human race. We know that God constituted man as the head and gave him a dignity and preeminence above that of the woman. . . . It is true that the image of God is imprinted on all; but still woman is inferior to man."[51] In his treatment of 1 Timothy 2:12–14, Calvin

[48] Stjerna, *Women and the Reformation*, 219–20.

[49] Mary Potter, "Gender Equality and Gender Hierarchy in Calvin's Theology," *Signs*, vol. 11, no. 4 (Summer, 1986): 726.

[50] Potter, "Gender Equality and Gender Hierarchy in Calvin's Theology," 727.

[51] "Les hommes sont préférez aux femmes au genre humain. Nous savons que Dieu a constitué l'homme comme chef, et luy a donné une dignité et preeminence par dessus la femme. . . . Il est vray que l'image de Dieu est bien inprimee par tout:

attributed this inferior status of women not to the fall of Adam and Eve but to God's design for their original creation: "Woman is more guilty than the man, because she was seduced by Satan, and so diverted her husband from obedience to God that she was an instrument of death leading all to perdition. It is necessary that woman recognize this, and that she learn to what she is subjected; and not only against her husband. This is reason enough why today she is placed below and that she bears within her ignominy and shame."[52] More clearly, Calvin commented, "Moses teaches that women are created to be a kind of appendage to the man on the express condition that woman should be ready to obey him. Thus, God did not create two 'beings' of equal standing, but added to man a lesser helpmeet."[53]

Returning to our four questions and using Martin Luther as an example, the Reformation generally held that (1) men and women are opposites because men are hot and women are cold; thus, men are the more active sex and women are the more passive sex; (2) in sexual intercourse, both men and women produce and release "seed" that unite to form a child (though the details of fertilization and *in utero* development still remained unknown);

---

mais si est-ce que la femme est inférieure à l'homme." John Calvin, *Sermons on Job*, 11th sermon. *Calvini opera selecta*, ed. Peter Barth and William Niesel, 5 vols. (Munich: Christian Kaiser Verlag, 1974), 33:146.

[52] "Il faut que la femme cognoisse qu'elle est plus coulpable que l'homme, pource qu'elle a esté séduite par Satan, et a tellement diverti son mari de l'obéissance de Dieu, qu'elle a esté un instrument de mort pour mener tout à perdition. Il faut donc que la femme cognoisse, et qu'elle apprene que c'est de s'assuièttir: puis qu'elle s'est ainsi élevée contre son créateur, et non pas seulement contre son mari: c'est bien raison que maintenant elle soit mise bas, et qu'elle porte comme une note d'gnominie et de honte en soy." John Calvin, *Sermon on 1 Timothy 2:12–14. Calvini opera selecta*, ed. Peter Barth and William Niesel, 5 vols. (Munich: Christian Kaiser Verlag, 1974), 53:11.

[53] "Moses autem docet, ita posteriore loco creatam esse mulierem, ut sit quasi viri accessio: et faac lege fuisse viro adiunctam, ut praesto adsit ad exhibenda obsequia. Quum ergo non duo capita Deus aequa potestate creaverit, sed viro addiderit adiumentum inferius." John Calvin, *Commentary on 1 Timothy 2:13. Calvini opera selecta*, ed. Peter Barth and William Niesel, 5 vols. (Munich: Christian Kaiser Verlag, 1974), 52:277.

(3) men have a stronger nature because they are more rational than are women, who are accordingly weaker;[54] and (4) as another result of their differences in nature, men are more virtuous than are women and thus should rule women.

In conclusion, "The Reformation does not appear to have instigated any drastic changes in gender roles and expectations. Instead, Reformation teachings managed to give new meanings to the traditional roles of women while at the same time reinforcing a hierarchical view of human relations with a theology that taught created equality with natural differences between the sexes, as well as spiritual equality with hierarchically ordered gender roles."[55] Thus, both traditional sex polarity and sex complementarity were operative in the Protestant Reformation. One could critique the Reformers for not making significant strides away from polarity and toward complementarity. At the same time, in the triage of doctrinal matters that were swirling at the time, theological anthropology lagged behind the five *solas*, the material principle of justification, the formal principle of Scripture's ultimate authority, the sacraments, the papacy, purgatory, and more. Furthermore, it may be argued that doctrines such as the priesthood of all believers and the clarity of Scripture provided a solid foundation for later developments in terms of equal dignity, significant difference, and flourishing interdependence among women and men.

To conclude, Chapter 7 has addressed the expansion of all five sex identity views from 1250 to 1550: traditional sex polarity, sex unity, sex complementarity, sex neutrality, and reverse sex polarity. Movements such

---

[54] It appears that Luther attributed this difference in nature, which began with Eve in relation to Adam, to the fall rather than to the original creation. "Had the woman not been deceived by the serpent, she would have been equal to Adam in all things. That which she is now subjected to is a punishment which was inflicted upon her after and because of her sin, just as she has also sorrows and troubles, such as labor in travail and the like. Therefore Eve [in her original state of nature] was not as women are today. She was far more excellent so that she was behind Adam in no bodily or spiritual gift." Martin Luther, *Commentary on Genesis*, trans. J. Theodore Mueller (Grand Rapids: Zondervan, 1958), 55.

[55] Stjerna, *Women and the Reformation*, 214.

as humanism and the Reformation, and individuals like Christine de Pizan and Nicholas of Cusa, contributed to these developments. Like earlier epochs, this period continued to witness the dominance of traditional sex polarity.

CHAPTER 8

Early Modern to Postmodern Views of Men and Women (1550–Present)

As Prudence Allen highlights, an important advancement took place in the sixteenth century concept of women and men: "the discovery and articulation of masculine and feminine characteristics, rooted in a woman's and in a man's psyche and way of acting in the world." She describes this development as "a movement from a two-dimensional understanding of gender identity as female-woman and male-man to a three-dimensional understanding of gender identity as female-(feminine and masculine)-woman and male-(masculine and feminine)-man." Allen qualifies: "This advance was not to an androgenous or unisex model of gender, because the woman always had a different starting point *qua* female + feminine than the man *qua* male + masculine." This advance anticipated "a further development that will build on female-feminine and male-masculine ways of being and acting in the world rather than to attribute masculine characteristics to women or feminine characteristics to men."[1]

[1] Prudence Allen, *The Concept of Woman, Volume 3: The Search for Communion of Persons, 1500–2015* (Grand Rapids: Eerdmans, 2016), 94–95.

This movement or advancement of the concept of men and women is the subject of this chapter that takes us from the mid-sixteenth century to the present day. Through the contributions of key figures such as Lucrezia Marinella, René Descartes, Immanuel Kant, and Jacques Maritain, the development of all five sex identities—traditional sex polarity, sex equality, sex neutrality, reverse sex polarity, and sex complementarity in both its fractional and integral versions—will be traced.

This epoch's female-feminine and male-masculine development seems to stand in opposition to Teresa of Ávila's (1515–1582) traditional Aristotelian/Thomistic framework of sex polarity that considered women to be naturally weak and rationally underdeveloped while men are naturally strong and rational. For example, Teresa deemed her own tears to be "womanish and without strength" and portrayed herself as "a poor little woman like myself, weak and with hardly any fortitude."[2] As a solution to this inherent female weakness of nature and mind, Teresa encouraged women to develop masculine characteristics and virtues such as a strong will and intellectual abilities. They should heed Teresa's warning that their soul is "not to be conquered. . . . Let the soul be manly."[3] Teresa granted the attributes of strength and courage as belonging to men and exhorted women to be brave like men and not like women.[4]

At the same time, such conceptualization pioneered the aforementioned development of female-feminine and male-masculine ways of being and acting in the world, especially as related to spiritual matters. For example, John of the Cross questioned how it is possible for him as a man to identify himself as (part of) the Bride of Christ, which is a female-feminine way of relating to Jesus and his church. As Allen describes this phenomenon:

---

[2] Allen, *Concept of Woman*, vol. 3, 96. Her citation is Teresa of Ávila, *The Book of Her Life*, in *The Collected Works of St. Teresa of Avila*, 2 vols. (Washington, DC: Institute of Carmelite Studies, 1976), 1:73, 84.

[3] Allen, *Concept of Woman*, vol. 3, 97. Her citation is Teresa of Ávila, *The Interior Castle*, in *The Collected Works of St. Teresa of Avila*, 2 vols. (Washington, DC: Institute of Carmelite Studies, 1976), 2:300.

[4] Allen, *Concept of Woman*, vol. 3, 97.

> *On the horizontal level* of ordinary life, a bride would accord with the female human being and a bridegroom would accord with the male human being. *On the transcendental level* of spiritual life, a woman only has to make a single spiritual analogy between being a bride in relation to a particular man in the world, and being a bride in relation to Christ in heaven. It is more complicated for a man: he has to die, so to speak, to his male identity spiritually to identify himself as a member of the corporate or collective bride, or church, and then made the further analogy with the relation of the bride to husband on earth being like the relation of spiritual bride to Christ.[5]

Teresa of Ávila underscored a similar movement for women who must identify themselves as sons of God in baptism (Gal 3:25–27). In other words, rather than attributing a feminine characteristic to men who identify themselves with the Bride of Christ, we should view them as expressing a female-feminine way of being and acting in the church according to Scripture. Similarly, rather than attributing a masculine characteristic to women who identify themselves with sonship in the Son of God, we should view them as expressing a male-masculine way of being and acting in the church according to Scripture. This development is a new addition to our discussion of the concepts of men and women.

While the overturning of the traditional sex polarity position, the rise of the sex complementarity positions, and the initial articulation of the reverse sex polarity position have been traced thus far, the demise of the first position and the advancement of the second and third positions continued with vigor in the early modern and postmodern eras. Baldassare Castiglione (1478–1529) questioned the metaphysics upon which the traditional sex polarity position was grounded and defended. Against that view that women are imperfect creatures, having less dignity and being less virtuous than men, and being generated by accident

[5] Allen, *Concept of Woman*, vol. 3, 108–9. (original italics)

as mistakes of nature, Castiglione employed two arguments.[6] First, he disagreed that the concept of substance can be patient of degree, affirming instead that

> one man [i.e., the species of human being] cannot be more perfectly man than another; and consequently the male [i.e., a man as one type of the species human being] will not be more perfect than the female [i.e., a woman as one type of the species human being] as regards their formal substance, because the one and the other are included under the species man [i.e., the species of human being], and that in which the one differs from the other is an accident [i.e., not a mistake, but a secondary characteristic] and is not of the essence.[7]

Castiglione then listed robustness, quickness, agility, and endurance in toil as accidental, not essential qualities, noting that even men differ among themselves in those characteristics (e.g., some men are stronger than other men) without esteeming one man (e.g., the stronger one) above another man (e.g., the weaker one). Thus, Castiglione rejected the common foundation of the traditional sex polarity position.

Second, he disagreed with the Aristotelian/Thomistic distinction between (1) universal nature, which intends to generate both men and women (for the expansion of the human race), and (2) particular nature, which intends to generate men only but accidently generates women (who are accordingly defective men). Appealing to the natural cycle of life—men and women generate children who, when their parents are old, maintain them, which pattern continues on and on—Castiglione averred, "since woman is as necessary in this as man, I do not see why one would be made

[6] Allen, *Concept of Woman*, vol. 3, 114. The list is constructed from Baldesar Castiglione, *The Book of the Courtier*, trans. Charles S. Singleton (Garden City, NY: Anchor Books, 1959), bk. 3, sec. 11, pp. 213–14.

[7] Allen, *Concept of Woman*, vol. 3, 115. Her citation is Castiglione, *The Book of the Courtier*, bk. 3, sec. 12, p. 214.

more by chance than the other."[8] Then, he used the soul/body unity of an individual person as an analogy of the male/female unity for the expansion of humanity: "for just as there results from body and soul a composite more noble than its parts, which is man [i.e., an individual human being], so from the union of male and female there results a composite which preserves the human species, and without which its parts would perish. And hence male and female are by nature always together, nor can the one be without the other." He concluded his argument with an appeal to Scripture: "we read in Holy Writ that God created man male and female in his own likeness" (Gen 1:26–27).[9]

By these two arguments, Castiglione exposed the errors of the traditional sex polarity position. Using empirical evidence, he also provided a hint of the reverse sex polarity view: "to return to the praises of women, I say that, for every admirable man that [one] finds me, I will show you a wife or daughter or sister of equal and sometimes greater merit."[10] Castiglione concluded from many such examples: "If you will compare the worth of women in every age to that of men, you will find that they have never been, and are not now, a whit inferior to men in worth."[11]

Henricus Cornelius Agrippa also articulated and defended this position of reverse sex polarity in his *Declamation on the Nobility and Preeminence of the Female Sex* (1529). His first argument drew upon the biblically and theologically sound affirmation that both men and women are created in the divine image. From this, Agrippa maintained that the two are differentiated only on the basis of reproductive bodily organs, while they have an identical

[8] Allen, *Concept of Woman*, vol. 3, 115–16. Her citation is Castiglione, *The Book of the Courtier*, bk. 3, sec. 14, pp. 215–16.

[9] Allen, *Concept of Woman*, vol. 3, 116. Her citation is Castiglione, *The Book of the Courtier*, bk. 3, sec. 14, p. 216.

[10] Allen, *Concept of Woman*, vol. 3, 118. Her citation is Castiglione, *The Book of the Courtier*, bk. 3, sec. 21, p. 222.

[11] Allen, *Concept of Woman*, vol. 3, 116. Her citation is Castiglione, *The Book of the Courtier*, bk. 3, sec. 34, p. 235.

soul that is not differentiated by these sexual characteristics. Accordingly, and reflecting Neo-Platonism, Agrippa maintained that "woman has been allotted the same intelligence, reason, and power of speech as man and tends to the same end he does, that is [eternal] happiness, where there will be no restriction by sex."[12]

His second argument set forth four reasons for reverse sex polarity:

> (1) the name "woman" signifying life, was superior to the name "man," signifying only lifeless earth; (2) woman, who was created last in order of creation, is comparable to the end, goal or perfection in the circle of creation, while man, who was created second to last, was only created as a step toward the end; (3) the first woman was made from the purified material of the bone of man, while the first man was made from inanimate clay; and finally, (4) because that which is more beautiful is closer to the transcendental beauty, woman, whose body is more beautiful than man's, is closer to God.[13]

Agrippa was joined by others in arguing against traditional sex polarity and in favor of reverse sex polarity, including Thomas Elyot, *The Defense of Good Women* (1540), Moderate Fonte, *The Worth of Women: Wherein is Clearly Revealed Their Nobility and Their Superiority to Men* (1600), and Lucrezia Marinella, *The Nobility and Excellence of Women and the Defects and Vices of Men* (1601).

Specifically in regard to this last contribution, Lucrezia Marinella championed reverse sex polarity by first arguing that, in terms of virtues, those of women are better than those of men, and, second, in terms of vices, those of men are worse than those of women.

---

[12] Allen, *Concept of Woman*, vol. 3, 121. Her citation is Henry Cornelius Agrippa, *Declamation on the Nobility and Preeminence of the Female Sex*, ed. and trans. Albert Rabil, Jr. (Chicago: University of Chicago Press, 2005), 43.

[13] Allen, *Concept of Woman*, vol. 3, 122.

As for her first claim, Marinella surveyed the etymology of five words for "woman"—*donna*, *femina*, *eva*, *isciah*, and *mulier*—averring that each term highlights the superiority of woman over man.[14] She drew the conclusion:

> These are the names with which this honorable sex is adorned. . . . [T]hey are among the most illustrious and remarkable that can be expressed by man [humanity]. Such rare, wondrous, worthy names, which denote every excellent quality that is found, or can be found, in the world! All other names must yield to them, signifying, as they do, procreation and generation, earthly fire and light, soul, life, divine radiance, delicacy [in the sense of gracefulness] and mercy, and, finally, lordly dominion.[15]

Marinella also appealed to the philosophical notion of forms or ideas: "According to Platonists, Ideas are the eternal exemplars and images of things, whose proper place lies in the mind of the supreme power before creation."[16] From her perspective, then, these eternal ideas in the divine mind can be distinguished in the case of the two sexes: "Ideas of women are nobler than those of males, as their beauty and their virtue demonstrates."[17] In other words, the outward beauty and evident virtues of women, reflective as they are of the higher perfection of the eternal female forms in God's mind, signify that women are superior to men. To put it differently, Marinella maintained "that women's souls were created nobler than men's as can be

[14] Allen, *Concept of Woman*, vol. 3, 141–42.

[15] Allen, *Concept of Woman*, vol. 3, 142. Her citation is Lucrezia Marinella, *The Nobility and Excellence of Women and the Defects and Vices of Men*, ed. and trans. Anne Dunhill (Chicago: University of Chicago Press, 1999), 51.

[16] Allen, *Concept of Woman*, vol. 3, 143. Her citation is Marinella, *The Nobility and Excellence of Women*, 53.

[17] Allen, *Concept of Woman*, vol. 3, 143. Her citation is Lucrezia Marinella, *La nobiltà et l'eccellenza delle donne co'diffetti et mancamenti de gli huomini* (Venice: Gio. Batista Ciotti Sanese, 1601), 10; Marinella, *The Nobility and Excellence of Women*, 53.

seen from the effect they have and from the beauty of their bodies."[18] She also borrowed one of Henricus Cornelius Agrippa's arguments for female superiority: "because a woman is made of a man's rib and a man made of mud, she is nobler than he because the rib is nobler than mud."[19]

Marinella's second argument focused on the relative evil of male and female vices. She addressed this difference from the perspective of Aristotle's sex polarity position that men are characterized by greater heat than are women:

> All learned men are convinced that males are nobler than females because they are warmer by nature. . . . I would add that it renders men unstable and inconsistent because "warmth shakes the body". . . . What great faults are those that spring from such a warmth that they praise and exalt so much, for because of it, the reasonable soul is bent and led astray from the right path of virtue, and allows itself to precipitate in dishonesty and lust, out of which infinite other errors and enormous misdemeanors are born; this cannot happen to the womanly sex, because being by nature warm and humid, their senses are ruled by reason. They are more temperate, more constant, more steadfast, more just, and more prudent than men. This happens because reason stays in its own seat, which does not happen in the male.[20]

Using Aristotle's view of opposites against him, Marinella championed reverse sex polarity.

As emphasized through the repeated discussions of philosophical views of generation and the specific contributions of men and women in the reproductive process, the traditional sex polarity view was profoundly based on an

---

[18] Allen, *Concept of Woman*, vol. 3, 145. Her citation is Marinella, *The Nobility and Excellence of Women*, 55; *La nobiltà et l'eccellenza delle donne*, 11.

[19] Allen, *Concept of Woman*, vol. 3, 144. Her citation is Marinella, *The Nobility and Excellence of Women*, 54.

[20] Allen, *Concept of Woman*, vol. 3, 148. Her citation is Marinella, *La nobiltà et l'eccellenza delle donne*, 137.

incorrect belief that only men, through their provision of a seed/sperm, have a role in procreation; women, who do not have seed/ova, only play the (passive) role of a receptacle of the male seed in their menstrual fluid. In the seventeenth century, philosophers and scientists began to question this reproductive theory, hypothesizing that women too contribute seed. Full confirmation of this suggestion awaited nineteenth-century discoveries, yet even the earliest of these serendipitous findings continued to be interpreted in a traditional way: the male seed was active—metaphorically, an "adventurous sperm"—while the female seed was passive—metaphorically, a "passive ovum."[21]

Antoni van Leeuwenhoek (1632–1723) rightly identified "animalcules" (i.e., sperm) in semen, but wrongly postulated the existence of "male animalcules" and "female animalcules." If a father's male sperm fertilized the mother, the offspring would be male; if a father's female sperm fertilized the mother, a female child would be conceived. Van Leeuwenhoek underscored the importance of his "discovery": "by this explanation, that received view [on which traditional sex polarity was based] would fall to the ground: namely, that if the male semen has prevailed over the female, male offspring will be born; if the female semen has prevailed over the male, female offspring will be born."[22] His idea overturned (1) the nearly universally dismissed ancient two-seed theory that both the man and the woman contribute seed in the generation of offspring, and (2) the Aristotelian view that the man's contribution was only the (immaterial) form of the offspring and not their (physical) matter. As we understand today, van Leeuwenhoek correctly identified the man's determining role of the sex of the offspring by supplying either (1) an X chromosome, thus producing a female offspring when united with the X chromosome supplied by the woman, or (2) a Y chromosome, thus producing a male offspring when united with the X chromosome supplied by the woman.

---

[21] Allen, *Concept of Woman*, vol. 3, 241.

[22] Allen, *Concept of Woman*, vol. 3, 241. Her citation is Antoni van Leeuwenhock, "Epistola 30," in Arthur William Meyer, *The Rise of Embryology* (Palo Alto, CA: Stanford University Press, 1939), 173.

Oscar Hertwig made this scientific discovery in 1875/6, paving the way for the sex complementarity view based on equal yet different contributions on the part of men and women to the generation of children. Still, the old sex polarity position and its accompanying devaluation of women, refused to disappear or die.

Specifically, sex neutrality gained momentum through René Descartes (1596–1650) and his substance dualism: "With the 'Cartesian turn to the subject,' the human being is characterized as a 'thinking thing' with no reference to gender differentiation."[23]

Specifically, "Descartes argued that the identity of a human being is located in the rational mind, and that both women and men have this unisex kind of mind."[24] His position, clearly that of sex neutrality, arose from his metaphysical view of human nature as consisting of mind—a "thinking thing"—and body—an "extended thing." He averred, "I am, then, in the strict sense only a thing that thinks, that is, I am a mind, or intelligence, or intellect, or reason. . . . I am not that structure of limbs which is called a human body."[25] As a consequence, Descartes maintained there are "only two ultimate classes of things: first, intellectual or thinking things, i.e., those which pertain to mind or thinking substance; second, material things, i.e.,

---

[23] Allen, *Concept of Woman*, vol. 3, 247.

[24] Allen, *Concept of Woman*, vol. 3, 248.

[25] Descartes added, "[F]rom the fact that I know that I exist, and that at the same time I judge that obviously nothing rightly else belongs to my nature or essence except that I am a thinking thing, I rightly conclude that my essence consists entirely in my being a thinking thing. And although perhaps (or rather . . . assuredly) I have a body that is very closely joined to me, nevertheless, because on the one hand I have a clear and distinct idea of myself, insofar as I am merely a thinking thing and not an extended thing, and because on the other hand I have a distinct idea of a body, insofar as it is merely an extended thing and not a thinking thing, it is certain that I am really distinct from my body, and can exist without it." Allen, *Concept of Woman*, vol. 3, 255–56. Her citation is René Descartes, *Meditations on First Philosophy: In Which the Existence of God and the Distinction of the Soul from the Body are Demonstrated*, 3rd ed., trans. Ronald A. Cress (Indianapolis: Hackett, 1993), *Meditation* 6, #78, 51.

those which pertain to extended substance or body."[26] Thus, every human reality and experience must be considered solely according to one or the other of these two substances; in the one case, the mind (soul) or thinking substance only, in the second case, the body or extended substance only.[27] Importantly for our discussion, the mind/soul, which is one's personal identity, is sexless and is completely separate from the body, which is either male or female. Equal dignity, yes; but significant differentiation, no. The slow and sporadic movement toward sex complementarity would be interrupted by this novel Cartesian philosophy. Indeed, sex neutrality can trace its modern origins to this Cartesian philosophy.

While many philosophers adopted this Cartesian dualism, some objected to its fierce division between thinking and extended substances. For example, Elizabeth of Bohemia (1618–1680)[28] questioned Descartes about how the two substances could interact in a person. His response pointed to a small area of the brain—"the part which is said to contain the 'common sense'"[29]—rather than all parts of the body. Integration occurred uniquely in "the innermost part of the brain, which is a certain very small gland situated in the middle of the brain's substance,"[30] or, as he would later identify, the "pineal gland," from which the soul "radiates through the rest of the body by means of the animal spirits, the nerves, and even the blood."[31] The pineal gland could be affected by the soul (which is immaterial), and it could be

---

[26] Allen, *Concept of Woman*, vol. 3, 256. Her citation is René Descartes, *Principles of Philosophy* #48, in *The Philosophical Writings of Descartes*, trans. John Cottingham, Robert Stoothoff, and Dugald Murdoch, 3 vols. (Cambridge: Cambridge University Press, 1989–1991), 1:208–209.

[27] Allen, *Concept of Woman*, vol. 3, 256.

[28] Descartes dedicated his *Principles of Philosophy* to Princess Elizabeth, indicative of his desire to write philosophy not only for men but for women as well.

[29] Allen, *Concept of Woman*, vol. 3, 266. Her citation is Descartes, *Meditations on First Philosophy*, *Meditation* 6, #78, p. 59.

[30] Allen, *Concept of Woman*, vol. 3, 266. Her citation is René Descartes, *The Passions of the Soul*, #31, in *The Philosophical Writings of Descartes*, 1:340.

[31] Allen, *Concept of Woman*, vol. 3, 266–67. Her citation is Descartes, *The Passions of the Soul*, #34, in *The Philosophical Writings of Descartes*, 1:341.

affected by these "animal spirits" (which are material), but Descartes did not explain how the immaterial soul could affect material substances. Ultimately, Cartesian dualism failed to explain the interaction of mind/soul and body, though it pushed forward the sex neutrality view. Indeed, according to this position, little attention is given, nor needs to be given, to the concept of men and women.[32]

Without significant differentiation between the sexes or even attention given to the sexes, two movements—one favoring access to education for women alongside of men, the other advocating for the equal participation of women in citizenship—gained momentum.[33] Some historians see these developments as part of an early first wave feminism in the late eighteenth and mid-nineteenth century.

As an example of the first movement, Mary Astell (1666–1731), in *A Serious Proposal to the Ladies for the Advancement of Their True and Greatest Interest* (1694), advocated for the inauguration of a women's college offering higher education that would be the equivalent of the training available to men in England.[34]

As an example of the second movement, Antoine Caritat, Marquis de Condorcet (1743–1794), encouraged the full participation of women as citizens of the newly founded United States of America: "We want a constitution [in the state of Virginia], the principles of which would be based solely upon the natural rights of man [humanity], anterior to social institutions. We call these rights *natural* because they are derived from man's [human] nature. . . . Is it not as sensitive [sentient = living] beings, reasonable, having moral ideas, that men have rights? Women must then have absolutely the same; and yet never, in any so-called free constitution, have women exercised the right of citizenship."[35] As another example,

[32] Allen, *Concept of Woman*, vol. 3, 295.

[33] Allen, *Concept of Woman*, vol. 3, 297.

[34] Allen, *Concept of Woman*, vol. 3, 311.

[35] Allen, *Concept of Woman*, vol. 3, 317–18. Her citation is Marie Jean Antoine Marquis de Condorcet, *Recherches historiques et politiques sur les Etats-unis de L'Amérique septentrionale, avec quatre lettres d'un bourgeois de New Haven*

Elizabeth Cady Stanton's "Declaration of Sentiments" (1848), patterned after the U.S. Declaration of Independence, insisted that women, like men, are endowed with the inalienable rights of life, liberty, and the pursuit of happiness. Furthermore, women should be free from patriarchal oppression as evidenced by the absence of women's suffrage, exclusion from government, lack of property rights for married women, restrictions on access to educational and employment opportunities, and more. The Declaration called for women to be recognized as full citizens of the United States with the same rights as accorded to men.

An appeal to the common human capacity of reason became a standard part of advocacy for citizenship rights of women, as illustrated by Mary Wollstonecraft's (1759–1797) *A Vindication of the Rights of Woman* (1792).[36] She underscored "the gift of reason" shared equally by men and women and a "parity of reason" between the two sexes, concluding: "If women are to be excluded, without having a voice, from a participation of the natural rights of mankind, prove first, to ward off the charge of injustice and inconsistency, that they [women] want [lack] reason—else this flaw in your New [French] Constitution will ever show that man must, in some shape, act like a tyrant, and tyranny, in whatever part of society it rears its brazen front, will ever undermine morality."[37]

Despite this advocacy for equal rights and equal access to education for women, significant resistance arose to challenge and deny such promotion. Two examples are Jean-Jacques Rousseau and Immanuel Kant, both of

---

sur l'unité de legislation, trans. Christiane Teasdale (Paris: A. Colle, 1788), 280–81. Similarly, Olympe de Gouges, "Les Droits de la Femme" (Paris, 1791), outlined seventeen rights of women, including liberty, possession of property, security, resistance to oppression, participation in government, voicing of public opinion, naming publicly the father of their children, passing on property to their children, and more.

[36] She wrote to extend the discussion of rights beyond those of men as advocated by Edmund Burke (*Reflection on the French Revolution*, 1790) and Thomas Paine (*The Rights of Man*, 1791).

[37] Allen, *Concept of Woman*, vol. 3, 323–24. Her citation is Mary Wollstonecraft, *A Vindication of the Rights of Woman* (New York: Norton, 1975), 5.

whom favored fractional sex complementarity together with a sex-polarity-grounded devaluation of women.

Jean-Jacques Rousseau (1712–1778) continued the millennia-old portrayal of the difference between men as "focused on ideas and arguments, abstract judgments, and planning for the future" and women as focused on "the emotions, practical decisions in the present, and the general categories of taste, sentiments, and the senses."[38] As Rousseau himself asserted, "Consult the women's opinions in bodily matters, in all that concerns the senses; consult the men in matters of morality and all that concerns the understanding."[39]

Immanuel Kant (1724–1804) addressed the differences between men and women in his chapter "Of the Distinction of the Beautiful and Sublime in the Interrelations of the Two Sexes": "It is not to be understood . . . that woman lacks noble qualities, or that the male sex must do without beauty completely. On the contrary, one expects that a person of either sex brings both together, in such a way that all the other merits of a woman should unite solely to enhance the character of the beautiful, which is the proper reference point; and on the other, among the masculine qualities, the sublime clearly stands out as the criterion of his kind."[40] In other words, a woman is distinguished by the beautiful, her senses, and feelings; a man, by the sublime and his noble understanding of excellence, rationality, and principles.

Moreover, Kant proposed a fractional complementarity as seen in his explanation of marriage: "In matrimonial life the united pair should, as it were, constitute a single moral person, which is animated and governed

---

[38] Allen, *Concept of Woman*, vol. 3, 340. This quotation has been modified slightly for grammatical purposes.

[39] Allen, *Concept of Woman*, vol. 3, 340. Her citation is Jean-Jacques Rousseau, *Emile* (London: Dent, 1984), 306.

[40] Allen, *Concept of Woman*, vol. 3, 341. Her citation is Immanuel Kant, *Observations on the Feeling of the Beautiful and Sublime*, trans. John T. Goldthwait (Berkeley: University of California Press, 1963), 76–77.

by the understanding of the man and the taste of the wife."[41] That is, a woman is ontologically incomplete in herself, and a man is ontologically incomplete in himself; thus, when they join together in marriage, they become ontologically one person made up of two fractional parts. They are never—before marriage or after marriage—two ontologically complete, differentiated persons. Before marriage, each is an ontologically incomplete person; after marriage, they compose one ontologically complete person, not two.[42] Moreover, Kant's description of that single person as animated by the wife's taste relegated the female sex to inferior status, as Kant expressed elsewhere: women are typically engaged in storytelling, jesting, and arguing; they are subordinated in nature to their female sexual identity ("human nature is thereby sacrificed to sex"); and they are incapable of rational thinking and acting.[43]

Finally, if we consider Kant's "An Answer to the Question: What is Enlightenment?", it appears that women cannot be enlightened:

> Enlightenment is man's emergence from his self-imposed immaturity. Immaturity is the inability to use one's understanding without guidance from another. This immaturity is self-imposed when its cause lies not in lack of understanding, but in lack of resolve and courage to use it without guidance from another. Sapere Aude! "Have courage to use your own understanding!"—that is the motto of enlightenment.[44]

If women cannot gain understanding, or if they are irresolute and fearful to use their understanding apart from the leadership of a man, then they

---

[41] Allen, *Concept of Woman*, vol. 3, 341. Her citation is Kant, *Observations*, 95.

[42] Allen, *Concept of Woman*, vol. 3, 342.

[43] Allen, *Concept of Woman*, vol. 3, 343. Her citation is Immanuel Kant, "Duties towards the Body in Respect of Sexual Impulse," in *Lectures on Ethics*, trans. Louis Infield (New York: Harper & Row, 1963), 164.

[44] Immanuel Kant, "An Answer to the Question: What is Enlightenment?"

cannot become mature, that is, enlightened.[45] Consequently, Kant wedded a type of fractional complementarity (at least in marriage) with a traditional demeaning posture toward women.

One of his students critiqued Kant's framework. Theodor Gottlieb von Hippel (1741–1796) embraced fractional complementarity but somewhat shed of its sex polarity and belittling of women. At times, he championed the equality of women and men: "As soon as women are considered to be human beings and given credit for possessing the power of reason, one can no longer place limitations on their intellectual faculties."[46] Respect for the full humanity, rationality, and intellectual capacities of women should translate into equal rights—"women, just like men, are human beings, and . . . therefore, equal rights are due them as well"[47]—and citizenship for women.[48] Hippel also blamed the persistent and pervasive oppression of women for the inequality that actually exists between them and men.[49]

At other times, however, Hippel slipped into sex polarity while also attempting to affirm a fractional complementarity. Echoing his mentor Kant, Hippel described the marriage relationship: "In marriage the woman finally attains completion through the man—to the same degree that he is completed through her. Man and woman together constitute a complete human being. The distribution of human characteristics between the two sexes leaves no doubt as to the veracity of this conclusion."[50] Two ontologically fractional, or partial, persons—the man with his masculine characteristics, the woman with her feminine characteristics—exist before contracting

---

[45] Immanuel Kant, "An Answer to the Question."

[46] Allen, *Concept of Woman*, vol. 3, 356. Her citation is Theodor Gottlieb von Hippel, *On Improving the Status of Women*, trans. Timothy E. Sellner (Detroit: Wayne State University Press, 1979), 190.

[47] Allen, *Concept of Woman*, vol. 3, 352. Her citation is Theodor Gottlieb von Hippel, *On Marriage*, trans. Timothy E. Sellner (Detroit: Wayne State University Press, 1994), 170.

[48] Allen, *Concept of Woman*, vol. 3, 355.

[49] Allen, *Concept of Woman*, vol. 3, 352–53.

[50] Allen, *Concept of Woman*, vol. 3, 354. Her citation is Hippel, *On Marriage*, 144.

a marriage. Afterwards, they are one ontologically complete person with the full distribution of both masculine and feminine characteristics. Hippel affirmed a fractional sex complementarity.

The emphatic calls for equal rights and full citizenship of women flowered in the women's suffrage movement in the late nineteenth and early twentieth century. A key result was the passage of the Nineteenth Amendment (1920), granting women in the United States the right to vote.

Good developments such as this were contradicted by an ongoing traditional sex polarity and its accompanying devaluation of women in the field of psychology. For example, Sigmund Freud (1856–1939) underscored one biological element that men possess and that women lack—a penis—as the foundation for his view that women seek to recuperate that absent anatomical element and do so by becoming passive in relation to men/fathers/husbands. The similarities to Aristotelian sex polarity are striking: the one aspect of human materiality—for Aristotle, the male's ability to produce seed (sperm); for Freud, the male penis—is key to all valuation of sex identity and is the fundamental Aristotelian philosophical or Freudian psychological basis for the evaluation of men as superior to women. Additionally, both key figures affirmed the traditional view that men are naturally active and women are naturally passive.[51]

The twentieth century witnessed the rise of integral sex complementarity. One example was Dietrich von Hildebrand (1889–1977): "[The] difference between man and woman is a metaphysical one. . . . [F]or the human species, this difference represents two manifestations of the person. . . . These two types, man and woman, have a unique capacity for *complementing* each other. Their meaning for one another is something quite unique. They are made for the other in a special way, and they can, purely as spiritual persons, form a unity in which they reciprocally complement one."[52]

---

[51] Allen, *Concept of Woman*, vol. 3, 360.

[52] Allen, *Concept of Woman*, vol. 3, 369. Her citation is Dietrich von Hildebrand, *Marriage: The Mystery of Faithful Love* (Manchester, NH: Sophi Institute Press, 1982, 1991), 14–15 (von Hildebrand's italics). Though von Hildebrand affirmed

A second example is Jacques Maritain (1882–1973), who grounded integral sex complementarity, equal dignity, and significant differentiation in the two creation accounts (Genesis 1–2):

> First of all, we must go back to the text of Genesis. I think that the two accounts of the creation of man must be taken together and refer to two complementary truths both of which must be safeguarded: the first of these accounts has for its object to emphasize the unity of human nature and the equality in nature and dignity of man and of woman (from the very creative act by which man appeared on the earth, human nature was male in one and female in the other); the second account . . . presenting the creation of Eve as posterior to that of Adam . . . has for its object to emphasize the way in which God willed and brought it about that women be differentiated from man.[53]

Hildebrand and Maritain voiced key themes that will echo throughout this book: biblical and theological foundations for complementarity; an emphasis on the nature or essence of men and women; the unity of human nature as the large category of humankind with two types, women and men, who are equal in dignity; their capacity for complementing one another; divinely willed differentiation between the sexes; and a unity that is characterized by reciprocity.

In conclusion, Chapter 8 has traced the development of the concept of women and men from the mid-sixteenth century to the present day, focusing on the contributions of key figures such as Lucrezia Marinella, René Descartes, Immanuel Kant, and Jacques Maritain. This period witnessed

---

this complementarity for men and women in a marital relationship, I will take it beyond that one relationship and affirm it for men and women in general.

[53] Allen, *Concept of Woman*, vol. 3, 374. Her citation is Jacques Maritain, "Let Us Make for Him a Helpmate Like to Himself," in *Untrammeled Approaches*, trans. Bernard Doering (Notre Dame: University of Notre Dame Press, 1997), 156–57.

the development of all five sex identities—traditional sex polarity, sex equality, sex neutrality, reverse sex polarity, and sex complementarity in both its fractional and integral versions. These sex identities continue at the present time, defended by proponents and critiqued by opponents, the lived experiences of both women and men, and influential for both sexes relationally, familially, vocationally, and ecclesially.

This extensive survey brings us to our contemporary context, with further discussion to follow later.

CHAPTER 9

Summary and Implications for the Church, and My Thesis

Largely through the life-long writings of Sister Prudence Allen, I have traced the history of the concept of woman and its corollary concept of man. Often, this history has sought to answer four questions:

1. The metaphysical question of *opposites*: in what ways are male and female opposites? The various answers to this question will be summarized below.
2. The natural philosophy question of *generation*: what are the respective functions of mothering and fathering in reproduction or the generation of children? A pervasive and persistent misunderstanding of human anatomy and physiology—especially when it comes to sperm, ova, menstruation, and the way reproduction occurs—erroneously led to the conclusion that a woman is an inferior, or deformed, man.
3. The epistemological question of *wisdom*: do women and men relate to wisdom in the same way? The tradition has associated the higher capacities of rationality, reason, judgment, and the like with men, and the lower functions of passion, bodily desire, appetite, and the

like with women. Wisdom, then, has been traditionally viewed as more the domain of men.

4. The question of moral philosophy or *virtue*: do women and men have the same or different virtues? Largely because of the third point, the tradition has held that men and women have or are capable of different virtues: for men, the active virtues of reason, wisdom, speech, public activity, and ruling; for women, the passive virtues of opinion, silence/listening, private (home) management, and obedience/submission.

Returning to the first question about men and women as opposites, Allen proposes five basic theories of sex identity.

- *sex unity*: Women and men are equal, and they are not significantly different. This view is often accompanied by a devaluation of the materiality/embodiment of human beings.
- *sex neutrality* (which may be a derivative of sex unity): Women and men are equal and not significantly different. This theory ignores differences between the sexes rather than arguing directly for the equality of women and men.
- *traditional sex polarity*: Women and men are significantly different, and men are superior to women. Often, as a foundation for this view, one aspect of human materiality is key to all valuation of sex identity and is the fundamental basis for the evaluation of men as superior to women.
- *reverse sex polarity*: Women and men are significantly different, and women are superior to men. Often, as a foundation for this view, one aspect of human materiality is key to all valuation of sex identity and is the fundamental basis for the evaluation of women as superior to men.
- *sex complementarity*: Women and men are significantly different, and they are equal. Historically, this view was often accompanied by the realization that both the mother and the father contribute one-half of the seed/reproductive material that is needed for the

production of the fetus—that is, through the union of differentiated, equal, and necessary male sperm and female ovum, a child is generated. This category can be divided into two types:

- *fractional sex complementarity*: As with complementarity in general, women and men are significantly different, and they are equal; additionally, this subgroup "ascribes specific masculine and feminine characteristics to the two sexes, dividing them so that a woman may have one, a man the other," and through their complementarity they as fractional (i.e., incomplete, partial) beings constitute one being.[1]
- *integral sex/gender complementarity*: in addition to the principles of complementarity in general, this subgroup considers a woman and a man "as two separate and complete human individuals who are equal in dignity and worth and who have philosophically significant differences. They are not fractional beings who together make up one being. Instead, they are two whole beings who, together, synergetically generate more than just the sum of themselves."[2]

This brief historical journey has alerted us to the ebb and flow of these various theories of sex identity and how the concepts of women and men have expressed themselves in philosophy, theology, and ecclesiology.

These views of women and men have had, and continue to have, many implications for the church during its two-thousand-year existence and ministry. The following four implications (which correspond to Allen's four questions) are of the church overall throughout its lengthy history.[3]

---

[1] Allen, *Concept of Woman*, vol. 2, 18.

[2] Allen, *Concept of Woman*, vol. 2, 18.

[3] I acknowledge the ambiguity in my use of the word "church." By it I refer as broadly as possible to the institution at the core of Christendom and its three historical branches of Roman Catholicism, Eastern Orthodoxy, and Protestantism. Though an all-encompassing concept, this institution manifests itself in particular churches that are characterized by both a "mere orthodoxy" in terms of "the faith that was once for all delivered to the saints" (Jude 3 ESV) as well as specific theological,

First, the church has embraced—either explicitly as a studied conviction or implicitly by its repeated mistreatment of women—traditional sex polarity, considering men to be superior to women. Complementarity, while occasionally occurring and exerting an influence, has largely been a contemporary development that is still questioned and, in some quarters, opposed today. Second, a significant reason for the dominance of traditional sex polarity (and the accompanying rejection of complementarity) was an entrenched misunderstanding of human anatomy and physiology (e.g., only men contribute seed [sperm] to the generation of children, while women play a passive role). Such error, which was not definitively overturned until the middle of the nineteenth century by scientific discoveries, has led to the conclusion that a woman is an inferior, or deformed, man. Even when a corrected view of procreation is removed as a support for male superiority and female inferiority, other reasons for traditional sex polarity bolster its retention. Third, the church has associated the higher capacities of rationality, reason, judgment, and the like with men, and the lower functions of passion, bodily desire, appetite, and the like with women. Wisdom, then, is more the domain of men. Fourth, and largely because of the third point, the church has held that men and women have or are capable of different virtues: for men, the active virtues of reason, wisdom, speech, public activity, and ruling; for women, the passive virtues of opinion, silence/listening, private (home) management, and obedience/submission.

---

liturgical, sacramental, hierarchical/structural, denominational, and practical emphases that differentiate them. Such "mere orthodoxy" is witnessed by a common affirmation of the Creed of Nicaea (325), the Nicene-Constantinopolitan Creed (381), the Apostles' Creed, the Athanasian Creed, and the Chalcedonian Creed (451). Distinctives include matters such as the nature of divine revelation (e.g., *sola Scriptura* or Scripture, Tradition, and the Magisterium), Trinitarian processions (e.g., double or single procession of the Holy Spirit), justification (e.g., a forensic declaration or a transformative process), the nature and number of sacraments (e.g., means of communicating infused grace, seven or two), church government (e.g., episcopalianism, presbyterianism, congregationalism), and much more. Accordingly, as I discuss implications of this long historical development of different views of sex identity and the demeaning of women for the church, I am generalizing as broadly as possible.

The overall conclusion that arises from this consideration is that the Western philosophical/theological/ecclesiastical concept of women is demeaning of and disparaging toward women, whom men consider to be inferior in terms of nature, procreation, wisdom, and virtue. While the primary focus has been on the effects of this deprecating concept of women on women and the many restrictions placed on them as a result, Vern Bullough offers a convicting corollary: "What is sometimes overlooked is that they also put limitations on male development."[4] This lament corresponds well with the notion of complementarity, which calls for both sexes to fill out and mutually support one another. When one sex discounts or dismisses the other, half of the partnership that is needed for mutual reliance and collaboration is missing or abandoned. Complementarity cannot exist. Tragically, then, the church's historical conditioning has been to view women as inherently inferior to men, deeply impacting both sexes and their proper development and defrauding the divinely designed complementarity between men and women of its requisite contributors.

Consequently, my thesis is that this perspective continues to dominate our contemporary Western ecclesial and social context; we are saddled with this tragic view and, even though we may point to positive (and actual) developments that have taken us beyond that view, it continues to haunt even our best efforts and to devastate our resolve. Examples are legion and include toxic versions of masculinity, the marginalization of women within the workforce, illegitimate restrictions of women in certain spheres of church leadership, and relational difficulties between men and women and between husbands and wives. The deep and pervasive stain of two-and-a-half millennia of gender confusion and male-female conflict is not and cannot be easily or quickly removed. Moreover, this stain may express itself in subtle and not-so-subtle ways. Furthermore, this influence affects both complementarianism and egalitarianism alike.

---

[4] Vern L. Bullough, "On Being a Male in the Middle Ages," in *Medieval Masculinities: Regarding Men in the Middle Ages*, ed. Clare A Lees, Medieval Cultures 7 (Minneapolis: University of Minnesota Press, 1994), 33.

PART THREE

Contemporary Context

Part Two traced the historical development of the various positions on sex identity: sex unity, sex neutrality, traditional sex polarity, reverse sex polarity, and sex complementarity, with its two types of fractional sex complementarity and integral sex complementarity. It stopped with twentieth-century developments. Part Three completes that survey by focusing on several key developments over the course of the last century: modern feminist movements, contemporary complementarianism, and contemporary egalitarianism.[1]

[1] I will address each of these terms in chapters 10, 11, and 13.

CHAPTER 10

Modern Feminist Movements

First Wave Feminism

At the end of Part Two, I noted the rise of what may be considered to be early first wave feminism in the late eighteenth and mid-nineteenth century. In particular, two movements arose that championed access to education for women alongside of men and the equal participation of women in citizenship. Advancing on these developments was the women's suffrage movement—what may be recognized to be later first wave feminism—in the late nineteenth and early twentieth century. Fueled by the advocacy of women's rights and appeals for their full citizenship, as well as abolitionist and the temperance movements, this largely social and political movement championed the cause of equal political rights for women. An example in the United States was women's right to vote, which was granted by the Nineteenth Amendment in 1920. Advocates for suffrage were mostly white, Christian, anti-abortion, middle-class women.[1] In relation to the following developments, women's suffrage is generally referred to as first wave feminism.

[1] Abigail Favale, *The Genesis of Gender: A Christian Theory* (San Francisco: Ignatius, 2022), 57.

In terms of modern feminist movements, discussion often follows along the lines of three more numbered feminist movements: second, third, and (perhaps) fourth wave feminism.

Second Wave Feminism and Simone de Beauvoir

Second wave feminism of the 1960s and 1970s was a widespread, anti-patriarchal, cultural movement that opposed systemic sexism against women. Such sexism manifested itself in several areas: (1) denying women certain employment opportunities, exclusion from which was warranted by the traditional insistence that a woman's place is in her home;[2] and (2) limiting certain emerging social rights for women—for example, reproductive freedom through access to birth control and abortion—that put them at a socio-economic-vocational-educational disadvantage in relation to men.

In some arguments in its support, second wave feminism relied on the newly (1968) coined phrase "gender identity,"[3] by which biological "sex"—what one is physiologically, anatomically, chromosomally—could be distinguished from "gender"—one's perceived or imagined identity, which could be that of the opposite sex from that with which one was born (i.e., a biologically sexed male feeling that he is a gendered woman trapped in a man's body). Accordingly, "gender" became one's self-identification and began to be considered, for the most part, as socially constructed and malleable. If such is the case, argued second wave feminists, then the female sex should not be conflated with the traditional gender roles that were so oppressive of women. Women could and should have access to all professions—e.g., business, education, politics, law, religion—that were once the sole domain of men.

---

[2] This pervasive insistence of a well-defined domestic role for women was the subject attacked by Betty Friedan's *The Feminine Mystique* (New York: Norton, 1963).

[3] Robert J. Stoller, *Sex and Gender: On the Development of Masculinity and Femininity* (New York: Science House, 1968).

Accordingly, women may make themselves, and may make of themselves, as they wish. One aspect of this self-designation and self-determination involves rejection of the traditional sex polarity view that men are superior to women, who are defective, inferior men. Simone de Beauvoir (1908–1986) exposed some of the ways that men define women: "For him, she is sex—absolute sex, no less. She is defined and differentiated with reference to man and not he with reference to her; she is the incidental, the inessential as opposed to the essential. He the Subject, he is the Absolute—she is the Other."[4] As she underscored, "One is not born, but rather becomes, a woman. No biological, psychological, or economic fate determines the figure that the human female presents in society; it is civilization as a whole that produces this creature, intermediate between male and eunuch, which is described as feminine."[5] Tamped down by male superiority and defined as inferior by male arrogance, women are not women by nature or status (nor, Christians would add to this list [though not mentioned by Beauvoir], are they created by God as women). Rather, they exist and act only in relation to and for men who, as leaders of society, produce women as they so determine. It was against such portraits of women that second wave feminism rebelled, fighting for the right to be and act as and for themselves, including working in once male-only professions.

In the process, what seems to have developed is an even deeper disrespect for women. Ironically, however, it was not men's disrespect for women, but women's disrespect for themselves and for other women. As Beauvoir opined about female identity, "Better that she identify herself as a human being who happens to be a woman. It's a certain situation which is not the same as men's situation, of course, but she shouldn't identify herself as a

[4] Prudence Allen, *The Concept of Woman,* Volume 3*: The Search for Communion of Persons, 1500–2015* (Grand Rapids: Eerdmans, 2016), 392. Her citation is Simone de Beauvoir, *The Second Sex,* trans. and ed. H. M. Parshley (New York: Knopf, 1957), xvi and 142.

[5] Allen, *The Concept of Woman,* vol. 3, 392. Her citation is Beauvoir, *Second Sex,* 267.

woman."[6] To do so would be to passively concede to her nature and not act responsibly: "to give birth and to breastfeed are not *activities* but natural functions; they do not involve a project, which is why the woman finds no motive there [in childbearing] to claim a higher meaning for her existence; she passively submits to her biological destiny."[7] Women may settle for being mothers, breastfeeding their babies, and raising children, but such is not a conscientious choice that will propel them to a more mature level of existence. Rather, it is a passive condescension to their biological nature, a non-choice leading to an inferior future. Second wave feminism made certain advances for women, particularly with respect to career paths, but also demeaned certain aspects of womanhood.

Third Wave Feminism and Judith Butler

Third wave feminism, beginning in the 1990s and ongoing, is a hard-to-define, diffuse movement that (1) battled against sexual harassment in the workforce and in marriage, and (2) worked to elect women to places of political power. Some aspects of this approach can be traced to the 1980s feminist debate, "an internal conflict between feminists who opposed pornography and prostitution as forces of female oppression, and the so-called 'sex-positive' feminists who viewed these as liberating."[8] To a large degree, third wave feminism embraced this second perspective. Yet, at the same time, it also denounced the pervasive evil of sexual harassment against women at their jobs and married women in their homes. Joining women in their battle against sexual harassment were several men's movements. For example, White Ribbon was founded in 1991 in response to the heinous

[6] Allen, *Concept of Woman,* vol. 3, 393. Her citation is Margaret Simons, "Two Interviews with Simone de Beauvoir (1982)," *Hypatia* 3, no. 3 (Winter 1989): 19.

[7] Favale, *The Genesis of Gender*, 64. Her citation is Simone de Beauvoir, *The Second Sex* (New York: Vintage, 2011), 73.

[8] Favale, *The Genesis of Gender*, 59.

slaughter of fourteen women students at École Polytechnique by the misogynist Mark Lévine in 1989.[9] MenEngage Alliance was founded in 2004 and aims at "transforming patriarchal masculinities and rigid, harmful norms around 'being a man,'" and "working with men and boys on gender justice through intersectional feminist approaches."[10]

As for women in politics, a comparison of the number of women in the U.S. Congress one hundred years ago to today reveals the significant strides that third wave feminism made. In the 66th Congress from 1923 to 1925, no woman served in the Senate and only one woman served in the House of Representatives. At the halfway point in our survey, the 93rd Congress (1973–1975) had no woman senators and sixteen representatives in the House. The 103rd Congress (1993–1995) featured seven women in the Senate and forty-seven in the House, leaping ahead to a total of fifty-four women. That number reached an even one hundred two decades later: the 113th Congress numbered twenty female Senators and eighty female Representatives. The current 119th Congress (2025–2027) totals one hundred fifty women, twenty-five of whom are Senators and one hundred twenty-five of whom are Representatives.[11]

A major figure in this period was Judith Butler, who modified the sex-gender division—with gender being a social construct—into the position that the category of sex itself is a social construct, and one that is oppressive to the marginalized in society. That is, the traditional binary structure of male human beings and female human beings itself is socially constructed

---

[9] For further discussion see White Ribbon USA, https://www.whiteribbonusa.org/.

[10] These are two of the four elements of the mission of Men Engage Alliance; https://menengage.org/about/.

[11] Center for American Women and Politics (accessed December 2, 2024); https://cawp.rutgers.edu/election-watch/2024-election-results-tracker. "Record counts were updated to include U.S. Representative Erica Lee Carter (D-TX), who was sworn into the 118th Congress on November 12, 2024."

to oppress women, and the traditional binary sexual relationship permitting sexual intercourse between a man and a woman only, is itself socially constructed to promote heteronormativity and oppress homosexuals. Rather than any "givenness" for sex and gender (Butler insisted that the use of these two terms as being differentiated is counterproductive), there is only performance. As Butler famously opined, gender is performative in that it "is real only to the extent that it is performed."[12] In other words, there is no such reality as gender identity before a person engages in a gendered act. Again, she offered: "gender proves to be performative—that is, constituting the identity it is purported to be. In this sense, gender is always a doing, though not a doing by a subject who might be said to preexist the deed."[13] Butler rejected the notion that the gender identity of a person leads to or produces gendered attitudes, behavior, and acts. Rather, she maintained that those gendered attitudes, behaviors, and acts, in their being expressed, constitute the gender identity of that person. If identity is constructed, and if that construction is ever (even if so slightly) changing, then there is and can be no solidity to the concepts of men and women, male and female, masculinity and femininity, and human sexuality. Butler destroyed all "givenness" to human reality.

Conjoin Butler's radical deconstruction with the emerging concept of intersectionality, and even more challenges arose.[14] "The concept of intersectionality describes the ways in which systems of inequality based on

---

[12] Judith Butler, "Performative Acts and Gender Constitution: An Essay in Phenomenology and Feminist Theory," *Theatre Journal* 40.4 (1988): 527.

[13] Judith Butler, *Gender Trouble: Feminism and the Subversion of Identity* (New York: Routledge, 1990), 33. For a critique of the social construction of gender in general and that of Judith Butler in particular, see Fellipe do Vale, *Gender as Love: A Theological Account of Human Identity, Embodied Desire, and Our Social Worlds* (Grand Rapids: Baker Academic, 2023), 48–68.

[14] The origin of intersectionality is attributed to Kimberle Crenshaw, "Demarginalizing the Intersection of Race and Sex: A Black Feminist Critique of Antidiscrimination Doctrine, Feminist Theory and Antiracist Politics," *University of Chicago Legal Forum*, vol. 1989, issue 1, article 8. The contemporary uses of her term may diverge significantly from her original intention; https://chicagounbound.uchicago.edu/cgi/viewcontent.cgi?article=1052&context=uclf.

gender, race, ethnicity, sexual orientation, gender identity, disability, class and other forms of discrimination 'intersect' to create unique dynamics and effects."[15] Intersectionality divides human beings into two fixed categories: the haves/powerful/privileged and the have-nots/powerless/disenfranchised. "Examples of the first category of individuals are wealthy, straight, educated, English-speaking, native-born, white, Christian males. Examples of the second are poor, lesbian (or transgendered), uneducated, non-English-speaking, born elsewhere, Muslim women of color."[16] Importantly for our discussion, this hierarchical framework (almost) always places men in the privileged category and women in the underprivileged category.[17] This framework results in a fixed division while insisting that men denounce and deprive themselves of their prized patriarchal characteristics and prompting women to revolt against men and claim their right to female power and prestige. Clearly, intersectionality is a contemporary expression of reverse sex polarity and is the opposite of complementarity.

---

[15] This is the answer to the question "What is Intersectionality?" supplied by the Center for Intersectional Justice; https://www.intersectionaljustice.org/what-is-intersectionality. Accessed October 19, 2023.

[16] Gregg R. Allison, *Embodied: Living as Whole People in a Fractured World* (Grand Rapids: Baker, 2021), 60. I assembled these descriptors from the intersectionality score calculator, https://intersectionalityscore.com/. Analyzing these elements reveals that among them, some are ontological (e.g., biological male or female), some ethnic (e.g., Italian- or Peruvian-born), some economical (e.g., rich or poor), and some social (e.g., city dweller or rural resident) identities. Thus, people are *born* with some of these identities (and the intersectionality score calculator underscores this point) and others are the result of *being born* into a particular socio-economic context. Despite this fact, the calculator curates all the identities equally to determine one's intersectionality score.

[17] This point can be further nuanced with reference to womanism (a specific development within feminism), which offered a critique of both feminism in general (as proposed and developed largely by white women) and black liberation theology (as proposed and developed by black men); both movements reprehensibly ignored black women and their particular struggles for respect and social progress. For further discussion see Alice Walker, *In Search of Our Mothers' Gardens: Womanist Prose* (New York: Harcourt, 1983); Delores Williams, *Sisters in the Wilderness: The Challenge of Womanist God-Talk* (Maryknoll, NY: Orbis, 1993).

Fourth Wave Feminism

Some observers add a fourth wave as a present-day feminist development. This fourth wave feminism is an eclectic movement featuring #MeToo, Time's Up, SlutWalks, and the like. A key development that distinguishes this wave from its predecessors is the use of social media to spread its ideology and activate social change. For example, #MeToo (2017–present) spread awareness of sexual harassment against women worldwide by providing a platform for abused women to tell their experiences to a global audience. Its founder, Tarana Burke, described #MeToo: "This is a movement that deals specifically with sexual violence. And it is a framework for how to do the work of ending sexual violence."[18] As a second example, Christy Haubegger, creator of "Time's Up," explained, "Time's Up was founded on the premise that everyone, every human being, deserves a right to earn a living, to take care of themselves, to take care of their families, free of the impediments of harassment and sexual assault and discrimination."[19] This movement focuses on issues in the workplace where power imbalances and pay inequities dominate. It seeks to enact legislation for equal pay, equal work conditions, and equal access to employment opportunities for women in low paying jobs and women of color.[20] A third example is SlutWalk, which defines itself as "a rally, march, protest, and movement aimed to make visible the prevalence of victim-blaming, rape-culture, street harassment, and

---

[18] Alix Langone, "#MeToo and Time's Up Founders Explain the Difference Between the 2 Movements—And How They're Alike" (March 22, 2018), time.com, https://time.com/5189945/whats-the-difference-between-the-metoo-and-times-up-movements/.

[19] Alix Langone, "#MeToo and Time's Up Founders."

[20] Alix Langone, "#MeToo and Time's Up Founders." While the Time's Up movement was supported by actresses such as Ashley Judd, Oprah Winfrey, and Meryl Streep, it experienced a precipitous decline several years after its founding in 2017 and is in the process of reorganizing itself.

sexual violence."[21] Founded in 2011, it "began in response to Toronto police officer, Michael Sanguinetti, and his remarks that 'women should avoid dressing like sluts' in order to prevent being sexually assaulted. To combat this slut-shaming and rape culture in general, founders formed SlutWalk to speak out against victim blaming and slut shaming."[22] Since its beginning, SlutWalk has expanded its concerns to include harassment and violence due to sexism, classism, racism, homophobia, transphobia, and more.

Parallel to the ebb and flow of these waves of feminism has been the development of men's movements in response, with at least three varieties: (1) those that supported feminist causes and championed such issues as women's right to vote and the creation of safe workplace environments for women; (2) oppositely, those that opposed all things feminist and all focused attention on women and their concerns; and (3) those that opposed feminist movements in general but supported women and their particular causes. Examples of the first variety have already been mentioned: White Ribbon and MenEngage Alliance. Out of respect for readers, no examples of the second will be mentioned. An example of the third type is A Voice for Men, whose mission statement articulates the movement's purpose. After affirming the half century of "remarkable change" that has advanced the "freedom and identity" of women and their role, the statement warns that this change

> will not be complete until the same standards find their way into the lives of the average man. The absence of that complementary change in the lives of men has created an imbalance that erodes the autonomy of both sexes. Unless that changes, the imbalance will only worsen. Freedom from sex-based expectations for just one sex

---

[21] The University of Arizona Women and Gender Resource Center, "SlutWalk," https://wgrc.arizona.edu/slutwalk.

[22] Gender and Resource Center, "SlutWalk," https://wgrc.arizona.edu/slutwalk.

> will never result in freedom for either sex. It is simply a foundation of exploitation on which tyranny is built and administered.

The movement's statement continues,

> As a society, we are already on that path. The noble idea of freedom and equity between the sexes has been corrupted. It has become a malignancy on our social consciousness. What used to be cooperation between sexes is now gynocentric parasitism that inhabits every level of men's existence, from cradle to coffin. The efforts to enhance the rights of women have become toxic efforts to undermine the rights of men.

A Voice for Men's mission statement concludes: "It is time for a movement that truly favors humanity, not a particular sex. It is time for feminism to fulfill its promise of equity, and to quit making a mockery of it."[23]

From this statement, it appears that A Voice for Men applauds the many advances in terms of women's identity and freedom, that is, the overturning of traditional sex polarity. At the same time, it decries the bad fruit of (some of the waves of) feminism, particularly critiquing reverse sex polarity and its support for and practice of the superiority of women at the expense of men, who are relegated (either intentionally or unintentionally) to a status of inferiority in the process. Moreover, A Voice for Men urges the advancement of all human beings, both women and men, so that equality between the sexes is truly achieved. In this way, it supports sex complementarity.

Summary of the Four Waves of Feminism

In summary, four waves of feminism have resulted in three types of developments: (1) Positive developments through the championing of sex complementarity leading to substantial gains for the unity of men and women;

[23] "A Voice for Men Mission Statement," https://avoiceformen.com/featured/mission-statement/.

(2) Negative developments through the triumph of a reverse sex polarity that substitutes women for men in Prudence Allen's four arenas (opposites, generation, wisdom, and virtue), thus continuing the millennia-old superiority-inferiority framework that pathetically divides men and women; (3) Mixed developments through the overturning of traditional sex polarity to some degree and in some areas for the promotion of women's freedom and identity, with still a long way to go.

Christian Feminism

One development that has not been discussed is Christian feminism, a variation of feminism that considers women and men from a biblical perspective. Christian feminism traces its roots to the Evangelical Women's Caucus (EWC; modified to Evangelical and Ecumenical Women's Caucus in 1990; renamed Christian Feminism Today in 1990), founded in 1974 under the auspices of Evangelicals for Social Action, at whose consultation that women's caucus was one of six task forces. Its proposals included "endorsement of the Equal Rights Amendment, support for inclusive language in Bible translation and Christian publications, affirmation of the ordination of women, and criticism of discriminatory hiring policies in Christian institutions."[24]

A seismic shift occurred in 1986 when Evangelical Women's Caucus passed by a two-to-one margin the following resolution: "Whereas homosexual people are children of God, and because of the biblical mandate of Jesus Christ that we are all created equal in God's sight, and in recognition of the presence of the lesbian minority in EWCI [Evangelical Women's Caucus International], EWCI takes a firm stand in favor of civil rights protection for homosexual persons."[25] Conservative EWC members such as Catherine Kroeger withdrew from that caucus and created Christians for Biblical Equality (CBE).

---

[24] Evangelical and Ecumenical Women's Caucus, "Our Origin," https://eewc.com/about/#origin.

[25] Randall Balmer, "Evangelical and Ecumenical Women's Caucus," in *Encyclopedia of Evangelicalism*, 2nd ed. (Waco: Baylor University Press, 2004), 237.

At this point, two key movements—Council for Biblical Manhood and Womanhood (CBMW) and CBE—arose and began to dominate the evangelical landscape on the matters of complementarianism and egalitarianism. Their stories are told next.

But first, a bit of explanation of my terminology. The use of terms plays an important role in our discussion. I have chosen to use the labels *complementarianism* and *egalitarianism* rather than other possible terms for these frameworks and their proponents. I use the word *complementarianism* for that framework rather than *traditionalism*, *hierarchicalism*, or *patriarchalism*, and I use the term *complementarian* to describe proponents of that framework rather than *traditionalist*, *hierarchicalist*, or *patriarchalist*.[26] Similarly, I use the term *egalitarianism* for that framework rather than *progressivism*, *feminism*, or *biblical equality*, and I use the term *egalitarian* to describe proponents of that framework rather than *progressivist*, *feminist*, or *biblical egalitarian*.[27]

My goal in choosing these terms is to avoid causing division before any discussion can go forward. Relying on Charles Long's notion of "signification," Alice Mathews explains, "To signify is to name, and often by attaching pejorative names to movements or individuals, we can so color the perception of

---

[26] My terminology finds approbation from leading complementarians such as John Piper and Wayne Grudem. Commenting on their choice of terms in *Recovering Biblical Manhood and Womanhood*, the two offer: "If one word must be used to describe our position, we prefer the term *complementarian*, since it suggests both equality and beneficial differences between men and women. We are uncomfortable with the term 'traditionalist' because it implies an unwillingness to let Scripture challenge traditional patterns of behavior, and we certainly reject the term 'hierarchicalist' because it overemphasizes structured authority while giving no suggestion of equality or the beauty of mutual interdependence." John Piper and Wayne Grudem, eds., *Recovering Biblical Manhood and Womanhood: A Response to Evangelical Feminism* (Wheaton: Crossway, 1991, 2006), xiv. The editors of *Discovering Biblical Equality* have a fine discussion and advocate a use of terms similar to mine. Ronald W. Pierce, Cynthia Long Westfall, and Christa L. McKirland, "Introduction," in *Discovering Biblical Equality: Biblical, Theological, Cultural, and Practical Perspectives*, 3rd ed., ed. Ronald W. Pierce and Cynthia Long Westfall, assoc. ed. Christa L. McKirland (Downers Grove: IVP Academic, 2021), 4–7.

[27] I do discuss "feminism" and "feminists" in the preceding historical section.

our opponents that it becomes impossible to carry on meaningful dialogue."[28] I readily admit that these terms are controversial and debated. Much is made today of the ill-defined nature of the term *complementarianism*, due to its (alleged) association with June Cleaver of Leave It to Beaver fame,[29] its (purported) dependence on a certain view of the Trinity (Eternal Functional Subordination, or Eternal Relations of Authority and Submission),[30] as well as its (perceived) association with sexual abuse. As a result, many (even complementarians) advocate for not using the term. Some complain about the term *egalitarianism*, noting its (alleged) denial of the inerrancy and authority of Scripture, its (supposed) elimination of all differences (e.g., biological, roles) between men and women, and its (purported) support for the LGBTQIA2S+ agenda. Aware of these pitfalls, for better or worse, I will use *complementarianism* and *egalitarianism* (with definitions to follow shortly).

In conclusion and building on Part Two's lengthy presentation of historical development of the concept of women and men, Chapter 10 has traced the late-eighteenth to twenty-first-century emergence of first, second, third, and (perhaps?) fourth wave feminism, along with Christian feminism, to bring us up to the present time. Importantly, these recent developments fostered an environment in which contemporary complementarianism and contemporary egalitarianism arose. The stories of those two frameworks, which serve as my interlocutors, are recounted next.

---

[28] Alice P. Mathews, "Toward Reconciliation: Healing the Schism," in *Discovering Biblical Equality: Complementarity Without Hierarchy*, ed. Ronald W. Pierce and Rebecca Merrill Groothuis (Downers Grove: InterVarsity, 2004), 499. She references Charles Long, *Signification: Signs, Symbols and Images in the Interpretation of Religion* (Philadelphia: Fortress, 1988).

[29] Rachel Held Evans, *A Year of Biblical Womanhood* (Nashville: Nelson, 2012). An example of her use of June Cleaver is page 216.

[30] For a strong refutation of this alleged association of complementarianism with EFS/ERAS, see Stephen Wellum, "Does Complementarianism Depend on ERAS?: A Response to Kevin Giles, 'The Trinity Argument for Women's Subordination,'" *Eikon: A Journal for Biblical Anthropology* (June 22, 2023), https://cbmw.org/2023/06/22/does-complementarianism-depend-on-eras-a-response-to-kevin-giles-the-trinity-argument-for-womens-subordination/.

CHAPTER 11

The Rise of Contemporary Complementarianism

This section will begin with a definition of complementarianism, trace its development in the 1980s, discuss the concept of complementarianism according to *Recovering Biblical Manhood and Womanhood*, and present the spectrum of applications of complementarianism. As discussed earlier, complementarity goes beyond complementarianism to express and encourage the interdependence and reciprocity of men and women, who fill out and mutually support one another in terms of their relationships, family dynamics, collaborative work, and church ministries. Thus, complementarity is a broader framework than complementarianism, grounding that position even as it distinguished itself from the other position of egalitarianism (which will be the topic of the next chapter). Because complementarianism is a key framework both theoretically and practically for women and men in both the home and the church (as is egalitarianism), a deeper understanding of it and its spectrum of applications in those two spheres is important.

Definition of Complementarianism

Complementarianism is the perspective that men and women are complementary or correspond to one another, being equal to one another in several ways and significantly differentiated from one another in certain relationships and roles. Women and men are equal in three principal ways: being created in the image of God, enjoying access to salvation through Jesus Christ, and receiving the gifts of the Holy Spirit. That is, men and women alike bear the divine image, sharing equal dignity and honor. Men and women alike may be rescued from sin by Christ and, united together, may be incorporated into his one body, the church. And men and women alike receive the full range of spiritual gifts; that is, there are no gender-specific gifts.

At the same time, men and women are significantly differentiated from one another in relationships and roles. Such distinctions may appear in several realms. With respect to the home, husbands lead, and their wives submit to them. In the church, leadership (e.g., elder/pastor) responsibilities are reserved for qualified and called men.[1] Women, while participating in many ministries, may not hold the office of elder/pastor. While many complementarians do not hold to differences in roles in the societal realm, some maintain that men should lead governments and companies and women should serve in positions of lower authority. For example, women, while working as teachers and educational designers in a high school, may not lead as its principal. These distinctions come in various combinations. By contrast, egalitarianism denies some or all distinctions.[2] Furthermore, as will be discussed shortly, complementarianism has a spectrum of applications in the church and the home.

---

[1] For simplicity's sake, I use the words *elder* and *pastor* interchangeably as well as placeholders for other possible terms—e.g., *overseer*, *bishop*, *minister*, *priest*—that are commonly used for church leaders.

[2] For further discussion see Gregg R. Allison, *The Church: An Introduction* (Wheaton: Crossway, 2021), 132–33.

The Development of Complementarianism in the 1980s

To trace the development of complementarianism in the 1980s, I rely on a 2019 article from Denny Burk, president of the Council on Biblical Manhood and Womanhood, titled "What's in a Name: The Meaning and Origin of Complementarianism."[3] According to Burk, "Complementarianism was not first and foremost a sociological descriptor or movement. Nor was it describing an ethos or a set of extrabiblical stereotypes. The term emerged as a shorthand to describe the theological vision of the Danvers Statement," which summarized the need for the Council on Biblical Manhood and Womanhood (CBMW) and served as an overview of its core beliefs.[4] Burk recounts the origin of the Danvers Statement:

> In 1986, John Piper, Wayne Grudem, Susan Foh, Wayne House, and a handful of others met in Atlanta, Georgia to strategize a biblical response to a rising tide of feminism that they perceived within evangelicalism. A year later, in 1987, they met again, this time in Danvers, Massachusetts to finalize a theological statement of principles for a new organization that they wished to found. That statement became known as the Danvers Statement, which summarizes the Bible's teaching about male and female roles within the church and the home.[5]

Still without a term for the position advocated by the Danvers Statement and the movement it spawned, a nascent council (of the soon-to-be-launched CBMW) coined the term *complementarian* at the Evangelical

---

[3] Denny Burk, "What's in a Name: The Meaning and Origin of Complementarianism," cbmw.org (August 1, 2019), https://cbmw.org/2019/08/01/whats-in-a-name/.

[4] Danvers Statement (November 1987), https://cbmw.org/about/danvers-statement/.

[5] Burk, "What's in a Name?"

Theological Society's annual meeting at Wheaton College in 1988. As Burk details, "The group [including John Piper, Wayne Grudem, Bruce Waltke, Wayne House, Kent Hughes, and a few others] specifically coined 'complementarian' to refer to the theological position summarized in the Danvers Statement. For this reason, the Danvers Statement has been the touchstone of complementarian conviction ever since."[6]

Burk rightly wonders, "Why did they choose such a strange neologism to describe their position? It's not because the theological position was new. It was quite ancient actually. They settled on this word because there simply wasn't another one that adequately described their view. The term has a profound exegetical and linguistic root in the Hebrew of Genesis 2:18 (*kenegdo*), which the lexicons define as 'corresponding to.'"[7] To avoid misunderstanding of the origin of the term, Burk underscores "that while *complementarianism* emerged in a particular sociological context, it cannot be reduced to sociological categorization. Complementarianism is first and foremost a theological position that is rooted in a long history of exegesis of biblical texts such as Genesis 1–3, 1 Timothy 2:12, 1 Corinthians 11:2–16, etc."[8]

Accordingly, *complementarianism* expresses the framework of equal dignity and significant differentiation as promoted by the Danvers Statement and the Council on Biblical Manhood and Womanhood. This Statement and this Council continue to be pillars of complementarianism today.

The Concept of Complementarianism according to *Recovering Biblical Manhood and Womanhood*

To a significant degree, the Council on Biblical Manhood and Womanhood arose in response to evangelical feminism. Piper and Grudem distinguish proponents of evangelical feminism from advocates of secular feminism in the following:

[6] Burk, "What's in a Name?"
[7] Burk, "What's in a Name?"
[8] Burk, "What's in a Name?"

> [Evangelical feminists] differ from secular feminists because they do not reject the Bible's authority or truthfulness, but rather give new interpretations of the Bible to support their claims. We may call them "evangelical feminists" because by personal commitment to Jesus Christ and by profession of belief in the total truthfulness of Scripture they still identify themselves clearly with evangelicalism. Their arguments have been detailed, earnest, and persuasive to many Christians.[9]

The Council on Biblical Manhood and Womanhood proposed the *Danvers Statement* (1988) and Piper and Grudem edited *Recovering Biblical Manhood and Womanhood* (*RBMW*, 1991). The latter work defines biblical manhood: "At the heart of mature masculinity is a sense of benevolent responsibility to lead, provide for, and protect women in ways appropriate to a man's differing relationships."[10] This definition stands in conjunction with that of biblical womanhood: "At the heart of mature femininity is a freeing disposition to affirm, receive and nurture strength and leadership from worthy men in ways appropriate to a woman's differing relationships."[11] *RBMW* affirmed these concepts of mature manhood and mature womanhood as essential features of complementarianism.

Five observations follow, but first a clarification is needed. *RBMW* articulated these derived definitions in the context of a repeated and biblically grounded affirmation of the equality of men and women in terms of essence.[12] For example, men and women alike are created in the divine image; thus, even if role differences between men and women exist, by

---

[9] John Piper and Wayne Grudem, eds., *Recovering Biblical Manhood and Womanhood: A Response to Evangelical Feminism* (Wheaton: Crossway, 1991, 2006), xiii. Henceforth, *RBMW*.

[10] *RBMW*, 35. This definition is explained in detail, pp. 36–45.

[11] *RBMW*, 36. This definition is explained in detail, pp. 46–52.

[12] The following discussion is adapted from Gregg R. Allison, "What is a Man? Looking at a historical, contemporary, and essential answer," The Ethics and Religious Liberty Commission (June 6, 2022), https://erlc.com/resource-library/articles/what-is-a-man/. Used with permission.

nature the sexes are equal. This perspective is a far cry from, and a much needed corrective to, the traditional sex polarity position and reverse sex polarity position presented earlier in the historical section.

The five observations are: First, the definition focuses on a man's *roles*: leadership, provision, and protection.[13] Second, these roles are primarily (though not exclusively) for a man who is a husband. Third, *RBMW* noted that this "roled" approach is a secondary matter, with the more fundamental matter being a man's nature (though it did not treat this latter aspect).[14] Might this omission indicate that *RBMW* assumes man's innate nature from his roles and functions? Fourth, the definition of a woman is formulated in relationship to the definition of man.[15] Fifth, these points underscore the fact that *RBMW*, while well-meaning for the context it addresses, did not penetrate below the surface to actually define manhood and womanhood in

---

[13] The *Danvers Statement* underscores this focus: "Distinctions in masculine and feminine roles are ordained by God as part of the created order, and should find an echo in every human heart" (Affirmation 2).

[14] As for points 2 and 3, *RBMW* offers, "We are persuaded from Scripture that masculinity and femininity are rooted in who we are by nature. They are not simply reflexes of a marriage relationship. Man does not become man by getting married. Woman does not become woman by getting married." *RBMW*, xxvi. One wishes that the book would have developed those two concepts beginning with nature. An improper approach is to define a thing by listing its roles, activities, and functions. Rather, a proper definition is about the nature or essence of that thing. For critiques of this "roled" approach (and, by extension, other "roled" approaches), see Jordan L. Steffaniak, "Saving Masculinity and Femininity from the Morgue: A Defense of Gender Essentialism," *Southeastern Review* 12.1 (2021): 15–35; Patrick Schreiner, "Man and Woman: Toward an Ontology," *Eikon*, vol. 2.2 (Nov 20, 2020).

[15] As *RBMW* explains, "A significant aspect of femininity is how a woman responds to the pattern of initiatives established by mature masculinity." *RBMW*, 45–46. It appears that this initiative/responsive dynamic applies not only to husbands and their wives but to all men in relation to all women. This observation is the center of many critiques of the *RBMW* approach. For example, David C. Freeman, "The Search for Biblical Manhood and Womanhood: A Preliminary Response to the Council on Biblical Manhood and Womanhood," Alliance Studies at Ambrose University College (November 1999), available at https://online.ambrose.edu/alliancestudies/.

terms of nature or essence. As my concept of complementarity focuses on the nature of men and women (ontology precedes functions and roles), the relationships among them without concentration on marital relationships, equal dignity, significant differentiation, and interdependence, it is substantially different from *RBMW*'s purpose and emphasis.

A Spectrum of Applications of Complementarianism

As complementarianism has been lived out in churches and in homes (and, for some complementarians, society), it has led to a spectrum of applications. Complementarianism in churches and homes serves as my focus as I present minimum complementarianism, moderate complementarianism, and maximum complementarianism.[16]

Minimum Complementarianism

In agreement with the other two varieties of complementarianism, minimum complementarianism holds that women are excluded from holding the office of pastor/elder. At the same time, qualified women may preach on occasion; for example, deliver the sermon during the principal Sunday morning service. They may give an exhortation or admonition; for example, following the sermon, present a message to the mothers in the church on Mother's Day. Women may preside over the worship service; for example, superintend the celebration of baptism and the Lord's Supper. They may teach on any topic in mixed-gender settings; for example, teach Romans to an adult Sunday school class (with both men and women present) or teach

[16] This discussion is adapted from Allison, *The Church*, 140–43. Though many contributors to this discussion work with a spectrum of complementarian that has two varieties (e.g., soft vs. hard, broad vs. narrow, weak vs. strong), my observations of actual churches and marriages lead me to affirm the existence of three varieties in terms of applications of complementarianism. Moreover, each of these varieties has its nuances.

the doctrines of sin and salvation in an equipping class. Additionally, qualified women may hold the office of deacon as deaconesses.

To concentrate on one element, how could women teach as part of the Sunday morning worship service? Some advocates of minimum complementarianism argue for their view with an understanding of Paul's charge—"I do not allow a woman to teach or to have authority over a man" (1 Tim 2:12)—to be a prohibition of women teaching with authority. To paraphrase the proscription, "I do not permit a woman to teach with authority over a man."[17] In other words, women may not teach with the church's authority. Only pastors have this responsibility, and women cannot be pastors. Additionally, women may not convey official, authoritative church doctrine and any other teaching that binds the conscience of its members. The pastors, however, may permit a qualified woman to teach under their authority (and it should be evident to the church that she is under their auspices), but she cannot instruct nor exhort in an authoritative manner, nor can she do so on a topic that constitutes authoritative teaching.[18]

With respect to the home, while husbands lead and wives submit to them, practically speaking, this hierarchical relationship is minimally operative as most if not all decision-making and direction-setting are shared, cooperative efforts. Still, there are times when the wife defers to the husband's position.

Moderate Complementarianism

In agreement with the other two varieties of complementarianism, moderate complementarianism holds that women are excluded from holding the office of pastor/elder. Specifically, they may not preach, exhort, or preside over the worship service. However, qualified women may design and play a prominent role in the liturgy; for example, read Scripture publicly, pray,

---

[17] This rendering of 1 Tim 2:12 will be discussed later in the book.

[18] What constitutes authoritative teaching will differ between minimally complementarian local churches.

lead responsive readings, and be the main singer. In mixed-gender adult settings, they may not teach on topics mostly focused on biblical exposition (for example, Romans) and/or theology (for example, the doctrines of sin and salvation) but may teach on other subjects such as missions, mercy ministries, and counseling. Additionally, qualified women may hold the office of deacon as deaconesses.

Some advocates of moderate complementarianism defend their view by pointing to Paul's instructions to a woman "who prays or prophesies" in the worship service (1 Cor 11:4–5). According to the apostle, women properly engage in public praying. Furthermore, if Paul's idea of prophecy is the spontaneous reception and communication of a divine revelation, and women engage in prophecy, then by extension, women may rightly read written Scripture in the public worship service. Additionally, Paul's prohibition of women from teaching sound doctrine and exercising authority at the highest level (1 Tim 2:12) implicitly gives those responsibilities to the elders/pastors (1 Tim 3:1–7). Accordingly, the church should guard against illegitimately prohibiting women from engaging in teaching and leading activities that are not elder-level duties.

With respect to the home, husbands lead and wives submit to them, and within this moderately hierarchical relationship, the husband is engaged in the majority of decision-making and direction-setting, considering his wife's input and support.

Maximum Complementarianism

In agreement with the other two varieties of complementarianism, maximum complementarianism holds that women are excluded from holding the office of pastor/elder. Furthermore, they may not engage in any public ministry that is a mixed-gender adult setting; rather, their ministries should be focused on women and children. Generally speaking, churches who embrace this position only have the office of deacon, which in those churches is limited to qualified men; thus, the issue of deaconesses is moot. Some churches that distinguish between elders/pastors and deacons may still restrict women from serving as deaconesses. Other churches allow women to hold this office.

Some advocates of maximum complementarianism justify their view with appeal to 1 Cor 14:33–35: "As in all the churches of the saints, the women should be silent in the churches, for they are not permitted to speak, but are to submit themselves, as the law also says. If they want to learn something, let them ask their own husbands at home, since it is disgraceful for a woman to speak in the church." The all-encompassing nature of Paul's prohibition of women speaking in the public assembly means that his ban is to be observed in all the churches. Furthermore, Paul supports his proscription with an appeal to "the law," which may refer to the perspective of the entire Old Testament. Moreover, women have a ready provision for learning about issues they hear and question in the worship service: wives have their husbands and, by extension and in light of first-century culture, single women and girls have their fathers with whom to consult.

With respect to the home, husbands lead and wives submit to them, and within this maximally hierarchical relationship, the husband is engaged in (almost) all the decision-making and direction-setting, (in many cases) with little or no consideration for his wife's input and support.

Accordingly, the three varieties of contemporary complementarianism have their biblical support, more of which will be presented in later chapters. Without taking time to discuss them, each position also has its drawbacks. Tragically, constructive discussion of these varieties is for the most part lacking; what could be a beneficial conversation has devolved largely into a strident and disrespectful debate. With so much ministry in which to engage, churches can ill afford to be racked by division and discord.

CHAPTER 12

Contemporary Patriarchalism

Not included in this presentation on the spectrum of complementarianism is so-called Christian patriarchy. Though a hard-to-define movement, it should not be identified with complementarianism (in any of its varieties); while there are certain similarities, complementarianism and Christian patriarchy are distinct frameworks, and to identify the two is both naïve and prejudicial. If Susan Mathew's definition of patriarchy—"the project of male self-definition 'apart from woman'"—is on target, then patriarchy is not complementarianism.[1]

Christian patriarchy is represented by Bill Gothard (1934–present) and the movement Quiverfull. Bill Gothard's version of patriarchy is well known through his popular Institute in Basic Youth Conflicts, which he founded in 1974 and whose name was changed to Institute in Basic Life Principles in 1989. His version of patriarchy is perhaps best known for his "umbrella of authority" (or "umbrella of protection"), his teaching that in order to be protected from Satan, Christians must submit themselves to people who are

[1] Susan Mathew, *Women in the Greetings of Romans 16:1–16: A Study of Mutuality and Women's Ministry in the Letter to the Romans* (London: Bloomsbury, 2013), 13. Mathew considers the opposite of patriarchy to be feminism, which she describes as "the other extreme of female self-definition 'apart from man,'" 13.

in authority over them. With reference to the family, the chain of authority means that husbands submit to Christ, wives submit to their husbands, and children submit to their mothers and fathers:

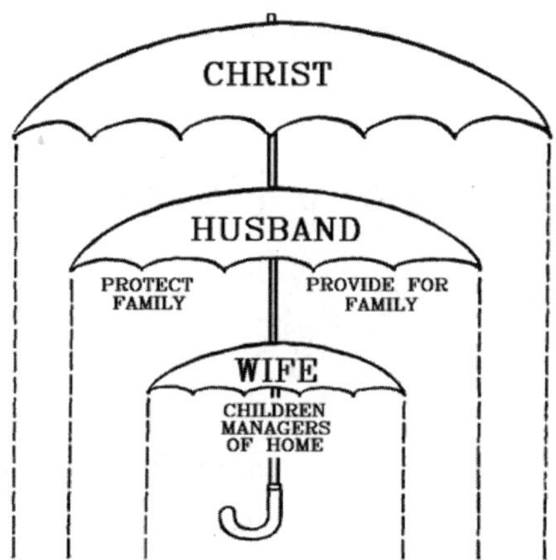

Obedience to this chain of authority comes with a promise: "As long as you are under God-given authority, nothing can happen to you that God does not design for your good."[2] Failure to live according to this hierarchical structure comes with a dire warning: "Getting out from under the protection of the Scriptural direction of parents, church, employers, or government allows Satan to bring destruction."[3]

Criticisms of Gothard's model abounded, not the least of which is its denial that all Christians, regardless of their gender or position in a family, have direct access to Christ and are responsible to submit to his authority. Moreover, the structure fomented abuse of "submitted"

[2] Gothard appealed to texts such as the centurion's encounter with Jesus (Matt 8:5–13) to encourage obedience to those in authority, with the promise of blessing if one does.

[3] Gothard appealed to texts such as Samuel's rebuke of the disobedient King Saul—"rebellion is like the sin of divination, and defiance is like wickedness and idolatry" (1 Sam 15:23)—to discourage disobedience to those in authority, with the warning of destruction if one does.

Christians (for example, women and children) at the hands of those (for example, husbands/fathers as well as church leaders) in unmitigated authority over them.[4]

The second example of Christian patriarchalism coalesces around the Quiverfull movement and features (some or more of) the following elements and values:[5] All men have authority over all women, not just husbands over their wives. Men have the duty to work and provide for their wives and children, and families should be debt-free and self-supporting even if the husband's income is insufficiently low. Wives are not allowed to, and thus do not, work outside their homes, and any domestic work they do that is income-producing should come from a home-based business, industry, or service. Men take responsibility as husbands and fathers, and they command the respect of their wives and children. Specifically with regard to their daughters, fathers may regard them as their property until such time as "ownership" is transferred to their husbands. Married couples are expected to have a large number of children; some proponents see this fruitfulness as necessary in order to "redeem" anti-Christian culture and/or as a solution to the large families of non-Christians (e.g., Muslims) by simply outnumbering them by outpacing them reproductively.

---

[4] Gothard himself exemplified unmitigated authority over his staff personnel. For example, Gothard believed (on the basis of a private revelation from the apostle Paul to himself) that God's ideal plan for Adam was for the man to find complete satisfaction in God and never need a woman companion. However, due to Adam's discontentment with God's friendship, God instituted a secondary (and inferior) plan and reluctantly conceded to create Eve. Thus, singleness rather than marriage is God's ideal. On this basis, Gothard had to approve (or disapprove) of any of his staff wishing to get married. (Personal correspondence with Bill Ritchie, a former Gothard staff member.) More tragically, Gothard has been sued for sexual abuse. Sarah Eekhoff Zylstra, "More Women Sue Bill Gothard and IBLP, Alleging Sexual Abuse," *Christianity Today* (January 28, 2016).

[5] Some of the following is adapted from Kathryn Joyce, *Quiverfull: Inside the Christian Patriarchy Movement* (Boston: Beacon, 2009). This book is limited in its helpfulness because of the author's conflation of patriarchy with complementarianism and fundamentalism with evangelicalism.

Parents homeschool their children, and those young adults who pursue education outside the home should be boys only because advanced learning is unproductive for girls who will be married and bear numerous children. In the church, only qualified men may hold the office of pastor/elder, from which office all women are excluded. Women may not engage in any public ministry; rather, their ministries should be focused on women and children. Furthermore, in some churches, women are not allowed to even speak during worship services, Bible study, prayer meetings, and the like. Ecclesially, a preference for house churches, in which the husband/father is the elder/pastor of the church, enforces the home-centeredness and patriarchal heart of the movement.

Again, contemporary Christian patriarchy, being grounded on a different framework, is not and should not be associated with any variety of complementarianism. In many respects, Christian patriarchy is an attempt to retrieve Old Testament patriarchy, thereby confusing a cultural reality with a biblical reality, and an old covenant framework with a new covenant framework.

In his post "Death to the Patriarchy? Complementarity and the Scandal of 'Father Rule,'"[6] Kevin DeYoung interacts with patriarchy, complementarity, and complementarianism. While he uses these terms differently than I do (for DeYoung, for example, *complementarity* is the vision embraced by *complementarianism*), he urges that "there is something in the broader idea of patriarchy—no matter how sinister the word itself has become—that is worth claiming." Specifically, he (correctly) underscores that "*patriarchy* is simply the Greek word meaning 'father rule.' There is nothing in its etymology to make the term an epithet of abuse." What DeYoung seems most concerned about losing if patriarchy "dies" is the divinely designed sexual differentiation between men and women and a proper kind of order that derives from it: "God created the world with sexual differentiation at the

---

[6] Kevin DeYoung, "Death to the Patriarchy? Complementarity and the Scandal of 'Father Rule,'" Desiring God (July 19, 2022), https://www.desiringgod.org/articles/death-to-the-patriarchy.

heart of what it means to be human beings made in his image. We cannot understand the created order as we should until we understand that God made us male and female." These innate sexual differences manifest themselves—and are clearly seen—in physiological, procreational, developmental, and relational distinctions, as well as in divisions in traditional roles (e.g., "traditional patterns of male initiative and female domesticity").

While my concept of complementarity broadly agrees with DeYoung in affirming significant differentiation between women and men, it does not incorporate the term *patriarchy*. Interestingly, complementarity, as I define it, rejects the term for the same reasons that DeYoung urges hesitancy about its use: in our contemporary society, the term is used pejoratively (often in conjunction with words such as *domination*, *exploitation*, and *oppression*), prompts negative association with sexual and other types of abuse, conjures up notions of "bad male leadership," and perpetuates the traditional sex polarity position of male superiority and female inferiority. Additionally, as noted above, I maintain that patriarchy and complementarianism are significantly different frameworks. Moreover, I think that as it is currently used, "patriarchy" (as a descriptive rather than a pejorative term) does *not* reflect "innate differences between the sexes." For these reasons, I disagree with its use in these discussions.

To conclude, Christian patriarchy is not a fourth category on the spectrum of complementarianism.

CHAPTER 13

The Rise of Contemporary Egalitarianism

This section will begin with a definition of egalitarianism, trace its development in the 1980s, discuss the concept of egalitarianism according to Christians for Biblical Equality, and present the spectrum of applications of egalitarianism. As discussed earlier, complementarity goes beyond egalitarianism to express and encourage the interdependence and reciprocity of men and women, who fill out and mutually support one another in terms of their relationships, family dynamics, collaborative work, and church ministries. Thus, complementarity is a broader framework than egalitarianism, grounding that position even as it distinguished itself from the other position of complementarianism (which was the topic of the last chapter). Because egalitarianism is a key framework both theoretically and practically for women and men in both the home and the church (as is complementarianism), a deeper understanding of it and its spectrum of applications in those two spheres is important.

Definition of Egalitarianism

Egalitarianism is the perspective that men and women are complementary or correspond to one another, being equal in nature, relationships, and roles, while still significantly differentiated from one another, but not as complementarianism projects those differences. In agreement with complementarianism, egalitarianism affirms that women and men are equal in three principal ways: being created in the image of God, enjoying access to salvation through Jesus Christ, and receiving the gifts of the Holy Spirit. That is, men and women alike bear the divine image, sharing equal dignity and honor. Men and women alike may be rescued from sin by Christ and, united together, be incorporated into his one body, the church. And men and women alike receive the full range of spiritual gifts; that is, there are no gender-specific gifts.

In contrast to complementarianism, egalitarianism affirms equalities in other realms as well. With respect to the home, husbands and wives share equal authority (or responsibility) and mutually submit (or defer) to each other. In the church, elder/pastor responsibilities are accessible to both qualified men and qualified women; women and men alike may hold the office of elder/pastor. In society, men and women alike lead governments and companies. Moreover, these equalities come in various combinations. At the same time, egalitarianism embraces the differences that women and men bring to relationships and to familial, ecclesial, and societal engagement, some of which may involve differences in roles that are not gender-determined. Egalitarianism stands in contrast to complementarianism.[1] Furthermore, as will be discussed shortly, egalitarianism has a spectrum of applications in the church and the home.

The Development of Egalitarianism in the 1980s

As discussed above, the Evangelical Women's Caucus (EWC; retitled Evangelical and Ecumenical Women's Caucus in 1990), emerged in 1974

---

[1] For further discussion see Gregg R. Allison, *The Church: An Introduction* (Wheaton, IL: Crossway, 2021), 135.

under the auspices of Evangelicals for Social Action. It endorsed the Equal Rights Amendment, supported inclusive language in Christian literature, promoted the ordination of women, and battled against discrimination in hiring practices at Christian institutions.[2] In 1986, when the EWC embraced "civil rights protection for homosexual persons,"[3] conservative EWC members left that caucus and established Christians for Biblical Equality (CBE) with Catherine Clark Kroeger as its first president. Additionally, Gretchen Gaebelein Hull, CBE's first editor of its academic journal, while theologically connected to first wave feminism, "distinguished CBE from the second wave by noting that CBE locates women's leadership and mutuality within Scripture, an obligation that secular feminists ignore."[4]

To trace the development of egalitarianism in the 1980s, I rely on its history as recounted by CBE International:

> Disturbed by the shallow biblical premise used by churches, organizations, and mission groups to exclude the gifts of women, evangelical leaders assembled in 1987 to publish their biblical perspective in a new scholarly journal, Priscilla Papers. Included in the group were Gilbert Bilezikian, W. Ward Gasque, Stanley Gundry, Gretchen Gaebelein Hull, Catherine Clark Kroeger, Jo Anne Lyon, and Roger Nicole. The group determined that a national organization was needed to provide education, support, and leadership about biblical equality.
>
> With the help and vision of these individuals, CBE International (founded as Christians for Biblical Equality) was established on January 2, 1988. Catherine Clark Kroeger served as the first

---

[2] Evangelical and Ecumenical Women's Caucus, "Our Origin," https://eewc.com/about/#origin.

[3] Randall Balmer, "Evangelical and Ecumenical Women's Caucus," in *Encyclopedia of Evangelicalism*, 2nd ed. (Waco: Baylor University Press, 2004), 237.

[4] CBE International, "Setting a Movement Aflame: The Power of CBE's Founders," https://www.cbeinternational.org/resource/power-cbes-founders/.

> president of the organization, and Alvera Mickelsen served as the first chair of the board of directors. Since 2001, Mimi Haddad has served as CBE's second president.
>
> CBE's first major project was the creation of a statement, "Men, Women, and Biblical Equality,"[5] which laid out the biblical rationale for equality as well as its application in the community of believers and the family. CBE hosted its first international conference in Saint Paul, Minnesota, in July of 1989.[6]

In summary, Christians for Biblical Equality arose from the Evangelical Women's Caucus when that movement affirmed protection for the civil rights of homosexual persons. Furthermore, it distanced itself from second wave feminism by affirming women's leadership and mutuality on the basis of Scripture.

The Concept of Egalitarianism according to Christians for Biblical Equality

According to Christians for Biblical Equality, key elements of the concept of egalitarianism include the following: CBE emphasizes "leading together, serving as equals" as it "advances the gospel by equipping Christians to use their God-given talents in leadership and service regardless of gender, ethnicity, or class."[7] In terms of leadership opportunities for both sexes, CBE "believes the Bible, properly interpreted, calls women and men to lead and serve as equals, based on Scriptures such as Galatians 3:28." As for the scope of its labors, CBE's "three-fold work features"

---

[5] CBE International, "Men, Women, and Biblical Equality," https://www.cbeinternational.org/wp-content/uploads/2023/06/DefiningBiblicalGenderEquality-1.pdf.

[6] CBE International, "History of CBE," https://www.cbeinternational.org/primary_page/cbes-history/.

[7] These points are taken from the Christians for Biblical Equality website: https://www.cbeinternational.org.

(1) "*building a global community*" by seeking "to eliminate gender-based violence and human trafficking, and improve girls' access to education by raising the status of women;" (2) "*preventing abuse*" as global statistics show that one-third of all women are "victims of physical abuse by an intimate partner, and studies show abuse is as common in the church as in society;" and (3) "*offering healing and hope* . . . for Christian women and men around the world."

CBE affirms the following in terms of its mission, envisioned future, and core values: Its purpose is "to promote the biblical message that God calls women and men of all cultures, races, and classes to share authority equally in service and leadership in the home, church, and world" and "to eliminate the power imbalance between men and women resulting from theological patriarchy." As for its hope, "CBE envisions a future where all believers are freed to exercise their gifts for God's glory and purposes, with the full support of their Christian communities." Its core values (those that relate directly to our topic) are:

- Patriarchy (male dominance) is not a biblical ideal but a result of sin.
- Patriarchy is an abuse of power, taking from females what God has given them: their dignity, freedom, and leadership, and often their very lives.
- While the Bible reflects patriarchal culture, the Bible does not teach patriarchy as God's standard for human relationships.
- Christ's redemptive work frees all people from patriarchy, calling women and men to share authority equally in service and leadership.
- The unrestricted use of women's gifts is integral to the work of the Holy Spirit and essential for the advancement of the gospel in the world.
- Followers of Christ are to oppose injustice and patriarchal teachings and practices that marginalize and abuse women, or restrict women's access to leadership in the home, church, and the world.

Though CBE is not solely responsible for producing *Discovering Biblical Equality: Biblical, Theological, Cultural and Practical Perspectives*, that important book for the egalitarian perspective acknowledges its indebtedness to CBE.[8]

A Spectrum of Applications of Egalitarianism

As egalitarianism has been lived out in the home, in churches, and in society, it has led to a spectrum of applications. Egalitarianism in churches and homes again serves as my focus as I present minimum egalitarianism, mixed egalitarianism, and maximum egalitarianism.[9]

Minimum Egalitarianism

In agreement with the other two varieties of egalitarianism, minimum egalitarianism maintains that both qualified men and qualified women may hold the office of elder/pastor. Still, in the case of women, they may not be the lead elder/pastor, serving in associate roles but not as the senior minister. These women elders may occasionally preach. They may occasionally preside over the worship service; for example, they may oversee the administration of baptism and the Lord's Supper. They may teach on any topic in mixed-gender settings; for example, they may teach Romans to an adult Sunday school class (with both men and women present) and/or teach the doctrines of sin and salvation in an equipping class. Additionally, qualified women may hold the office of deacon as deaconesses.

With respect to the home, husbands and wives share equal authority and mutually submit to each other. Still, in times when the two come to

---

[8] *Discovering Biblical Equality: Biblical, Theological, Cultural, and Practical Perspectives*, 3rd ed., ed. Ronald W. Pierce and Cynthia Long Westfall, assoc. ed. Christa L. McKirland (Downers Grove: IVP Academic, 2021), xvii.

[9] As with the spectrum of complementarianism, each of these varieties has its nuances.

an impasse over an important decision or action, the wife defers to the husband's lead.

Mixed Egalitarianism

In agreement with the other two varieties of egalitarianism, mixed egalitarianism maintains that its application is normally made to both the church and the home. In this form of egalitarianism, however, its practical outworking is seen in either (1) the church but not the home, or (2) the home but not the church. With respect to the first scenario, in the church, qualified men and qualified women may hold the office of elder/pastor. At the same time, in the home, husbands lead and their wives submit to them. With respect to the second scenario, in the home, husbands and wives share equal authority and submit to each other. At the same time, in the church, elder/pastor responsibilities are reserved for qualified men. Women, while participating in many ministries, may not hold the office of elder/pastor. Additionally, qualified women may hold the office of deacon as deaconesses.

Maximum Egalitarianism

In agreement with the other two varieties of egalitarianism, maximum egalitarianism maintains that both qualified men and qualified women may hold the office of elder/pastor, with the senior/lead minister position accessible to both women and men. Moreover, to rectify the illegitimate restrictions on women in ministry in the past, the church should give preference to advancing qualified women to the pastoral office. This preference may extend to having the entire pastoral staff be composed of women. Additionally, qualified women may hold the office of deacon as deaconesses.

With respect to the home, and in agreement with the other forms of egalitarianism, maximum egalitarianism maintains that husbands and wives share equal authority and mutually submit to each other. Still, to correct the illegitimate restrictions of wives from leading and providing for their family in the past, the couple should give preference to the wife in terms of decision making, career choices and moves, and financial support of the family. In times when the two come to an impasse over an important decision or action, the husband defers to the wife's position.

Importantly, the three varieties of contemporary egalitarianism have biblical support, which will be presented in later chapters. Without taking time to discuss them, each position also has its drawbacks. Tragically, constructive discussion of these varieties is for the most part lacking; what could be a beneficial conversation has devolved largely into a strident and disrespectful debate. With so much ministry in which to engage, churches can ill afford to be racked by division and discord.

Putting together the spectrums of complementarianism and egalitarianism, we have the following diagram:

COMPLEMENTARIANISM			EGALITARIANISM		
maximum	moderate	minimum	minimum	mixed	maximum

To be noted is the fact that these spectrums represent *applications* of the two frameworks to the two spheres of church and home. Formally, complementarianism grounds itself on specific biblical interpretations and theological positions, and its proponents are in widespread agreement on those matters. Similarly, egalitarianism grounds itself on specific biblical interpretations and theological positions, and its proponents are in widespread agreement on those matters. Notably, such formal agreements are applied concretely in different ways by different proponents/churches/husbands and wives/scholars and scholarly societies. Again, it is these specific and diverse applications that are represented by the spectrums of complementarianism and egalitarianism and the above diagram. Importantly, while there may be similarities in the applications of minimum complementarianism and minimum egalitarianism, for example, the two applications stem from formally different frameworks and should be understood appropriately.

In conclusion, Part Three has traced modern feminist movements (Chapter 10), the rise of contemporary complementarianism (Chapter 11), contemporary patriarchalism (Chapter 12), and contemporary egalitarianism (Chapter 13). As explained earlier, my choice of complementarianism and egalitarianism as my conversation partners is because they both develop from complementarity. Though they primarily treat roles of men and women in the church and in the home, and thus are more limited in their scope than is complementarity, they are of deep concern for most of my readers and thus worthy interlocutors. Accordingly, Part Three has rehearsed their definitions, origins, primary proponents, and spectrums of application. The foundation has thus been laid for upcoming discussions of complementarity and how it relates to these interlocutors.

PART FOUR

Biblical Considerations

Having rehearsed at length the historical development and contemporary context for my presentation of complementarity, I turn now to biblical considerations for complementarity. Before treating Scripture itself, however, I address the framework and setting for the ensuing biblical discussions. Accordingly, Chapter 14 includes three important topics: hermeneutics, the canonical and covenantal framework of Scripture, and Genesis 1–3 as setting the stage for the lengthy biblical discussion to follow.

CHAPTER 14

Framework and Setting

The first framework issue is hermeneutics, or principles of interpretation for understanding Scripture. This topic is important because different approaches to interpreting Scripture result in different understandings. Whether it is evident or not, all readers have their ways of interpreting Scripture, and some approaches are better than others because, for example, they understand the words, phrases, and sentences in keeping with lexical and grammatical principles operative at the time of the writing of Scripture. Or those approaches follow the narrative flow of the stories in Genesis and trace the arguments of Paul in his letters. Hermeneutical issues are often decisive for the development of the differences between complementarianism and egalitarianism.

Hermeneutics

Any interaction with Scripture necessarily includes a discussion of how it is to be interpreted. My approach is to focus on interpretive principles where complementarianism and egalitarianism differ in developing their perspectives on men, women, church leadership, roles, and the like. By identifying certain principles with an egalitarian approach to Scripture and other principles with a complementarian approach, I do not mean that *all* egalitarians appropriate those certain principles in understanding the Bible or that *all* complementarians follow those other principles.

To clarify from the outset, I do not treat hermeneutical approaches and principles that move away from a traditional doctrine of Scripture that affirms its canonicity, inspiration, authority, truthfulness (or inerrancy), sufficiency, necessity, clarity, and transformative power. All these attributes can be defended, but that is not my current task. Scripture itself, as well as the *consensus theologicum* of the church, affirms these characteristics, and I do not interact with any interpretive framework that is not grounded on them.[1] For example, interpretations of 1 Tim 2:11–14 that are based on a rejection of that letter's canonical status as part of the Pauline corpus,[2] and treatments of the Gospels that deny the resurrection of Jesus—and thus dismiss narratives of his post-resurrection appearances to women—will not be considered. Moreover, as one who has written extensively on the perspicuity of Scripture, I admit a personal distaste for hermeneutical approaches that concede that biblical passages are so unclear as to be incomprehensible.[3] Such a personal concern applies as well to a number of the passages—often viewed as obscure—that are at

---

[1] For further discussion see Gregg R. Allison, "The *Corpus Theologicum* of the Church and Presumptive Authority," in *Revisioning, Renewing, and Rediscovering the Triune Center: Essays in Honor of Stanley J. Grenz*, ed. Derek Tidball, Brian Harris, and Jason S. Sexton, (Eugene, OR: Wipf & Stock, 2014).

[2] Thus, I applaud Cynthia Long Westfall's insistence, in regard to the key Pauline passages on gender, that "The starting point should be to explore the interpretation of the texts according to their own terms as part of the Pauline corpus, within the narrative of Paul's life and within a viable Pauline theology." Cynthia Long Westfall, "Interpretive Methods and the Gender Debate," in *Discovering Biblical Equality: Biblical, Theological, Cultural, and Practical Perspectives*, ed. Ronald W. Pierce and Cynthia Long Westfall, 3rd ed. (Downers Grove: IVP Academic, 2021), 434.

[3] Gregg Allison, "The Protestant Doctrine of the Perspicuity of Scripture: A Reformulation on the Basis of Biblical Teaching" (PhD thesis, Trinity Evangelical Divinity School, Deerfield, Illinois, 1995).

the heart of the debate over men and women and their roles in the home and the church.

The hermeneutical principles to be treated are the following: regulative principle vs. normative principle; biblical language: descriptive (or situational) vs. prescriptive; single meaning vs. multiple meanings; consideration of eschatology; the weightiness and slightness of biblical material; Scripture only (or primarily) or Scripture supplemented with extra-biblical sources (e.g., archaeology); and preunderstanding and the biblical text.

Regulative Principle vs. Normative Principle

While these contrasting principles usually appear in ecclesiological discussions about what elements are required and what elements are permitted in worship services,[4] they also operate in differing approaches between complementarianism and egalitarianism. Providing a clear contrast between the two principles and frameworks, Aida Besançon Spencer notes that a hermeneutical presupposition of some evangelicals "seems to be that the Bible's teaching is limited to whatever is explicitly stated. In effect, if the text does not specifically say you *may* do something, then you may not."[5] This presupposition closely resembles the regulative principle of hermeneutics. She uses H. Wayne House's point as an example of this regulative principle: "The biblical record says nothing at all about Christ considering a woman's role in ministry leadership or spiritual headship indistinguishable from a man's. There is no evidence that any woman was commissioned as one of the seventy-two or the Twelve."[6] Spencer draws the implication for House's use of the regulative principle: "Silence on this matter means that women

---

[4] For further discussion see Gregg R. Allison, *Sojourners and Strangers: The Doctrine of the Church* (Wheaton: Crossway, 2012), 428–33.

[5] Aida Besançon Spencer, "Jesus' Treatment of Women in the Gospels," in *Discovering Biblical Equality*, 98.

[6] Spencer, "Jesus' Treatment of Women in the Gospels," 98. Her citation is H. Wayne House, *The Role of Women in Ministry Today* (Grand Rapids: Baker, 1995), 21.

may not be ordained as overseers."[7] Urging that this hermeneutical stance is not more valid than its opposite merely because it is asserted, Spencer articulates the normative principle: "If the text does not actually prohibit something, either explicitly or in principle, one may well choose to do it—especially given the way Jesus explicitly affirms women. Nowhere does Jesus ever say—or even imply in anything he says—that only men can be leaders in the church."[8]

The regulative principle, then, insists on specific—explicit or appropriately implicit—warrant for contemporary application of texts, and the normative principle insists that as long as Scripture does not explicitly or implicitly prohibit something, it permits contemporary application of texts.

Biblical Language: Descriptive (or Situational) vs. Prescriptive[9]

A key principle at the heart of the debate is whether so-called "hierarchical" passages that present (or seem to present) male authority and female submission should be understood to be descriptive or prescriptive in nature. In the first case, Scripture *describes* a certain posture or action, but such *description* is not normative for believers and churches today. In the second case, Scripture *prescribes* a certain posture or action, and such *prescription*—coming with imperatival or exemplary force—is and must be normative for believers and churches today. Alternatively, Scripture prescribed a certain attitude or stance but because it called for such positions in a certain ancient context or in a particular situation, such situational prescriptions may have been superseded or transcended by other considerations and may not be normative for today. More specifically, in contemporary cultures that are

---

[7] Spencer, "Jesus' Treatment of Women in the Gospels," 98.

[8] Spencer, "Jesus' Treatment of Women in the Gospels," 98–99.

[9] For further discussion see Allison, *Sojourners and Strangers*, 43–50; J. Scott Duvall and J. Daniel Hays, *Grasping God's Word: A Hands-on Approach to Reading, Interpreting, and Applying the Bible*, 4th ed. (Grand Rapids: Zondervan, 2020).

close ideologically to the worldview of Scripture and/or to the situations it addressed, its prescriptive texts may still be normative for believers and churches in those cultures and situations. Such is not the case, however, for contemporary cultures that are far removed from the biblical worldview and situations the Bible addressed. Its prescriptions, while normative in the past, are no longer so today.

As an example of the first case, some egalitarians may trace the reason for Paul's directives for women to learn in quietness rather than teach men in the church, and to be in submission rather than to exercise authority over men in the church, to a particular situation in the church of Ephesus (e.g., the threat of false teaching by female members of the church, or the constant disruption of worship services by overly talkative women). The apostle did in fact offer a prescription to quell these problems, and the Ephesian church was duty bound to obey his normative commands. However, in contemporary churches that do not face these crises but feature women who are doctrinally sound and gifted teachers, Paul's directives are no longer prescriptive, but only descriptive, in nature. They do not bind believers and churches today.

Alternatively, some egalitarians hold that Paul's instruction bears all the marks of capitulation to social norms and structures that are outdated and thus should no longer direct women and men in the church today.[10] The reasons for such capitulation are several, including the desire not to cause unnecessary tension between the Greco-Roman society and the emerging church and/or a missional impetus for Christians to exhibit impeccable conduct as they bore witness to the gospel before non-Christians (e.g., Titus 2:10).[11]

---

[10] A. Padgett, "The Pauline Rationale for Submission: Biblical Feminism and the ἵνα clauses of Titus 2:1–10," *Evangelical Quarterly* 59 (1987): 39–52. For further discussion see Andreas J. Köstenberger, *1–2 Timothy and Titus*, Evangelical Biblical Theology Commentary (Bellingham, WA: Lexham, 2020), 333n105.

[11] Padgett refers to David Balch as a proponent of the first rationale and Peter Lippert as an advocate for the second rationale. Padgett, "The Pauline Rationale for Submission," 46–47. His references are to David L. Balch, *Let Wives Be Submissive:*

As an example of the second case, in his commentary on 1 Tim 2:11–14, Andreas Köstenberger avers, "The fact that Paul is rooting his directive in the order of creation [v. 13] rather than providing a cultural rationale strongly suggests that vv. 11–12 are permanently applicable," that is, normative in the past as well as for today.[12] Accordingly, the perspective that Paul's directives are addressed to particular situations in the Ephesian church or the Greco-Roman culture in the first century, while certainly a proper interpretive consideration, do not change the normativity of those directives. Köstenberger concludes: "The fact that Paul grounds the command in the order of creation, not only the fall [v. 14], also contradicts the argument that female submission to male leadership in the church is solely a result of the fall. . . . In applying and extending God's order of creation to the church and in attempting to avoid the negative consequences of the fall, Paul places ultimate responsibility for teaching and exercising authority in the church on qualified men."[13]

Single Meaning vs. Multiple Meanings

While certainly part of a much broader hermeneutical debate, the issue of the meaning/meanings of Scripture provides another contrast between complementarian and egalitarian approaches to Scripture. On the one hand are proponents of a single meaning, which is the traditional Protestant/evangelical hermeneutical principle; their insistence on a sole meaning arose early on during the Reformation in contrast to the Roman Catholic fourfold sense of Scripture.[14] On the other hand are proponents of multiple meanings. As noted by Dorothy Lee, they criticize those on the other side for their

---

The Domestic Code in 1 Peter (Chico: Scholars, 1981) and Peter Lippert, *Leben als Zeugnis* (Stuttgart: Katholisches Bibelwerk, 1968).

[12] Köstenberger, *1–2 Timothy and Titus*, 117.

[13] Köstenberger, *1–2 Timothy and Titus*, 117–18.

[14] For further discussion see Gregg R. Allison, *Historical Theology: An Introduction to Christian Doctrine* (Grand Rapids: Zondervan, 2011), 169–78.

insistence "on one meaning of the Bible, crystal clear but allowing for no different or opposing view."[15] If this one meaning is the traditional view of women's restrictions in the home and ministry, then no room is left for alternative interpretations that favor women's equal participation in both arenas. But, according to Lee, multiple meanings of Scripture should be considered. Indeed, "Our cultural framework can open new doors of meaning for us from these ancient texts. It is (part of) the meaning of Scripture as inspired by the Holy Spirit: the capacity to speak anew through the One who inspired and inspires."[16] It may be the case that Lee's "multiple meanings" may actually refer to new applications of Scripture rather than to heretofore undiscovered meanings; but such specificity is a matter for another day.

Consideration of Eschatology in the Interpretation and Application of Scripture

Cynthia Long Westfall offers a significant discussion of the importance of eschatology for the interpretation and application of biblical texts that address gender issues. She proposes that "the human destiny of male and female [eschatology] reflects the purpose of God's creation of humanity. Life in the Christian community is supposed to be an eschatological reflection of believers' status, seen in their ethics, their spiritual experience, and the ministry of the Holy Spirit."[17] Her thesis can be framed around a typical four-point sketch—creation, fall, redemption, and consummation—of the metanarrative of Scripture. Skipping the third point for now, the diagram of her position regarding gender is as so:

[15] Dorothy A. Lee, *The Ministry of Women in the New Testament* (Grand Rapids: Baker Academic, 2021), xi.

[16] Lee, *The Ministry of Women in the New Testament*, xi. To be clear, Lee underscores the fact that she is not claiming that her work is inspired by the Spirit. She discusses this issue of interpretation at greater length (8–9).

[17] Cynthia Long Westfall, *Paul and Gender: Reclaiming the Apostle's Vision for Men and Women in Christ* (Grand Rapids: Baker Academic, 2021), 143.

creation	**fall**	**redemption**	**consummation**
men and women are created alike for authority and rule	sin destroyed this creational equality of authority and rule		men and women share a common destiny of authority and rule

Westfall explains that if a shared, common destiny of authority and rule for both men and women "is consistent with the purposes of God at the foundation of the world, with the creation of Adam and Eve, . . . then women could not have been created to be subject to men. In other words, women cannot have a final destiny that was not their intended purpose or function at creation. Rather, it is a transcendent norm for men and women to share dominion. The loss of authority and rule for women is a consequence of the fall in Genesis 3:16."[18]

Filling in the third point underscores why her discussion is so important for the church:

creation	**fall**	**redemption**	**consummation**
men and women are created alike for authority and rule	sin destroyed this creational equality of authority and rule	*men and women share equal authority and rule now in the church*	men and women share a common destiny of authority and rule

Westfall further explains "that no believer is banned from that future because of inherent distinctions or divisions among humans, including . . . gender; in Christ, all are heirs of this inheritance and moving toward this future, which is the accomplishment of God's will and his purpose at creation. . . . Any case or claim for male priority and entitlement in Christ fades before this transcendent norm."[19] Westfall applies this norm to men and women

---

[18] Westfall, *Paul and Gender*, 147.

[19] Westfall, *Paul and Gender*, 151.

in the church: "the distinction between male and female is not erased into some homogenous identity, but it does not follow that there are 'role distinctions' in the church that are determined by gender."[20]

Westfall's thesis represents an egalitarian approach to interpreting and applying texts addressing gender in the light of biblical eschatology. From the other perspective, a complementarian approach warns about interpretive error due to over-realized eschatology, the "view that realities that are reserved for the future, after Christ returns, should be prematurely brought into and actualized in the present. For example, some people insist that because human beings, in the future age, will not be married, they should forego marriage in this present age."[21] Other examples of over-realized eschatology include a triumphalist view of victory over sin (granted to all believers in the eschaton but not in the present age) and claims that complete healing from sickness is available now to those who have faith (promised to all believers in the age to come but not so presently). As Thomas Schreiner notes, "Some of the orders and structures of the present age won't exist when the age to come is consummated. Certainly, when the end comes, there will be no need for elders, pastors, and overseers. Life in the new creation, life in the world to come, isn't necessarily continuous with the structures and practices of the present time. Appealing to eschatology doesn't resolve the matter definitely."[22] According to complementarianism, then, equality of authority and rule for men and women in the eschaton does not constitute a transcendent norm governing the church today as it considers church leadership. Rather, the new covenant norm is set forth in 1 Tim 2:11–14, which

---

[20] Westfall, *Paul and Gender*, 171.

[21] Gregg R. Allison, *The Baker Compact Dictionary of Theological Terms* (Grand Rapids: Baker, 2016), s.v. "over-realized eschatology." I disagree with Westfall's idea that the term "refers to incorrect/false eschatological teaching;" it may so refer (her example "that the resurrection has already occurred [2 Tim 2:18]" is correct), but that is hardly the usual way that theologians use it.

[22] Thomas R. Schreiner, "Paul and Gender: A Review Article," *Themelios* 43.2 (2018): 178–92, https://www.thegospelcoalition.org/themelios/article/paul-and-gender-a-review-article/.

grounds the differentiation in authority and role (e.g., teaching) not only in the fall (v. 14) but also in creation (v. 13).

Weightiness and Slightness of Biblical Material

This hermeneutical issue focuses on the quantity of biblical material relevant to the issue of gender, church leadership, roles, and the like. Egalitarianism maintains that "the biblical basis some claim for disqualifying women is a handful of texts, and in asserting this claim, these interpreters blithely ignore the weight of New Testament theology and the basic principles of the gospel."[23] Complementarianism, by contrast, appeals to the canonical nature of that handful of texts, an official categorization that renders them authoritative and normative despite their slight amount. Furthermore, it underscores that male headship originated at creation and is therefore part of the creation order, and nature itself reflects such divinely designed purpose, making it evident to all human beings.[24]

Scripture Only (or Primarily) or Scripture Supplemented with Extra-Biblical Sources (e.g., Archaeology)[25]

As this principle is quite complex, I begin with an example of the second view that appropriates supplemental material for a proper interpretation of Scripture. Carol Meyers, admitting the scarcity of Old Testament material about the lives and roles of women, turns to Iron Age archaeology to uncover the daily realities that Israelite men and women faced.[26] As she notes, "the great majority of Israelites—as many as 90 percent—were rural farmers,

---

[23] Lee, *The Ministry of Women in the New Testament*, xi.

[24] Colin Smothers, "Why I am a Complementarian," CBMW.org (August 10, 2020), https://cbmw.org/2020/08/10/why-i-am-a-complementarian/.

[25] This topic was briefly treated in the excursus at the end of Chapter 5.

[26] Carol L. Meyers, "The Importance of Bread: Archaeology, the Bible, and Women's Power in Ancient Israel," in *The Biblical World of Gender: The Daily Lives*

not city dwellers. Fortunately, many archaeologists now pay attention to the setting for the farm families of ancient Israel. . . . They can reconstruct the daily life of ordinary Israelites by analyzing the material culture of their settlements."[27] Combining archaeology with contemporary ethnography and its studies of "pre-modern societies similar to ancient Israel," Meyers offers descriptions of a typical Israelite household, "the most important economic, social, and religious unit."[28] For example, she highlights the production of bread and other grain-based foods. This important daily activity involved the use of stone grinding tools (mentioned in Judg 9:53–54; 2 Sam 11:21; Isa 47:1–2; Matt 24:41, par. Luke 17:35) and domed clay ovens and consumed several hours each day. Further archaeological evidence shows that women from multiple households worked together for hours each day, probably in public areas between dwellings.[29]

From these discoveries, Meyers concludes that women were channels of social communication, mutual helpers, contributors to "household religious activities" (Num 15:19–21; Ezek 44:30), and (in regard to the senior women) skillful household managers.[30] Importantly for our purposes:

> Preparing bread was not simply a domestic chore; it was a life-sustaining activity. It was no less important to household survival than was the work of men in growing grain. While men and women were not equal in all aspects of community life, they made equally important contributions to household life. Both women and men were "breadwinners." In fact, women dominated many household activities and men dominated others. This is called gender complementarity.[31]

---

of Ancient Women and Men, ed. Celina Durgin and Dru Johnson (Eugene, OR: Cascade, 2022), 5–6.

[27] Meyers, "The Importance of Bread," 5.

[28] Meyers, "The Importance of Bread," 5.

[29] Meyers, "The Importance of Bread," 7.

[30] Meyers, "The Importance of Bread," 7–9.

[31] Meyers, "The Importance of Bread," 9–10.

Meyers concludes, "Recognizing gender complementarity in ancient Israel challenges views . . . that men controlled women in all respects. Moreover, it overturns the idea that women's work was not valued."[32] She provides biblical snapshots of women exercising household power: the Shunammite woman (2 Kgs 4:8–37; 8:1–6), Abigail (1 Samuel 25), Micah's mother (Judges 17), and the woman of Prov 31:10–31. Such biblical materials, along with archaeological findings, "call into question the suitability of the term *patriarchy*, a term used to denote male domination, to designate Israelite society. Men did not dominate women in all aspects of household life in ancient Israel."[33]

Cynthia Shafer-Elliott similarly employs ethnoarchaeology to reconstruct the ancient Israelite social world of households, concluding that men were primarily responsible for the protection of the household and hospitality (e.g., Genesis 18), women were primarily responsible for procreation, and (perhaps surprisingly) both were responsible for the aspect of production (except in the case of war, in which this productive duty fell to women). "Every able-bodied member" of the household contributed to agricultural activities, animal husbandry, the manufacture of goods and utensils (e.g., pottery and fabric), and whatever else was essential to the daily survival of rural agro-pastoral households.[34] She concludes, "The social world of ancient Israel was not the massively patriarchal system we typically imagine, nor was it an egalitarian system. Rather, it seems that the social world of ancient Israel was more like a heterarchy, where power and authority, at least on a household level, is more fluid."[35]

Proponents of the first view of the primacy or exclusivity of Scripture do not necessarily object to the second view's use of archaeology and ethnographic

---

[32] Meyers, "The Importance of Bread," 10.

[33] Meyers, "The Importance of Bread," 11.

[34] Cynthia Shafer-Elliott, "The Material World of Women and Men in Scripture: Gender and the Ancient Israelite Household," in *The Biblical World of Gender*, 15–19.

[35] Cynthia Shafer-Elliott, "The Material World of Women and Men in Scripture," 21.

studies to rightly interpret Scripture. Indeed, they (should) welcome such supplemental material as informing the historical setting for biblical texts. For example, these studies shed light on the enterprising woman of Prov 31:11–31 who, though exceptional in outpacing other similarly industrious women (v. 29), was not—and thus should not be seen as—an exception to the rule. This means that complementarians do not need to dismiss her as an outlier, nor should they understand her industriousness within a traditional patriarchal framework that severely restricted her activities to chores carried out in her home. Clarity that emerges from supplemental material as it sheds light on biblical backgrounds and cultures can and should be appreciated by both complementarians and egalitarians. And it may be the case that such extra-biblical insights provide a corrective to contemporary readers'/hearers' wrong presuppositions that hinder a correct interpretation of Scripture. On a note of caution, biblical scholars and theologians who employ such supplemental resources should take care to use it appropriately by ensuring their studies are accurate and properly applied to the biblical texts.[36]

[36] Moreover, from the perspective of the perspicuity of Scripture—the doctrine that the Bible is comprehensible to those who read/hear it—the readers/hearers of Scripture are not dependent on these important points of background to understand divine revelation. While they provide greater depth—and may help to correct wrong interpretations (see next point)—supplemental materials are not necessary for even simple readers/hearers of Scripture to grasp its meaning and live out its intended application. As an example from another field, uninitiated viewers of Michaelangelo's *The Final Judgment* (1541) understand that it is portraying some kind of decisive verdict, resulting in the central figure's separation of a group of people rising on the left side of the painting from a group descending on its right side. Art aficionados and Renaissance experts, knowing the idea of scales of judgment, Greek mythology, and the details of those whom Michaelangelo portrayed, appreciate the finesse and nuance of his masterpiece more than do amateurs. One understanding is certainly more profound than the other, but that does not mean the one group comprehends the painting while the other does not. In an analogous way, even simple believers and new Christians understand Scripture and are not dependent on archaeological and ethnographic background information to do so. At the same time, when such supplemental material sheds light on the historical context of Scripture, its readers/hearers should appreciatively embrace that material.

Preunderstanding and the Biblical Text

To oversimplify this issue, most interpreters approach Scripture with an acknowledgment that their preunderstanding—"the worldview, cultural framework, theological tradition, religious experience, and more that readers bring to the task of interpreting Scripture"—impacts their interpretation.[37] Reflecting on Rudolph Bultmann's important essay "Is Exegesis without Presuppositions Possible?"[38] a negative answer (nuancing Bultmann's own discussion) means that presuppositionalist-free exegesis is not possible in the sense that all interpreters bring their above-noted preunderstandings to the exegetical task, which is accordingly influenced by those "presuppositions."[39] A positive answer means that prejudging biblical texts is not necessary. It is possible to approach biblical texts without prejudging their meaning. While presuppositionalist-free exegesis is not possible, this fact does not spell doom for a correct interpretation of Scripture. Whereas an improper preunderstanding may render the interpretive task difficult, a proper preunderstanding fosters a correct interpretation. Of course, this begs the question of what constitutes a proper and improper preunderstanding of biblical texts.

For our purposes, egalitarians criticize complementarians for bringing wrong preunderstandings to texts that address gender, church leadership, roles, and the like. Oppositely, complementarians criticize egalitarians for bringing wrong preunderstandings to those same texts. Broadly speaking,

---

[37] Gregg R. Allison, *The Baker Compact Dictionary of Theological Terms* (Grand Rapids: Baker, 2016), s.v. "Preunderstanding."

[38] Rudolf Bultmann, "Is Exegesis without Presuppositions Possible?" in *Existence and Faith, Shorter Writings of Rudolph Bultmann*, ed. and trans. Schubert M. Ogden (New York: Meridian, 1960), 289–96.

[39] For Bultmann, his presupposition had to do with the historical method of interpretation: "Historical method includes the presupposition that history is a unity in the sense of a closed continuum in which individual events are connected by the succession of cause and effect." Bultmann, "Is Exegesis without Presuppositions Possible?" 291–92. This specific presupposition is not my concern here, which is limited to his overall point about presuppositions (of any kind) and the interpretative task.

egalitarian criticism focuses on complementarian readings that presuppose gender essentialism, restrictions of church leadership to men, traditional understandings of male/husband and female/wife roles (with, for example, "head" [κεφαλή, *kephalē*] signifying "authority" rather than "source"), and even traditional sex polarity and patriarchalism. With such preunderstandings contributing strongly to their interpretations of key biblical texts, of course complementarians will understand and apply those texts within a complementarian framework. According to egalitarians, such complementarian presuppositions and, thus, complementarian conclusions, are incorrect.[40]

Broadly speaking, complementarian criticism focuses on egalitarian readings that presuppose something other than gender essentialism (e.g., rejection of stereotypical assignment of certain traits and abilities to women and men so as to differentiate the genders, social constructionist views of gender), accessibility of church leadership to both men and women, mutual authority and submission between men/husbands and women/wives (with, for example, "head" [κεφαλή, *kephalē*] signifying "source" rather than "authority"), and even (some forms of secular) feminism and Western liberal egalitarian visions of society. With such preunderstandings contributing strongly to their interpretations of key biblical texts, of course egalitarians will understand and apply those texts within an egalitarian framework. According to complementarians, such egalitarian presuppositions and, thus, egalitarian conclusions, are incorrect.[41]

---

[40] Celina Durgin and Dru Johnson offer the following: "Recent discussions of 'biblical manhood and womanhood' tend to reflect our current concepts of masculinity and femininity, and less the lived world of the biblical authors. . . . We suggest that our current paradigms of masculinity and femininity can run interference and prevent us from considering what the biblical authors implicitly assumed about men and women." Celina Durgin and Dru Johnson, eds., "Introduction," in *The Biblical World of Gender*, xvi.

[41] Ray Ortlund, Jr., identifies the equating of personal worth and dignity with personal roles and responsibilities as one of the key presuppositions of egalitarianism, with this result: "a limitation in role reduces or threatens personal worth. But why? What logic is there in such a claim? Why must my position dictate my

What, then, constitutes a proper and improper preunderstanding of biblical texts? Egalitarianism and complementarianism, by answering this question differently and in accordance with their perspective, demonstrate the key point of this discussion: both sides of the debate come to biblical texts about gender, church leadership, roles, and similar matters with a preunderstanding—worldview, context, tradition, experience—and this preunderstanding impacts their interpretation. Biblical interpretation without presuppositions is not possible, but this fact does not rule out a correct understanding of Scripture, partial as it may be (1 Cor 13:12). Accordingly, as Craig Blomberg advises: "We all need regular reminders of the role presuppositions play in our interpretation, and we must moderate our opinions with healthy doses of humility. We must study all of the Scriptures relevant to a topic like men's and women's roles and affirm a position that we believe does adequate justice to all of the biblical data. In short, we must agree to disagree at times."[42]

In summary, this section has treated key hermeneutical principles as a framework for understanding Scripture and how in part to account for the substantial differences between complementarian and egalitarian interpretations of biblical texts on gender, church leadership, roles, and more. These are the regulative principle vs. normative principle; biblical language: descriptive (or situational) vs. prescriptive; single meaning vs. multiple meanings; consideration of eschatology; the weightiness and slightness of biblical material; Scripture only (or primarily) or Scripture supplemented with extra-biblical sources (e.g., archaeology); and preunderstanding and the biblical text. While this section has concentrated on these seven principles,

---

significance?" His criticism continues with a denial "that my personal significance is measured according to my rung on the ladder, and my opportunity for personal fulfillment enlarges or contracts according to my role." Raymond C. Ortlund, Jr., "Male-Female Equality and Male Headship: Genesis 1–3," in *Recovering Biblical Manhood and Womanhood: A Response to Evangelical Feminism*, ed. John Piper and Wayne Grudem (Wheaton: Crossway, 1991, 2006), 111–12.

[42] Craig Blomberg, "1 Corinthians" in *NIV Life Application Bible* (Grand Rapids: Zondervan, 1994), 226.

other hermeneutical issues (e.g., contextualization or application of biblical meaning) and positions (e.g., William Webb's trajectory hermeneutic)[43] are other areas to explore.[44]

The Canonical and Covenantal Framework of Scripture

At the heart of this issue is how the Bible presents itself in terms of its form—the canon of Scripture, that is, the writings that properly belong in Scripture—and its matter—the progressive development of God's relationship with his people according to six covenants. I develop my proposal of complementarity from canonical Scripture and through a particular understanding of the relationship between the covenants of Scripture.

For Protestants, Scripture is the ultimate authority for issues of faith, doctrine, and holy living (*sola Scriptura*). Moreover, the canon consists of sixty-six books and is closed—that is, after the completion of the New Testament, God is no longer inspiring written revelation to be added to the Bible. Complementarity is grounded on and advanced within this closed canon of sixty-six books.

Furthermore, Scripture itself sets forth a covenantal framework for properly understanding its divinely inspired, authoritative, and canonical revelation.[45] By covenant I mean "an enduring agreement which establishes [or formalizes] a defined relationship between two parties involving a solemn, binding obligation to specified stipulations on the part of a least one of the parties toward the other, which is taken by oath under threat of divine

---

[43] William J. Webb, *Slaves, Women, & Homosexuals: Exploring the Hermeneutics of Cultural Analysis* (Downers Grove: InterVarsity, 2001).

[44] For a complementarian response to Webb's position, see Benjamin Reaoch, *Women, Slaves, and the Gender Debate: A Complementarian Response to the Redemptive Hermeneutic Movement* (Phillipsburg, NJ: P&R Publishing, 2012).

[45] According to Michael Horton, the covenants are "the architectural structure that we believe the Scriptures themselves to yield." Michael S. Horton, *God of Promise: Introducing Covenant Theology* (Grand Rapids: Baker, 2006), 13.

curse, and ratified by a visual ritual."[46] Each of the six biblical covenants features four elements: a covenant (1) is unilateral in that God and God alone establishes it; (2) establishes or formalizes a structured relationship between God and his partners; (3) presents binding obligations on the part of God and on the part of his covenant partners; and (4) is ratified by a sign or the swearing of oaths.[47] A covenantal framework, then, means that Scripture sets forth (and is properly interpreted by discerning) the structured ways that God has related, and continues to relate, to his people.

The six covenants are the Adamic covenant (Gen 1–3), the Noahic covenant (Gen 6–9), the Abrahamic covenant (Genesis 12–17), the Mosaic or old covenant (Exodus 19–24), the Davidic covenant (2 Samuel 7; Psalm 89), and the new covenant (e.g., Jer 31:31–34; Matt 26:26–29; Heb 8:6–10:18; 2 Cor 3).[48]

There are three key issues to note: First, God always relates to his people through a covenant. Second, the six covenants revealed in Scripture progressively unfold the way in which God relates to his people differently at different junctures in salvation history.

Third, biblical scholars and theologians put together these covenants in different ways. Our focus will be on the two contrasting covenants: the old covenant and the new covenant. Scholarly division is usually along the lines of more continuity or more discontinuity between these covenants.[49]

---

[46] Daniel C. Lane, "The Meaning and Use of the Old Testament Term for 'Covenant' (berît): With Some Implications for Dispensationalism and Covenant Theology" (PhD diss., Trinity International University, 2000), 314. I have inserted the verb "formalizes" because a covenant may not establish a new agreement but may enact or solemnize an already existing relationship between two parties.

[47] Some of the following discussion is adapted from Gregg R. Allison, *Sojourners and Strangers: The Doctrine of the Church* (Wheaton: Crossway, 2012), 64–78.

[48] For further discussion of Scripture's canonical structure see Peter J. Gentry and Stephen J. Wellum, *Kingdom Through Covenant: A Biblical-Theological Understanding of the Covenants*, 2nd ed. (Wheaton: Crossway, 2018).

[49] Proponents of absolute continuity (theonomy, for example) and absolute discontinuity (classical dispensationalism, for example) will not be considered. For further discussion, see John S. Feinberg, ed., *Continuity and Discontinuity:*

As for more continuity, proponents maintain that much of old covenantal material—for example, Mosaic law—continues to be in force today for new covenant believers, though it has been significantly transformed by Jesus Christ and New Testament Scripture. To take one example, continuity proponents look to the rules and regulations about circumcision, the sign of the old covenant, as somehow applicable to the corresponding new covenant sign of baptism. By contrast, more discontinuity proponents hold that the binding nature of old covenant material—again, for example, Mosaic law—depends on what Jesus and the New Testament writers do with it. Proponents maintain that there is more discontinuity than continuity for new covenant believers. For example, aspects of old covenant law that continue in force today are the Ten Commandments and the law of love (illustrated in Rom 13:9). Elements that have been rendered obsolete include the dietary prohibitions of the Mosaic code (Mark 7:10; 1 Tim 4:3–4), the Levitical priesthood (Heb 7:11–12), and instructions regarding the sacrificial system (Hebrews 8–10). Facets that have been significantly modified or clarified include the commands that Jesus "fulfilled" (Matt 5:17–48) and Sabbath regulations (Rom 14:5–9; Col 2:16–17).

This continuity-discontinuity discussion influences complementarity. From a moderate continuity perspective, there is one overarching "covenant of grace" with two primary aspects—the old covenant and new covenant—with a significant degree of continuity between them. Proponents may be inclined to emphasize continuity between certain aspects of old covenant patriarchy and new covenant marital and familial structures. Regulations concerning the rights of inheritance, division of labor, and (apparently) favorable treatment of men may—though not necessarily—continue to have application for new covenant believers. From a moderate discontinuity perspective (the view that I hold), the proposal of an overarching

---

Perspectives on the Relationship between the Old and New Testaments: Essays in Honor of S. Lewis Johnson, Jr. (Wheaton: Crossway, 1988); Benjamin L. Merkle, *Discontinuity to Continuity: A Survey of Dispensational and Covenantal Theologies* (Bellingham, WA: Lexham, 2020).

"covenant of grace" seems to flatten the distinctions between the old covenant and new covenant and thus render them overly continuous.[50] Discontinuity proponents dismiss old covenant patriarchy as irrelevant for new covenant marital and familial structures because the covenant framework that fostered patriarchy has been rendered obsolete. Old covenant laws of clean and unclean have no binding authority and application today because Jesus and the New Testament rendered those laws null and void (e.g., Mark 7:1–23). Accordingly, accusations that Christians treat women as inferior in nature and lesser in dignity because the Bible—that is, the Old Testament—is misogynistic completely fail from a moderate discontinuity perspective.

Setting the Stage: Genesis 1–3

Given the importance of the opening chapters of Genesis, perhaps it should come as no surprise that many foundational elements for complementarity are narrated in the creation of divine image bearers as male and female, the formation of the first man and the first woman, the fall of Adam and Eve and its consequences, and the beginning of God's redemptive work to rescue his fallen image bearers. Perhaps equally unsurprising, egalitarianism and complementarianism differ significantly on their interpretation of the key passages that address men and women and their relationships.[51] In this section, then, I highlight those key passages for discussions of complementarity, egalitarianism, and complementarianism.[52]

---

[50] My proposal of complementarity, while flowing from this approach to biblical covenants, can be embraced by those who hold to a moderate continuity perspective.

[51] As noted in the opening pages of this book, though I interact significantly with these two positions, I do not adjudicate between their interpretations of Scripture, their theological foundations, and their applications. Such assessment is beyond the purpose and scope of this book.

[52] As I treat these biblical passages, I do not mean to indicate that the perspectives of complementarity, egalitarianism, and complementarianism are the *meaning*

Genesis 1:26–28

While most expositions of this passage focus on the identity of the divine image in which both men and women were created, I will focus on the words *'adam* and *ha'adam* and whether they refer to man in general, to humankind or humanity in general, or to a particular man, the man named Adam.[53]

At the apex of the creation account—in which God's establishment of the earth and everything in it in anticipation of and preparation for his formation of human beings—is the broad account of human creation. First, Gen 1:26 narrates the divine deliberation or plan:

> Then God said, "Let us make *'adam/man* [*mankind*, NIV] in our image, after our likeness. And let *them* have dominion over the fish of the sea and over the birds of the heavens and over the livestock and over all the earth and over every creeping thing that creeps on the earth."

Some Bible versions translate *'adam* as *man*, with the masculine noun being rendered literally as *man* while referring in the singular to the human race corporately (in "Let us make *man*," the singular *'adam* refers to the whole of the human race). Other versions also translate *'adam* as *man*, with the masculine noun being rendered literally as *man* while referring in the singular to the human race corporately; additionally, the masculine noun *'adam* or *man* is interpreted as implying something about the hierarchy of men in relationship to women. Still other versions translate *'adam* as *mankind* or *humanity* or *humankind*, with the masculine singular noun referring first

---

of these passages. Rather, in most if not all cases, they are implications or applications of these passages by the three frameworks.

[53] There seems to be overall agreement on the part of all sides that the divine image is the central biblical proposal for human identity. Certainly, differences continue about the precise nature of the image—substantive/structural, relational, functional, holistic—but those intramural debates seldom detract from the broad consensus that the key to human identity is creation in the divine image.

to the human race corporately (in "Let us make *humankind*," the singular *'adam* refers to the whole of the human race) and second to individual human beings (in "let *them* have dominion," the plural refers to individual human beings who, it will be specified in v. 27, are either male or female image bearers).

Second, Gen 1:27 presents the actualization of the divine plan:

> So God created *ha'adam/man* [literally, *the man*] in his own image,
> in the image of God he created him;
> male and female he created them.

According to some interpretations, God's creation of *ha'adam* (literally, *the man* with the definite article) refers to the first man as opposed to the first woman, neither of whom has been introduced in the narrative. Other interpretations take God's creation of *ha'adam* to refer to *the man* who is referenced in v. 26: God created that *man*, whom he purposed to create, with the similar options listed for that verse:

- *man/the man*, with the masculine noun being rendered literally as *man/the man* while referring in the singular to the human race corporately
- *man/the man*, with the masculine noun being rendered literally as *man/the man* while referring in the singular to the human race corporately, and with the masculine noun implying something about the hierarchy of men
- *mankind* or *humanity* or *humankind*, with the masculine singular noun referring, first, to the human race corporately ("in the image of God he created *him*," with the singular pronoun referring to the whole of the human race, perhaps with the additional implication about the hierarchy of men), and, second, to individual human beings ("male and female he created *them*," with the plural pronoun referring to individual persons who are either male or female image bearers).

Third, Gen 1:28 recounts the divine blessing and mandate:

> God blessed them, and God said to them, "Be fruitful, multiply, fill the earth, and subdue it. Rule the fish of the sea, the birds of the sky, and every creature that crawls on the earth."

To be underscored is the divine address that is directed to the two image bearers together.[54] First God blessed them (plural), then God communi-

[54] Peter Gentry structures Gen 1:26–28 and offers an interpretation of image bearing:

> God created mankind in his image
> according to his likeness;
>
> A in the image of God he created him
> B male and female he created them
> B` be fruitful and increase in number and fill the earth
> A` and subdue it and rule over the fish/birds/animals

He explains, "Binary sexuality, i.e., duality of gender, is the basis for being fruitful, while the divine image is correlated with the command to rule as God's viceroy." More specifically, he underscores that human beings, created *as* divine image bearers, *are* the divine images, an ontological affirmation that means that representation of God and ruling functions are products of creation in the divine image and not the image itself. In fact, "As servant king and son of God mankind will mediate God's rule to the creation in the context of a covenant relationship with God on the one hand and the earth on the other." Such is true for both female image bearers and male image bearers. Peter J. Gentry, "Understanding the Image of God: A Response to Mary L. Conway, 'Gender in Creation and Fall,'" *Eikon: A Journal for Biblical Anthropology*, vol. 5 issue 1 (June 22, 2023); and Peter J. Gentry and Stephen J. Wellum, *Kingdom through Covenant: A Biblical-Theological Understanding of the Covenants* (Wheaton: Crossway, 2012), 197–202. Whether or not Christa McKirland rightly engages with Gentry's view is one matter, but her conclusion is a bit puzzling: "This does not make sexed embodiment inconsequential, but it does position it as secondary (at best) to being made in the image of God and being tasked with dominion. All humankind is given the commission to have dominion over the rest of the creation." Christa L. McKirland, "Image of God and Divine Presence: A Critique of Gender Essentialism," in *Discovering Biblical Equality: Biblical, Theological, Cultural, and Practical Perspectives*, 3rd ed., ed. Ronald W. Pierce and Cynthia Long Westfall, assoc. ed. Christa L. McKirland (Downers Grove: IVP Academic, 2021), 291–92. From my perspective, because sex (maleness and femaleness) maps onto human embodiment (I bracket the issue of intersex conditioned human beings), and because every human being is

cated to them (plural) what is usually referred to as the cultural mandate to build society, that is, expanding the human race through procreation—"be fruitful" (plural), "multiply" (plural), "fill the earth" (plural)—and advancing the race through vocation: "subdue" (plural) the earth and "rule" (plural) the rest of the created order. While it may be common to consider this complementarity as required for the first aspect—multiplying divine image bearers through sexual intercourse, childbearing, and child rearing—it is equally needed for the second aspect: developing skills and engaging in work to produce what human beings need for life. As emphasized by the plural verbs as aspects of the cultural mandate, both procreation and vocation are to be carried out by both men and women and are designed for the purpose of human flourishing.[55]

Several elements of Gen 1:26–28 emerge in the debate between complementarianism and egalitarianism while also providing important points for complementarity. As for the debate, disagreement exists over the referent of *'adam* (v. 26) and *ha'adam* (v. 27). Again, the options are:

- *man/the man*, with the masculine noun interpreted as a nongendered/collective term for humankind—men and women—in general, being rendered literally as *man/the man* while referring in the singular to the human race corporately; this option is found in complementarianism;

---

embodied, and because every human being is created in the divine image, even though maleness and femaleness is not the divine image, all human beings are either female embodied image bearers or male embodied image bearers, which ties the concepts of sex, embodiment, and image bearing much more tightly together than it appears that McKirland does. For further discussion see Gregg R. Allison, *Embodied: Living as Whole People in a Fractured World* (Grand Rapids: Baker, 2021), chs. 1–2.

[55] For further discussion see Mary L. Conway, "Gender in Creation and Fall, Genesis 1-3," in *Discovering Biblical Equality: Complementarity Without Hierarchy*, ed. Ronald W. Pierce and Rebecca Merrill Groothuis (Downers Grove: InterVarsity, 2004), 38–39; and Gentry, "Understanding the Image of God: A Response to Mary L. Conway, 'Gender in Creation and Fall.'"

- *man/the man*, with the masculine noun, interpreted as a gendered collective term for mankind—men and women—in general, being rendered literally as *man/the man* while referring in the singular to the human race corporately, and with the masculine noun implying something about the hierarchy of men; this option is found in complementarianism;
- *humanity* or *humankind* or *mankind*, with the masculine noun, interpreted as a nongendered/collective term for humankind—men and women—in general, referring, first, to the human race corporately ("in the image of God he created *him*," with the singular pronoun referring to the whole of the human race), and, second, to individual human beings ("male and female he created *them*," with the plural pronoun referring to individual persons who are either male or female image bearers); this option is found in egalitarianism, which draws the implication that no hierarchy between men and women exists.

As for the egalitarian preference for this last option, Mary Conway argues, "It is important to note that the Hebrew lexis *'adam* is most often a nongendered/collective term for a specific human or humanity in general, male and/or female, unless its meaning is restricted by context."[56] With regard to older translations, she adds, "the gendered term *man* was used to indicate humanity in general, but this term obscures the Hebrew meaning and is no longer accepted in most contemporary contexts."[57] As the contemporary use of the word *man* encounters some problems, and as the terms *humanity* and *humankind* avoid those problems, egalitarianism opts for the use of the latter words; for example, "Let us make *humankind* in our image" (NRSVA, NRSVACE, NRSVue).[58] Importantly, some complementarians

---

[56] Conway, "Gender in Creation and Fall: Genesis 1–3," in *Discovering Biblical Equality*, 36.

[57] Conway, "Gender in Creation and Fall," 36.

[58] NRSVA text is from New Revised Standard Version Bible: Anglicised Edition, copyright © 1989, 1995 the Division of Christian Education of the

may also favor this option for the same reasons offered by Conway, yet they do not deny hierarchy between men and women as established elsewhere in Scripture as noted next.

Many (most?) complementarians choose either the first or the second option. Given that (1) the word *man* is the traditional translation of *'adam*; (2) the context makes it clear that the word refers to the human race and not to a particular male human being; and (3) other biblical passages make a stronger case for male hierarchy, complementarians may choose the first option.

As for the second option, Bruce Ware explains its rationale, arguing from Gen 5:2 (God "created them male and female. When they were created, he blessed them and called them mankind;" it seems that his argument would also be supported by Gen 1:26–27):

> In Genesis 5:2 God chooses to name *both* male *and* female with a name that functions as a masculine generic (i.e., the Hebrew term *'adam* is a masculine term that can be used exclusively for a man, especially in Genesis 1–4, but here it is used as a generic term in reference to male and female together). [Additionally,] "when they were created he called *them* '*man*'" (emphasis added). It appears that God intends the identity of *both* to contain an element of priority given to the male, since God chooses as their *common* name a name that is purposely masculine. . . . As God has so chosen to create man as male and female, by God's design her identity as female is inextricably tied to and rooted in the prior identity of the male.[59]

---

[59] Bruce Ware, "Male and Female Complementarity and the Image of God," *Journal for Biblical Manhood and Womanhood* 7 (2002), 19.

Similarly with reference to Gen 5:1–2, Wayne Grudem calls attention to the fact that "God named the human race 'Man,' not 'Woman.'"[60] Referring to the word *'adam*, Grudem avers "this is by no means a gender-neutral term in the eyes of the Hebrew reader, because in the four chapters prior to Genesis 5:2, *'adam* has been used many times to speak of a male human being in distinction from a female human being" (he lists Genesis 2:22, 23, 25; 3:8, 9, 12, 20).[61] Thus, Grudem affirms, in "the naming of the human race in Genesis 5:2 . . . , it was evident to the original readers that God was using a name that had clear male overtones or nuances."[62] While acknowledging that *'adam*, like the English word *man*, "can either mean a male human being or can refer to the human race in general," he opts for the second sense in Gen 5:2.[63] Accordingly, he concludes that *'adam/man* "does give a hint of male leadership, which God suggested in choosing this name" rather than calling the human race "Woman" or "humanity," the latter of "which would have no male connotations and no connection with the man in distinction from the woman."[64]

The interpretation of Gen 5:2 (similarly in Gen 1:26–27) by Ware and Grudem is the second option: the presence of the masculine noun *'adam/ha'adam* hints at or implies something about male hierarchy—authority of men and submission of women—in the human race.

This complementarian option is challenged by egalitarianism: "It should be pointed out that Old Testament Hebrew has no common term for 'humanity' other than *'adam*. . . . Therefore it is somewhat inaccurate to suggest that there was a conscious divine decision to use a masculine term to describe the human race. No other term was available. . . . It should also be noted that Hebrew has only two genders, masculine and

[60] Wayne Grudem, *Evangelical Feminism and Biblical Truth* (Sisters, OR: Multnomah, 2004), 34.

[61] Grudem, *Evangelical Feminism and Biblical Truth*, 34.

[62] Grudem, *Evangelical Feminism and Biblical Truth*, 34.

[63] Grudem, *Evangelical Feminism and Biblical Truth*, 35.

[64] Grudem, *Evangelical Feminism and Biblical Truth*, 35.

feminine; there is no neuter. . . . In short, [these points] all argue against the presumption that God's naming of the race 'man' whispers male headship."[65] Moreover, linguistically, it is wrongheaded to jump from a grammatically masculine term or a grammatically feminine term to a conclusion about ontology.[66]

Because of their differences over the issue of *'adam* as *man* or *humankind/humanity*, the two sides of the debate understand the cultural mandate differently (Gen 1:28). Both complementarianism and egalitarianism agree that this divine charter with God's image bearers is directed at and must be obeyed by all human beings *qua* human beings; that is, flowing from verses 26 and 27, and being affirmed explicitly by the plural verbs (God blessed them [plural] and God communicated the mandate to them [plural]), the mandate is the responsibility of all male and female embodied image bearers.

The division comes over whether this mandate is given to women and men alike without any hierarchy being implied, or whether it is given with a priority of men in relationship to women. Noting that the terms *zakar* and *neqebah* (*male* and *female*; v. 27) are biological descriptions that do "not indicate any social or functional superiority or inferiority of either male or female," Mary Conway offers the egalitarian view that both women and men are "given the same functions" in their joint exercise of dominion over the created order.[67] Likewise, Gilbert Bilezikian contends that the mandate does not differentiate on the basis of sex nor hints at a division of

[65] Richard S. Hess, "Equality With and Without Innocence: Genesis 1–3," in *Discovering Biblical Equality: Complementarity Without Hierarchy*, ed. Ronald W. Pierce and Rebecca Merrill Groothuis (Downers Grove: IVP Academic, 2004), 80. His citation is from Raymond C. Ortlund Jr., "Male-Female Equality and Male Headship: Genesis 1–3," in *Recovering Biblical Manhood and Womanhood: A Response to Evangelical Feminism*, ed. John Piper and Wayne Grudem (Wheaton: Crossway, 1991, 2006), 98.

[66] For example, in Italian, *il tavolo* (masc.) and *la tavola* (fem.) have nothing to do with a male table and a female table; tables are not gendered.

[67] Conway, "Gender in Creation and Fall," 38–39.

responsibilities.[68] Similarly, Linda Belleville, while noting the distinction between the sexes in Genesis 1–2, underscores "the sameness of male and female" in that both are divine image bearers and both are named *'adam*. Such sameness can also be seen in their function in that both sexes are given the cultural mandate—which means "there is not even a division of labor (e.g., domestic versus nondomestic)"—and both have the same family function, being "given responsibility in the bearing and rearing of children. The idea that it is the woman's job to produce and raise the children and the man's job to work the land is simply not found in the creation accounts."[69]

To summarize the egalitarian perspective, both men and women alike contribute equally to the fulfillment of the cultural mandate, which has no hint of hierarchy. As will be discussed shortly, egalitarianism maintains that hierarchy was introduced as a result of the fall but did not exist in the prefall relationship between men and women.

From a complementarian perspective, the cultural mandate contains within itself the seed of hierarchy, that is, male authority and female submission. Grudem appeals to Genesis 2 (e.g., the order and purpose of creation; Adam's naming of Eve) and its presentation "that Adam and Eve were to relate to one another in different ways, with a leadership role given to Adam."[70] His interpretive approach is to read Genesis 1 through the lens of Genesis 2. George Knight turns to Genesis 3 to draw implications for the cultural mandate. "God relates the effects of the curse respectively to that portion of His creation mandate . . . that most particularly applies to the woman on the one hand and to the man on the other hand. . . . In short, God speaks to her [concerning her pain in childbirth and the struggles in

---

[68] Gilbert Bilezikian, *Beyond Sex Roles* (Grand Rapids: Baker, 1990), 24. Cited in Grudem, *Evangelical Feminism and Biblical Truth*, 106–107.

[69] Linda L. Belleville, "Women in Ministry: An Egalitarian Perspective," in *Two Views on Women in Ministry*, ed. James R. Beck, rev. ed., Zondervan Counterpoints Series (Grand Rapids: Zondervan, 2005), 25–26.

[70] Grudem, *Evangelical Feminism and Biblical Truth*, 107. He discusses the particular aspects that support Adam's leadership role on pp. 29–45, with a summary on p. 109.

the husband-and-wife relationship] about what is unique to her as a woman, namely, being a mother and a wife. To the man He speaks of the difficulties" he will encounter in working the land. "Thus He delineates what is the main calling for man, namely the responsibility of breadwinner and provider for his wife and family."[71] Knight's interpretive approach is to read Genesis 1 through the lens of Genesis 3.

To summarize the complementarian perspective, both men and women alike contribute to the fulfillment of the cultural mandate, but they do so within a hierarchical framework in which men exercise authority over women, who submit to their leadership at particular points. As will be discussed shortly, complementarianism maintains that such hierarchy was not introduced as a result of the fall, but its expression among men and women was and is corrupted by sin.

My proposal of complementarity emphasizes in Gen 1:26–28, whatever the translation of *'adam* may be—as *man* or as *humankind*, *humanity*, or *mankind*—the fact remains that, according to God's purpose and as actualized by his creative work, both women and men alike are created in the divine image. This affirmation highlights both their equal dignity and their significant differentiation. Complementarity denounces any hint of superiority or inferiority, all suggestion of advantage or disadvantage, between the sexes. Men and women are to fill out and mutually support one another relationally. Complementarity insists on embracing this perspective over against both traditional sex polarity and reverse sex polarity while also decrying sex unity and sex neutrality. Sadly, it detects the presence of both versions of sex polarity—the first in complementarianism, the second in egalitarianism—even as it regrets the contemporary cultural dominance of both sex unity and sex neutrality.

Moreover, my vision for complementarity underscores the cultural mandate as given to both sexes and thus the responsibility of both men

---

[71] Knight III, "The Family and the Church: How Should Biblical Manhood and Womanhood Work Out in Practice?" in *Recovering Biblical Manhood and Womanhood*, 347.

and women to obey it. As divine image bearers, they are to fill out and mutually support one another familially (through procreation) and vocationally (through work) for both individual and corporate flourishing. Complementarity takes issue with (some expressions of) egalitarianism that there is no division of labor between the sexes. Such a view violates the element of significant differentiation of men and women. The two sexes are not interchangeable, and in the haste to emphasize equal dignity, unguarded affirmations of such interchangeability are confusing as well as unnecessary.

My idea of complementarity also takes issue with (some expressions of) complementarianism that read back Genesis 2 and 3 into Genesis 1. To be recalled is that these chapters narrate the first two created human beings with two unique modes: Adam is both the first man and the first husband, and Eve is both the first woman and the first wife. In regard to the second of these two modes, a complementarian approach of reading Genesis 1 in the light of Genesis 2 may obscure the fact that divine image bearing and the cultural mandate are true of male and female human beings *qua* male and female human beings and not of male human beings *qua* husbands and female human beings *qua* wives. Such an approach misses the point that image bearing is first and foremost about identity rather than function. Husband/wife is a role, not an identity. Correlatively, such an approach overlooks single people. Single women and single men are full image bearers and as such responsible for the cultural mandate whether or not they ever get married. To take two obvious examples, a single woman is not confined to child raising and housework, and a single man works and provides for himself, his church, the poor, and more, but not for his family and not necessarily in any leadership role. Finally, reading back Genesis 2 and 3 into Genesis 1 may blunt the intended point of Scripture's opening chapter: God's design for his male image bearers and female image bearers to fill out and mutually support one another for individual and corporate flourishing.[72] Whether or not that design is hierarchical (and, if hierarchical,

---

[72] What I am *not* saying is that it is illegitimate to read earlier Scripture in the light of latter Scripture; I affirm the hermeneutical principle that Scripture is its best

to what extent), may emerge from later Scripture, and it may or may not emerge without affecting the foundational affirmation of complementarity in Genesis 1.

Genesis 2:7–8, 18–25

Following this broad account of God's creation of his image bearers comes the narrow account of his formation of the first man and the first woman. As for the first man's creation, Gen 2:7–8 narrates:

> Then the LORD God formed *ha'adam/the man* (*man*, RSV; *a man*, NIV) of dust from the ground and breathed into his nostrils the breath of life, and *the man* became a living creature. And the LORD God planted a garden in Eden, in the east, and there he put *the man* whom he had formed. (Gen 2:7–8; so throughout Genesis 2–3)

Some Bible versions translate *ha'adam* (literally, *the man* with the definite article in Hebrew) as *man* or *a man* (with the non-definite article in English) with the masculine singular noun referring to the first created male human being, whose creation will be followed by that of the first woman (2:18–25). Other versions translate *ha'adam* as *the man* (definite article) with the masculine singular noun being rendered literally as *the man*, referring to the first created male human being, whose creation will be followed by that of the first woman. Apparently, no versions translate *ha'adam* as Adam. In fact, the first appearance of the name of *the man* does not appear until 3:21 (cf. 4:25; 5:1). Accordingly, throughout Genesis 2 and 3, *the man* refers to the first created male human being and, while his name is *Adam*, he is not named until later in the Genesis narrative.

---

interpreter and that, as Christians, we read every part of Scripture canonically, that is, in light of all the rest of Scripture. What I *am* saying is that such reading must not be allowed to blunt or change the meaning of earlier Scripture, which has its own integrity that must be respected.

As to the actual creation of *the man*, God formed his material aspect (body) "out of the dust from the ground." His creation was not *ex nihilo* but mediately through already existing material; indeed, God formed *ha'adam* from the dust of *ha'adamah*.[73] He was not a heavenly being but an earthy, "grounded" creature, wholly dependent on God for his existence. God also "breathed into his nostrils the breath of life." While the traditional interpretation identifies this act as God's impartation of the immaterial aspect (soul), another interpretation holds that it is God's communication of the energizing principle, the "spark of life" that characterizes all living beings (Gen 1:30; 6:17; 7:15, 22), by which "the [lifeless] man became a living creature." Moreover, as human embodiment implies emplacement, God established this first living male human being in "a garden in Eden, in the east," a well-watered garden full of pleasant, nourishing trees in which the man would work and over which he would watch (vv. 9–16). Two particular trees—one of life, the other of the knowledge of good and evil—were distinguished by a divine command: "You are free to eat from any tree of the garden [including the tree of life], but you must not eat from the tree of the knowledge of good and evil, for on the day you eat from it, you will certainly die" (vv. 16–17).

As for the first woman's creation, Gen 2:18–25 narrates a much lengthier account:

> Then the LORD God said, "It is not good for the man to be alone. I will make a helper corresponding to him." The LORD God formed out of the ground every wild animal and every bird of the sky, and brought each to the man to see what he would call it. And whatever the man called a living creature, that was its name. The man gave names to all the livestock, to the birds of the sky, and to every wild animal; but for the man no helper was found corresponding to

[73] Accordingly, if we read back Genesis 2 into Genesis 1, it seems that *'adam* (v. 26) emphasizes man's formation from the ground and not male hierarchy. See Belleville, "Women in Ministry: An Egalitarian Perspective," 29.

> him. So the LORD God caused a deep sleep to come over the man, and he slept. God took one of his ribs and closed the flesh at that place. Then the LORD God made the rib he had taken from the man into a woman and brought her to the man. And the man said:
>
> > This one, at last, is bone of my bone
> > and flesh of my flesh;
> > this one will be called "woman,"
> > for she was taken from man.
>
> This is why a man leaves his father and mother and bonds with his wife, and they become one flesh. Both the man and his wife were naked, yet felt no shame.

The discordant words "it is not good" recall the earlier, repeated divine assessment ("it was good"/"it was very good") and underscore not that the loneness of the first man was sinful or evil, but that it was not according to the divine plan for humankind, which was to consist of both male image bearers and female image bearers.

God's stated resolution of this loneness was for him to "make a helper corresponding to" ("meet for," KJV; "fit for," ESV; "suitable for," NIV) the man. As I will return to a more detailed discussion shortly, it is sufficient to note here a significant disagreement over the meaning of the phrase. Complementarianism takes it to refer to one who is in a subordinate role in certain contexts, such that the woman whom God intends to make for the man will be in submission to him even as she helps as his equal in nature. Egalitarianism maintains that the phrase, as it is used elsewhere of God providing help for human beings and Israel, emphasizes strength and competence and is far removed from notions of submission.

The divine solution would not come from the animal kingdom but from a special creation by God himself. The exhibition of the animals before the first man, and his naming of each of them, was not a failed attempt to fulfill the divine promise to provide a helper corresponding to the man. Rather, it was to awaken in the man an awareness of his loneness and his need to be filled out, not in the sense of an individual incompleteness but in terms of an unfinished humankind responsible for the cultural mandate. As a result of this display and naming of the animals, "for the man no helper was found corresponding to him." As promised, God undertook to provide for the man's need. As he put the man to sleep, God removed a rib and formed it "into a woman and brought her to the man." The man's poetic response highlighted both his delight in her and the exactness of the divine provision of her: the woman, unlike the animals, was indeed of the same nature as the man, a helper corresponding precisely to him, reflected in her being called אִשָּׁה (*'ishshah*) because she was taken out of אִישׁ (*'ish*). This divinely designed and executed complementarity—the basis for all subsequent human marriage—was reflected in the total openness of their relationship, displayed in the shamelessness of their nakedness.

Several aspects of Genesis 2 emerge in the debate between complementarianism and egalitarianism while also providing important points for complementarity. As for the debate, disagreement exists over the significance of the *order* of creation, the *manner* of creation, and the *purpose* of creation.

As for the *order* of creation, Genesis 2 narrates the formation of the first man occurring before that of the first woman. Later Scripture draws out the significance of this order (1 Tim 2:12–13):

> I do not allow a woman to teach or to have authority over a man; instead, she is to remain quiet. For Adam was formed first, then Eve.

Egalitarianism and complementarianism disagree over the significance of this creation order.

Egalitarianism discounts the order of creation as having any significance for male and female relationships and roles. Some object to the argument because, to follow its logic, the animals, which were created before the first man and the first woman, should have authority over human beings.[74] Some egalitarians object to the concept of primogeniture—the priority of the firstborn

[74] Belleville, "Women in Ministry: An Egalitarian Perspective," 30.

son—being invoked by complementarians on this issue, with the application that the man, being created first, enjoys primogeniture status—and, thus, hierarchal authority—over the woman, who was created second. Egalitarians dismiss its application on the basis that Scripture narrates God's overriding of the principle as "the norm among the patriarchs" as at times he blesses "the second or third born (e.g., Isaac over Ishmael, Jacob over Esau, Joseph over his brothers, Ephraim over Manasseh, etc.)."[75] Moreover, they note, only Deut 21:15–17 articulates the principle of primogeniture, and its application is to a context very different from Genesis 2 (and, by extension, 1 Tim 2:12–13).[76] What, then, does the order of creation signify, if anything, for egalitarianism? Appealing to Genesis 1 and 2, Linda Belleville notes its emphasis on "the human completeness that occurs after the creation of woman" and, turning to 1 Tim 2:12–13 ("Adam was formed *first*"), she offers that "the notion of hierarchy simply does not appear in Paul's language of 'first.'"[77]

Complementarianism, represented by Thomas Schreiner, understands this creation order differently: "When Paul read Genesis 2, he concluded that the order in which God created Adam and Eve signaled an important difference in the role of men and women. Thus, he inferred from the order of creation in Genesis 2 that women should not teach or exercise authority over men."[78] Additionally, responding to egalitarian objections to primogeniture attached to 1 Tim 2:13, Schreiner offers this complementarian response:

> In referring to primogeniture, complementarian scholars are scarcely suggesting that the cultural practice of primogeniture should be enforced today, nor do they think that Paul is endorsing

---

[75] Richard S. Hess, "Equality With and Without Innocence: Genesis 1–3," in *Discovering Biblical Equality: Complementarity Without Hierarchy*, ed. Ronald W. Pierce and Rebecca Merrill Groothuis (Downers Grove: IVP Academic, 2004), 84.

[76] Hess, "Equality With and Without Innocence," 84.

[77] Belleville, "Women in Ministry: An Egalitarian Perspective," 30.

[78] Thomas R. Schreiner, "A Dialogue with Scholarship," in *Women in the Church*, ed. Andreas J. Köstenberger and Thomas A. Schreiner, 3rd ed. (Wheaton: Crossway, 2016), 201.

> primogeniture per se. Nor would they deny the many examples from the Old Testament . . . in which God overturned primogeniture. Instead, they appeal to primogeniture to explain that Paul's readers would have easily understood the notion of the firstborn having authority. . . . To the original readers, the priority of Adam in creation would naturally have suggested his authority over Eve. Paul does not endorse primogeniture per se in 1 Timothy 2:13; he appeals to the creation of Adam first in explaining why women should not teach men.[79]

Additionally, Wayne Grudem disagrees with Belleville's dismissal of "first" in relation to Adam's creation. He underscores that Paul employs the temporal sequence (narrated in Genesis 2 and referenced in 1 Tim 2:13) as a reason for (γάρ, *gar*) his prohibition of women teaching and exercising authority over a man (1 Tim 2:12). According to complementarianism, the creation order *does* have significance for male authority (and the prohibition of female authority) in the church.[80]

Turning to the *manner* of creation, Genesis 2 recounts God's formation of the first man from the dust of the ground and his formation of the first woman from the man's rib. Paul later alludes to this diversity in the manner of creation and draws out its significance (1 Cor 11:7–8):

> A man should not cover his head, because he is the image and glory of God. So too, woman is the glory of man. For man did not come from woman, but woman came from man.

Egalitarianism and complementarianism disagree over the significance of this manner of creation.[81]

---

[79] Schreiner, "A Dialogue with Scholarship," 203.

[80] Grudem, *Evangelical Feminism and Biblical Truth*, 122–25.

[81] As we have seen, opponents of traditional sex polarity (e.g., Christine de Pizan, Henricus Cornelius Agrippa, Lucrezia Marinella) stood against the common view of the inferiority of women by appealing to the manner of creation, with a twist: "because a woman is made of a man's rib and a man made of mud, she is

Egalitarianism does not find any sense of female subordination from the fact of the first woman's formation from the first man. On the contrary, noting that she was not taken from the dust of the ground, as was the man, but from the man himself, egalitarianism concludes that the emphasis is on sameness of nature and thus equality, with no hint of authority and submission between the sexes.[82]

Complementarianism may view the manner of creation as affirming male authority and female submission. While I will return to this discussion later, Bruce Ware holds that God's creation of the first man was immediate and underived but the creation of the first woman was mediated and derived, as she was taken from the man. He applies this (original) differentiation in the manner of creation to today, explaining that the nature of women, and thus their image bearing, while being equal to that of men, continues to be mediated and derived. Specifically, "man is a human being made in the image of God first; woman becomes a human being bearing the image of God only through the man. While both are fully and equally the image of God, there is a built-in priority given to the male that reflects God's design of male headship in the created order."[83]

Regarding the *purpose* of creation, Genesis 2 narrates the first man's loneness and God's intention to "make a helper corresponding to him." In the same Pauline passage cited above, the apostle appeals to this divine purpose for the woman's formation and explains its significance (1 Cor 11:7, 9):

> A man should not cover his head, because he is the image and glory of God. So too, woman is the glory of man. . . . Neither

---

nobler than he because the rib is nobler than mud." Prudence Allen, *The Concept of Woman, Volume 3: The Search for Communion of Persons*, 1500–2015 (Grand Rapids: Eerdmans, 2016), 144. Her citation is Lucrezia Marinella, *The Nobility and Excellence of Women*, 54.

[82] Grudem refers to Gilbert Bilezikian as expressing this view in *Beyond Sex Roles*, 29–30. Grudem, *Evangelical Feminism and Biblical Truth*, 121.

[83] Bruce Ware, "Male and Female Complementarity and the Image of God," *Journal of Biblical Manhood and Womanhood* 7 (2002), 20–21. See further discussion in ch. 18.

> was man created for the sake of woman, but woman for the sake of man.

Egalitarianism and complementarianism disagree over the significance of this purpose of creation.

Egalitarian interpretations of עֵזֶר כְּנֶגְדּוֹ (*'ezer kenegdo*) focus on biblical passages that refer to God as the *'ezer* for individuals or Israel. According to Mary Conway, "The use of the term *helper* does not imply subordination or inferiority, since Yahweh himself often 'helps' or provides 'help' (e.g., Gen 49:25; Ex 18:4; Deut 33:7; Ps 20:3, 21:1–2; 115:9–11; 146:5)."[84] Moreover, according to Linda Belleville, *'ezer* always has "to do with the assistance that one of strength offers to one in need (i.e., help from God, the king, an ally, or an army)." Applying this observation to Gen 2:18, she affirms that the first man's "situation was that of being 'alone,' and God's evaluation was that it was 'not good.' The woman was hence created to relieve the man's aloneness through *strong partnership*."[85] Rebecca Groothuis adds, "If the term 'helper' most frequently refers to God, whose status is clearly superior to ours . . . then there is no justification for inferring [as complementarians do] a subordinate status from the woman's designation as 'helper.'"[86] Finally, as Conway offers, "The phrase *kenegdo* is best translated as 'corresponding to him,' a term that implies competence and equality, rather than subordination or inferiority."[87]

Complementarian interpretations understand the expression as referring to a person in a subordinate role. More specifically, the purposed female partner would be fully equal to the first man, but her creation as a "helper corresponding to" him would also mean that she would be different from

[84] Conway, "Gender in Creation and Fall," 41.

[85] Belleville, "Women in Ministry: An Egalitarian Perspective," 27 (emphasis original).

[86] Rebecca Merrill Groothuis, *Good News for Women: A Biblical Picture of Gender Equality* (Grand Rapids: Baker, 1997), 134. The citation is taken from Grudem, *Evangelical Feminism and Biblical Truth*, 117.

[87] Conway, "Gender in Creation and Fall," 41.

him in terms of her submissive role. Importantly, complementarian interpreters bemoan the fact that egalitarian discussions like those above insert the notion of inferiority into the debate, as complementarianism does not believe that *'ezer kenegdo* means or implies that the woman as a "helper corresponding to" the man is inferior in nature to him or that she plays a lesser role in relationship to him. For example, Grudem, echoing Conway, underscores, "the Hebrew word *kenegdo* means a helper '*corresponding to him*,' that is 'equal and adequate to himself.' So Eve was created as a helper, but as a helper who was Adam's equal, and one who differed from him, but who differed from him in ways that would exactly complement who Adam was."[88]

Complementarianism notes the helpful studies of the word *'ezer* and even agrees that the term is often used in reference to God and the help that he provides for his people (e.g., Ps 33:20; 121:2). Indeed, Grudem highlights "the fact that God calls Himself our 'helper' imparts dignity and honor to this role and this title."[89] At the same time, he offers a clarification: "A person who helps can be superior to, equal to, or inferior to the person being helped. Sometimes God is called our helper . . . and He is superior to us. On the other hand, the 'helper' can be one of lesser rank or authority [he appeals to Ezek 12:14 in support] . . . or can be used of an equal, as when one army helps another [he appeals to Jer 37:7 in support]. . . . So *helper* (*'ezer*) itself cannot settle the issue for us; it has to be decided on other grounds."[90] One of those grounds, for Grudem, is explicitly stated in the

---

[88] Grudem, *Evangelical Feminism and Biblical Truth*, 119 (emphasis original). His citation is from Francis Brown, S. R. Driver, and Charles A. Briggs, *A Hebrew and English Lexicon of the Old Testament* (Oxford: Clarendon, 1968), 617.

[89] Grudem, *Evangelical Feminism and Biblical Truth*, 118.

[90] Grudem, *Evangelical Feminism and Biblical Truth*, 118. As Craig Blomberg explains, such usage of *'ezer* "proves that the term itself does not inherently imply subordination, but it does not prove that it *cannot* imply subordination. Some helpers are authority figures, others are peers, many others are subordinates." Craig Blomberg, "1 Corinthians," 75. Similarly commenting on the woman as *'ezer*, Gentry adds, "The woman has strengths that match the man's weaknesses, and vice versa. They will have to work as a team, but this does not rule out the possibility of the man having a primary responsibility or servant leadership in the relationship."

verse (v. 18): "I will make a helper corresponding *to him*." God purposed to and then created the first woman specifically as a helper *for the man.* Paul echoes this in 1 Cor 11:9: "Neither was man created for the sake of woman, but woman *for the sake of man*."[91]

My proposal of complementarity highlights a few points from this narrow account of God's formation of the first man and the first woman. The first point is the two are designed and created to fill out and mutually support one another relationally (and eventually, as the narrative continues, familially) as well as vocationally. Whereas Genesis 1 calls attention to the nature and responsibilities of human beings as human beings, Genesis 2 provides an inaugural focus on the first husband in relationship to the first wife, with the narrative addressing the order, manner, and purpose of their creation. This point cautions us to apply Genesis 2 thoughtfully: What of it applies to marital relationships only? What applies to those relationships primarily with a secondary application to men and women in general? What applies primarily to women and men in general? For example, what is the application to men and women of the first woman's creation as overcoming the first man's loneness and as a "helper corresponding to him"? Is this applicable to all women in relationship to all men? Does the phrase provide support for the general notion of "community" between all human beings, who are "lonely" apart from others?

The second point focuses on marriage. As the narrator steps outside of the story (2:24), he elaborates on the nature of human marriage and how those who are to be married should practice it. Whatever one's understanding of hierarchy or non-hierarchy between the two may be (and how that works out in the marriage/family), the equality of dignity along with significant differentiation between husband and wife must be manifested. They are designed and created to fill out and mutually support one another relationally.

Gentry, "Understanding the Image of God: A Response to Mary L. Conway, 'Gender in Creation and Fall.'"

[91] Grudem, *Evangelical Feminism and Biblical Truth*, 118–19.

The third point addresses vocation. However one understands the word *'ezer* and its sense of "helper," Genesis 2 emphasizes that the first man and the first woman together were designed to fulfill the command to work as articulated in the cultural mandate (Gen 1:28). This is the labor to which men and women are called: the expansion of the human race so that they may individually and corporately flourish in the vocational realm.

Genesis 3

The broad account of God's creation of his image bearers (Genesis 1) and the narrow account of his formation of the first man and the first woman (Genesis 2) both conclude with high points: the entire creation is assessed as "very good," and the man and the woman are "naked, yet felt no shame." How long this idyllic experience endured is unknown, and the ensuing narrative recounts the undoing of the created order and its created couple.

As Gen 3:1–7 presents this demise, the subtle/shrewd (and not obviously evil) serpent approached the woman who, at least narratively, had not heard the prohibition that God gave to the first man (with second person masculine singular verbs: "*you* are free to *eat*," "on the day *you eat* from it," and "*you will* certainly *die*;" 2:17).[92] Though he approached the woman, the serpent's interchange with her has been transposed to second person masculine plural verbs ("*you* can't *eat*," "*you will* certainly not *die*," "when *you eat* it," "*you will be* like God) to include the man in the trap. She at first repulsed his misconstrual of the divine prohibition, though her additional exclusion of touching the fruit ("You must not eat it *or touch it*, or you will die") might indicate that she was not rightly taught (by God himself? by the man?) the prohibition or that she (wrongly) added to a divine directive, or it might have simply been her expression of a growing frustration with the troublesome conversation.

[92] Conway, "Gender in Creation and Fall," 40.

Contradicting that prohibition with a promise that she and the man will not die (again, a second person masculine plural verb) if they eat the fruit, the serpent sought to deceive the woman with good grounds to violate the prohibition: "your eyes will be opened and you will be like God, knowing good and evil." Though she saw rightly that "the tree was good for food and delightful to look at, and that it was desirable for obtaining wisdom" (2:8–9), she wrongly took and ate the fruit, disobeying the divine proscription; "she also gave some to her husband, who was with her, and he ate it." Why the man did not intervene in the situation is a mystery. What we do know from later Scripture (1 Tim 2:14) is that while the woman was deceived by the serpent and fell, the man sinned with his eyes wide open.

Curses and punishments were the result of, and correspond to, the misdeeds of the serpent, the woman, and the man (Gen 3:8–19). God addressed the man first, calling him to account for his fear due to nakedness and its signaling that he had violated the prohibition. The man shifted the blame to the divine gift of the woman, who in turn assigned fault to the serpent who had deceived her. Each of these futile attempts to avoid responsibility and place it on another had some truth to it: the woman did offer the fruit to her husband, God had given the woman to the man, and the serpent did deceive the woman. But these were half-truths: The man knew the prohibition, and his wife did not coerce him into violating it. The man had joyfully received the divine gift and experienced with his wife a complementary relationship full of integrity. And the serpent was part of the created order over which both the man and the woman were to rule as viceregents of God.

Upon the serpent, God pronounced a curse, the denouement of which courses throughout the rest of human history. Upon the woman, God pronounced two judgments: intensified pain in childbirth, a disruptive element in the procreative aspect of the cultural mandate; and a disordered marital relationship (3:16): "Your desire will be for your husband, yet he will rule over you" (CSB) or "Your desire shall be contrary to your husband, but he shall rule over you" (ESV). With regard to the man, God pronounced an indirect judgment and a direct judgment: a cursed ground that would require painful (and sometimes futile) labor for it to yield its produce, a disruptive element in the vocational aspect of the cultural mandate; and death, a return to the dust from which he was taken. That vocational aspect would now take place outside of the garden of Eden, and the threat of death would not find relief from the tree of life in the center of the garden, as access to it would now be shuttered.

As dismal as these curses and punishments might seem, the narrative inaugurates two hopeful themes. The major hope is the protoevangelium—the hostility between the serpent and his offspring and the woman and her offspring would climax in a male figure who would strike a death blow to the head of the serpent, who would inflict only a wound to the figure's heel (3:15). The other hope is found in the statement, "The man named his wife Eve because she was the mother of all the living" (3:20). Though death would reign because of the fall, physical human life would continue and, for those rescued from the curse, eternal life would restore the destiny of men and women created in the image of God.

This passage raises four key issues: the disordered relationship and the woman, the disordered relationship and the man, the reason that God addressed the man first and the woman second, and Adam's naming of Eve.

The first issue concerns the nature of the disordered marital relationship that God pronounced on the woman for her part in the fall (3:16).[93] Two interpretive points arise: (1) The translation of the verse. The CSB rendering is the traditional one: "Your desire will be *for* (אֶל, *'el*) your husband, yet he will rule over you" (CSB). The ESV translation, which from its release in 2001 until its revision in 2014 followed this tradition, now uniquely translates it "Your desire shall be *contrary to* (אֶל, *'el*) your husband, but he shall rule over you" (ESV 2016). As noted, the change involves the translation of one word (אֶל, *'el*) as either *for* (CSB) or *contrary to* (ESV).

[93] My thanks to my colleagues Denny Burk, Duane Garrett, Peter Gentry, and Kaspars Ozolins for their work on this passage and suggestions for how to interpret it.

(2) The nature of the woman's "desire" and of her husband's "ruling over her," with four divergent views:[94] (2a) A sexual desire: The woman still sexually desires her husband even though sexual intercourse may lead to intense pain in conception and childbirth. He "rules over her" in that he sexually satisfies her desire.[95] (2b) A desire for protection: The woman yearns for her husband to care for and shelter her, and he "rules over her" by protecting her. Some scholars consider this desire to be a good desire, in keeping with the pre-fall order, manner, and purpose of the woman's creation to be under her husband's protection, even though now he expresses his role sinfully. Other scholars consider it to be an evil desire that is due to the fall, which corrupted the original egalitarian relationship of the woman and her husband. As part of the curse, then, she now subjects herself to him as he "rules over her."

---

[94] The first three views are summarized in Susan T. Foh, "What is the Woman's Desire," *Westminster Theological Journal* 37 (1974/75): 376–83. She argues for (2c)—the adversarial view—by strongly linking Genesis 3:16 with the sense of sin's "desire" for Cain, who in turn must "rule over it," in Gen 4:7. She concludes that "the desire of the woman in Genesis 3:16b does not make the wife (more) submissive to her husband so that he may rule over her. Her desire is to contend with him for leadership in their relationship. This desire is a result of and a just punishment for sin, but it is not God's decretive will for the woman. Consequently, the man must actively seek to rule his wife." (p. 383). Foh's adversarial view is disputed, and (2d)—the (re)turn view—is championed by Janson C. Condren, "Toward a Purge of the Battle of the Sexes and 'Return' for the Original Meaning of Genesis 3:16b," *JETS* 60.2 (2017): 227–45. For further discussion see Irvin A. Busenitz, "Woman's Desire for Man: Genesis 3:16 Reconsidered," *Grace Theological Journal* 7.2 (1986): 203–12.

[95] A version of (2a) is that a woman in her post-fall reality will have an inordinate sexual desire for her husband. Alternatively, focusing on men, "Men want women sexually, and since they are bigger and stronger, they dominate women, 'ruling over them' to get what they want." M. Elizabeth Lewis Hall, "Gender Differences and Biblical Interpretation: A View from the Social Sciences," in *Discovering Biblical Equality: Biblical, Theological, Cultural, and Practical Perspectives*, ed. Ronald W. Pierce and Cynthia Long Westfall, 3rd ed. (Downers Grove: IVP Academic, 2021), 634.

(2c) An adversarial desire. The woman combatively opposes the desire and will of her husband yet capitulates to him as he "rules [treacherously] over her." Moreover, both postures are a result of the fall and the divine punishment for sin. (2d) A desire to (re)turn: The woman moves toward or moves back to her original reality of being divinely created to remove her husband's loneness, to be a helper corresponding to him, to be joined to him through sexual intercourse, to procreate with him, and together to fulfill the cultural mandate. In terms of her husband who "rules over her" post-fall, she continues to (re)turn toward her husband—to relieve his loneliness, help him, fulfill the cultural mandate through multiplication—but sin will distort its actualization by producing pain and suffering in childbirth and relational distress among them as he will seek to rule over her.

On a popular level, it seems difficult to understand how (2c)—the adversarial view—fosters a woman's submission to her husband, because her posture toward him is actually a surrender of evil yearnings. As Wendy Alsup and Hannah Anderson conclude, this perspective may paralyze women as they regret that their desire for their husbands is sinful and seek to limit its damage. Moreover, it may lead to men mistrusting women, whom they view as sinfully motivated and thus dangerous to them.[96]

The second issue concerns the man's part in the disordered marital relationship as reflected in the expression "he will rule over you." Two alternatives exist: it is either descriptive or prescriptive. As a description, the expression presents the reality of a post-fall world with respect to marital relationships. Pre-fall, hierarchy between husband and wife did not exist; authority and submission are the tragic results of sin that destroys the original harmony and mutuality in married life. As Linda Belleville explains,

[96] Wendy Alsup and Hannah Anderson offered a popular three-part discussion of the ESV's translation change: "Toward a Better Reading: Reflections on the Permanent Changes to the Text of Genesis 3:16 in the ESV," Practical Theology for Women (September 2016). The series was originally, but is no longer, available at https://theologyforwomen.org/2016/09/toward-better-reading-reflections-permanent-changes-text-genesis-316-esv.html.

"The context of Genesis 3 is human disobedience and its impact, so it is not difficult to see the male's . . . domination as something different from the divine intent of Genesis 1–2. The divine intent was that of partnership—a co-dominion over the earth and a co-responsibility to bear and raise children. Dominion of one over the other was not the intent. This is gender dysfunction, not gender normalcy."[97]

As a prescription, the expression affirms male authority and female submission within the marriage relationship. What has been devastated by the fall—wives seek to usurp their husband's authority and rule over them—becomes restored through salvation, which returns the role differentiation to what it was divinely designed to be: husbands rule and wives submit to them. This creation hierarchy, originally good and functioning with integrity, is now marred by sin such that male leadership is harsh and domineering and female submission is resisted and disobeyed.[98]

To summarize, egalitarianism and complementarianism view differently the first and second issues about disordered marital relationships. Egalitarianism considers hierarchy to be a sinful structure that was not part of the original creation but tragically and devastatingly entered into human relationships at the fall and continues to poison those relationships today.[99]

---

[97] Belleville, "Women in Ministry: An Egalitarian Perspective," 34–35.

[98] According to Bruce Ware, "the male/female relationship would now, because of sin, be affected by mutual enmity. In particular, the woman would have a desire to usurp the authority given to man in creation, leading to man, for his part, ruling over woman in what can be either rightfully-corrective or wrongfully-abusive ways. . . . [T]he man would be inclined to misuse his rights of rulership, either by sinful abdication of his God-given authority, acquiescing to the woman's desire to rule over him (and so fail to lead as he should), or by abusing his rights to rule through harsh, cruel and exploitative domination of the woman." Bruce Ware, "Summaries of the Egalitarian and Complementarian Positions," CBMW online (June 26, 2007).

[99] John Chrysostom locates the introduction of authority and submission at the time of the fall: "For with us indeed the woman is reasonably subjected to the man: since equality of honor causes contention. And not for this cause only, but by reason also of the deceit (1 Timothy 2:14) which happened in the beginning. Wherefore you see, she was not subjected as soon as she was made; nor, when He

In Christ, men and women resist any and all hierarchy. Complementarianism maintains that hierarchy was a divinely designed framework that originated at the time of human creation for the flourishing of God's image bearers.[100] The fall thoroughly wreaked havoc with human relationships of authority and submission, and the hope is that salvation restores them to what they are intended to be.

The third issue concerns the reason that God addressed the man first and the woman second in calling out the couple for their fall into sin (vv. 8–13). Mary Conway offers a common egalitarian answer: "That God addresses the man (*ha'adam*) first in Genesis 3:9 need not be an example of his greater responsibility or superior status as representative of the family. It could equally well be because he is more culpable, or because he was the first to have received the prohibition."[101]

Complementarianism, to the extent that it functions within a covenantal framework,[102] appeals to the fact that God had unilaterally established a covenant—the so-called Adamic covenant or covenant with creation—with Adam. This pact designated him as the federal head or representative of all humanity before God, such that as Adam went—in integrity or in

---

brought her to the man, did either she hear any such thing from God, nor did the man say any such word to her: he said indeed that she was bone of his bone, and flesh of his flesh (Genesis 2:23) but of rule or subjection he no where made mention unto her. But when she made an ill use of her privilege and she who had been made a helper was found to be an ensnarer and ruined all, then she is justly told for the future, your turning shall be to your husband (Genesis 3:16)." Chrysostom, *Homilies on 1 Corinthians* 26.3, https://www.newadvent.org/fathers/220126.htm.

[100] As noted earlier, Calvin commented, "Moses teaches that women are created to be a kind of appendage to the man on the express condition that woman should be ready to obey him. Thus, God did not create two 'beings' of equal standing, but added to man a lesser helpmeet." John Calvin, *Commentary on 1 Timothy 2:13. Calvini opera selecta,* ed. Peter Barth and William Niesel, 5 vols. (Munich: Christian Kaiser Verlag, 1974), 52:277.

[101] Conway, "Gender in Creation and Fall," 46.

[102] See earlier discussion of covenants (pp. 187–90).

disobedience to the divine prohibition (2:15–17)—so would go the human race: remain upright or fall into sin, guilt, shame, and death. Biblical support for this covenantal approach to Adam being addressed first includes Hos 6:7 ("they [Ephraim/Judah], like Adam, have violated the covenant; there they have betrayed me") and Paul's attribution of the devasting consequences of sin to the one sin of the one man, Adam (Rom 5:12–21). Thus, though the woman was the first to sin, Adam was addressed first and held responsible not only for the fall of the first couple, but for the guilt and corruption of all subsequent human beings.

The fourth issue focuses on Adam's naming of Eve. The theme of naming or calling appears throughout these early chapters of Genesis. For example, "God called the light 'day' and the darkness he called 'night'" (1:5), "God called the expanse 'sky'" (1:8), "God called the dry land 'earth,' and the gathering of the water he called 'seas'" (1:10). Prior to the creation of the first woman, "The LORD God formed out of the ground every wild animal and every bird of the sky, and brought each to the man to see what he would call it. And whatever the man called a living creature, that was its name. The man gave names to all the livestock, to the birds of the sky, and to every wild animal" (2:19–20). Using the same word for "call," the first man exclaimed in reference to the divine gift, "this one will be called 'woman,' for she was taken from man" (2:23). Before their banishment from God's presence in the garden of Eden, "The man named his wife Eve because she was the mother of all the living" (3:20). Egalitarianism and complementarianism disagree over the significance of Adam's naming of Eve.

From an egalitarian perspective, Mary Conway offers, "That the man (*ha'adam*) names the woman, as he previously did the animals, however, is also not a sign of the man's superiority or dominance. Naming in the Old Testament is an act of discerning a trait or function or ability that already exists in the person being named, not a sign of authority over that person."[103] Accordingly, the narrative point of "the man named his wife Eve because

[103] Conway, "Gender in Creation and Fall," 48.

she was the mother of all the living" (3:20)—with the Hebrew name "Eve" (חַוָּה, *ḥawwah*) being related to the verb חי (*ḥayah*) "to live"—is that Adam recognized the life-giving nature/capacity of his wife and thus named her accordingly but not authoritatively.

From a complementarian perspective, Peter Gentry disagrees with Conway, first appealing to the context in which such naming occurs: "In Genesis 1, God names entities and structures created on Days 1–3 while Adam names entities filling the structures created on Days 4–6. It is difficult not to see Adam in imitation of the rule of his Creator and fulfilling the divine image here." Gentry also draws attention to the man's response to the woman's creation (a point that Conway overlooks): "this one will be called 'woman,' for she was taken from man" (2:23). Gentry notes that "Adam names the woman but the name he gives her is perceived as the feminine form of *'îš* (man, male, husband). He sees her as ontologically equal."[104] Equal in nature, but different in that Adam exercised an authoritative role in naming Eve. Thus, complementarianism underscores the presence of hierarchy—which is a divinely designed structure established before the fall—in this act: "Adam's naming of the woman signifies that he bears the leadership role."[105]

In summary, four key issues—the disordered relationship and the woman, the disordered relationship and the man, the reason that God addressed the man first and the woman second, and Adam's naming of Eve—prompt significant disagreement between egalitarianism and complementarianism.

My proposal of complementarity urges several key points. First, from a perspective removed from the debates, complementarity applauds the fact that both egalitarianism and complementarianism denounce the elevation

---

[104] Gentry, "Understanding the Image of God: A Response to Mary L. Conway, 'Gender in Creation and Fall.'"

[105] Thomas R. Schreiner, "Another Complementarian Perspective," in *Two Views on Women in Ministry*, ed. James R. Beck, rev. ed., Zondervan Counterpoints Series (Grand Rapids: Zondervan, 2005), 295. He responds (pp. 295–97) to a substantive critique of this issue raised by Phyllis Trible, *God and the Rhetoric of Sexuality* (Philadelphia: Fortress, 1978), 99–100.

of "he will rule over her" to a divine prescription that foments the dehumanization of women, sexual abuse, rape, and other heinous crimes.[106] Such application of Scripture—however the expression may be understood—is the opposite of complementarity.

Second, however one parses out the responsibility for the disordered relationship between them, both husbands and wives live out their marriage as sinful people in a broken world that presently in our society is hellbent in opposition to marital flourishing. Complementarity is particularly needed and deserving of attention as it directs husbands and wives to fill out and mutually support one another relationally (and, in many cases, familially) for their individual and corporate flourishing.[107] How they live out such divine design is largely left to their wisdom-aided and Spirit-empowered discretion. Both complementarians and egalitarians should use caution and discernment when their applications of complementarity are different from those of others. Certainly, there are expressions within both camps that violate complementarity, and married couples must forego such expressions. At the same time, a wide diversity of applications exists and should be respected.[108]

This section introduced several chapters dedicated to the consideration of many biblical texts. It addressed three broad topics: hermeneutics, the canonical and covenantal framework of Scripture, and setting the stage for what is to come by focusing on the opening three chapters of Genesis. To sum up in one sentence a major theme from this chapter, Alice Mathews

---

[106] Mimi Haddad, "Human Flourishing: Global Perspectives," in *Discovering Biblical Equality: Biblical, Theological, Cultural, and Practical Perspectives*, ed. Ronald W. Pierce and Cynthia Long Westfall, 3rd ed. (Downers Grove: IVP Academic, 2021), 634. She seems to be directing her denunciations against patriarchy.

[107] Brad Wilcox, *Get Married: Why Americans Must Defy the Elite, Forge Strong Families, and Save Civilization* (Broadside Books, 2024).

[108] The applicability of Genesis 3 to people other than husbands in relationship to their wives focuses on the major theme of that chapter: the fall. All human beings, regardless of marital status, are infected with sin, influenced by Satanic/demonic forces, and live in a fallen world. All these factors contribute to relational brokenness and cry out for redemption leading to male-female relationships characterized by complementarity.

underscores David Scholer's identification of the central problem for biblical scholars: "The biblical text one chooses for one's starting point in the study of a doctrine or issue in Scripture becomes the lens through which one looks at all other texts."[109]

[109] Alice P. Mathews, "Toward Reconciliation: Healing the Schism," in *Discovering Biblical Equality*, 496. She references David Scholer, "1 Timothy 2:9–15 and the Place of Women in the Church's Ministry," in *Women, Authority, and the Bible*, ed. Alvera Michelsen (Downers Grove: InterVarsity, 1986), 193–219. The examples she provides are 1 Tim 2:12 (a restrictive Pauline instruction as one's starting point) and Gal 3:28 (a "no distinctions" statement as one's starting point). Mathews, "Toward Reconciliation," 496–97.

CHAPTER 15

Old Testament Considerations

For her undergraduate course on Israelite women, Carol Meyers asked her students to describe their view of women in the Hebrew Bible. Some examples from those students are that women are "shrouded and quiet," "oppressed," "vastly inferior to men," and "subservient." Meyers commented,

> Perhaps these negative views were to be expected, given that, until relatively recently, the main source of information about ancient Israelite women was the Hebrew Bible. Yet the Hebrew Bible is hardly a balanced repository of information on this topic. For one thing, women are not very visible. Fewer than 10 percent of the named individuals in the Hebrew Bible are women. Also, those who do appear tend to be exceptional women—royal women, the matriarchs, a few female prophets—not representative of most ordinary women.[1]

---

[1] "Carol L. Meyers, "The Importance of Bread: Archaeology, the Bible, and Women's Power in Ancient Israel," in *The Biblical World of Gender: The Daily Lives of Ancient Women and Men,* ed. Celina Durgin and Dru Johnson (Eugene, OR: Cascade, 2022), 3–4.

In light of the relative scarcity of Old Testament treatment of women, and with complementarity's emphasis on engaging with both women and men, this chapter will give extensive attention to nineteen narratives in which both sexes are featured, concluding with an exposition of a poem lauding the wife of noble character (Prov 31:10–31).

Major Male and Female Characters in the Old Testament

As just discussed, it is a widely recognized fact that the Old Testament was written in and reflects the context of patriarchalism. Accordingly, a second fact—that male characters play the major roles in Old Testament narratives—comes as no surprise. A correlative question may be raised: Why, then, are female characters included in these narratives, with only ten percent of these stories containing them? Do they only play the role of minor characters? Is their part only to act as foils to male accomplishments and virtues? Do the female characters display achievements and traits that are unique to women or that are common human capacities and common human properties that are expressed in typical and fitting female ways? Together with the male characters, do the female characters fill out and mutually support one another relationally, familially, vocationally, and (not ecclesially but) nationally?

Given the sizable amount of material with which to interact, a strict selection is necessary; thus, attention will be focused on nineteen narratives in which key male and female characters are in relationship and/or engaged with one another, for better or worse. We will see that these biblical stories of both men and women affirm and applaud faith, courage, steadfastness, hope, self-sacrifice, goodness, and love. We will also see the opposite traits portrayed: faithlessness, despondency, disobedience, hate, and sheer evil. These narratives demonstrate either the blessings achieved through complementarity or the harm brought through its absence. After discussing these narratives, and after presenting the "woman of noble character" of Prov 31:10–31, we will look at a few principles that are drawn by complementarianism and egalitarianism. Finally, we will note some key points for complementarity.

Abraham and Sarah

Because we've already discussed Adam and Eve in the previous chapter, I begin this section with Abraham and Sarah. Of the narratives about the patriarchs of the people of Israel, none are more foundational than those regarding Abraham and Sarah (Genesis 12–25). Canonically, Abraham is the quintessential example of justification by grace through faith in the divine promise (Gen 15:2–6), after whose pattern followers of Jesus are justified (Rom 4:22–25).

In establishing circumcision as the sign of his covenant with Abram, the Lord promised, "You will become *the father of many nations*. Your name will no longer be Abram; your name will be Abraham, for I will make you *the father of many nations*. I will make you extremely fruitful and will make *nations and kings come from you*" (17:4–6, emphasis added). As a mirror image to this promise, God continued, "As for your wife Sarai, do not call her Sarai, for Sarah will be her name. I will bless her; indeed, I will give you a son by her. I will bless her, and *she will produce nations; kings of peoples will come from her*" (17:15–16, emphasis added). Of course, the promise of a son for Sarah was met with laughter on the part of both one-hundred-year-old Abraham (17:17–22) and ninety-nine-year-old Sarah (18:9–15); as it could only happen, the promise was miraculously fulfilled. The two also encountered pressures and tragically failed: Abraham fearfully mischaracterized his relationship with Sarah as brother-sister rather than as husband-wife (12:10–20; 20:1–18), and the two attempted to bring about the fulfillment of the divine promise of a child through human machination (16:1–6).

New Testament reflections on this couple include Sarah's exemplary hope in God through obedient submission to her husband (1 Pet 3:1–6; see later discussion) and the participation of Christians in the Abrahamic covenant (Rom 3:29). Specifically, this incorporation comes through faith, of which Abraham is a model:

> He did not weaken in faith when he considered his own body to be already dead (since he was about a hundred years old) and also the deadness of Sarah's womb. He did not waver in unbelief at God's promise but was strengthened in his faith and gave glory to God (Rom 4:19–20).

Likewise, and for the same reason, Sarah is a model of faith: "By faith even Sarah herself, when she was unable to have children, received power to conceive offspring, even though she was past the age, since she considered that the one who had promised was faithful" (Heb 11:11).

Justification by faith. Obedience in the face of the unknown. Forefather and foremother of God's people. Sinful failures. Hope in a hopeless situation. Faith despite physical impossibilities. Abraham and Sarah exemplify complementarity—filling out and mutually supporting one another in the relational, familial, and national (not ecclesial) realms—mostly as it functions properly but also as it misfires.

Isaac and Rebekah

As the fulfillment of the divine promise to Abraham and Sarah, Isaac was a significant figure in the narratives of Israel's patriarchs. After being spared from being sacrificed to the Lord (22:1–18), Isaac appeared in association with God's provision of Rebekah as his wife (Genesis 24). For nearly two decades, the couple did not have children. The narrative continues, "Isaac prayed to the LORD on behalf of his wife because she was childless. The LORD was receptive to his prayer, and his wife Rebekah conceived. But the children inside her struggled with each other" (25:21–22). The twins to whom she gave birth eventually produced two nations: Esau (also named Edom) gave rise to the Edomites, archenemies of Israel, and Jacob (later renamed Israel) continued the development of the nation of Israel. The couple contributed to the mutual hatred of their sons through Isaac's preference for game-eating Esau and Rebekah's love for Jacob (25:27–28). She aided and abetted the (usurped) blessing of second-born Jacob (whose name means "to usurp") over firstborn Esau (27:1–45). In the aftermath of this disaster, Isaac passed on the Abrahamic blessing and covenant to Jacob as further contributing to the people of Israel.

A divinely designed marriage. Prayer to overcome childlessness, answered with kindness by the Lord. Parental failures that led to national enmity. Continued blessing for the people of God. Isaac and Rebekah contribute to complementarity in the relational, familial, and national realms, positively for the most part, yet with failures as well.

Jacob and Rachel and Leah

The narratives about the final patriarch begin with Jacob (or Israel) and feature his two wives, Rachel and Leah, the first of whom Jacob loved more than the second (Genesis 28–35).

This disparity did not escape divine detection: "When the Lord saw that Leah was neglected [unloved, even hated], he opened her womb; but Rachel was unable to conceive" (Gen 29:31). Three times through having children Leah attempted to change her husband's neglect of her—more forcefully, Jacob's lack of love or even hate of her—into love, mindfulness, and affection. But each time she remained disappointed, unfulfilled, and unloved (vv. 32–24).

Leah's fourth attempt was decidedly different from the first three failed attempts: "She conceived again, gave birth to a son, and said, 'This time I will praise [sounds like *Judah*] the Lord.' Therefore she named him Judah. Then Leah stopped having children" (v. 35). Though neglected and unloved by her husband, Leah discovered this time—the narrative provides no details of her change of heart—the Lord's attentive care for and constant mindfulness of her. Having experienced such unconditional divine love, Leah ceased to futilely seek the human love of her husband.

Filled with jealousy for the fruitfulness of her sister, especially shameful in light of her own barrenness, Rachel concocted a plan to have children through her slave Bilhah. As seen by the names of her two sons, vindication and victory at the expense of her sister motivated Rachel's childbearing through her surrogate (30:6–8). Discontented with the end of her own childbearing, especially painful in light of Rachel's surrogate-conceived sons, Leah had more children (30:9–21). Finally, the Lord remembered Rachel and she herself conceived a son (Joseph), saying, "God has taken away my disgrace" (30:23). The birth of another son came at the cost of Rachel's own life (35:16–18).[2]

Tragically, Jacob's only daughter Dinah was raped by Shechem (34:1–2). Jacob's sons devised a plan for revenge, tricking Shechem and his men to be circumcised. "On the third day, when they were still in pain, two of Jacob's sons, Simeon and Levi, Dinah's brothers, took their swords, went into the unsuspecting city, and killed every male;" they reclaimed Dinah and, joining with their other brothers, destroyed Shechem's city "because their sister had been defiled" (34:25–27).

The legacy of Jacob, Rachel, and Leah continues with narratives about the exploits—both good and bad—of their children.

The positive narrative about Jacob's pursuit of Rachel highlights the beauty of genuine love between husband and wife, one aspect of complementarity. The negative narrative about Leah also affirms, by way of reversal, what should be the positive reality of the mutual love between husband

---

[2] The lengthy narratives concerning Jacob and his family continue with more drama. He wrestled with a man all night, and at daybreak refused to let the man go without being blessed. The man conceded: "'Your name will no longer be Jacob,' he said. 'It will be Israel [sounds like *he struggled with God*] because you have struggled with God and with men and have prevailed. . . . Jacob then named the place Peniel, 'For I have seen God face to face,' he said, 'yet my life has been spared'" (32:24–30). In a second renaming, God again substituted the name "Israel" for "Jacob," promising that the patriarch would inherit the Abrahamic blessing and covenant (35:9–15).

and wife when their marital relationship is characterized by complementarity. The disparity in Jacob's affection for Rachel and Leah underscores the negative consequences of an imbalance in complementarity.[3] Though certainly it is by divine design that Leah is enabled to bear children, her efforts (as revealed in her choice of names for her offspring) are futile attempts to secure Jacob's love, which never transpires. Ultimately, Leah learns to cherish the unconditional love of God and finally experiences satisfaction. But not so with her sister, who is motivated for childbearing by the hope of vindication and victory at the expense of her sister. When God's design for complementarity between one man and one woman in marriage is ignored, it is replaced by jealousy, competition, and ungodly motivations. Even more disconcertedly, when complementarity collapses, heinous acts such as rape darken the world.

Judah and Tamar

The narrative of Jacob's son Judah (Genesis 38) recounts another perversion of complementarity. Judah found a wife for his firstborn son, Er; her name was Tamar. Because Er was evil, the Lord put him to death, leaving Tamar a widow. When Judah's second son, Onan, refused to perform the duty of Levirate marriage with her, the Lord put Onan to death as well. Faced with an abandoned daughter-in-law, Judah brought her into his house with the intention that she would remain a widow until Judah's youngest son Shelah would be able to marry her. That intention never materialized. Imagining Tamar to be a cult prostitute whom he chanced upon while travelling, Judah engaged in sexual intercourse with her, and his double sin was exposed: he did not properly care for Tamar by timely giving her to his son Shelah, and he committed sexual immorality.

---

[3] The complications due to Jacob having multiple wives might also indicate the propriety of marriage between one man and one woman for the rightful functioning of complementarity.

This narrative is the opposite of the vision of complementarity between male and female family members, who are to fill out and mutually support one another rather than take advantage of one another.

Joseph and Potiphar

A reverse episode—the refusal to engage in sexual immorality—is narrated from the life of another son of Jacob (Genesis 39). Through the Lord's blessing, Joseph had successfully risen into a position of renown in Potiphar's house. In another instance of complementarity gone awry, we see Potiphar's wife attracted to Joseph, who "was well-built and handsome" (39:6); Potiphar's wife repeatedly sought to seduce him, and Joseph equally refused her enticements. In her last failed attempt to seduce him, Potiphar's wife grabbed a piece of Joseph's clothing and screamed loudly, accusing Joseph of raping her. "When his master heard the story his wife told him—'These are the things your slave did to me'—he was furious and had him thrown into prison, where the king's prisoners were confined. So Joseph was there in prison" (39:19–20). Though clearly a miscarriage of justice, the event was just one instance contributing to Joseph's rise to power in Egypt.

Through Joseph's elevation and his contribution to Potiphar's growing status, human flourishing took place not only for one member of the people of God but also for pagans whose lives he touched. When immoral designs (appear to) win and complementarity is eroded, evil may prevail. Even then, through divine intervention, evil may give way to good as the Lord honors those who walk in his ways and reverses their fortunes.

Moses, Shiphrah and Puah, Jochebed (Moses's Mother), Moses's Sister, and Pharaoh's Daughter

Moving beyond the narratives of the patriarchs of Israel, the next major figure who emerges as leader of the burgeoning nation was Moses.

Narratively, his birth is set up by the account of the Hebrew midwives Shiphrah and Puah. Against the orders of the Egyptian Pharaoh, these women refused to kill newborn sons, at whose births they assisted, by drowning them in the Nile (Exod 1:8–22). Though it (apparently) was not assisted by midwives, Moses's birth meant that his mother (Jochebed, Exod 6:20; Num 26:59) had to disobey the Pharaoh's decree of death: "The woman became pregnant and gave birth to a son; when she saw that he was beautiful, she hid him for three months. But when she could no longer hide him, she got a papyrus basket for him and coated it with asphalt and pitch. She placed the child in it and set it among the reeds by the bank of the Nile" (2:2–3). As the baby's sister watched from a distance, Pharaoh's daughter discovered the floating basket in which was "one of the Hebrew boys" (2:6). Volunteering to find a Hebrew woman to nurse the boy, his sister "went and called the boy's mother," who cared for him until, at the appropriate time, "she brought him to Pharaoh's daughter, and he became her son. She named him Moses, 'Because,' she said, 'I drew him out of the water'" (2:8–10).

The God-fearing courage of these midwives (who, unusually for ancient literature, are named) and Moses's mother, her industrious and sacrificial provision for her son's safety, his sister's clever and timely intervention on his behalf, and the pity of Pharaoh's daughter that prompted her to save a Hebrew boy's life and raise him as her son—in stark contrast with Pharaoh's unrelenting oppression and ruthless attempts to control the Israelite people—are stellar examples of female hope, bravery, faith, fearlessness, kindness, obedience, and ingenuity.[4]

Complementarity applauds such women and their virtues and heroism, and it calls for both women and men today to follow their example.

---

[4] The book of Hebrews underscores the importance of faith in this incident in Moses's life: "By faith Moses, after he was born, was hidden by his parents for three months, because they saw that the child was beautiful, and they didn't fear the king's edict" (Heb 11:23).

Moses and Zipporah

Though speculation abounds with regard to this narrative, it is significant because of its covenantal importance and for the action of Moses's wife Zipporah. As Moses and his family traveled back to Egypt in response to God's appearance in the burning bush and directive to Moses to lead the people of Israel out of captivity there (Exod 3:1–4:17), "the LORD confronted him and intended to put him to death. So Zipporah took a flint, cut off her son's foreskin, threw it at Moses's feet, and said, 'You are a bridegroom of blood to me!' So he let him alone. At that time she said, 'You are a bridegroom of blood,' referring to the circumcision" (Exod 4:24–26).

Apparently, the reason for God's intent to kill his chosen leader was Moses's failure to have circumcised his son. Circumcision, as the sign of the Abrahamic covenant that God had established with the people of Israel, was required for all Israelite males when they were eight days old (Gen 17:12–14). Absence of this covenantal sign on the part of a member of Moses's own family would have created confusion for Moses's leadership of the people; more importantly, it disqualified him from playing such a key role in their redemption. For this reason, God sought to eliminate Moses, either through some kind of illness or injury. Zipporah, understanding this reason, rectified the evil by circumcising her son.

Though in some circles confusion abounds about the roles of husbands and wives, this narrative highlights the complementary nature of the marriage relationship: both spouses are to do their utmost for the sake of the other. Even though disgusted at their spouses' failure and revulsed by certain actions they are called to perform, wives and husbands fill out and mutually support one another even in dark times so they may flourish.

Miriam, Aaron, and Moses

The central theme of the Old Testament is the Lord's deliverance of his people out of Egypt by means of the crossing of the Red Sea. Whereas Moses sings of that divine rescue (Exod 15:1–18), its last phase is recounted as a narrative ending in a song of triumph (15:19–21):

> Then the prophetess Miriam, Aaron's sister, took a tambourine in her hand, and all the women came out following her with tambourines and dancing. Miriam sang to them:
>
> Sing to the Lord, for he is highly exalted;
> he has thrown the horse and its rider into the sea.

Miriam is probably referred to as a prophetess because of her song praising God for his defeat of Israel's enemies.[5] As a chronicler of the exodus, she played a crucial role in leading the Lord's rescued people in recognition of his mighty act.

Her crucial role sadly shifts to a critical one, as "Miriam and Aaron criticized Moses because of the Cushite woman he married (for he had married a Cushite woman). They said, 'Does the LORD speak only through Moses? Does he not also speak through us?' And the LORD heard it" (Num 12:1–2). As her name appears first in order before that of her brother, Miriam may have been the leader of this revolt against Moses, a revolt that featured their arrogance over Moses's humility (v. 3). Demanding to be heard, God reminded Aaron and Miriam of the superiority of his revelation to Moses and rebuked them for speaking against Moses. As God's righteous anger burned against the co-conspirators, resulting in a skin disease for Miriam, Aaron begged for forgiveness for Miriam and for himself and Moses prayed for her healing. The Lord answered this prayer and healed Miriam, though he required that she be shamed for a week's time for rebelling against Israel's leader (vv. 14–15).[6]

---

[5] As I argue elsewhere, when the Holy Spirit falls upon people, they engage in some kind of utterance, whether that be prophecy, praise, proclamation, and/or prayer. On this basis I think that Miriam is called a prophetess because of her exclamation of praise. Gregg R. Allison and Andreas J. Köstenberger, *The Holy Spirit* (Nashville: B&H Academic, 2022), 286–89.

[6] The fact that Aaron did not become leprous and have to be shamed possibly underscores Miriam's principal role in the rebellion against Moses (v. 1).

The narrative's ending—"the people did not move on until Miriam was brought back in" the camp (v. 15)—can be understood in two ways: (1) Positively: "The congregation of Israel viewed her role as essential to its mission, refusing to move ahead . . . until she was restored to leadership after her criticism of Moses (Num 12:15)."[7] (2) Negatively: Given the disapproving portrait of Miriam and her shameful role in the rebellion, together with the narrative's emphasis on the uniqueness and superiority of Moses's leadership of the nation, it is doubtful that the congregation took the lead by refusing to move on until Miriam regained her leadership role. That they did not move on was a negative result of her rebellion that slowed down the people's exodus to the promised land.

When affirmed and practiced properly, complementarity results in praise to God for his mighty acts that lead to national flourishing. When pride and jealousy of one another reign, however, complementarity gives way to suffering that leads to personal and corporate loss.

Rahab and the Spies

The New Testament's summaries of Rahab call attention to her faith: "By faith Rahab the prostitute welcomed the spies in peace and didn't perish with those who disobeyed" (Heb 11:31). At the same time, the letter of James clarifies that the type of faith that she exhibited supports the truth "that a person is justified by works and not by faith alone. In the same way, wasn't Rahab the prostitute also justified by works in receiving the messengers and sending them out by a different route?" (James 2:24–25). Faith that is expressed in good works is the central point of the narrative about Rahab and the spies.

[7] Linda L. Belleville, "Women Leaders in the Bible," in *Discovering Biblical Equality: Biblical, Theological, Cultural, and Practical Perspectives*, ed. Ronald W. Pierce and Cynthia Long Westfall, 3rd ed. (Downers Grove: IVP Academic, 2021), 71.

Highlights include Rahab hiding the spies and misdirecting the scouts who were searching for them (Josh 2:1–7); acknowledging that the Lord had given Jericho into the hands of the Israelites; rehearsing the widely known stories of God's rescue of his people through the Red Sea and their subsequent destruction of two Amorite kings; and requesting that the spies reciprocate the kindness she had shown them by being kind to her and her family (vv. 8–13).

They swore, "We will give our lives for yours. If you don't report our mission, we will show kindness and faithfulness to you when the LORD gives us the land." Then Rahab helped them escape from Jericho and, at the spies' prompting, tied a scarlet cord as the sign of their arrangement (vv. 14–21).

The spies kept their promise. The narrative concludes: "Joshua spared Rahab the prostitute, her father's family, and all who belonged to her, because she hid the messengers Joshua had sent to spy on Jericho, and she still lives in Israel today" (6:25).

Rahab's faith, which she expressed by her courageous protection of the spies and her acknowledgement of the Lord, is the key lesson from these narratives. However, attention should also be drawn to the complementarity expressed by the unlikely cohort of Rahab, the spies, and Joshua: one woman (a prostitute) who feared God and trusted her life and the lives of her family to male spies and the male leader of all Israel, was honored for her faith in action, as the men kept their promise to her. Such cooperation and mutual respect should be exhibited by women and men today.

Hannah and Samuel

This narrative features a faithful woman whom "the LORD had kept . . . from conceiving" (1 Sam. 1:5). Hannah vowed, "LORD of Armies, if you will take notice of your servant's affliction, remember and not forget me, and give your servant a son, I will give him to the LORD all the days of his life, and his hair will never be cut" (v. 11). Moved by her desperation, Eli the priest prayed, "Go in peace, and may the God of Israel grant the request you've made of him" (v. 17). And so it came to pass: "The LORD remembered her. After some time, Hannah conceived and gave birth to a son. She named him Samuel, because she said, 'I requested him from the LORD'" (vv. 19–20). Hannah fulfilled her vow by giving Samuel to Eli in the Lord's house in Shiloh (v. 28). This narrative is followed by Hannah's joyful prayer that exalts her promise-keeping Lord for his salvation and his sovereign righting of all wrongs (2:1–10). And in later narratives, Samuel plays a major role in leading the people of Israel.

When trust in the Lord is strong, when vows to him are kept, when God shows favor, and when women and men express mutuality, such faithfulness and obedience foster an atmosphere in which complementarity abounds, and this leads to praising God for his mighty works and results in both individual and corporate flourishing.

Phinehas's Wife

Introduced in the Hannah-Samuel narrative, Eli the priest faced the tragedy of the death of his two sons, Hophni and Phinehas, and the capture of the ark of God by the Philistines. At the news of the latter crisis, Eli himself died. The narrative continues:

> Eli's daughter-in-law, the wife of Phinehas, was pregnant and about to give birth. When she heard the news about the capture of God's ark and the deaths of her father-in-law and her husband, she collapsed and gave birth because her labor pains came on her. As she was dying, the women taking care of her said, "Don't be afraid. You've given birth to a son!" But she did not respond or pay attention. She named the boy Ichabod, saying, "The glory has departed from Israel," referring to the capture of the ark of God and to the deaths of her father-in-law and her husband. "The glory has departed from Israel," she said, "because the ark of God has been captured." (1 Sam 4:19–22)

This ancient event preceded the much later departure of the glory of God from the temple (Ezek 11:22–25), a disaster of epic proportion. It underscores the devotion of a woman who lamented such loss. She stands as an example for us of honoring the Lord above all else as well as putting the welfare of others above her own personal blessing. Though not a direct model of complementarity, this woman's good character and sacrifice exemplify postures that are at the heart of complementarity.

Deborah, Barak, Jael, and Sisera

This narrative (Judg 4:4–24) features a courageous female prophetess/judge, a hesitant male army leader, an indomitable woman avenger, and a shamefully defeated man. Because of controversy over the interpretation of certain aspects of this narrative, I will include a discussion of the complementarian and egalitarian understandings of it before offering applications from the perspective of my proposal of complementarity.

The major character is Deborah, a prophetess who judged Israel by settling disputes among the Israelites. She challenged Barak to obey the Lord's command concerning Israelite troop deployment to defeat Sisera and his army (vv. 6–7). Barak agreed to act only if Deborah would accompany him (v. 8), prompting her response, "I will gladly go with you . . . but you will receive no honor on the road you are about to take, because the LORD will sell Sisera to a woman" (v. 9). The two join forces with ten thousand men.

As they encountered Sisera and his army, "Deborah said to Barak, 'Go! This is the day the LORD has handed Sisera over to you. Hasn't the LORD gone before you?'" Leading his men, Barak thoroughly defeated their enemies; only Sisera escaped destruction by fleeing "on foot to the tent of Jael. . . . Jael went out to greet Sisera and said to him, 'Come in, my lord. Come in with me. Don't be afraid.'" After (seemingly) caring for him, Jael feigned standing guard as Sisera slept and killed Sisera by hammering a tent peg into his temple (vv. 14–24). She triumphantly showed off the slain enemy to Barak, who had been in pursuit of Sisera. God's power continued to be displayed through the Israelites.

This narrative is accompanied by the song of Deborah and Barak (Judg 5). Except for two mentions of the latter character, the song rehearses the mighty deeds of the prophetess/judge (vv. 6–9) and Jael (vv. 24–27). The song concludes with a prayer: "LORD, may all your enemies perish as Sisera did. But may those who love him [the LORD] be like the rising of the sun in its strength" (v. 31). As a postscript, the narrative notes that peace ensued for Israel for forty years (v. 31).

The roles of Deborah and Jael, the hesitancy of Barak, and the violent death of Sisera at the hands of a woman raise much debate. On the one hand, some (many?) complementarians view this episode in the life of the nation of Israel in a negative manner because it disrupts the normal pattern of male leadership and teaching responsibilities, which they hold is firmly established throughout Scripture. Moreover, this position maintains that the narrative provides pointers that the two women "followed their unusual paths in a way that endorsed and honored the usual leadership of men, or indicated they failed to lead."[8]

With regard to the first point, Deborah's posture and behavior with respect to Barak in particular and the people of Israel in general is key: Though other judges in Israel were military warriors and conquerors, Deborah as judge was instructed by the Lord that Barak would function in that capacity (Judg 4:6–7). So, "she handed over the leadership, contrary to the pattern of all the other judges, to a man."[9] At the crucial moment, "Deborah said to Barak, 'Go! This is the day the LORD has handed Sisera over to you. Hasn't the LORD gone before you?'" (4:14). Challenging Barak

---

[8] John Piper and Wayne Grudem, "An Overview of Central Concerns," in *Recovering Biblical Manhood and Womanhood: A Response to Evangelical Feminism*, ed. John Piper and Wayne Grudem (Wheaton: Crossway, 1991, 2006), 72.

[9] Thomas R. Schreiner, "The Valuable Ministries of Women in the Context of Male Leadership: A Survey of Old and New Testament Examples and Teaching," in Piper and Grudem, eds., *Recovering Biblical Manhood and Womanhood*, 216.

to fulfill his divinely appointed mission (in which she promised to join him), Deborah acknowledged that mission and Barak as the one who had to carry it out. Moreover, whereas other prophets in Israel exercised their ministry publicly, Deborah prophesied privately as "she would sit under the palm tree of Deborah" and individual "Israelites went up to her to settle disputes" (4:5).[10]

With regard to the second point, the complementarian position holds that the prophetess Deborah, along with Jael, "was a living indictment of the weakness of Barak and other men in Israel who should have been more courageous leaders (Judges 4:9)."[11]

In general, this complementarian position urges hermeneutical caution in drawing lessons from the book of Judges: "The period of the judges is an especially precarious foundation for building a vision of God's ideal for leadership. In those days God was not averse to bringing about states of affairs that did not conform to His revealed will in order to achieve some wise purpose."[12] Accordingly, pointing to Deborah's prophetic and judicial leadership of the people of Israel, her initiative with respect to (inappropriately weak) Barak, and Jael's bold action in killing Sisera, have nothing to say in terms of principles regarding male and female roles in the church today.

---

[10] Schreiner, "The Valuable Ministries of Women in the Context of Male Leadership," 216.

[11] Piper and Grudem, "An Overview of Central Concerns," 72. Linda Belleville critiques this view: "It is sometimes remarked that God permitted women to lead at times when Israel lacked adequate male leadership. But the examples of Miriam, Deborah, and Huldah, who ministered in the context of other renowned male figures (Moses, Barak, Josiah, Jeremiah, etc.), demonstrate the opposite. Others plead exceptional circumstances. They argue that Israel's nomadic existence during the wilderness years and a leadership vacuum after years of slavery in Egypt called for exceptional measures. The period of the judges, they point out, was a unique time when everyone did whatever was deemed right in their own eyes. Yet if there was any time when wise spiritual counsel was in evidence, strong leadership was in place and the nation was on an even keel, it was during King Josiah's reign—and Huldah's tenure." Belleville, "Women Leaders in the Bible," 74.

[12] Piper and Grudem, "An Overview of Central Concerns," 72.

On the other hand, some (many?) egalitarians view this narrative in a positive manner because it illustrates the legitimate leadership of women, a pattern that they hold is also firmly established throughout Scripture. Of note are the various roles that Deborah plays: prophetess, judge, and mother of Israel.[13] That her prophetic ministry was from God, though not mentioned specifically, is implied in Barak's response to her question to him, "Hasn't the LORD, the God of Israel, commanded you?" (4:6).[14] She seems to be speaking the word of the Lord to Barak because that word had come to her; thus, she teaches with divine authority.[15] And he responds positively by promising to execute his duty if she will assist him in doing it. Furthermore, as judge, Deborah solved difficult disputes involving both men and women. Moreover, it may be that, though not directly stated, she served as commander-in-chief of Israel's armies, as evidenced by Barak's deference to her: "If you will go with me, I will go. But if you will not go with me, I will not go" (4:8).[16]

Though the complementarian position may view Barak's submission as an (inexcusable) evidence of his weakness in relation to Deborah, the egalitarian position maintains that Barak's insistence on being accompanied by Deborah was due to the fact he highly respected and deeply depended on her prophetic ministry. Additionally, whereas the first position may understand Deborah's response to Barak—"I will gladly go with you . . . but you

---

[13] Belleville, "Women Leaders in the Bible," 111.

[14] Belleville, "Women Leaders in the Bible," 111.

[15] This view differs from the first position, which holds (correctly) that "in the case of Deborah, there is no explicit statement that the Lord raised her up," making her prophetic ministry (which was in any case legitimate, as evidenced by the many blessings that Israel experienced from it) different from that of many of the other significant judges such as Othniel (3:9), Ehud (3:15), Gideon (6:14), Jephthah (11:29), and Samson (12:25; 14:6). Schreiner, "The Valuable Ministries of Women in the Context of Male Leadership," 216. Though this point is correct textually, it is hard not to see Deborah's role as prophetess—which required the Spirit's empowerment—as favoring the view that God raised her up for Israel's redemption.

[16] Belleville, "Women Leaders in the Bible," 111–12n6.

will receive no honor on the road you are about to take, because the Lord will sell Sisera to a woman" (4:9)—as an (indefensible) demonstration of his (wrongful) deference to women, the second position holds that Deborah's reply is an enthusiastic acknowledgement of her (rightful) leadership in uniting the armies of Israel to defeat their archenemies.

The egalitarian position underscores several other points: (1) the significance of the order of the names—Deborah and Barak—at the head of the song (Judg 5:1); (2) the immense change that occurred in Israel—"the main roads were deserted because travelers kept to the side roads [and] villages were deserted, they were deserted in Israel, until I, Deborah, arose, a mother in Israel" (5:6–7)—as a result of Deborah's effective prophesying, judging, and leading; (3) and (as just cited) the importance of her title—"a mother in Israel"—that highlighted the honor with which she was recognized.[17]

In addition to acknowledging this debate, other points need to be made from the perspective of my proposal of complementarity. First (and foregoing any framework of male-female roles outside this narrative and the question of the propriety or impropriety of her ministry), Deborah was a divinely chosen and directed, highly and gratefully respected, and much needed woman at one of the worst junctures in Israel's history. Indeed, she is presented as one of the few good judges in an awful array of weak or evil leaders. As a prophetess, she received and communicated revelation from God for the people of Israel. As a judge, she adjudicated difficult, disputed cases, bringing settlements to her people. Summoning Barak, she exhorted him to carry out his God-ordained mission, and whether he responded to her in weakness or in strength, Deborah pointed to him as the one before whom the Lord would go and lead his people in defeat of their enemies. As a mother in Israel, Deborah redirected her nation such that it worshiped the Lord and changed for the better. When prominent women exercise their divinely given gifts for their divinely established tasks in concert with important men engaging missionally to

[17] Belleville, "Women Leaders in the Bible," 112–13.

accomplish the Lord's plan, complementarity as men and women filling out and supporting one another relationally, vocationally, and nationally leads to flourishing.

Second, if Barak exemplifies male weakness, complementarity insists that a wrong application is for contemporary churches to prioritize teaching and discipling for men over those same activities for women. Certainly, churches need strong men, but complementarity underscores that they certainly and similarly need strong women. Church ministry is not a competition between the sexes, nor is it a zero-sum game in which attention to one sex necessarily results in inattention to the other. Churches should instruct and shepherd both men and women so that they fill out and mutually support one another ecclesially for their individual and corporate flourishing.

As for Jael, though little debate centers on her, the narrative presents her as a courageous, resourceful, and divinely appointed agent in ending the life of a treacherous enemy of Israel. The details of her deed—whether narrated or sung—are quite striking, reinforcing her enforcement of justice. As prophesied by Deborah, Jael rather than Barak received honor for Sisera's elimination. From her part in this story, we learn that each woman (and each man, for that matter) should accomplish the duty to which she is beholden, even *in extremis*. Only in this way, as complementarity insists, will women and men fill out and mutually support one another for both individual and corporate flourishing.

David, Abigail, and Nabal

While the narratives about David and his kingship are extensive, and whereas the story of Bathsheba is well known, this section focuses on two lesser-known accounts involving David and women. The first engages with Abigail and her husband Nabal (1 Samuel 25). The narrative describes her as "intelligent and beautiful" and him as "harsh and evil in his dealings" (v. 3). During a heightening conflict between David and Nabal (vv. 4–17), Abigail attempted an intervention to calm down the tension (vv. 18–31).

David blessed the Lord for Abigail's discernment and praised her for her intervention to ward off bloody revenge on his part (vv. 32–35).

When Abigail told Nabal about her encounter with David, "the Lord struck Nabal dead" (v. 38). This second account rehearses David's response to Nabal's death: "Blessed be the Lord who championed my cause against Nabal's insults and restrained his servant from doing evil. The Lord brought Nabal's evil deeds back on his own head.' Then David sent messengers to speak to Abigail about marrying him" (vv. 39). And the two were married.

Though we often think of complementarity as only applicable to marriage (which only comes at the end of this story), this narrative reminds us that the appropriate interaction between a resourceful, discerning woman and a wise, God-honoring man who responds to her provides an outstanding example of complementarity that courts divine blessing and leads to human flourishing. This narrative also underscores the disaster that may arise within marriage when one of the two partners neglects to uphold his responsibility—that is, fails to be a complement to his spouse.

Tamar, Amnon, Jonadab, and Absalom

If the preceding narrative emphasized the beauty of complementarity while also exposing the tragedy that arises when men and women fail to practice complementarity, this next narrative (2 Samuel 13) focuses solely on that second aspect. The main characters are three half-siblings—the beautiful Tamar, Amnon, and Absalom—along with Jonadab, Amnon's wicked friend.

Amnon was lovesick (i.e., consumed with lust) for "his sister Tamar because she was a virgin, but it seemed impossible to do anything to her" (v. 2). To rectify his friend's infatuation, Jonadab hatched a plan for Amnon to feign sickness and thereby lure Tamar to his bedside to take care of him (vv. 3–7). Taking food to her bedridden brother, Tamar innocently walked into Amnon's trap (vv. 8–10) as he forced himself upon her. In desperation she begged him to stop: 'Don't disgrace me, for such a thing should never be done in Israel. Don't commit this outrage! Where could I ever go with my humiliation? And you—you would be like one of the outrageous fools in Israel!' . . . But he refused to listen to her, and because he was stronger than she was, he disgraced her by raping her" (vv. 12–14).

Amnon's "love" for Tamar was replaced with contempt for her. He demanded that she leave him (to which Tamar objected as an evil worse than his raping her) and had her removed from the scene of the crime (vv. 15–18). Tamar righteously mourned the evil inflicted on her (vv. 18–19), which her brother Absalom correctly perceived to indicate that Amnon had raped their sister. He urged Tamar to be silent for the moment, possibly because he anticipated that David, who himself had committed a similar evil against Bathsheba, would do nothing about the rape. The consequences of Amnon's sin were widespread: "Tamar lived as a desolate woman in the house of her brother Absalom" (v. 20), and he, after a two-year wait, got revenge for Tamar by murdering Amnon (vv. 21–33).

The heinousness of rape and similar acts of violence against female image bearers is an awful consequence of disregarding complementarity, which decries such evils. Rather than filling out and mutually supporting one another, perverse men tear down and undermine women, resulting in desolation rather than flourishing. Moreover, complementarianism and egalitarianism alike condemn such acts.

Joab and the Two Wise Women

The narratives of 2 Samuel 14; 20:14–22 feature Joab, the general over David's troops, and two unnamed wise women, the first from Tekoa and the second from Abel of Beth-maacah.

In the first narrative, which follows the preceding story of Absalom's revenge against his brother Amnon, Joab sought to discern David's plan for resolving the conflict created by this retaliation by Absalom, his son and heir to his throne. Joab summoned a "wise woman" from Tekoa and dispatched her to King David. She fabricated a story—a legal case—that clearly paralleled the actual events of Absalom's revenge against his brother Amnon, with the hope that David would recognize the predicament he was in. Should he settle for Absalom's banishment or bring him home? The woman made her appeal: "Please, may the king invoke the LORD your God, so that the avenger of blood will not increase the loss, and they will not eliminate my son!" David responded by vowing, "As the LORD lives, not a hair of your son will fall to the ground." She boldly applied the story to the king with a strong reprimand, "Why have you devised something similar against the people of God? When the king spoke as he did about this matter, he has pronounced his own guilt. The king has not brought back his own banished one. . . . But God would not take away a life; he would devise plans so that the one banished from him does not remain banished" (14:11–14). In other words, when David ruled in the case of the woman's fictious case—exempting her son from revenge—he was effectively ruling in his own actual case: he exempted Absalom his son from revenge. Accordingly, the king should recall Absalom from exile, which he did indeed do.

In the second narrative (2 Sam 20:14–22), Joab led David's troops in besieging Sheba, leader of the rebel forces against the king, in the fortified city of Abel of Beth-maacah. As before, an unnamed "wise woman" of the city played a decisive role. As the siege persisted, the woman summoned Joab and wisely cautioned him: "In the past they used to say, 'Seek counsel in Abel,' and that's how they settled disputes. I am one of the peaceful and faithful in Israel, but you're trying to destroy a city that is like a mother in Israel. Why would you devour the LORD's inheritance?" Joab denied that his intention was to destroy the city; rather, it was to force out the rebel leader Sheba. Joab proposed, "'Deliver this one man, and I will withdraw from the city.' The woman replied to Joab, 'Watch! His head will be thrown over the wall to you.' The woman went to all the people with her wise counsel, and they cut off the head of Sheba son of Bichri and threw it to Joab." The general called off the siege and spared the city.

The Old Testament portrays wisdom as a woman in Proverbs (3:13–18; 4:5–9; 7:4–5; 9:1–6) and 2 Samuel narrates two stories of wise women who helped to resolve difficult matters of national interest. Complementarity draws attention to David's deference to the wise woman of Tekoa's (veiled) confrontation. Though she appealed to the king to invoke the Lord's will to rectify the challenging situation, the woman underscored what that will was, and the king acted accordingly. Similarly, complementarity applauds Joab's esteem for the wise woman of Abel of Beth-maacah. She described herself as "one of the peaceful and faithful in Israel," and it would have been unconscionable for the general to dismiss her wise counsel. Through the woman's faithful and sage intervention and the man's willingness to listen to her, an entire city was preserved from destruction and enjoyed peace. This is complementarity between men and women for human flourishing on a national level.

Jehosheba

This narrative (2 Kgs 11:1–3) underscores that the evil rehearsed in the preceding stories is not confined to men acting evilly against women. In this case, Ahaziah, the son of Jehoram and Athaliah, was the king of Judah for one year (2 Kgs 8:25–27). He had a sister named Jehosheba and a young son named Joash. The narrative features a rampage that is thwarted by a courageous deed:

> When Athaliah, Ahaziah's mother, saw that her son was dead, she proceeded to annihilate all the royal heirs. Jehosheba, who was King Jehoram's daughter and Ahaziah's sister, secretly rescued Joash son of Ahaziah from among the king's sons who were being killed and put him and the one who nursed him in a bedroom. So he was hidden from Athaliah and was not killed. Joash was in hiding with her in the LORD's temple six years while Athaliah reigned over the land. (2 Kgs 11:1–3)

As we have seen, when complementarity fails, the pursuit of one's selfish advancement may come at the expense of others, as exemplified by Athaliah.

At the same time, when complementarity prospers, courageous resourcefulness may win the day, as embodied in Jehosheba.

Ruth, Boaz, and Naomi

One of two Old Testament books named for its female main character, Ruth follows Proverbs canonically and thus may be interpreted as the quintessential example of the woman of Prov 31:10–31. This connection is supported by the adjective חַיִל (*ḥayil*), which occurs only four times in the Hebrew Bible: twice in respect to a wife's *noble* character (Prov 31:10; 12:4), once in a description of Boaz as "a prominent man of noble character" (Ruth 2:1), and once in Boaz's admiration for Ruth as "a woman of noble character" (Ruth 3:11). The noble character of Ruth and Boaz points us in the direction of two contributions that this book makes to complementarity.

First, this book portrays the mutual respect, grace, and honor that are at the heart of complementarity. As the narrative continues, the noble Boaz encountered Ruth as she gathered grain and immediately cared for and protected her (2:8–9). Puzzled by his gracious treatment of her, Ruth asked Boaz to explain his care, which he did: "Everything you have done for your mother-in-law since your husband's death has been fully reported to me: how you left your father and mother and your native land, and how you came to a people you didn't previously know. May the LORD reward you for what you have done, and may you receive a full reward from the LORD God of Israel, under whose wings you have come for refuge" (2:11–12). The respect that Boaz accorded her was well deserved, as Ruth's reputation had become widely known. By the providence of God, Boaz also turned out to be a close relative of Naomi who could serve as a family redeemer (2:20).

Because of this family connection, Naomi directed Ruth to position herself physically close to Boaz as he slept. Startled by her presence at his feet, Boaz blessed her for her kindness, and promised, "I will do for you whatever you say, since all the people in my town know that you are a woman of noble character" (3:10–11). A man of noble character together with a woman of noble character, and propriety reigning between them. Indeed, decorum dictated that Boaz yield to a closer kinsman redeemer (3:12–18). Skillfully, Boaz secured the right of redemption of Naomi's land (4:1–9) and, together with it, Ruth, "to perpetuate the deceased man's name on his property, so that his name will not disappear among his relatives or from the gate of his hometown" (4:10). The concern not for himself but for Naomi and the reputation of her family, was evident in Boaz, who also gained a wife who exemplified Prov 31:10–31. Consummating their marriage, Boaz and Ruth had a son named Obed, "the father of Jesse, the father of David" (4:17) and, eventually, "Jacob the father of Joseph the husband of Mary, of whom Jesus was born, who is called Christ" (Matt 1:16 ESV).

This book highlights the mutual respect, gracious treatment, and honorable devotion that is expected in complementary relationships between male and female image bearers, leading to flourishing in relational, familial, and national areas.

Second, and most importantly, the fruit of the complementary relationship between Boaz and Ruth is the Messiah himself, Jesus Christ. Certainly, his genealogy is full of names that invoke guilt and shame, concern and consternation. Not so with the names of Ruth and Boaz, ancestors of noble character and models of complementarity.

Esther and Mordecai

The book of Esther, again one of two biblical writings that bear the name of a woman, is set in the fortress of Susa—the palace of Ahasuerus (or Xerxes I), king of the Persians—during the exile of the people of Israel under the reign of Nebuchadnezzar of Babylon. The story features four main characters. The first was King Ahasuerus, who was contradicted and shamed by his wife, Queen Vashti (1:10–12). To quell any possible momentum of wives despising rather than honoring their husbands to gather steam from this incident, Ahasuerus commissioned a search for "a beautiful young virgin" as Vashti's replacement (2:2–4).

The second main character was "a Jewish man named Mordecai" (v. 5) who "was the legal guardian of his cousin Hadassah (that is, Esther), because she had no father or mother" (v. 7).

Esther, then, was the third character. Because of her lovely appearance, Esther was handpicked and aesthetically groomed to be a candidate for Queen Vashti's privileged position, joining other beautiful contenders in the palace harem. "Every day Mordecai took a walk in front of the harem's courtyard to learn how Esther was doing and to see what was happening to her" (vv. 10–11).

As part of the selection process to find his new queen, King Ahasuerus would bring one embellished woman at a time to spend the night with him in his quarters; "she never went to the king again, unless he desired her and summoned her by name" (v. 14). When her turn arrived, Esther was taken to the palace. "The king loved Esther more than all the other women . . . and made her queen in place of Vashti" (v. 17). Throughout this process, "Esther still did not reveal her family background or her ethnicity, as Mordecai had directed. She obeyed Mordecai's orders, as she always had while he raised her" (v. 20; cf. v. 10).

Mordecai's constant watchfulness of Esther bore unexpected fruit. Learning of a plot by two eunuch-guards to assassinate the king, "he reported it to Queen Esther, and she told the king on Mordecai's behalf." The co-conspirators were hanged (vv. 20–23) and Mordecai saved Ahasuerus's life.

The fourth main character appears at this point in the narrative. Haman, being honored by the king, held the highest position among all the king's officers, who "bowed down and paid homage to Haman, because the king had commanded this to be done for him. But Mordecai would not bow down or pay homage" (3:2). Incensed by Mordecai's disrespect, and learning "of Mordecai's ethnic identity, . . . Haman planned to destroy all of Mordecai's people, the Jews, throughout Ahasuerus's kingdom" (vv. 5–6).

When the lot (the *pur*) was cast and fell to Haman, permitting him to approach the king, he used his opportunity to expose the presence of the Jewish people and prevailed upon the king to decree and finance the destruction of these troublemakers. Their destruction was scheduled for "a single day, the thirteenth day of Adar, the twelfth month" (v. 13).

"When Mordecai learned all that had occurred, he tore his clothes, put on sackcloth and ashes, went into the middle of the city, and cried loudly and bitterly" (4:1). He was joined in mourning by the Jewish people throughout the kingdom. As Esther became aware of the news about her people's fate, she became overwhelmed with fear. Mordecai commanded her "to approach the king, implore his favor, and plead with him personally for her people" (4:8). Esther explained her legal predicament to Mordecai: unless summoned by the king, she would face the death penalty if she approached him. And she had not been summoned (v. 11).

At the climax of this narrative comes Mordecai's well-known reply to Esther: "Don't think that you will escape the fate of all the Jews because you are in the king's palace. If you keep silent at this time, relief and deliverance will come to the Jewish people from another place, but you and your father's family will be destroyed. Who knows, perhaps you have come to your royal position for such a time as this" (4:13–14). Courageously, Esther ordered Mordecai to call for the Jews to fast, promising, "After that, I will go to the king even if it is against the law. If I perish, I perish. So Mordecai went and did everything Esther had commanded him" (v. 17).

True to her word, Esther (illegally) approached the king, with whom she gained favor. At a dinner, Mordecai was honored for his long-forgotten exposure of the plot to assassinate the king. Haman was shamed, ordered the construction of gallows on which he planned to hang Mordecai, and was prophetically warned, "Since Mordecai is Jewish, and you have begun to fall before him, you won't overcome him, because your downfall is certain" (6:13). When promised by Ahasuerus to grant her wish, Esther asked for the king to spare her life. Even more, she interceded, "And spare my people; this is my desire. For my people and I have been sold to destruction, death, and annihilation" (7:3–4). The king asked for the identity of the plotter of this devious scheme, to which Esther answered, "The adversary and enemy is this evil Haman" (v. 6). As the narrative tersely notes, "They hanged Haman on the gallows he had prepared for Mordecai" (v. 10).

In the aftermath of these events, Esther received "the estate of Haman, the enemy of the Jews. Mordecai entered the king's presence because Esther had revealed her relationship to Mordecai. The king removed his signet ring he had recovered from Haman and gave it to Mordecai, and Esther put him in charge of Haman's estate" (8:1–2). Most importantly, Esther prevailed upon Ahasuerus to issue a new edict reversing the earlier decree to annihilate the Jewish people. They were spared and their enemies were destroyed. Esther and Mordecai, with equal and full authority (9:29), inaugurated the celebration of Purim[18] as two "days of feasting, rejoicing, and of sending gifts to one another and to the poor" (9:22). Additionally, "many of the ethnic groups of the land professed themselves to be Jews because fear of the Jews had overcome them" (8:17). Finally, Mordecai was elevated in rank to become "second only to King Ahasuerus" and achieved many "powerful and magnificent accomplishments. . . . He was famous among the Jews and highly esteemed by many of his relatives. He continued to pursue prosperity for his people and to speak for the well-being of all his descendants" (10:1–3).

The book of Esther illustrates complementarity throughout its pages. Though significantly differentiated—Esther is a woman, a queen, and an adopted daughter, in stark contrast with Mordecai as a man, a commoner, and her guardian—they shared equal dignity. He cared for her as she cared for him. She constantly obeyed his orders (e.g., by not revealing her Jewish ethnicity), even in the face of death (e.g., her uninvited appearance before the king could cost Esther her life), and he obeyed her orders (e.g., to call a palace-wide fast for her to find favor with the king). With equal and full authority, Esther and Mordecai established the festival of Purim. Both played decisive roles in the good outcome of the story. Their interdependence resulted in both individual flourishing—Esther remained the exalted

[18] *Purim*, or *lots*, recalls the *lot*—the *pur* that was cast and fell to Haman (3:7).

queen and Mordecai became second in rank to the king—and corporate flourishing: the Jewish people were not annihilated but prospered greatly as "fear of them fell on every nationality" (9:2). Similarly, despite their many differences, Esther and Ahasuerus exhibited complementarity in their relationship. Even if contemporary readers are repulsed by the details of his dismissal of Queen Vashti and his harem of beautiful young virgins whom he "tested" to be her substitute as queen, King Ahasuerus granted Esther an unprecedented breadth of relational and national favor for the good of many: her own life was spared, Haman and his evil influence (exemplifying the opposite of complementarity) was destroyed, the Jewish people were saved, and Mordecai powerfully and magnificently accomplished much.

As biblical scholars and theologians commonly note, God is not a major character or even mentioned in this book. As they also regularly underscore, however, his sovereign presence and providential work is everywhere to be found in the unfolding of the narrated events, many of which seem impossible on a human level. This point reminds us that complementarity, as defined, is *God's design* for his male and female gendered image bearers to fill out and mutually support one another relationally, familially, vocationally, and ecclesially for their individual and corporate flourishing. His purpose was at the heart of, and accomplished by, the complementary engagements of Ahasuerus, Esther, Mordecai, and (negatively) Haman.

Huldah

Another narrative of a prophetess holds lessons about complementarity (2 Kgs 22:11–20). As before, because of controversy over the interpretation of certain aspects of this narrative, I will include a discussion of the complementarian and egalitarian understandings of it before offering applications from the perspective of my proposal of complementarity.

As the narrative begins, King Josiah had been repairing the temple only to discover "the book of the law," probably Deuteronomy. As Josiah listened to the reading of the book, he "tore his clothes" and gave orders to some leaders to "inquire of the LORD. . . . For great is the LORD's wrath that is kindled against us because our ancestors have not obeyed the words of this book in order to do everything written about us" (v. 13). The group "went to the prophetess Huldah, wife of Shallum son of Tikvah, son of Harhas, keeper of the wardrobe" (v. 14). She directed them to return to the king with this prophecy about Jerusalem: "This is what the LORD says: I am about to bring disaster on this place and on its inhabitants, fulfilling all the words of the book that the king of Judah has read, because they have abandoned me and burned incense to other gods in order to anger me with all the work of their hands. My wrath will be kindled against this place, and it will not be quenched" (vv. 15–17). She also prophesied about Josiah who, because of his tenderheartedness, humility, and repentance, would die before the promised destruction of Jerusalem (v. 20). The group delivered Huldah's report to the king (v. 20).

Like the prophetess Deborah, Huldah the prophetess is viewed in two contrasting ways. On the one hand, some (many?) complementarians deny that her prophetic ministry contradicts the common biblical pattern of male leadership and teaching. Specifically, in contrast with other Old Testament prophets, who exercised their ministry publicly, Huldah used her prophetic gift privately and in deference to male leaders: "She did not publicly proclaim God's word. Rather, she explained in private the word of the Lord when Josiah sent messengers to her. She exercised her prophetic ministry in a way that did not obstruct male headship."[19]

On the other hand, some (many?) egalitarians view this narrative as an illustration of the legitimate leadership and teaching roles of women. Of particular note are the various ways in which the narrative highlights Huldah's renown: As the wife of the court official "Shallum son of Tikvah, son of Harhas, keeper of the wardrobe" (v. 14), Huldah would have been "at the center of public affairs." Moreover, her reputation as a "religious

---

[19] Schreiner, "The Valuable Ministries of Women in the Context of Male Leadership," 216.

counselor" was such that, at the discovery of the book of the law, the king discharged his emissaries to find Huldah. These men were high-level officials: "the high priest (Hilkiah), the father of a future governor (Ahikam), the son of a prophet (Achbor), the secretary of state (Shaphan), and the king's officer (Asaiah)."[20] Their stature is indicative of the high status of Huldah, whose prophecies were taken seriously, thus leading to Josiah's covenant renewal with the people and major reforms of Israelite worship, including the reinstitution of the Passover (2 Kgs 23:1–27).

Two points about complementarity stand out in this narrative. First (and foregoing any framework of male-female roles outside this narrative and the question of the propriety or impropriety of her ministry), Huldah was a woman of substantial renown whom the Lord directed and empowered to use her prophetic gift to bring about repentance from sin, covenant renewal, and religious reform. Israel was in dire straits, and the discovery of the book of the law served to expose its plight. The proper course of action came at the prophetic instruction that Huldah communicated from the Lord. Her valued gift led to both individual and corporate flourishing, which is the expected outcome of complementarity.

Second, the respect of leading men for this woman is notable and to be applauded. While debates may continue between the sexes and their different positions on the roles of men and women, the lesson of esteeming one another must not be allowed to be muted. Complementarity urges such mutual honor.

Conclusion

A final narrative in which the complementarity of women and men is highlighted ends and sums up this section on Old Testament men and women. It is the story (emphasis added) of what took place after Moses instructed the entire Israelite community about the construction of the tabernacle:

---

[20] Belleville, "Women Leaders in the Bible," 73.

> *Everyone* whose heart was moved and whose spirit prompted him came and brought an offering to the Lord for the work on the tent of meeting, for all its services, and for the holy garments. *Both men and women came; all who had willing hearts* brought brooches, earrings, rings, necklaces, and all kinds of gold jewelry—*everyone* who presented a presentation offering of gold to the Lord. *Everyone* who possessed blue, purple, or scarlet yarn, fine linen or goat hair, ram skins dyed red or fine leather, brought them. *Everyone* making an offering of silver or bronze brought it as a contribution to the Lord. *Everyone* who possessed acacia wood useful for any task in the work brought it. *Every skilled woman* spun yarn with her hands and brought it: blue, purple, and scarlet yarn, and fine linen. And *all the women whose hearts were moved* spun the goat hair by virtue of their skill. The leaders brought onyx and gemstones to mount on the ephod and breastpiece, as well as the spice and oil for the light, for the anointing oil, and for the fragrant incense. So the Israelites brought a freewill offering to the Lord, *all the men and women whose hearts prompted them* to bring something for all the work that the Lord, through Moses, had commanded to be done. (Exod 35:20–29, emphasis added)

This narrative displays the beauty of complementarity as both women and men freely offer their gifts to the Lord, encouraging one another by their wholehearted participation. Complementarity is God's design for both women and men to fill out and mutually support one another for human flourishing.

Proverbs 31:10–31

Scripture's most notable treatment of wives comes at the conclusion of the book of Proverbs. Not to be overlooked is the first part of the chapter, which contains "the words of King Lemuel, a pronouncement that his mother taught him" (31:1). These instructions particularly address the avoidance of dangerous women and alcoholic drinks, the consumption of which may lead to the perversion of justice. Moreover, several themes that course throughout the book of Proverbs appear for their last time in this final chapter, as will be noted. As with my discussion of Old Testament narratives, because of controversy over the interpretation of certain aspects of this poem, I will include a discussion of the complementarian and egalitarian understandings of it before offering applications from the perspective of my proposal of complementarity.

Bruce Waltke outlines this acrostic poem, which he titles "The Valiant Wife:"[21]

- I. Introduction: her value (vv. 10–12)
  - A. Her general worth inferred from her scarcity (v. 10)
  - B. Her worth to her husband (vv. 11–12)
- II. Body: her activities (vv. 13–27)
  - A. Her cottage industry (vv. 13–18)
  - B. Seam (or janus) (v. 19)
  - C. Her social achievements (vv. 20–27)
- III. Conclusion: her praise (vv. 28–31)
  - A. By her family (vv. 28–29)
  - B. By all (vv. 30–31)

As to the specific type of poetry, opinions vary. Al Wolters classifies it as heroic poetry, a genre that narrates heroic deeds, usually of a military sort. As a heroic poem featuring a woman, it is a polemic against Near Eastern literature and its fascination "with the physical charms of women from an erotic point of view," countering it with a celebration of "her activity in the ordinary affairs of family, community and business life."[22] He also sees in this heroic poem a critique of the Hellenistic intellectual ideal as it highlights "concrete practical wisdom rooted in the fear of the LORD" over against

---

[21] Bruce K. Waltke, *The Book of Proverbs: Chapters 15–31*, New International Commentary on the Old Testament (Grand Rapids: Eerdmans, 2005), 515. Much of the following discussion follows Waltke's commentary.

[22] Waltke, *The Book of Proverbs: Chapters 15–31*, 517. His citation is Al Wolters, "Proverbs XXI 10–31 as Heroic Hymn: A Form-Critical Analysis," *Vetus Testamentum*, 38 (1988): 456–57.

hypothetical wisdom grounded in objective rationality.[23] Alternatively, Maryse Waegeman views the poem as a polemic against Classical and Hellenistic Greek literature's portrait of an ideal wife as embodying the virtues of silence, obedience, and keeping to management of the home. The heroic wife in this poem is, by stark contrast, communicative, ambitious, and active both inside and outside her home.[24] More likely is the view that this poem, rather than a polemic against other cultural/literary perspectives on women/wives, is a portrait of an ideal woman/wife who embodies Hebrew Scripture's acclamation and affirmation of godly virtues such as industriousness, wisdom, fortitude, generosity, and skillfulness.

Another interpretive issue is whether this wife is the personification of wisdom, similar to "woman wisdom" elsewhere in Proverbs (1:20–33; 8:1–36; 9:1–6), or if she exemplifies for a real woman what an ideal wise wife is to be. In favor of the first view is the parallelism between this wife and "woman wisdom" elsewhere in this book:[25]

the wife	*"woman wisdom"*
valiant (v. 10)	14:1
rare (v. 10)	1:28; 3:13; 4:22; 8:17, 35
precious (v. 10)	3:13; cf. 12:4; 16:16; 18:19; 21:15
trustworthy (v. 11)	3:1–6; 4:6, 8, 9, 12; 10:9
energetic, not a sluggard (vv. 13, 27b)	6:6–11; 26:13–16
resourceful (v. 16)	1:4
strong (v. 17)	24:5
prosperous/wealthy (v. 18)	3:10; 13:9
kind to the poor (v. 20)	3:27; 11:24–25; 14:21
fortified (v. 21)	1:26–7; 30:25
wise and loving teacher (v. 26)	8:14, 32
pious (v. 30)	1:7

---

[23] Waltke, *The Book of Proverbs: Chapters 15–31*, 517. His citation is Wolters, "Proverbs XXI 10–31 as Heroic Hymn," 457.

[24] Waltke, *The Book of Proverbs: Chapters 15–31*, 517. His citation is Maryse Waegeman, "The Perfect Wife of Proverbia 31:10–31," *Goldene Apfel*, 101–107.

[25] Waltke, *The Book of Proverbs: Chapters 15–31*, 518.

Given this clear parallelism, proponents of this first option consider this wife to be the personification of wisdom.

In favor of the second option is the poem's subsequent canonical connection to the real, historical Ruth, the "valiant woman" (v. 10; Ruth 3:11); accordingly, the wife in Proverbs is an actual woman whose virtues appear canonically in the woman/wife Ruth. As to the literary parallelism with "woman wisdom," Waltke explains, "although these similarities show that this heroine incarnates wisdom, they do not establish that she is fictitious. The echoes of this portrait of the valiant wife with Woman Wisdom, who is portrayed on the purely symbolic register in the Prologue [Prov 1:20–33], are wholly compatible with an ideal wife on the historical register."[26] Accordingly, proponents of this second option maintain that this wife actually embodies the many godly virtues rehearsed throughout Proverbs.

As we come to the poem itself, a final interpretive consideration is the proper descriptor of the featured character. Biblical scholars have offered various translations of the adjective חַיִל (*ḥayil*) modifying *wife* (v. 10a): *virtuous* (KJV), *worthy* (ASV), *excellent* (ESV, NASB), *capable* (HCSB), and *good* (RSV). The CSB and NIV go in a different direction, preferring *noble character* in their translation of the first phrase; for example, "Who can find a wife of *noble character*?" (CSB). In all cases, the second phrase indicates the great value of such a wife: "She is far more precious than jewels" (v. 10b). Though such a woman/wife is indeed rare, the wife portrayed in this poem is one such treasure.

The fact that "the heart of her husband trusts in her" (v. 11)—not in contrast with the biblical insistence that one's trust should be wholly and only in the Lord, but along with that righteous posture—"elevates the valiant wife, who herself fears the LORD, to the highest level of spiritual and physical competence. The claim implies that this husband and wife enjoy

[26] Waltke, *The Book of Proverbs: Chapters 15–31*, 518.

a robust spiritual relationship."[27] The reason for his trust in her is that "he will not lack anything good. She rewards him with good, not evil, all the days of her life" (vv. 11–12). The first "good" refers to all the necessities of life, which she provides for him. The second "good" refers generally to all the benefits and blessings for her husband's flourishing, and particularly to all the economic help needed for his well-being.

The poem rehearses her many activities (vv. 13–27), both her cottage industry (vv. 13–18) and her social achievements (vv. 20–27). From raw materials, she manufactures textiles; from the profits of this cottage industry, she trades for luxurious foods from far off (vv. 13–14). Putting her own comfort after that of others, she rises very early to resourcefully provide food for her immediate family as well as her female servants (v. 15). Her manufacturing profits further permit her to strategically plan and purchase a field in which, after removing its stones and tilling its soil, she plants a vineyard (v. 16, which probably includes building a watchtower and a winepress).

She is competent to engage in these activities because of her well-developed strength and endurance to do them all (v. 17). From this tenacious potency, her financial gain is significant and lasting. The specialty foods from foreign lands and the wine from her vineyard satisfy her and those who depend on her industriousness. "Her lamp that is never extinguished" probably refers to the consistency of her finances; her supply of wealth never dries up (v. 18).

The poem's seam or janus (v. 19) completes the portrayal of the wife's textile manufacturing (done manually with her hands on the spinning staff/the spindle). This production is the foundation for her other activities. The seam of v. 19 is related chiastically to v. 20, which begins the poem's rehearsal of this wife's social achievements (vv. 20–27). This noble wife cares for the poor and marginalized from the fruit of her hard-earned profits.

---

[27] Waltke, *The Book of Proverbs: Chapters 15–31*, 521.

The spreading out of her hands refers either to her invitation (beckoning) to the disenfranchised to come to her home or to her offer (bequeathing) of material help. In either case, "The hands that grasp to produce open wide to provide."[28]

Whereas the opening lines of the poem highlight the wife's industriousness through a cottage industry in order to build a solid financial foundation, the poem pivots to underscore another use for her textile manufacturing: through it, she fearlessly provides the costly, warm clothes that her family needs in the challenging winter months (v. 21). In addition to, yet in contrast with, those stiff, functional garments, she also manufactures soft, comfortable, expensive, and plush coverings for her bed and attire for herself (v. 22).

In an ascending scale of beneficiaries of this wife's productivity—from the poor (v. 20), to her household (v. 21), to herself (v. 22)—the climactic recipient is her husband, who "is known at the city gates, where he sits among the elders of the land" (v. 23). She has freed him up from household duties. She has established a fine reputation regarding the affluence of his household. She enhances his public image by clothing him in expensive garments. And she brings him honor through her own widely known good reputation (v. 31). As a result, he is part of the region's authoritative, wise leadership.

As she makes bed coverings and clothes for herself (v. 22), she also "makes and sells linen garments and . . . delivers belts to the merchants" (v. 24); her productive clothing enterprise extends beyond her family and herself to traders in similar business ventures. Metaphorically, her clothing is "strength and honor," and just as "she is not afraid" to face the challenges of winter, so "she can laugh at the time to come" (v. 25).

The wife's social achievements conclude with a new aspect: "Her mouth speaks wisdom, and loving instruction is on her tongue" (v. 26). Such activity is not occasional but a lifestyle of imparting wisdom to others from her

---

[28] Waltke, *The Book of Proverbs: Chapters 15–31*, 527. His citation is R. Van Leeuwen, *The Book of Proverbs* (New Interpreter's Bible 5; Nashville: Abingdon, 1997), 262.

own wellspring of wisdom and instructing others from her own loving character. Alternatively, she may teach a particular body of loving instruction, which would likely consist of the directives of the book of Proverbs. She vigilantly guards her family so that they follow those directives, disciplining them when they fail (13:24; 22:6) and maintaining proper order and relationships within the household. Her diligence is admirable; she never imitates the way of the sluggard (24:30–34; 26:13).

The poem concludes (vv. 28–31) with a rehearsal of praise for this woman/wife/mother on the part of her household (vv. 28–29) and her community (vv. 30–31). The reciprocity is notable: she blesses her household and her husband, and in turn they bless her; she blesses her community, and in turn it blesses her. "In sum, the woman so concerned for others now becomes the central concern and praise of others."[29] As to her household, "Her children rise up and call her blessed; her husband also praises her: 'Many women have done noble deeds, but you surpass them all!'" (vv. 28–29). Rising to publicly honor their mother, her children "esteem her and declare her as one living life optimally, as the Creator intended, and so endowed with wisdom's benefits."[30] Joining in this chorus is her husband, whose acclamation is a superlative that is actually cited. Interestingly, the poem begins with an acknowledgement of the rarity of "a wife of *noble* character" (v. 10), penultimately affirms that many women have engaged in *noble* works, then concludes with yet another acknowledgement of the rarity of this woman/wife whose *noble* nature surpasses them all. Such idealization of her does not minimize or mitigate the expectation that this woman should serve as a model for all wives.

Shifting from the husband's praise to the poet's final accolade, a contrast is offered: what might be attractive in the eyes of the world—womanly charm and beauty—turns out to be deceptive and fleeting, "but a woman

---

[29] Waltke, *The Book of Proverbs: Chapters 15–31*, 533. His reference is to Thomas P. McCreesh, "Wisdom as Wife: Proverbs 31:10-31," *Revue biblique* 92 [1985], 36.

[30] Waltke, *The Book of Proverbs: Chapters 15–31*, 534.

who fears the LORD will be praised" (v. 30). While physical characteristics are not evil in and of themselves, and husbands and wives are to be attracted sexually to one another (e.g., Song of Songs), those features can attract wrongly and fail to deliver enduring satisfaction.[31] Not so with "the fear of the LORD, which is the beginning of wisdom" (1:7; 9:10). "By definition, the fear of the LORD means in part living according to the wisdom revealed in this book. This woman's itemized, self-sacrificing activities for others exemplify the fear of the LORD (see 1:7)."[32]

The poem turns outwardly to exhort the Israelites at the gates: "Give her the reward of her labor, and let her works praise her at the city gates" (v. 31). "Her works" refers to this woman's many enterprising activities, the fruit of her cottage industry, and to her many philanthropic initiatives, that is, her social achievements for the poor and marginalized.

This beautiful poem has been the center of debate between egalitarianism and complementarianism. Egalitarianism offers several points: The first is "that the idealized imagery here points to a woman who complements her husband. She lives not for her own accomplishments but for [the] happiness and wellbeing of her husband and family. It would be a little anachronistic to say that the poem assumes a complementarian framework but it certainly does not contradict that thinking."[33] Second, and by contrast, "the poem also makes it clear that a woman has standing, value, worth. She can be described positively as strong. She can be successful in business. She is a leader in the home and in the wider world."[34] To be noted is the vast distance between the culture in which this woman lived

[31] In his first letter, Peter affirms something similar: "Don't let your beauty consist of outward things like elaborate hairstyles and wearing gold jewelry or fine clothes, but rather what is inside the heart—the imperishable quality of a gentle and quiet spirit, which is of great worth in God's sight" (1 Pet 3:3–4).

[32] Waltke, *The Book of Proverbs: Chapters 15–31*, 536.

[33] Dave Williams, "The Ideal Wife?" *Faithroots* (June 24, 2023), https://faithroot.com/2023/06/24/the-ideal-wife/.

[34] Williams, "The Ideal Wife?"

and worked and our contemporary context, cautioning us from reading it from our present viewpoint.

Third, egalitarianism proposes that the poem seems to contradict the model of marriage that complementarianism endorses. Specific aspects of the poem that appear to present problems include the following: (1) "She evaluates a field and buys it; she plants a vineyard with her earnings" (v. 16), apparently without checking with her husband. (2) "She makes and sells linen garments; she delivers belts to the merchants" (v. 24), an occupation that takes her outside of her home, which is her proper place (e.g., "working at home," Titus 2:5). (3) "Her mouth speaks wisdom, and loving instruction is on her tongue" (v. 26), in seeming contradiction to prohibitions against women teaching (e.g., 1 Tim 2:12). (4) "She watches over the activities of her household and is never idle" (v. 27), apparently replacing or usurping her husband's role as head of the household. (5) While "her husband is known at the city gates, where he sits among the elders of the land" (v. 23), the poem also encourages the citizens, "Give her the reward of her labor, and let her works praise her at the city gates" (v. 31), again seeming to applaud her activities that take her away from her home. (6) Rather than correcting his wife and these various "non-complementarian" activities, her husband actually lauds her with superlative praise (vv. 28–29).

Complementarianism also makes several points: The first underscores that this woman "does not live her life gripped by the expectations of mere men" because she fears God above all else.[35] Second, "She is a vivid picture of the God-centered 'helper' [Gen 2:18], for her husband 'trusts in her' even as he sits with the elders at the city gates (31:11, 23). He has the call to go and lead the people; while he is not home, he knows that she" is providing for him and their children.[36] Thus, her role is that of support for her husband as he engages in his responsibilities outside the home. Third, and adding to the second point, "her burden is her family and home. She

[35] Owen Strachan, *Reenchanting Humanity: A Theology of Mankind* (Fearn: Mentor, 2019), 141–42.

[36] Strachan, *Reenchanting Humanity*, 142.

strengthens it through economic activity (31:13, 16, 24), cooking for her household (31:15), clothing her loved ones (31:21), and speaking truth and wisdom (31:25). The care and nurture of her family and her home occupy her attention constantly (v. 27)."[37]

This valiant wife of noble character underscores numerous aspects important for complementarity. First, "the heart of her husband trusts in her" (v. 11) because she provides him with all the necessities of life; these benefits are blessings for his flourishing, the intended outcome of complementarity in the relational arena. Second, as she sees to the wellbeing of her husband, she does also for her entire household, who are well provided for—even with expensive, luxurious garments. Such flourishing—even though not necessarily to such an extent—is the desired result of complementarity within the familial realm.

Third, she is an industrious worker, excelling in various areas such as manufacturing, foreign trade, buying land, viticulture, and more. The fact that she engages in these activities not only in the domestic sphere but also outside her home is of no concern, particularly as the mobility of contemporary women enables them to work with ease outside their home or even to work virtually from home. Such flourishing is the anticipated outcome of complementarity in the vocational sphere. Fourth, through her industriousness and entrepreneurship, this woman has resources to share with the poor and disenfranchised of her land. Furthermore, she frees up her husband so that he may make a significant contribution to the region's leadership. Moreover, her people acknowledge her outstanding works. Such flourishing is the intended outcome of complementarity in the national (replacing ecclesial) arena.

Finally, three qualities or postures are foundational for the noble character of this woman (not in any order): She works hard and rejects idleness. She fears the Lord. And she is full of wisdom. When women (and men, for that matter) are similarly noble of character, they fill out and mutually support

[37] Strachan, *Reenchanting Humanity*, 142.

men (and men, for that matter, mutually support women) relationally, familially, vocationally, and ecclesially (nationally). This noble woman/wife/ mother exemplifies the qualities or postures necessary for complementarity.

In summary, this chapter on Old Testament Considerations has explored nineteen Old Testament narratives in which men and women are featured in some kind of proximity to complementarity, and the Proverbs 31 poem about a noble woman/wife. Accompanying these presentations have been discussions of how complementarianism and egalitarianism view these Old Testament matters, as well as how complementarity draws from them.

Having explored these Old Testament considerations, I now turn to New Testament considerations. Given the vast amount of material to cover, I devote the next four chapters to it. Chapter 16 treats the Gospels, focusing on Jesus's interactions with women and men. Chapter 17 explores the book of Acts, concentrating on men and women believers in the early church. Chapter 18 is an eclectic handling of the so-called "controversial passages" in the Pauline corpus that figure prominently in the complementarian-egalitarian debate. Chapter 19, the concluding part of these New Testament considerations, treats a final "controversial passage" in 1 Peter and ends with a study of Paul's greetings to a number of leading women at the end of his letter to the Romans.

CHAPTER 16

New Testament Considerations: Gospels

Introduction

In contemporary scholarship on gender as it relates to ministry in general and leadership in particular, it is common and helpful to focus on Jesus and his interaction with women as narrated in the Gospels. Interestingly, as Aída Besançon Spencer underscores, "Recognizing that Jesus both affirmed and elevated the status of women has now become commonplace on both sides of the women-in-leadership debate."[1] As this book is on complementarity,

[1] Aída Besançon Spencer, "Jesus' Treatment of Women in the Gospels," in *Discovering Biblical Equality: Biblical, Theological, Cultural, and Practical Perspectives*, ed. Ronald W. Pierce and Cynthia Long Westfall, assoc. ed. Christa L. McKirland, 3rd ed. (Downers Grove: IVP Academic, 2021), 91. She cites writers who oppose women in senior leadership roles in church yet who highlight Jesus's regular and radical affirmation of women. These writers include Michael J. Wilkins, "Women in the Teaching and Example of Jesus," in *Women and Men in Ministry: A Complementary Perspective*, ed. Robert L. Saucy and Judith K. TenElshof (Chicago: Moody, 2001), 91–112; James A. Borland, "Women in the Life and Teaching of Jesus," in *Recovering Biblical Manhood and Womanhood*, ed. John Piper and Wayne

such concentration can be only part of the discussion; indeed, a presentation of Jesus's ministry to and with both women and men is appropriate. Accordingly, this section treats Gospel narratives that portray Jesus's healing, teaching, calling, rebuking, and serving both men and women. It also explores the Gospels' portrayal of Mary, his mother.

Historically speaking, studies such as these do not underscore the gender of those whom Jesus helps, as the sex of the recipients of his compassion and grace is not thought to be a significant feature. As this point is usually taken for granted, I begin with a survey of Gospel stories about Jesus's interaction with men, after which I present the narratives of Jesus's interaction with women, whose sex is indeed a significant feature of the Gospels. The main point I underscore throughout this material is the reception (or, in some cases, the rejection) of Jesus and what postures (e.g., faith in him) and/or qualities (e.g., perseverance in trial) are positively (or, in some cases, negatively) portrayed through the male and female characters in their interaction with Jesus. From these two points that emerge from the Gospels—Christology and characteristics of Christ's followers—I will address two issues for the contemporary church: how Christ's engagements with his followers inform our understanding of men and women in ministry in general and leadership in particular, and how these stellar examples of his followers form Christian disciples—both women and men. Unlike the previous section on Old Testament male and female characters, my treatment of Gospel narratives will not concentrate on applications for complementarity but will focus on Christology and model disciples. Complementarity, then, will emerge from these themes.

Grudem (Wheaton: Crossway, 1991, 2006), 144, 146, 148; H. Wayne House, *The Role of Women in Ministry Today* (Grand Rapids: Baker, 1995) 21, 82; and Samuele Bacchiocchi, *Women in the Church: A Biblical Study on the Role of Women in the Church* (Berrien Springs, MI: Biblical Perspectives, 1987), 47–50. She also references positively James B. Hurley, *Man and Woman in Biblical Perspective* (Grand Rapids: Zondervan, 1981), 82–111.

Jesus and the Centurion (Luke 7:1–10; Matthew 8:5–13)

The occasion that prompted this encounter with Jesus was the imminent death of a highly valued servant of a centurion. According to Luke's detailed account, Jesus engaged indirectly with the man through two groups of emissaries.[2] The first group were Jewish elders whom the centurion sent to bring Jesus to heal the servant. They appealed to the propriety of Jesus's involvement with the centurion because of the soldier's worthiness: "He is worthy for you to grant this, because he loves our nation and has built us a synagogue" (Luke 7:4–5). The second group consisted of friends whom the centurion sent to intercept Jesus as he approached the leader's home. His message to Jesus contradicted the elders' earlier appeal in that it emphasized the man's unworthiness to engage with Jesus: "Lord, *don't trouble yourself*, since *I am not worthy* to have you come under my roof. That is why *I didn't even consider myself worthy* to come to you" (vv. 6–7, emphasis added). His humility expressed itself in extraordinary faith, as the centurion continued: "But say the word, and my servant will be healed. For I too am a man placed under authority, having soldiers under my command. I say to this one, 'Go,' and he goes; and to another, 'Come,' and he comes; and to my servant, 'Do this,' and he does it" (vv. 7–8). Unprecedently, Jesus "marveled at him" (ESV), underscoring, "I tell you, I have not found so great a faith even in Israel" (v. 9). At the return of the centurion's friends, "they found the servant in good health" (v. 10).

This story highlights the importance of remarkable faith, narrating its very definition as obediently trusting the authoritative word of Jesus. The centurion himself was under authority. He had soldiers under his authority. In such a structure, issuing commands—"Go," "Come," "Do

[2] The Matthean account narrates the interaction as taking place directly between Jesus and the centurion.

this"—resulted in appropriate actions of obedience. The centurion trusted that if Jesus, even at a distance, issued a command for his servant to be healed, the servant would be healed. As Jesus told the soldier, "Go. As you have believed, let it be done for you" (Matt 8:13). The centurion's expression of faith prompted amazement on the part of Jesus.

Also highlighted is the value of humility. Though the Jewish elders pleaded with Jesus because of the worthiness of the centurion, he himself reversed their claim: he was unworthy for Jesus to trouble himself and would never presume on the Lord's presence to bless.

To be noted is Jesus's response to humility and remarkable faith: astonishment and healing. These expressions of unworthiness and obedient trust should characterize all of Jesus's disciples, both men and women.

Jesus and the Royal Official (John 4:46–54)

Having performed his first Johannine sign/miracle—turning water into wine—at the wedding in Cana, Jesus returned to that town and encountered "a certain royal official whose son was ill at Capernaum." The man "pleaded with him to come down and heal his son, since he was about to die." Jesus challenged the official, "Unless you people see signs and wonders, you will not believe." Not to be deterred, "the official said to him, 'come down before my boy dies.'" Jesus instructed him to leave, assuring the man, "'your son will live.' The man believed what Jesus said to him" and his son's health began to improve precisely at "the very hour at which Jesus had told him, 'Your son will live.'" Together with his household, the official "himself believed."

This narrative underscores the importance of a tenacious faith. Even when faced with the impending death of his son as well as Jesus's rebuke that believing in him is often (and wrongly) associated with miracles, the official believed that Jesus could heal his son and insisted in faith that Jesus does so. Such persistent faith in the face of obstacles is the proper response of all Jesus's followers, whether men or women.

Jesus and the Man with Leprosy (Mark 1:40–45)

In the midst of his busy ministry, Jesus encountered a leprous man who, falling "on his knees, begged him, 'If you are willing, you can make me clean.' Moved with compassion, Jesus reached out his hand and touched him. 'I am willing,' he told him. 'Be made clean.' Immediately the leprosy left him, and he was made clean." Though Jesus gave the cleansed man strict instructions that he not spread the news of the healing but show himself "to the priest, and offer what Moses commanded for [his] cleansing, as a testimony to them," the man "began to proclaim it widely and to spread the news, with the result that Jesus could no longer enter a town openly." Still, people came to Jesus from everywhere.

This story highlights Jesus's compassion toward a desperate man, a leper whose disintegrating skin Jesus touched, breaking a law of uncleanness. No Jew could touch a leper without becoming ritually unclean. Moreover, the narrative underscores the importance of bearing testimony to Jesus and his work. Though warned by Jesus not to do so, the restored man announced widely the good news of his cleansing. Flowing from a heart of deep gratitude, such proclamation is the appropriate action at the appropriate time (which was not so in this case) of all those who encounter Jesus, whether men or women.

Jesus and the Blind Man/Men (Mark 10:46–52; par. Matt 9:27–31; 20:29–34; Luke 18:35–43)

Another example of Jesus healing people—an intervention that propelled them to bear testimony about him and his work—is his restoring of sight to the blind. While Jesus healed many blind people in his ministry, one narrative, with several different details supplied by the Gospel writers, serves to illustrate.

In this story, Jesus and his disciples were in the vicinity of Jericho when they came upon a blind beggar. According to Mark's account, this man was "Bartimaeus (the son of Timaeus)." In Luke's version, the blind man is unnamed, while in Matthew's narratives, Jesus's encounter is actually with two men.[3] When the protagonist discovers that Jesus was approaching, his cry for help—"Jesus, Son of David, have mercy on me!"—reaped warnings for him to be quiet, to which he responded with further pleas for help. Summoning the man, who "threw off his coat, jumped up, and came," Jesus posed the surprising question, "What do you want me to do for you?", with the thunderous answer obviously being "I want to see." Accordingly, Jesus declared, "Go, your faith has saved you." In the narrative of the two blind men, "Jesus said to them, 'Do you believe that I can do this?' They said to him, 'Yes, Lord.' Then he touched their eyes, saying, 'Let it be done for you according to your faith" (Matt 9:28–30). The narrative concludes with the man's transformation: "Immediately he could see and began to follow Jesus on the road." Luke's version adds that the man glorified God as the crowd of onlookers, "when they saw it, gave praise to God" (Luke 18:43). Additionally, Matthew's account of the two healed men notes that, though Jesus "warned them sternly, 'Be sure that no one finds out'" (Matt 9:30), "they went out and spread the news about him throughout that whole area" (Matt 9:31).

Once again, this narrative underscores the importance of faith. The blind man believes that Jesus can restore his sight, the need that he forcefully articulates when questioned by Jesus, who in turn emphasizes that the man's faith has saved him. In the narrative of the two blind men, Jesus explicitly questions the men as to their faith: "Do you believe that I can

[3] These diverse accounts should not lead to the conclusion that the Bible contains contradictions, resulting in a dismissal of the inerrancy of Scripture. Each Gospel author had his own purpose for writing, reasons for including details (e.g., "Bartimaeus [the son of Timaeus]"; Mark 10:46) or not giving them (e.g., "a blind man"; Luke 18:35). For further discussion see Gregg Allison, "How do we explain seeming inconsistencies between accounts in Scripture?" *Christianity Today Bible Studies*, https://www.christianitytoday.com/biblestudies/bible-answers/theology/inconsistenciesbetweenaccountsscripture.html.

do this?" They believe, their sight is restored, and Jesus underscores, "Let it be done for you according to your faith." Furthermore, the story emphasizes that healing from blindness leads to following Jesus, glorifying God (on the part of both the one healed and those who witnessed the healing), and (even against Jesus's directions) telling others the news about Jesus. Such vivid faith, obedient following, glory giving, and proclamation are the appropriate posture and actions of all those who encounter Jesus, whether men or women.

Jesus and the Deaf and Mute Man (Mark 7:31–37)

A final narrative that presents proclamation as the result of healing is the story of a deaf and (nearly) mute man whom Jesus, taking him from the crowd who accompanied him, drew aside in private. Because the man could not hear, Jesus approached him in an understandable manner: Jesus put "his fingers in the man's ears," spat, and "touched his tongue. Looking up to heaven, he sighed deeply and said to him, 'Ephphatha!' (that is, 'Be opened!'). Immediately his ears were opened, his tongue was loosened, and he began to speak clearly." Though Jesus repeatedly ordered the man and his companions (who were "extremely astonished" by the healing) not to speak of it, they joyfully proclaimed it by praising Jesus: "He has done everything well. He even makes the deaf hear and the mute speak."

As before, Jesus's encounter with this man highlights his personalized compassion, here with a heightened sense: Jesus "sighed deeply" and spoke directly to the man's ears with the command "Be opened!", probably indicating that some demonic activity had devastated the man's ability to hear and speak, a fiendish condition from which Jesus released him. Additionally, as seen before, Jesus's command for silence regarding the miracle went unheeded; joy and praise are very difficult to restrain in the light of such healing on Jesus's part. Accordingly, the restored man and his companions model the proclamation of the good news by all Jesus's followers, both women and men: "He has done everything well."

Jesus and Another Blind Man (Mark 8:22–26)

In another healing of blindness that includes an unusual action on the part of Jesus, a crowd led a blind man and begged Jesus "to touch him. He took the blind man by the hand and brought him out of the village. Spitting on his eyes and laying his hands on him, he asked him, 'Do you see anything?' He looked up and said, 'I see people—they look like trees walking.' Again Jesus placed his hands on the man's eyes. The man looked intently and his sight was restored and he saw everything clearly." The point is not to seek to resolve questions like why Jesus met privately with the man and why Jesus's healing took two steps.[4] Rather, this narrative highlights Jesus's personal, solitary attention for the man and his particular expression of compassion: a physical application to the afflicted eyes of one who could not see. As for the man himself, his response to Jesus's instruction—"Don't even go into the village" (v. 26)—as he sent the man home is ambiguous. If the man's response was to return home without saying a word, then obedience to Jesus is implied—a proper action for both male and female followers of Jesus. Alternatively, knowing the conclusion of narratives that end similarly with an unheeded prohibition about spreading the news of Jesus's healings, and imagining the joy of the crowd who brought the man to Jesus for healing in the first place, one might expect that this restored man and his companions proclaimed the good news everywhere. Again, though prohibited in this case, announcing the good news about Jesus is proper for all Jesus's followers.

Jesus and Still Another Blind Man (John 9:1–7)

This story recounts the travails of "a man blind from birth" whose misfortune prompted a question about whose sin was responsible for his disability.

---

[4] This latter point is probably illustrative of the myopic disciples who continuously "failed to see" Jesus's mission correctly and thus required repeated instruction from him before they could "see" perfectly. C. Clifton Black, *Mark*. Abingdon New Testament Commentaries (Nashville: Abingdon, 2011), 191.

Jesus's redirection of the question to an affirmation about the glory of God's works included a statement about his identity: "I am the light of the world." As such, Jesus performed a glorious divine work: "He spit on the ground, made some mud from the saliva, and spread the mud on his eyes. 'Go,' he told him, 'wash in the pool of Siloam' (which means 'Sent'). So he left, washed, and came back seeing."

The remainder of the lengthy narrative rehearses several confrontations between Jesus's opponents and the man. The Pharisees denounced the miracle because it occurred on a Sabbath (v. 14), further reasoning that Jesus "is not from God, because he doesn't keep the Sabbath" (v. 16). As they interrogated the man as to how his sight was restored, he attributed the miracle to a prophet. Not believing they have a formerly blind man before them, the Pharisees also interrogated his parents, who confirmed that the blind man who now sees was indeed their son. As to the how and the who of the miracle, the parents directed the Pharisees to inquire of their son himself, "because they were afraid of the Jews, since the Jews had already agreed that if anyone confessed him as the Messiah, he would be banned from the synagogue" (v. 22). Summoning the man before them again, the Pharisees asserted that Jesus "is a sinner" (v. 24), to which the healed man answers, "Whether or not he's a sinner, I don't know. One thing I do know: I was blind, and now I can see!" (v. 25). The Pharisees promptly expelled him from the synagogue.

"Jesus heard that they had thrown the man out, and when he found him, he asked, 'Do you believe in the Son of Man?' 'Who is he, Sir, that I may believe in him?' he asked. Jesus answered, 'You have seen him; in fact, he is the one speaking with you.' 'I believe, Lord!' he said, and he worshiped him" (vv. 35–38). The narrative concludes with Jesus leveraging the opportunity to teach about his mission to judge blinding sin (vv. 39–41).

This story portrays much about Jesus himself (the light of the world, the Messiah), the glorious outworking of his mission, his intense confrontation with his enemies, his particular expression of compassion (as with the preceding narrative, Jesus physically applied saliva to the eyes of a blind man), and his theology of sin and divine judgment. The narrative also underscores the steadily progressing faith of the healed man as he moves from ignorance of Jesus's identity to imagining that Jesus is a prophet, and from defending Jesus's restoration of his sight to believing in him as the Son of Man, the Lord, whom he worships. Such growth in knowledge and development of faith is commended for all Jesus's followers, both men and women.

Jesus and the Paralytic Man and Friends (Mark 2:1–12)

In Jesus's hometown of Capernaum, "so many people gathered together that there was no more room, not even in the doorway, and he was speaking the word to them. They came to him bringing a paralytic, carried by four of them. Since they were not able to bring him to Jesus because of the crowd, they removed the roof above him, and after digging through it, they lowered the mat on which the paralytic was lying. Seeing their faith, Jesus told the paralytic, 'Son, your sins are forgiven.'" This pronouncement ignited a storm of protest from the religious leaders, who charged Jesus with blasphemy for his scandalous absolution of the man's sins. Jesus was ready with a frontal challenge: "So that you may know that the Son of Man has authority on earth to forgive sins"—he told the paralytic—"I tell you: get up, take your mat, and go home." As the man—forgiven and healed—walked away, the crowd glorified God for his good work.

As before, this narrative emphasizes the importance of a resolute faith, a believing posture that persists in the face of seemingly insurmountable obstacles, both physical (the man's lameness), logistical (the friends' lack of access to Jesus), and religious (the scribes' charge of blasphemy). This latter hindrance also underscores Jesus's willingness to confront his opponents who, because of their misunderstanding of his divine person and work, sought to interfere with his mission. Such unwavering faith in the God-man and his divine work of healing and forgiving broken people is both the proper posture and the right Christological understanding incumbent upon all Jesus's followers, both men and women.

Jesus and the Man with the Withered Hand (Luke 6:6–11; par. Matt 12:9–14; Mark 3:1–6)

Jesus's opponents not only condemned his claim to forgive sins as blasphemous, they also denounced the healings that he performed on the Sabbath. One example is Jesus's encounter with the man "whose right hand was shriveled." Perceptively aware of the religious leaders' spying on his activities to find cause for accusing him, Jesus asked them, "Is it lawful to do good on the Sabbath or to do evil, to save life or to destroy it?" Though their Sabbath tradition prohibited the Jewish people from working on that day, Jesus's pointed contrast between doing good/saving life (i.e., healing the withered hand) or evil/destroying life (i.e., leaving the man in his disabled condition) left them speechless. Not Jesus, however; he told the man, "Stretch out your hand." As the man obeyed, his shriveled hand was restored to wholeness. By contrast, the religious leaders "were filled with rage and started discussing with one another what they might do to Jesus."

While this story portrays this man in favorable light, its emphasis is on Jesus's compassion and courage to confront a religious system that had devolved from one that bestowed God's grace upon the Jewish people to one that deprived them of divine mercy. According to Mark's account, such a desacralized framework prompted Jesus to be filled "with anger" and be "grieved at the hardness of their hearts" (3:5). With his withered hand deliberately and manifestly restored, the man stood in the center of controversy firmly on the side of Jesus, the proper location for all Jesus's followers, whether men or women.

Jesus and the Disabled Man (John 5:5–16)

Another example of Sabbath-breaking healings involves a man who had been disabled for thirty-eight years. Out of a crowd of infirm people hoping to be healed by being lowered into the pool of Bethesda when its water was stirring,[5] Jesus picked out this man, who responded wrongly to Jesus's surprising invitation: "Do you want to get well?" Commanding the man, "Jesus told him, 'pick up your mat and walk.' Instantly the man got well, picked up his mat, and started to walk." Because this healing occurred on the Sabbath, Jesus's religious critics "said to the man who had been healed [not to Jesus], 'This is the Sabbath. The law prohibits you from picking up your mat.'" The man did not know the identity of his healer, because immediately after healing the man, "Jesus had slipped away into the crowd that was there." Moreover, the restored man seemed to blame Jesus for the fact that his healing took place on the Sabbath, telling his Jewish interrogators, 'The man who made me well told me, 'Pick up your mat and walk.'" Tracking the man down in the temple, Jesus "said to him, 'See, you are well. Do not sin anymore, so that something worse doesn't happen to you.' The man went and reported to the Jews that it was Jesus who had made him well. Therefore, the Jews began persecuting Jesus because he was doing these things on the Sabbath."

This story of healing on the Sabbath illustrates what Jesus affirms elsewhere: "The Sabbath was made for man and not man for the Sabbath. So then, the Son of Man is Lord even of the Sabbath" (Mark 2:27–28).[6] To

---

[5] The text provides the explanation for this hope (John 5:2–3): "By the Sheep Gate in Jerusalem there is a pool, called Bethesda in Aramaic, which has five colonnades. Within these lay a large number of the disabled—blind, lame, and paralyzed." The CSB adds a footnote about the insertion of additional material (vv. 3b–4): "waiting for the moving of the water; because an angel [of the Lord] would go down into the pool from time to time and stir up the water. Then the first one who got in after the water was stirred up recovered from whatever ailment he had."

[6] Another Gospel narrative of Jesus breaking the Sabbath is Luke 14:1–6. Because the narrative is similar to the other stories of healing on the Sabbath treated in this section, it will not be discussed.

teach and restore this truth, Jesus had to violate the pervasive Sabbath tradition that acted as a straitjacket, constricting the Jewish people's flourishing. As for the healed man, his posture of faith (at least implied by the immediacy of his obedience to Jesus's command) was admirable. At the same time, his blaming Jesus for breaking the Sabbath while performing his healing, and his reporting to Jesus's Jewish opponents once he became aware of Jesus's identity, demonstrate the man's remaining obtuseness, which was a culpable offense as it led to the Jews persecuting Jesus. This two-fold theme of faithful reception of Jesus's work intermixed with disconcerting dimwittedness is a regrettable feature of the Gospel characters who are helped by Jesus.

Jesus and the Man with a Demon Possessed Son (Luke 9:37–43)

Several Gospels present narratives of Jesus's encounter with demonically influenced or demon possessed people. While some accounts do not portray any human agency contributing to the good outcome of the story (e.g., Mark 1:21–27; Matt 8:28–33, par. Mark 5:1–20; Luke 8:26–39; Matt 9:32–34; Matt 12:22–32),[7] this story of a man with a son who is demonized serves our purpose well.

Jesus was approached by a man whose only son was demonically tyrannized. Having begged the disciples to cast out the demon—a task at which

[7] Only in Luke's account of the Gerasene demoniac (8:26–39) does the conclusion include human agency, as "the man from whom the demons had departed begged him [Jesus] earnestly to be with him. But he sent him away and said, 'Go back to your home, and tell all that God has done for you.' And off he went, proclaiming throughout the town how much Jesus had done for him" (vv. 38–39). Though so devastatingly influenced by demonic activity that he lacked all human agency, once the man was restored, he sought to stay with Jesus. Sending the man back home, Jesus instructed him—note the difference of directives in this narrative from other narratives in which Jesus enjoined silence—to bear witness to his restoration. In this case, the man used his new agency to obey Jesus and proclaim the good news, a model for all Jesus's followers, both men and women.

they failed—the father implored Jesus to exorcise it. Before ordering the son be brought to him, Jesus scolded, "You unbelieving and perverse generation, how long will I be with you and put up with you?" As the demon launched one last assault on the boy, "Jesus rebuked the unclean spirit, healed the boy, and gave him back to his father. And they were all astonished at the greatness of God."

This narrative, like others involving demonic oppression or possession, underscores Jesus's work of casting out demons. His authority and power—which he exercises "by the Spirit of God" (Matt 12:22–32)—over the demonic realm conquers its dehumanizing evil, liberates the afflicted from torment, and returns them to normal life.[8] That those who follow his ministry—especially his disciples—and who witnessed his many exorcisms continue to fail to understand Jesus and his powerful work perturbs Jesus and calls forth his specific reprimand for their unbelief, their perverse faithlessness. Indeed, when the disciples later question Jesus as to why they were not able to cast out the demon, he chastised them, "Because of your little faith" (Matt 17:20).[9]

This confrontation sets up the contrasting narrative featuring Jesus and the father (Mark 9:21–24):

> "How long has this been happening to him?" Jesus asked his father.
> "From childhood," he said. "And many times it has thrown him into fire or water to destroy him. But if you can do anything, have compassion on us and help us."
> Jesus said to him, "'If you can'? Everything is possible for the one who believes."
> Immediately the father of the boy cried out, "I do believe; help my unbelief!"

---

[8] The narrative details of Mark's account portray the intensity of battle with demonic forces and the wonder of liberation from them.

[9] A textual variant has "because of your unbelief." Some manuscripts include v. 21: "However, this kind [of demon] does not come out except by prayer and fasting."

Jesus rebuked the demon, banished it forever from tormenting the boy, restored the nearly dead boy, and gave him to his father (Luke 9:42).

This narrative underscores that faith is essential. The man's (seemingly innocent) request for compassion—"if you can" exorcise the demon, please intervene—leads to Jesus's focus on and call for faith: "'If you can'? Everything is possible for the one who believes." Unlike the other characters in this story, the father exercises faith, even though he confesses that his belief needs to be strengthened and completed. At the conclusion of Matthew's account, Jesus again underscores this point: "Truly I tell you, if you have faith the size of a mustard seed, you will tell this mountain, 'Move from here to there,' and it will move. Nothing will be impossible for you" (Matt 17:20). Moving from unbelief to belief with Jesus's help, exercising even little faith in an all-powerful Lord, resisting the all too pervasive and culpable mistrust in Jesus's promise of the invincibility of faith—such faithfulness should characterize all Jesus's followers, both women and men.

Though the textual fact stands that the Gospel writers give less prominence to female characters than to male characters, the Gospels clearly underscore the proximity and value of women in the life and ministry of Jesus.[10] As with the preceding treatment of Jesus and male characters, so with this section on Jesus and female characters the main point is the reception (or, in some cases, the rejection) of Jesus and what postures (e.g., faith in him) and/or qualities (e.g., perseverance in trial) are positively (or, in some cases, negatively) portrayed through the female characters in their interaction with Jesus. From these two points that emerge from the Gospels—Christology and characteristics of Christ's followers—I will address two issues for the contemporary church: how Christ's engagements with his followers inform our understanding of men and women in ministry in general and leadership in particular, and how these stellar examples of his followers form Christian disciples—both women and men. As before, my treatment of Gospel narratives will not concentrate on applications for complementarity

---

[10] Much of the following is adapted from Dorothy A. Lee, *The Ministry of Women in the New Testament* (Grand Rapids: Baker Academic, 2021), 15–95.

but will focus on Christology and model disciples. Complementarity, then, will emerge from these themes.

Jesus and His Mother Mary

The biblical portrait of Mary the mother of Jesus is complex and, because of nearly two millennia of tradition and Marian devotion that influences the interpretation of texts narrating her relationship with Jesus, astoundingly diverse. Moreover, unlike the following texts about Jesus and women, the passages that narrate Jesus's interaction with Mary are in a category by themselves because of the mother-son relationship. Keeping these points in mind, I focus on four key areas: (1) the birth narratives (Matt 1:18–25; Luke 1:26–38; 2:1–20); (2) Jesus as an enigma to Mary (John 2:1–12; Luke 8:19–21; Mark 3:20–35); (3) Mary at the cross (John 19:25–27); and (4) Mary in the upper room (Acts 1:12–14).[11]

The Birth Narratives (Matt 1:18–25; Luke 1:26–38; 2:1–20)

The incarnation of the eternal Second Person of the Trinity, God the Son, as the God-man Jesus Christ has both a divine (and primary) aspect and a human (and derivative) aspect, as confessed in the Creed: "he was conceived by the Holy Spirit and born of the virgin Mary." The conception by the Spirit, the divine aspect, is emphasized several times in two Gospels (Matt 1:18; Luke 1:35). Mary's virginity, the human aspect, is affirmed several times as well (Luke 1:26; Matt 1:18, 23, 25).[12]

---

[11] For discussion of Roman Catholic Marian doctrines (e.g., Mary's immaculate conception and bodily assumption), see *Catechism of the Catholic Church*, Part 1, Section 2, Chapter 2, Article 3, Paragraph 2 (484–511) and Part 1, Section 2, Chapter 2, Article 9, Paragraph 6 (963–75). For an evangelical assessment of these doctrines, see Gregg R. Allison, *Roman Catholic Theology and Practice: An Evangelical Assessment* (Wheaton: Crossway, 2014), 132–43, 202–5.

[12] Luke narrates the actual birth of Jesus (2:1–20), which is presented as normal in every way, reminding readers that the miraculous event was Jesus's conception in

These birth narratives emphasize three important points about her. First, her role as *theotokos* should be acknowledged and applauded: Mary, uniquely and wonderfully, is the woman who bore the Son who was fully God.[13] Second, Mary's response of faith and obedience to God's design

---

the womb of the virgin Mary and not his birth. The drama of Mary's traveling while pregnant to Bethlehem, the unavailability of room in the inn, the delivery in the manger, the angel's appearance and proclamation of the good news to the nearby shepherds, the revelation of the multitude of the heavenly host and their voicing praise to God before the shepherds, the shepherds' visit and report to Mary and Joseph, and the shepherds' praising God for his mighty work (which was confirmation by their visit to the manger) underscore the glory of the miraculous event. For Mary's part, Luke offers this simple statement: "Mary was treasuring up all these things in her heart and meditating on them" (2:19).

[13] The affirmation of Mary as *theotokos* prompts me to question the following: "Most extraordinary still is at the end of a list of male begettings[,] God bypasses the male line altogether and effects the incarnation—the presence of Emmanuel, 'God with us,'' (Matt 1:22–23)—through the female line alone (1:16). As a virgin, Mary is the guarantor of Jesus's humanity; he is not half-human and half-divine but wholly human in and through her femaleness, as well as wholly divine. The genealogy is significant for Jesus's adopted father and for the traditions of Abraham and David, which shape Jesus's identity throughout the Gospel [of Matthew]—but his humanity is dependent solely on his mother. Though a man, he is conceived, nurtured, and born only of a woman. That gives the Matthean (and Lukan) Jesus a profound connection with women that other men do not possess. The virginal conception is a key theological point in understanding not only the incarnation but also Jesus's relationship to women." Lee, *The Ministry of Women in the New Testament*, 23. Certainly, and as *theotokos* acknowledges, Jesus's humanity comes from Mary and Mary alone; there is no human father (Joseph) involved. At the same time, *theotokos* in particular, and Christology in general, propose two points for consideration: First, the eternal generation of the Son from the Father (and this classical Trinitarian doctrine has nothing to do with gender but everything to do with begottenness) uniquely, eternally, and profoundly connects the incarnate Son to the Father and, through the redemptive work of adoption, uniquely, eternally, and profoundly connects all Jesus's followers—both women and men—to the triune God—Father, Son, and Holy Spirit. Second, though Scripture does not indicate the physical process by which Mary conceived Jesus, at least some consideration should be given to the view that the Holy Spirit, in overshadowing Mary, provided a sperm with the male chromosome (Y) that fused with Mary's ovum with her female chromosome (X) to produce the fully human male Jesus (XY). If such

for her as communicated through his word should be emulated. To the angel's announcement of divine favor for her and her particular role in God's work of redemption, Mary replies, "Behold, I am the servant of the Lord; let it be to me according to your word" (v. 38 ESV). In Elizabeth's words to her cousin, "Blessed is she who has believed that the Lord would fulfill what he has spoken to her!" (Luke 1:45). This "obedience of faith" is proper for all Jesus's followers, both women and men. Third, Jesus's followers should bless Mary for her stellar example of trusting the Lord. As her Magnificat rehearses,

> My soul magnifies the Lord, and my spirit rejoices in God my Savior,
> because he has looked with favor on the humble condition of his
> servant.
> Surely, from now on all generations will call me blessed, because
> the Mighty One has done great things for me, and his name is
> holy. (Luke 1:46–49)

Mary is blessed because of her role in (the human aspect of) the incarnation, yielding to the work of the Holy Spirit in (the divine aspect of) the redemption of sinful people by the person and work of Jesus Christ.[14]

---

were the case—and there could be no true human Jesus without both X chromosome and Y chromosome—then on one level it would be an overstatement that "God bypasses the male line altogether and effects the incarnation . . . through the female line alone." Certainly, given the absence of sexual intercourse between Mary and Joseph, there is no male contribution in the usual way. But on one view of the working of the Spirit in Mary's conception of Jesus, there is a "male contribution" (a sperm) by way of supernatural provision. Indeed, without that contribution (however it was provided), Jesus could not have been fully human like all other human beings.

[14] As a Jewish son, "when the eight days were completed for his circumcision, he was named Jesus—the name given by the angel before he was conceived" (Luke 2:21). As the ritual of circumcision was being performed, another righteous and devout man, Simon, entered the scene under the guidance of the Holy Spirit, who had revealed to Simon "that he would not see death before he saw the Lord's Messiah" (Luke 2:25–26). Praising God for the fulfillment of that Spirit-given promise, he was now ready for a peaceful death, "For my eyes have seen your salvation. You have

Jesus as an Enigma to Mary (John 2:1–12; Luke 8:19–21; Mark 3:20–35)[15]

Two examples of Mary's misunderstanding of Jesus suffice. First, in John's account of Jesus's first miracle/sign, Mary played an important role at the wedding at Cana (John 2:1–12). "When the wine ran out, Jesus's mother told him, 'They don't have any wine.' 'What has this concern of yours to do with me, woman?' Jesus asked. 'My hour has not yet come.' 'Do whatever he tells you,' his mother told the servants" (vv. 3–5). Though Mary appealed to her maternal relationship with her son to secure his favor, he would not

---

prepared it in the presence of all peoples—a light for revelation to the Gentiles and glory to your people Israel" (2:29–32). At such redemptive-historically significant praise, Jesus's "father and mother were amazed at what was being said about him" (v. 33). Simon then trained his attention on Mary and offered a prophecy: "Indeed, this child is destined to cause the fall and rise of many in Israel and to be a sign that will be opposed—and a sword will pierce your own soul—that the thoughts of many hearts may be revealed" (vv. 34–35). Though righteous and devout, and partially sensing the enormity of the future universal ministry of her infant son, Mary also became painfully aware of what her son's destiny would mean for her own destiny—a shared road of suffering. Luke's narrative closely ties Mary and Jesus together.

Paired with Simon and his prophecy was "a prophetess, Anna, a daughter of Phanuel, of the tribe of Asher. She was well along in years, having lived with her husband seven years after her marriage, and was a widow for eighty-four years. She did not leave the temple, serving God night and day with fasting and prayers. At that very moment, she came up and began to thank God and to speak about him to all who were looking forward to the redemption of Jerusalem" (Luke 2:36–38). Luke presents Anna as a righteous and devout Jewish woman who had foregone remarriage as a widow and faithfully served God in the temple, trusting in his salvation for herself and all who hoped in it.

Though the timing of the visit of the wise men to Bethlehem (Matt 2:1–12) is difficult to establish with certainty (probably within two years after Jesus's birth; 2:13–18), Matthew's account mentions that "they saw the child with Mary his mother" (v. 11). She is in the background as these men worship Jesus and offer gifts to him.

[15] Because the account of Jesus at the age of twelve (Luke 2:41–50) presents him as an enigma not only to his mother but to his father as well, I skip it in favor of presenting Jesus's enigmatic character for Mary in the next discussion.

be thrown off course. In another example (Luke 8:19–21),[16] Jesus was told of his family's wish to see him and responded, "My mother and my brothers are those who hear and do the word of God" (v. 21). Jesus established the true and decisive basis for relating to him: not motherhood or familial bonds but obedient attention to the word of God.

In Mark's Gospel, this incident follows two other narratives that create an even greater distance between Jesus and his misguided mother and family. In the first (Mark 3:20–21), Jesus's family astonishingly believed "He's out of his mind" and sought to restrain him. In the second story (Mark 3:22–30), Jesus's opponents rebukingly announced, "He is possessed by Beelzebul," and, "He drives out demons by the ruler of the demons" (v. 22). Accordingly, Jesus's family considered him to be insane and desired to isolate him socially, and Jesus's enemies attributed his work to demonic empowerment. Importantly for our point, Mary does not understand Jesus and his work.

Accordingly, these Gospel accounts present a profile of Mary that is similar in many respects to the profiles of most characters in the Gospels, including the apostles. She, like Jesus's other disciples, partially grasped his identity, work, and purpose. And she, like Jesus's other disciples, misunderstood his person, ministry, and mission. In one sense, such disconcerting combination of positives and negatives is due to the redemptive-historical moment narrated in the Gospels: Jesus's mother and apostles are on the old covenant/pre-cross side of God's unfolding work, and thus unable to understand.[17] In another sense, this amalgam portrays

---

[16] For a similar rebuke by Jesus referring to Mary but without her being present, see Luke 11:27–28. In an incorrect interpretation, however, Pope John Paul II's *Redemptoris Mater* notes the apparent contrast in Jesus's statement but then rejects it: "Thus we can say that the blessing proclaimed by Jesus is not in opposition, despite appearances, to the blessing uttered by the unknown woman but rather coincides with the blessing in the person of this Virgin Mother" (§20).

[17] For this redemptive-historical reason, caution is urged with respect to the affirmation (based on Luke's birth narrative) that Mary "is, in effect, the first Christian in Luke's narrative, the first to believe in, and respond wholeheartedly

the experience of all Jesus's followers in the already/not-yet reality on this side of the age to come.

Mary at the Cross (John 19:25–27)

Though no other Gospel recounts Mary's presence at the crucifixion, John's Gospel places Mary "standing by the cross of Jesus" along with other women (v. 25). "When Jesus saw his mother and the disciple he loved standing there, he said to his mother, 'Woman, here is your son.' Then he said to the disciple, 'Here is your mother.' And from that hour the disciple took her into his home" (vv. 26–27).

Much Marian tradition and devotion may influence the interpretation of this text, leading to an exaggerated understanding of her person (Mediatrix), status (motherhood of all humanity), and ecclesial role (mother of the Church). However, the leanness of the narrative and its position at the critical moment of Jesus's redemptive-historical work should chasten wrong attributions to Mary and highlight Jesus's atoning sacrifice on behalf of Mary, his disciples, and all women and men since then who follow him.

Mary in the Upper Room (Acts 1:12–14)

Canonically and chronologically, the last narrative about Mary occurs in Luke's second volume of Acts. He lists the names of the eleven apostles (v. 13) and places them in an upstairs room where "they all were continually united in prayer, along with the women, including Mary the mother of Jesus, and his brothers" (1:14). Importantly, their presence assures us that despite their earlier misunderstandings of Jesus and wrongheaded attempts to frustrate his mission, Jesus's family members have become his true disciples, seeking

---

to, God's calling (1:26–38)." Lee, *The Ministry of Women in the New Testament*, 41. From one perspective, not only Mary, but no other follower of Jesus, could be a "Christian" until after his passion, death, burial, resurrection, ascension, and exaltation, and the outpouring of the Holy Spirit on the day of Pentecost.

to do the word and will of God.[18] Luke's additional mention of Mary as part of a group of "the women"—probably including Mary Magdalene, Joanna, Mary the mother of James, and more (Luke 24:10)—is in keeping with his narrative strategy to emphasize the important role women played in the life and ministry of Jesus (e.g., Luke 8:1–3). Thus, while Mary plays an important role at the inauguration of the church, other women make a significant contribution as well.

In summary, these Marian texts call attention to five key points. First, Mary is *theotokos* and should be affirmed by both men and women alike as the unique and wonderful woman who bore the incarnate Son who was fully God. Second, in her response to God's will for her as revealed through his word, Mary through her obedience of faith is to be emulated by both women and men alike. Indeed, third, both male and female followers of Jesus should bless Mary for her stellar example of trusting the Lord, specifically for her role in the incarnation and her yielding to the work of the Holy Spirit.

Fourth, a key reason why the person and work of Christ was an enigma to Mary and most others who interacted with him during his earthy ministry is the salvation-historical reality of pre-cross time and work. Simply put, prior to Jesus's death, burial, resurrection, ascension, and exaltation, along with the outpouring of the Holy Spirit on the day of Pentecost, no one—not even Mary at the foot of the cross—could grasp the nature of Jesus and his mission. Being on this side of the Christ event, however, and aided by divine grace, both men and women may embrace the salvation he accomplished. There is no difference whatsoever between the sexes in terms of access to the gospel and the redemption it brings. Fifth, the presence of the apostles, joined with the participation and prayers of Mary and a number of other key women in the upper room, underscores that from its very outset, the church has consisted of both men and women who make significant contributions to its growth and expansion throughout the world.

---

[18] This happy outcome was left in doubt in both Luke's Gospel (8:19–21) and John's Gospel, which specifies that Jesus's brothers had not believed in him during his lifetime (7:9).

Jesus and Peter's Mother-in-Law (Matt 8:14–15; par. Mark 1:29–31; Luke 4:38–39)

Peter's mother-in-law exhibited disciple-like engagement in hospitality/service when healed by Jesus: "Jesus went into Peter's house and saw his mother-in-law lying in bed with a fever. So he touched her hand, and the fever left her. Then she got up and began to serve (διακονέω, *diakoneō*) him" (Matt 8:14–15; par. Mark 1:29–31). Luke's account supplies three details: the woman (1) suffered from "a high fever" that (2) apparently was caused in some way by demonic activity, as Jesus "stood over her and rebuked [his normal action with respect to demons] the fever, and it left her,"[19] at which release (3) "she got up immediately and began to serve them"—not only Jesus but also those who were with him (Luke 4:38–39). According to many biblical scholars, these narratives underscore the expected, traditional role of female hospitality or/and exemplify the selfless ministry of service, which is the proper response to Jesus on the part of all his followers.[20]

Jesus and the Disabled Woman (Luke 13:10–17)

As seen in narratives of Jesus's restoration of health on the Sabbath, this story involves the Sabbath-healing of a woman who was listening to Jesus's teaching in a synagogue. She was in dire straits, described as having "been disabled by a spirit for over eighteen years. She was bent over and could not straighten up at all." Jesus saw her, called to her ("Woman, you are free of your disability"), and laid his hands on her. "Instantly she was restored and began to glorify God." The synagogue leaders became angry, publicly rebuked Jesus for healing on the Sabbath—the one day in which work should not be done—and directed the awestruck attendees to come for

---

[19] In the preceding narrative, Jesus "rebuked" (ἐπιτίμαω, *epitimaō*) the demonic spirit (Luke 4:35), and in the present narrative he "rebuked" (ἐπιτίμαω, *epitimaō*) the fever, implying that the high fever was caused or at least influenced by demonic activity.

[20] Lee, *The Ministry of Women in the New Testament*, 17–18.

healing on the other six days. Jesus replied with the charge of hypocrisy, as even his opponents "worked" on the Sabbath by caring for their animals. Creating a parallel with the current crisis, Jesus explained, "Satan has bound this woman, a daughter of Abraham, for eighteen years—shouldn't she be untied from this bondage on the Sabbath day?" At Jesus's rebuke, "all his adversaries were humiliated" while the crowd rejoiced at the healing.

This narrative underscores the compassion of Jesus as he singled out a long-suffering woman among the synagogue attendees. Though teaching the crowd, he focused on this particular attendant. From one perspective, Jesus broke the traditional taboo of speaking to and touching a woman. From another perspective, he acted rightly and tenderly toward "a daughter of Abraham," a beloved member of the covenant who had for too long endured demonic torment. Jesus had indeed come to save his Jewish people from both physical disability and demonic debilitation, so his liberation of this dear woman from longstanding demonically caused suffering was proper and worthy of praise.

The restored woman acknowledged Jesus's praiseworthiness, instantly giving glory to God for healing her. In this she was not alone, as "the whole crowd was rejoicing over all the glorious things he was doing." Though her faith is not made explicit, her actions toward Jesus—her agonizingly painful journey to the synagogue to listen to his teaching, her restoration at Jesus's liberation of her disability—bespeak her belief in him. Such faith and praise are models for all Jesus's followers—both women and men.

Jesus and the Hemorrhaging Woman and Jairus's Daughter (Matt 9:18–26; par. Mark 5:21–43; Luke 8:40–56)

The intertwined narratives of two female characters—the one a woman who suffered at length from a hemorrhage, the other a twelve-year-old girl who suffered death—illustrate Jesus's disregard for the religious and cultural taboos of his day and his mercy toward women in desperate need. To summarize the narrative: (1) A distraught man named Jairus, a leader of the Jewish synagogue, pleaded with Jesus, "My daughter just died, but come and lay your hand on her, and she will live." (2) As Jesus went to Jairus's house to tend to the girl, a large crowd pressed against Jesus. (3) An incurably sick woman—she was "suffering from bleeding for twelve years had endured much under many doctors. She had spent everything she had and was not helped at all. On the contrary, she became worse" (Mark 5:25–26)—touched Jesus's outer garment, imagining "If I can just touch his robe, I'll be made well" (Matt 9:21).

(4) Jesus responded, "Have courage, daughter. . . . Your faith has saved you" (Matt 9:22). Immediately, the woman's flow of blood stopped, and she physically sensed that she was healed. (5) Following the woman's touch, Jesus sensed "that power had gone out from him" (Mark 5:30) and inquired as to whom had touched him. "The woman, with fear and trembling, knowing what had happened to her, came and fell down before him, and told him the whole truth. 'Daughter,' he said to her, 'your faith has saved you. Go in peace and be healed from your affliction'" (Mark 5:33–34).

(6) As Jesus was now free to travel with Jairus to confront the earlier trouble, people from the synagogue informed Jairus that his daughter was dead; thus, there was no longer any need to bother Jesus. Even as professional mourners lamented the daughter's death, Jesus urged Jairus, "Don't be afraid. Only believe" (Mark 5:36) and told the crowd to leave "because the girl is not dead but asleep" (Matt 9:24). (7) Taking with him only Jairus, the daughter's mother, Peter, James, and John, Jesus went into the dead girl's room. "Then he took the child by the hand and said to her, 'Talitha koum' (which is translated, 'Little girl, I say to you, get up')" (Mark 5:41–42). Though Jesus "gave strict orders" to the witnesses of the girl's resurrection "that no one should know about this and told them to give her something to eat" (Mark 5:43), they did not heed his command but spread the good news everywhere.

These miraculous stories underscore key considerations for understanding and appreciating women in the life and ministry of Jesus. For one thing, the hemorrhaging woman displayed exemplary faith in the face of seemingly insurmountable obstacles: After twelve years no one had succeeded in healing her, so why should she have expected a different outcome this time? Furthermore, because of her flow of blood, she was ritually unclean, meaning that Jesus, a Jew, could have nothing to do with her without violating religious protocol. Additionally, being a woman, she was an obstacle herself—her very sex—to ever speaking to and being helped by Jesus, a man. Moreover, she was prevented from readily approaching Jesus because of the surging crowd surrounding him. Despite these physical, cultural, and religious hindrances, the woman pushed her way toward Jesus, believing that she would be healed by simply touching his clothing.

Added to this story is the account of the daughter of Jairus. Jesus exhorted this synagogue leader to resist the dread he was feeling at his little girl's tragic death and to trust Jesus instead. Jairus's response of faith, though not made explicit in the text, is assumed as she is raised to life. These accounts highlight the kind of overcoming faith that should characterize all Jesus's followers.

Secondly, these accounts underscore Jesus's compassion for women, a posture that, as just noted, entailed his breaking of numerous taboos. His address to the hemorrhaging woman—"Daughter, your faith has saved you" (Mark 5:34)—expressed his nearness to her and her plight. His tender care for the dead girl (he addressed her with a term of endearment and directed her parents to feed their once-dead daughter) highlights what is found throughout the Gospels: Jesus sees and saves those who are barely present to others.[21]

Jesus and the Syrophoenician Woman (Matt 15:21–28; par. Mark 7:24–30)

Surprisingly, Jesus himself seemed to contradict this point in his conversation with the Canaanite woman who approached him for healing for her

[21] In one of very few instances of Aramaic in his Gospel, Mark provides the *ipsissima verba* of Jesus.

demon-possessed daughter. Jesus initially ignored her, and when his disciples urged him to send her and her bothersome crying away, he responded, "I was sent only to the lost sheep of the house of Israel" (Matt 15:24). Undeterred, she repeated her cry for help. "He answered, 'It isn't right to take the children's bread and throw it to the dogs.' 'Yes, Lord,' she said, 'yet even the dogs eat the crumbs that fall from their master's table.' Then Jesus replied to her, 'Woman, your faith is great. Let it be done for you as you want.' And from that moment her daughter was healed" (Matt 15:26–28).

At first glance, this narrative seems to portray a different stance of Jesus toward outsiders, those who are easily overlooked by everyone else. On further inspection, however, this is an incorrect understanding of what transpired between Jesus and this desperate woman, who "was a Gentile, a Syrophoenician by birth" (Mark 7:26), that is, a stranger to the old covenant people of God. What is more, she is identified as a Canaanite, a descendant of Israel's longtime adversaries. Quite remarkably, then, she pleaded with Jesus with Messianic awareness, calling him "Lord, Son of David!" Both Jesus and his disciples were less than welcoming.

Moreover, Jesus's exchange with the woman began with his appeal to the restricted scope of his mission ("I was sent only to the lost sheep of the house of Israel"), exclusive and exclusionary words that were intended to silence her and send her away (a futile attempt!). Drawing a metaphorical application from his specific mission, Jesus underscored the impropriety of feeding the bread that properly belongs to the children—that is, healing for the Jewish people whom he came to save—to the dogs, that is, Gentiles like this woman. Rather than taking offense or getting angry, the woman masterfully completed Jesus's metaphor—even the dogs get the breadcrumbs—with its implied application: Jesus can carry out his mission unabated while still healing her daughter. Her unexpected response prompted Jesus to send her away ("Because of this reply, you may go"; Mark 7:29), not empty-handed as was the original plan but satisfied with the granting of her entreaty: "The demon has left your daughter" (Mark 7:29). What accounts for the change of outcomes? In one of only two cases (the other is the centurion, Matt 8:10) in which Jesus emphasized the unusual quality of people's response to him, "Jesus replied to her, 'Woman, *your faith is great.* Let it be done for you as you want'" (Matt 15:28).[22] The woman's daughter was healed/released from demonic oppression.

As with the other narratives of Jesus and women, this story highlights a woman's exemplary faith despite several cultural barriers as well as attempts to deter her from obtaining what she desperately wanted. The specific cultural hurdles were her gender (a woman in a highly male-dominant society), her race/ethnicity (a member of the hated Canaanites), and her religion (a Gentile rather than Jew). The attempts to detour her were at the hands of Jesus and his disciples. Though initially rejecting her overtures on account of his missional purposes, Jesus was won over. Indeed, he is presented as engaging meaningfully with the woman—an interaction unheard of in their context—and responding to her exemplary faith with exceptional commendation—exactly as is narrated of him throughout the Gospels. Furthermore, her faith in Jesus's power to rescue her daughter corresponded to her unexpected knowledge of his messianic identity and was exhibited as resilient faith by her verbal sparring with him. She affirmed his exclusive messianic mission while underscoring that Jesus can also minister mightily to people other than those whom he specifically came to heal/save. Her "great faith" was nearly unprecedented, shared narratively with only one other Gospel character, himself a gentile like she was.

Moreover, as with the other narratives of Jesus and women, this story underscores Jesus's compassion for women, a posture that required him to violate several cultural norms. As a man, he should not speak with a woman; as a Jew, he should not engage with a Gentile; as the Jewish Messiah on an exclusive mission, he should not reach out to a Gentile woman who was a stranger to the covenant people of God. Yet, breaking cultural taboos is

[22] In both cases of Jesus's commendation of "great faith," the Roman centurion and the Syrophoenician woman are non-Jews, increasing the unlikelihood of their trust. On more occasions, Jesus rebukes his disciples as "men of little faith" (Matt 6:30; 8:26; 14:31; 16:8).

exactly what Jesus did. Yes, this story is one of the few narrated that portrays Jesus going outside his (purposefully) restricted ministry.[23] But Jesus's healing of the Syrophoenician woman's daughter was a foretaste of the mission that he would give to his church: the Great Commission, making disciples of men and women, Jews and Gentiles, outsiders and insiders, and all other differences that are contrary to his gospel (Matt 28:18–20).

Jesus and the Widowed Woman (Luke 7:11–17)

Another narrative about Jesus and women is the story of his interaction with the woman of Nain, to whom he showed deep concern. Approaching the town of Nain, Jesus came upon a funeral procession of an only son of a widow. Moved with compassion, he halted the procession and said, "Young man, I tell you, get up!" Jesus gave back the restored man to his mother, prompting fear and praise for God's kindhearted intervention.

Once again, this story emphasizes the compassion of Jesus toward a woman who, in this case, was a widow without the support of a husband and who had just lost her only son; thus, she was without any assistance in her life. Jesus sought to relieve her burden ("Don't weep," possibly a call to her to have faith in him), halted the funeral procession, and raised the man from the dead. Tenderly, Jesus gave the resurrected son to his helpless mother, whose only worldly hope was thereby restored. As Dorothy Lee explains, "Jesus shows deep concern for the particular vulnerabilities of an unsupported woman in a male-oriented world."[24] Furthermore, she and the crowd of mourners, awestruck with fear, turned their attention to

---

[23] As Christopher Wright explains, "Jesus' earthly ministry was launched by a movement that aimed at the restoration of *Israel*. But he himself launched a movement that aimed at the ingathering of the *nations* to the new messianic people of God. The *initial impetus* for his ministry was to call Israel back to their God. The *subsequent impact* of his ministry was a new community that called the nations to faith in the God of Israel." Christopher J. H. Wright, *The Mission of God: Unlocking the Bible's Grand Narrative* (Downers Grove: IVP Academic, 2006), 506.

[24] Lee, *The Ministry of Women in the New Testament*, 45.

the one who had divinely intervened with this miracle: they glorified God, acknowledging (even without a full understanding) that the miracle working Jesus was in some way the fulfillment of the messianic hopes: a prophet who would bring divine revelation and who himself, as Immanuel, would be God with his people.

While the narrative largely focuses on Jesus and his work of resurrecting the widow's son, the woman herself reacts to this intervention with (implied) faith, praise directed to God, and acknowledgement of Jesus's identity as prophet and Immanuel. Such responses, even if partial, are proper for all Jesus's followers, both women and men.

Jesus and the Samaritan Woman (John 4:1–42)

As "God among us," Jesus pursued his divinely ordained work into Samaria ("He had to travel through Samaria") where he (alone, because of his disciples' departure to obtain food) met a solitary Samaritan woman at Jacob's well about noontime. Because he was thirsty after a long journey, Jesus asked for a drink from the woman. Expressing common protocol for such a conversation, she wondered why he, a Jewish man, was asking for a drink from her, a Samaritan woman ("for Jews do not associate with Samaritans"). Speaking enigmatically about a non-physical water that would lead to eternal life, Jesus uncovered the truth about the woman's husband or, better, five husbands. After the ensuing discussion about the location of divinely approved and divinely sought worship, "the woman said to him, 'I know that the Messiah is coming' (who is called Christ). 'When he comes, he will explain everything to us.' Jesus told her, 'I, the one speaking to you, am he.'"

Upon their return, the disciples "were amazed that he was talking with a woman," who promptly "left her water jar, went into town, and told the people, 'Come, see a man who told me everything I ever did. Could this be the Messiah?' They left the town and made their way to him." Following a conversation between Jesus and his disciples about feeding on physical food or feeding on food that "is to do the will of him who sent me [Jesus] and to finish his work"—that is, sowing and reaping "fruit for eternal life"—the narrative concludes with an acknowledgment that much fruit had been harvested because of the woman's testimony about her encounter with Jesus. Jesus himself spoke the good news to the Samaritans, who relayed to the woman, "We no longer believe because of what you said, since we have heard for ourselves and know that this really is the Savior of the world."

This narrative features the divinely ordained nature of Jesus's mission: Geographically speaking, he did not have to travel through Samaria. In fact, commonly, Jews would take a longer route so that they would not have to journey through that region. But missionally speaking, Jesus had to take that route. Such compulsion was due to his Father's will, which was the food that Jesus longed to eat. Shockingly, this mission led to an encounter that was rife with taboos: First, Jesus as a lone man should not have been talking with a woman (his disciples represented this taboo, as "they were amazed that he was talking with a woman" 4:27) who, in this particular case, may have been of questionable character due to her highly unusual, solo appearance at the well at noon rather than earlier in the day in the company of other women. Second, Jesus as a Jew should not have been engaging with a Samaritan. But Jesus broke such taboos, despite the shame and complaints such an encounter could bring his way. His mission to fulfill his Father's will in regard to this woman required him to confront such cultural, ethnic, and religious prohibitions—and overturn them.

As for this woman herself, the narrative highlights both her perplexedness as she encounters Jesus—she drew attention to his violation of protocol, and she was baffled by his knowledge of her relationships with men—and her halting understanding of Jesus: She misunderstood his lesson about water and eternal life, then she recognized him as a prophet. Next, she wondered with him about the nature of proper worship, then she made a vague reference to the future Messiah, who Jesus affirmed himself to be. Whatever her wavering understanding may have been, it was enough for others to believe in Jesus. Spectacularly, her simple testimony yielded to Jesus's own testimony about himself, which in turn yielded a great harvest of people who "know that this [Jesus] really is the Savior of the world." Then and now, both women and men—hearing personal testimonies, hearing the good news of Jesus—come to faith in Jesus.

General Narratives about Jesus Healing Men and Women (Luke 4:40–41; par. Matt 8:16–17; Mark 1:32–34)

While the above narratives specifically recount Jesus's intervention to heal either a man or a woman, several summaries in the Gospels underscore that Jesus's ministry was directed at hundreds, if not thousands, of people, both women and men without distinction. As Luke recaps, "When the sun was setting, all those who had anyone sick with various diseases brought them to him [Jesus]. As he laid his hands on each one of them, he healed them. Also, demons were coming out of many, shouting and saying, 'You are the Son of God!' But he rebuked them and would not allow them to speak, because they knew he was the Messiah."[25]

Jesus and the Women at his Death and Resurrection

The four Gospels narrate the events of Jesus's death and resurrection and recount the important role that several women exercised in these happening. The four accounts describe in detail Jesus's death (Matt 27:50; Mark

---

[25] In a particular narrative rather than a summary, Matthew recounts, "When they [Jesus and his disciples] had crossed over, they came to shore at Gennesaret. When the men of that place recognized him, they alerted the whole vicinity and brought to him all who were sick. They begged him that they might only touch the end of his robe, and as many as touched it were healed" (Matt 14:34–36). Whether the phrase "the men of that place" (οἱ ἄνδρες τοῦ τόπου ἐκείνου; *hoi andres tou topou ekeinou*) refers to men only as the initiators of the alert, the entire locale—probably both men and women—was informed and that extensive group—probably both men and women—brought the sick to Jesus, who healed all—probably both men and women—who touched the end of his robe.

15:37; Luke 23:44–46; John 19:28–37),[26] with the Synoptic Gospels noting that "all who knew him, including the women who had followed him from Galilee, stood at a distance, watching these things" (Luke 23:49). Matthew's Gospel lists a few of these women: "Mary Magdalene, Mary the mother of James and Joseph, and the mother of Zebedee's sons" (27:55–56). Mark has them as "Mary Magdalene, Mary the mother of James the younger and of Joses, and Salome [whom some commentators understand to be "the mother of James and of Joses]," adding the detail that "in Galilee these women followed him and took care of him [literally, "ministered to/served him," διηκόνουν αὐτῷ, *diēkonoun autō*]. Many other women had come up with him to Jerusalem" (Mark 15:40–41).[27]

Next, Joseph of Arimathea attended to the lifeless body of Jesus, placing it in his tomb (Matt 27:57–60; Mark 15:42–46; Luke 23:50–53; John 19:38).[28] Again, the Synoptic Gospels note the presence of women at this event, with Luke giving the most details: "It was the preparation day, and the Sabbath was about to begin. The women who had come with him from Galilee followed along and observed the tomb and how his body was placed.

---

[26] John's Gospel includes the details of not breaking Jesus's bones, the piercing of Jesus's side, and the issue of water and blood, in fulfillment of Scripture (John 19:31–37).

[27] Given the semantic range of "to minister/serve" (διακονεῖν, *diakonein*), Lee may overstate the case: "This is the same verb we have found elsewhere to describe the core work of Christian ministry. It is the same ministry that defines the work of Jesus, including not only his teaching and healing but also his journey to the cross. It sums up what it means for Jesus to live and die as Savior, and it articulates the form and practice of the ministry bequeathed to his community of disciples." Lee, *The Ministry of Women in the New Testament*, 28–29. Certainly, *diakonein* may have this connotation, but it may also be used with respect to angels *caring for* Jesus after his temptation (Matt 4:11), Peter's mother-in-law *serving* Jesus after he healed her (Matt 8:15), and the unrighteous seeing "Jesus" (i.e., "the least of these") "hungry, or thirsty, or a stranger, or without clothes, or sick, or in prison" yet failing *to help* him (Matt 25:44). The specific connotation of *diakonein* is not brought out in this context.

[28] John's Gospel includes the details of Joseph and Nicodemus preparing Jesus's body in light of the approaching Sabbath (John 19:39–42).

Then they returned and prepared spices and perfumes. And they rested on the Sabbath according to the commandment" (Luke 23:54–56). The other two Synoptics specify that Mary Magdalene and Mary the mother of Joses were facing the tomb and watching where Jesus was laid (Matt 27:61; Mark 15:47). The last event prior to resurrection Sunday was the securing of Jesus's tomb by the guard, narrated only by Matthew (27:62–66).

Turning to the events narrated after Jesus's resurrection, a summary follows: Several women—Mary Magdalene, Mary the mother of James the younger and of Joseph/Joses, and Salome [perhaps "the mother of James and of Joses"]—came to his tomb after the Sabbath ready to anoint his body for burial. Discovering the stone had been rolled away from the tomb's opening (Mark 16:1–4),[29] and being addressed by an angel/angels, the women became terrified (Luke 24:3–5).[30] The angel's/angels' announcement to the women assured them that the once crucified Jesus had risen from the dead, in accordance with his promise/prophecy (Matt 26:32) to them after the Last Supper and before the garden of Gethsemane (Luke 24:5–8; Matt 28:5–6; Mark 16:6–7). Commissioned to tell the news to Jesus's disciples, the women left the tomb to report to the Eleven (Luke 24:9–10).[31] Filled with fear and great joy, they became the first to announce the resurrection. Jesus himself appeared to them, also instructing them to direct his many followers to meet him in Galilee. While Matthew's account (Matt 28:8–10) of Jesus's appearance seems redundant, echoing the angelic instructions given to the women, its repetitive nature seems to underscore "the importance of the women's commission. They are the first to meet the

---

[29] This event did not let Jesus's resurrected body out of the tomb but made it possible for the women to enter and observe that the tomb no longer contained the body of the resurrected Jesus.

[30] Mark's Gospel focuses on "one man" (i.e., angel): "When they entered the tomb, they saw a young man dressed in a white robe sitting on the right side; they were alarmed" (Mark 16:5).

[31] Mark's Gospel ends surprisingly: "They [the women] went out and ran from the tomb, because trembling and astonishment overwhelmed them. And they said nothing to anyone, since they were afraid" (Mark 16:8).

Risen Lord, to fall at his feet in worship, and to be given the commission to proclaim the resurrection."[32]

The women did as Jesus charged them: "Mary Magdalene, Joanna, Mary the mother of James, and the other women with them were telling the apostles these things. But these words seemed like nonsense to them, and they did not believe the women" (Luke 24:9–11). Because of the cultural rejection of testimonies by women, the disciples did not believe them. Thus, Peter and John confirmed for themselves the empty tomb (John 20:3–10; Luke 24:12).[33]

John's Gospel narrates Jesus's specific appearance to Mary Magdelene. Discovering the stone's removal from the tomb's entrance, and assuming its displacement meant that someone had stolen Jesus's body such that it could not be properly anointed with spices and buried, Mary wept for her loss (John 20:11–13). Jesus appeared to Mary, though she failed to recognize him, mistaking him for the gardener (vv. 14–15). When Jesus called her by her name, Mary recognized him as "Teacher" and clutched him, apparently to prevent him from leaving her. As his ascension was still a way off, Jesus told her not to cling to him but to tell his disciples that he is present but would be departing (v. 17). Obediently, Mary Magdalene announced to the disciples "I have seen the Lord!" and recounted his post-resurrection words to her.

In the climactic events of Jesus Christ's ministry, his death as an atoning sacrifice for sin and his resurrection for the justification of sinful people, women played such an important role that the four Gospels prominently

---

[32] Lee, *The Ministry of Women in the New Testament*, 31.

[33] John's Gospel details that Peter and John ran to the tomb, with John being the first to arrive and to see Jesus's graveclothes and head wrapping no longer clothing a body but simply lying in the tomb. The narrative continues: "The other disciple [John], who had reached the tomb first, then also went in, saw, and believed. For they did not yet understand the Scripture that he must rise from the dead" (John 20:8–9). In his narrative of Jesus's appearance to the two disciples on the road to Emmaus, Luke includes this detail of the women's report to the disciples and their confirmation of the empty tomb (Luke 24:21–24).

highlight who they were and what they did. Their presence in these earth-shattering events was not unique or unexpected, as these women had followed and served/ministered to Jesus from his earliest days in Galilee. While the disciples (John was the lone exception) had fled before Jesus was executed, these women (including his own mother, Mary) had courageously looked on as the ghastly crucifixion unfolded. To be recalled is the fact that one of these women, the mother of Zebedee's sons, was the one who earlier had made the wrongheaded request that Jesus might promise to install her sons in positions of authority in his kingdom (Matt 20:20–23).[34] As Lee points out, "There is a small parable here. The sons disappear at Jesus's arrest along with the other male disciples and are not present at the cross (Matt 26:56b). Their mother, by contrast, remains courageously with Jesus in his suffering and death. Her understanding has changed since her first appearance. She has now grasped the message of the cross that James and John have as yet failed to understand."[35]

These women had observed Jesus's entombment, prepared spices for his burial, approached the tomb to anoint his body, heard the angel's/angels' announcement of Jesus's resurrection, seen the risen Lord, embraced the commission to report to his disciples, and were the first to proclaim the resurrection. However, the disciples, who had stood far off from the reality of these events, did not believe their testimony.

To our modern sensitivities, the disciples' rejection of the women's testimony to the resurrection is both harsh and demeaning. Given the context, however, their dismissal of the report may have been motivated by several factors, not all of which were disgraceful. One reason was due to the obvious fact that dead people do not rise from the dead and live again. Thus, for the women to assert such a miracle in regard to Jesus would have been incredible, seeming like nonsense to the disciples. A second reason was that the disciples, throughout Jesus's three-year ministry, did not grasp that his

---

[34] The parallel in Mark's Gospel does not mention their mother but recounts "James and John, the sons of Zebedee" making the request of Jesus (Mark 10:35).

[35] Lee, *The Ministry of Women in the New Testament*, 26.

mission would entail his death and resurrection. On multiple occasions when Jesus taught on his impending crucifixion and subsequent resurrection, the disciples did not believe him (e.g., Matt 16:21–23; Luke 9:44–45; 18:31–34). Accordingly, when the women testified that Jesus had risen from the dead, the disciples thought it was nonsense.

A third reason was typical and even culturally appropriate for the disciples: any testimony from a woman was considered to be unreliable and thus to be rejected. According to Josephus, "But let not a single witness be credited, but three, or two at the least, and those such whose testimony is confirmed by their good lives. But let not the testimony of women be admitted, on account of the levity and boldness of their sex."[36] Celsus, a second century critic of Christianity, chastised it for being grounded on untrustworthy testimony to Jesus's resurrection:

> But who really saw this [the resurrection]? A hysterical woman, as you admit and perhaps one other person—both deluded by his sorcery, or else so wrenched with grief at his failure that they hallucinated him risen from the dead by a sort of wishful thinking. . . . When he was in the body, he was disbelieved but preached to everyone; after his resurrection, apparently wanting to establish a strong faith, he chooses to show himself to one woman and a few comrades only.[37]

Incredible as it seemed at the time, the women's announcement of the resurrection of Jesus was the truth. Peter and John confirmed its factuality. The

---

[36] Flavius Josephus, *Antiquities of the Jews*, trans. William Whiston (St. Paul, MN: Wilder Publications, 2018), 4:219. Not only were women excluded from giving testimony, as the legal notice next in order states: "Nor let servants be admitted to give testimony, on account of the ignobility of their soul; since it is probable that they may not speak truth, either out of hope of gain, or fear of punishment." Josephus, *Antiquities* 4:219.

[37] Origen, *Contra Celsum* 2.59, 70, in Henry Chadwick, *Origen: Contra Celsum* (Cambridge: Cambridge University, 1953), 112, 120. R. Joseph Hoffmann, *Celsus on the True Doctrine* (New York: Oxford University Press, 1987), 67–68.

Eleven minus Thomas believed it to be true (John 20:24–25). The Eleven including Thomas affirmed its truth (vv. 26–29). Jesus "appeared to over five hundred brothers and sisters at one time," confirming his resurrection (1 Cor 15:6). The resurrection of Jesus, first proclaimed by his women followers and subsequently announced by his apostles, is at the core of the gospel that both women and men continue to proclaim throughout the world today.

Conclusions from Jesus's Engagement with Men and Women in the Gospels

The Gospels recount Jesus's engagement with men and women to teach all who read these narratives two principal points: first, the identity of Jesus as Messiah and Savior and the work that he accomplished, which included breaking religious and cultural taboos that marginalized many people from divine blessing and human flourishing; and second, the responses of those who encountered Jesus as demonstrating the attitudes and actions that should characterize all of Jesus's followers.

First, as for the identity of Jesus as Messiah and Savior, these narratives encourage us to make several affirmations: (1) At the heart of Jesus's healing was compassion, but of a particular kind. The details of these miracles prompt us to appreciate Jesus's personalized compassion, that is, his specific approach to healing that depended on the illness, oppression, or suffering of those whom he sought to heal. For our purposes, Jesus loved both men and women not as gendered categories but as individual male and female image bearers. In the latter case, he saw and rescued divinely loved women who were barely present to others. (2) In most cases, Jesus directed those who were healed not to broadcast their miracle but to remain silent. This unexpected silencing of the recipients of his care reminds us that Jesus's ultimate work was not physical restoration, as good as that might be, but redemption for incorporation into the kingdom of God. Indeed, he warned people not to misconstrue his healing, underscoring the wrongheadedness of reliance on miracles and pushing people to believe in himself. Jesus healed both women and men so they would become citizens of the kingdom that he was building.[38]

(3) This was the mission on which he was sent by the Father; thus, Jesus's inclusion of both men and women in his glorious good works reveals the Father's love for both women and men. The popular notion that, by his crucifixion, the loving and merciful Jesus won over the just and wrathful Father is wrong not only as applied to the Son's death but also to his entire life, as demonstrated by his healings.[39] (4) As his healings provoked the outrage of his opponents, Jesus exhibited fearlessness in carrying out his mission and courage to confront and denounce his enemies. He challenged insidious taboos by reaching out and restoring the castaways of the religious and social systems of his day. These misguided protocols included the laws of uncleanness (e.g., the leper), Sabbath restrictions (e.g., the man by the pool of Bethesda), proscriptions of speaking with and touching women (e.g., the Samaritan woman), the religious/ethnic division between Jews and Gentiles (e.g., the Syrophoenician woman), and social disregard for the poor and disenfranchised (e.g., the widow of Nain). By his courageous compassion, Jesus rescued many people who were marginalized, cut off from divine blessing and human flourishing. For our purpose, Jesus healed both men and women, and while the first type did not elicit concern because Jesus was male, the second type cost Jesus because it entailed breaking barriers that prohibited him from such contact.

Second, as for the responses of those who encountered Jesus, these narratives underscore the attitudes and actions that should characterize all of Jesus's followers. They include the following: (1) A tenacious/persistent/marvel-provoking/great faith in Jesus, one that resists and overcomes the

---

[38] According to Mark's Gospel, Jesus told his disciples who urged him to meet a growing crowd of people who desired healing, "Let's go on to the neighboring villages so that I may preach there too. This is why I have come" (Mark 1:38).

[39] These healings, then, are another reason to reject the common "Jesus versus the Father" caricature.

dread of potential and/or actual loss. At the same time, a little faith may be adequate, with the expectation that it will lead to a steadily progressive understanding of Jesus and a growing trust in him. (2) Bearing witness to Jesus and giving glory to God by proclaiming what Jesus did in saving them. (3) Serving Jesus and his people, with hospitality particularly emphasized (e.g., Peter's mother-in-law). (4) Deep gratitude and joy. (5) Obedience in following Jesus. (6) Embracing the forgiveness extended by Jesus. (7) Attention to and trust in the word of God. (8) Yielding to the Holy Spirit and the will of God. More than just the narrated responses to encountering Jesus, these characteristics and conducts emerge from the stories as indicators of the expected and proper responses to the Savior and the salvation he offers for all his followers.[40]

This substantial treatment of Gospel stories that present the proximity and value of women in the life and ministry of Jesus intersects with complementarity, complementarianism, and egalitarianism. (1) For some, these narratives reinforce the stereotypical concept of women and their roles that was pervasive in the Greco-Roman world of Jesus and his followers. (2) Others, while starting with the first consideration, add that these stories are primarily if not exclusively Christological in orientation; that is, they affirm important aspects of the character and mission of Jesus who, in their estimation, breaks numerous cultural barriers to reach out to women in his context. These narratives underscore who Jesus is and what Jesus does: he is compassionate toward women in desperate, life-threatening situations; tender with respect to women in their brokenness; and sharply aware of women's vulnerabilities and deep needs. In both (1) and (2), the women's responses to Jesus are typical of (a) what would be expected in light of his

[40] Though not the focus of our attention, wrong reactions to Jesus and his work arise from these narratives and serve as counter examples, warnings to readers as to how not to respond to Jesus. They include the following: (1) A lack of understanding or a misunderstanding of Jesus and his mission. (2) An absence of faith. (3) Hardness of heart. (4) Capitulation to religious and cultural taboos that opposed Jesus's mission.

divine intervention (faith, thanksgiving) and/or (b) what would be expected of women in that first century context (service, hospitality).

(3) Still others consider these narratives as portraying both Christological truths and female models of faith and discipleship—models that are instructive for all followers of Jesus, both female and male. (4) Finally, these narratives lead some to affirm that (a) just as Jesus included them in all aspects of his ministry, despite the cost to him in terms of challenging contemporary cultural norms and breaking taboos in the process of including women in his life and ministry, so (b) the church today should include women in all aspects of its ministry, not only to and for other women, but even the highest positions of leadership, whether those are the pastorate/eldership, priesthood, bishopric, and/or diaconate.

On this last position, which is still highly debated today and not advancing adequately in the way envisioned by those who advocate for full inclusion of women in the highest church offices, I suggest that it needs some clarification. If rendered as a logical argument, the position requires several steps between its premise and its conclusion. That is:

> *premise*: according to narratives in the Gospels, Jesus fully included women in his life and ministry;
>
> *conclusion*: the contemporary church should include women in all aspects/highest levels of its leadership.

The explicit steps to be inserted between the premise and conclusion are something along these lines:

> *step 1*: a justification for moving from Gospel narratives, which highlight the exemplary faith and discipleship of Jesus's followers (both women and men), not only to a conclusion about women as consummate believers but especially to their inclusion in ministry in general;
>
> > *step 1a*: certainly, women were significantly involved in Jesus's ministry, but their involvement was never at the level of

engagement by the Twelve, who were specifically chosen and being prepared to minister in and exercise leadership for the post-Pentecost church;

step 1b: moreover, the nature of Jesus's ministry changed significantly from his earthly work to that of his post-Pentecost church, so an explanation is needed for how this significant transition affects women and their engagement in this altered, ongoing ministry;

step 1c: given that the emphasis in the Gospels is the person and work of Jesus Christ, warrant is needed for the move from this prevalent Christology to ecclesiology, which directly addresses the matter of women in ministry;

step 2: a justification for moving from the inclusion of women in ministry in general to their inclusion in all aspects/highest levels of church leadership;

step 2a: certainly, the ministries of these Gospel women focused on hospitality, financial support, and other forms of service, and the women were exemplary followers of Jesus for these very activities, but warrant is needed for transposing these commendable ministries in general into ministry in all aspects/the highest levels of church leadership;

step 2b: certainly, women were the first recipients of Jesus's post-resurrection appearances, preceding even those to the Twelve, but justification is needed for how such a phenomenon translates into women serving in all aspects/highest levels of church leadership;

By providing these steps, the gap between premise and conclusion will be removed.

Further work is also needed with regard to the position that it is incoherent to embrace both men and women in full membership of the church and at the same time prohibit women from all aspects/highest levels of church leadership. A biblical example questions the incompatibility of these two realities: Was it incoherent to embrace the full and equal inclusion of both female and male Israelites in the old covenant people of God *and* acknowledge the divinely directed restriction of the priestly ministry/office to male only members of the Aaronic/Levitical tribe? According to old covenant stipulations, there was no discrepancy in this regard; indeed, the limitation was God-ordained. If membership in Israel and the restriction of the priesthood to men were not incompatible, some warrant needs to be provided for the charge that membership in the church and the restriction of its leadership to men is incoherent.[41]

By means of these steps and the resolution of the matter of incompatibility, the conclusion holds.

At the same time, the position that views that these Gospel narratives as portraying both Christological truths and female models of faith and discipleship has significant work to do to ensure that such models are actually instructive for all followers of Jesus, both female and male. Again, if rendered as a logical argument, the position requires several steps between its premise and its conclusion. That is:

> *premise*: according to narratives in the Gospels, the women with whom Jesus interacted were exemplary models of faith and discipleship;
>
> *conclusion*: the contemporary church should look to and teach about these consummate believers, holding them up as examples for both women and men.

The explicit steps to be inserted between the premise and conclusion are something along these lines:

> *step 1*: a justification for moving from Gospel narratives, which highlight the exemplary faith and discipleship of Jesus's followers

[41] One such warrant could be the change from the old covenant to the new covenant.

(both women and men), to a specific view of women as consummate believers;

> *step 1a*: to be noted is a phenomenon in the Gospel of Mark that all its women characters are unnamed and are the heroines of their stories, eclipsing by far its male characters, so this emphasis supports viewing Gospel women as model followers of Jesus Christ;[42]
>
> *step 1b*: also to be noted is a phenomenon in the Gospel of Luke, which "seems to accord women a high status, with significantly more female characters than any of the other Gospels," thus confirming the above step (*1 a*) in support of viewing Gospel women as consummate believers;[43]
>
> *step 1c*: the disproportionately lesser presence of faithful, heroic male characters in the Gospels should not lead to the conclusion that no male characters provide exemplary models of faith and discipleship (such is in fact not the case [e.g., the centurion; Matt 8:5–13; Luke 7:1–10], and reverse sex polarity is not a viable solution in light of complementarity), but it does provide a background for viewing the Gospel women as stellar examples;[44]

step 2: a justification for moving from the specific view of women as consummate believers to embracing them as examples for both women and men in the contemporary church;

---

[42] As noted by Abraham Kuruvilla: "Indeed, the women in this Gospel shine far brighter than the Twelve men. See on the woman with the hemorrhage (5:25–34), the Syrophoenician woman (7:25–30), the widow and her coins (12:38–44), and the woman who anoints Jesus (14:1–11)—all positive models of discipleship. Abraham Kuruvilla, *Mark: A Theological Commentary for Preachers* (Eugene, OR: Cascade, 2012), 38n13.

[43] Lee, *The Ministry of Women in the New Testament*, 37.

[44] These thoughts have their origin in a personal conversation with my colleague, Abraham Kuruvilla, on August 29, 2023.

step 2a: to be overcome is a more or less pronounced valuation of the Gospels as historical presentations that are true (inerrant), primarily or exclusively about the person and work of Christ, and thus only slightly applicable (or inapplicable) in terms of their narrative characters for the contemporary church's faith and discipleship;

step 2b: to be overcome is a more or less prominent view that Gospel narratives that feature women characters are primarily if not exclusively for women in the church today but not men;

By providing these steps, the gap between premise and conclusion will be removed and the conclusion holds.

CHAPTER 17

New Testament Considerations: Acts

The Acts of the Apostles highlights the valued ministries of both men and women in the early church. As she compares Luke's treatment of women in his first writing with that in his second volume, Dorothy Lee notes, "Women are significantly less prominent in Acts than they are in the Gospel in terms of number and visibility. . . . [A] key question here is whether Luke ultimately gives any place to women's leadership in the community or whether he reflects a later context where patriarchal control is being reestablished and projected back onto the past in the story of the early church."[1] While that question will not occupy our attention, it contributes to the debate between egalitarians and complementarians and will be raised at the end of this chapter. As always, my focus will be Acts' contribution to complementarity. Unlike my approach to Jesus's interactions with characters in the four Gospels, where I first treated his engagement with men followed by his encounters with women, in this section I will

[1] Dorothy A. Lee, *The Ministry of Women in the New Testament* (Grand Rapids: Baker Academic, 2021), 59.

move textually through Acts highlighting Luke's narratives of both men and women in the early church.

At the start of Acts, Luke extends the concluding narrative of his first writing into his second volume. Particularly germane to our topic, both the conclusion of the Gospel and the opening of Acts focus on Jesus and his (male) apostles. Luke reminds readers that Jesus had chosen these men, presented himself alive to them by means of his post-resurrection appearances, taught them about the kingdom of God over the course of forty days, and commanded them to remain in Jerusalem until the baptism with the Holy Spirit had occurred, a long-expected event that was not far off in time (Acts 1:1–5). Correcting the apostles' conception of his mission, Jesus's affirmed that their upcoming work would be that of being his Spirit-empowered witnesses throughout the world (vv. 6–8). In recounting Christ's last "appearance" to them, Luke specifies that they were "men of Galilee" (ἄνδρες Γαλιλαῖοι, *andres Galilaioi*, with *andres* referring not to human beings in general but to men specifically). This was the ascension, which marked the end of his embodied presence with his followers (vv. 9–11).[2]

After watching him depart, the apostles obeyed Jesus's command and congregated in Jerusalem (vv. 12–14). Not only were the eleven disciples (who are named to set up the subsequent "replacement of Judas" narrative) in attendance in an upper room, they who patiently and obediently awaited the outpouring of the Holy Spirit incorporated "the women, including Mary the mother of Jesus, and his brothers" (v. 14). "The women" were those who had faithfully followed Jesus during his ministry, ministered to and with him, and had as eyewitnesses endured his death and burial: Mary Magdalene, Joanna, Mary the mother of James/Joses, and other women (Luke 24:10; Matt 27:61; Mark 15:47). They were joined by "Mary the mother of Jesus" (whose mention here is the last time she is named in the New Testament narratives) "and his brothers,"[3] a surprising and encourag-

[2] Lee, *The Ministry of Women in the New Testament*, 61.

[3] Lee offers that ἀδελφοῖς (*adelphois*) could be a reference to both the brothers and sisters of Jesus. Lee, *The Ministry of Women in the New Testament*, 60n3.

ing note, given that during Jesus's earthly ministry, they had not believed in him (John 7:5). As Luke details, "the number of people who were together was about a hundred twenty" (v. 15), composed of both men and women, long-time apostles, new followers, and family members of Jesus.

Of course, the group of apostles with whom Jesus engaged in this forty-day period was not identical to the group he had led during his three-year ministry. Abandoning his apostolic ministry, Judas Iscariot "left to go where he belongs" (v. 25), a euphemism for his earthly demise and eternal destiny. Thus, in accordance with several inspired scriptural writings, and guided by the Lord as they prayed, the apostles filled his position so as to restore "the Eleven" to "the Twelve." As Peter rehearsed, the selection for this restoration was "from among the men who have accompanied us [the apostles] during the whole time the Lord Jesus went in and out among us—beginning from the baptism of John until the day he was taken up from us—from among these, it is necessary that one become a witness with us of his resurrection" (vv. 21–22). Through divine directive, Matthias "was added to the eleven apostles" (v. 26).

These opening narratives underscore what is clear and repeated in the Gospels: Jesus's apostolic band consisted of twelve men. This fact is not in conflict with what we have seen earlier, that Jesus's followers who ministered with him and to him included many women.

Luke's narrative of the baptism with the Holy Spirit underscores that this event on the day of Pentecost was a fulfillment of Jesus's promise of a fresh, unprecedented outpouring of the Spirit (a promise itself based on several Old Testament prophecies; e.g., Ezek 36:25–27; Joel 2:28–32).[4] As noted previously, the recipients of this Spirit baptism "were all together in one place" (2:1). Whether "they" were the reconstituted apostolic group or the one hundred and twenty disciples is

---

[4] For further discussion see Gregg R. Allison and Andreas J. Köstenberger, *The Holy Spirit*, Theology for the People of God (Nashville: B&H Academic, 2020), 383–95.

uncertain.[5] In either case, "devout people from every nation under heaven" (v. 5), both men and women who were not yet followers of Jesus, equally experienced the effects of the outpouring of the Spirit upon the Twelve/ the one hundred twenty: they heard "the magnificent acts of God" being rehearsed in their own languages (v. 11) by the Spirit-filled disciples who spoke in tongues (vv. 4, 11). Peter's explanation of this phenomenon was a citation from Joel's promise, which, as the Magna Carta of the new covenant, was breathtaking in its inclusiveness:

> And it will be in the last days, says God, that I will pour out my Spirit on all people; then your sons and your daughters will prophesy,
> *your young men* will see visions,
> and *your old men* will dream dreams.
> I will even pour out my Spirit on *my servants* in those days, *both men and women*
> and they will prophesy. (vv. 17–18; emphasis added)

Whatever one may think of prophecy and other revelatory occurrences (dreams and visions), such manifestations as enabled and empowered by the Holy Spirit came through both men and women on the day of Pentecost with its initial outpouring of the Spirit.[6]

---

[5] In favor of the first option is the immediately preceding narrative about Matthias's addition to "the Eleven" (1:26) and the subsequent narrative about Peter and "the Eleven" (2:14). In favor of the second option is Luke's earlier reference to the larger group gathered together in the upper room (1:12–15) and his later reference to the fulfillment of Joel's prophecy—which was all-inclusive as to its promise of the Spirit's outpouring, certainly not limited to the apostles, nor to men, but it was open to all male and female disciples (2:16–21).

[6] For all who believe such gifts continue today because the Spirit continues to distribute them to the church, they should expect and welcome their expression from both male and female church members. For those who believe such gifts have ceased, the point still stands as to its historical expression.

Through this startling outpouring of the Spirit that enabled Peter to preach the gospel (v. 33), and in response to the convicting work of the Spirit, both women and men who were listening to Peter's message "were pierced to the heart" (v. 37), repented of their sins (v. 38), believed in Jesus as Messiah (v. 44), were forgiven of their sins (v. 38), received the gift of the Holy Spirit (v. 38), and were baptized in Jesus's name (v. 38)—three thousand new followers of Jesus (v. 41). These men and women "devoted themselves to the apostles' teaching, to the fellowship, to the breaking of bread, and to prayer" (v. 42), experienced signs and wonders by the apostles' hands (v. 43), gave sacrificially (vv. 44–45), daily met together in the temple and house assemblies (v. 46), worshiped God and "enjoyed the favor of all the people" (v. 47), and grew in number every day (v. 47). Again, for our purposes, this narrative of the emerging early church included both men and women.

Subsequently, Luke narrates the first of several healing miracles (Acts 3). "A man who was lame from birth" was begging at the temple's Beautiful Gate "when he saw "Peter and John about to enter the temple [and] asked for money" (3:1–3). Invoking "the name of Jesus Christ of Nazareth," Peter (along with John) took the lame man's hand, raised him up, "and at once his feet and ankles became strong. So he jumped up and started to walk, and he entered the temple with them—walking, leaping, and praising God" (vv. 6–8). As with the recipients of similar miracles performed previously by Jesus and narrated in the Gospels, the healed man appropriately glorified God, a response that was echoed by "all the people" who recognized him as the former beggar whose wholeness had been restored: "So they were filled with awe and astonishment at what had happened to him" (vv. 9–11). This miracle became the occasion for Peter to again preach the gospel (vv. 11–23). The apostle highlighted the timeliness of his announcing the good news—a new age has dawned just as Scripture foretold (v. 24)—with this gospel as key to the fulfillment of the Abrahamic covenant and promise: "And all the families of the earth will be blessed through your offspring," who is "the servant" of God, Jesus (vv. 25–26; cf. Gen 12:3; 18:18; 22:18).

The gospel as this Abrahamic blessing came to both believing women and men alike, whose number had rapidly climbed to about five thousand (4:4).

As with the miracles of Jesus, this miracle by Peter and John provoked persecution of the apostles (ch. 4). Taking advantage of the opportunity to explain that it was Jesus Christ of Nazareth who accounted for the healing of the lame man, Peter again preached the gospel, underscoring, "There is salvation in no one else, for there is no other name under heaven given to people [men and women alike] by which we must be saved" (v. 12). The persecutors of the apostles, who were the very same persecutors of Jesus (e.g., Luke 22:4, 52; Matt 22:23), were confounded by the miraculous sign and its connection to the Jesus whom they believed to be dead. Despite being warned to cease and desist from speaking and teaching in the name of Jesus (v. 18), the apostles refused to obey a human command above the divine command to preach the gospel. Returning to "their own people" (v. 23), the apostles and these new believers faced the crisis by praying in accordance with Scripture's emphasis on the sovereignty of God and pleading with the Lord to "'grant that your servants may speak your word with all boldness, while you stretch out your hand for healing, and signs and wonders are performed through the name of your holy servant Jesus.' When they had prayed, the place where they were assembled was shaken, and they were all filled with the Holy Spirit and began to speak the word of God boldly" (vv. 29–31). The tangible filling with the Spirit and the fierce boldness in proclaiming the gospel characterized both men and women in the church, which also featured oneness in heart and mind (v. 32), sacrificial giving (v. 32), palpable grace (v. 33), and the absence of need within the community of believers (vv. 34–35).

This sacrificial generosity was splendidly exhibited by Barnabas, the "Son of Encouragement" (vv. 36–37), and sinfully contradicted by the couple Ananias and Saphira (5:1–11). Divine discipline was exercised without partiality on both this husband and wife as they co-conspired to lie to the church/lie to the Holy Spirit. If Acts commends both men and women for the good they do, so it chastises both women and men for the evil they do.

In another narrative exemplifying the commendation of both sexes, Luke recounts, "Believers were added to the Lord in increasing numbers—multitudes of both men and women" (5:14). Such belief was fostered significantly by amazing miracles (e.g., healings occurred when Peter passed by the sick and his shadow fell on some of them; v. 15) that were numerous (e.g., "a multitude . . . from the towns surrounding Jerusalem" brought the sick and demon-tormented so that "they were all healed"; v. 16). Despite renewed and intensified persecution (vv. 17–41), the apostles "continued teaching and proclaiming the good news that Jesus is the Messiah" (v. 42).

Expansive growth led to a pressing problem: how to care for widowed disciples. When a complaint arose about partiality in the treatment of Hellenistic Jewish widows and Hebrew Jewish widows, the Twelve proposed a solution, the appointment of table waiters, whom the disciples would select on the basis of certain criteria (6:1–4). Though (apparently) women and men together were part of the selection process, seven servants, all of whom were men, were chosen and commissioned by the apostles (vv. 5–7). Whether these seven were the first "deacons" in the official sense of that term or "servants" in the general sense that is true of all Jesus's followers and not just church officers, it seems significant that the seven were men rather than women as the widows were women whom the men served.[7]

Expansive growth of the Christian movement also led to persecution, with two narratives as examples. Luke recounts at length and in great detail Stephen's Spirit-empowered denunciation of the people of Israel, which resulted in his martyrdom (6:8–7:60). Then Luke introduces Saul as a proponent of Stephen's death, which sparked "a severe persecution [that] broke out against the church in Jerusalem, and all except the apostles were scattered

---

[7] For a discussion of these two options, see Gregg R. Allison, *Sojourners and Strangers: The Doctrine of the Church*, Foundations of Evangelical Theology (Wheaton: Crossway, 2012), 240–42. As for the selection of men only, in this case the exclusivity may have been due to (1) the greater likelihood that men would serve these conflicted women impartially or/and (2), from a cultural perspective, the widows would have more likely respected the service of men.

throughout the land of Judea and Samaria" (8:1). Luke specifies that the devasting wrath of Saul was directed against the house churches everywhere, such that he would "drag off men and women (ἄνδρας καὶ γυναῖκας, *andras kai gynaikas*) and put them in prison" (v. 3).

Counterintuitively, such fierce persecution of women and men resulted in even further expansion of the gospel and multiplication of churches. Philip proclaimed the good news and performed signs and wonders in "a city in Samaria" (8:4–13), bearing fruit in many new followers of Jesus as confirmed by the many healings (v. 7), the "great joy in that city" (v. 8),[8] and the fact that "both men and women were [water] baptized" (v. 12). The (delayed) baptism with the Spirit of these Samaritans through the laying on of the hands of Peter and John (vv. 14–17),[9] even though misinterpreted by Simon Magus (vv. 9–13, 18–24), meant that the initial ministry of the gospel and the foundation of the church, with its concentration on Jewish background believers in Jesus, had now expanded to Jewish-Gentile followers of Jesus, both men and women.

The next people group to hear and embrace the gospel were the Gentiles. Directed first by an angel and then by the Holy Spirit (vv. 26, 29), Philip proclaimed "the good news about Jesus" (v. 35) to an Ethiopian eunuch in service to "Candace, queen of the Ethiopians" (v. 27). This inchoate Gentile mission took a decisive turn with the conversion of Saul, who had persisted in his persecution of the churches. This enemy's strategy was simple: "He went to the high priest and requested letters from him to the synagogues in Damascus, so that if he found any men or women who belonged to the Way, he might bring them as prisoners to Jerusalem" (9:1–2). Saul engaged in gender-blind hounding of Jesus's followers. As

---

[8] A Lukan expression signaling salvation; e.g., Luke 19:6, 9; Acts 8:39.

[9] For further discussion of the unusual nature of this delayed conferring of the baptism with the Spirit, see Gregg R. Allison, "Baptism with and Filling of the Spirit," *Southern Baptist Journal of Theology* 16.4 (2012): 4–21, https://equip.sbts.edu/publications/journals/journal-of-theology/baptism-with-and-filling-of-the-holy-spirit/.

Saul had targeted both women and men in the churches for persecution, so God would redirect Saul's targets to be men and women among "Gentiles, kings, and Israelites" (v. 15) who would establish new churches as Saul proclaimed the name of Jesus Christ, the name for which he would suffer severe persecution (v. 16). "So the church throughout all Judea, Galilee, and Samaria had peace and was strengthened. Living in the fear of the Lord and encouraged by the Holy Spirit, it increased in numbers" of both men and women (v. 31).

A pair of healing miracles—one involving a man, another involving a woman—continue Luke's emphasis on signs and wonders as accompanying and confirming the proclamation of the gospel. In Lydda, Peter "found a man named Aeneas, who was paralyzed and had been bedridden for eight years. Peter said to him, 'Aeneas, Jesus Christ heals you. Get up and make your bed,' and immediately he got up" (9:32–34). Two details stand out: It was not Peter, but Jesus Christ through Peter, who healed Aeneas. And Peter's directive for him to make his bed recalls Jesus's words to the paralyzed man: "so that you may know that the Son of Man has authority on earth to forgive sins"—he told the paralyzed man, "I tell you: Get up, take your stretcher, and go home" (Luke 5:24). Forgiveness and healing come through Jesus as announced in the gospel. The impact of this miracle was extensive, as all the citizens of Lydda and the neighboring region "saw him and turned to the Lord" (9:32–35).

In Joppa (a port city in that region, twelve miles from Lydda, v. 38), "there was a disciple named Tabitha (which is translated Dorcas)" (v. 36). Luke uses the hapax legomenon μαθήτρια (*mathētria*) to highlight that Tabitha/Dorcas was a "female disciple," a fact that she clearly demonstrated by her life of good works and love (v. 36). At her death, unspecified caretakers—possibly (women) disciples or widows who had benefited from Dorcas's good deeds—prepared her body, which they placed in an upper room (v. 37). Apparently with hope for a miraculous intervention, some (unspecified, but including at least two male) disciples appealed to Peter to come to Joppa without delay (v. 38), a summons that Peter heeded (v. 39).

Upon his arrival, "all the widows approached him, weeping and showing him the robes and clothes that Dorcas had made while she was with them" (v. 39). As with the following narrative about Cornelius, this vast display of evidence of love and good works was intended to communicate an appreciation of Tabitha's godly life and thus the appropriateness of divine intervention. Dismissing the disciples and humbly posturing himself before the woman's body, Peter urged, "'Tabitha, get up.' She opened her eyes, saw Peter, and sat up. He gave her his hand and helped her stand up. He called the saints and widows and presented her alive" (vv. 40–41). Though no mention is made of this miracle being done in the name of Jesus, its narrative location among other miracle stories in Acts in which Jesus's name is invoked (e.g., 9:34), and its similarity to the narratives of the widow of Nain's son (Luke 7:11–17) and of Jairus's daughter (Luke 8:40–42, 49–56) by Jesus himself, leaves no doubt as to the actual source of Tabitha's restoration to life. Moreover, its impact was felt among "the saints and widows," that is, all the disciples with particular reference to the women who could now continue to benefit from Tabitha's extended beneficence.

As with other such miraculous interventions, "this became known throughout Joppa, and many believed in the Lord" (v. 42). For our purposes, these two healing narratives underscore that the power of the gospel at work in the early church knew no gender boundaries but decisively reached both women and men.

Though the Ethiopian eunuch was technically the first Gentile to embrace the gospel (8:26–40), Luke's two-chapter narrative (10:1–11:18) about Cornelius underscores the pivotal nature of his conversion for the early church's mission to the Gentiles. Specifically for our purposes, Cornelius was joined by his family—"his whole household" (10:2)—and "his relatives and close friends" (v. 24), both male and female Gentiles who gathered to hear the gospel. "While Peter was still speaking these words, the Holy Spirit came down on all those who heard the message [both women and men]. The circumcised believers who had come with Peter were amazed because the gift of the Holy Spirit had been poured out even on the Gentiles. For they heard them speaking in tongues and declaring the greatness of God" (vv. 44–46). Though, previously, these Gentiles would have been prevented from becoming fully incorporated into the (old covenant) people of God, not so any longer: As they had received the baptism with the Spirit just as the circumcised believers had received it on the day of Pentecost, so Cornelius and his family and friends could be baptized with water and thus fully incorporated into the new covenant people of God through the gospel of Jesus Christ (vv. 47–48).

Perhaps a small yet easily overlooked point should be made here. What Peter learned from the vision of unclean animals (vv. 9–16) was "that God doesn't show favoritism, but in every nation the person who fears him and does what is right is acceptable to him" (vv. 34–35). Clearly, the lesson was about God's acceptance of Gentiles as part of his new covenant people, a revelation with which Peter initially struggled. But there is neither here, nor elsewhere in Acts, any indication that the early church struggled with the inclusion of women. Indeed, the gospel broke through and eliminated ethnic and religious barriers as it advanced from "Jerusalem, in all Judea and Samaria, and to the ends of the earth" (1:8), but it never needed to breach and eradicate gender barriers as it progressed because the church was already composed of both women and men.[10] From its inauguration, the gospel of Jesus Christ was fully inclusive: "through his name everyone who believes in him receives forgiveness of sins" (v. 43).

Luke next reminds us about the scattering of believers "as a result of the persecution that started because of Stephen" (11:19, referring to 8:1–4).

[10] The question about the possibility of baptism was raised, first, in the case of the Ethiopian eunuch (8:36–39) and, second, in the case of Cornelius and his people. In the first case, baptism would have been denied to the eunuch because he was an incomplete man; yet, because the gospel changes everything, he was baptized. In the second case, baptism would have been denied to Cornelius and the others with him because they were Gentiles; yet, because the gospel changes everything, they were baptized. This issue of the appropriateness of baptism for women was never raised.

Whereas this dispersion led to the disciples "speaking the word to no one except Jews" (v. 19, with the occasional exception of, for example, Philip and the people of Samaria, 8:5–8), "there were some of them, men from Cyprus and Cyrene, who came to Antioch and began speaking to the Greeks also, proclaiming the good news about the Lord Jesus. The Lord's hand was with them, and a large number who believed turned to the Lord" (11:21–22). One specific impact of this initiative was the inauguration of the church of Antioch, which was blessed and helped by Barnabas (v. 23)—"a good man, full of the Holy Spirit and of faith" (v. 24)—who in turn brought Saul to join him in teaching "large numbers" of the disciples, who "were first called Christians at Antioch" (vv. 25–26).

In the midst of this advancement of the gospel, difficulties continued to mount for the expanding church. These included a famine (11:27–30) and persecutions such as the martyrdom of James (12:1–2) and the imprisonment of Peter (12:3–5). For our purposes, attention falls on the location of the fervent intercession that was being offered on behalf of incarcerated Peter: it was "the house of Mary, the mother of John who was called Mark, where many had assembled and were praying" (v. 12). Moreover, Mary's household included at least one female slave, Rhoda (vv. 13–16). For Mary to host a prayer meeting in her house and be served by at least one servant girl indicates at minimum that she was a wealthy woman who, like other wealthy women before her, invested significantly in the ministry of Jesus (Luke 8:1–3) and the church that arose after him. Whether or not she was "most likely both the host and the leader" of this house church[11] requires us to assess the limited amount of narrative detail that Luke provided here, but such a judgment would certainly be in keeping with other New Testament indications of house churches in the homes of women: Lydia (Acts 16:40), Nympha (Col 4:15), Prisca and Aquila (Rom 16:3, 5; 1 Cor 16:19), possibly Apphia with Philemon (Philemon 2), possibly Chloe (1 Cor 1:11), and possibly some of the

[11] Lee, *The Ministry of Women in the New Testament*, 64.

women in the list of Paul's greetings at the end of his letter to the Romans (Romans 16).[12]

Returning to his narrative about the church of Antioch (11:19–26), Luke details the presence of "prophets and teachers: Barnabas, Simeon who was called Niger, Lucius of Cyrene, Manaen, a close friend of Herod the tetrarch, and Saul. As they were worshiping the Lord and fasting, the Holy Spirit said, 'Set apart for me Barnabas and Saul for the work to which I have called them.' Then after they had fasted, prayed, and laid hands on them, they sent them off. So being sent out by the Holy Spirit" (13:1–4) and commissioned by the church of Antioch, these men—and no female name is included in the list—embarked on what is commonly known as Paul's first missionary journey. This trip, like the other missionary travels recounted later in Acts (chs. 13–14; 15:36–18:22; 18:23–20:38), featured the apostle and male leaders: Barnabas (Acts 13:2), Timothy (16:1–3), Silas (15:40), Luke (16:10),[13] John Mark (13:5), Erastus (19:21), Gaius and Aristarchus (19:29), Sopater the Berean, son of Pyrrhus (20:4); Aristarchus and Secundus (20:4); Gaius of Derbe (20:4); and Tychicus and Trophimus (20:4). Clearly Priscilla and Aquila were Paul's co-workers in Corinth (18:1–4) and Ephesus (18:24–28), even risking their own lives for his sake (Rom 16:4). How the hardworking women whom Paul commends in his letter to the Romans—Mary (16:6), Tryphaena and Tryphosa (16:12), and Persis (16:12)—fit into these missionary journeys is unclear.[14] While Luke emphasizes the primary involvement of men in these missionary journeys, this focus does not contradict his other narratives that feature a prominent role of women in early church ministry.

Specifically, attention should be given to Paul's gospel message on the Sabbath in the synagogue of Pisidian Antioch. He addressed his audience as

[12] Possible mention of men who led house churches include Jason in Thessalonica (Acts 17:5–9) and Titius Justus and/or Crispus in Corinth (Acts 18:7–8).

[13] Though not mentioned by name, Luke includes himself ("we") as a late addition to the missionary team of Paul, Timothy, and Silas (16:10).

[14] See the later discussion of Paul's list at the end of Romans.

Ἄνδρες, ἀδελφοί, υἱοὶ γένους Ἀβραὰμ καὶ οἱ ἐν ὑμῖν φοβούμενοι τὸν Θεόν (*Andres, adelphoi, huioi genous Abraam kai hoi en hymin phoboumenoi ton theon*), literally "Men, brothers, sons of the family of Abraham, and those among you who fear God" (13:26). While his male-only addressees were contextually proper, Paul's message was not and could not be exclusively restricted to that original audience of men only. On the contrary, in at least two places, Paul textually indicated the universality of the gospel: it is directed not only to men but also to women. First, speaking of the once-crucified Jesus, the apostle continued, "God raised him from the dead, and he appeared for many days to those who came up with him from Galilee to Jerusalem, who are now his witnesses to the people" (13:30–31). As we have seen earlier in our discussion of the Gospels, Jesus's first appearances to those who accompanied him to his crucifixion and thus who became his witnesses to others were the women Mary Magdalene, Mary the mother of James [the younger] and Joseph/Joses, the mother of Zebedee's sons, Salome [possibly the mother of Zebedee's sons], and perhaps others (Matt 27:55–56; Mark 15:40–41; Luke 24:10). Second, Paul urged his audience to respond to the gospel: "let it be known to you, ἄνδρες ἀδελφοί (*andres adelphoi*), that through this man forgiveness of sins is being proclaimed to you. Everyone who believes is justified through him from everything that you could not be justified from through the law of Moses" (13:38–39). Again, the literal translation is "men brothers," appropriate contextually for his male listeners. At the same time, the forgiveness of sins and justification were not and cannot be reserved for men only; on the contrary, to both men and women alike is offered salvation in Jesus Christ.

Furthermore, the conclusion of Luke's narrative underscores the jealousy-provoked rejection of the gospel and Paul and Barnabas's resulting turn to the Gentiles (vv. 44–47). "When the Gentiles heard this, they rejoiced and honored the word of the Lord, and all who had been appointed to eternal life believed. The word of the Lord spread through the whole region" (vv. 48–49). This joyful and honorific response was not confined to men but included women as well, as confirmed by the subsequent narrative: "But the Jews incited the prominent God-fearing women and the leading men of the city. They stirred up persecution against Paul and Barnabas and expelled them from their district" (vv. 49–50). As both prominent God-fearing women and men believed the gospel, so their counterparts stirred up trouble for the gospel and its heralds. Undeterred, "the disciples [both women and men] were filled with joy and the Holy Spirit" (v. 52).

Similar scenes repeated themselves in Iconium (14:1–7), Lystra (vv. 8–19), and Derbe (vv. 20–21). In the second town, Paul encountered a profoundly lame man who "listened as Paul spoke. After looking directly at him and seeing that he had faith to be healed, Paul said in a loud voice, 'Stand up on your feet!' And he jumped up and began to walk around" (14:8–10). Though no mention is made of Jesus Christ in this narrative, Paul's recognition of the man's sufficient faith implies that the lame man was healed by Jesus. As with other signs and wonders, this miracle ignited religious fervor among the Lycaonians and attracted the attention of jealous Jews, who stoned the apostle and left him for dead. Tended to by the disciples, Paul went with Barnabas to Derbe.

Having "made many disciples"—women and men—in Derbe, the missionary band "returned to Lystra, to Iconium, and to Antioch, strengthening the disciples by encouraging them to continue in the faith and by telling them, 'It is necessary to go through many hardships to enter the kingdom of God.' When they had appointed elders for them in every church and prayed with fasting, they committed them to the Lord in whom they had believed" (vv. 21–23). While the churches consisted of both men and women followers of Jesus, the question at the heart of the debate is whether the office of elder was restricted to men only or accessible equally to both men and women. In favor of the first option are (1) probable parallels in leadership structures between the Jewish synagogue (the masculine emphasis of the narrative of 13:13–41 has already been noted) and those of the inchoate Christian churches; (2) Pauline instruction elsewhere about eldership; and (3) the fact that the New Testament never names a woman in association with this office.[15] In favor of the second option is this section's sustained narrative on the inclusion of both men and women in salvation and their standing as disciples in the church.

With the door to the Gentiles fully open, the mission awakened a controversy about the nature of the salvation of these Gentiles (Acts 15). Some Judaizing believers insisted, "Unless you are circumcised according to the custom prescribed by Moses, you cannot be saved" (v. 1). This particular rule about circumcision, which would have singled out Gentile men, was part of a broader legalistic framework that threatened to undue both male and female Gentile Christians: "It is necessary to circumcise them and to command them to keep the law of Moses" (v. 5). At the Jerusalem Council—which included the participation of the church of Jerusalem as well as representatives from the church of Antioch (and possibly from the churches of Syria and Cilicia; v. 23), the apostles, elders, and church members reiterated and defended the gospel of grace alone by faith alone in Christ alone.[16] The Council's communication of its decision was sent by a letter from "the apostles and the elders, with the whole church" (v. 22) through selected men: Paul and Barnabas; Judas, called Barsabbas; and Silas (v. 22, 25). Again, though the prominent role of male leaders is not to be overlooked, women also played an important part in this monumental decision about the nature of salvation. Furthermore, the reception of this message brought joy and

---

[15] In each of these cases, the question of whether these practices were simply capitulation to existing cultural mores and expectations and thus would eventually change as the gospel transformed Christian conceptions of men and women, or whether these practices were correct from the outset and were not intended to change, also enters into this discussion with the first view being advocated generally by egalitarianism and the second generally by complementarianism.

[16] Peter's affirmation is startling: "We are saved through the grace of the Lord Jesus in the same way they are" (v. 11). One would have expected just the opposite statement: "They [the Gentiles] are saved through the grace of the Lord Jesus in the same way that we [Jews] are." It was so necessary to make this emphatic point about the nature of Gentile salvation—that their salvation is solely by grace through faith alone without circumcision and the Mosaic law—that it even became the touchstone for Jewish salvation.

encouragement "to the brothers and sisters among the Gentiles in Antioch, Syria, and Cilicia" (vv. 23, 30–35).

Following this decisive soteriological affirmation, plans developed for a second missionary journey that would feature Paul along with Timothy and Silas (and later Luke). Though called by God and commissioned by the church of Antioch to preach the gospel and plant churches, this team was forbidden by the Holy Spirit from ministering in Asia, taking instead a detour north into Phrygia and Galatia. Next, they were prevented by the Spirit of Jesus from ministering in Bithynia, being redirected west to Troas, a port city in which God gave Paul a vision of a man of Macedonia, a region northwest and across the sea from Troas. The apostle concluded that it would be in Macedonia that God's call to preach the gospel should be actualized (16:6–10). The group traveled four hundred miles by foot and by boat until they came to the city of Philippi in Macedonia, as the narrative continued:

> On the Sabbath day we went outside the city gate by the river, where we expected to find a place of prayer. We sat down and spoke to the women gathered there. A God-fearing woman named Lydia, a dealer in purple cloth from the city of Thyatira, was listening. The Lord opened her heart to respond to what Paul was saying. After she and her household were baptized, she urged us, "If you consider me a believer in the Lord, come and stay at my house." And she persuaded us (vv. 13–15).

According to her name, Lydia was a Gentile, and she had become a God-fearer who was attracted to the Jewish faith and thus attached herself not to a synagogue but to a Jewish prayer group. She was a wealthy businesswoman who worked in the luxury industry of dyed purple cloth. After months of being forbidden to preach the gospel, Paul at long last proclaimed the good news to Lydia, who became a believer and, together with her household, was baptized. As Paul agreed to take up residence in her home, he completed his missionary task of planting a house church in Philippi.

Luke pairs the female convert Lydia with a male convert, the Philippian jailor, who oversaw the imprisonment of Paul and Silas. After the violent earthquake that shook the foundations of the prison in which the two had been bound (vv. 19–23), the jailor escorted them out of the prison while asking, "Sirs, what must I do to be saved?" (v. 30). The newly freed duo "spoke the word of the Lord ['Believe in the Lord Jesus, and you will be saved—you and your household'; v. 31] to him along with everyone in his house" (v. 32). After the jailor tended to Paul and Silas's injuries (v. 33), "Right away he and all his family were baptized. He brought them into his house, set a meal before them, and rejoiced because he had come to believe in God with his entire household" (vv. 33–34). While from very different socio-economic classes as well as having very different religious backgrounds, Lydia and the jailor both believed in the gospel and were baptized, both were joined in such belief and baptism by their entire household, and both showed hospitality to their newfound Christian friends. The gospel and saving faith along with baptism is for both women and men.

Not to be overlooked in this discussion is the intervening narrative of a female antihero. She was a slave girl possessed by a demonic spirit by which she engaged in a soothsaying business that was very profitable for her owners. Though she fictitiously foretold the future to deceive her clients, the girl honestly revealed the true identity of Paul and Silas as well as the genuine nature of their mission: "These men, who are proclaiming to you a way of salvation, are the servants of the Most High God" (vv. 16–18). Annoyed by the girl's persistent clamor, and "turning to the spirit [tormenting the girl]," Paul urged, "'I command you in the name of Jesus Christ to come out of her!' And it came out right away" (v. 18). With their devious source of illegitimate profit now dried up, the slave girl's owners wreaked havoc for Paul and Silas (vv. 19–22), leading to their imprisonment (vv. 22–24).

As this narrative is the only exorcism in Acts, conclusions must be drawn with caution. However, the transformation that undoubtedly took place in her life—from slave girl to free, from demonically controlled to an agent in her own right, from an instrument for cheating and deceiving others to (possibly) a contributor to good—this young woman may have embraced the "way of salvation" through the gospel and become a follower "of the Most High God." Perhaps she became another founding member of the church of Philippi in addition to Lydia, the jailor, and their households. Whatever may have ensued with this girl, after Paul and Silas's escape from jail, "they came to Lydia's house, where they saw and encouraged the brothers and sisters, and departed" (v. 40). This house church, born through the unlikely conversions of a wealthy woman and a male jailor, was the first church in Europe.

Luke continues with such pairings of women and men in salvation. In Thessalonica, through Paul's preaching in the synagogue, "some of them were persuaded and joined Paul and Silas, *including a large number of God-fearing Greeks, as well as a number of the leading women*" (17:4). Similarly, in the synagogue of Berea, as the two proclaimed the gospel, members of the synagogue "received the word with eagerness and examined the Scriptures daily to see if these things were so. Consequently, many of them believed, *including a number of the prominent Greek women as well as men*" (vv. 11–12). At the Areopagus in Athens, as Paul announced the gospel while urging that "God now commands all people [men and women] everywhere to repent" (v. 30), "some people joined him and believed, *including Dionysius the Areopagite, a woman named Damaris, and others with them*" (v. 34). As he began his ministry in Corinth, Paul was joined by the husband-and-wife team of Aquila and Priscilla (18:1–2). The response to the apostle's turning from the Jews to the Gentiles was notable: "So he left there and went to the house of a man named Titius Justus, a worshiper of God, whose house was next door to the synagogue. Crispus, the leader of the synagogue, believed in the Lord, along with his whole household. Many of the Corinthians, when they heard, believed and were baptized" (vv. 6–8). Men and women alike joined themselves to this emerging Corinthian church, recipients of two of Paul's letters.

At this juncture, Luke introduces a new character: "Now a Jew named Apollos, a native Alexandrian, an eloquent man who was competent in the use of the Scriptures, arrived in Ephesus. He had been instructed in the way of the Lord; and being fervent in spirit, he was speaking and teaching accurately about Jesus, although he knew only John's baptism. He began to speak boldly in the synagogue" (vv. 24–26). While Luke presents Apollos in a favorable light, this new character had serious limitations in terms of salvation-historical location. Luke notes relief from these inadequacies: "After Priscilla and Aquila heard him, they took him aside and explained the way of God to him more accurately" (v. 26). Being corrected and furnished with a more truthful understanding of the gospel, Apollos was welcomed by the church in Achaia and proved himself to be "a great help to those who by grace had believed. For he vigorously refuted the Jews in public, demonstrating through the Scriptures that Jesus is the Messiah" (vv. 27–28).

Much is made of Priscilla and Aquila's intervention with Apollos, including the following three positions: (1) The order of the couple's names is important, with the woman/wife being given prominence as first in the list. Such order contradicts (and perhaps even reverses) traditional sex polarity—men are superior to women—and supports sex complementarity (perhaps even reverse sex polarity)—men and women are equal yet different (or women are superior to men). (2) The teaching of a man by a woman is significant, with at least four perspectives arising from it: (2a) Because Priscilla taught Apollos privately and not in a formal worship service in a church, she becomes a model of such personal but not corporate ministry for women in relation to men. (2b) Because Priscilla taught Apollos privately and not in a formal worship service in a church, she provides no warrant for the incorporation of women in the church's worship service. (2c) Because Priscilla taught Apollos (whether privately or not is irrelevant), women may teach men in mixed-gendered adult church ministries (e.g., Sunday school classes). (2d) Because Priscilla taught Apollos (whether privately or not is irrelevant), women may serve as pastors/elders in churches.[17]

---

[17] Dorothy Lee seems to suggest this point as she comments on Priscilla and Aquila's ministry to Apollos in Ephesus: "It is ironic that Ephesus is the same location at which Timothy is ministering, where women are supposedly instructed

(3) The co-involvement of both Priscilla and Aquila—"*they* took him aside and explained the way of God to him [Apollos] more accurately" (v. 26)—is important. Accordingly, collaboration of wife and husband in ministry is encouraged, with the particular application to their partnership in "discipling" men and, by extension, their partnership in "discipling" women.

As the book of Acts continues with nearly exclusive focus on the ministry of Paul, a few passages draw our brief attention. (1) Paul's unusual experience with the salvation-historically challenged disciples of John the Baptist, "about twelve men in all" (19:1–7). (2) The apostle's daily lecturing in the hall of Tyrannus for two years so as to reach "all the residents of Asia, both Jews and Greeks" with the gospel (19:9–10). (3) Paul's return trip through Macedonia during which he was accompanied by male coworkers: "Sopater son of Pyrrhus from Berea, Aristarchus and Secundus from Thessalonica, Gaius from Derbe, Timothy, and Tychicus and Trophimus from the province of Asia" (20:3–4). (4) The miracle of the resurrection of Eutychus (20:7–12). (5) The apostle's farewell to the elders of the church of Ephesus (20:17–38).

(6) The leading of the Holy Spirit for Paul, who resolved through the Holy Spirit to go to Jerusalem and face great persecution, and the same leading for the apostle's friends—disciples in Tyre and in Caesarea—who through the Spirit attempted to persuade him to desist from his dangerous journey (Acts 21–23). Luke describes the group of friends in Tyre as the disciples "with their wives and children" (21:5). Furthermore, Luke details that at Caesarea, Paul "entered the house of Philip the evangelist, who was one of the Seven, and stayed with him. This man had four virgin daughters who prophesied" (21:8–9). This comment narrates the ongoing fulfillment of the promised new covenant work of the Holy Spirit for both women and men in the church (2:16–18, citing Joel 2:28–29).

(7) Paul's payment for the purification of four men, together with his own purification, to (unsuccessfully) ward off charges against him of

---

to be silent and forbidden to teach." Lee, *The Ministry of Women in the New Testament*, 67.

abandoning the law of Moses (21:17–30). (8) The apostle's testimony that, before being confronted by Jesus on the road to Damascus, he had "persecuted this Way to the death, arresting and putting both men and women in jail" (22:4–5; cf. 26:10–11). (9) The brief mention of Felix and "his wife Drusilla, who was Jewish" and who may have heard Paul speak about "faith in Christ Jesus" (24:24–26). (10) Similarly, the account of Paul's testimony before King Agrippa, his wife Bernice, and the governor Festus, who determined that the apostle had done nothing to deserve death or imprisonment (25:13, 23; 26:30–31). (11) As he traveled to Rome, Paul stayed with "brothers and sisters" (ἀδελφοι, *adelphoi*; here, referring to both sexes) for a week in Puteoli (28:13–14), after which he finally "came to Rome. Now the brothers and sisters (ἀδελφοι, *adelphoi*; again, referring to both sexes) from there had heard the news about us and had come to meet us as far as the Forum of Appius and the Three Taverns" (28:14–15).

Recalling that Acts is the second of a two-volume work, several points need to be highlighted from Luke's narratives of men and women and their interaction with Jesus (in the Gospel) and their engagement in the early church. On the one hand, complementarians might underscore the difference in Luke's attention to women in his two volumes, with significantly more narrative space being dedicated to women in the Gospel (which also gives more treatment to women than do the other Gospels) than in Acts. Their conclusion: whereas Jesus (rightly, by divine design) embraced women in terms of ministering with them and to them, and being ministered by them, this inclusion of women (rightly, by divine design) did not extend to incorporation of them in the leadership of the early church and (rightly, by divine design) does not extend to such leadership in contemporary churches.

On the other hand, egalitarians might note the difference in Luke's narrative focus and conclude that he "added women to the Gospel only in order to hammer home their subservience" in Acts.[18] Alternatively, egalitarians might conclude that the early church only gradually incorporated the

---

[18] Lee, *The Ministry of Women in the New Testament*, 69.

transformation of "human lives and human community at every level"—including full participation of women in the leadership of the church—as promised in the gospel. As Craig Keener explains,

> If the church could not immediately surmount ethnic and cultural barriers, we should not be surprised if the earliest communities developed egalitarian sensitivities only gradually and not everywhere at once. . . . [J]ust as the Spirit eventually led most Jerusalem Christians beyond their ethnocentrism . . . , the promise of Pentecost in 2:17–28 suggests similar crossing of gender barriers in the future, an ideal that the earliest community about which Luke writes had not fully attained.[19]

In either case, egalitarians underscore the emergence of women in church leadership as flowing from Jesus's engagement with many women in the Gospel of Luke and as either (temporarily) diminished (through oversight? through traditional disregard? through insipient patriarchalism?) in Acts or inchoately present there such that women's leadership will later surface as the church gradually overcomes not only ethnocentrism but also sexism.

---

[19] Lee, *The Ministry of Women in the New Testament*, 72. The citation is Craig S. Keener, *Acts: An Exegetical Commentary*, 4 vols. (Grand Rapids: Baker Academic, 2012–2015), 1:600, 603. I note two considerations: First, whereas Acts directly addresses the overcoming of ethnocentrism in several substantial narratives (the Samaritans, 8:4–25; the Ethiopian eunuch, 8:26–40; the Gentiles, 10:1–11:18; 11:19–24; and Paul's turning to the Gentiles, 13:44–49; 18:1–5; 28:23–28), it never addresses the overcoming of sexism. Flowing from this is the second point, that though Luke narrates relatively less about women in Acts, when he does, it is without fanfare or unusual in any way, because his treatment of women is the same as his treatment of men, as I have tried to build the case: He pairs the healing of Aeneas with the healing of Tabitha/Dorcas. He pairs the conversion of Lydia with the conversion of the Philippian jailor. He underscores the wife and husband team of Priscilla and Aquila in their ministry to Apollos. As almost an aside, Luke highlights the ongoing fulfillment of Acts 2:17–18 with a brief mention of Philip's four daughters who are prophetesses.

In terms of complementarity, I emphasize one point. As many commentators have proposed, a better title for Luke's second volume would be "the Acts of the Holy Spirit"; thus, even though "the characters of Acts, female as well as male, are 'subservient to the larger story of divine activity,'" the presence of both means that men and women are the stars of the book under the agency of the Holy Spirit.[20] Certainly, the selective nature of the writing highlights, relatively speaking, the ministries of male disciples guided and empowered by the Spirit. Yet, it would be wrong to conclude or even seek to imply that the promise of the Holy Spirit—that he would guide and empower the church in its missional endeavors (Acts 1:8), that he would give gifts to both women and men (2:17–18), that he would save through the gospel all varieties of fallen human beings (Acts 10), and more—is somehow more true of and fulfilled in men than in women.

[20] Lee, *The Ministry of Women in the New Testament*, 71. The citation is Beverly Roberts Gaventa, *Acts of the Apostles*, Abingdon New Testament Commentaries (Nashville: Abingdon, 2003), 27.

CHAPTER 18

New Testament Considerations: Pauline Instructions

This chapter offers an eclectic handling of the so-called "controversial passages" in the Pauline corpus that figure prominently in the complementarian-egalitarian debate: 1 Tim 2:11–14; 1 Tim 3:11; 1 Cor 11:3–16; 1 Cor 14:26–40; Eph 5:22–23; Gal 3:26–28; Col 3:16; and Titus 2:1–6. As these eight texts feature male and female roles in the church and husband and wife roles in the home, the two sides divide significantly in both their interpretations and applications. Interactions with these passages are legion, and my contribution will be to compare and contrast the complementarian positions and the egalitarian positions while drawing out principles and applications for complementarity.

1 Timothy 2:11–14[1]

Without a doubt, the following Pauline instructions are at the heart of the controversy between complementarianism and egalitarianism. The Christian Standard Bible offers this version:

> A woman is to learn quietly with full submission. I do not allow a woman to teach or to have authority over a man; instead, she is to remain quiet. For Adam was formed first, then Eve. And Adam was not deceived, but the woman was deceived and transgressed.

The New International Version is a bit different:

> A woman should learn in quietness and full submission. I do not permit a woman to teach or to assume authority over a man; she must be quiet. For Adam was formed first, then Eve. And Adam was not the one deceived; it was the woman who was deceived and became a sinner.

Key Issues of Interpretation

Generally speaking, six interpretive issues fuel the different understandings and applications of Paul's directives: (1) the context for and tenor of

[1] While verse 15 is clearly a part of this passage, I. Howard Marshall makes the point "that the precise interpretation of this verse does not alter the main thrust of the passage which rests upon the authoritative command in 1 Timothy 2:12 that forbids women from teaching and exercising authority in the church." I. Howard Marshall, "Women in Ministry: A Further Look at 1 Timothy 2," in *Women, Ministry, and the Church: Exploring New Paradigms*, ed. Mark Husbands and Timothy Larsen (Downers Grove: IVP Academic, 2007), 71. Cynthia Long Westfall disagrees with Marshall's assessment, arguing that this passage is directed at husbands and their wives in the home. A key reason for her position is v. 15. Cynthia Long Westfall, *Paul and Gender: Reclaiming the Apostle's Vision for Men and Women in Christ* (Grand Rapids: Baker Academic, 2021). Accordingly, though the following discussion of this passage at times interacts with interpretations of v. 15, it will not be accorded as much attention as vv. 11–14.

Paul's instruction (i.e., whether "negative" or "positive"); (2) the nature of the quietness/silence and submission enjoined upon women as they engage in learning; (3) the type of teaching that Paul embargoes for women; (4) the meaning of the difficult infinitive *authentein* (αὐθεντεῖν) and whether it is a second activity that Paul prohibits for women or a mode of teaching; (5) the function of the construction *ouk . . . oude* ("neither . . . nor") that links the infinitives *didaskein* and *authentein* and whether Paul prohibits one or two activities for women; and (6) the reasons for Paul's instruction, with particular attention to vv. 13–14. From these six interpretive issues flow different applications of the Pauline instructions for the contemporary church, with significant differences between complementarian and egalitarian applications.

(1) the context for and tenor of Paul's instruction (i.e., whether "negative" or "positive")

I begin with the view that the context and tenor is negative. Expressing a common egalitarian perspective, Linda Belleville notes that throughout this letter, Paul's instructions are not "routine" but "corrective." He exposes desperate situations and proposes a way forward to rectify them. As she explains,

> Paul was reacting to a situation that had gotten out of hand. False teachers needed silencing (1:3–7, 18–20; 4:1–8; 5:20–22; 6:3–10, 20–21). Certain widows were going from house to house, speaking things they ought not (5:13); others had turned away from the faith altogether to follow Satan (v. 15). Certain elders needed public rebuking on account of their continuing sin . . . [v. 20] . . . The men of the congregation had become angry and quarrelsome (2:8); the women were dressing inappropriately (v. 9) and learning in a disruptive manner (vv. 11–12). . . . Overall, it was an alarming scenario.[2]

[2] Linda L. Belleville, "Women in Ministry: An Egalitarian Perspective," in *Two Views on Women in Ministry*, ed. James R. Beck, rev. ed., Zondervan Counterpoints Series (Grand Rapids: Zondervan, 2005), 78–79.

As a corrective to this disastrous situation, Paul's second chapter urges peace (vv. 2, 8, 11, 12). His correction was in direct response ("then," v. 2; "therefore," v. 8) to the false teaching and divisiveness that he addressed in the first chapter of his letter (1:3–7, 18–20).

In terms of his specific corrective of women in 2:11–14, Paul's command for them to "learn quietly with full submission" (v. 11) and "to remain quiet" (v. 12) "suggests that women were disrupting worship. The men were too . . . (v. 8). Since Paul targets women who teach men (v. 12) and uses the example of Adam and Eve as a corrective, it would be a fair assumption that there was a battle of the sexes going on in the congregation."[3] Given this situation, Paul exposes these problems and sets forth a trajectory for rectifying the disaster.

Belleville raises the question about the reason for these women's behavior. She proposes that they were under the influence of "the cult of Artemis, where the female was exalted and considered superior to the male."[4] She maintains that this interpretative framework makes sense of Paul's subsequent discussion:

> An Artemis influence would certainly explain Paul's correctives in verses 13–14. While some may have believed that Artemis appeared first and then her male consort, the true story was just the opposite. For Adam was formed first, then Eve (v. 13). And Eve was deceived to boot (v. 14)—hardly a basis on which to claim superiority. It would also explain Paul's statement (v. 15) that "women will be kept safe through childbirth" . . . ; for Artemis was the protector of women. Women turned to her for safe travel through the childbearing process.[5]

---

[3] Belleville, "Women in Ministry: An Egalitarian Perspective," 80.

[4] Belleville, "Women in Ministry: An Egalitarian Perspective," 89. Belleville did not originate the idea of an Artemis cult as the key to interpreting this passage. For further discussion see Richard Clark Kroeger and Catherine Clark Kroeger, *I Suffer Not a Woman: Rethinking I Timothy 2:11–15 in Light of Ancient Evidence* (Grand Rapids: Baker, 1992).

[5] Belleville, "Women in Ministry: An Egalitarian Perspective," 90.

More recently, Sandra Glahn has argued for the cult of Artemis as the source of the Ephesian church's troubles.[6]

This egalitarian perspective understands the context and tenor of Paul's directive in our passage to be one of correction. This view influences the interpretation of the other five elements of this text and generally leads to dismissing Paul's instructions as normative for churches today because the contemporary context is so different from the one that Paul confronted with his correctives.

As for the view that the context and tenor is positive, a typical complementarian position sees this Pauline teaching as part of his overall positive instructions to Timothy about "how people ought to conduct themselves in God's household, which is the church of the living God" (1 Tim 3:15). Andreas Köstenberger, for example, notes the context (2:1–3:16) as Paul's directives about the appropriate conduct of believers in the church, underscoring the movement from the apostle's teaching about proper prayer for government authorities (2:1–8) to women and men in ecclesial leadership (2:9–15). This is followed by specific instructions given about elders/pastors/overseers (3:1–7) and deacons (3:8–13), concluding with a brief exposition of the great mystery of godliness (3:14–16).[7] Köstenberger underscores Paul's central concern in this section: "leading a tranquil and quiet life in all godliness and dignity" (2:2). Certainly, such concern prompts Paul to offer correction, which involves, negatively, men avoiding "anger or argument" (v. 8) and women eschewing immodesty in dress in favor of "good works, as is proper for women who profess to worship God" (vv. 9–10). But such negative orientation does not dominate the context and tenor of Paul's instructions.

---

[6] Sandra Glahn, *Nobody's Mother: Artemis of the Ephesians in Antiquity and the New Testament* (Downers Grove: IVP Academic, 2023). See the review of Glahn's book by Denny Burk, "Artemis Can't Undermine Complementarianism" (April 10, 2024); www.thegospelcoalition.org/reviews/nobody's-mother/

[7] Andreas J. Köstenberger, *1–2 Timothy and Titus*, Evangelical Biblical Theology Commentary (Bellingham, WA: Lexham, 2020), 107.

This complementarian perspective understands the context and tenor of Paul's directive in our passage to be one of positive instruction. This view influences the interpretation of the other five elements of this text and generally leads to embracing Paul's instructions as normative for churches today because, even though the contemporary context is different, churches must continue to hear and be shaped by Paul's prescriptive teaching.

(2) the nature of the quietness/silence and submission enjoined upon women as they engage in learning

This element focuses on Paul's use of ἡσυχία (*hēsychia*; quietness or silence) and ἐν πάσῃ ὑποταγῇ (*en pasē hypotagē*; full submission) in vv. 11–12 (from both the CSB and NIV versions): "A woman is to learn quietly [NIV "in quietness"] with full submission. . . . [S]he is to remain [NIV "must be"] quiet." To begin with, Linda Belleville disagrees with the traditional translation of the word as "silence," exemplified by the KJV: "Let the women learn in silence. . . . [She is] to be in silence" (KJV). Belleville explains that this translation ends up "prohibiting women from all forms of public speaking," which is problematic for two reasons.[8] First, the prohibition is incompatible with the Socratic method of question and answer to impart instruction and foster learning. If early church sermons employed such an approach, commanding women to be silent as they learned would be nonsensical. Second, she maintains that Paul does not use *hēsychia* to mean silence; rather, his preferred term is σιγάω (*sigaō*; Rom 16:25; 1 Cor 14:28, 30, 34). He uses *hēsychia* to signal "quiet behavior" (e.g., "quiet life," 1 Tim 2:2). Her conclusion: rather than commanding women to be silent in terms of public speaking, Paul instructs them "to learn quietly" (v. 11).

Köstenberger agrees on this point: ἡσυχίᾳ (*hēsychia*) does not mean total silence on the part of women but refers to the apostle's central concern

---

[8] Belleville, "Women in Ministry: An Egalitarian Perspective," 80.

for tranquility and peacefulness (2:2). Differing from Belleville, he underscores that women are to learn quietly rather than to be engaged in public teaching. As Köstenberger explains, such an injunction reflects traditional Jewish and Greco-Roman expectations for women; it was not common for women at the time to be permitted to learn anything.[9] In keeping with this last point, some would add that the fact that Paul envisions and prescribes a woman learning (μανθανέτω) is quiet notable for his first century context. Indeed, his description of the manner of their learning indicates his inclusion of women members in the public assembly for the purpose of being instructed in sound doctrine and practice.

Additionally, the apostle's emphasis on the manner of learning is twofold: in quietness and [full] submission. As to this latter instruction, Belleville dissents from the traditional understanding that Paul has in mind wives submitting to their husbands.[10] She offers two alternatives, both of which are suitable to the context of learning: either submission to teachers or self-control.[11] Again differing from Belleville, Köstenberger underscores that women are to be in full submission rather than have/exercise authority over a male believer.[12] So his parallelism—combining "quietness" and "with full submission" (v. 11) with "teaching" and "exercising authority" (v. 12)—is the following: women are to learn quietly rather than to be engaged in public teaching, and women are to fully submit rather than exercise authority over men.

---

[9] Köstenberger, *1–2 Timothy and Titus*, 113.

[10] She doesn't provide references in support of this interpretation commonly being that of traditional interpreters.

[11] Belleville, "Women in Ministry: An Egalitarian Perspective," 80–81. As noted in the interpretation above, a strong case can be made for the elders, who have the responsibility of teaching and leading the congregation (1 Tim 3:1–7), being the ones from whom the women (as well as all non-elder men) should learn and to whom all should be submissive. But Belleville, for reasons discussed next, would not accept this idea.

[12] Köstenberger, *1–2 Timothy and Titus*, 114–15.

(3) the type of teaching that Paul embargoes for women; (4) the meaning of the difficult infinitive* authentein *(αὐθεντεῖν) and whether it is a second activity that Paul prohibits for women or a mode of teaching; and (5) the function of the construction* ouk . . . oude *("neither . . . nor") that links the infinitives* didaskein *and* authentein *and whether Paul prohibits one or two activities for women

Combining the discussion of these three key issues, the two prohibitions about a woman teaching and exercising authority can be diagrammed as follows:[13]

> *I do not permit* (οὐκ ἐπιτρέπω, *ouk epitrepō*, a negated imperative)
> *a woman* (γυναικας, *gynaikas*, with reference to a woman in the church assembly)
>
> *to teach* (διδάσκειν, *didaskein*, the first of three infinitives)
>
> *or* (οὐδὲ, *oude*, a contrastive connector)
>
> *to exercise authority over* (αὐθεντεῖν, *authentein*, the second infinitive)
> *a man* (ἀνήρ, *anēr*, with reference to a man in the church assembly)
>
> *but* (ἀλλα, *alla*, another contrastive connector)
>
> *to remain quiet* (εἶναι ἐν ἡσυχίᾳ, *einai en hēsychia*, the third infinitive that, as discussed above, indicates the posture for learning and submitting)

I first look at a typical complementarian interpretation of this verse, followed by a typical egalitarian understanding of it.

Because of the grammatical structure—(5) the construction *ouk . . . oude* ("neither . . . nor") that links the infinitives *didaskein* and *authentein*—Köstenberger understands Paul's reference to teaching and

[13] Adapted from Andreas J. Köstenberger, "A Complex Sentence: The Syntax of 1 Timothy 2:12," in *Women in the Church*, ed. Andreas J. Köstenberger and Thomas A. Schreiner, 3rd ed. (Wheaton: Crossway, 2016), 121–22.

exercising authority to be two activities that are positive in and of themselves. As he explains, the syntax allows for two patterns:

> Pattern 1: Two activities or concepts are viewed positively in and of themselves, but their exercise is prohibited, or their existence is denied due to circumstances or conditions made clear by the context.
>
> Pattern 2: Two activities or concepts are viewed negatively, and consequently their exercise is prohibited, or their existence is denied, or they are to be avoided.[14]

The limitation of this grammatical structure to these two patterns means that interpretations that understand these two activities—teaching and exercising authority—as one activity only, or that understand that one of these activities is positive and the other is negative, are wrong. Moreover, for Köstenberger, the proper way to view these two activities is that they are positive, given, for example, the fact that Paul's overwhelming use of διδάσκειν (*didaskein*, to teach) is positive (1 Tim 3:2; 4:11, 13, 16; 5:17; 6:1, 2). Furthermore, had he intended to indicate teaching as a negative activity, Paul could have used another word—ἑτεροδιδασκαλεῖν (*heterodidaskalein*) as he did in 1 Tim 1:3—to indicate wrong teaching or false doctrine.[15] Accordingly, (3) the type of teaching that Paul embargoes is the positive communication of biblical truth and sound doctrine.

With teaching being the positive transmission of the truths of Scripture and theology, it follows that (4) the exercise of authority (αὐθεντεῖν, *authentein*) must also be a positive activity, a second activity that Paul embargoes for women;[16] "it has no necessary negative connotation" such as "usurp authority from" or "domineer over" a man (ἀνήρ, *anēr*; singular, for men

---

[14] Köstenberger, "A Complex Sentence: The Syntax of 1 Timothy 2:12," 122–23.

[15] In 1 Tim 6:3, Paul uses both ἑτεροδιδασκαλεῖν (*heterodidaskalein*) and διδάσκειν (*didaskein*) as a contrast between false teaching and true teaching.

[16] Al Wolters, "The Meaning of Αὐθεντέω," in *Women in the Church*, 3rd ed., 65–115. This traditional study is highly contested by egalitarian interpreters.

generically).[17] Paul's directive, then, is that "women are not to occupy positions in the church that involve permanent ruling functions over men; these are reserved for [qualified] males."[18] To be emphasized is that Paul's prohibition is not applicable to women ministering to other women (commanded in Titus 2:3–5), instructing children (commanded for mothers in Eph 6:4; 2 Tim 1:5; 3:14–15), and training men in conjunction with their husbands (exemplified in Priscilla and Aquila in Acts 18:24–28).[19] As will be discussed with 1 Tim 3:11, Paul's proscription of women does not prevent them from serving as women deacons in the church. This interpretation is a typical complementarian understanding of v. 12.

As for a typical egalitarian view, Linda Belleville interacts with the three key elements. (3) The type of teaching that Paul embargoes for women. Admitting the difficulty of interpreting Paul's prohibition of women teaching, Belleville addresses both the kind of teaching he had in mind and the type of authority such teaching possessed in Paul's context. First, she disagrees with the traditional understanding that Paul means "a teaching office or other position of authority."[20] Her reason: the New Testament presents teaching as an activity and a gift but does not link it with an office and position of authority. Indeed, she maintains that all church members, not

---

[17] Köstenberger, *1–2 Timothy and Titus*, 115. Douglas Moo offers three key points in regard to *authentein*: "First, the frequent appeal to etymology . . . must always remain a precarious basis for conclusions. . . . Second, the occurrences of this word—the verb—that are closest in time and nature to 1 Timothy mean 'have authority over' or 'dominate' (in the neutral sense of 'have dominion over,' not in the negative sense 'lord it over'). Third, the objection that, had Paul wanted to say 'exercise authority,' he would have used the word *exousiazō* does not bear up under scrutiny. . . . For these reasons, we think the translation 'have authority over' is the best English rendering of this word." Douglas Moo, "What Does It Mean Not to Teach or Have Authority over Men? 1 Timothy 2:11–15," in *Recovering Biblical Manhood & Womanhood: A Response to Evangelical Feminism*, ed. John Piper and Wayne Grudem (Wheaton: Crossway, 2006), 186.

[18] Köstenberger, *1–2 Timothy and Titus*, 115.

[19] Köstenberger, *1–2 Timothy and Titus*, 115.

[20] Belleville, "Women in Ministry: An Egalitarian Perspective," 81.

just leaders, are called to teach (Col 3:16; Heb 5:12). Second, she avers that authority resides neither in the activity of teaching nor in the teacher; rather, it resides in "the truths of the faith" or "the faith" that is taught (1 Tim 3:9; 4:1, 6; 5:8; 6:10, 12, 21). Indeed, *exousia* ("authority;" v. 12) "is simply not used of either local church leadership or the activity of teaching."[21] She dismisses the traditional claim that "teaching" in 1 Timothy (one could add the other two pastoral epistles; see below) "takes on the more official sense of 'doctrine'—and teaching doctrine is something that women can't do."[22] Belleville dissents from the idea of doctrine as a theological system; such a notion is foreign to 1 Timothy and can be blamed on a flawed translation of *hygiainousē didaskalia* as "sound doctrine" rather than (the correct) "sound teaching" (1 Tim 1:10; *kalē didaskalia*, 4:6; 2 Tim 4:3; Titus 1:9).[23]

(4) The meaning of the difficult infinitive *authentein* (αὐθεντεῖν). According to Belleville, the hapax legomenon *authentein* does not easily mean "to exercise authority over." She suggests various words that Paul could have chosen if he had intended that ordinary idea. Appealing to numerous extra-biblical sources,[24] she avers that Paul's use of *authentein* likely means "to dominate;" therefore, she concludes that his prohibition should be translated "I do not allow women . . . to dominate men."[25] She bolsters her view with an appeal to Paul's word order in v. 12: he first addresses teaching, then authority, but would have reversed the order had he intended a proper use of authority rather than dominating power. In addition, she provides a lengthy list of versions of the Bible (e.g., Old Latin, Vulgate, Geneva,

---

[21] Belleville, "Women in Ministry: An Egalitarian Perspective," 81.

[22] Belleville, "Women in Ministry: An Egalitarian Perspective," 82.

[23] Belleville, "Women in Ministry: An Egalitarian Perspective," 82.

[24] She references the LXX of Wisdom of Solomon 12:6 and 3 Maccabees 2:28–29; Josephus, *Jewish War* 1:582; 2:240; Diodorus, *Bibliotheca Historia* 17.5.4.5; Polybius, *Histories* 22.14.2.3; the commentator on Aeschylus's *Eumenides*; Aristonicus, *On the Signs of the Iliad* 9.694; Philodemus, *Rhetoric* II, 133; Dorotheus, *Carmen Astrologicum*, 346; Ptolemy, *Tetrabiblos* III.13; and more. See Belleville, "Women in Ministry: An Egalitarian Perspective," 82–85.

[25] Belleville, "Women in Ministry: An Egalitarian Perspective," 82–85.

KJV) that render Paul's expression "to dominate a man" or "to usurp authority over a man."[26] She faults "a hierarchical, noninclusive understanding of leadership," operative in mid-twentieth century English translations (e.g., RSV, NRSV, NASB, CSB, ESV, NIV), for their erroneous rendering "I do not permit a woman . . . to have [exercise, assume] authority over a man."[27]

(5) The function of the construction *ouk . . . oude* ("neither . . . nor") that links the infinitives *didaskein* and *authentein*. As the CSB renders it, "I do *not* allow a woman to teach *or* to have authority over a man" (v. 12, emphasis added). Belleville holds that this construction indicates movement from an idea to its purpose or goal.[28] Thus, she renders the verse, "I do *not* permit a woman to teach *in order* to gain mastery over a man" or "I do *not* permit a woman to teach *with a view* to dominating a man."[29] That is, Paul moves from the idea of a woman teaching to the purpose that she entertains ("in order to," "with a view to") for such teaching: to prevail over a man; it is such getting the better of a man that Paul prohibits. Belleville points to the conclusion of the verse—"but to have a quiet demeanor" (CSB: "instead, she is to remain quiet")—in support of her rendering: rather than attempting to gain mastery over or dominate a man, a woman should exhibit quiet behavior.[30] This interpretation is a typical egalitarian understanding of v. 12.

---

[26] Belleville, "Women in Ministry: An Egalitarian Perspective," 86–87.

[27] Belleville, "Women in Ministry: An Egalitarian Perspective," 87.

[28] She cites an example using her own translation of Matt 6:20: "where thieves neither break in nor steal [i.e., break in to steal]." Belleville, "Women in Ministry: An Egalitarian Perspective," 88.

[29] Belleville, "Women in Ministry: An Egalitarian Perspective," 88.

[30] Belleville, "Women in Ministry: An Egalitarian Perspective," 89. In a change from his original (egalitarian) interpretation that is similar to the one just outlined, Craig Keener posits that "Paul probably prohibits not simply 'teaching authoritatively' but both teaching Scripture at all and having (or usurping) authority at all. In other words, women are forbidden to teach men—period. (How one teaches Christian Scripture without exercising the authority involved in instructing others how to live, seems difficult to understand in any case!)" In other words, Keener understands the *ouk . . . oude* ("neither . . . nor") construction linking the infinitives *didaskein* and *authentein* to indicate two distinct activities (teaching, exercising

(6) The reasons for Paul's instruction, with particular attention to vv. 13–14. From a complementarian perspective, the question arises why Paul "does not permit" women from engaging in these two distinct yet related good ministries. Following Köstenberger's interpretation, the apostle's prohibition is due to two reasons (vv. 13–14): the γάρ (*gar* = "for"; v. 13) after the prohibition offers a reason for it, and the καὶ (*kai* = "and"; v. 14) linked to γάρ provides a second explanation.[31] Both reasons refer to the earliest parts of Scripture. Alluding to Genesis 2, Paul's first reason is based on the order of creation: Adam's creation preceded Eve's (1 Tim 2:13). According to the flow of the creation account in Genesis 2, God first created Adam (v. 7) then created Eve (vv. 18–25). This creation order substantiates Paul's prohibition of women teaching and exercising authority.

Alluding to Genesis 3, Paul's second reason is based on the manner of Eve's fall into sin: "Adam was not deceived, but the woman was deceived and transgressed" (1 Tim 2:14). According to the account of the fall, Satan in the guise of a serpent tricked Eve by his evil machinations (twisting God's original prohibition, contradicting God's actual words, and questioning the goodness of God). Deceived, she violated the divine prohibition not to eat of the tree of knowledge: "The woman saw that the tree was good for food and delightful to look at, and that it was desirable for obtaining wisdom. So she took some of its fruit and ate it; she also gave some to her husband, who was with her, and he ate it" (Gen 3:6). As a consequence of the specific type of Eve's sin—transgression through deception—or as a result of her sin through deceit, Paul prohibits women from teaching and exercising authority in the gathered assembly. Alternatively, according to Douglas Moo,

> [V]erse 14, in conjunction with verse 13, is intended to remind the women in Ephesus that Eve was deceived by the serpent in the Garden (Genesis 3:13) precisely in taking the initiative over the

---

authority) that are prohibited to women. Craig S. Keener, "Women in Ministry: Another Egalitarian Perspective," in *Two Views on Women in Ministry*, 231.

[31] Köstenberger, *1–2 Timothy and Titus*, 116n171.

> man whom God had given to be with her and to take care of her. In the same way, if the women at the church at Ephesus proclaim their independence from the men of the church, refusing to learn "in quietness and full submission" (verse 11), seeking roles that have been given to men in the church (verse 12), they will make the same mistake Eve made and bring similar disaster on themselves and the church.[32]

In either case, to be ruled out is the idea that Paul is suggesting that "Eve was more gullible than Adam" and/or that women are more easily deceived than are men.[33]

A more complete diagram from a complementarian viewpoint can now be offered:

I do not permit (οὐκ ἐπιτρέπω, *ouk epitrepō*, a negated imperative) *a woman* (γυναικας, *gynaikas*, with reference to a woman in the church assembly)

to teach (διδάσκειν, *didaskein*, the first of three infinitives, meaning the positive communication of biblical truth and sound doctrine)

or (οὐδὲ, *oude*, a contrastive connector)

to exercise authority over (αὐθεντεῖν, *authentein*, the second infinitive, meaning the positive role of proper church leadership) *a man* (ἀνήρ, *anēr*, with reference to a man in the church assembly)

but (ἀλλα, *alla*, another contrastive connector)

---

[32] Moo, "What Does It Mean Not to Teach or Have Authority over Men?" 190.

[33] Köstenberger, *1–2 Timothy and Titus*, 117; cf. Moo, "What Does It Mean Not to Teach or Have Authority over Men?" 189–90.

> *to remain quiet* (εἶναι ἐν ἡσυχίᾳ, *einai en hēsychia*, the third infinitive, indicating the positive posture for learning and submitting)

for two reasons (alluding to the narratives of Genesis 2–3)

> the order of creation (Adam was created first, then Eve)
> the type of the sin of Eve (Eve was deceived by Satan and transgressed)

As Köstenberger urges, "the fact that Paul is rooting his directive in the order of creation rather than providing a cultural rationale strongly suggests that vv. 11–12 are permanently applicable. The fact that Paul grounds the command in the order of creation, not only the fall, also contradicts the argument that female submission to male leadership in the church is solely a result of the fall."[34]

From an egalitarian perspective, on the basis of her above cited interpretation of v. 12—"Paul [is] prohibiting teaching that tries to get the upper hand (not teaching per se)"—Belleville offers "a reasonable reconstruction . . . : The women at Ephesus (perhaps encouraged by false teachers) were trying to gain an advantage over the men in the congregation by teaching in a dictatorial fashion. The men in response became angry and disputed what the women were doing."[35] As noted above, Belleville posits the reason for these women's behavior by appealing to "the cult of Artemis, where the female was exalted and considered superior to the male."[36]

Moreover, Belleville takes issue with a common complementarian understanding of these verses. First, she dissents from the idea that the order of creation—Adam first, then Eve (v. 13)—has to do with male leadership.

---

[34] Köstenberger, *1–2 Timothy and Titus*, 117–18.

[35] Belleville, "Women in Ministry: An Egalitarian Perspective," 89.

[36] Belleville, "Women in Ministry: An Egalitarian Perspective," 89. See also Sandra Glahn, *Nobody's Mother: Artemis of the Ephesians in Antiquity and the New Testament* (Downers Grove: IVP Academic, 2023).

On the contrary, Paul's language of "first . . . then" "does nothing more than define a sequence of events or ideas."[37] Thus, she dismisses the notion that Paul is giving the creation order as a cause for the church to acknowledge that men teach (because Adam was created first, men are to lead women) and to prohibit women from doing so.[38]

Second, Belleville disagrees with the traditional idea that Paul is "using Eve as an example of what can go wrong when women usurp the male's created leadership role" (v. 14).[39] She points to the reason for Eve's deception and fall into sin: she was deceived by Satan into disobeying God's command, not into taking the lead in her relationship to Adam, who was her head. Belleville concludes: "The language of deception calls to mind the activities of the false teachers at Ephesus. If the Ephesian women were being encouraged to assume the role of teacher over men as the superior sex," then Paul's explanation in vv. 13 and 14 makes sense. "The relationship between the sexes was not intended to be one of female domination and male subordination; but neither was it intended to be one of male domination and female subordination. Such thinking is native to a fallen creation order (Gen. 3:16)" and not to an original creation (Gen. 2:7, 18–25) that has nothing to do with hierarchy between men and women.[40]

I have discussed six key interpretive issues for 1 Timothy 2:11–14:

---

[37] She underscores that the same "first . . . then" construction appears in 1 Tim 3:10 and signifies nothing more than steps in a process. Belleville, "Women in Ministry: An Egalitarian Perspective," 91.

[38] Belleville, "Women in Ministry: An Egalitarian Perspective," 90n134, 91.

[39] Belleville, "Women in Ministry: An Egalitarian Perspective," 91.

[40] Belleville, "Women in Ministry: An Egalitarian Perspective," 91. Keener understands Paul's appeal to Eve as "simply drawing a local analogy between Eve and the easily deceived women in Ephesus (or the majority of women in his day who were uneducated, hence easily deceived)." He refers to a similar Pauline analogy between the Corinthian church's members—both men and women—and Eve (2 Cor 11:3). Keener concludes that Paul's appeal to Scripture does not signify that his prohibition in v. 12 is a transcultural proscription of women teaching and exercising authority. Keener, "Women in Ministry: Another Egalitarian Perspective," 237.

(1) the context for and tenor of Paul's instruction;
(2) the nature of the quietness/silence and submission enjoined upon women;
(3) the type of teaching that Paul embargoes for women;
(4) the meaning of *authentein* (αὐθεντεῖν) and whether it is a second activity that Paul prohibits for women or a mode of teaching;
(5) the function of the construction *ouk . . . oude* ("neither . . . nor") that links the infinitives *didaskein* and *authentein* and whether Paul prohibits one or two activities for women; and
(6) the reasons for Paul's instruction, with particular attention to vv. 13–14.

From these six interpretive issues flow different applications of the Pauline instructions for the contemporary church, with significant differences between complementarian and egalitarian applications.

From a typical complementarian perspective, women are not permitted to teach (biblical truth and sound doctrine) but should learn (such good instruction) quietly, and they are not to exercise (proper church) authority but to obey submissively. These prohibitions invite two important questions to be asked: From whom are women to learn? And to whom are women to submit? As though anticipating such inquiries, Paul (indirectly) answers them in his subsequent instructions about elders/pastors (1 Tim 3:1–7). Because these overseers must be "able to teach" (v. 2), women are to learn from them; elders/pastors bear the responsibility to teach biblical truth and sound doctrine to the church. This application regarding learning is also true for all the men who do not hold the office of elder/pastor. Additionally, because these overseers "take care of God's church" (v. 5, as evidenced by their competency in managing their own household, v. 4), women are to submit to them; elders/pastors bear the responsibility to lead the church. This application regarding submitting is also true for all men who do not hold the office of elder/pastor. All women and all non-elder men are to learn from and submit to the pastors of the church (Heb 13:7, 17). As we have seen, the application of these Pauline instructions in contemporary complementarian churches stretches across a spectrum from minimum to moderate to maximum.

Several approaches to this Pauline instruction are common within an egalitarian framework. One approach is to agree overall with it while denying its application to our contemporary situation. Several examples follow. A first example is the view of Gordon Fee that this letter is an ad hoc correspondence in which Paul does not intend to specifically teach church order. Therefore, to draw contemporary application of 1 Tim 2:11–14 to our contemporary context is a precarious venture, fraught with difficulties compounded by personal inconsistency and exegetical ambiguity.[41]

For a second example, some maintain that Paul's treatment is primarily, if not exclusively, concerned with the context of the Ephesian church. That context may be viewed through the lens of unique problems in that church. As we have seen, Linda Belleville points to "the cult of Artemis, where the female was exalted and considered superior to the male."[42] Also, Gordon Fee underscores the problem of false teaching that was rampant in the Ephesian church, averring that "the whole of 1 Timothy in fact is dominated by this singular concern."[43] Once that particular evil has been removed, the Pauline directives that were intended to eliminate it no longer apply to churches today. Alternatively, that context may be seen from the perspective of general cultural realities—for example, a lack of education for women in the ancient world—that rendered women unfit for teaching and leading the church at that time. When the context changes and that particular cultural limitation disappears, then Paul's prohibitions of women teaching and leading are no longer operative in churches today.

---

[41] Gordon D. Fee, "Reflections on Church Order in the Pastoral Epistles, with Further Reflections on the Hermeneutics of Ad Hoc Documents," *Journal of the Evangelical Theological Society* 28 (1985): 141–51. While Fee rehearses this view throughout his article, the specific points noted here are from p. 150.

[42] Belleville, "Women in Ministry: An Egalitarian Perspective," 89. See also Glahn, *Nobody's Mother*.

[43] Fee, "Reflections on Church Order in the Pastoral Epistles," 142.

A second approach is found in Cynthia Long Westfall's book, *Paul and Gender: Reclaiming the Apostle's Vision for Men and Women in Christ*, which offers a unique interpretation of this passage and therefore warrants a more extensive treatment. Rather than addressing problems among men and women in the church or church gatherings, Paul's instructions seek to rectify domestic difficulties between husbands and wives.[44] As is our pattern, Westfall's presentation will be outlined according to the six key interpretive issues.[45]

(1) the context for and tenor of Paul's instruction

Westfall identifies the purpose for this letter as the apostle's effort to instruct Timothy in the prevention of false teaching in the church of Ephesus

---

[44] Westfall, *Paul and Gender*. Though I call her position "unique" in the sense that it differs significantly from the interpretations at the heart of the complementarianism-egalitarianism debate, it is not novel. For a brief history of the interpretation that Paul addresses husbands and wives in particular and not men and women in general, see Gordon P. Hugenberger, "Women in Church Office: Hermeneutics Or Exegesis? A Survey of Approaches to 1 Tim 2:8–15," *Journal of the Evangelical Theological Society* 35.3 (1992): 350–51.

[45] She is highly critical of the traditional interpretation, which is her "primary dialogue partner" for her book: "[T]he traditional interpretation of 1 Timothy 2:12 is often treated as a citadel that dominates biblical interpretation, church polity, and praxis on gender, which can be overturned (hypothetically) only with incontrovertible proof or a rejection of the canonical status of 1 Timothy and ultimately a rejection of the Bible as an authority for life and practice. This study will try to show that the traditional interpretation of 1 Timothy 2:12 and other passages on gender are based on information, assumptions, and inferences that are imposed on the text, part of the interpreter's embedded theology, and/or the direct and inevitable outcome of how the understanding of the passage has been taught, preached, and discussed in various venues by teachers, preachers, parents, and companions. Consequently, the traditional assumptions and inferences are often unacknowledged and even conferred with an inspired status of being 'what God says.' These assumptions have been combined with atomistic readings that are removed from the biblical situation, time, and culture." Westfall, *Paul and Gender*, 3.

(1:3–4).[46] As for the tenor of the letter, then, Westfall maintains that it is corrective.[47] Surprisingly, Westfall does not believe that Paul's corrective measures are directed at the church when it is gathered together for worship.[48] Rather, she locates his instruction as a solution to problems within marriage. Specifically, women should "engage in spiritual formation in the home:" that is, wives should receive personal instruction quietly and submissively from her husband in the context of her home.[49]

Noting four parallels between Paul's directives here and his instructions in 1 Cor 14:34–35—(1) silence or quietness; (2) the prohibition of

---

[46] Westfall, *Paul and Gender*, 279–80. Cf. 298–99.

[47] Westfall, *Paul and Gender*, 286.

[48] She lists several problems with this scholarly consensus. First, she underscores the lack of any signal in 2:1 and 8 that prayer is taking place in the assembly or should be limited to such gatherings. Indeed, Paul commands the men to pray "in every place" (v. 8), which can hardly be confined to church meetings (which, it should be recalled, took place in homes rather than public buildings such as those most churches have today). Moreover, Paul's comment on childbearing (v. 15) seems out of place if he were addressing a worship service. Second, Westfall highlights the fact that Paul's instructions to women about proper attire cannot be restricted to gatherings of the church. Add to that his solution to women's improper clothing: they should clothe themselves with good works (v. 10). Again, such instruction does not apply to the specific context of worship. Third (and this point is not specified in what is otherwise a clearly enumerated list), Westfall connects Paul's directives about female attire to his earlier concern for prayer so that the Ephesian Christians "may lead a tranquil and quiet life in all godliness and dignity" (2:2). If improper female adornment was hindering prayer (which, again, was not confined to church meetings) and thus thwarting the divine goal of peace and quiet, Paul seeks to correct their sartorial error, which would not be limited to those church gatherings. Fourth, Westfall draws attention to the textual shift from the plurals of "men" and "women" (vv. 8–10) to the singular "woman" and "man" (vv. 11–14; v. 15 singular "she"). To address a problem of a woman teaching men, or women teaching men, in a public setting makes sense, but it is not so "of a woman teaching 'a man' in a group setting. Rather, the use of the singular signals some private interaction between a woman and a man" (p. 289), which Westfall applies to communication between a wife and her husband. Fifth, Westfall again points to the unusual reference to salvation through childbearing (v. 15). While appropriate to a familial context (the last discussion), it is unfitting to an ecclesial context. Westfall, *Paul and Gender*, 286–89.

[49] Westfall, *Paul and Gender*, 305.

talking or teaching; (3) submission or self-control; (4) Paul's antidote of learning at home[50]—Westfall avers that Paul's antidote of wives learning from their husbands at home, and their husbands taking the responsibility to instruct and answer their wives' questions at home, would have been well accepted and rightly expected cultural behavior in the first century context of Ephesus. She details the three specific concerns that Paul addresses with his prohibition. First, by men teaching their wives at home, the female-sourced problem of spreading myths and attending to genealogies in the Ephesian church would be averted. Second, any possible negative cultural reaction to a role reversal in a believing household—fodder for rejection of Christianity as a subversive, anti-family movement—would be forestalled. Third, by prohibiting all tendency toward domination and abuse in the exercise of authority—and Westfall maintains that Paul's instructions to wives concerning their misuse of authority pertains equally to husbands and their mishandling of authority in relation to their wives—Paul offers a countercultural model of marriage, church leadership, and authority.[51]

(2) the nature of the quietness/silence and submission enjoined upon women.

From the above, Westfall concludes that "women who are demonstrably in need of teaching should assume the 'posture and attitude of learners' at home."[52] Accordingly, wives are to quietly and responsively learn from the teaching of their husbands through private home instructions.

---

[50] Westfall, *Paul and Gender*, 306

[51] Westfall offers a fourth possible concern addressed by Paul: by prohibiting a role reversal fueled by disobedient wives, any possible sexual abuse such as wives withholding sex from their husbands (an abuse within the semantic range of αὐθεντέω, she claims), would be corrected. This point is highly speculative. Westfall, *Paul and Gender*, 308; cf. 301–302.

[52] Westfall, *Paul and Gender*, 307. Her citation is Philip Towner, *The Letters to Timothy and Titus*, New International Commentary on the New Testament (Grand

(3) the type of teaching that Paul embargoes for women; (4) the meaning of **authentein** *(αὐθεντεῖν); and (5) the function of the construction* **ouk . . . oude** *("neither . . . nor") and whether Paul prohibits one or two activities for women*

Though she does not comment specifically on this grammatical construction, Westfall's view emerges from this summary of the kind of teaching that Paul prohibits (v. 12): "Paul does not permit (or is not currently permitting) any exception of a wife reversing the roles and becoming the designated spiritual guide and mentor of her husband's spiritual formation in the home."[53] Westfall posits that such instruction could be Paul's general approach to the reversal of the teaching role among husbands and wives, or it could be the context-specific antidote for the Ephesian problem of female false teaching and other destructive practices.[54] In either case, she views the activity of teaching as central to Paul's concerns: "The prohibition is in the prime position of emphasis, then Paul adds the prohibition of a wife 'controlling' or 'domineering' her husband, or 'forcing him against his will.'"[55] Accordingly, Westfall understands the grammatical structure as underscoring that wives are not to be the domineering instructors responsible for their husbands' spiritual growth.

As for the meaning of *authentein* (αὐθεντεῖν), Westfall notes the division of contemporary scholarship into two groups: One understands it in a positive or neutral sense, exemplified in its translation as "exercise authority"

Rapids: Eerdmans, 2006), 216.

[53] Westfall, *Paul and Gender*, 307.

[54] Westfall, *Paul and Gender*, 307. Westfall finds further support for her domestic interpretation of Paul's prohibition in v. 15. Childbirth would have been a well-recognized concern for husbands and wives, and Paul encourages them both to trust God for protection so that wives will come safely through the dangerous experience of childbirth as both they and their husbands continue in faith, love, and holiness, with good sense" (CSB). Given the domestic context of 2:11–15, Westfall interprets "both they" as a reference to husbands and wives. Westfall, *Paul and Gender*, 311.

[55] Westfall, *Paul and Gender*, 307.

or "master." The other group interprets it in a negative or pejorative sense, expressed in its translation as "usurp," "domineer," "control," or "initiate violence."[56] Convinced of its negative connotation, Westfall avers that "Paul uses the word αὐθεντέω to criticize the behavior of wives toward their husbands in a case of role reversal, where the woman would assume an authority that may be comparable to a paterfamilias and behave in an abusive or controlling manner."[57]

(6) the reason for Paul's instruction, with particular attention to verses 13–14.

Westfall dismisses the traditional interpretation that Paul alludes to Genesis 2 and 3 in order to provide a transcendent norm for his prohibition in verse 12.[58] Flowing from her interpretation of Paul's prohibition as an antidote for the false teaching among women—and thus a call for husbands to provide spiritual formation for their wives in their homes—Westfall reframes the apostle's allusions to Genesis 2 and 3 in vv. 13–14. She underscores two typological parallels: (1) the creation order (Genesis 2)—Adam's (physical) formation was first, then Eve's (v. 13)—parallels Paul's prescription that husbands offer spiritual formation for their wives; and (2) the deception of Eve by the serpent/Satan (Genesis 3) parallels the deception of the Ephesian women by Satanic/demonic false teachers (5:15).

In summary, decisions about the six interpretive issues in 1 Tim 2:11–14 result in different applications of the Pauline instructions for the

---

[56] Westfall, *Paul and Gender*, 291.

[57] Westfall, *Paul and Gender*, 293.

[58] Westfall, *Paul and Gender*, 294. She claims that Adamic priority, as inferred by Thomas Schreiner, "was not a norm for Paul in other temporal relationships" (without reference to any examples) and notes that "Moving from a simple statement of the order of creation to the priority of men is a logical leap that has seemed transparent to male scholars historically." Westfall, *Paul and Gender*, 295. Her interaction is with Thomas Schreiner, *Paul, Apostle of God's Glory in Christ: A Pauline Theology* (Downers Grove: InterVarsity, 2001), 408.

contemporary church, with significant differences between complementarian and egalitarian applications.

In concluding this discussion of 1 Tim 2:11–14, it is evident that at the center of the controversy is the very practical matter of church leadership and its accessibility either to men only or to men and women alike. Given the vast chasm between complementarian and egalitarian understandings, and focusing on this central practical issue, what if any contribution may complementarity make?

A good place to start is with a clarification of what the issue is not about and what it is about. As for what the issue is not about, two varieties bear consideration: the ontological view and the functional view. The first view is that only men can be in church leadership because of (ontological) male superiority. Certainly, the Western philosophical, theological, and ecclesiastical tradition claimed that men are (ontologically) superior to women and women are (ontologically) inferior to men. On the basis of this inequality, then, 1 Tim 2:11–14 was interpreted as Paul's prohibition of women from being in church leadership; only (ontologically superior) men may be in church leadership. Although there are some exceptions, almost everyone today on both sides of the debate (rightly) rejects this rationale. The (ontological) inequality of women and men is not the reason for the restriction of church leadership to men. Inequality between the sexes is not what the issue is about.

The second view (of what the issue is not about) is that only men can be in church leadership because men are divinely designed and equipped (functionally) for teaching and leading and women are not. Certainly, the Western philosophical, theological, and ecclesiastical tradition claimed that men are (functionally) different from women and women are (functionally) different from men, and this functional difference pertains in particular to the roles of teaching and leading. On the basis of this role differentiation, then, 1 Tim 2:11–14 was interpreted as Paul's prohibition of women from church leadership; only men (who are functionally designed and equipped for teaching and leading) may hold church leadership positions. But is this functional difference what the issue is about?

I. Howard Marshall critiques this "role" rationale for the exclusion of women from church leadership, but I think he misses the point and ends up demonstrating instead that functional differentiation is not what the issue is about. To diagram his view:

	church activities	*church activities*
forbidden to men	none	
forbidden to women		church leadership (because teaching and leading are male functions)

As Marshall explains it, "men apparently do not have a different role from women except in that they are permitted to do not only all that women do but also more in the church." He then cautions complementarians who

> assert that God has given complementary roles to men and women that are both needed in order that the church may have the fullness of God's blessing. . . . But if we have a situation in which the men can do all that the women do and more in the church, then it is surely the case that the women are not doing anything complementary to what the men do. In that case the self-description of supporters of this position as "complementarians" is misleading since the women are not complementing the men by doing things that the latter are forbidden or unable to do.[59]

[59] Marshall, "Women in Ministry: A Further Look at 1 Timothy 2," 72–73.

But this is not what the issue is about. Despite what the Western tradition held, not only men may be functionally designed and equipped for teaching and leading. Women may be so functionally designed and equipped as well.[60] Specifically, there are no gender-specific gifts. Accordingly, women and men alike may receive from the Holy Spirit the gifts of teaching and leading and thus be functionally equipped for teaching and leading. In what ways they may exercise their gifts—and here we enter a discussion of church offices and go beyond our point about gifts—is the issue that divides complementarianism and egalitarianism.

To highlight what the issue is really about, these two diagrams represent the complementarian position and the egalitarian position:

The Complementarian Position

	church activities	*church activities*
forbidden to men	church leadership if they are unable to teach and lead	
forbidden to women		church leadership (because of Paul's prohibition; 1 Tim 2:11–14)

[60] Moreover, Marshall's view of the complementary functioning of men and women is incorrect. "Complementary" does not only mean, for example, that a man is called to do what a woman cannot do, or that a woman is called to do what a man cannot do. Each may be functionally able to do what the other may be functionally able to do, but when they work together, such complementary functioning produces a synergy that would be absent had they each worked alone.

The Egalitarian Position

	church activities	*church activities*
forbidden to men	church leadership if they are unable to teach and lead	
forbidden to women		church leadership if they are unable to teach and lead

The issue is a much narrower one focused on qualifications for the leadership office (1 Tim 3:1–3; Titus 1:5–9). Among these qualifications are a divine call (1 Tim 3:1), certain character qualities (e.g., self-control, respectability, blamelessness, godliness; 1 Tim 3:2–7; Titus 1:7–8), and specific competencies (e.g., ability to teach and lead; 1 Tim 3:2, 4–5; Titus 1:8–9).[61] According to complementarianism, only men who possess and consistently exhibit these virtues and skills may be in church leadership; all other men are prohibited from holding the office. So, this is not a case of men may be church leaders and women may not be church leaders, as only a select few men may be church leaders. The rest of the men may not be church leaders, and women may not be church leaders on the basis of Paul's prohibition in 1 Tim 2:11–14. Again, complementarianism does not maintain that only men may be functionally designed and equipped for teaching and leading, as women may also be so designed and equipped for their ministries to other women and children, their diaconal responsibilities, and more.

[61] I am assuming broad agreement that 1 Tim 3:1–7 and Titus 1:5–9 present the calling, character, and competencies that are required for those in the highest level of church leadership (pastor/elder/bishop/overseer). Diaconal matters, which are set forth in 1 Tim 3:8–13, will be covered in the next section.

The issue is a similarly narrower one for egalitarianism, with the only difference being the conviction that 1 Tim 2:11–14 does not prohibit women from church leadership. According to egalitarianism, only men and women who possess and consistently exhibit the above-listed virtues and skills may be in church leadership; all other men and all other women are prohibited from being in church leadership. So, this is not a case of men may be church leaders and women may be church leaders, as only a select few men and a select few women may be church leaders, while the rest of the men and the rest of the women may not be church leaders. Moreover, 1 Tim 2:11–14 does not prohibit women from church leadership.

To conclude, the issue of the very practical matter of church leadership and its accessibility either to men only or to men and women alike is not about ontological inequality between men and women, nor is it about functional differentiation between men and women. Rather, the issue is a narrower one: the qualifications for church leadership and its responsibilities. For complementarianism, only a select few men who meet those qualifications may be in church leadership, and for egalitarianism, only a select few men and a select few women may be qualified for church leadership.

1 Timothy 3:11[62]

As part of his specific instructions so that Timothy "will know how people ought to conduct themselves in . . . the church" (1 Tim 3:15), Paul discusses the calling, character, and competencies of those who hold (the) two ecclesial offices: elders/pastors/bishops/overseers and deacons (3:1–13).[63] The structure of Paul's presentation is the following: Paul first

---

[62] Some of the following is adapted from Gregg R. Allison, *Sojourners and Strangers: The Doctrine of the Church* (Wheaton: Crossway, 2012), 240–47; Gregg R. Allison, *The Church: An Introduction* (Wheaton: Crossway, 2021), 85–91; Gregg Allison and Ryan Welsch, *Raising the Dust: How to Equip Deacons to Serve the Church* (Louisville: Sojourn Network, 2019), 11–15.

[63] The interchangeability of New Testament terms for those serving in the eldership or pastorate—"elder" or "presbyter" (Gk. *presbyteros*), "bishop" or "overseer"

addresses the office of elder (vv. 1–7), commencing with one's aspiration or desire to be an overseer (v. 1), then treating the qualifications (both character and capability) for the officer. Specifically, Paul's prescription is "an overseer . . . must be" such and such, followed by a lengthy list of requirements (vv. 2–7). The Greek δεῖ . . . τὸν ἐπίσκοπον . . . εἶναι (*dei . . . ton episkopon . . . einai*) establishes the pattern for the discussion to follow.

Second, Paul addresses the office of deacon (vv. 8–13), building upon that pattern: "deacons, likewise" (διακόνους ὡσαύτως, *diakonous hōsautōs*), *should be* (CSB) or *must be* . . . (ESV), with the italicized words being supplied by the translators. The additional words are properly inserted because (1) they convey the sense of "likewise" and (2) they carry forward the pattern established in verse 2, to be specific δεῖ . . . τὸυς διακόνους . . . εἶναι (*dei . . . tous diakonous . . . einai*). To amplify, "in a similar way as elders must meet certain requirements for their office, deacons must meet certain requirements for their office."

This structural discussion is important for the interpretation of v. 11, with two possibilities for the Greek phrase γυναῖκας ὡσαύτως (*gynaikas hōsautōs*): The first option is "Wives, likewise," *should be* (CSB) or *must be* . . . (ESV), again with the italicized words rightly supplied by the translators because (1) they convey the sense of "likewise" and (2) they carry forward the pattern established in v. 2, to be specific δεῖ . . . τας γυναῖκας . . . εἶναι (*dei . . . tas gunaikas . . . einai*).[64] To amplify, "in a similar way as elders must meet certain requirements for their office, and in a similar way as deacons must meet certain requirements for their office, wives must meet certain requirements." As to the identity of these "wives," given the word's placement in Paul's discussion of the diaconate, they are probably the "wives of deacons;" accordingly, along with their deacon-husbands, the wives of deacons must meet certain qualifications.

(Gk. *episkopos*), and "pastor" (Gk. *poimēn*)—can be demonstrated by appeal to Acts 20:17–35 (esp. vv. 17, 28), 1 Tim 3:1–2 with 5:17, Titus 1:5 and 7, and 1 Pet 5:1–4 (esp. vv. 2, 5).

[64] CSB, ESV, NIV 1984.

The second option is "Women, likewise," *should be* (CSB) or *must be* . . . (ESV), again with the italicized words rightly supplied for the same reasons.[65] In this case, the amplification would be "in a similar way as elders must meet certain requirements for their office, and in a similar way as deacons must meet certain requirements for their office, women must meet certain requirements for their office." As to the identity of these "women," given the word's placement in Paul's discussion of the diaconate, they are probably "women deacons" or "deaconesses;" consequently, deacons who are women, like deacons who are men, must meet certain (additional) qualifications.

Arguments for the first interpretation are the following: (1) As Paul has a sustained presentation of elders/pastors (vv. 1–7) and is in the midst of a sustained presentation of deacons (vv. 8–13), why would he interject a brief mention of deaconesses?[66] Moreover (2), if he were to discuss deaconesses, we would expect a much more robust treatment of them and their qualifications, akin to his discussions of the other two officers. (3) Paul's earlier use of γυνή (*gynē*) in relation to elder requirements (an overseer must be "the husband of one *wife*; v. 2), and his subsequent use of the word in relation to deacon requirements ("deacons are to be the husbands of one *wife*;" (v. 12) would seem to favor the sense of "wives" of deacons in v. 11. (4) It seems appropriate, if the wives of deacons assist their deacon-husbands in their ministry, that Paul lists the expectations for those "wives."

Arguments for the second interpretation are these: (1) The structure of the passage favors this view:

(v. 2) δεῖ . . . τὸν ἐπίσκοπον . . . εἶναι (*dei . . . ton episkopon . . . einai*)
(v. 8) διακόνους ὡσαύτως (*diakonous hōsautōs*); that is, δεῖ . . . τοὺς διακόνους . . . εἶναι (*dei . . . tous diakonous . . . einai*)

[65] CSB alternative reading; also NASB, NIV 2011.

[66] The second interpretation poses the same question of the first interpretation: In the midst of a sustained presentation of deacons (vv. 8–13), why would Paul interject a brief mention of deacons' wives? If the interruptive nature of v. 11 is a problem for one interpretation, it is a problem for the other.

(v. 11) γυναῖκας ὡσαύτως (*gynaikas hōsautōs*); that is, δεῖ . . . τας γυναῖκας . . . εἶναι (*dei . . . tas gynaikas . . . einai*)

As Paul discusses the officers of the church, he first addresses overseers, who must meet certain requirements for the pastorate/eldership (v. 2). Second, Paul addresses deacons; they must similarly exhibit certain qualifications for the diaconate (v. 8). Third, he addresses deaconesses; they likewise must meet certain conditions for the diaconate (v. 11). The structure, then, favors the view that, like elders and deacons, so too women must meet certain criteria to hold the office of deaconess.

(2) Connected to the first point is the parallelism between the list for deaconesses and that for deacons. Both women deacons and male deacons must be worthy of respect or dignified (σεμνός [*semnos*] for a male deacon, σεμνή [*semnē*] for a woman deacon), vigilant with their speech, temperate with respect to alcohol, and "faithful in everything," or "holding the mystery of the faith" (vv. 11, 9). The similarity of the list for women and the list for deacons supports the interpretation that these are women deacons.

(3) Had Paul intended to address wives (of deacons) rather than women (deacons), he could have written γυναῖκες διακόνων (*gynaikes diakonōn* = wives of deacons) or γυναῖκες αὐτῶν (*gynaikes autōn* = their wives). Certainly, some translations have "wives" (CSB)—with the assumption that the context of the verse indicates that these are wives of deacons rather than all wives—or "their wives" (ESV, NIV 1984, KJV). In this case it should be noted that the word αὐτῶν (*autōn*) is not in the Greek text but inserted as "their" by the translators to indicate that it is deacons' wives who are being addressed. The absence of these markers favors the second interpretation.

(4) The reason that Paul did not clarify his referent by using the word διάκοναι (*diakonai*, feminine noun) to indicate women deacons is that this feminine form of διάκονος (*diakonos*, masculine noun) did not exist at the time of his writing. Accordingly, in the midst of his instructions about διάκονοι (*diakonoi*), Paul selects γυναῖκες (*gynaikes*) to signal a switch from his discussion of deacons to either "women" in regard to deaconesses or "wives" in regard to the spouses of deacons. (5) If the first interpretation is

correct, an anomaly arises: "It seems quite strange that he [Paul] would give the requirements for wives of deacons but not the wives of elders, particularly because elders have more responsibility. But this problem would be avoided if Paul refers here to deaconesses."[67] This absence of any mention of elders' wives favors the second interpretation.

If the second interpretation is correct, then the New Testament supports both male and female deacons.[68] Biblical examples include the seven deacons in the church of Jerusalem (Acts 6:1–6) and Phoebe in the church of

---

[67] Thomas Schreiner, personal correspondence, April 30, 2008.

[68] Even if one takes the first interpretation of 1 Tim 3:11 and understands it to refer to wives of deacons rather than to women deacons, it is possible to affirm the office of deaconess on other bases (e.g., Phil 1:1 indicates two ecclesial offices: ἐπισκόποι καὶ διακόνοι [*episkopoi kai diakonoi*], bishopric and diaconate). Though a thorough discussion of the diaconate is beyond the scope of this book, whatever else one may affirm of it, the concept of service should be at the center. Because it is an office that involves responsibility for members of the church, the diaconate as consisting of *leading* servants is a justified and better concept. As to the exact nature of diaconal leadership, caution is warranted. The diaconate is certainly a leadership position, but of what type is not detailed in Scripture. As Mathew observes, "The term [διακόνος, *diakonos*] is referring to a special office, but the nature of the special office is not clearly depicted in the New Testament." Susan Matthew, *Women in the Greetings of Romans 16:1-16: A Study of Mutuality and Women's Ministry in the Letter to the Romans* (London and New York: Bloomsburg, 2013), 71. Accordingly, she affirms "the responsibilities of a διάκονος involve some form of leadership, which probably includes teaching and preaching." Her hesitancy attached to the latter claim is appropriate. Mathew, *Women in the Greetings of Romans 16:1–16*, 73.

For complementarianism, because deacons are not responsible for teaching and leading the church at the highest level of human authority (functions that are the duties of male elders), nothing in the responsibilities of the diaconate would exclude women from holding that office. Justification for this view includes the fact that in 1 Timothy 3, Paul requires (male) elders to be able to teach (v. 2) and to demonstrate their leadership competency at the microcosmic level of the family as an indicator of their leadership competency at the macrocosmic level of "God's church" (vv. 4–5), but he does not so require those competencies of deacons (vv. 8–13; there is no corresponding explanation for successful household management by deacons as there is for elders; v. 12 compared with vv. 4–5). For egalitarianism, there are no obstacles to women being deacons in the church. For further discussion of these two approaches, see Mathew, *Women in the Greetings of Romans 16:1–16*, 70.

Cenchreae (Rom 16:1–2).[69] According to Origen, "This text teaches . . . two things: that there are . . . women deacons in the church, and that women, who have given assistance to so many people and who by their good works deserve to be praised by the apostle, should be accepted in the diaconate."[70] In the early church, deacons ministered to and served bishops, distributed the communion elements at the Lord's Supper, cared for the weak, and visited the sick.[71] Deaconesses, working in tandem with deacons, engaged in ministry for women. They accompanied women church members when they spoke with deacons or bishops, primarily to avoid bringing reproach upon the church for (even the appearance of) sexual immorality between male clergy and women. Similarly, to avoid scandal, deaconesses administered baptism to women converts, who during the ritual were stripped of their clothes—to symbolize the removal of their old nature and the restoration to the innocence (nakedness) of Adam and Eve before the fall—before being baptized.[72]

As I favor the second interpretation, I note several considerations for complementarity. Whatever one may decide about the accessibility of the office of pastor/elder to men and women, the office of deacon is accessible to qualified church members of both genders. Accordingly, as current church leaders search to identify and disciple future leaders, they should equally

---

[69] See the later discussion of Phoebe in the treatment of Paul's greetings at the end of his letter to the Romans.

[70] Origen, *Commentary on the Epistle to the Romans*, 16:1–2, cited in Ruth Tucker and Walter Liefeld, *Daughters of the Church* (Grand Rapids: Zondervan, 1987), 106.

[71] Cyprian, *Letter* 64.3, in *ANF*, 5:366; Hippolytus, *The Apostolic Tradition of Hippolytus*, 43.9, in Ray C. Petry, ed., *A History of Christianity: Readings in the History of the Church*, vol. 1: The Early and Medieval Church (Grand Rapids: Baker, 1990), 29; *Apostolic Constitutions*, 2.4.26 (*ANF*, 7:410); 2.6.44 (*ANF*, 7:410); 8.3.28 (ANF, 7:494); 3.2.19 (*ANF*, 7:432).

[72] *Apostolic Constitutions*, 2.4.26 (*ANF*, 7:410); 3.2 between 15 and 16 (*ANF*, 7:431). For further discussion of the roles of deaconesses in the early church see Gregg R. Allison, *Historical Theology: An Introduction to Christian Doctrine* (Grand Rapids: Zondervan, 2011), 594–95.

consider women and men who demonstrate Christlike character, are experienced in proven ministry, have demonstrated servant leadership of others who serve in ministry, and who desire to be leading servants, that is, deaconesses and deacons. Additionally, and taking our cue from the early church, men and women work in complementary fashion in diaconal ministry. Not only because of the reprehensible rise in church scandals involving inappropriate male-female relationships, but especially because of the siblingship of Christians (e.g., Paul instructs believers to consider "the younger women as sisters with all purity;" 1 Tim 5:2), male deacons should lead particular ministries and female deacons should lead particular ministries. In this diaconal way, male image bearers and female image bearers fill out and mutually support one another ecclesially for both individual and corporate flourishing.

1 Corinthians 11:3–16

In one of the more difficult passages on which debate between complementarians and egalitarians focuses, Paul addresses men and women participating in public worship services, treats an important (but largely unknown to us contemporary readers) issue about hair/head coverings and honor/shame, underscores image bearing and glory, alludes to the manner of the creation and the purpose of the creation of Adam and Eve as narrated in Genesis 2, emphasizes the interdependence of men and women in the church, and concludes with a return to the issue about hair/head coverings and honor/shame and glory. Though controversial, this passage has important points regarding complementarity.

Key Issues of Interpretation

Generally speaking, eight interpretive issues fuel the different understandings and applications of Paul's instructions: (1) the meaning of κεφαλή (*kephalē*) as either "authority over" or "source," and what Paul affirms by his statement "the man is the head of the woman" (v. 3); (2) the point of the parallel instruction: (a) every man who prays or prophesies with his head covered dishonors his head and (b) every woman who prays or prophesies with her head uncovered dishonors her head (vv. 4–5); (3) Paul's reasons for insisting that a woman has her head covered; (4) Paul's reason for insisting that a man not cover his head, "because he is the image and glory of God. So too, woman is the glory of man" (v. 7); (5) the manner of creation and the purpose of creation (vv. 8–9); (6) what it is for women to have [a sign or symbol of] authority "because of the angels" (v. 10); (7) the interdependence of men and women (vv. 11–12); and (8) proper judgment, nature's "teaching" about long hair as disgraceful for a man but the glory for a woman, and common ecclesial practice (vv. 13–16).

1. *the meaning of* κεφαλή (**kephalē**) *as either "authority over" or "source," and what Paul affirms by his statement "the man is the head of the woman" (v. 3)*

The debate seems to be at an impasse, with two firmly entrenched and reasoned positions affirming it means "authority over" or "source."[73] Dorothy

[73] The literature is dauntingly massive and includes: Stephen Bedale, "The Meaning of *kephalē* in the Pauline Epistles," *Journal of Theological Studies* 50 (1954): 211–15; Gilbert Bilezikian, "A Critical Examination of Wayne Grudem's Treatment of *Kephalē* in Ancient Greek Texts," appendix in *Beyond Sex Roles*, 2nd ed. (Grand Rapids: Baker, 1985), 215–52; Richard S. Cervin, "Does *Kephalē* Mean 'Source' or 'Authority Over' in Greek Literature? A Rebuttal," *Trinity Journal* 10 (1989): 85–112; Joseph A. Fitzmyer, "Another Look at *Kephalē* in 1 Corinthians 11:3," *New Testament Studies* 35 (1989): 503–11; idem., "*Kephalē* in 1 Corinthians 11:3," *Interpretation* 47 (1993): 52–59; Wayne Grudem, "Does *kephalē* (Head) Mean 'Source' or 'Authority Over' in Greek Literature? A Survey of 2,336 Examples," *Trinity Journal* 6 (1985): 38–59; idem., "The Meaning of *Kephalē* ('Head'): A Response to Recent Studies," in *Recovering Biblical Manhood and Womanhood*, ed. John Piper and Wayne Grudem (Wheaton: Crossway, 1991), 425–68; idem., "The Meaning of *Kephalē* ('Head'): An Evaluation of New Evidence, Real and Alleged," *Journal of the Evangelical Theological Society* 44 (March 2001): 25–66; Judith M. Gundry-Volf, "Gender and Creation in 1 Corinthians 11:2–16: A Study in Paul's Theological Method," in *Evangelium, Schriftauslegung, Kirche Feschrift für Peter Stuhlmacher*, ed. Jostein Ådna, Scott

Lee summarizes the two views: "Those who opt for 'source' argue that Paul's meaning is not one of submission but rather of origin, recalling the second creation account, where Eve is created from Adam. Those who see some notion of headship argue that it is part of the order of creation or that it indicates patriarchal assumptions on Paul's part. Both sides point to examples in Greek literature that support their interpretations."[74]

Linda Belleville argues for *kephalē* as "source" by appealing to the four other instances of Paul's use of the word to present Christ's relationship to his church: "Paul's language is thoroughly biological. The church is a living organism that draws its existence and nourishment from Christ as *kephalē.* Christ is *kephalē* and 'savior' of the church, 'his body' (Eph. 4:16; 5:22–23; Col. 1:18; 2:19); he is its 'beginning' and 'firstborn' (Col. 1:18). 'From him' (*ex hou*) the church is supported, held together, and grows (Eph. 4:16; Col. 2:19). As *kephalē* of the church, Christ 'feeds and cares' for it as people do for 'their own bodies' (Eph. 5:29)."[75] Belleville avers that a theology of creation explains Paul's biological orientation: "*Kephalē*

Hafemann, and Otfried Hofius (Göttingen, Germany: Vandenhoeck & Ruprecht, 1997), 151–71; Catherine C. Kroeger, "The Classical Concept of *Head* as 'Source'" in Gretchen Gaebelein Hull, *Equal to Serve* (Old Tappan, N.J.: Fleming Revell, 1987), 267–83; idem, "Toward an Understanding of Ancient Conceptions of 'Head,'" Priscilla Papers 20, no. 3 (summer, 20026); Walter L. Liefeld, "Women, Submission & Ministry in 1 Corinthians," in Mickelsen, *Women, Authority & the Bible*, 134–53; Berkeley and Alvera Mickelsen, "What Does *Kephalē* Mean in the New Testament?" in *Women, Authority and the Bible*, ed. Alvera Mickelsen (Grand Rapids: Zondervan, 1986), 97–132; Jerome Murphy O'Connor, "Sex and Logic in 1 Corinthians 11:2-16," *Catholic Biblical Quarterly* 42 (1980): 482–500; "Interpolations in 1 Corinthians," *Catholic Biblical Quarterly* 48 (1986): 81-94; Andrew C. Perriman, "The Head of a Woman: The Meaning of *Kephalē* in 1 Cor. 11:3," *Journal of Theological Studies* 45 (1994): 602–22; Thomas Schreiner, "Head Coverings, Prophecies and the Trinity: 1 Corinthians 11:2-16," in R*ecovering Biblical Manhood and Womanhood*, ed. John Piper and Wayne Grudem (Wheaton: Crossway, 1991), 124–39.

[74] Dorothy A. Lee, *The Ministry of Women in the New Testament* (Grand Rapids: Baker Academic, 2021), 116.

[75] Belleville, "Women in Ministry: An Egalitarian Perspective," 100.

as 'source' goes back to the creation of male and female [Gen 2:21–23]. It derives from the theological notion of the first man as the 'source' (*kephalē*) of the first woman."[76]

In his pioneering article, "Does Κεφαλη ('Head') Mean 'Source' Or 'Authority Over' in Greek Literature? A Survey of 2,336 Examples," Wayne Grudem concluded "that 'source, origin' is nowhere clearly attested as a legitimate meaning for κεφαλή, and that the meaning 'ruler, authority over' has sufficient attestation to establish it clearly as a legitimate sense for κεφαλή in Greek literature at the time of the New Testament. Indeed, it was a well-established and recognizable meaning, and it is the meaning that best suits the New Testament texts that speak of the relationship between men and women by saying that the man is the 'head' of a woman and the husband is the 'head' of the wife."[77]

Belleville and Grudem represent, respectively, the understanding of *kephalē* as "source" and *kephalē* as "head" or "authority over."

Between these two opposite understandings is the position that sees both connotations as possibly applying to Paul's use of *kephalē* in 1 Cor 11:3. For example, Dorothy Lee appeals to Anthony Thiselton's suggestion of ambiguity of the term in Paul such that it could mean either "authority over" or "source."[78] She then proposes, "Even if 'source' is the dominant meaning here, it still implies at least a sense of dependence, whether or not it includes submission."[79] Similarly, Craig Blomberg notes that "even if Paul

---

[76] Belleville, "An Egalitarian Perspective," 100.

[77] Grudem, "Does Κεφαλη ('Head') Mean 'Source' Or 'Authority Over' in Greek Literature? A Survey of 2,336 Examples," (59); followed by other articles: Grudem, "The Meaning of Kephalē ('Head'): A Response to Recent Studies," *Trinity Journal* 11 n. s. (1990): 3–72; republished as appendix 1 in Piper and Grudem, eds., *Recovering Biblical Manhood and Womanhood*, 425–68; Grudem, "The Meaning of κεφαλή ("head"): An Evaluation of New Evidence, Real and Alleged," *JETS* 44.1 (2001): 25–65.

[78] Anthony Thiselton, *First Epistle to the Corinthians*, NIGTC (Grand Rapids: Eerdmans, 2000), 823–33.

[79] Lee, *The Ministry of Women in the New Testament*, 116.

is talking only about origins in verse 3, he does so to set up his subsequent commands about honoring those in authority over us."[80]

Thomas Schreiner also discusses this "both . . . and" option, noting that "even if *kephalē* should be defined only as 'source' (which is very unlikely), it would still support male leadership."[81] For warrant, he appeals to Eph 5:22–24 and explains that the reason that Paul gives for his command that wives submit to their husbands is "because (ὅτι, *hoti*) the husband is the head of the wife as Christ is the head of the church" (v. 23). Schreiner offers, "even if *kephalē* means 'source,' wives are to fill a supportive and submissive role, and husbands, as the 'source,' are to function as leaders."[82] He proposes that as in Ephesians, so also in 1 Cor 11:3: "If *kephalē* means 'source,' then women are to defer to their source by adorning themselves properly."[83] He concludes with a denial that "authority" can be jettisoned from either passage.[84]

In summary and generally speaking, egalitarianism understands *kephalē* as "source" and denies any sense of male hierarchy, whereas complementarianism takes *kephalē* to mean "authority over" with respect to men in relation to women in the church. Moreover, if the "both source and authority" view is warranted, then *kephalē* underscores both an organic unity between men and women (i.e., the latter comes from and is thus linked to the former) and authority.

---

[80] Craig L. Blomberg, *1 Corinthians* (Grand Rapids: Zondervan Academic, 1995), 71. Cf. Blomberg, "Women in Ministry: A Complementarian Perspective," in *Two Views on Women in Ministry*, 155–56.

[81] Thomas R. Schreiner, "Women in Ministry: Another Complementarian Perspective," in *Two Views on Women in Ministry*, 301.

[82] Schreiner, "Women in Ministry: Another Complementarian Perspective," 302.

[83] Schreiner, "Women in Ministry: Another Complementarian Perspective," 302.

[84] He adds further support for "the concept of obedience is involved in submission" with appeal to 1 Pet 3:5–6, in which Peter connects submission to Sarah's obedience to Abraham (303).

2. *the point of the parallel instruction (vv. 4–5)*

every man
  who prays or prophesies with his
    head covered
      dishonors his head
and
every woman
  who prays or prophesies with her
    head uncovered
      dishonors her head (vv. 4–5)

To begin with, an important yet largely unclear matter in v. 4 is the referent of the phrase κατὰ κεφαλῆς ἔχων (*kata kephalēs echōn*). Fee proposes "an external cloth covering,"[85] noting that the key point in this hypothetical situation is "that such a covering for men would bring shame to Christ."[86] Working from the phrase's literal rendering "having down from the head," Blomberg concurs that the reference may be to an external covering. Based on Paul's later discussion (vv. 14–15), however, Blomberg opts for the apostle's prohibition being a reference to the relative length of a man's hair, with Paul's prohibition stemming from such long hairstyle as indicative of homosexual behavior or some other (bad) cultural practice.[87]

Similarly, in v. 5, the referent of the phrase ἀκατακαλύπτῳ τῇ κεφαλῇ (*akatakalyptō tē kephalē*) is obscure. Fee notes three views: (1) the traditional view is similar to his proposal for men (v. 4) and refers to "some kind of external covering;" (2) long hair; and (3) "loosed hair", or women letting down their hair in public and thus provoking shame.[88]

[85] Gordon D. Fee, *The First Epistle to the Corinthians*, rev. ed., NICNT (Grand Rapids: Eerdmans, 2014), 507. He notes the nearly universal absence of men covering their heads.

[86] Fee, *The First Epistle to the Corinthians*, 508.

[87] Blomberg, *1 Corinthians*, 72.

[88] Fee, *The First Epistle to the Corinthians*, 496–97.

He offers a modified first view: the external covering "is a loose shawl, not a veil."[89]

3. *Paul's reasons for insisting that a woman has her head covered*

Blomberg presents two possibilities for Paul directing women to be covered when praying and prophesying: (1) Paul instructs women in the church to wear some kind of external covering, as was the practice of Greek women in public. By wearing a shawl, Christian women would distinguish themselves from other women who, during pagan worship services, uncovered themselves to flaunt "their temporary transcendence of human sexuality."[90] (2) Paul directs women in the church to keep their hair up, as was the practice of married women in public. To wear loose and flowing hair would be a sign of being unmarried, an adulteress, or part of pagan prophetic activity; additionally, by having short hair, women signal that they are the "male" partner in a lesbian relationship.[91] In either case, if Christian women ignore Paul's directive to be covered (by not wearing a shawl or by not wearing their hair up), they might as well go all the way and shave off their hair completely: baldness would send the unequivocally wrong signal.

---

[89] Fee, *The First Epistle to the Corinthians*, 497n20. Schreiner concurs with the covering being a shawl rather than a veil, as Paul's later use of περιβόλαιον (*peribolaion*, v. 15) refers to some type of wrap around garment and not to a veil. Schreiner, "Head Coverings, Prophecies, and the Trinity," 126. Schreiner also notes that Paul's reference in v. 15 to a woman's long hair being given to her for a covering does not contradict or overturn his directives to women to wear a shawl as a covering (vv. 4–6). In such case, those directives would be "awkward and even misleading." Accordingly, he interprets the phrase ἡ κόμη ἀντὶ περιβολαίου δέδοται (*hē komē anti peribolaiou dedotai*) not as "her long hair is given *as a substitute for* (or *instead of*) a covering" (thus rendering Paul's insistence on women being covered meaningless) but as "her long hair is given as an *equivalence* of a covering," that is, "an indication that she needs to wear a covering" (126).

[90] Blomberg, *1 Corinthians*, 72.

[91] Blomberg, *1 Corinthians*, 72–73.

Blomberg urges: "What all these phenomena share is that Paul was concerned that Christian men and women at worship do not appear as though they were either religiously unfaithful to God or sexually unfaithful to their spouses."[92] Fee adds another possible wrong outcome: "a breakdown in the distinction between the sexes."[93] Whatever reason might be the case, disobedience to Paul's directives would result in shaming their *kephalē*: for men, Christ who is their authority or source; for women, men, who are their authority or source.

4. *Paul's reason for insisting that a man not cover his head, "because he is the image and glory of God. So too, woman is the glory of man" (v. 7)*

Harking back to Genesis 1 and 2, another reason for (γάρ, *gar*) Paul's directions for women to cover themselves when praying and prophesying in the corporate assembly has to do with image bearing and glory. Paul sets up a simple contrast: "on the one hand, a man . . . on the other hand, the woman" (ἀνὴρ μὲν . . . ἡ γυνὴ δὲ, *anēr men . . . hē gynē de*). When participating in the public gathering of the church, men should not be covered (repeating v. 4) but women should be covered. This instruction for "a man" is "because he is the image and glory of God," alluding to Gen 1:26–28 though leaving out the textual fact that image bearing belongs equally to a woman while also not affirming that the woman is the image of a man. Paul's instruction for "a woman" is because she "is the glory of man."

Fee rejects the interpretation that Paul is continuing his argument (v. 3) about male headship/authority; instead, he locates Paul's concern with man's relationship to God.[94] "By creating man in his own image, God set his own glory in the man. Man, therefore, exists to God's praise and honor, and is to

---

[92] Blomberg, "Women in Ministry: A Complementarian Perspective," 137.

[93] Fee, *The First Epistle to the Corinthians*, 510, 511.

[94] Fee, *The First Epistle to the Corinthians*, 515.

live in relationship to God so as to be his 'glory.'"[95] Similarly, Fee sees Paul's concern not with woman per se—"Paul does not hereby deny that woman was created in God's image, or that she, too, is God's glory"—but with a woman's relationship to men: "She is related to man as his glory, a relationship that somehow appears to be jeopardized by her present action" of not being covered.[96]

Interestingly, instead of making the above point explicitly—that women should be covered—and rather than clarifying how her being covered is the appropriate application of a woman being the glory of a man, Paul expounds in more detail why she is a man's glory. Fee rejects the traditional explanation that Paul addresses or implies the subordination of women to men. Such a reason "makes little sense of the argument itself. Appearance does not mark roles of authority or subservience, at least not in this text. Furthermore, at the crucial point, their praying and prophesying, they are clearly not in hierarchical roles."[97] They are men's glory, which is the opposite of "disgrace" or "dishonor" (vv. 4–6, 14–15), in the sense of "esteem" or "honor": a woman is man's glory in that she should honor him (see next discussion of vv. 8–9).[98] Throughout his discussion, Fee articulates a common egalitarian understanding: Paul's framework is not hierarchical—with a man as *kephalē*, that is, the authority over a woman—but relational: a man in an honorific relationship to God and a woman in an honorific relationship to man.

A typical complementarian understanding of v. 7 underscores several points (the first two points are shared broadly with egalitarian interpretations). First, Paul does not deny that women are created in the divine image; among other problems if this were the case, the apostle would blatantly contradict Gen 1:27, which is the biblical background for his

---

[95] Fee, *The First Epistle to the Corinthians*, 516.

[96] Fee, *The First Epistle to the Corinthians*, 516.

[97] Fee, *The First Epistle to the Corinthians*, 516n15.

[98] For further discussion see Schreiner, "Head Coverings, Prophecies, and the Trinity," 133.

present discussion of men and women. Second, and flowing from his first point, Paul does not affirm an essential inferiority of women to men; among other problems, if this were the case, the apostle would blatantly contradict an implication (equal dignity) of both sexes being created in the divine image, as well as controvert his later affirmation of the interdependence of women and men. Third (and here is the divergence between complementarian and egalitarian understandings), Paul does in some sense highlight the submission of women to men by his description of a woman as the glory of man. Some complementarians envision this submission to apply to all women in relation to all men, with ανήρ (*anēr*, singular "man") referring to all men and γυνή (*gynē*, singular "woman") referring to all women. As demonstrated by women covering themselves in the public assembly, all female members of the church express submission to all its male members. Other complementarians consider this submission to apply restrictively to all married women in relation to their husbands, with ανήρ (*anēr*, singular "man") referring to all married men and γυνή (*gynē*, singular "woman") referring to all married women. As demonstrated by married women covering themselves in the public assembly, all wives express submission to their husbands.[99] In either case, complementarianism emphasizes some sense of male/husband authority and female/wife submission in v. 7, an interpretation bolstered by its understanding of *kephalē* as "head" or "authority over" as setting the tone of the entire passage.

---

[99] Blomberg argues for this latter interpretation, noting "it is much harder to understand how Paul could have claimed that every man is an authority over every woman and much easier to interpret the passage if husbands and wives are meant throughout (e.g., v. 5)." The preference for "man" and "woman" arises from Paul's later discussion of Adam and Eve (vv. 8–9), "but Adam and Eve were not only the prototypical male and female but also the first 'married' couple." If he is correct, "husband" and "wife" would significantly restrict the application of Paul's entire discussion: rather than instructing all women to be covered when praying and prophesying, Paul would be directing wives to participate appropriately in the assembly. Blomberg, *1 Corinthians*, 71.

5. *the manner of creation and the purpose of creation (vv. 8–9)*

Paul offers two explanations for his point that, in her relationship with man, a woman is his glory. The two reasons allude to the narratives of Genesis 2:

> verse 8: For man did not come from woman, but woman came from man (the *manner* of creation: Eve was taken from Adam's side; Gen 2:21–23)
>
> verse 9: Neither was man created for the sake of woman, but woman for the sake of man (the *purpose* of creation: Eve was created to remove Adam's lack of companionship and to be his helper; Gen 2:18)

From an egalitarian perspective, as he reflects on these two Genesis narratives, Paul affirms that (1) "the man is the *kephalē* of the woman" (v. 3), that is, he is her source, in that she has her life from him; and (2) "woman is the glory of man" (v. 7), that is, she was created for his sake. Fee does not view these passages as indicating a woman's subordination to man, especially because verses "11–12 make clear that Paul did not intend them to be" taken in that way.[100] Specifically, Fee maintains that "for the sake of man" (v. 9) cannot mean "for his dominion" or "for him to exercise authority over" a woman.[101] Rather, the phrase alludes to and affirms Gen 2:18: "Man by himself is not complete; he is alone, without a companion suitable to him."[102] Flowing from this lack is the woman's reality: "She is thus man's glory because she 'came from man' and was created 'for him.' She is not thereby subordinate to him, but necessary for him. She exists to his honor as the one who having come from man is the one companion suitable to him, so that he might be complete and that they together might form humanity."[103] Accordingly, a common egalitarian interpretation of

[100] Fee, *The First Epistle to the Corinthians*, 517.
[101] Fee, *The First Epistle to the Corinthians*, 517.
[102] Fee, *The First Epistle to the Corinthians*, 517.
[103] Fee, *The First Epistle to the Corinthians*, 517.

this section emphasizes "source" and "glory": the man is the source of the woman, who came from man (v. 8), and the woman is the glory of man (v. 7), for whose sake the woman was created in order to complete the divine design for humankind (Gen 1:27).

From a complementarian perspective, Paul alludes to the Genesis narratives and draws from both points—the manner of creation and the purpose of creation—further support for his different directives regarding covering one's head while praying and prophesying, all of which is tied into male authority and female submission.

> the man is the head of the woman
>
> [when praying and prophesying]
>
> the man does not pray with his head covered
>
> [reasons]
>
> 1. such would dishonor his head, Christ
> 2. the man is the image and glory of God
>
> the woman does not pray with her head uncovered
>
> [reasons}
>
> 1. such would dishonor her head, the man
> 2. she is the glory of man
>
> further reasons from creation for these instructions
>
> 1. man did not come from woman, but woman came from man (manner of creation)
> 2. man was not created for the sake of woman, but woman for the sake of man (purpose of creation)
>
> ultimately this is tied to the fact that the man is the head of (authority over) the woman (who is to be submissive to him)

While agreeing with egalitarian affirmations about the incompleteness of man apart from woman, the fittingness of the first woman for the first man, and the creation of the original human beings as actualizing the divine design for humanity, complementarianism underscores the Genesis narrative's emphasis on the manner and purpose of creation as expressing the hierarchical relationships between men/husbands and women/wives. Flowing from the apostle's use of *kephalē* as "authority over" and his affirmation that a woman/wife is the glory of a man/husband, complementarianism underscores the fact that Paul's allusions to the manner and purpose of creation—vv. 8–9, which continue his argument—further support male authority and female submission.

6. *what it is for women to have [a sign or symbol of] authority "because of the angels" (v. 10)*

A further reason (διὰ τοῦτο, *dia touto*) for Paul's directive is (literally) "the woman ought to have authority on her head" (ὀφείλει ἡ γυνὴ ἐξουσίαν ἔχειν ἐπὶ τῆς κεφαλῆς, *opheilei hē gynē exousian echein epi tēs kephalēs*). The CSB renders it "a woman should have a symbol of authority on her head." Fee rejects the traditional view that finds an affirmation of female submission by taking ἐξουσίαν ἔχειν (*exousian echein*) in a passive sense—"the woman ought to have authority *over* her head"—meaning that her husband is the authority over her and her head covering (though not mentioned) is the sign or symbol of his authority and her submission. Cautiously, Fee understands Paul's point to mean that a woman is to exercise her newfound freedom to pray and prophesy yet continue to be covered "as a sign of her new liberty in Christ,"[104] or that she has "the freedom over her head to do as she wishes."[105] In either case, though she is free, a woman should not be uncovered, which would bring shame on man, but she should use her freedom appropriately, due to the interdependence between the sexes (see next discussion).[106]

For Blomberg, v. 10 should not include the additional words "a symbol/sign on" when translated (e.g., CSB, NIV). Instead, he maintains "'to

---

[104] Fee, *The First Epistle to the Corinthians*, 520. Fee notes the lack of textual support for this view.

[105] Fee, *The First Epistle to the Corinthians*, 520.

[106] Fee, *The First Epistle to the Corinthians*, 522–23.

have authority' most naturally means something the woman would actively exercise. So a popular recent view has been that the woman's head covering indicates her authority to pray and prophesy."[107] For Blomberg, this interpretation is incorrect, as he seeks to demonstrate with appeals to other New Testament passages in which ἐξουσίαν ἔχειν ἐπί (*exousian echein epi*) occurs; in every one of those instances, the sense is "to have authority (or control) over."[108] Thus, the proper rendering should be something like, "For this reason . . . a wife should exercise control over her head [i.e., keep the appropriate covering on it]."

As for Paul's reference to "the angels," Blomberg opts for the idea that angels watch over creation and protect Christian worship; accordingly, "They in particular would want to see services proceed with appropriate dignity and decorum."[109] Fee appeals to the three other uses of "angels" in 1 Cor 4:9; 6:3; 13:1 and offers three possibilities: (1) similar to Blomberg's view, angels are present when the church assembles publicly, thus requiring women to have some kind of sign of authority as they are being watched by angels (4:9); (2) because believers will judge angels in the future, women should exercise freedom over their heads now (6:3); and (3) suffering from an over-realized eschatology, the Corinthian women were arguing that they may exercise their authority to participate in the public assembly without being covered because they were already like the angels (13:1).

For both complementarianism and egalitarianism, this verse remains quite obscure. Still, in keeping with the framework of the entire passage, complementarianism understands Paul to be giving further support for some kind of hierarchical relationship between men and women in the church while egalitarianism dismisses this point.

---

[107] Blomberg, *1 Corinthians*, 73.

[108] His list is Matt 9:6 [par. Mark 2:10; Luke 5:24]; Rev 11:6; 14:18; 16:9; 20:6; cf. similar constructions with *epano* for *epi* in Luke 19:17 and with *peri* for *epi* in 1 Cor 7:37. Blomberg, *1 Corinthians*, 73.

[109] Blomberg, *1 Corinthians*, 73.

7. *the interdependence of men and women (vv. 11–12)*

Paul's following point qualifies his preceding arguments and establishes a contrast—"however" (πλήν, *plēn*). Whether the apostle has been addressing hierarchical relationships between men and women or emphasizing female freedom, he now clarifies his meaning or provides a corrective to any possible misunderstanding.

Fee notes the chiastic structure of the two sets of verses (vv. 8–9, 11–12, modified for CSB):

A a man did not come from woman,
A b but woman came from man;

B a neither was man created for the sake of woman,
B b but woman for the sake of man.

however

B′ b woman is not independent of man, } in the Lord
B′ a and man is not independent of woman. }

for

A′ b just as woman came from man,
A′ a so man comes through woman,
and all things come from God

Fee's conclusions are: (1) He denies that Paul "means that woman exists for man's purposes, as though in some kind of subordinate position to his aims and will. To the contrary, God has so arranged things that 'in the Lord' the one cannot exist without the other."[110] Interdependence, not authority and submission, is affirmed. (2) Paul does not mean that men and women are equal in terms of salvation in Christ, as that, while true, is not the apostle's

[110] Fee, *The First Epistle to the Corinthians*, 523. He clarifies that Paul does not insist that every man and every woman must be married.

point in this discussion. (3) Rather, Paul's emphasis is on the mutual dependence of women and men in terms of creation. He starts with the original creation, underscoring Eve's creation from Adam (the manner of creation):

A b	woman came from man

and not the reverse:

A a	man did not come from woman

Paul next underscores Eve's creation for Adam (the purpose of creation):

B b	woman [was created] for the sake of man

and not the reverse:

B a	neither was man created for the sake of woman

Paul then combines the original creation with all subsequent creation of human beings:

A′ b	just as woman came from man (the original creation of Eve from Adam)
A′ a	so man comes through woman (all subsequent creation: every man [and woman] since that original creation is born of a woman/mother)

The apostle concludes with the general statement that, ultimately, God is the Creator of all things, including all men and all women.

While complementarianism and egalitarianism may largely agree with this structure and development of Paul's presentation, they draw different conclusions. Fee offers an egalitarian perspective: "Both man and woman, not just man, are from God. God made the one from dust, the other through man, and finally both through woman. This seems clearly designed to keep the earlier argument from being read in a subordinationist way."[111]

---

[111] Fee, *The First Epistle to the Corinthians*, 524.

Egalitarianism emphasizes interdependence without hierarchy. Blomberg presents a complementarian viewpoint. By contrast with (πλήν, *plēn*) what he has presented thus far about men/husbands and women/wives in hierarchical relationships, Paul reminds both groups of their fundamental interdependence. Certainly, the order of creation started with a man (Adam) from whom a woman (Eve) was taken; thus, the first woman came from a man. This order has, in every subsequent procreation, been reversed; all men (and all women, for that matter) come from a woman/mother.[112] Accordingly, "whatever hierarchies remain are significantly tempered by the fact that God is the origin of everything that belongs to redemption. He is therefore our ultimate and most important authority."[113] Complementarianism emphasizes interdependence with hierarchy.

8. *proper judgment, nature's "teaching" about long hair as disgraceful for a man but the glory for a woman, and common ecclesial practice (vv. 13–16).*

As Paul returns to his earlier discussion of head covering (vv. 13–16), which is the main idea of the entire passage (vv. 3–16), he poses two rhetorical questions:[114] (1) "Is it proper for a woman to pray to God with her head uncovered?" The expected reply is negative, which is the response that the Corinthians should give (though at least some were not so responding) because "every woman who prays or prophesies with her head uncovered

---

[112] Could this also be Jesus's point when he identifies John the Baptist: "among those born of women no one greater that John the Baptist has appeared, but the least in the kingdom of heaven is greater than he" (Matt 11:11)? Jesus's contrast seems to be that of all human beings (among whom John the Baptist is the greatest) and those who have entered the kingdom through following Jesus. As for the first category, Paul affirms that "man comes from woman" (1 Cor 11:12) in the sense that all humanity, or all men and all women, come from a woman/mother. Similarly, in Jesus's expression, all humanity, or all men and all women, are "born of women/mothers."

[113] Blomberg, *1 Corinthians*, 73.

[114] Fee, *The First Epistle to the Corinthians*, 525.

dishonors her head" (v. 5). (2) "Does not even nature itself teach you that if a man has long hair it is a disgrace to him, but that if a woman has long hair, it is her glory?" The expected reply is positive, with this second question and its response intended to reinforce the first question and its response.

Paul makes three points as he directs the Corinthians to judge for themselves the truthfulness of his position:[115] (1) "propriety" argues for appropriate head covering; (2) "nature" supports appropriate head covering; and (3) the pervasive "custom" (CSB, ASV, KJV) or "practice" (ESV, RSV) of the early churches does so as well. Both Fee and Blomberg hold that "nature" refers to a long-standing convention or well-established pattern. According to Fee, "'nature' itself has thus distinguished between the sexes" and the Corinthians should be aware of that fact and thus maintain that gender distinctiveness in their corporate worship service.[116] As for hair length, what is customary in their culture should indicate to them the unnaturalness—and, thus, the disgrace—of men wearing their hair long and, oppositely, the naturalness—and, thus, the glory—of women wearing their hair long, which functions as their natural covering. Such glory, being the opposite of "disgrace" or "dishonor" (vv. 4–6), means "esteem" or "honor": "Long hair does not give her glory; it functions as something that distinguishes the splendor of the woman."[117] As the conclusion to Paul's sustained discussion of hair, shame, glory, dishonor, and the like, it seems that the apostle's point reinforces "the preceding arguments that the woman should not be 'uncovered' when praying or prophesying."[118] Because women naturally have long hair as a covering, that fact underscores Paul's directive for them to be covered when participating in the public assembly. Moreover, if anyone in the

---

[115] Blomberg, *1 Corinthians*, 73.

[116] Fee, *The First Epistle to the Corinthians*, 525.

[117] Fee, *The First Epistle to the Corinthians*, 527.

[118] Fee, *The First Epistle to the Corinthians*, 528. Fee offers this as one of two alternatives, the other having to do with the specific issue of hair as the key idea all along. He discusses the preposition ἀντί (*anti*) and rejects this alternative interpretation as fatally flawed for various reasons. Fee, *The First Epistle to the Corinthians*, 528–29.

Corinthian church dissents from Paul's instruction (for example, women who pray and prophesy while being uncovered), he appeals to the universality of this custom among all "the churches of God," as he did earlier in his letter (4:17; 7:17) and as he will do later on (14:33).

From these eight interpretive issues flow several implications. From an egalitarian perspective, Fee believes that Paul's intent "is not to put women in their place, as it were, but to maintain a cultural tradition that has the effect of serving as a gender distinctive, even while 'in the Lord' neither is independent of the other (1 Cor 11:11)."[119] As for the ministry of men and women, Philip Payne, taking κεφαλή (*kephalē*) as "source," maintains that "men and women should show respect to each other, honoring the opposite sex as their source. As Paul stresses in the climax of this passage, believers must affirm the equal rights and privileges of women and men in the Lord. Women as well as men may lead in public Christian worship. Since in the Lord woman and man are not separate, women who are gifted and called by God ought to be welcomed into ministry just as men are."[120] Egalitarianism emphasizes interdependence without hierarchy.

From a complementarian perspective, three implications flow. One focuses on the hierarchical structure of male-female relationships. As discussed above, some complementarians apply female submission to all women in relation to all men; thus, broadening Paul's discussion, such submission is exhibited by female members not preaching, teaching, or leading the church and by obeying the directives of all the male members. Other complementarians apply female submission restrictively to all married women in relation to their husbands; thus, broadening Paul's discussion, such submission is exhibited by female members not preaching, teaching,

---

[119] Gordon D. Fee, "Praying and Prophesying in the Assemblies: 1 Corinthians 11:2–16," in *Discovering Biblical Equality: Biblical, Theological, Cultural, and Practical Perspectives*, ed. Ronald W. Pierce and Cynthia Long Westfall, 3rd ed. (Downers Grove: IVP Academic, 2021), 145.

[120] Philip B. Payne, "Wild Hair and Gender Equality in 1 Corinthians 11:2–16," *Priscilla Papers* 20. 3 (2006), https://www.cbeinternational.org/resource/wild-hair-and-gender-equality-1-corinthians-112-16/.

or leading the church while only obeying the directives of their husbands rather than all men (with the exception of the elders/pastors who preach, teach, and lead the church).

A second implication flows from Paul's appeal to the manner and purpose of creation. I will return to the first point shortly. In terms of the second point, and as Blomberg notes, Paul's expression "the woman was created for the sake of the man" (v. 9) indicates that the purpose for Eve's creation was that she would be Adam's helper. Some commentators highlight the fact that עֵזֶר (*'ezer*) is often used with reference to God as helper of his people, concluding that just as God as helper does not indicate his subordination to human beings, neither does Eve as helper indicate her submission to Adam. Blomberg agrees—while adding an important qualification—that such usage "proves that the term itself does not inherently imply subordination, but it does not prove that it *cannot* imply subordination. Some helpers are authority figures, others are peers, many others are subordinates."[121] However, in the case of vv. 3–7, it is difficult to deny that Paul establishes a hierarchy among men/women or husbands/their wives.[122] Accordingly, complementarianism understands Paul's allusion to the purpose of Eve's creation for Adam's sake to indicate a male-female hierarchy in the church.

A third implication, as articulated by Blomberg, concerns a warning about interpreting vv. 11–12, with Paul's emphasis on interdependence rather than hierarchy among men or women (or at least among husbands and their wives), as cancelling out vv. 8–9, with the apostle's attention to the manner of creation and the purpose of creation, with some implications for hierarchy among the sexes or at least among married couples.[123] Such an interpretation (a) threatens to render vv. 8–9 meaningless; (b) fails

[121] Blomberg, *1 Corinthians*, 75.

[122] Blomberg, *1 Corinthians*, 75.

[123] He disagrees specifically with Judith Gundry-Volf, "Gender and Creation in 1 Corinthians 11:2–16: A Study in Paul's Theological Method," in *Evangelium, Schriftauslegung, Kirche*, ed. J. Ådna, S. J. Hafemann, and O. Hofius (Göttingen: Vandenhoeck & Ruprecht, 1997), 152. Blomberg, "Women in Ministry: A Complementarian Perspective," 160–61n112.

to note the contrasting "however" as v. 11 begins, underscoring that Paul is turning his attention from a discussion of hierarchy (vv. 3–10) to a new focus on interdependence without minimizing or contradicting that earlier discussion; and (c) is actually contradicted by Paul's directive that women/wives not dishonor men/their husbands (v. 5 and the implication of v. 7).[124] Complementarianism embraces interdependence with hierarchy.

As noted, I turn to Paul's appeal to the manner of creation and join it to the apostle's unparalleled affirmations that a man "is the image and glory of God. So too, woman is the glory of man" (v. 7). The question is: Are men and women alike created in the image of God, or are they created in the divine image with some differences? Additionally, does the manner of creation answer this question in some way?

Bruce Ware, in his essay "Male and Female Complementarity and the Image of God," offers, "Complementarians and egalitarians have agreed that the creation of male and female as the image of God indicates the equal value of women and men as being fully human, with equal dignity, worth and importance."[125] Yet, in his essay, Ware maintains that the creation of the first man and the first woman was different and, because of that difference in their original creation, the creation of all men and all women ever since then has continued and continues today to be different. Accordingly, though both are fully in the image of God and equally in the image of God, they are not constituted in the image of God in the identical way; the manner of their creation differentiates them.

Specifically, Ware proposes the following:

> [I]t might be best to understand the original creation of male and female as one in which the male was made in the image of God first, in an unmediated fashion, as God formed him from the dust of the ground, and the female was made in the image of God second, in

---

[124] Blomberg, *1 Corinthians*, 75.

[125] Bruce Ware, "Male and Female Complementarity and the Image of God," *JBMW* 7 (2002): 18.

> a mediated fashion, as God chose not mere earth, but the very rib of Adam by which He would create the woman fully and equally the image of God. In the very formation of the woman, it was to be clear that her life, her constitution, her nature, was rooted in and derived from the life, constitution, and nature of the man.[126]

Ware extends this idea of the man's creation as being immediate and underived and the woman's creation as being mediate and derived (from the man) to all men and women today. He works not only from the woman's creation "through (and by God's design, *only* through) her origination from the man and as the glory of the man," but also from Seth's creation in the divine image through his origination from his father (Gen 5:2).[127] "What this suggests, then, that not only is the concept of male-headship relevant to the question of how men and women are to relate and work together, but it seems also true that male-headship is part of the very constitution of the woman being created in the image of God. Man is a human being made in the image of God first; woman becomes a human being bearing the image of God only through the man. While both are fully and equally the image of God, there is a built-in priority given to the male that reflects God's design of male headship in the created order."[128] He takes this priority to support "the principle of male headship as functioning as the image of God persons both men and women are."[129]

Before assessing this proposal, I note Ware's clear affirmation that God's creation of men and women as his image bearers signifies their full humanity and equal value, dignity, and importance. Moreover, he pleads for women and men to collaborate by working together to achieve God's purposes, and he denounces any disparagement of women by men and of men by women.[130]

---

[126] Ware, "Male and Female Complementarity and the Image of God," 18.
[127] Ware, "Male and Female Complementarity and the Image of God," 20.
[128] Ware, "Male and Female Complementarity and the Image of God," 20–21.
[129] Ware, "Male and Female Complementarity and the Image of God," 21.
[130] Ware, "Male and Female Complementarity and the Image of God," 21.

At the same time, Ware distinguishes between the two as to the divinely designed priority of men. It seems to me that if this principle is applied to society (and it seems like it should be applied, given its overarching vision of human creation), logical consistency would dictate that it be applied to all men and all women, that is, in every sphere of life. Ware does indicate that "this male-headship principle ought to be exhibited generally among men and women."[131] Leaving that issue, Ware specifically applies this principle to men and women in the home and church and, to a lesser degree, to single men and single women relating to each other. As for the home, he denies that all women should submit to all men, because it is not all men who have authority over all women, but only husbands have authority over their wives (justified by appeal to Eph 5:22). Regarding the church, female members should submit not to all men but to the elders only (the same would hold true for all non-elder men). With respect to relationships between singles, "there should be a deference offered to the men by the women in the group, which acknowledges the women's reception of her human nature in the image of God through the man, but which also stops short of a full and general submission of women to men. Deference, respect, and honor should be shown to men, but never should there be an expectation that all the women must submit to the men's wishes. And for single men, there should be a gentle and respectful leadership exerted within a mixed group" without it becoming an authority like that of husbands or church elders.[132]

I raise three areas of concern. First, I am not sure what Ware means by God's direct creation of the nature of men in an unmediated fashion. As for the original man, God did not create Adam *ex nihilo* but employed dust from the ground, which is certainly a mediated material. In terms of all men since Adam, God does not create men (or women, for that matter) directly or in an unmediated manner (I'll return to this point shortly). Second, I am not sure what Ware means by God's indirect creation of the nature of women in a mediated fashion. As for the original woman, God did indeed

[131] Ware, "Male and Female Complementarity and the Image of God," 22.

[132] Ware, "Male and Female Complementarity and the Image of God," 22.

create Eve indirectly through Adam, that is, derivatively from his body. But in terms of all women since then, how is it that their nature comes indirectly or derivatively from or through a man?

Third, and more importantly still, 1 Cor 11:11–12 seems to explicitly contradict Ware's proposal: "In the Lord, however, woman is not independent of man, and man is not independent of woman. For just as woman came from man, so man comes through woman, and all things come from God."[133] Paul's point amends ("however" or "nevertheless") the notion of independence of woman from man or of man from woman, and his correction is certainly not only that woman is dependent on man (that would be true in the first creation of Eve from Adam: "for just as woman was made from man," v. 12) but also that man is dependent on woman ("so man comes through woman," v. 12), because every man since Adam has been born of woman, and every man currently is born of woman. Yes, "woman was made from man." If this refers to Eve's mediate and indirect creation in the divine image, then "man comes through woman" refers to every male (as well as female) human being's mediate and indirect creation from their mother, which then does not speak of male headship functioning in divine image bearing.

What lessons for complementarity can be gleaned from 1 Cor 11:3–16? As just emphasized, God has designed his female and male image bearers to be interdependent. Sharing equal dignity and being significantly differentiated from one another, they interdependently fill out and mutually support one another relationally, familially, vocationally, and ecclesially. Such interdependence was and is forged out of mutual dependence: Eve was dependent on Adam for her existence, and from that point on every man is dependent on a woman for his existence, and this divinely designed reality underscores the organic unity of women and men. Even more importantly, God has designed men and women to be dependent on him, from whom are all things.

---

[133] Would Ware's proposal have been different if he had continued to interact with vv. 11–12? I would think so.

Moreover, both women and men engage in praying and prophesying in the church. While cessationism maintains that the Holy Spirit has ceased to distribute the gift of prophecy today, one wonders that if women in the early church could receive revelations from God and communicate them to the church, could/should they now read written divine revelation in the worship service, i.e., through the public reading of Scripture? And cessationism affirms that prayer should be a major element of worship. So, do churches that hold to cessationism engage women in public prayer during their services? As for continuationism, which affirms that the Spirit continues to distribute the gift of prophecy today, do churches that embrace this view engage women in both public prophesying and praying in their worship services?

Furthermore, complementarity promotes maintaining the clear distinction between men and women and denounces the contemporary phenomena of transgenderism and unigenderism. As I have written elsewhere, the proper state of human existence is embodiment, and as divinely created embodied persons, we are either women or men.[134] While there are many factors contributing to the erasure of such distinctives and/or the move to transition from one's biological sex to one's imagined gender, such confusion violates God's design for his male and female image bearers and is to be resisted. Paul's two-thousand-year-old directive for men and women being uncovered or covered in the public assembly serves to reinforce this distinction. Though the cultures in which churches exist today are in many cases quite different from the context that Paul addressed, his allusions to Scripture (Genesis 1–2) and appeals to sound judgment, nature, and ecclesial custom urge churches throughout the world to speak and act courageously to promote the equal dignity and significant differences between women and men who flourish individually and corporately through their interdependence on one another and dependence on God.

---

[134] Gregg R. Allison, *Embodied: Living as Whole People in a Fractured World* (Grand Rapids: Baker, 2021), chs. 1–2.

1 Corinthians 14:26–40

As Paul concludes his teaching about spiritual gifts (1 Corinthians 12–14), he explains the proper purpose for the gifts of prophecy and speaking in tongues (14:1–25), then addresses the proper expression of these two gifts to correct what seems to be a confusing and chaotic situation in assemblies in the Corinthian churches.[135] The structure of the passage is as follows:

v. 26	general statement: congregational activities are for the edification of the church
vv. 27–28	instructions about speaking in tongues
v. 27	two/three tongue speakers plus an interpreter
v. 28	if no interpreter, silence in the church; speak to oneself and God
vv. 29–33a	instructions about prophecy
v. 29	two/three prophets speak, plus others evaluate
v. 30	if a second person receives a revelation, the first speaker is to be silent
v. 31	orderly prophecy benefits the church
v. 32	prophets are in control of speaking their prophecies
v. 33a	because God does not favor disorder but peace
vv. 33b–40	
v. 33b	these instructions are for all the churches

[135] The debates over the nature and the continuation or cessation of the gifts of prophecy and speaking in tongues are legion. I consider prophecy to be the reception of a divine revelation directly from God, and the communication of that message to the congregation, which (either in the persons of its leaders or by its members themselves) in turn evaluates it. I define speaking in tongues as "involving communication in languages or encoded speech" and may consist of rehearsing the mighty acts of God in languages never before spoken (Acts 2:11), uttering divine mysteries that no one understands (1 Cor 14:2, 9), and expressing prayers that bypass one's mind (1 Cor 14:13–17). Continuationism holds that both gifts continue today, while cessationism believers that both have ceased.

v. 34	women are to be silent, not speaking but submitting, as the Law indicates
v. 35	women/wives should learn from their husbands at home because it is disgraceful for women to speak in the church
vv. 36–38	Paul's authority to issue the Lord's command takes precedence over others
vv. 39–40	conclusion: be eager to prophesy, don't despise speaking in tongues, do everything decently and in order

From this structural outline, three key points are to be noted. First, Paul addresses three speaking activities: speaking in tongues, speaking prophecies, and speaking the interpretation of prophecies. Second, he issues three calls for silence: there is to be no speaking in tongues in the absence of an interpreter, no continuation of speaking a prophecy if a revelation comes to another, and no speaking by women in the interpretation of prophecies. Third, Paul employs strong language regarding women:

- the women should *be silent* in the churches, for *they are not permitted to speak, but are to submit themselves*, as the law also says (v. 34)
- it is *disgraceful* for a woman to speak in the church (v. 35)

How is both speaking and silence to be understood?

I begin with the reason for Paul's dramatic language and how his call for silence squares with his earlier instructions (just discussed) about men and women participating in the public assembly (1 Cor 11:4–5). Clearly, men pray and prophesy (this is completely uncontroversial) and, clearly, women pray and prophesy, which would also be completely uncontroversial except for Paul's command for them to be silent (14:34, 35). Even more immediately, Paul describes congregational activity—"What then, brothers and sisters? Whenever you come together, each one has a hymn, a teaching, a revelation, a tongue, or an interpretation" (v. 26)—in which there does not seem to be any distinction between men and women participating in those worship elements. How should these various streams be considered?

Linda Belleville offers an egalitarian understanding of v. 34–35.[136] The context of these two verses indicates three points: "First, the setting is public worship. . . . Second, the command for silence is not absolute." She points to 14:26 as indicative of women speaking in the assembly; she also points to 11:2–5 as indicative of women praying and prophesying in the worship service. "Third, Paul's comments are corrective (versus informational) in nature." She points to the bookends of the passage—vv. 26, 40—as being imperatival regarding order in the assembly, grounded on Paul's affirmation that "God is not a God of disorder but of peace" (v. 33a). She then sees Paul's limitations on speaking in tongues and prophesying as corrective of the disorder in the Corinthian church.

As for the nature of the disorderly speaking in which the Corinthian women were engaged, she rejects the idea that Paul "is prohibiting women from taking part in evaluating prophetic speech," which he earlier addressed (v. 29). She posits that the reason complementarians favor this interpretation is a matter of male authority: "to evaluate the prophecies of men (so it is argued [by complementarians]) would be for the woman to usurp the man's created role as leader."[137] Rather, Belleville holds that Paul restricts his address to married women: "The women creating the disturbance are those who could 'ask their own husband at home' (v. 35)."[138] She notes that these women wanted to learn (14:35); thus, Paul is not prohibiting women from singing, teaching, presenting a revelation (prophesying), speaking in tongues, interpreting tongues speech or even participating in the evaluation

---

[136] Belleville, "Women in Ministry: An Egalitarian Perspective," 70–78. She dismisses Grosheide's interpretation that Paul permits women to pray and prophesy in informal settings but not in formal, public church services. F. W. Grosheide, *The First Epistle to the Corinthians*, NICOT (Grand Rapids: Eerdmans, 1953), 341–43.

[137] Belleville, "Women in Ministry," 72. She references James Hurley, E. Earl Ellis, Wayne Grudem, and D. A. Carson.

[138] Belleville, "Women in Ministry," 73. She disagrees with Carson, who broadens Paul's address to all the Corinthian women.

of prophecies (v. 29). "These are, rather, women in the congregation who are asking questions because they want to learn ('they should ask . . .' [v. 35]). Their fault was not in the asking per se but in the corporate disorder their asking produced."[139] Such disruptive speech would rightly earn Paul's dramatic rebuke: "it is *disgraceful* for a woman to speak in the church" (v. 35). The Corinthian women's disruptive speech was reprehensible, primed to cause a scandal.[140]

Belleville explains why this particular group of married women would have engaged in disruptive speech of this kind and thus court Paul's strong rebuke. They had stopped their formal education when they got married (sometime between fourteen and eighteen years old) to their older, more mature, and better educated husbands who were well positioned to rule. "Add to this the all-consuming task of raising children and running a household, and we have a group who, tasting freedom in Christ to expand their minds, grabbed at the opportunity—albeit in a less than suitable fashion."[141]

Belleville summarizes her interpretation: "Married women, in exercising their newly acquired freedom to learn alongside the men, were disturbing the orderly flow of things by asking questions during the worship service. Paul instructs them to ask these questions of their own husbands at home (v. 35) so that worship can progress in orderly fashion."[142] She concludes with two observations: "Paul affirms the right of women to learn and be instructed. This, in and of itself, is a progressive, not a restrictive, attitude. He also affirms the right of women to ask questions. He does not question

---

[139] Belleville, "Women in Ministry," 74.

[140] Belleville, "Women in Ministry," 74. For this background material, she references her own work, *Women Leaders in the Church*.

[141] Belleville, "Women in Ministry," 75. She acknowledges that D. A. Carson calls her interpretation "unbearably sexist" (D. A. Carson, "'Silent in the Churches': On the Role of Women in 1 Corinthians 14:33b-36," in *Recovering Biblical Manhood and Womanhood*, 147.). Her rejoinder emphasizes that, given the cultural background of the first century, her interpretation stands and is not sexist.

[142] Belleville, "Women in Ministry," 78.

the what (women asking questions) but the how/where (during the worship service)."[143] Importantly, her interpretation (the same would be true of other egalitarian understandings) of Paul's prohibition, being specific to the disruptive situation in the church of Corinth, means that once the context changes—women are no longer engaged in disorderly speech—the apostle's ban on women speaking in church is lifted. Though once normative and binding for a particular setting, Paul's embargo is now descriptive and thus non-binding for churches today.

The complementarian response to Linda Belleville's egalitarian interpretation is offered by Craig Blomberg.[144] Appealing to Anthony Thiselton's commentary on 1 Corinthians,[145] Blomberg avers, "we need not choose between the complementarian approach to women's silence in the church being understood in the context of the evaluation of prophecy and the egalitarian approach that sees uneducated wives asking disruptive questions. The two may have, in fact, been combined when overseers' wives were challenging the prophecies of their husbands in public."[146] Blomberg's continuation is more pointed: "At any event, if these are merely intrusive questions asked by untutored women, then Paul is hopelessly sexist by barring all women from speaking and no men (notwithstanding the fact that there would have been plenty of uneducated men as well)."[147]

---

[143] Belleville, "Women in Ministry," 78. For a similar interpretation, see Keener, "Women in Ministry: Another Egalitarian Perspective," 205–48.

[144] Craig L. Blomberg, "A Response to Linda Belleville," in *Two Views on Women in Ministry*, 117.

[145] Anthony C. Thiselton, *The First Epistle to the Corinthians: A Commentary on the Greek Text*, NIGTC (Grand Rapids: Eerdmans, 2000).

[146] Blomberg, "A Response to Linda Belleville," 117.

[147] Blomberg, "A Response to Linda Belleville," 117. His citation is from Carson, "'Silent in the Churches'", 147. Noting the theme of false teaching, with specific indications that it was fostered by men (e.g., Hymenaeus and Alexander; 1:20), Schreiner questions, "Since men are specifically named as purveyors of the heresy, would it not make more sense if Paul forbade all false teaching by both men and women?" Thomas R. Schreiner, "A Dialogue with Scholarship," in *Women in the Church*, 173.

Positively, Blomberg articulates the common complementarian understanding of these verses: Paul prohibits women from engaging in the evaluation of prophecies. "He is telling the women (at least in his day) to be silent merely in that one specific context. They are not to usurp the authority of the male leaders in pronouncing authoritatively on any disputed prophecy."[148] Blomberg calls attention to the fact that the immediately preceding verses (vv. 29–33) address prophecies and their evaluation. Thus, Paul's prohibition is restricted, not to women prophesying (clearly, they prophesy in the assembly; 11:5; 14:26), but to women evaluating prophecies that both they and the men communicate. Blomberg offers a variation on this theme: "It is even possible to combine this interpretation with elements of the third view . . . that women were asking disruptive questions as part of the evaluation of prophecies. Among other problems, this could have led to wives contradicting their husbands, including their husbands' prophecies, in a way that compromised their submission (v. 34)."[149]

Accordingly, Thomas Schreiner denies that Paul's instructions are confined to the particular situation at Corinth.[150] He appeals to the universal nature of Paul's teaching: "As in all the churches of the saints, the women should be silent in the churches . . ." (vv. 33b–34).[151] And he takes Paul's appeal to the "law" (the women "are to submit themselves, as the law also says;" v. 34) to be a reference to the Old Testament and, more specifically, to Genesis 1–2 in which Adam is given the responsibility to lead and Eve the duty to submit.[152]

---

[148] Blomberg, "Women in Ministry: A Complementarian Perspective," 164.

[149] Blomberg, "Women in Ministry: A Complementarian Perspective," 164–65.

[150] Thomas R. Schreiner, "Women in Ministry: Another Complementarian Perspective," in *Two Views on Women in Ministry*, 320–21.

[151] Belleville notes the debate over whether the phrase "as in all the churches of the saints" continues Paul's preceding thought—"since God is not a God of disorder but of peace, as in all the churches of the saints"—or introduces his next idea: "As in all the churches of the saints, the women should be silent in the churches." Belleville, "Women in Ministry: An Egalitarian Perspective," 75.

[152] Belleville understands Paul's reference to be Roman law, not Old Testament law. Belleville, "Women in Ministry: An Egalitarian Perspective," 77. Given Paul's many references to "the law" being to the Old Testament, Blomberg

Schreiner concludes: "The women are not to speak in such a way that they arrogate leadership. As in all the other churches, they are to behave submissively, so that the leadership of the church belongs to men."[153]

While resolution of this debate awaits another day, at minimum the two sides agree that Paul's directive, according to which

- the women should *be silent* in the churches, for *they are not permitted to speak, but are to submit themselves,* as the law also says (v. 34); and
- it is *disgraceful* for a woman to speak in the church (v. 35),

is not an absolute prohibition of women speaking in the public assembly. On the contrary, his other textual discussions about women praying, prophesying, singing, teaching, speaking in tongues, and more enjoin on women (as well as men) these responsibilities as they come together to worship the Lord. As to the exact nature of the apostle's proscription—whether it was disorderly speaking, disruptive speech, culturally shameful asking of questions, learning too loudly, or participating in the evaluation of prophecies—disagreement continues.

Complementarity underscores and is exhibited by the full participation (minus whatever Paul's prohibition singles out) of both women and men in public worship services. Egalitarians and complementarians, and their corresponding churches, will parse out differently the nature of those various activities and the extent to which their expression in the public worship service is available to all members. For example, egalitarian churches engage men and women alike in all areas of ministry yet may restrict the activity of teaching and the administration of the sacraments/ordinances to those in church leadership only. As another example, complementarian churches restrict women from church leadership yet may engage them in planning

---

considers Belleville's understanding to be untenable. Blomberg, "A Response to Linda Belleville," 117.

[153] Schreiner, "Women in Ministry: Another Complementarian Perspective," 321.

and leading many areas—praying, reading Scripture, leading responsive readings—of the liturgy.[154]

Complementarity, when fully functioning among men and women in the church, leads to that which Paul envisions:

- everything is done for building up (v. 26), done decently and in order (v. 40), that everyone may learn and be encouraged (v. 31)
- exhibits that God is not a God of disorder but of peace (v. 33)
- eschews speaking by women (whatever such speech means) that promotes anything and everything that is disgraceful (v. 35)
- recognizes that what Paul writes is the Lord's command and thus must be obeyed (v. 37).

This vision intersects closely with complementarity and its emphasis on men and women filling out and mutually supporting one another ecclesially for individual and corporate flourishing.

Ephesians 5:22–33[155]

Debate rages over the proper interpretation and application of Paul's instructions to husbands and wives. Complementarians insist that Paul presents a hierarchical structure of authority for husbands and submission for wives, and egalitarians contend that the apostle promotes mutuality rather than a hierarchical structure. I will first discuss the passage's connection to the preceding verse (v. 21), then present the four sections of the passage: vv. 22–24 about wives and the model of Christ; vv. 25–27 about husbands and the model of Christ; vv. 28–32 about husbands and their bodies; and v. 33 in conclusion. Next, I will discuss some considerations for

---

[154] For further discussion, see the spectrums of complementarianism and egalitarianism in ch. 11.

[155] Because of its similarities of directives for both wives and husbands with Eph 5:22–33, Col 3:18–19 will not be treated separately, though occasional reference to it will be made.

and by complementarians and egalitarians, concluding with implications for complementarity.

The passage's connection to v. 21

Before discussing the passage itself, understanding its connection to the preceding context is important. Flowing from his command to "be filled with the Spirit" (5:18), Paul lists four gerunds (participles in Greek) that present either the results of being filled with the Spirit, commands that correlate with being filled with the Spirit, actions that attend being filled with the Spirit, or means by which Christians are filled with the Spirit.[156] Whereas the first three results/directives/actions/means concern the church as it worships corporately, the final point—"submitting to one another in the fear of Christ" (v. 21)—functions both as continued instructions for corporate worship through the fullness of the Holy Spirit as well as detailed mandates for specific relationships within the new covenant community: husbands and wives, parents and children, and masters and slaves.[157]

Biblical scholars offer two competing interpretations of how "submitting to one another" relates to the passage under our consideration.[158]

---

[156] Clinton E. Arnold, *Ephesians*, ZECNT 10 (Grand Rapids: Zondervan Academic, 2010), 351.

[157] Frank Thielman underscores the unprecedented nature of Paul's addresses to the subordinate members of these pairs. Ancient philosophical and political literature simply directed the principal members—e.g., husbands, parents, masters—and ignored their counterparts. Not only does the apostle engage with both the principal and subordinate members, but he begins his engagement with the pairs with the subordinate members. Frank Thielman, *Ephesians*, BECNT (Grand Rapids: Baker Academic, 2010), 370, 375.

[158] As Thielman notes, a third interpretation is "that 'submitting to one another' refers to mutual submission and states the author's real view, but that the traditional pattern of subordination in the household codes contradicts this view." Paul, then, allowed an authoritarian framework to creep into his treatment of the husband-wife relationship, though he himself embraced an egalitarian perspective. How readers would detect such slippage is difficult to know, and the apostle's sustained, positive

One interpretation is that the gerund/participial phrase "states a general and comprehensive principle before Paul moves to the specific roles of husbands and wives, parents and children, and masters and slaves, so that the specific is considered in light of the general. On this view, Paul reminds all in the congregation of their need for mutual submission in the Body of Christ before writing of the specific duties each has in his particular situation."[159] Support for this interpretation includes (1) the reciprocal pronoun "one another" (ἀλλήλούς, *allēlous*), a reference to the entire congregation—not specific believers or groups of believers—as the recipients of the command "be filled with the Spirit" (v. 18);[160] and (2) parallel passages elsewhere (e.g., Phil 2:3; 1 Pet 5:5) that address church members generally and collectively while also giving specific and individual directives to certain categories of members. In this case, Paul's general principle of mutual submission, for which all believers are responsible, is followed by specific instructions for wives and husbands (vv. 22–33), children and their parents (6:1–4), and slaves and their masters (6:5–9).

In what sense is "submitting to one another" due to people—e.g., wives, children, and slaves—under whose authority the other paired members—husbands, parents, and masters—have been placed? Paul's directives to those three subordinate pairs never reverse the authority-submission framework, such that husbands are to submit to the authority of their wives, parents are to submit to the authority of their children, and masters are to submit to the authority of their slaves. Such an understanding would clearly elevate the general principle of mutual submission over the specific instructions that follow in Paul's treatment, thus contradicting them.

More fruitful is the idea that the mutual submission that flows from the filling of the Spirit may approach what the apostle urges elsewhere:

---

treatment of this marital relationship seems to belie such a notion. Thielman, *Ephesians*, 372.

159 George W. Knight III, "Husbands and Wives as Analogues of Christ and the Church: Ephesians 5:21–33 and Colossians 3:18–19," in *RBMW*, 167. Thielman, *Ephesians*, 372.

160 Thielman, *Ephesians*, 373.

believers are "not to think of [themselves] more highly than [they] should think" (Rom 12:3); they should "take the lead in honoring one another" (Rom 12:10); they should "not be proud; instead, associate with the humble. Do not be wise in your own estimation" (Rom 12:16); they are to "do nothing out of selfish ambition or conceit, but in humility consider others as more important than yourselves. Everyone should look not to his own interests, but rather to the interests of others" (Phil 2:3–4). Accordingly, even within the authority-submission structure, relationships between believers are to be characterized by proper consideration of oneself, showing honor, renunciation of pride, humble wisdom, eschewing of selfishness, and respecting, deferring to, and ministering to others. The model for such mutual submission—"the household of Stephanus"—receives apostolic commendation: "They are the firstfruits of Achaia and have devoted themselves to serving the saints. I urge you also to submit to such people, and to everyone who works and labors with them" (1 Cor 16:15–16). As Thielman proposes, "There may be a difference between placing oneself in the service (εἰς διακονίαν . . . τάσσω, *eis diakonian . . . tassō*) of others and submitting to others (ὑποτάσσω, *hupotassō*), but it is not large."[161] Importantly, Paul's phrase, "submitting to one another," allows for it to be both a result/directive/action/means of being filled with the Spirit that is applicable to all church members (v. 21) as well as to initiate his subsequent instructions about wives in relation to their husbands.

Another interpretation is that "submitting to one another" "is a general statement of the specifics spelled out for wives, children, and servants. That is, certain ways in which Christians are to submit to others are then specified."[162] In this case, the directive "does not teach mutual submission at all, but rather teaches that we should all be subject to those whom God has put in authority over us—such as husbands, parents, or employers. In this way, Eph 5:21 would be paraphrased, 'being subject to one another

[161] Thielman, *Ephesians*, 374.

[162] Knight, "Husbands and Wives," 167.

(that is, *to some others*), in the fear of Christ.'"[163] Support for this interpretation includes (1) the word "submit" (ὑποτάσσω, *hypotassō*) "always implies a relationship of submission to an authority. . . . The word is never 'mutual' in its force; it is *always one-directional* in its reference to submission to an authority;" and (2) the reciprocal pronoun "one another" (ἀλλήλων, *allēlōn*) does not have to be "completely reciprocal (that it must mean 'everyone to everyone'). . . . There are many cases where it rather means 'some to others;' . . . Similarly, in Ephesians 5:21, both the following context and the meaning of *hupotassō* require *allēlous* here to mean 'some to others.' . . . [I]t would seems best to say that it is not mutual submission but submission to appropriate authorities that Paul is commanding in Ephesians 5:21."[164]

The four sections of the passage: vv. 22–24 about wives and the model of Christ; vv. 25–27 about husbands and the model of Christ; vv. 28–32 about husbands and their bodies; and v. 33 in conclusion

Following his directive about submission in v. 21, Paul addresses submission on the part of wives (v. 22). In this case, the finite verb ὑποτασσέσθωσαν

---

[163] Editor's note to Knight, "Husbands and Wives," 167, in *RBMW*, 493–94n6. Thielman, *Ephesians*, 373.

[164] Editor's note to Knight, "Husbands and Wives," 167, in *RBMW*, 493–94n6. Clint Arnold lists four problems with this interpretation: "(1) It fails to recognize that this participle is dependent on the main verb of this section, "be filled with the Spirit," which is addressed to all believers; (2) it fails to recognize how this admonition provides a fitting conclusion to the previous section by calling all believers to the radical form of self-denial and love that Christ has modeled for the church; (3) it unduly restricts the unqualified reciprocal pronoun (ἀλλήλοις) to members of the household addressed in the next section; and (4) it does not take into account that the primary verbal element in the household code shifts from 'submit' (ὑποτάσσω) to 'obey' (ὑπακούω) when Paul moves his focus away from wives to children and slaves." Arnold emphasizes that "the mere fact that Paul calls every believer to an attitude of submission to others does not obviate the truth that we live these relationships out in a set of socially structured relationships—and this by God's design." Arnold, *Ephesians*, 356–57.

(*hypotassesthōsan*) or ὑποτάσσεσθε (*hypotassesthe*)[165] is inferred from the participle ὑποτασσόμενοι (*hypotassomenoi*) in v. 21.[166] To be underscored is the exclusivity of this submission: it is only to their own (ἴδιος, *idios*) husbands, not to all men in general, that women are to adopt this posture.[167]

As Clinton Arnold diagrams this section of Ephesians:

> *Be filled with the Spirit . . . (5:18)*
> *by submitting to one another (5:21)*
> *and, specifically, by wives submitting to their husbands (5:22)*[168]

Arnold divides the passage into four parts. He takes section one (vv. 22–24) as a chiasm:[169]

wives, submit to your husbands	a
as to the Lord	b
the husband is the head of the wife	c
Christ is the head of the church	c'
as . . . to Christ	b'
wives [submit] to their husbands	a'

By means of this chiasm, Paul directs wives to submit to their husbands (a and a'), provides a Christocentric pattern for their submission (b and b'), and underscores the reason—the matter of κεφαλή (*kephalē*, headship or

[165] ὑποτάσσεσθε (*hypotassesthe*) is the verb that Paul employs in his parallel instruction in Col 3:18.

[166] Peter J. Gurry, "The Text of Eph 5.22 and the Start of the Ephesian Household Code," New Testament Studies, vol. 67, issue 4 (September 6, 2021): 560–81. Cf. Thielman, *Ephesians*, 392–93.

[167] Later, Paul will make a similar point with regard to husbands: they are to love their own wives (vv. 28, 32). Thus, his discussion is limited to the marriage relationship. Thielman, *Ephesians*, 375.

[168] Arnold, *Ephesians*, 365. As noted, Arnold opts for the first interpretation of the relationship of v. 21 to v. 22. This is borne out in his rendering of the second phrase as "by submitting to one another" rather than as "by some submitting to others."

[169] Arnold, *Ephesians*, 365.

source)—for such submission (c and c'). Inserted into this discussion is a parenthetical statement that Christ "is the Savior of the body" (v. 23).

Moving from the directive to wives, section two (vv. 25–27) is a complementary directive to husbands, who are commanded to "love your wives." As more will be discussed later, a notable point is that this complementary command to husbands is not "exercise authority over/lead your wives." The apostle explains that such husbandly love should be comparable (as far as human imitation is possible) to the sacrificial love Christ had for the church (v. 25). Moreover, his atoning sacrifice had both a main purpose and a subordinate purpose. The main purpose of his saving death was in order to (ἵνα, *hina*) render the church holy or sanctified, made so by his cleansing of the church "with the washing of water by the word" (v. 26). The subordinate purpose of his sacrifice was in order to (ἵνα, *hina*) "present the church to himself" gloriously perfect (v. 27);[170] this purpose features an eschatological dimension. Christ's atoning sacrifice and ongoing work of sanctifying the church is oriented toward the future in which it will be his perfect and perfected bride.

Section three (vv. 28–32) returns to the directive to husbands to love their wives, with some modifications.[171] First, rather than repeating the command to love (ἀγαπᾶτε, *agapate*), Paul presents the directive in terms of oughtness (ὀφείλουσιν . . . ἀγαπᾶν, *opheilousin . . . agapan*): "husbands are to [i.e., ought to] love their wives." Second, Paul offers a different comparison: not "as Christ loved the church" (v. 25) but "as their [husbands'] own bodies" (v. 28). Paul reflects Jesus's teaching on the second great commandment: "love your neighbor as yourself" (Matt 5:43; cf. Lev 19:18; Rom 13:9; Gal 5:14) becomes "love your wife as you love yourself." The apostle explains (γάρ, *gar*) his comparison: no person (a general principle for all human beings, set in the specific context of husbands) hates their own body; rather, they tend to their physical needs (one can imagine proper

---

170 Arnold, *Ephesians*, 365, 368.

171 Arnold, *Ephesians*, 368.

nutrition and rest).[172] At the same time, Paul advances beyond the idea of "love someone *as* oneself" to the idea that a husband is to "love his wife because she *is* himself."[173]

Paul makes another comparison: the attentiveness of husbands for *their own bodies* (physically speaking) parallels Christ's helpfulness for the church (v. 29), which is *his own body* (metaphorically speaking; v. 30).[174] In another Christological parallel, Paul urges husbands to nourish and cherish their wives as Christ nourishes and cherishes his church. The reason (ὅτι, *hoti*) is because "we"—each Christian is included as Paul personalizes his discussion—"are members of his body" (v. 30). So, Christ cares for his body; husbands care for their own body; thus, husbands are to care for their wives.[175] Citing Gen 2:24 (v. 31)—Mosaic instructions about God's design and purpose for human marriage—Paul emphasizes that the "one flesh" union of two people in marriage, which is a profound mystery, "is relevant not only for urging men to love their wives, but perhaps even more importantly, for expressing the union between Christ and the church" (v. 32).[176]

Paul finishes this section with a startling affirmation: "This mystery is profound, but I am talking about Christ and the church" (v. 32). As Arnold underscores: "Paul sees a typology present in the divine institution of marriage that finds its antitype in the relationship between Christ and the church."[177] Thielman adds that "the union of husband and wife in 'one flesh' was originally intended to prefigure and illustrate the union that Christ now has with the church."[178] Accordingly, until Christ accomplished his work so as to establish his church with whom he would be

---

[172] Arnold, *Ephesians*, 391.

[173] Thielman, *Ephesians*, 387.

[174] Arnold discusses the switch from "body" (σῶμα, *sōma*) to "flesh" (σάρξ, *sarx*), maintaining they are interchangeable terms in this context, with the latter being used to set up the citation (v. 31) of Gen 2:24 [the LXX uses σάρξ (*sarx*)].

[175] Arnold, *Ephesians*, 392.

[176] Arnold, *Ephesians*, 368.

[177] Arnold, *Ephesians*, 396.

[178] Thielman, *Ephesians*, 389.

united, that reality remained a mystery, awaiting God's revelation of it, primarily through the work of his Son but secondarily through the present writing about it by the apostle Paul ("*I am talking about* Christ and the church;" v. 32).[179]

Section four (v. 33) is a summary of Paul's two directives. As for husbands (whom the apostle directly addresses with an emphatic individuality), "each one of you is to love his wife as himself." As for wives (whom Paul indirectly addresses with a milder tone), "the wife is to respect her husband."[180] The singular addressees—to each husband, to his wife—underscore that the individual man and the individual woman in a marital relationship is responsible for obeying the apostle's specific command.[181] Returning to the general instruction "*submitting* to one another in the *fear* of Christ" (v. 21) that led into this passage, Paul does not direct the wife with the (implied) imperative "to *submit*" (ὑποτάσσω, *hypotassō*) but with the verbal form of "*fear*" (φοβέω, *phobeō*). Better rendered "respect" (CSB, ESV, NIV, NASB, RSV) than "fear" (ASV) because of the negative and improper connotations of the latter translation, the command to the wife is clearly associated with the notion of submission as that which is voluntarily offered and underscores her responsibility to respond to her husband's love with proper regard and right honor. Moreover, according to Thielman, the imperatival nature of Paul's directive to wives is clear. At the same time, the apostle's engagement with wives—he requires that they supply the verb "submitting" with its implied rather than stated imperatival force (vv. 22, 24)—may reveal his awareness of the precarious position that wives in the Greco-Roman world inhabited. Their vulnerability that called for "a household code that had been transformed by the gospel not to be heavy-handed in its instructions to the less-powerful partner."[182]

---

[179] Thielman, *Ephesians*, 390.

[180] Thielman, *Ephesians*, 390–91.

[181] Arnold, *Ephesians*, 398.

[182] Thielman, *Ephesians*, 391.

Some considerations for and by complementarians and egalitarians

Key points to underscore include the following: (1) The nature of the submission (ὑποτάσσω, *hypotassō*) that Paul enjoins on wives (v. 22). Arnold makes three comments on this verb. First, the verb occurs in the context of "ordered relationships in a social structure."[183] As Lynn Cohick emphasizes, in the "stratified Greco-Roman culture . . . submitting to authorities was as natural as breathing, and just as critical for the existence of ordered society."[184] Thus, Paul's call for wives to submit to their husbands corresponded with cultural expectations, was acknowledged as necessary for harmony and social order, and contributed to the flourishing of society as the church lived it. At the same time, whatever the influence of Greco-Roman household codes may have been, the apostle's directive is thoroughly cast (or recast) within the Christian worldview and approach to the husband-wife relationship. Specifically, his employment of this household code structure was not "an affirming nod to traditional cultural values that domesticate the gospel."[185] On the contrary, his discussion is countercultural, a Christological rather than cultural model.[186]

Second, the verb "submit" is different from the verb "obey" (ὑπακούω, *hypakouō*). Thus, the response of wives in relation to their husbands differs from the responses of children to their parents and slaves to their masters (6:1,5); their obedience could be demanded, even coerced in some situations, but such compliance is different from the submission of wives to

---

[183] Arnold, *Ephesians*, 380.

[184] Lynn Cohick, *Ephesians*. New Covenant Commentary Series (Eugene, OR: Cascade, 2010), 135. Her more recent commentary goes into greater detail: Lynn Cohick, *The Letter to the Ephesians*, NICNT (Grand Rapids: Eerdmans, 2020), 257–58.

[185] Lynn Cohick, "Loving and Submitting to One Another in Marriage: Ephesians 5:21–33 and Colossians 3:18–19," in *Discovering Biblical Equality: Biblical, Theological, Cultural, and Practical Perspectives*, 3rd ed., ed. Ronald W. Pierce and Cynthia Long Westfall, assoc. ed. Christa L. McKirland (Downers Grove: IVP Academic, 2021), 193.

[186] Arnold, *Ephesians*, 380.

their husbands. Third, this non-coercive attribute of submission is highlighted by the fact that ὑποτασσόμενοι (*hypotassomenoi*; v. 21) is in the middle voice, indicating that the action of submission is a voluntary, rather than forced, choice.[187]

Specifically, the submission of wives to their husbands should reflect their submission to Christ himself; as they respond to Christ, so should they respond to their husbands.[188] Of course, in the former case, their response should be complete and unhesitating, but not so in the latter case: wives must never submit to their husbands if they direct them to sin, break the law, or passively yield to abuse.[189] "To submit to their husbands in everything" (v. 24) could be taken as the optimistic Paul painting an idealized portrait of marital relationships, but more likely the realistic Paul, fully aware of the still sin-tainted nature of those relationships, intends for readers to use their common sense when it comes to actual application of his directive.[190]

In greater detail, Thielman offers two interpretations of the phrase "as to the Lord." One interpretation is that wives are to submit to their husbands as if their husbands are Christ, similar to Paul's parallel of a husband's role with the role of Christ (vv. 23–24). A second interpretation is that by submitting to their husbands, wives are submitting to Christ in terms of

---

[187] Arnold, *Ephesians*, 380; Thielman, *Ephesians*, 372. As Cohick explains, "The participle can be interpreted as either middle or passive (being submissive or submitting yourselves), which affects the interpretation. The passive voice would imply that the person instructed has little say in the matter, while the middle implies some agency. This latter sense is preferred, as it matches the other active participles' voice [in vv. 19–20] and it fits Paul's point that believers should not act as though drunk (passively under the influence of another source) but actively make choices following the Spirit's leading." Cohick, *Ephesians*, 136–37.

[188] Scot McKnight notes that wives are instructed to submit, not to obey, their husbands, and offers a reason that obedience is not in view: "the grounding here is neither the husband's authority nor some supposed creation order nor his role as leader" but "in the Lord." Scot McKnight, *The Letter to the Colossians*, NICNT (Grand Rapids: Eerdmans, 2018), 347.

[189] Arnold, *Ephesians*, 380.

[190] Thielman, *Ephesians*, 380.

doing his will for them (par. Eph 6:7; Col 3:18): "The person to whom they submit does not have the authority of Christ, except in the case of marriage, and then only by analogy, not in reality. Christ is the submissive party's authority, and when wives, children, and slaves render obedience, they do so out of obedience to Christ, not because of any innate authority in the male head of the household."[191]

(2) The nature of the word κεφαλή (*kephalē*). Because this term was discussed earlier, I summarize the issues here. Scholars proffer two views: "authority over" and "source." According to the first understanding (κεφαλή = "authority over"), wives are to submit to their husbands as they submit to the Lord "because the husband is the head of [that is, 'the authority over'] the wife as Christ is the head of [that is, 'the authority over'] the church. He is the Savior of the body" (v. 23). Specifically, as Christ exercises his authority by leading the church, which responds to him by submitting to his direction, so husbands exercise their authority by leading their wives, who respond to them by submitting to their direction.[192]

According to the second understanding (κεφαλή = "source"), "the husband is the head [that is, 'the source'] of the wife as Christ is the head [that is, 'the source'] of the church. He is the Savior of the body" (v. 23). According to Arnold, "The implication of this view is that Eph 5:23 does not entail any God-ordained leadership that husbands have in relationship to their wives."[193] Rather, "the husband is the *source* of goodness and help for his wife. The term 'Savior' used to describe Christ is understood to reflect

---

[191] Thielman, *Ephesians*, 376.

[192] Cohick cautions about a potential overreach in applying the metaphor of head and body if head is understood literally and body figuratively: "First, it ignores Paul's argument, which relies on metaphor to create a new meaning. Second, it allows us to import notions of head (or even worse, headship) into the conversation. Paul's focus in the metaphor is to help believers better understand Christ as Savior, and it is the descriptor of savior that should guide our thinking." Cohick, "Loving and Submitting to One Another in Marriage," 199. As will be seen in the following discussion, Arnold similarly warns about misunderstanding the metaphorical framework of Paul's discussion, but from a different perspective.

[193] Arnold, *Ephesians*, 381.

the husband's role as protector for the wife, who did not have at that time the legal and social protections of a man."[194]

The debate continues seemingly unabated, though as noted in our discussion of 1 Cor 11:3–16, a third possibility that is sometimes offered is that κεφαλή has the sense of both "head" and "source."

(3) A third key point is that the follow-up to Paul's appeal to Christ as the head of the church is "He is the Savior of the body." The asyndeton (the lack of a conjunction to the preceding sentence), the statement's close tie to the preceding statement, and the strong contrast (ἀλλὰ, *alla*) to introduce the following verse (v. 24) should prompt interpreters to understand the statement to be a Christological affirmation only without indicating "an additional feature of the husband's role."[195] That is, Paul does not intend to urge husbands to imitate Christ as Savior of the church by "saving," that is, "protecting," their wives. Additionally, Christ does not exercise his authority to control the church but to redeem it through his sacrificial death.[196] Σωτήρ (*Sōtēr*) does not connote "protector" or "the one who controls" but means "Savior" in the sense of the one who died to pay the penalty for sin, which is Paul's point later on (v. 25). As Cohick notes, "This phrase clearly distinguishes Christ's headship from the husband's headship, thus narrowing the application of the latter. . . . In 5:22–24, Christ as head is explained in part as Christ the Savior, a quality that is not characteristic of husbands."[197]

(4) Fourth, in her interpretation of the head-body metaphor (which appears to express a common egalitarian understanding), Cohick seems to place the emphasis on unity and the analogical relationship between husband and wife and Christ and the church rather than on ethical injunctions to husbands and wives about how to live their marital relationship.[198] She avers that "although in his discussion of marriage, Paul first notes the

[194] Cohick, *Ephesians*, 138 (author's emphasis).
[195] Arnold, *Ephesians*, 382.
[196] Thielman, *Ephesians*, 378.
[197] Cohick, *Ephesians*, 137–38.
[198] Cohick, *Ephesians*, 137.

distinction between head and body, his conclusions in the second half of the argument stress unity, from which distinctions can be made. The quality of difference makes Paul's claim of unity so outstanding."[199]

As she concludes, Cohick maintains that "this description of marriage speaks not at all of roles for women and men, even less about headship or leadership. Instead, it presents a reversal of patriarchal assumptions by focusing on self-sacrificial love by the husband to the wife, and submission expressed as honor and respect by the wife to her husband. Both actions are characteristics incumbent on believers, to love each other as Christ loved the church and to submit to each other out of reverence for Christ."[200]

Implications for complementarity

Despite the wide divide in interpretations of these Pauline directives for husbands and wives, I note several applications for complementarity. First, both the directives to wives and the directives to husbands must necessarily be heeded for marriages to flourish as the apostle envisions. If the wife does not do her part in relation to her husband, that marital relationship will struggle. If the husband does not do his part in relation to his wife, that marital relationship will flounder. Importantly, Paul instructs wives in such a way that they must personally and from their heart activate his directives toward them; their husbands are not to cajole, coerce, or demand their wives' submission, honor, and respect. Likewise, the apostle instructs husbands in such a way that they must personally and from the heart activate his directives toward them; their wives are not to manipulate, browbeat, or intimidate their husbands' love, nurture, and care. But when Paul's instructions are carried out consistently and winsomely, marriages flourish. Complementarity in marital relationships has this divinely designed and human-promoting fruit.

Second, the person and work of Christ—he is the Savior of the body who gave himself up for the church and is sanctifying her with an

[199] Cohick, *Ephesians*, 140.

[200] Cohick, "Loving and Submitting to One Another in Marriage," 203.

eschatological orientation—stands at the heart of Christian marriages. Both wives and husbands are to be Christ-centered in their relationships with each other. Yes, complementarians and egalitarians differ as to whether these Pauline instructions are one-directional or reciprocal. From a complementarian perspective, wives are to submit to their husbands as to the Lord in terms of doing his will for them. For their part, husbands are to love their wives "as Christ loved the church and gave himself for her" (v. 25); that is, through self-sacrifice that is appropriate for human beings in differentiation from the Savior and his atoning death, husbands unselfishly give themselves for their wives, cherishing, nurturing, and caring for them. From an egalitarian perspective, Paul's commands to love, submit, sacrifice oneself, treasure, and nourish are mutually obeyed by husbands and wives. In either case, Christ-centered marriages that live out this divinely designed unity of husbands and wives reveal the profound mystery of the church's union with Christ. Such complementarity fosters both the individual flourishing of the husband and the wife and the corporate flourishing of the church.

Galatians 3:26–28

This Pauline passage has been described in various ways to indicate that "of all the texts that support Biblical equality, Galatians 3:26–28 is probably the most important."[201] For example, Paul Jewett calls v. 28 "the magna carta of humanity,"[202] and David Scholer maintains that v. 28 is "the fundamental Pauline theological basis for the inclusion of women and men as equal and mutual partners in all the ministries of the church."[203] Over forty years ago, before the debate began, Steven Clark opined, "Nowadays many assume

---

[201] Rebecca Merrill Groothuis, *Good News for Women: A Biblical Picture of Gender Equality* (Grand Rapids: Baker Books, 1997), 25.

[202] Paul Jewett, *Man as Male and Female: A Study in Sexual Relationships from a Theological Point of View* (Grand Rapids: Eerdmans, 1975), 142.

[203] David M. Scholer, "Galatians 3:28 and the Ministry of Women in the Church," *Theology News and Notes* (Pasadena, CA: Fuller Theological Seminary, 1998): 20.

that Gal 3:28 is the place in which we find the heart of the scriptural teaching about the roles of men and women. Moreover, many interpret Gal 3:28 to mean that ideally in Christ there are no role differences between men and women."[204] In treating this important passage, I begin with a general interpretation (helped by Douglas Moo),[205] turn to complementarian understandings and egalitarian understandings of it, and conclude with some applications for complementarity.

General Interpretation

At the center of his letter to the Galatians, Paul rehearses several of the themes—faith in Christ, sonship status, union with Christ, seed, inheritance, and promise—that have dominated his instruction to the church. Moo identifies vv. 26–28 as the climax of the apostle's argument of Gal 3:7–25.[206] As he begins his argument, Paul highlights that "those who have faith, these are *Abraham's sons*" (v. 7), and as he ends his argument, Paul underscores "if you belong to Christ, then you are *Abraham's seed*" (v. 29).

Moo rightly notes that the use of the male term "sons" (CBS, ESV) may cause misunderstanding (seemingly, at least from a linguistic view, excluding female Christians) when Paul clearly intends to include both men and women under this rubric. Some translations, then, opt for translating "sons" (υἱοί, *huioi*) as "children" (e.g., KJV, NIV, NRSV). Moo cautions against this move, because the generic "children" misses out on the full sense of "sons" both in the patriarchal structure of Greco-Roman society and (most importantly) the Old Testament and Christology.[207] In the former case, "sonship" signified high status and the legal prerogative of inheritance. In

[204] Steven B. Clark, *Man and Woman in Christ: An Examination of the Roles of Men and Women in Light of Scripture and the Social Sciences* (Council of Biblical Manhood and Womanhood website, http://www.cbmw.org/resources/books/clark/), ch. 6, para. 3.

[205] Douglas J. Moo, *Galatians*, BECNT (Grand Rapids: Baker Academic, 2013).

[206] Moo, *Galatians*, 248.

[207] Moo, *Galatians*, 250.

the second case, the Old Testament applies the term "sonship" to Israel: God is "Israel's Father," and Israel is God's "firstborn son" (Jer 31:9; Exod 4:22); Yahweh addresses Israel with "you are sons of the LORD your God" (Deut 14:1), calling them "sons of the Living God" (Hos 1:10). Moreover, the Christological connection is evident: "the language of 'sons' also highlights the significant organic connection between Christ as '*the* son' and Christians."[208] Given the canonical and covenantal structure of Scripture (as discussed earlier), even though the term "sons" seems exclusionary, I will retain it here so that the apostle's Christological and (both old and new) covenant intent is preserved in a way that rendering it "children" misses.

It is "in Christ" that this sonship/heir status is conferred through union with Christ, which is by faith.[209] This is true for "as many of" (ὅσοι, *hosoi*) those who are united with Christ; no one—not even Gentiles—is excluded, for "all [are] sons" (πάντες υἱοὶ, *pantes huioi*; v. 26).

Such union with Christ, which comes by faith, is vividly portrayed as true by water baptism, a point that the apostle makes elsewhere (Col 2:12).[210] As the initiatory rite of Christianity, baptism strikingly depicts salvation, associating new converts with the Triune God (Matt 28:18–20), identifying them with the death, burial, and resurrection of Christ (Rom 6:1–11), and more.[211] As incorporated into *the* Son by baptism, Christians are "sons."[212] Furthermore, all who have been "baptized into Christ have been clothed with Christ," a concept of "putting on" the "new self" (Col 3:10–11; Eph 4:24) and "the Lord Jesus Christ" (Rom 13:14).[213]

---

[208] In 4:1–7, Paul connects the Father's sending of his Son, Christians' adoption as sons, the Father's sending of the "Spirit of his Son" to Christians so they acknowledge God as "'Abba', Father," and the privilege of inheritance for being sons. For further discussion see Fred Sanders, *The Deep Things of God: How the Trinity Changes Everything*, 2nd ed. (Wheaton: Crossway, 2017).

[209] Moo, *Galatians*, 250–51.

[210] Moo, *Galatians*, 251.

[211] For further discussion see Gregg R. Allison, *Sojourners and Strangers: The Doctrine of the Church* (Wheaton: Crossway, 2012), 353–57.

[212] Moo, *Galatians*, 252.

[213] Moo, *Galatians*, 252.

Coming to the key point for our purposes, Moo notes the asyndeton of verse 28: it is not linked to the preceding context by means of a particle or conjunction. This fact compels interpreters to understand its emphasis on "the way traditional religious, social, and gender barriers are transcended in Christ" with help from other passages and theological frameworks.[214] Though not clearly connected to its immediate context, the main idea of the verse is found in two other Pauline passages:

- For in one Spirit we were all baptized into one body—*Jews or Greeks, slaves or free*—and all were made to drink of one Spirit. (1 Cor 12:13 ESV)[215]
- In Christ there is not *Greek and Jew, circumcision and uncircumcision, barbarian, Scythian, slave and free*; but Christ is all and in all. (Col 3:11)

Diagrammatically:[216]

Galatians 3:28	*1 Corinthians 12:13*	*Colossians 3:11*
Jew or Greek	Jews or Greeks	Greek and Jew, circumcision and uncircumcision, barbarian, Scythian,
slave or free	slaves or free	slave and free
male and female	X	X
oneness in Christ	one body by one Spirit	Christ is all in all

[214] Moo, *Galatians*, 252.

[215] The change to the ESV reflects my disagreement with the CSB's "we were all baptized *by one Spirit* into one body," which attributes this baptism to the Holy Spirit—he is the agent of baptism—rather than (correctly) to Jesus Christ. He is the agent who baptizes new believers with the Spirit, as affirmed in all the other biblical passages that affirm this baptism (John 1:33; Acts 1:4–5; 2:1–4, 33). The point for our discussion—the pairs of opposites—is not affected by this change in Bible versions.

[216] The diagram is adapted from Moo, *Galatians*, 253–54.

The similarities are striking: the pairs of opposites, with the Jew/Greek pair and the slave/free pair appearing in all three contexts, and the application drawn about oneness in the body of Christ brought about by (baptism in/with) the one Spirit such that Christ may be all in all.

Moo assesses these pairs of opposites: "'Neither Jew nor Greek' depicts the key distinction among humans from the Jewish perspective: between those who were chosen to be God's people and all others."[217] Because the erasure of this distinction is thematized in this letter, Paul's mention of this pair fits this context well. His reference to the other pairs of opposites is less clear, though his use of the slave/free pair in both 1 Cor 12:13 and Col 3:11 could account for it here. Whatever the reason, "slave or free" underscores the elimination of the pervasive and persistent Greco-Roman distinction of socio-economic status through faith in and union with Christ. Though the "slave/free" distinction is noted in the other two passages, neither one lists the final male/female pair, raising the question of why Paul includes it here. As Moo notes,

> The choice of the distinctive gender words ἄρσεν [*arsen*] and θῆλυ [*thēly*] (in contrast to ἀνήρ [*anēr*, man/husband] and γυνή [*gynē*, woman/wife], which can connote marital roles) suggests an allusion to Gen. 1–2. . . . The influence of the creation account could also account for the change in construction between the first two pairs and the third: the conjunction καὶ [kai] is found also in Gen. 1:27 (LXX: ἄρσεν καὶ θῆλυ ἐποίησεν αὐτούς, *arsen kai thēlu epoiēsen autous*, male *and* female he made them).[218]

In other words, this appeal to Genesis 1 possibly accounts for the similarity in the first two pairs—"Jew *or* Greek" and "slave *or* free"—and their difference from the third pair "male *and* female." Moo continues: "One reason, then, for Paul to include this third pair is to emphasize his concern in Galatians

[217] Moo, *Galatians*, 254.

[218] Moo, *Galatians*, 254.

to recast the fundamental nature of the world in light of Christ: his coming means a 'new creation,' 'in which neither circumcision nor uncircumcision means anything' (Gal. 6:15)."[219] Following on this biblical reference, Moo offers that "the mention of circumcision may be a subsidiary reason for the inclusion of this third pair: by putting so much stress on circumcision, Paul suggests, the agitators are effectively marginalizing women."[220]

Of course, the apostle's "elimination" of these pairs of opposites does not mean that the pairs no longer exist in reality. The traditional religious distinction between Jew and Gentile/Greek remains to this day. The same is true of the difference between slave and free. Enslavement stubbornly persists and, though dissimilar in many ways, the employer/employee status differential continues. Importantly for our purpose, the sex/gender differentiation of male and female continues today. Men and women alike are justified through faith so that they "are all one in Christ Jesus." What is discontinued—at least according to the new order in Christ—is the hostility and division that these traditional categories enflame.

Before returning to this topic of men and women in the body of Christ, a brief comment on v. 29 is in order: "if you belong to Christ, then you are Abraham's seed, heirs according to the promise." Specifically, Abraham's seed (σπέρμα, *sperma*, singular) is Christ (3:16) and, when the singular is taken in a corporate sense, includes all Christians. Without distinction, all of Jesus's followers—Jews and Gentiles/Greeks, slaves and free, men and women—are "in Christ" and "in Abraham" and thus heirs of a rich inheritance.[221]

---

[219] Moo, *Galatians*, 254.

[220] Moo, *Galatians*, 254. He lists Witherington, Martin, and Schreiner as concurring with this idea. Ben Withington III, *Grace in Galatia: A Commentary on Paul's Letter to the Galatians* (Grand Rapids: Eerdmans, 1998), 279–80; T. W. Martin, "The Covenant of Circumcision (Genesis 17:9–14) and the Situational Antithesis in Galatians 3:28," *JBL* 122 (2003): 111–25; Thomas R. Schreiner, *Galatians*, ZECNT 9 (Grand Rapids: Zondervan Academic, 2010), 258.

[221] Moo, *Galatians*, 255–56.

Complementarian and egalitarian understandings

Broadly speaking, complementarianism understands the "male and female" pair of opposites as pertaining to salvation in Christ—women and men alike have equal access to redemption—and incorporation into Christ's body, but not in reference to ministry in general or leadership in particular in the church. Oppositely, egalitarianism interprets this pair of opposites as pertaining to both salvation and ministry, with church leadership equally accessible to both qualified men and qualified women.

Moo's commentary addresses both perspectives, beginning with egalitarianism. Once again he underscores the passage's theme of "you are all one in Christ Jesus," with "one" (εἷς, *heis*) being masculine, thereby indicating a possible Christological focus with "the one new man" ("new man," Eph 4:24; cf. "new self," Col 3:10) referring to Jesus with whom all believers are united as one *person*, not *thing*.[222] As he addresses this blessing of oneness in Christ, Moo wonders, "But how far reaching is this new reality? It is easy to quote the saying in this verse as a slogan that proclaims the erasure of any distinctions within the Christian community. But of course Paul recognizes the continuing reality of the male/female distinction among human beings."[223] Moo notes and comments: "These continuing realities, then, lead many other scholars [i.e., complementarians] to suggest a rather severe delimitation in applying the principle that Paul announces here: only one's access to grace in Christ is in view. . . . But this would be to go too far in the other direction. Paul obviously applies the principle here to the basic matter of status within the people of God; but the principle itself, being a general claim about the new reality created by and in Christ, extends beyond this particular application."[224]

Then Moo notes and comments on the perspective of complementarianism: "The saying in this verse is rightly prized as a far-reaching and fundamental claim about the way in which the distinctions that 'matter' in the

---

[222] Moo, *Galatians*, 254.

[223] Moo, *Galatians*, 254–55.

[224] Moo, *Galatians*, 255.

world we live in are to be left at the door of the church. But this 'adiaphorizing' [considering it an indifferent matter, neither moral nor immoral] of difference within the Christian community does not entail erasure of difference . . . and cannot be used arbitrarily to rule out any distinctions in roles that Paul may teach elsewhere."[225]

More directly, Robert Fung opines, "It seems precarious to appeal to this verse in support of any view of the role of women in the Church, for two reasons: (a) Paul's statement is not concerned with the role relationships of men and women within the Body of Christ but rather with their common invitation into it through (faith and) baptism; (b) the male/female distinction, unlike the other two, has its roots in creation, so that the parallelism between the male/female pair and the other pairs may not be unduly pressed."[226] S. Lewis Johnson adds some nuance: "There is no reason to claim that Galatians 3:28 supports an egalitarianism of function in the church. It does plainly teach an egalitarianism of privilege in the covenantal union of believers in Christ. The Abrahamic promises, in their flowering by the Redeemer's saving work, belong universally to the family of God. Questions of roles and functions in that body can only be answered by a consideration of other and later New Testament teaching."[227] Getting more specific, Richard Hove formulates a key question from a complementarian perspective: "How does one get 'equality' from a verse that only mentions being 'one in Christ'?"[228]

Perhaps the best answer from an egalitarian perspective is provided by Cynthia Long Westfall in her treatment of Gal 3:26–29.[229] Her key points

---

[225] Moo, *Galatians*, 255. He references Schreiner, *Galatians*, 258–59.

[226] Ronald Y. K. Fung, *The Epistle to the Galatians*, NICNT (Grand Rapids: Eerdmans, 1988), 170.

[227] S. Lewis Johnson, "Role Distinctions in the Church: Galatians 3:28," in *RBMW*, 164.

[228] Richard W. Hove, *Equality in Christ: Galatians 3:28 and the Gender Dispute* (Wheaton: Crossway, 1999), 146.

[229] Cynthia Long Westfall, "Male and Female, One in Christ: Galatians 3:26–29," in *Discovering Biblical Equality: Biblical, Theological, Cultural, and Practical*

include: (1) Paul's discussion emphasizes that the believers' "primary or *salient* identity" is that "of being baptized and placed 'within Christ.'"[230] (2) As opposed to Moo, Westfall supports the translation of υἱοὶ (*huioi*) as "children who have the status of sons."[231] This translation avoids language that would confuse readers by (seemingly) excluding women from their rightful status as children, which is not about authority (Paul does not use the Greco-Roman authority structure of husband and wife) but emphasizes siblingship with equal standing in Christ.[232]

(3) Interpreting *huioi* within the cultural context of Greco-Roman society, Westfall understands Paul to define offspring "as the status of a free adult male who is an heir of property (an estate);"[233] thus, her translation of the term as "children who have the status of sons" is necessary to capture both Paul's emphasis on both siblingship and freepersons/inheritors. Her application to the complementarian/egalitarian debate is clear: "According to this passage, men cannot have any sort of primogeniture status over women in the church or the people of God because of the order of creation."[234] (4) Westfall underscores that this new status of primogeniture is due to justification by faith, being "in Christ," and being "wrapped in Christ." The implication of such membership means several important changes must take in the "social practices in the church,"[235] applications that extend to matters far beyond salvation and incorporation into the church.

(5) Reminding us that the salient identity of all believers is their membership "in Christ," Westfall avers, "The identification of the scope of what changes for Greeks/Gentiles determines the scope of what changes for slaves and women. . . . We may confidently conclude that the ways and contexts in

---

Perspectives, 3rd ed., ed. Ronald W. Pierce and Cynthia Long Westfall, assoc. ed. Christa L. McKirland (Downers Grove: IVP Academic, 2021), 159–84.

[230] Westfall, "Male and Female, One in Christ," 163 (author's emphasis).

[231] Westfall, "Male and Female, One in Christ," 164.

[232] Westfall, "Male and Female, One in Christ," 164.

[233] Westfall, "Male and Female, One in Christ," 164.

[234] Westfall, "Male and Female, One in Christ," 165.

[235] Westfall, "Male and Female, One in Christ," 166–67.

which 'there is no male and female inside him' will correspond to the ways and contexts that Paul is talking about in Galatians in which 'there is no Jew or Greek inside him'" (and, as she adds, those same ways and contexts must also affect the relationship between slave and free).[236]

(6) What does this point mean specifically for Paul's third pair of male/female? One area of Westfall's application is the following: "This does not override any identity of male and female that may be legitimately drawn from the creation account, but it overrides certain theological constructs about the significance of what is differentiated in creation, and negates the assumed correlation between the various functions in the church and gender roles."[237] Specifically, Westfall points to Paul's emphasis on spiritual gifts and believers being identified according to those gifts, which are not distributed or empowered according to ethnicity, socio-economic status, and/or gender. In this realm, however, particular men and women may exercise their gifts differently; "it should have nothing to do with inherent disqualifications from any function in the church. . . . Consequently, those who have authority or influence in the church should never restrict anyone with a priori rules that discriminate against another group [e.g., women] because of their identity."[238]

To summarize an egalitarian perspective of Gal 3:26–28, F. F. Bruce maintains, "It is not their [women and men] distinctiveness, but their inequality of religious role, that is abolished 'in Christ Jesus.'"[239] As for other Pauline instructions about (apparent) male and female roles, they "are to be understood in relation to Gal. 3:28, and not vice-versa."[240] Practically speaking, then, both qualified men and qualified women alike may engage in church leadership, and the church should not make any distinction for the officeholders on the basis of gender.

---

[236] Westfall, "Male and Female, One in Christ," 168–69.

[237] Westfall, "Male and Female, One in Christ," 176.

[238] Westfall, "Male and Female, One in Christ," 177, 178.

[239] F. F. Bruce, *The Epistle to the Galatians: A Commentary on the Greek Text*, NIGTC (Grand Rapids: Eerdmans, 1982), 169.

[240] Bruce, *The Epistle to the Galatians*, 190.

To summarize a complementarian rejoinder to this egalitarian perspective, the question arises as to why this passage should take precedence over other Pauline instructions that (apparently) restrict access to church leadership to qualified men (e.g., 1 Tim 2:11–14). The answer is divided along perspectival lines:[241] Complementarians consider such directives as prescriptive, universal, and thus normative for the church today. They underscore the transcultural and transtemporal reasons for which Paul issues the prohibition of women being church leaders: the creation order (v. 13) and the fall (v. 14). Egalitarians view these instructions as (1) either prescriptive for leadership in the early church but now for various reasons transcended, thus being localized and not normative for today; or (2) prescriptive not for church leadership but for marital relationships in the early church but now for various reasons transcended, thus being localized and not normative for today. Additionally, complementarians raise the question of why a restriction in the roles of women in church leadership is thought to diminish or jeopardize their personal dignity and worth, and why it renders them somehow unequal to men.[242] Finally, complementarianism draws a distinction between church offices and spiritual gifts, two matters that are usually collapsed by egalitarians: i.e., the non-genderedness of spiritual gifts equates to non-genderedness in church leadership.

Applications for Complementarity

In the midst of this debate, complementarity offers three applications. First, Gal 3:26–28 underscores the equal dignity of men and women, all of whom alike participate in sonship and share union with Christ the Son through faith in him as vividly portrayed in baptism. Beyond being equally created as divine image bearers, women and men are equally re-created through

[241] For an explanation of these hermeneutical issues, see the earlier discussion in chapter 14.

[242] Raymond C. Ortlund, Jr., "Male-Female Equality and Male Headship: Genesis 1–3," in *RBMW*, 111–12.

salvation in Christ and incorporated into his body. Specifically, there is no "male and female; since [men and women] are all one in Christ Jesus." Second, this passage highlights the significant differentiation that, even if sinful forces of division and enmity associated with it still raise their ugly head to disrupt unity and peace in the church, there remains a divinely designed demarcation from the outset of human creation as male and female image bearers to eternity future. Paul's affirmation that there is no "male and female" does not mean that the God-ordained differences between them are erased; on the contrary, they are to be celebrated as they form the basis for honorable relationships between women and men. Third, such shared blessings and oneness in Christ lead to both individual flourishing for men and women and corporate flourishing for the church.

Colossians 3:16

Though not a major passage with a significant contribution to our discussion, Col 3:16 raises a point about the complementarity of its outworking in the church. After Paul's exhortation to focus one's attention on the heavenly Christ (Col 3:1–4) and his embargo of numerous earthly sins of one's old self (vv. 5–11), the apostle describes what it means to put on one's new self. Ten virtues should characterize Christians: compassion, kindness, humility, gentleness, patience, forbearance, forgiveness, "love, which is the perfect bond of unity," peace, and thankfulness (vv. 12–15).

Paul's next exhortation is our focus: "Let the word of Christ dwell richly among you, in all wisdom teaching and admonishing one another through psalms, hymns, and spiritual songs, singing to God with gratitude in your hearts." The thorough and constant abiding of the word of Christ is not an indwelling of the good news within one's self but among "one another," that is, in the community of the redeemed. It is not an interiority but an externally proclaimed word in the midst of the church.[243] The modali-

---

[243] For further discussion of whether "word of Christ" should be viewed as a subjective genitive or objective genitive, see Nijay K. Gupta, *Colossians* (Macon,

ties of such instruction are "psalms, hymns, and spiritual songs" gratefully directed toward God. This singing is not centered on the church itself nor its members but rehearses the goodness and greatness of the Lord and his mighty acts of salvation.

Who is responsible for such proclamation? Members of the congregation are responsible for wisely "teaching and admonishing one another." On one interpretation, these members are church leaders, elders who are "pastors and teachers" (Eph 4:11), who must be "able to teach" (1 Tim 3:2; Titus 1:9), and who "work hard at preaching and teaching" (1 Tim 5:17). The venue envisioned for such instruction is (primarily, if not exclusively) the church's worship service. Thus, from a complementarian perspective, those responsible for obeying Paul's exhortation are the qualified male elders/pastors who lead the church; Paul does not direct his instruction to women and non-elder men. From an egalitarian viewpoint, those responsible are both qualified men and qualified women who are in church leadership; Paul does not admonish women and men who are not church leaders.

On another interpretation (with which both egalitarianism and complementarianism may agree), all church members—men and women alike—are duty bound to mutually teach and admonish one another.[244] Given the audience (all members of the Colossian congregation) to whom Paul gives instructions about Christ-centeredness, the avoidance of sins, and the inculcation of virtues, his exhortation about the indwelling word is also directed to the congregation as a whole. A Pauline parallel is his description of a worship service that featured the wide participation of the Corinthian church members (1 Cor 14:26).

Paul's qualification "in all wisdom" could be a vague hint that only church leaders are to teach and admonish (the first interpretation), but it is far more likely that it points to the more mature women and men of the church as being responsible for this community-wide, public and private

GA: Smyth & Helwys, 2013), 145.

[244] McKnight, *Colossians*, 299.

ministry.[245] Moreover, Paul's concluding exhortation—"And whatever you do, in word or in deed, do everything in the name of the Lord Jesus, giving thanks to God the Father through him" (v. 17)—reinforces the second interpretation. In terms of our earlier discussion of biblical covenants (specifically, the difference between the old and new covenants), "In the new covenant there are no longer different categories among God's people such as priests who mediate between God and his people, and 'ordinary' lay people. Rather, all of God's new covenant people 'know the Lord' and in this sense all, on the basis of the word of Christ, can teach and admonish one another."[246]

The mutuality of such teaching and admonishing is an outworking of complementarity among church members as they fill out and mutually support one another ecclesially for the flourishing of each member and of the church as a whole.

Titus 2:1–6

In his letter to Titus, Paul corrects false teachers and their teaching with instructions to Titus "to proclaim things consistent with sound teaching" (2:1). The apostle describes these insidious instructors (vv. 10–15) as false teachers who are living contradictions, with their evil works belying their claim to know God; indeed, "they are detestable, disobedient, and unfit for any good work" (v. 16).

---

[245] If this is the case, the category of "more mature members" is not a limitation to an elite group within the church but a recognition of Scripture's constant emphasis on wisdom (e.g., Col 1:9–12, 28–29; cf. Prov 1:1–7) and spiritual maturity that brings with it the privilege of instructing others (e.g., Heb 5:11–14). Moreover, the "one another" does not necessarily mean that everyone without distinction should teach and admonish everyone else. To encourage immature, foolish, and/or doctrinally unsound church members to engage in these activities would be the opposite of Paul's directive to teach and admonish with all wisdom.

[246] Alan J. Thompson, *Colossians and Philemon: An Introduction and Commentary*, TNTC (Downers Grove: IVP Academic, 2022), 147.

Paul counters this dangerous situation with instructions to Titus to be a true teacher instructing the church in Crete in sound doctrine (2:1).[247] Titus is to direct his teaching to four specific groups of church members according to their age and gender: older men (v. 2), older women (v. 3), young women (vv. 4–5), and young men (v. 6).

First, older men (πρεσβύτας, *presbytas*) "are to be self-controlled, worthy of respect, sensible, and sound in faith, love, and endurance" (v. 2). These qualities are typical virtues expected of Christians generally; for example, *sensibility* (σώφρων, *sōphrōn*) is also enjoined on young women (v. 5), young men (v. 6), and all believers (v. 12). They are also standard character traits required of church leaders in particular, as in the case of *self-control* or *sober-mindedness* (νηφαλίος, *nēphalios*), which is demanded of both male elders and female deacons (1 Tim 3:2, 11).[248] Similarly, *respectability* or *dignity* (σεμνός, *semnos*) is to characterize both deacons and deaconesses (1 Tim 3:8, 11). *Soundness* in faith, love, and endurance is again a common Christian character trait (e.g., 1 Tim 1:5; 6:11) as well as proper to Christian teaching (Titus 2:1).

Second, and "in the same way" (v. 3) that Paul makes clear to older men, "older women (πρεσβύτιδας, *presbytidas*) are to be reverent in behavior, not slanderers, not slaves to excessive drinking.[249] "They are to teach what is good, so that they may encourage the young women to love their husbands and to love their children, to be self-controlled, pure, workers at home,

---

[247] Some of the following discussion adapts material in Andreas J. Köstenberger, *1–2 Timothy and Titus*, EBTC (Bellingham, WA: Lexham, 2020), 327–35.

[248] For arguments for understanding 1 Tim 3:11 as referring to women deacons/deaconesses, see the previous discussion of that verse in this chapter.

[249] Schreiner notes that some commentators understand Paul's reference to be to *women elders* rather than *older women*. However, the word πρεσβύτιδας (*presbytidas*), rather than signifying *female elders*—the word for which would have been πρεσβύτερα (*presbytera*)—refers to *older women*. They stand in contrast with the πρεσβύτοι (*presbytoi*), *older men*, who are "older" in a chronological sense without any reference to a church office. Thomas R. Schreiner, "The Valuable Ministries of Women in the Context of Male Leadership: A Survey of Old and New Testament Examples and Teaching," in *RBMW*, 220–21.

kind, and in submission to their husbands, so that God's word will not be slandered" (vv. 3–5). Titus is to encourage older women to develop in two positive areas—reverence (ἱεροπρεπής, *hieroprepēs*) in demeanor and teachers of the good—and to avoid two negative areas—slander and addiction to alcohol. Given Paul's earlier recitation of a common proverb—"Cretans are always liars, evil beasts, lazy gluttons" (1:12)—such character and conduct on the part of older women would distinguish them and their church from the surrounding immorality and pagan religions.

Older women are specifically "to teach what is good," with several qualifiers. First, the content of their instruction should be sound doctrine (1 Tim 1:10; Titus 1:9) or sound words (1 Tim 6:3; 2 Tim 1:13) rather than false teaching (Titus 1:10–16). Second, such instruction should inculcate not only orthodoxy but also orthopraxy, that is, godliness and good works, as emphasized throughout this letter to Titus (1:1, 16; 2:12, 14; 3:1, 8, 14). Third, as teachers of the good, older women (not Titus himself) bear a particular responsibility for the young women, whom they are to "encourage" (σωφρονίζω, *sōphronizō*).[250] As Köstenberger notes, "it's unusual that the role of the older women is cast in almost priestly terms (ἱεροπρεπεῖς, v. 3)."[251] Girls and women did serve as priestesses in the Greco-Roman world, offering cultic sacrifices and engaging in ritual acts of worship.[252] In a priestly way, then, older women should minister to and disciple the young women (who constitute the third category of believers that Paul addresses, vv. 4–5).

Such discipleship features several areas. The first area concerns the young women's devotion: they are to be taught to love their husbands and their

---

[250] As Köstenberger explains, the proper translation of the hapax legomenon σωφρονίζω, related as it is to σώφρων (sensible), should be "instill self-control and sensibility in young women (the suffix -ίζω may convey a causative notion). The NIV's, ESV's, and NLT's 'train' evokes unwarranted associations with other kinds of training (e.g., of pets). The CSB's, NASB's, and NRSV's 'encourage' is better. Perhaps best is the CEB's "mentor."

[251] Köstenberger, *1–2 Timothy and Titus*, 331.

[252] S. M. Baugh, "A Foreign World: Ephesus in the First Century," in *Women in the Church*, 45–52.

children, with the imperative to love adding to similar directives for wives to submit to and respect their husbands (Eph 5:22–33; Col 3:18; 1 Pet 3:1). The second rehearses their personal qualities: like older men, young men, and all believers, young women are to learn to be sensible or self-controlled (σώφρωναι, *sōphrōnai*) as well as pure (similar to Peter's injunction to wives, 1 Pet 3:2) and kind (as in "doers of the good;" 1 Thess 5:15). The third area has to do with their contribution and compliance: young women should be instructed to be busy at home and submissive to their husbands. As to their contribution, they are to be οἰκουργούς (*oikourgous*), with several interpretations. One is that young women should do their work inside their home and not engage in work outside it; as housewives, they are restricted to their home, being wholly dedicated to raising their children and caring for household matters.[253] A second interpretation is that of homemakers: "the essence of the phrase is that wives are managing their households well," without restrictions as to the location of such household management.[254] Thus, Paul's emphasis is not so much one of location—workers *at home*—but one of diligent industriousness—*workers* at home.[255] Placing the apostle's instructions into a broader biblical theology of work, such labor is the God-honoring fulfilment of the original cultural mandate (Gen 1:28).

Not to be missed in this debate about young women is the purpose to which Paul points for their uprightness: "so that God's word will not be slandered" (v. 5). Not only do his instructions indicate and advocate for the divine will for the people of God; they also embrace and promote compliance to the common social expectations for women/wives and men/

---

[253] This view must wrestle with the canonical presentation of the idealized wife (Prov 31:10–31), whose industrious practices are multifaceted and multilocated, as well as archaeological and ethnographic sketches of rural women's production of food and provision of sustenance for their family.

[254] Köstenberger, *1–2 Timothy and Titus*, 332n104. This view points to Paul's warning that young widows tend toward idleness, gossip, and being busybodies, and thus should get married, have children, and "manage their households" (1 Tim 5:13–14; in a more general sense, 2 Thess 3:11).

[255] Such industriousness offers a startling contrast to the slothful Cretans (1:12).

husbands in the Greco-Roman world. In one sense, there is nothing exceptional about Paul's teachings here. Still, there is another framework within which these instructions work—divine revelation—rather than social convention that, as argued in the historical part of the book, was grounded on and flourished because of wrongful and harmful concepts of women. Accordingly, some (many?) complementarians maintain that such teaching continues to be applicable to men and women in the church today, with some consideration of how their applications need to be modified in light of the differences between first century culture and the current context. By contrast, some (many?) egalitarians hold that such instruction bears all the marks of capitulation to social norms and structures that are outdated and thus should no longer direct women and men in the church today.[256] The reasons for such capitulation are several, including the desire not to cause unnecessary tension between the Greco-Roman society and the emerging church or/and a missional impetus for Christians to exhibit impeccable conduct as they bore witness to the gospel before non-Christians (e.g., Titus 2:10).[257] Only in cases in which contemporary churches face similar situations should they practice these Pauline instructions.

The last category that Paul addresses is the young men (v. 6). Titus is to encourage them to be self-controlled (σώφρωνοι, *sōphrōnoi*), just as older men (v. 2), older women (v. 3), and young women (vv. 4–5) are to be.[258]

Complementarity underscores two key ideas. First, Paul addresses both men (older and younger) and women (both older and younger), reinforcing

---

[256] A. Padgett, "The Pauline Rationale for Submission: Biblical Feminism and the ἵνα clauses of Titus 2:1–10," *Evangelical Quarterly* 59 (1987): 39–52. For further discussion see Köstenberger, *1–2 Timothy and Titus*, 333n105.

[257] Padgett refers to David Balch as a proponent of the first rationale and Peter Lippert as an advocate for the second rationale. Padgett, "The Pauline Rationale for Submission," 46–47. His references are to David L. Balch, *Let Wives Be Submissive: The Domestic Code in 1 Peter* (Chico: Scholars, 1981), and Peter Lippert, *Leben als Zeugnis* (Stuttgart: Katholisches Bibelwerk, 1968).

[258] A grammatical point: *in everything*, which is numbered as v. 7, actually modifies *self-controlled*, specifying the completeness of the self-discipline that should characterize young men.

the point of equal dignity together with significant differences. As I will discuss later, even when identical virtues (e.g., sensibility) and traits (e.g., sober-mindedness) are prescribed for them, women and men as thoroughly sexed/gendered will inherently and naturally express these properties in female and male ways. Second, when the church practices complementarity, both male image bearers and female image bearers fill out and mutually support one another relationally (e.g., being respectful of one another), familially (embracing alike husbands/fathers, wives/mothers, and their children), vocationally (e.g., being diligently industrious workers), and ecclesially (e.g., "God's word will not be slandered") for their flourishing.

In summary, this chapter has interacted with so-called "controversial passages" in the Pauline corpus (1 Tim 2:11–4; 3:11; 1 Cor 11:3–16; 14:26–40; Eph 5:22–33; Gal 3:26–28; Col 3:16; and Titus 2:1–6) that figure prominently in the complementarian-egalitarian debate.

CHAPTER 19

Other New Testament Considerations

Bringing to a conclusion this lengthy treatment of New Testament considerations (Gospels, Acts, and Pauline instructions), this chapter treats a final "controversial passage" in 1 Peter and ends with a study of Paul's greetings to a number of leading women and men at the end of his letter to the Romans.

1 Peter 3:1–7

First Peter addresses the relationship between husbands and wives, calling the latter group to submission to the former group, which is called to live in an understanding way with and give honor to the latter group. I first provide an exposition of the passage, then interact with egalitarian and complementarian perspectives on its key issues. While much attention is given to the disparity between husbands and wives in this passage, not to be overlooked is the sense of complementarity it underscores, which is my concluding section.[1]

In the immediate context, Peter first urges Christians to "submit to every human authority because of the Lord," with particular application to governmental authorities (2:13–15). He next exhorts household slaves to "submit to your masters with all reverence not only to the good and gentle ones but also to the cruel. For it brings favor if, because of a consciousness of God, someone endures grief from suffering unjustly" (vv. 18–19). Peter illustrates what he means by his instruction by pointing to the example of submission by Christ (vv. 20–25).

As his third directive, Peter admonishes wives to "submit yourselves to your own husbands" (3:1). "In a similar way" that Christians are submissive to every human authority and servants are submissive to their masters, and following the example of Christ's submission, wives are to be subject to their own husbands. Such submission is not the same, for example, as that of slaves to their masters: wifely submission is (intended to be) the willing yieldedness on the part of an equal agent to one in authority (i.e., wives submit themselves), while servile subjection may be the unwilling succumbing of a non-agent to a superior who wields authority. As a second example of difference, wifely submission is not the same as that of Christians to "every human authority." Wives are not directed to submit to all men indiscriminately, but only to their husbands. At the same times, wives similarly heed Peter's instructions "because of the Lord" (as Christians do in relation to governing authorities; 2:13), and because to do so is to accomplish God's will and court his favor through an attitude of godly reverence/fear (as slaves do in relation to their masters; 2:15, 18–20).

---

[1] The exposition of this text reflects the particular influence of Karen Jobes, *1 Peter*, 2nd ed. (Grand Rapids: Baker Academic, 2022), 202–212, along with other commentaries, including Edmund P. Clowney, *The Message of 1 Peter* (Downers Grove: InterVarsity, 1988), 98–106; Peter H. Davids, *The First Epistle of Peter*, NICNT (Grand Rapids: Eerdmans, 1990), 99–105; Greg W. Forbes, 1 Peter, EGGNT (Nashville: B&H Academic, 2014), 97–105; Wayne Grudem, *1 Peter*, TNTC (Downers Grove: IVP Academic, 1988), 134–46.

While submission is the prescribed posture of wives in relation to their husbands, obedience is the actualization or expression of that yieldedness. Peter's illustration of Sarah underscores this movement: Sarah submitted to her own husband (3:5), that is, she "obeyed Abraham, calling him lord" (v. 6). The stance or posture of submission is the ground for and prompts the action of obedience.

Such steady submission and actioned obedience on the part of wives was oriented toward an important purpose with regard to their husbands: "so that, even if some disobey the word, they may be won over without a word by the way their wives live, [specifically] when they observe your pure, reverent lives." While in most cases wives will be married to Christian husbands, in some cases ("even if some" of) their husbands are non-believers, men who "disobey the word" of the gospel.[2] Karen Jobes notes three problems that such religious disparity created. First, a wife's adoption of a religion—Christianity—different from that of her non-Christian husband "violated the Greco-Roman ideal of an orderly home."[3] Second, both her unbelieving husband and society at large "would perceive the wife's worship of Jesus Christ as rebellion, especially if she worshipped Christ exclusively."[4] Third, her gathering with other worshipping Christians outside her home would foster fellowship and friendship with people "who possibly were not her husband's friends," thereby violating social expectations.[5] Jobes underscores the significance of the fact "that Peter does not directly address any of these particulars," signifying that the couple is "to work out the specific way her submission is to be expressed."[6]

Whatever may be the details of their submission, the hope of believing wives is that their husbands will become Christians ("won over" in the sense of salvation; 1 Cor 9:19–22) not through their wives' ongoing

---

[2] Earlier in his letter, Peter describes unbelievers as those who "stumble" over the cornerstone of Christ "because they disobey the word" (1 Pet 2:6–8).

[3] Jobes, *1 Peter*, 203.

[4] Jobes, *1 Peter*, 203.

[5] Jobes, *1 Peter*, 203.

[6] Jobes, *1 Peter*, 203.

proclamation of the gospel but by their wives' consistent Christ-like conduct that bespeaks the gospel. Peter does not dismiss the importance of the announcement of the good news; indeed, he probably assumes that such verbal communication is going on in unequally yoked marriages. Rather, along with this verbalized gospel must come the enacted gospel, the good news that expresses itself convincingly through their Christian wives' "pure, reverent lives." Word and deed combine to win these unbelieving husbands to the Christian faith.

In what does that adornment of the gospel consist?[7] Peter contrasts that in which beauty does not consist—"outward things like elaborate hairstyles and wearing gold jewelry or fine clothes" (v. 3)—with that in which beauty does consist: "what is inside the heart—the imperishable quality of a gentle and quiet spirit, which is of great worth in God's sight" (v. 4). The outward adornment is what some segments of society value: elaborate, ostentatious, expensive clothing and an outward beauty (that will eventually perish). The proper adornment is what God values (and, certainly in the Greco-Roman world and still today, what many segments of society value): modest, decent, sensible clothes and an inward, imperishable beauty of the heart.[8]

Such gentleness and quietness of spirit does not mean several things, such as wimpy surrender (see later discussion) and inattention to one's clothes. Every culture and context has expectations of such external matters and, unless those norms for expression are sinful in terms of violating biblical standards, their influence is not evil and may rightly direct Christian wives in clothing, hairstyles, and other types of adornment.

By contrast, gentleness and quietness mean the following. First, gentleness is a fruit of the Holy Spirit, and thus a Christlike quality enjoined upon and expected of every believer, whether woman or man, wife or husband

---

[7] Jobes explains that Peter's call for such inner beauty as proper adornment for wives coincides with both the Old Testament vision (1 Sam 16:7; Prov 31:30) and Greek moral philosophy (e.g., Xenophon, *Oeconomicus* 7:43; Aristotle, *Oeconomica* 3.1).

[8] For further discussion see Gregg R. Allison, *Embodied: Living as Whole People in a Fractured World* (Grand Rapids: Baker, 2021), 201.

(Gal 5:23). Jesus himself modeled gentleness.[9] Accordingly, while wives are to adorn themselves with a gentle spirit in relationship to their husbands, such gentleness is not confined to them in that limited role but should characterize all followers of Jesus.

Second, quietness of spirit is similarly a highly prized quality for all Christians and of great value in many contexts. For example, because God "is not a God of disorder but of peace" (1 Cor 14:33), "everything is to be done decently and in order" in the church (1 Cor 14:40). Tranquility is to characterize the life of Christians generally; indeed, believers are commanded "to seek to lead a quiet life, to mind your own business, and to work with your own hands" (1 Thess 4:10–11; cf. 2 Thess 3:12). Social calmness is key for making progress in the ministry of the gospel; thus, Paul urges prayer for "all those who are in authority, so that we may lead a tranquil and quiet life in all godliness and dignity. This is good, and it pleases God our Savior, who wants everyone to be saved and to come to the knowledge of the truth" (1 Tim 2:1–4). Moreover, quietness of spirit on the part of wives is teamed with gentleness, hope in God, and fearlessness (1 Pet 3:4–6).

Accordingly, the priority of developing a gentle and quiet spirit for wives in relationship to their husbands is not an anomaly, a disappointing and debilitating deviation from divine norms elsewhere in Scripture and the overall biblical worldview. Submission and obedience to their husbands that flows from their gentle and quiet spirit "is of great worth in God's sight."

To exemplify this proper adornment, Peter first points to "the holy women who put their hope in God" as narrated in the Old Testament. While he could have appealed to—and probably had in mind—various examples (Rebecca and Isaac, Rachel and Jacob, Leah and Jacob, Abigail

---

[9] As he triumphantly entered Jerusalem, he fulfilled Zechariah's prophecy of a gentle king coming to his people, mounted on a donkey (Matt 21:1–11; cf. Zech 9:9). He proceeded to cleanse the temple of merchants and moneychangers (Matt 21:12–13). Furthermore, Jesus referred to himself as gentle as he beckoned wearied people to come to him for rest, adding "for I am gentle and lowly in heart, and you will find rest for your souls" (Matt 11:28–30 ESV).

and David),[10] Peter concentrates on the example ("just as") of Sarah with respect to her husband, Abraham. She submitted to him, obeying him and calling him lord.

A possible reason for Peter's selection of Sarah as an example of hope in God is her centrality in the Abrahamic covenant.[11] One covenantal feature was the divine promise that Abraham would become "a great nation" and the fount of blessing "for all the families of the earth" (Gen 12:1–3). The complementary (and necessary) covenantal counterpart was the divine promise that Sarah would become "the mother of nations" (Gen 17:16 NIV, RSV; "produce nations," CSB) through the eventual miraculous birth of Isaac (Gen 21:1–6). In her central role in this covenant fulfillment, Sarah exemplified hope in God: "By faith even Sarah herself, when she was unable to have children, received power to conceive offspring, even though she was past the age, since she considered that the one who had promised was faithful" (Heb 11:11).

As to her example of submission to her husband—with the specific detail, "Sarah obeyed Abraham, calling him lord"—some commentators understand a general reference to her pattern of obedience to Abraham, even when it was dangerous to do so (e.g., Gen 12:5)[12] and especially when he directed her wrongly (e.g., Gen 12:10–20).[13] Others focus on the incident in which Sarah laughed at the angel's promise that she would conceive a son (Gen 18:11–14).[14]

---

[10] See earlier discussions of each of these pairs of wives and husbands in chapter 15.

[11] See the earlier discussion of the covenantal framework of Scripture in chapter 14.

[12] Jobes, *1 Peter*, 205; she references A. B. Spencer, "Peter's Pedagogical Method in 1 Peter 3:6," *BBR* 10 (2000): 113, as exemplifying this view.

[13] Jobes, *1 Peter*, 205; she references M. Kiley, "Like Sara: The Tale of Terror behind 1 Peter 3:6," *JBL* 106 (1987): 692, as exemplifying this view.

[14] Jobes, *1 Peter*, 205. Several problems arise if this incident is taken as the example of Sarah's obedience to Abraham. For one thing, she expressed her amazement to herself, though the omniscient Lord "heard" her laughter. Moreover, Sarah did not address Abraham as lord if by "calling him lord" is meant a verbal affirmation directed to him. Rather, she referred to him as "my lord" as an expression of

Whether Peter's reference is to the general pattern of Sarah's submission to Abraham or to a specific incident of her obedience to him, Peter's point stands: Sarah is an example of a holy woman who put her hope in God, submitting herself to her own husband.[15]

A specific application concludes Peter's exhortation to wives: "You have become her children when you do what is good and do not fear any intimidation" (v. 6). To be Sarah's daughters should not be taken in a physical sense—Jewish descendants by ethnicity—but in a covenantal sense as "children of promise" (Gal 4:28; 3:29) through faith in Jesus Christ. As Paul explains, "it is not the children by physical descent who are God's children, but the children of the promise are considered to be the offspring" (Rom 9:8).

More specifically, wives become Sarah's daughters as they maintain a life of goodness and refuse to fearfully succumb to intimidation. Peter's encouragement may generally point to suffering persecution for righteousness' sake as Jesus's followers (1 Pet 3:13–14). Stellar wives should continue doing good and trust in God rather than fear human threats. Alternatively, Peter's encouragement of wives may have specific reference to mistreatment by their husbands: demanding that they engage in sin, coercing them to violate God's will, abusing them physically, manipulating them emotionally, and more. As discussed later, submission does not mean capitulation to evil in any form it may take. Still, as wives resist such harm, they themselves should not engage in evil; rather, as Peter again urges, "let those who suffer according to God's will entrust themselves to a faithful Creator while doing what is good" (1 Pet 4:19).

In a complementary conclusion to his exhortation ("in the same way"), Peter addresses husbands, directing them to "live with your wives

---

respect for him as she contemplated her infertile body and her husband's advanced age, the combination of which made fulfillment of the Lord's promise of a child a laughable matter.

[15] For Jobes, Peter draws on Jewish tradition and its high regard for Sarah rather than on any specific Old Testament passage for his reference to this matriarch. Jobes, *1 Peter*, 206.

in an understanding way, as with a weaker partner, showing them honor as coheirs of the grace of life, so that your prayers will not be hindered" (v. 7).[16] Radically unlike husbands in the surrounding Greco-Roman context, Christian husbands are not to consider their wives as inferior persons to be treated disgracefully as possessions but to cohabit considerately (κατὰ γνῶσιν, *kata gnōsin*, lit. "according to knowledge") with them. Peter illumines the reason for such proper regard for a wife (ὡς ἀσθενεστέρῳ σκεύει, *hōs asthenesterō skeuei*): a wife is "as a weaker partner" (CSB), variously translated as "the weaker partner" (NIV), "the weaker vessel" (ASV, ESV, KJV, NKJV), and "the weaker sex" (RSV).[17]

Some interpreters consider the wife's weaker quality ("weaker" is a comparative) to be her lesser bodily strength; in comparison with her husband, she is weaker physically. Accordingly, husbands are to live with their wives in a way that is considerate of their physical liability in relation to the husbands' strength. Other interpreters understand the phrase to refer to the wives' posture of submission, a stance that renders them vulnerable to their husbands' abuse of (rightful) authority in leading them. If this is the case, husbands are to live with their wives in a way that is mindful of their wives' greater susceptibility to mistreatment; thus, husbands are to be circumspect with regard to their leadership in the marriage. Still other interpreters maintain that the wives' greater weakness refers to any frailty or susceptibility—for example, "in the sense of social entitlement and empowerment"—they may have in relation to their husbands.[18] In this case, husbands are to live with their wives with an awareness of their greater feebleness and exposure to harm.

---

[16] In an unusual interpretation, Jobes cautions against assuming these husbands are believers. Jobes, *1 Peter*, 207–209.

[17] The word σκεῦος (*skeuos*) is used here metaphorically, not in the sense of an actual (non-human) vessel but in the sense of a human being created by God and thus dependent on him for his/her existence and sustenance (e.g., 2 Cor 4:7).

[18] Jobes, *1 Peter*, 209.

To be recalled in this discussion is that "weaker" is a comparative; thus, both husbands and wives are characterized by whatever quality is decided upon for one's interpretation, whether physicality, vulnerability, frailty, and/or susceptibility, with wives experiencing a more pronounced weakness.

Peter continues his directives to husbands, urging them to bestow honor upon their "wives," the unusual adjective γυναικεῖος (*gynaikeios*), literally "feminine" or, if a nominative, "female" or "feminine one." Again, in a radical departure from first century marital relationships in which demeaning and dishonoring women was the cultural norm, Peter's instruction stands out. While the pagan treatment of women arose from a degrading concept of women as inferior to men, Peter's exhortation is grounded in the gospel: husbands are to honor their wives "as coheirs of the grace of life." Through salvation in Jesus Christ—a redemption which is graciously and equally provided for both men and women—husbands and wives are joint participants in eternal life. To be banished in Christian marriages is any and all sense of superiority and inferiority, of favoritism and partiality, of advantage and disadvantage.

Compliance in heeding the complementarity that Peter urges is so "that your prayers will not be hindered." Some interpreters understand the pronoun "your" to refer to the prayers of both husbands and wives, particularly when they pray together. In such case, they should not expect God to hear and answer their supplications. Other interpreters take the pronoun to refer exclusively to the prayers of husbands. If this is the case, then husbands who do not live with their wives in an understanding way and who do not show them proper honor should not expect God to respond to their prayers.

Briefly entering into the debate between complementarianism and egalitarianism in regard to 1 Pet 3:1–7, the former framework clearly appeals to it for support. For example, Wayne Grudem presents submission with three points: "1. Submission is an inner quality of gentleness that affirms the leadership of the husband," demonstrated by a wife willingly affirming her husband's authority and honoring him even when she disagrees. Next, "2. Submission involves obedience like Sarah's." Last, "3. Submission acknowledges an authority that is not totally mutual" because a wife "has to submit to her husband's authority and leadership in a way that the husband does not have to—indeed, should not—submit to his wife's authority or leadership."[19] Though his focus, as is Peter's, is on wives, Grudem explains what considerate leadership on the part of husbands is *not*: "harsh or domineering use of authority . . . equal sharing of leadership in the family . . . lesser importance for a wife . . . always giving in to a wife's wishes . . . [and] optional for husbands."[20]

An example of an egalitarian engagement with 1 Pet 3:1–7 is that of Peter Davids. He makes two points. First, he draws attention to its apologetic tenor, as a Christian wife is hoping to influence her non-believing husband for Christ by her godly and pious lifestyle. Thus, Peter's directives to wives must be interpreted and applied with this particular context in mind. Second, Davids explains that the Greco-Roman world at that time upheld virtues such as submission, silence, and obedience; such virtues were also approved by God and thus served well as the focus of the apostle's instructions. Such is not the case with contemporary (Western) societies that "generally do not give exclusive authority to husbands [but expect] marriage to be a partnership with a significant degree of intimacy." Putting together his two points, Davids warns, "interpretations that focus on the unilateral obedience or submission to husbands, regardless of cultural context, achieve the opposite of Peter's intention. Rather than promoting harmony with culture, they heighten the tension, and Christianity is perceived as undermining culture in a retrogressive way. First Peter might agree that this tension should exist, but only if the virtues are present in both men and women."[21]

---

[19] Wayne Grudem, "Wives Like Sarah, and the Husbands Who Honor Them: 1 Peter 3:1–7," in *RBMW*, 196–201. Italics removed. His points diverge from the egalitarian understanding as articulated by Gilbert Bilezikian, *Beyond Sex Roles* (Grand Rapids: Baker, 1990), 191.

[20] Grudem, "Wives Like Sarah, and the Husbands Who Honor Them," 206–7.

[21] Peter H. Davids, "A Silent Witness in Marriage: 1 Peter 3:1–7," in *Discovering Biblical Equality: Biblical, Theological, Cultural, and Practical Perspectives*, 3rd ed.,

As for an egalitarian application for contemporary husbands, Davids raises the question: "Will men/husbands insist on an authority over their wives that once was given them by the surrounding culture but now for the most part they no longer have? Or will they follow Christ and the way of the cross and drop power, treating their wives as equal, reaping not only a more intimate marriage relationship but also divine pleasure?"[22]

Complementarity underscores several points, the first of which is the life-changing character of conversion to Christ that is the hope of believing wives for their non-Christian husbands. Though not Peter's point, elsewhere in his letter (as well as throughout the New Testament), the proclamatory power of both the verbal gospel (e.g., 1 Pet 1:23–25) and the lived gospel (e.g., Titus 2:10) operates in all unequally yoked marriages as well as Christian marriages. In the former case, the unbelieving spouse experiences conversion through the believer, and in the latter case, both husband and wife complementarily experience sanctification through one another. Second, complementarity highlights the promise of covenant attachment to the matriarch Sarah along with the blessings that come through her to wives. While Scripture makes much of the Abrahamic covenant for both men and women (complementarity), the unique "Sarahonic" covenant is grounded on the divine promise that Sarah would become "the mother of nations" (Gen 17:16), a promise that she believed (Heb 11:11) and that is now fulfilled as Christian wives "become her children" as they fearlessly do good. Third, complementarity emphasizes the honorable and understanding way of husbands with their wives motivated by the fact of their co-inheritance. Husbands and wives alike may be saved and inherit present blessings (answered prayers) and future blessings (eternal life). These spouses fill out and mutually support one another relationally and familially for their personal flourishing and the wellbeing of their marriage.

---

ed. Ronald W. Pierce and Cynthia Long Westfall, assoc. ed. Christa L. McKirland (Downers Grove: IVP Academic, 2021), 239–42.

[22] Davids, "A Silent Witness in Marriage," 244.

A final note on Peter's instructions to wives about gentleness and quietness of spirit: It does not mean wimpy surrender, that wives are to passively capitulate to their husbands' demands through a cowardly capitulation that necessitates or results in loss of their agency. Submission should never become an irresolute acquiescence. Obedience should never succumb to abuse and other evils. Indeed, weak, non-agential surrender and passive, enabling obedience is destructive of complementarity, which depends on the full collaboration of husbands and wives who submit to them.

Romans 16

Perhaps an unexpected conclusion to this lengthy section on New Testament considerations is a treatment of Paul's lengthy and detailed greetings to friends and acquaintances at the end of his letter to the church in Rome. I will first discuss Paul's commendation of Phoebe before making some general comments about the names of those on this list, noting the presence of both men and women. Then, I will focus on the highly disputed reference to Andronicus and Junia(s) and the different applications to church leadership that egalitarians and complementarians draw from their different interpretations of that reference. Finally, I will give some attention to points about complementarity that emerge from Romans 16.

Phoebe's appearance at the beginning of Paul's conclusion is likely because the letter served as the apostle's introduction of her to the Roman church.[23] He characterizes Phoebe in three ways, as a sister, as a servant or deacon, and as a benefactor or patron. As for the first descriptor, Phoebe's sisterhood reflects the pervasive New Testament metaphor of the church as a united family composed of fathers, mothers, brothers, and sisters. As Schreiner underscores, "The term 'sister' relays the intimacy and warmth characterizing the early church so that the relationship between family

[23] Dunn points to Συνίστημι (*Synistēmi*) as indicating a commendation as, for example, in the case of a letter of recommendation (2 Cor. 3:1). James D. G. Dunn, *Romans 9–16*, WBC 38B (Nashville: Nelson, 1988), 886.

members describes most appropriately the affiliation between Christians (cf. 1 Tim. 5:1–2)."[24]

In terms of the second descriptor, Phoebe was a διάκονος (*diakonos*), which may mean that she, in a general sense like all Christians are to be (Gal 5:13–14), was a servant who provided assistance to others (as did Christ, Rom 15:8, and as did Paul, 2 Cor 6:40). C. E. B. Cranfield affirms this sense for Phoebe, who was engaged in "the practical service of the needy."[25] Because of the modifying phrase "of the church of Cenchreae," it may be that Phoebe held the office of deacon in that particular church. As James Dunn argues, "διάκονος together with οὖσα [*ousa*] points more to a recognized ministry . . . or position of responsibility within the congregation." If this is the correct interpretation, he urges caution as "it would be premature to speak of an established office of diaconate, as though a role of responsibility and authority, with properly appointed succession, had already been agreed upon in the Pauline churches. We are still at the stage of ministry beginning to take regular and formal shape."[26]

Regarding the third descriptor, προστάτις (*prostatis*) is translated variously as "benefactor" (CSB, NIV), "patron" (ESV), "helper" (NASB, RSV), and "succorer" (KJV), with Paul and many others being the recipients of her sponsorship. Following Dunn, it is best to take the word in its normal sense of patronage: "Paul's readers were unlikely to think of Phoebe as other than a figure of significance, whose wealth or influence had been put at the disposal of the church in Cenchreae" and had even benefited the apostle himself.[27]

Egalitarians and complementarians are divided over the significance of Phoebe and Paul's commendation of her. From the first perspective, "deacon" and "patron" point in the direction of Phoebe holding a church office

---

[24] Thomas R. Schreiner, *Romans*, BECNT, 2nd ed. (Grand Rapids: Baker Academic, 2018), 759.

[25] C. E. B. Cranfield, *The Epistle to the Romans*, vol. 2, International Critical Commentary (London: T&T Clark, 1979), 781.

[26] Dunn, *Romans 9–16*, 886–87.

[27] Dunn, *Romans 9–16*, 888–89.

and thus being engaged in church leadership. Linda Belleville envisions Phoebe as an itinerant missionary, not only as the courier who brought the letter from Paul to the Roman church.[28] From the second perspective, and with reference to Phoebe as "patron," Schreiner admonishes that "the concept of leadership [should not] be read into the term here."[29] In support, he offers "the connection between the injunction to 'help' (παραστῆτε [*parastēte*]) Phoebe and her role as a 'benefactor' (προστάτις). Paul's argument is that the Romans should assist her because she has served as a benefactor to others. The link is severed if the latter term means 'leader,' for Paul is hardly enjoining the Romans to 'lead' Phoebe as she has been the 'leader' of others."[30]

Moving outside this debate, complementarity highlights three points from this discussion. First, Phoebe was an outstanding female believer who, as "our sister," was closely and affectionately commended by Paul to the Roman Christians. Second, whether as a servant in general or a deaconess in her church, she helped others through her ministry of assistance (as all followers of Jesus are called to do) or held one of two church offices (the other being pastor/elder/bishop/overseer; Phil 1:2; 1 Tim 3:1–7). Following Dunn, circumspect application of this latter sense of διάκονος (*diakonos*) is warranted, as church leadership structure and the nature of its authority was in its early stages of development when Paul wrote Romans.

Third, as a patron or benefactor to Paul and many others, Phoebe played a significant role in the early church. Through her wealth and/or influence, she stood out as advancing the ministry of the gospel; accordingly, she was deserving of complementary sponsorship from believers in Rome. As a female image bearer, she filled out and mutually supported

---

[28] There is widespread agreement that tradition ascribes this courier task to Phoebe. Linda L. Belleville, "Women Leaders in the Bible," in *Discovering Biblical Equality: Biblical, Theological, Cultural, and Practical Perspectives*, ed. Ronald W. Pierce and Cynthia Long Westfall, 3rd ed. (Downers Grove: IVP Academic, 2021), 82.

[29] Schreiner, *Romans*, 761.

[30] Schreiner, *Romans*, 761.

male image bearers and other female image bearers relationally (sisterhood) and ecclesially (patronage of other believers) for both individual and corporate flourishing.

I turn now from Paul's commendation of Phoebe to his greetings of many Christians as he concludes his letter. He expresses twenty-one greetings to twenty-six people, twenty-four of whom are mentioned by name and two of whom are left unnamed but whose relational connections individualize them. Most commentators agree that, of the names in this list, eighteen are Greek, eight are Latin, six or seven are Jewish, and several are probably slaves. All are Christians (e.g., vv. 9, 12) associated with the churches in Rome which Paul greets.[31] He thus loves them either directly through personal familiarity with them (e.g., v. 8), through their reputation (e.g., v. 6), or indirectly through their membership in the churches (e.g., v. 11). Accordingly, Paul does not personally greet those named but encourages (grammatically) second-person Christians to greet (grammatically) third-person Christians, thereby stimulating mutual engagement and strengthening personal relationships among the believers.[32]

Paul praises both men and women for their co-labors in the gospel. Prisca and Aquila (v. 3) and Urbanus (v. 9) are his coworkers in Christ, and Tryphaena, Tryphosa, and Persis are hard workers (v. 12).[33] Apelles is

---

[31] These "house churches"—like that of Prisca and Aquila (v. 5)—made up the church in Rome.

[32] Schreiner, *Romans*, 764. For further discussion, see Susan Mathew, *Women in the Greetings of Romans 16:1–16: A Study of Mutuality and Women's Ministry in the Letter to the Romans* (London: Bloomsbury, 2013), 39–40, 93.

[33] That Paul describes both men and women as co-workers here is not unique to this letter. He refers to both men—himself (1 Cor 3:9; 2 Cor 1:24); Timothy (Rom 16:21; 1 Thess 3:2); Titus (2 Cor 8:23); Epaphroditus (Phil 2:25); Philemon (Phlm 1); Mark, Aristarchus, Jesus called Justus, Demas, and Luke (Phlm. 24; Col 4:11)—and women—Euodia and Syntyche (Phil 4:3)—as συνεργούς (*synergous*). The reference in 3 John 8 describes coworkers as truth-promoting, itinerant missionaries "who set out for the sake of the Name, accepting nothing from pagans," and thus dependent on the support of churches. At other times, the nature of coworking may not be specified, meaning that the semantic range of *synergos* is varied.

singled out for his being proven through testing (v. 10). Focusing on the women, we find eight whom Paul names: Prisca, Mary, Junia, Tryphaena, Tryphosa, Persis, Rufus's mother, and Julia (though not named, Nereus's sister is singled out as well). As noted earlier, though not appearing in the list of greetings, Phoebe is named with instructions to the Roman church to welcome her (vv. 1–2).

In the New Testament, Prisca (or Priscilla) is associated with her husband, Aquila.[34] Here, in Paul's greetings, they are named first and acknowledged as "coworkers," a probable reference to their missionary labors. The order in which their names appears in Paul's letters—four times for Prisca/Priscilla, twice for Aquila—may indicate her predominant role in their missional efforts. Certainly, they played a vital part as co-laborers with Paul in Corinth (Acts 18:1–4) and Ephesus (Acts 18:24–28), even risking their own lives for his sake (Rom 16:4), and as hosts of the church that met in their home (Rom 16:5). Not only Paul, but "all the Gentile churches" (v. 4) are thankful for Prisca and Aquila, probably due to their fruitful ministry of the gospel among the Roman house churches.[35] They were joined by several other hardworking women—Mary, Tryphaena, Tryphosa, and

---

Additionally, Paul's use of the expression πολύς κοπιάω (*polys kopiaō*), extolling Mary (v. 6) and Persis (v. 12) for "working very hard," and the word κοπιάω (*kopiaō*; without the degree adverb πολύς), commending Tryphaena and Tryphosa (v. 12) for "working hard," occurs elsewhere in descriptions of his own labors (1 Cor 15:10; Gal 4:11; Phil 2:16; Col 1:29; 1 Tim 4:10) and those of others (1 Cor 16:16; e.g., the household of Stephanus, perhaps including Stephanus himself, Fortunatus, and Achaicus; v. 17), including church leaders (1 Thess 5:11) such as elders who preach and teach (1 Tim 5:17). The (very) hard work of these four women is not detailed but could have included missionary work such as church planting (the members of Stephanus's household were the first converts to the Christian faith and served the church of Corinth; 1 Cor 16:16–17). Again, the semantic range of (*polys*) *kopiaō* is broad, also referring to the (hard) labor of elders. Mathew, *Women in the Greeting of Romans 16:1–16*, 46–113.

[34] Rom 16:3; Acts 18:2, 18, 26; 1 Cor 16:19; 2 Tim 4:19.

[35] Mathew treats this couple at length. Mathew, *Women in the Greetings of Romans 16:1–16*, 85–96.

Persis—whom Paul greets. Beyond their mention in this list, nothing is known about Rufus's mother,[36] Julia, and Nereus's sister.

As discussed before, the structure of Paul's greetings is the following: he is the writer, the Christians in the churches in Rome are the addressees, and the persons named in the list are the third parties who are to be greeted by the Roman Christians. Assuming that the addressees were both men and women, Paul's greetings create and/or enhance a web of relationships between the two genders. Both women and men alike were "commissioned to pass on the welcome and greetings to others."[37] Minimally, according to Mathew, "It is very clear from Paul's praise of the women in the greetings of Romans, that he does not want to exclude their participation in the church."[38]

The reference to Andronicus and Junia(s) in v. 7 is highly disputed.[39] Overall agreement exists regarding Paul's description of them as "my fellow Jews and fellow prisoners" (συγγενεῖς μου καὶ συναιχμαλώτους μου). The first designation (*syngeneis mou*) refers to their shared Jewish ancestry. The second designation (*synaichmalōtous mou*) references either an actual shared prison experience with the apostle or a similar experience of imprisonment—at a different place and time—as the apostle. Moreover, the two had become Christians before Paul's conversion (v. 7).

Two disagreements arise as to whether Junia was a woman or a man and to the nature of their association with the apostles. As to the first, if the Greek accent falls on the last syllable—'Ιουνιᾶν (*Jounian*)—then the word is masculine, from the nominative 'Ιουνιᾶς (*Jounias*) and an abbreviation of

---

[36] Paul's reference to Rufus's mother as Paul's mother also is too obscure to know its meaning.

[37] Mathew, *Women in the Greetings of Romans 16:1–16,* 42.

[38] Mathew, *Women in the Greetings of Romans 16:1–16,* 41.

[39] Some translations use "Junia" (e.g., CSB, ESV [with footnote "Junias"], KJV, LEB [with footnote "Junias"], NASB [with footnote "Junias"], NIV, NKJV, NIrV, NRSV), while others use "Junias" (e.g., ASV, NASB1995 [with footnote "Junia"], RSV). Mathew treats this person at length. Mathew, *Women in the Greetings of Romans 16:1–16,* 96–108.

Junianus; accordingly, it is rendered "Junias," a man.[40] However, if the Greek accent falls on the middle syllable—'Ιουνίαν (*Jounian*)—then the word is feminine, and it is not an abbreviation of *Junianus* (which does not exist in abbreviated form in extant Greek literature). Accordingly, it is rendered "Junia," a woman. As the early church and medieval church (until the thirteenth century) interpreted Junia to be a woman, this view has strong support. Because the list links here to Andronicus, a man, it may be the case that Paul greets a husband and wife.

The second and more controversial disagreement is the nature of Andronicus and Junia's association with the apostles.[41] One interpretation—which Michael Burer and Daniel Wallace name the "exclusive" view—of οἵτινές εἰσιν ἐπίσημοι ἐν τοῖς ἀποστόλοις (*hoitines eisin episēmoi en tois apostolois*) is "they are noteworthy in the eyes of the apostles" (CSB) or "they are well known to the apostles" (ESV).[42] In this case, both Andronicus and Junia were not apostles themselves but were held in high esteem by them. Another interpretation—which Burer and Wallace name the "inclusive" view—is "they are outstanding among the apostles" (NIV) or "of note among the apostles" (ASV).[43] In this case, both Andronicus and Junia were themselves apostles, even to an exceptional degree.[44]

---

[40] Everett Harrison, without any indication of the gender debate, affirms that Junias was a man. Everett Harrison, "Romans," in *The Expositor's Bible Commentary*, vol. 10, ed. Frank E. Gaebelein, (Grand Rapids: Zondervan, 1976), 164.

[41] For further discussion see Michael Burer and Daniel B. Wallace, "Was Junia Really an Apostle? A Re-examination of Rom 16:7," *New Testament Studies* 47 (2001): 76–91. Their view is challenged by Linda L. Belleville, "Women Leaders in the Bible," in *Discovering Biblical Equality: Biblical, Theological, Cultural, and Practical Perspectives*, ed. Ronald W. Pierce and Cynthia Long Westfall, 3rd ed. (Downers Grove: IVP Academic, 2021), 80n29.

[42] Burer and Wallace, "Was Junia Really an Apostle?," 79.

[43] Burer and Wallace, "Was Junia Really an Apostle?," 79.

[44] To be noted is the change in translation between the NASB ("who are outstanding in the view of the apostles") and the NASB1995 ("who are outstanding among the apostles").

A key issue arises from this latter interpretation. As apostles, what was the nature of their apostolic authority and responsibility? On the one hand, did Andronicus and Junia possess the same type of apostolic authority and engage in the same kind of apostolic ministry as the Twelve (apparently concentrated in the church of Jerusalem; Acts 15) and (perhaps) a few others, the "apostolic circle" including Paul, Barnabas, and James?[45] In this case, they would have constituted the foundation of the church (Eph 2:20), wielded Christ-delegated authority to direct all the churches (2 Thess 2:15), established patterns of conduct for all the churches (e.g., 1 Cor 7:17–24, 14:29–35), and, if engaged in evangelistic ministry and church planting, appointed elders in all the churches (Acts 14:23). Alternatively, if "the apostles" with whom Andronicus and Junia(s) were associated were the same group of five hundred to whom Jesus appeared after his resurrection (1 Cor 15:6–7), the nature of their apostolic ministry and authority is quite vague.[46] On the other hand, did Andronicus and Junia possess a different type of apostolic authority and engage in a different kind of apostolic ministry as the Twelve and the apostolic circle (or the very large group of recipients of Jesus's post-resurrection appearance)? On occasion, the New Testament uses the term ἀπόστολος (*apostolos*) with the basic idea of a messenger (John 13:16; 2 Cor 8:23; Phil 2:25). Moreover, the Apostolic Fathers used it in reference to an itinerant missionary or evangelist.[47] Was this the type of authority and mission of Andronicus and Junia?

If their ministry was like that of the Twelve (or the apostolic circle, whether very small or large), then some scholars conclude that Junia, who was outstanding among the apostles, exercised the highest level of authority

---

[45] The case for the apostolic designation of these three leaders is the following: Paul (Acts 14:14; 26:12–18; his epistolary greetings), Barnabas (Acts 14:14; 1 Cor 9:6; Gal 2:9), and James (Gal 1:19; 2:9, Acts 15:12–21).

[46] Belleville, "Women Leaders in the Bible," 77. She has a lengthy discussion of Junia and how discussions of her/his gender and the nature of her/his authority have changed over the centuries (77–81).

[47] E.g., *Didache* 11:3–6; *Shepherd of Hermas*, Similitude 9, 16[92]:4; Similitude 9, 25[102]:2).

and engaged in the uppermost kind of ministry. Such eminent work supports the inclusion of qualified women in church leadership today. Other scholars maintain that Junia, as noteworthy among the apostles (of whatever this group might have consisted), engaged in itinerant missionary work, especially among other women.[48] Still other scholars hold that Junia, as prominent among the apostles (no matter the identity of this group) and functioning under the apostle Paul's restrictions of women in the church, particularly in the patriarchal Greco-Roman context in which she lived and ministered, would not have engaged in any ministry involving teaching and exercising authority over a man (1 Tim 2:12).[49]

The conclusion from this debate is as follows: With regard to the named women in the list, many (all?) egalitarians understand their contributions to include church leadership at the highest level. Consequently, Romans 16 supports full access for women today to church leadership at all levels, including the office of elder/pastor. By contrast, many (all?) complementarians, pointing to the broad and varied sense of such words/expressions as "coworker" (*synergos*) and "hard working" (*polys kopiaō*), and questioning their reference to church leadership, maintain that the named women likely engaged in itinerant missionary work but not (in accordance with

---

[48] Cranfield affirms the translation of the phrase as "outstanding among the apostles," then comments, "that is, 'outstanding in the group who may be designated apostles,' which is the way it was understood by the patristic commentators (it would seem, without exception). On this interpretation, 'the apostles' must be given a wider sense as denoting those itinerant missionaries who were recognized by the churches as constituting a distinct group among the participants in the work of spreading the gospel (cf., e.g., Acts 14:4, 14; 1 Cor 12:28; Eph 4:11; 1 Thess 2:7; also *Didache* 11:3–6). That Paul should not only include a woman . . . among the apostles but actually describe her, together with Andronicus, as outstanding among them, is highly significant evidence (along with the importance he accords in this chapter to Phoebe, Prisca, Mary, Tryphaena, Typhosa, Persis, the mother of Rufus, Julia and the sister of Nereus) of the falsity of the widespread and stubbornly persistent notion that Paul had a low view of women and something to which the Church as a whole has not yet given sufficient attention." Cranfield, *Romans*, 789.

[49] Schreiner, *Romans*, 770–71.

Paul's prohibition in 1 Tim 2:11–14) in the church office of elder/pastor. Accordingly, Romans 16 does not support full access for women today to church leadership.[50]

Not to be lost in these debated points about Junia's sex and the nature of the association that Andronicus and she enjoyed with the apostles is the obvious fact of complementarity that characterized the churches in Rome. Men and women loved one another as brothers and sisters, reciprocally serving and benefitting one another. They alike were self-sacrificial, (very) hardworking co-laborers in the gospel, a vital and risky ministry for which Paul and all the churches gave thanks. Men and women hosted churches in their homes, offering hospitality and spiritual encouragement to believers, whatever their gender or religious background or social status may have been. The enormity of such complementarity comes into relief when we consider the Greco-Roman context in which these women and men ministered. In brief, the men and women listed in this passage exemplify complementarity as God's design for his male and female image bearers to fill out and mutually support one another relationally and ecclesially for both individual and corporate flourishing.

[50] Harrison draws out another important point that arises from the prominence of women in Paul's list of greetings. "Evidently Paul esteemed them highly for their work's sake. His relation to them and appreciation for them makes suspect the verdict of those who would label him a misogynist on the basis of such passages as 1 Corinthians 14:34 and 1 Timothy 2:11–15." Harrison, "Romans," 166.

CHAPTER 20

Conclusion from Biblical Considerations

Part Four has ranged widely over both the Old Testament and the New Testament, treating about fifty passages that are relevant for complementarity. Specifically, Old Testament considerations focused on nineteen narratives in which men and women characters interacted in either complementary ways for flourishing or otherwise for destruction, and concluded with a detailed look at the woman of noble character in Prov 31:10–31. Similarly, New Testament considerations were broken down into four sections: over twenty narratives in the Gospels, Acts, eight Pauline instructions, and concluding with a reflection on 1 Pet 3:1–7 and the list of men and women whom Paul greets at the end of his letter to the Romans. In the process, attention was given to how complementarianism and egalitarianism view these biblical passages, often sharply dividing over their interpretation and/or application. Most importantly, these considerations highlighted principles and lessons for complementarity, demonstrating that Scripture is replete with a vision of and support for women and men filling out and mutually supporting one another relationally, familially, vocationally, and ecclesially (or nationally) for human flourishing.

PART FIVE

Theological Considerations

Having explored biblical considerations, ranging widely over both the Old Testament and New Testament and drawing principles for complementarity while also noting the diversity of interpretations of key biblical texts regarding gender, church leadership, roles, and the like between egalitarianism and complementarianism, I turn now to theological considerations that bear significantly on complementarity. Discussion points are my view of men and women as male and female gendered embodied image bearers (ch. 21), the contribution that biblical images/metaphors of the church make to our topic (ch. 22), and the offices of prophet, priest, and king and implications for complementarity (ch. 23).

CHAPTER 21

Men and Women as Male and Female Image Bearers

As complementarity is defined in terms of God's design for his male and female image bearers, more discussion about the nature and complementarity of these two sexed/gendered beings is appropriate at the start of theological considerations.

According to Gen 1:26–28, by divine design, human beings are created and exist as either female embodied image bearers or male embodied image bearers. Of course, this affirmation raises two questions: What is a man? What is a woman? Though it is common to define a man—and, equally applicable, to define a woman—by listing certain roles and responsibilities unique to both, my approach is an ontological one.[1] Before we consider function, we must begin with essence: What is the nature of a man? What is the nature of a woman? With this ontological starting point, I offer these definitions, first of a man and second of a woman.

[1] Much of the following discussion is from Gregg R. Allison, "What is a Man? Looking at a historical, contemporary, and essential answer," The Ethics and Religious Liberty Commission online (June 6, 2022), https://erlc.com/resource-library/articles/what-is-a-man/. Used with permission.

> A man is a human being created as the divine image in the male-type of humankind and who inherently expresses the common human capacities and the common human properties in ways that are typical of and fitting for a man.[2]

> A woman is a human being created as the divine image in the female-type of humankind and who inherently expresses the common human capacities and the common human properties in ways that are typical of and fitting for a woman.[3]

A brief justification follows in five points.

First, God created human beings in his image, and his image bearers are either male or female (Gen 1:26–27). In other words, there is the general *kind*—humanity, or humankind—of which there are two *types*: male sexed/gendered image bearers and female sexed/gendered image bearers.[4] Second, there is no such thing as a genderless or agendered human being. God created his image bearers as either men or women. He did not begin with some kind of generic human being then add on genderedness as a secondary characteristic or type. Everything about human beings as divine image bearers is gendered.

Third, the ground for the distinction between these two types is biological. Men and women are fundamentally different because of chromosomes, hormones, and other physiological particularities (e.g., genitalia; skeletal, muscular, and brain structures). Specifically, a man is a human being who is

---

[2] My thanks to Gracilynn Hanson for her work on female-gendered embodied image bearing, from which my definition is adapted. "Establishing a Framework for Female-Gendered Embodied Image Bearers in a Redemptive Context." (PhD diss., The Southern Baptist Theological Seminary, 2022).

[3] Again, Gracilynn Hanson pioneered this work on female-gendered embodied image bearing, from which my definition is adapted. "Establishing a Framework for Female-Gendered Embodied Image Bearers in a Redemptive Context".

[4] Though I am well aware of the contemporary use of the two terms to refer to biological sex and to perceived or socially constructed gender, for simplicity sake I use the terms synonymously.

characterized by a penis, testicles, the production of sperm, a general range of testosterone to estrogen ratio (T/E2) that is different from that range in women, a general range of muscle mass that is different from that range in women, and more.[5] From this biological foundation flows a man's capacity to impregnate women and his potential of being a father. Specifically, a woman is a human being who is characterized by a vagina, uterus, ovaries, the production of ova, a general range of estrogen to testosterone ratio (E/T) that is different from that range in men, a larger limbic system (associated with language, relationships, memory, and bonding) and, with regard to the brain, a larger *corpus callosum* as well as larger frontal and temporal lobes than those in men. From this biological foundation flows a woman's capacity to become pregnant and her potential of being a mother.[6] At the same time, this position is not what is generally considered to be gender essentialism in the sense of biological essentialism or determinism.[7]

---

[5] Helpful contributions include J. Budziszewski, "The Meaning of Sexual Differences," and Paul C. Vitz, "Men and Women: Their Differences and Their Complementarity; Evidence from Psychology and Neuroscience," in *The Complementarity of Women and Men: Philosophy, Theology, Psychology, and Art*, ed. Paul C. Vitz (Washington, DC: Catholic University of America Press, 2021), 9–34, 182–215. In discussions of biological differences, some people offer objections from the (alleged) ambiguity of intersex conditions. For responses to these objections, see Tomas Bogardus, "Evaluating Arguments for the Sex/Gender Distinction," *Philosophia* 48.3 (2020), 873–92; Preston Sprinkle, *Embodied: Transgender Identities, the Church, and What the Bible Has to Say* (Colorado Springs: David C. Cook, 2021), ch. 7; Fellipe do Vale, *Gender as Love: A Theological Account of Human Identity, Embodied Desire, and Our Social Worlds* (Grand Rapids: Baker Academic, 2023), 191–204.

[6] For further discussion see Budziszewski, "The Meaning of Sexual Differences," and, Vitz, "Men and Women: Their Differences and Their Complementarity," 9–34, 182–215; cf. Katie J. McCoy, *To Be A Woman: The Confusion over Female Identity and How Christians Can Respon*d (Brentwood, TN: B&H Publishing, 2023), 77–90

[7] My view has significant overlap with Jordan Steffaniak's proposal of the "causal" type of gender essentialism. Jordan L. Steffaniak, "Saving Masculinity and Femininity from the Morgue: A Defense of Gender Essentialism," *Southeastern Review* 12.1 (2021): 31. Moreover, in agreement with Fellipe do Vale, grounding a

Fourth, God created men and women alike with (1) human capacities: rationality, cognition, memory, imagination, emotions, feelings, volition, motivations, purposing, and more; and (2) human properties: gentleness, courage, initiative, nurturing, patience, protectiveness, goodness, and more. Some of these properties are fruits of the Spirit (Gal 5:22–23), while others are Christian virtues.[8] These are *common* capacities and *common* properties; there are no particular capacities and properties that belong exclusively to men or to women (and I am not talking about roles). At the same time, given the divinely created design of embodied genderedness, these common capacities and common properties must and will be inherently expressed in gendered ways that are appropriate to men and appropriate to women. Men typically and fittingly express these commonalities in male-gendered ways, and women typically and fittingly express these commonalities in female-gendered ways.

Fifth, articulating what these "typical and fitting" expressions look like is notoriously difficult.[9] Three errors must be avoided. The one is to so differentiate male and female expressions that the properties expressed become

---

definition of man or woman in biology does not reduce human nature in general nor the nature of man or woman in particular to biological factors. Nor does this point imply that the answer to our question is that a man or a woman is completely explained by biology. Do Vale, *Gender as Love*, 94–100. As he explains (71–75), biological essentialism destroys human freedom and moral responsibility, and dismisses the influence of culture and context on the expression of one's gender.

[8] As Celina Durgin and Dru Johnson offer from Scripture, "the biblical authors portray complex, praiseworthy women and men, with neither gender laying exclusive claims to what some might now think of as gendered virtues, such as bravery or family care." Celina Durgin and Dru Johnson, eds., "Introduction," in *The Biblical World of Gender: The Daily Lives of Ancient Women and Men* (Eugene, OR: Cascade, 2022), xix.

[9] A significant advance is underway in working through this issue of fittingness of gender expression. Jacob B. Percy and Torey J. S. Teer offer a framework in their "A Creation Essentialist Framework for God-Honoring Gender Expression," a paper presented at the annual meeting of the Evangelical Theological Society, November 14, 2023.

two distinct properties; for example, male goodness and female goodness.[10] The second error is to so stereotype these expressions that men and women who don't "fit the mold" become confused and doubt their maleness and femaleness. The third error is to consider "typical and fitting" to be anything that cultural context allows.

These definitions of a man and woman both affirm and reflect complementarity. In terms of complementarity's emphasis on equal dignity, all human beings are created as either female image bearers or male image bearers. Put differently, the general *kind*—humanity, or humankind—is of two *types*: female image bearers and male image bearers. Banished are any and all notions of superiority and inferiority, advantage and disadvantage, dominance and subservience, and the like. Men and women are equal as created, embodied, gendered image bearers of God.

Moreover, women and men alike are characterized by *common* human capacities and *common* human properties; there are no particular capacities and properties that belong exclusively to men or to women. Rationality, emotions, will, motivations, and purposing, along with goodness, courage, love, faithfulness, self-sacrifice, initiative-taking, gentleness, protectiveness, and humility (are to) characterize both men and women alike.

Complementarity affirms that women and men are equal in dignity.

As for complementarity's emphasis on significant differentiation, the sex of divine image bearers is the fundamental difference among the members of humanity. There is nothing more basic, more foundational, for the difference in humankind than these two types: male image bearers and female image bearers. Given this divinely created design, the *common* human capacities and *common* human properties must and will be inherently expressed in sexed ways that are appropriate to men and appropriate to women. These expressions are clear manifestations of the significant differentiation between women and men.

[10] My thanks to Marc Cortez for suggesting this problem in an external reader report.

At this point, someone might insist that another area of differentiation is the roles for men and women. While this insistence is surely correct, I offer a clarification. Certainly, complementarians underscore the differences in roles between husbands and wives in the home/family. They also reserve the role of church leadership for qualified men in the church and prohibit it for women. Some complementarians would extend this significant differentiation to the societal/civil realm as well, as all men are to lead all women in businesses, government agencies, educational institutions, the military-industrial complex, and much more.[11] While such delineation between the sexes is clear, this specific delineation does not mean that egalitarians dissolve the differentiation in roles between men and women in the home/family, church, and society. For example, egalitarianism believes that men as well as women may hold the office of elder/pastor in the church, but it does not deny the reality of church leadership for the church. The role of overseer is crucial for the church, and that affirmation is true whether the office is exercised by a man or by a woman. If a man is an overseer, his role is significantly differentiated from all other responsibilities and ministries in the church. If a woman is an overseer, her role is significantly differentiated from all other responsibilities and ministries in the church.

Complementarity affirms significant differentiation between men and women.

With respect to flourishing interdependence, these definitions of a man and of a woman underscore the two sexes' need for one another. As the two types of humankind, men and women are designed to fill out and mutually support one another relationally, familially, vocationally, and ecclesially for individual and corporate flourishing.

Complementarity affirms flourishing interdependence between men and women.

---

[11] Proponents of traditional gender essentialism—certain human properties and certain human capacities characterize men, while other human properties and other human capacities characterize women—would add these sexed/gendered properties and capacities to the list of significant differentiation.

CHAPTER 22

Images/Metaphors of the Church

Though it could be argued that this section belongs under biblical considerations, I discuss images and metaphors of the church under theological considerations because my treatment is less about exegesis and interpretive disputes and more about the implications of these descriptive literary devices for complementarity. While Scripture is rich in images and metaphors, I concentrate on four: the people of God, the body of Christ, the temple of the Holy Spirit, and the family of God.

The People of God

The descriptor "people of God" has two senses: (1) all human beings as divine image bearers created by God are his people in the sense of creation (Gen 1:26–28; Acts 17:24–28; Eph 4:5);[1] and (2) specific human beings

[1] In Acts 17, Paul alludes to the creation narrative of Adam (Gen 2:7) and cites the pagan poets Epimenides of Crete (6th–5th century BC) and Aratus ("Phaenomena"; 3rd century BC). In this way, the apostle affirms from Scripture and from the general human sense of a divine Creator the universal recognition that

who have experienced redemption through God are his people in the sense of salvation.[2] It is in the second sense that I discuss the implications of the image "people of God" for complementarity.

Turning first to the old covenant people of God, the image has particular reference to the people of Israel. From among all the nations of the earth, Yahweh chose Israel to be his particular people (Deut 7:6–8). This vision and call were for Israel to keep its covenant with Yahweh and thus be "a kingdom of priests and a holy nation" (Exod 19:3–6). Israel was the old covenant people of God.

With regard to the new covenant people of God, the image has particular reference to people who have been redeemed by Jesus Christ and incorporated into his church. They are, using the rich images for the people of Israel (just cited), "a chosen race, a royal priesthood, a holy nation, a people for [God's] possession" (1 Pet 2:9). They are the members of the new covenant church, a united rather than divided people, consisting of both Gentiles and Jews (Eph 2:13–19). All people who have been saved through God the Son have access to God the Father through God the Holy Spirit. Moreover, both Jews and Gentiles have been reconciled and incorporated together as one new man and one body into the church. This new unity pertains not only to ethnicity, but also to socio-economic status and gender: "There is no Jew or Greek, slave or free, male and female; since you are all one in Christ Jesus" (Gal 3:28; cf. Rom 10:12; 1 Cor 12:13; Rev 5:9–10).

All Christians incorporated into the church are the new covenant people of God. As discussed earlier, Gal 3:28 connects well with our emphasis: the image of the people of God, particularly as it applies to new covenant Christians in the church, underscores the complementarity of women and

---

all human beings have God as their Father. Consequently, all human beings are the people of God in the sense of creation. In Eph 4:5, Paul underscores a commonality that unites the church: there is "one God and Father of all, who is above all and through all." This is the Fatherhood of God in the sense of creation.

[2] For further discussion see Gregg R. Allison, *The Church: An Introduction*, Short Studies in Systematic Theology (Wheaton: Crossway, 2021), 23–29.

men.[3] In Christ, sex as a difference that commonly and sinfully divides women and men is no longer, and can no longer be, a separator. While the distinction between sexes remains, the division between sexes does not; even more, it must be eliminated from the church because of and for the sake of unity in Christ.

The Body of Christ

This Pauline metaphor is used to characterize the church in several places, two examples of which are "his [Christ's] body, that is, the church" (Col 1:24) and "the church, which is his [Christ's] body" (Eph 1:22–23). Paul expands on the metaphor bi-directionally, that is, (1) upwardly, in terms of its connection to a head: God the Father "subjected everything under his [the exalted Son's] feet and appointed him as head over everything for the church, which is his body" (Eph 1:22–23); and (2) inwardly, in terms of its composition of parts: Christians in the church "are the body of Christ, and individual members of it" (1 Cor 12:27). Whether "headship" is to be understood as "authority over" or "source of"[4]—in the first case, demanding submission as the body's proper response to its authoritative head, and in the second case, demanding dependence as the church's proper response to its divine source—the idea is that Christ is the one to whom the church responds (with either submission or dependence). Some kind of hierarchy or different status on the vertical level is operative. This dynamic is not so when it comes to the individual parts of the body or individual members of the church: on the horizontal level, all Christians are equal, all enjoy the same status. They are not related in some kind of hierarchy; they are not of different status. As Lynn Cohick comments,

[3] See the earlier discussion of this passage.

[4] The debate over whether "head" should be understood in terms of "authority over" or "source of" has been treated earlier in this book. As noted in those discussions, even if the headship of Christ in relationship to his body means that he is the source of the church, dependence upon him (rather than submission to him) is still required.

"Paul explains that the body of Christ, while it has many members, does not rank those members based on social status or value them based on their ancestry," or, complementarity would add, ascribe dignity to them based on their sex.[5]

This headship-member dynamic means that "the church submits to Christ" (Eph. 5:24). That same dynamic also means that the gifted leaders of the church—apostles, prophets, evangelists, pastors and teachers—exercise their gifts "to equip the saints for the work of ministry, to build up the body of Christ" as church members "grow in every way into him who is the head—Christ. From him the whole body, fitted and knit together by every supporting ligament, promotes the growth of the body for building itself up in love by the proper working of each individual part" (Eph 4:11–16). Paul's prescription is that all church members become equipped for ministry and lovingly build up the body by their individual contribution so that the church matures and multiplies.

Paul emphasizes that the individual contribution of each church member is essential for the church's development and expansion (1 Cor 12:12–14). This fact means that no gifted member can pretend she doesn't belong to the body, and no gifted member can belittle another gifted member as being inconsequential or dismiss another gifted member as being unnecessary (vv. 15–24). Paul assures the church that "God has arranged each one of the parts in the body just as he wanted" (v. 18) "so that there would be no division in the body, but that the members would have the same concern for each other" (v. 25).[6]

Two implications for complementarity stand out. First, the church is a united body that consists of many different parts, each of which is vital for its flourishing. Gifted women and gifted men alike are personally to take the initiative to engage in ministry for the edification of the church. The church, in turn, is to facilitate the involvement of all its members so they

---

[5] Lynn Cohick, *Ephesians*, New Covenant Commentary Series (Eugene, OR: Cascade, 2010), 136.

[6] For further discussion see Allison, *The Church: An Introduction*, 29–35.

may use their gifts in ministry. Importantly, there are no gender-specific gifts. Men and women alike receive from the Holy Spirit the gifts (which he empowers) of teaching, leading, helping, shepherding, exhorting, evangelizing, giving, and, from a continuationist perspective, prophesying, healing, speaking in tongues, interpreting tongues, and more.[7]

Second, and flowing from the first implication, a church should help its members identify their gifts, train them to use their gifts, and deploy them in ministries in accordance with their gifts. There is a dual dimensionality to spiritual gifts. The divine dimension is the sovereign distribution and empowerment of spiritual gifts by the Holy Spirit, a prerogative and work that belongs solely to him. The human dimension is church members' recognition and employment of their divinely given and empowered gifts: those with the gift of teaching teach; those with the gift of leading lead; those with the gift of administrating administer; those with the gift of prophecy prophesy; and so on. Churches who have not developed this aspect of church life and ministry should do so, and such training should not be reserved for a small number of men who might become or are church leaders. It pertains to all church members. Churches who have developed this aspect while largely overlooking their women members in such development should rectify this imbalance.[8]

---

[7] Whether women and men alike may exercise those gifts in certain offices of the church is part of the debate treated in this book. For further discussion see Gregg R. Allison, *Sojourners and Strangers: The Doctrine of the Church* (Wheaton: Crossway, 2012), 413–24; Gregg R. Allison, *The Church: An Introduction*, Short Studies in Systematic Theology (Wheaton: Crossway, 2021), 127–30; Gregg R. Allison and Andreas J. Köstenberger, *The Holy Spirit* (Nashville: B&H Academic, 2022), 426–34.

[8] This oversight is one of the key corrective points that Aimee Byrd makes in *Recovering from Biblical Manhood and Womanhood: How the Church Needs to Rediscover Her Purpose* (Grand Rapids: Zondervan Reflective, 2020), esp. ch. 6. As she critiques the church's lack of discipleship of its women members, "many women have given up trying to grow and serve in their local churches, as they have more opportunities to learn, teach, write, and speak in parachurch organization" (157). Her point (and mine): women should be discipled in and by their local churches, with one aspect of that discipleship being development of their spiritual gifts. If this does not happen, women will find a ready reception and many opportunities for ministry in parachurch movements.

A final thought. The metaphor of the body of Christ and its emphasis on unity takes on a regular appearance every time the church celebrates the Lord's Supper. Paul underscores this reality as he explains this rite of communion: "The cup of blessing that we bless, is it not a sharing in the blood of Christ? The bread that we break, is it not a sharing in the body of Christ? Because there is one bread, we who are many are one body, since all of us share the one bread" (1 Cor 10:16–17). As historically and presently administered, this rite includes three aspects: A loaf of bread is torn into two pieces, vividly displaying the broken body of Christ. A cup of wine is elevated, vividly portraying the shed blood of Christ. And the bread and the wine are consumed by church members for whom Christ made his sacrifice, vividly depicting their participation in (Gk. κοινωνία; *koinōnia* = fellowship, communion) Christ and his saving benefits (his blood and body). Often overlooked, however, is Paul's affirmation of a fourth sign: the one, singular loaf of bread (and the one cup of wine) of which all partake vividly displays the fact that the many church members compose the one body of Christ.[9] Beyond a display of unity, this common loaf and cup fosters that unity as women and men alike and together engage in the eating of the bread and drinking of the wine. Whatever disparity of status of men and women that may be true in the world, that register of superiority and inferiority disappears when the church gathers together and in particular as it celebrates the Lord's Supper. Appropriately, then, Augustine urges the assembly as it engages in this rite with one load of bread, composed of many grains, and one cup of wine, composed of many grapes, "Be what you can see, and receive what you are."[10] Women and men are the many who are united without disproportion of standing before God and/or discrepancy of rank or prestige before one another.

---

[9] Though not explicitly stated, I think Paul's presentation can be extended to include the one cup of wine that all members drink.

[10] Augustine, *Sermon* 272, in *Works of St. Augustine*, ed. John E. Rotelle, vol. 7: *Sermons*, trans. Edmund Hill (Hyde Park, NY: New City Press, 1993), 300–301.

The Temple of the Holy Spirit

This third biblical metaphor for the church has a rich Old Testament background.[11] Beginning with the temple-garden of Eden (Gen 2:8, 15, 22) and God's expulsion of Adam and Eve from it (Gen 3:23–24), a critical and persistent question arose: Will God ever again dwell with his people? The positive answer began with a promise from Yahweh: "I will dwell among the Israelites and be their God. And they will know that I am the LORD their God, who brought them out of the land of Egypt, so that I might dwell among them. I am the LORD their God" (Exod 29:45–46; cf. Lev 26:11–13).

The positive though partial answer became manifest in several ways: the tabernacle (Exodus 25–31, 35–40), Solomon's temple (1 Kings 5–7), and the postexilic temple (Ezra, Nehemiah, Haggai, Malachi), as well as the incarnate Son of God (John 1:14; 2:13–22) and, most importantly for our purpose, the church of Jesus Christ.[12] Speaking of Christ, Paul explains, "In him the whole building, being put together, grows into a holy temple in the Lord. In him you are also being built together for God's dwelling in the Spirit" (Eph 2:21–22). Here, the "whole building" is detailed as "a holy temple in the Lord" and "God's dwelling in the Spirit," emphasizing the two co-instituting principles of the church—the Son and the Spirit—as the temple of the Holy Spirit. Similarly, Paul addresses the Corinthian church as God's holy temple in which the Spirit of God lives (1 Cor 3:16–17). Accordingly, the church is holy and a holy dwelling for the divine presence through the Holy Spirit.

Though I have been tracing the temple of the Holy Spirit as a metaphor for the church, it deserves noting that the New Testament also applies the metaphor to individual believers: "Don't you know that your body is a

---

[11] For further discussion see Allison and Köstenberger, *The Holy Spirit* (Nashville: B&H Academic, 2022), 291–94.

[12] For a full biblical theology see G. K. Beale, *The Temple and the Church's Mission: A Biblical Theology of the Dwelling Place of God* (Downers Grove: IVP Academic, 2004).

temple of the Holy Spirit who is in you, whom you have from God?" (1 Cor 6:19).[13] Accordingly, each holy follower of Jesus, whether female or male, is a holy dwelling place for the divine presence as a temple of the Holy Spirit. This is in keeping with the pledge of Jesus Christ himself, who comforted his disciples prior to his departure with this promise: "If anyone loves me, he will keep my word. My Father will love him, and we will come to him and make our home with him (μονὴν παρ' αὐτῷ ποιησόμεθα; *monēn par' autō poiēsometha* = make our dwelling place)" (John 14:23). How would it be that the Father and the Son would come to dwell with Jesus's followers? A few lines above this promise, Jesus explained to the disciples that the Holy Spirit "remains with you and will be in you" (παρ' ὑμῖν μένει καὶ ἐν ὑμῖν ἔσται; *par' hymin menei kai en hymin estai*) indicating that the Spirit's current *dwelling with* the disciples would give way to his *indwelling* them (John 14:17). Jesus promised his followers that by the indwelling presence of the Holy Spirit, the Father and the Son would dwell with them. In other words, the presence of the Holy Spirit renders the presence of the triune God in Christians, making each one a temple of the Holy Spirit.

Considering both the corporate and individual sense of the temple of the Holy Spirit, several implications may be drawn for complementarity. Corporately, all church members—both men and women—when gathered together compose and live out this reality, without distinction of gender, status, gifting, and the like. There are no divisions as there were in former temples—the forecourt or porch, the sanctuary or main room, and the holy of holies. The Spirit of God dwells in the gathered assembly as women and men sing songs of praise, offer prayers of thanksgiving, hear Scripture read and preached, engage in baptism and the Lord's Supper, and more.

---

[13] Though Paul addresses his readers as a corporate audience with the plural personal pronoun "your" (ὑμῶν; humōn), the plural locative dative "in you" (ἐν ὑμῖν; *en humin*), and the plural verb "you have" (ἔχετε; *echete*), his use of the singular "body" (τὸ σῶμα; *to sōma*) and "temple" (ναὸς; *naos*) indicates his focus is on individual believers. Each Christian has been purchased by God to be a temple of the Holy Spirit and thus glorify God.

Individually, each church member—each man and each woman—experiences the presence of the triune God because each one is indwelt by the Holy Spirit. Though there are differences in maturity, awareness and enjoyment of the divine presence, faithfulness and obedience, and the like, such differences do not mean that the Spirit dwells more or less in each follower of Jesus. As he is promised to each Christian (Acts 2:38; Eph 1:13), he indwells each one (Rom 8:9). Certainly, his manifest presence in believers—and hence their dependence upon and delight in the triune God—may differ from person to person, from season to season, from circumstance to circumstance. But such diversity of experience cannot be accounted for by the appearance or disappearance of the Spirit, who dwells with believers "forever" (John 14:16). For our purposes, then, a female disciple of Jesus is a temple of the Holy Spirit in the same way as a male disciple is a temple of the Spirit. Both men and women alike are called to yield to the Spirit (Eph 5:18–21), grow in their reliance upon the Spirit (Rom 8:4–5), strengthen their walk by the Spirit (Gal 5:16–18), and keep up with the Spirit (Gal 5:25). This posture is equally true of women and men as temples of the Holy Spirit.

The Family of God

Soteriologically, all Christians are foreknown, predestined, called, justified, and glorified not primarily for their own glorious future but ultimately for the exaltation of their preeminent Savior, "the firstborn among many brothers and sisters" (Rom 8:29–30). Jesus himself identified his true family not as those who can claim a physical connection with him but as those who hear the word of God and do his will, gaining for themselves recognition as his brother, sister, and mother (Matt 12:46–49; Mark 3:31–35; Luke 8:19–21). Through the Holy Spirit, this familial bonding is both established and confirmed:

> For all those led by God's Spirit are God's sons. For you did not receive a spirit of slavery to fall back into fear. Instead, you received

> the Spirit of adoption, by whom we cry out, "'Abba,' Father!" The Spirit himself testifies together with our spirit that we are God's children, and if children, also heirs—heirs of God and coheirs with Christ. (Rom 8:14–17)

Whereas "sonship" language is thematized here (v. 14), "sonship" in new covenant salvation is not restricted to male disciples but includes both men and women followers of Christ. This inclusivity is confirmed by the work of "the Spirit of adoption, by whom we [clearly, both women and men] cry out "'Abba,' Father!" (v. 15) as well as the broader phrase "God's children, and if children, also heirs" (vv. 16–17). Brothers and sisters alike compose the covenantal "sonship" through the Holy Spirit.[14]

The phrases "the household of faith" (Gal 6:10) and "the household of God" (Eph 2:19)[15] clearly highlight the familial relationships of brothers and sisters in Christ. Collectively, they celebrate, portray, and foster their siblingship by "coming together to eat," that is, to participate in the Lord's Supper (1 Cor 11:33). As "dear brothers and sisters," they hear and obey the biblical exhortation to "be steadfast, immovable, always excelling in the Lord's work" (1 Cor 15:58). As we have seen, such outstanding "Lord's work" was exemplified by both men and women in the church in Rome (Rom 16:3–16).[16]

A familial atmosphere should characterize church members in general, as Paul instructs, "Don't rebuke an older man, but exhort him as a father, younger men as brothers, older women as mothers, and the younger women as sisters with all purity" (1 Tim 5:1–2). The church as brothers and sisters in Christ obeys the vision "that there may be no division in the body, but that the members may have the same care for one another. If one member suffers, all suffer together; if one member is honored, all rejoice together"

---

[14] See the earlier discussion of "sonship" in the treatment of Gal 3:26–28.

[15] Whereas this expression has particular reference to the inclusion of both Jews and Gentiles in the "holy temple" and "God's dwelling" (Eph 2:21–22), that is, the church, an extension for our purposes to both men and women is appropriate.

[16] See the earlier discussion of Paul's greetings in Romans 16.

(1 Cor 12:25–26). More broadly still, these familial relationships are at the heart of the New Testament's "one anothers," commands to love one another, accept one another, forgive one another, pray for one another, defer to one another, serve one another, submit to one another, show hospitality to one another, confess sins to one another, and more. Sisters and brothers, bound to one another through the work of Christ and the bond of the Holy Spirit, carry out their loving responsibilities to one another in God-honoring and others-respecting ways.

In conclusion, the four metaphors or images of the church—the people of God, the body of Christ, the temple of the Holy Spirit, and the family of God—highlight and support complementarity. Members of the new covenant, parts of the body, living stones in the temple, and siblings in the one family enjoy equal dignity even as they are significantly differentiated, though not according to hierarchical roles, which are not a feature of these images/metaphors. As they cooperate interdependently by divine design, men and women fill out and mutually support one another relationally and ecclesially for both individual and corporate flourishing.

CHAPTER 23

The Offices of Prophet, Priest, and King in the New Covenant

The *munus triplex*, or threefold office of Jesus Christ—prophet, priest, and king—has a long-standing history in the church and, importantly for our purposes, significant application for complementarity. I begin with a brief biblical overview of prophet, priest, and king, then turn to how each office intersects with complementarity.

According to the Old Testament, Yahweh established three offices in Israel: prophet, priest, and king. Inspired by the Holy Spirit, prophets spoke (and some wrote) divine revelation so the people of Israel might know the Lord and his ways (Mic 3:7; 2 Pet 1:16–21). Functioning as covenantal mediators, priests offered sacrifices according to the Law to atone for the sins of the people and interceded for them before the Lord (e.g., the high priest on the Day of Atonement; Leviticus 16). As representatives of Yahweh, kings ruled over the people (e.g., Saul, David, and Solomon).

Prophets, priests, and kings were distinct people, and prophesying, priesthood, and kingship were distinct roles. However, the Old Testament envisioned a future in which one person would be Prophet, Priest, and

King, joining these roles together into one triplex office. Moses offered hope that "the LORD your God will raise up for you a prophet like me" (Deut. 18:15). Yahweh himself promised, "I will raise up a faithful priest for myself. He will do whatever is in my heart and mind" (1 Sam 2:35). And the Lord promised to David and his descendants, "Your house and kingdom will endure before me forever, and your throne will be established forever" (2 Sam 7:16).

The Son of God incarnate fulfilled this Old Testament hope. He is the realization of the Moses-like prophet (Acts 3:22–24), acknowledged as a prophet by the Samaritan woman (John 4:19), the blind man (John 9:17), and many others (Matt 16:14). He revealed God by his words (John 7:16; 12:49–50; 14:10, 24), his works (John 5:19, 36; 10:37–38), and his very being (John 14:8–9). Additionally, God the Son incarnate is the fulfillment of Yahweh's "faithful priest," being "a priest forever according to the order of Melchizedek" (Heb 5:6; cf. Ps 110:4). Moreover, Jesus is the high priest who prays for his followers (John 17; Heb 7:24–25), interceding for them before God (Rom 8:34). Finally, the incarnate Son is the actualization of the long-awaited Davidic king. He is the son of David (Matt 1:1; 9:27; John 7:42), the Son of God (Mark 1:1; Luke 3:38; Matt 16:16), and, as both, the sovereign king: "Jesus Christ our Lord . . . was a descendant of David according to the flesh and was appointed to be the powerful Son of God according to the Spirit of holiness by the resurrection of the dead" (Rom 1:3–4). As this sovereign head over all creation, he is the head of the church, its king who directs his followers for the glory of God (Eph 1:19–23).

Prophet. Priest. King. As Jesus unites these three roles into one triplex office, he motions to his disciples to engage in prophetic, priestly, and kingly ministries. With appropriate consideration for the differences between Christ's threefold office and the threefold ministry delegated to church members, I examine each one in terms of men's and women's participation and how such equal contribution underscores complementarity between the two sexes.

The Prophetic Office

Unlike priesthood and kingship, prophesying was a role for both men and women, according to both the Old and New Testaments. Thus, the male-female distinction that we will see later with priesthood and kingship is not found with regard to who could prophesy.

According to the Old Testament, both men and women prophesied, that is, received and communicated divine revelation to the people of Israel. Among the male prophets are those who are well known because of their major writings (e.g., Isaiah, Jeremiah, Ezekiel), those who are well known though did not write (e.g., Elijah, Elisha), those who are lesser known because of their minor writings (e.g., Amos, Jonah, Joel), and those who are often overlooked as prophets (e.g., Ahijah, 1 Kgs 11:29–39; Azariah, 2 Chr 15:1–8; Jahaziel, 2 Chr 20:14). Though no female prophets wrote Old Testament Scripture, there were prophetesses: Miriam (Exod 15:20), Deborah (Judg 4:4), Huldah (2 Kgs 22:14; par. 2 Chr 34:22), and others (Neh 6:14; Isa 8:3).[1]

Similarly, as presented in the New Testament, both men and women prophesied. Zechariah was "filled with the Holy Spirit and prophesied" about his son, John the Baptist (Luke 1:67–79). Simeon, upon whom the Holy Spirit came, praised God for fulfilling Messianic promises and prophesied about the salvation and judgment that Jesus the Christ would bring (Luke 2:25–35). Named prophets in the church include "Barnabas, Simeon who was called Niger, Lucius of Cyrene, Manaen, a close friend of Herod the tetrarch, and Saul" who were part of the Antioch church group described as "prophets and teachers" (Acts 13:1); Judas and Silas, envoys from the Council of Jerusalem (Acts 15:27, 30–32); and Agabus, who prophesied Paul's demise in Jerusalem (Acts 21:10–12). Negative examples of prophets are Elymas Bar-Jesus, a sorcerer and Jewish false prophet (Acts 13:6–12); and the eschatological false prophet (Rev 16:13; 19:20; 20:10).

---

[1] See earlier discussions of these prophetesses.

Specific prophetesses include Elisabeth (Luke 1:41–42); Anna, who, while serving the Lord in the temple, came up to Mary and Joseph and spoke about the future redemption of Jerusalem (Luke 2:36–38); and the four daughters of Philip the evangelist (Acts 21:8–9).[2] A negative example is "the woman Jezebel, who called herself a prophetess" and led the church into idolatry (Rev 2:20).[3]

These specific prophets and prophetesses in the new covenant era are examples of the overall New Testament affirmations about prophecy. Citing the prophet Joel's foretelling of a fresh, unprecedented outpouring of the Holy Spirit (Joel 2:28–32), Peter announced,

> And it will be in the last days, says God, that I will pour out my
> Spirit on all people;
> then your sons and your daughters will prophesy, your young men
> will see visions, and your old men will dream dreams.
> I will even pour out my Spirit on my servants in those days, both
> men and women, and they will prophesy. (Acts 2:17–18)

This "Magna Carta" of the new covenant age of the Spirit twice underscores the ubiquitous nature of prophecy, a gift to be poured out by the Spirit "on all people . . . both men and women."

An example of such revelatory enablement is the church of Corinth, which was richly granted a plethora of spiritual gifts (1 Cor 1:7–8), including the gift of prophecy in which both men and women engaged (1 Cor 11:3–16; 14:26–40).

Paul underscores the essential role of prophets in the inauguration of the church. Together with the apostles, the prophets were "the foundation" upon which the church was constructed (Eph 2:20). Moreover, together

---

[2] Zechariah, Simeon, Elizabeth, and Anna were old covenant followers of Yahweh and thus different covenantally from the later examples of new covenant prophets and prophetesses.

[3] Because she is characterized as a woman "who calls herself a prophetess," Jezebel might not serve as a negative example because she was not actually a prophetess, no matter how evil she may have been.

with the apostles, evangelists, and pastors and teachers, the prophets were the gifted people whom Christ gave to the church for its multiplication and maturation (Eph 4:11–16). Though one may debate whether this group of prophets contained only men or consisted of both men and women, there can be no disputing that Scripture provides ample evidence for both prophets and prophetesses. Specifically, prophesying as a new covenant reality in the age of the Spirit is not restricted to men but a capacity given to both women and men for the edification of the church.

This prophetic office is a first aspect of complementarity. Adapting language from the following discussion, we embrace the prophethood of all believers, both women and men.

The Priestly Office

Though there was a priest-like patriarchal activity (e.g., Noah [Gen 8:20–22] and Job [Job 1:5] offered burnt offerings on altars), I present the Old Testament inauguration and development of this office with the Aaronic and Levitical priesthood. Intriguingly, before God gave the law to Israel, he promised that his covenant-keeping people would experience great blessings, among which was the following: "you will be my kingdom of priests and my holy nation" (Exod 19:6).[4] This promise of a royal priesthood, which would be left unfilled by the (disobedient) people of Israel, envisioned that all Israelites would "function as priests in ways similar to the Levitical priesthood," the official priesthood that Yahweh would institute for his people.[5]

---

[4] This theme is picked up by Isaiah in his vision of Israel's restoration: "you will be called the Lord's priests; they will speak of you as ministers of our God" (Isa 61:6).

[5] Uche Anizor, *Kings and Priests: Scripture's Theological Account of Its Readers* (Eugene, OR: Pickwick, 2014), 34. He asks and answers this insightful question: "How might readers of Exodus have understood Israel's calling as priests? It seems probably that what is less familiar (i.e., the notion of a universal priesthood) would have been read in light of what is more familiar (i.e., a professional priesthood)" (33). As we will see, the New Testament picks up the promise of Exod 19:6, applies

Specifically, the Lord commanded Moses to invite his "brother Aaron, with his sons, . . . to serve me as priest" (Exod 28:1). To help the Aaronic ministers carry out their responsibilities, God conscripted the Levites as representatives of the first born of Israel, who belonged to the Lord (Num 3:6–9).[6] Moses stipulated the divinely directed Levitical duties: "They will teach your [Yahweh's] ordinances to Jacob and your instruction to Israel; they will set incense before you and whole burnt offerings on your altar" (Deut 33:10). As Uche Anizor argues, "the priest is concerned primarily with the tabernacle, the Holy of Holies (דביר), as the place in which the Word (דבר) resided in the form of the Ten Words and book of the law. . . . Thus, it is difficult to conceive of the nature and role of priesthood in Israel apart from its connection to the Word of YHWH. Indeed, a priest *is* a minister of the Word."[7]

As just noted, a second priestly duty was assisting in the offering of sacrifices; for example: "The guilt offering is to be slaughtered at the place where the burnt offering is slaughtered, and the priest is to splatter its blood on all sides of the altar. . . . The priest will burn them on the altar as a food offering to the Lord; it is a guilt offering" (Lev 7:1–7).

Superintending the annual Day of Atonement was a third priestly responsibility. Specifically, Moses declared this to be "a permanent statute" for Israel on "the seventh month, on the tenth day of the month:" "Atonement will be made for you on this day to cleanse you, and you will be clean from all your sins before the LORD. . . . The priest who is anointed and ordained to serve as high priest in place of his father will make atonement. . . . This is

---

it to the church (with appropriate modifications), and thus sees its fulfillment in the priesthood of all believers in the new covenant.

[6] The Lord explained his choice of the Levites for priestly service: "See, I have taken the Levites from the Israelites in place of every firstborn Israelite from the womb. The Levites belong to me, because every firstborn belongs to me. At the time I struck down every firstborn in the land of Egypt, I consecrated every firstborn in Israel to myself, both man and animal. They are mine; I am the LORD" (Num 3:12–13).

[7] Anizor, *Kings and Priests*, 84.

to be a permanent statute for you, to make atonement for the Israelites once a year because of all their sins" (Lev 16:29–34).

A fourth and final duty was blessing the people of Israel, as the Lord directed Moses: "Tell Aaron and his sons, 'This is how you are to bless the Israelites. You should say to them,

> "May the LORD bless you and protect you;
> may the LORD make his face shine on you and be gracious to you;
> may the LORD look with favor on you and give you peace."'
>
> In this way they will pronounce my name over the Israelites, and I will bless them.'" (Num 6:22–27)

Tragically and reprehensibly, the priests and the Levites failed miserably in their duties of instruction, mediation, and intercession. The office of priesthood did not function as it was divinely intended to work.

As briefly noted above, the Old Testament sounded a faint theme of hope of a new and truthful prophet (Deut 18:15) and a new and obedient king (2 Sam 7:16). To this expectation was added the hope of a new and faithful priest: [Yahweh speaking] "I will raise up a faithful priest for myself. He will do whatever is in my heart and mind. I will establish a lasting dynasty for him, and he will walk before my anointed one for all time" (1 Sam 2:35). As we will see in the next section, this expectation combined the offices of king and priest, promised with striking symbolism by the crowning of "Joshua son of Jehozadak, the high priest." As Yahweh instructed Zechariah:

> You are to tell him: This is what the LORD of Armies says: Here is a man whose name is Branch; he will branch out from his place and build the LORD's temple. Yes, he will build the LORD's temple; he will bear royal splendor and will sit on his throne and rule. There will be a priest on his throne, and there will be peaceful counsel between the two of them. The crown will reside in the LORD's temple as a memorial. (Zech 6:12–14)

A royal priest, or a priestly king: such a remarkable development was the hope of Israel. Unlike the old covenant priesthood centered on Aaron and Levi, this fresh, unprecedented royal priest would be "a priest forever according to the pattern of Melchizedek" (Ps 110:4; cf. Gen 14:18).

God the Son incarnate fulfilled this Old Testament hope. The Letter to the Hebrews points out the need for a different type of priest: "Now if perfection came through the Levitical priesthood (for on the basis of it the people received the law), what further need was there for another priest to appear, said to be according to the order of Melchizedek and not according to the order of Aaron?" (Heb 5:11). In the incarnation, the Son appeared as "a priest forever according to the order of Melchizedek'" (v. 17). Jesus's priesthood, accomplished by his one for all time offering of himself for sin and because it is eternal, is superior in every way to the former priesthood; "therefore, he is able to save completely those who come to God through him, since he always lives to intercede for them" (7:25).

Jesus's priesthood is a heavenly one (Heb 8:1–6), and because of his superior ministry, "he is the mediator of a better covenant, which has been established on better promises" (8:6). In this new covenant, Jesus is the antitype of the type of priests of the old covenant: "he entered the most holy place once for all time, not by the blood of goats and calves, but by his own blood, having obtained eternal redemption" (9:12). God the Son incarnate fulfilled the Old Testament hope of a royal priest, becoming the antitype that perfectly realized the Levitical type of priest, offering once and for all the sacrifice for sins and interceding for his people as the mediator of the new covenant.

Through this decisive, covenant-changing work of the High Priest Jesus Christ, a new and better priesthood has been inaugurated. Specifically, Christ has made his followers "a kingdom, priests to his God and Father" (Rev 1:6; cf. 5:9–10). As "a spiritual house, they are being built to be a holy priesthood to offer spiritual sacrifices acceptable to God through Jesus Christ" (1 Pet 2:5). As Anizor underscores,

> The emphasis of the former phrase ["a spiritual house" or "house of the Spirit"] is on the collective nature of the priesthood, namely,

> that believers are a body or community of priests who, by virtue of God's election and the sanctifying work of the Spirit, together share the benefits of direct access to God. By implication, of course, this refers to the individuals that make up the priestly body. The latter phrase ["being built to be a holy priesthood to offer spiritual sacrifices"] lays stress on the idea that the multitudinous sacrifices offered by this priesthood are motivated or wrought by the Holy Spirit, thus making them acceptable to God.[8]

The church, then, is a "royal priesthood" (1 Pet 2:9), both the replacement of the old covenant Aaronic/Levitical priesthood and, in and through the royal priest Christ, the fulfillment of the Old Testament hope for a combination of the two offices of kingdom and priesthood.

Of what does this royal priesthood consist? First and foremost, as Anizor argues on the basis of 1 Pet 2:9 ("so that you may proclaim the praises of the one who called you out of darkness into his marvelous light"), "the *raison d'être* of the royal priesthood of believers is that they would declare God's ἀρετὰς (virtues, mighty acts, praises). . . . Royal priesthood is tied to the declaration of God's Word, in that God's promises (inscripturated or otherwise), and the fulfillment thereof, form the basis of the church's joyful proclamation."[9] Accordingly, all church members as royal priests are to obey Paul's directive: "Let the word of Christ dwell richly among you, in all wisdom teaching and admonishing one another through psalms, hymns, and spiritual songs" (Col 3:16). As will be discussed in the following section on kingship, kings (like priests) were to focus their attention on the Word of God and its proclamation. Accordingly, the royal priesthood is Word-centered.

Second, and tracing out the theme of presenting "spiritual sacrifices acceptable to God through Jesus Christ" (1 Pet 2:5), royal priests offer sacrifices consisting of praise and thanksgiving to the Lord (Heb 13:15); acts of

[8] Anizor, *Kings and Priests*, 38.

[9] Anizor, *Kings and Priests*, 41.

service and physical provisions for others (Heb 13:16), exemplified in financial gifts for the advancement of Paul's ministry (Phil 4:18); partnership in the ministry of the gospel, even being "poured out as a drink offering" to martyrdom (Phil 2:17; 2 Tim 4:6; Rev 6:9); and conversions to Christ through the announcement of the gospel (Rom 15:16–17). Third, because they "have boldness to enter the sanctuary through the blood of Jesus" (Heb 10:20), and because "they have a great high priest over the house of God" (v. 22), royal priests are to "consider one another in order to provoke love and good works" (v. 24) as they gather together for worship (v. 25).

Importantly for our purposes, this new covenant royal priesthood consists not only of (a very narrow swath of) men, for whom the Aaronic/Levitical priesthood was reserved, but of all men and all women who have been redeemed through the High Priest Jesus Christ. Women and men alike, together as members of the church, are called to be and function as priests. This new priesthood is the fulfillment of God's promise that if his covenant people would obey the law, he would constitute them—in an inclusive, corporate sense—as "my kingdom of priests and my holy nation" (Exod 19:6). In terms of the church, this all-encompassing new priesthood changes (1) the male-only system in which the patriarchs functioned as priests by offering burnt sacrifices through the erecting of altars, and (2) the male-only Aaronic/Levitical system in which the priests proclaimed the Word of God, offered sacrifices, blessed the people, and more. Without commenting on how different churches provide for the superintendence and leadership of their worship services, the key point to be made from this restructuring of the priesthood is that all church members—men and women together—participate together as priests of the new covenant.

This affirmation reflects Martin Luther's insistence on the priesthood of all believers.[10] For Luther, God's mighty work of justification—his dec-

---

[10] Some of the following is adapted from Gregg R. Allison and Rachel Ciano, "Roman Catholic Theology and Practice of the Priesthood Contrasted with Protestant Theology and Practice of the Priesthood," *Southern Baptist Journal*

laration that the ungodly are not guilty but righteous instead—necessarily results in Christians being constituted a priesthood. Such saving action on the part of God is displayed by the sacrament of baptism, so that "through baptism all of us are consecrated to the priesthood."[11]

As Luther championed the material principle of Protestantism and its implication for the priesthood, he also attacked the centuries-old Roman Catholic division of human reality into a "spiritual estate" (the realm of the Church's priestly caste) and a "temporal estate" (the realm of everyone else as the laity):

> It is pure invention that pope, bishop, priests, and monks are called the spiritual estate while princes, lords, artisans, and farmers are called the temporal estate. This is indeed a piece of deceit and hypocrisy. Yet no one need be intimidated by it, and for this reason: all Christians are truly of the spiritual estate, and there is no difference among them except that of office. Paul says in 1 Corinthians 12 [:12-13, paraphrased] that we are all one body, yet every member has its own work by which it serves the others. This is because we all have one baptism, one gospel, one faith, and are all Christians alike; for baptism, gospel, and faith alone make us spiritual and a Christian people.[12]

Accordingly, Luther sought to dismantle the Roman Catholic Church's exaltation of its priesthood above the laity, insisting instead on the equality of all

of Theology 23.1 (2019): 137–55. Luther's name for this doctrine was the "general priesthood of all baptized Christians." Martin Luther, *Selected Psalms II*, in *Luther's Works*, 55 vols., ed. Jaroslav Pelikan and Helmut T. Lehmann (St. Louis: Concordia, 1955–86), 13:332.

[11] Luther, "To the Christian Nobility of the German Nation," in *Luther's Works*, 44:127.

[12] Luther, "To the Christian Nobility of the German Nation," in *Luther's Works*, 44:127.

Christians rather than a hierarchy based on an essential difference between priests and laypeople.[13]

Specifically, Luther set forth seven priestly functions that may be carried out by laypeople as constituting the priesthood of all believers:[14] (1) Teach and preach the Word of God: "Even though not everybody has the public office and calling, every Christian has the right and the duty to teach, instruct, admonish, comfort, and rebuke his neighbor with the Word of God at every opportunity and whenever necessary."[15] (2) Administer baptism: In emergency situations, both men and women could administer the sacrament of baptism. (3) Administer the Lord's Supper: Just as the entire Corinthian congregation had received from Paul the words of institution (1 Cor 11:23–26), so all church members today may administer the sacrament of the Lord's Supper. (4) Exercise the keys by binding and loosing sins (Matt 16:19; 18:18), by which Luther meant announcing the forgiveness of sins or declaring the retention of sin. As it is the right of priests to announce forgiveness or to deny such forgiveness on the basis of the gospel, all Christians may exercise the keys of the church. (5) Pray for others: "We may boldly come into the presence of God in the spirit of faith and cry 'Abba, Father!', pray for one another, and do all things which we see done and foreshadowed in the outer and visible work of priests."[16] (6) Sacrifice: Not in the sense of Roman Catholic sacrifices (e.g., the Eucharist) but spiritual sacrifices such as praise and thanksgiving. (7) Judge doctrine: In accordance with congregation-wide instructions to test false teachers and discern false teaching (e.g., Matt 7:15; 1 Thess 5:21), and because of each believer's anointing with the Holy Spirit (e.g., John 14:26; 1 John 2:27), "it is the duty of the Christian

---

[13] Luther, "The Babylonian Captivity of the Church," in *Luther's Works*, 36:112-13. This essential difference is due to the fact that priests are consecrated by the Sacrament of Holy Orders, which confers an indelible mark by which the nature of its recipients is forever changed.

[14] This discussion is adapted from Anizor, *Kings and Priests*, 154–58.

[15] Luther, "Psalm 110 [:4]," in *Luther's Works*, 13:333.

[16] Luther, "The Freedom of a Christian," in *Luther's Works*, 31:355.

to espouse the cause of the faith, to understand and defend it, and to denounce every error."[17]

Still, Luther did not do away with all distinctions, retaining the office of ministry. In place of the Roman Catholic Church's elevated priesthood, Luther proposed priests as servants in and of the church, which selected them from among its priest-members: "We are all priests, as many of us as are Christians. But the priests, as we call them, are ministers chosen from among us. All that they do is done in our name; the priesthood is nothing but a ministry. This we learn from 1 Corinthians 4 [:1]: 'This is how one should regard us, as servants of Christ and stewards of the mysteries of God.'"[18]

Importantly for our purpose, Luther's proposal did not eliminate the priestly responsibilities of all the members—both women and men—of the church. On the contrary, offering and sacrifice, priest and priesthood, now belong to all who have faith in Christ. They are not reserved for a differentiated estate of ordained people, which includes in Protestant churches those who hold the office of pastor/elder/overseer/priest/bishop. Contemporary expressions of the priesthood of all believers will reflect various ecclesial and denominational distinctives such as the nature of the sacraments and the requirements for those who administer them, the responsibilities that are incumbent on congregational members or reserved for church officers, and the position on complementarianism or egalitarianism. Acknowledging these factors, concrete expressions of the priesthood may include announcing the gospel to one another, teaching and admonishing one another with Scripture, praying for one another, hearing one another's confession of sin and assuring one another of divine forgiveness, preaching and/or administering the sacraments/ordinances during worship services, guarding the church from false teachers and false teaching, choosing/electing church

[17] Luther, "To the Christian Nobility of the German Nation," in *Luther's Works*, 44:136.

[18] Luther, "The Babylonian Captivity of the Church," in *Luther's Works*, 36:113.

leaders, and engaging in the Great Commission through evangelism, planting churches, and supporting and serving as international missionaries.[19]

To be recalled in this discussion, the priesthood of all believers is made possible through the High Priest Jesus Christ who, as the one mediator between God and sinful humanity, has accomplished salvation through his atoning sacrifice. Such salvation, together with its entailment of the priesthood of all believers, pertains to men and women alike.

This priestly office is a second aspect of complementarity. We embrace the priesthood of all believers, both men and women.

The Kingly Office

As mentioned above, the Old Testament occasionally links together priesthood and kingship as a divinely designed, perfect reality. In its first appearance, this priesthood-kingdom is promised to the people of Israel as God is set to give the Ten Commandments as part of his covenant with them. By paying close attention to the old covenant, the people of Israel, out of all the people in the world, would graciously be priestly citizens of a holy kingdom/nation (Exod 19:5–6). Though, as we have seen, the Levites as a caste of consecrated men would serve in the office of priest (priesthood), and though, as we will see, some of Israel's anointed men would serve in the office of king (kingship), the Lord envisioned from early on, even as the old covenant was being instituted, a future priesthood/kingdom to which all of his people would belong.

---

[19] As Kevin Vanhoozer points out, the priesthood of all believers, particularly its emphasis on "the distinctly communicative nature of the priestly task," explains "the rise to prominence of certain distinctive forms of Protestant communication": translations of the Bible into the vernacular, transformation of the central (physical) feature of church buildings from the Roman Catholic altar (on which the Eucharistic sacrifice of Christ is offered) to the Protestant pulpit, and production of biblical commentaries for help in understanding and expositing Scripture. Kevin J. Vanhoozer, *Biblical Authority After Babel: Retrieving the* Solas *in the Spirit of Mere Protestant Christianity* (Grand Rapids: Brazos, 2016), 159.

Turning to the office of king, the Old Testament underscores that kingship in Israel was both a divinely ordained institution and a humanly—and, primarily, sinfully—expressed position. As part of the Deuteronomic command, a future king was envisioned for and enjoined upon Israel: "When you enter the land the LORD your God is giving you, take possession of it, live in it, and say, 'I will set a king over me like all the nations around me,' you are to appoint over you the king the LORD your God chooses. Appoint a king from your brothers. You are not to set a foreigner over you, or one who is not of your people" (Deut 17:14–15). Specific instructions provided details about the king and his kingship: he was not to acquire many horses, many wives, and much wealth (vv. 15–17). By contrast, the king was to focus on copying, reading, and obeying Torah (vv. 18–19), with the result that "his heart will not be exalted above his countrymen, he will not turn from this command to the right or the left, and he and his sons will continue reigning many years in Israel" (v. 20). As noted in the above discussion of the priestly office, its fundamental purpose was centered on the Word of God, an emphasis that was echoed here with respect to the kingly office.

Though a divinely ordained office for the flourishing of Israel, its actualization began as a sinfully generated demand on the part of the people against the explicit will of God himself. They demanded that the aged Samuel appoint a king to judge them, a structure that would mirror the monarchies of the surrounding nations. Samuel consulted the Lord, who instructed him to heed the people's wish; such an evil demand expressed their rejection of the Lord as king. He told Samuel, "Listen to them, but solemnly warn them and tell them about the customary rights of the king who will reign over them" (vv. 4–9). Samuel provided a list of the king's privileges, which appears to be diametrically opposed to the Deuteronomic list: Israel's king will conscript her sons, employ her daughters, confiscate Israel's land and harvest, exact tribute from her citizens, subjugate Israel's slaves and draft animals, and even enlist Samuel's listeners/readers themselves as the king's servants (vv. 11–18).

Sadly, "The people refused to listen to Samuel," insisting on a king, at which "the LORD told Samuel, 'Appoint a king for them'" (vv. 19–22). Importantly, then, kings and kingship in Israel, though divinely ordained and instructed, was wrongly demanded by its rebellious people against the revealed will of God. The office became a reluctant concession on the part of God to his heinously sinful people. Unsurprisingly, then, the Old Testament narrates only one example of a king—Josiah—who wholeheartedly obeyed the Lord by fixing his attention on his Word (2 Kgs 23:24–25).

Even given the improper imposition and constant failure of kingship, the Old Testament offers a magnificent hope for a righteous king ruling righteously over God's kingdom. As the Lord established his covenant with David, he presented this vision:

> "I will raise up after you your descendant, who will come from your body, and I will establish his kingdom. He is the one who will build a house for my name, and I will establish the throne of his kingdom forever. I will be his father, and he will be my son. When he does wrong, I will discipline him with a rod of men and blows from mortals. But my faithful love will never leave him as it did when I removed it from Saul, whom I removed from before you. Your house and kingdom will endure before me forever, and your throne will be established forever." (2 Sam 7:11–16)

This Davidic covenant was the promise of a future king and kingdom according to the will of God.

Tragically, this promise did not and could not arise from within the sinful people of Israel themselves. As narrated over and over in the historical books and denounced in the prophetic books of the Old Testament, kingship was for the most part a disaster. Of the thirty-nine kings after the division of the kingdom into its northern and southern parts, eight were good and thirty-one were evil. Only one woman ruled over Judah, and she was queen for six years (842–836 BC), though her tenure began through her usurpation of the throne that rightly belonged to her grandsons, whom she murdered (2 Kgs 11:1–3).

Importantly, then, for our purposes, the ruling office in Israel was the (nearly) exclusive domain of men who served as Israel's kings under the old covenant, and their kingship was often an utter failure.

But the promise itself of a Davidic covenant and king would not and could not fail; such hope was the subject of several Old Testament prophecies. Jeremiah pledged,

> "Look, the days are coming"—this is the LORD's declaration—"when I will fulfill the good promise that I have spoken concerning the house of Israel and the house of Judah. In those days and at that time I will cause a Righteous Branch to sprout up for David, and he will administer justice and righteousness in the land. In those days Judah will be saved, and Jerusalem will dwell securely, and this is what she will be named: The LORD Is Our Righteousness." For this is what the LORD says: "David will never fail to have a man sitting on the throne of the house of Israel. The Levitical priests will never fail to have a man always before me to offer burnt offerings, to burn grain offerings, and to make sacrifices." (Jer 33:14–18)

Salvation would arise for God's people by means of a "Righteous Branch" for David, for whom the promise of an eternal kingdom would never fail. A new unshakable item was added to this promise: an eternal priesthood that would offer worship and sacrifice. The hope of a priesthood-kingdom echoed once again. Specifically, Isaiah identified this hope with a divine child/son:

> For a child will be born for us, a son will be given to us, and the government will be on his shoulders. He will be named Wonderful Counselor, Mighty God, Eternal Father, Prince of Peace. The dominion will be vast, and its prosperity will never end. He will reign on the throne of David and over his kingdom, to establish

> and sustain it with justice and righteousness from now on and forever. (Isa 9:6–7)

The Lord himself promised to fulfill his covenant with David and place a righteous Davidic king on his eternal throne.

God the Son incarnate, as the Savior Jesus of Nazareth, was the fulfillment of this Davidic covenant of an eternal and righteous kingship. Such was the angel's message to Mary: "You will conceive and give birth to a son, and you will name him Jesus. He will be great and will be called the Son of the Most High, and the Lord God will give him the throne of his father David. He will reign over the house of Jacob forever, and his kingdom will have no end" (Luke 1:31–33). Jesus himself came preaching, "The time is fulfilled, and the kingdom of God has come near. Repent and believe the good news!" (Mark 1:15). Indeed, Jesus's ministry could be summed up simply: "he was traveling from one town and village to another, preaching and telling the good news of the kingdom of God" (Luke 8:1; cf. 4:43). In addition to teaching about it (e.g., Mark 4:30; Luke 13:18, 20; Acts 1:3), he embodied and inaugurated the kingdom as his mighty works (e.g., his exorcism of demons) manifested: "If I drive out demons by the Spirit of God, then the kingdom of God has come upon you" (Matt 12:28). Jesus addressed the nature of the kingdom, clarifying that it would not be a visible reign with physical rulers and activities because it centered on him (Luke 17:20–21) and required a spiritual, not a physical, rebirth for entrance into it (John 3:1–8). Moreover, the kingdom would not belong exclusively to Israel but would extend its boundaries to include the Gentiles worldwide (Matt 21:43; Acts 15:6–21).

The contrast between kingship and kingdom under the old covenant and its reality in the new covenant is striking. Exclusivity—the people of Israel, male kings—and calamity do not carry over into and plague the New Testament idea of kingship. Indeed, there is only one King, the Lord Jesus Christ, and no new covenant office of (human) king. Rather, kingship belongs to all of Christ's followers, both men and women. It is King Jesus who rules over his people, and male and female citizens of this kingdom do not rule over one another.

Additionally, the ancient promise of a priesthood-kingdom begins its fulfillment with the new covenant people of God. As John's trinitarian benediction for the churches of Revelation turns to Jesus Christ, the apostle blesses "him who loves us and has set us free from our sins by his blood, and *made us a kingdom, priests to his God and Father*" (Rev 1:5–6; emphasis added). Without distinction, female Christians and male Christians alike are incorporated into the kingdom of God as priests. Furthermore, Peter vividly portrays elect believers by means of striking Old Testament expressions: "you are a chosen race, a royal priesthood, a holy nation, a people for his [God's] possession" (1 Pet 2:9; reflecting Exod 19:6; Deut 7:6). Christians constitute a new humanity, a divinely chosen humankind consisting of two types: elect women and elect men. Believers compose a new nation, a sacred citizenry that includes both saintly men and saintly women. The people whom God owns comprise his new possession of treasured women and treasured men. Of particular importance for our discussion, "a royal priesthood"—the promised combination of priesthood-kingdom—presents priestly men and priestly women as sacrificing themselves and interceding for one another with kingly authority and power.

Radically transposed from its old covenant expression by the kingship of Jesus and the establishment of his kingdom, the new covenant reality of kingship and kingdom embraces both men and women in Christ.

This kingly office is a third aspect of complementarity. We embrace the kingship of all believers, both men and women.

In conclusion, the triplex office of prophet, priest, and king, as described and actualized among the new covenant people of God, underscores the equal dignity of women and men and does not exhibit any significant differentiation between them. Men and women alike are prophets and prophetesses. Women and men alike are priests. Men and women alike are kings (in the non-gendered sense of that term), perhaps rendered better co-regents of God and the kingdom of Christ. The prophethood, priesthood, and kingship of women and men have noting to do with hierarchy, at least not with authority and submission between them (as opposed to, for example, their joint authority over the creation, their co-regency according to the cultural mandate).

CHAPTER 24

Conclusion from Theological Considerations

Part Five has brought together a diverse spectrum of topics that contribute to our overall discussion of complementarity. Specifically, the opening task was to define what is a man and what is a woman, focusing on their nature rather than their roles because identity precedes function. Embracing common human capacities and common human properties, this definitional exercise affirms the equal dignity of women and men, and, because these capacities and properties are always expressed in a sexed way, also affirms significant differences between them. Attention was next directed to the images or metaphors for the church, specifically the people of God, the body of Christ, the temple of the Holy Spirit, and the family of God. Men and women as members of the new covenant community, parts of the body, living stones composing the temple, and siblings in the one family of God share equal dignity even as they are significantly differentiated (for example, each body part is gifted differently and assigned different places in the body), though not hierarchically. That is, in each of these metaphors, God—Father, Son, and Holy Spirit—is the authority to whom the members submit as they exist and minister side by side as, for example, living stones in the temple. The final focus was on the offices of prophet, priest, and king and their implications for complementarity. This emphasis underscored that both men and women alike compose the prophethood, priesthood, and kingship of all believers.

When men and women actualize the equal dignity and significant differences that these topics emphasize and that are reflective of the divine design for male and female image bearers, they fill out and mutually support one another relationally, familially, vocationally, and ecclesially for both corporate and individual flourishing.

PART SIX

Arenas of Application

Though it may seem odd, before I address areas of application between two or more people for human flourishing in four arenas, I need to say something about complementarity for one person, for personal flourishing. Though complementarity is interpersonal—"filling out and mutually supporting one another"—it is in a paradoxical sense intrapersonal: it addresses concerns of, and promotes flourishing for, the person herself or himself.

The fact of human sociality—"the universal human condition of desiring, expressing, and receiving human relationships"[1]—and its subset complementarity should never lead to disregard for and/or disrespect of oneself, one's own being and way in this world. Certainly, there is the biblical command to self-denial, which is not only part and parcel of devotion to the Lord, but the very heart of such piety. God the Son's entire incarnate existence was that of self-sacrifice, as Jesus declared: "the Son of Man did not

[1] Gregg R. Allison, *Embodied: Living as Whole People in a Fractured World* (Grand Rapids: Baker, 2021), 73.

come to be served, but to serve, and to give his life as a ransom for many" (Mark 10:45). To such self-denial Jesus calls every disciple: "If anyone wants to follow after me, let him deny himself, take up his cross daily, and follow me. For whoever wants to save his life will lose it, but whoever loses his life because of me will save it" (Luke 9:23–24). By such death to themselves, believers mimic Jesus's death to himself (2 Cor 5:14–15). Clearly, the core of the Christlike or cruciform life is self-denial.

But there are limits to such sacrifice. Self-denial is not a call to the annihilation of oneself as a divine image bearer whose identity is becoming progressively more conformed to the image of Christ. Self-denial is not an obliteration of oneself as designed and called by God to a station in life, a purpose, a vocation, mutual relationships and not isolation, and more. It is not an eradication of oneself that leads to passivity, a docility that suffers involuntarily even to the point of tolerating sin and evil that should be repulsed. Resignation in the face of wickedness that is done in the name of self-denial is a betrayal of true sacrifice, not an admirable application of it.

If there is no personal self, interpersonal complementarity is impossible. With the disappearance of one's person/self comes the disappearance of complementarity. An absent self cannot contribute to the filling out and mutual support of others.

But when we engage properly in self-denial, retaining our personal identity as female image bearers and male image bearers, complementarity has many applications as men and women fill out and mutually support one another as divinely-adopted siblings in Christ and (if applicable) covenanted husbands and wives (relationally); as mothers, fathers, sons, daughters, sisters, and brothers (familially); as colleagues laboring together at their jobs (vocationally); and as fellow citizens of the kingdom, ministers of the shared prophethood/priesthood/kingship, pastors/elders/overseers/bishops, deacons and deaconesses, and members of their church (ecclesially).

In detail, this concluding chapter explores complementarity as it leads to relational flourishing, familial flourishing, vocational flourishing, and ecclesial flourishing.

Complementarity for Relational Flourishing

Creation in the divine image highlights and is the ground for the equal dignity and the significant differentiation of men and women. Accordingly, complementarity decries any sense of superiority or inferiority, all trace of advantage or disadvantage, between the sexes. Moreover, it insists on the full participation of all women and men as their differences foster a much-needed synergy between them. Men and women are to fill out and mutually support one another relationally. This full-orbed connectiveness is reciprocal, embracing men in relation to women and women in relation to men. This complementarity stands over against other sex identities. Regretfully, it perceives the presence of both versions of sex polarity—traditional sex polarity in complementarianism, reverse sex polarity in egalitarianism—even as it bemoans the contemporary cultural supremacy of both sex unity and sex neutrality.

With specific attention to complementarity for relational flourishing between husbands and wives, the kind of sex identity that Prudence Allen calls *integral sex complementarity* seems the right option. This "integral" variety considers a woman and a man "as two separate and complete human individuals who are equal in dignity and worth and who have philosophically significant differences. They are not fractional beings who together make up one being. Instead, they are two whole beings who, together, synergetically generate more than just the sum of themselves" through interdependence.[2] This integral sex complementarity issues in Thomas Schreiner's sober warning: "Complementarians have too often made the mistake of envisioning the husband/wife relationship in one-dimensional terms, so that any idea of mutuality and partnership is removed and wives are conceived of as servants (or even as slaves) of husbands. . . . Indeed, any marriage relationship

---

[2] Prudence Allen, *The Concept of Woman, Volume 2: The Early Humanist Reformation, 1250–1500* (Grand Rapids: Eerdmans, 2006), 18.

that lacks such a sense of mutuality has serious problems!"[3] A similar caution is appropriate for egalitarians who so emphasize equal dignity between the sexes that they minimize the significant differences between men and women who, according to complementarity, are not interchangeable parts playing interchangeable roles.[4]

Though it is beyond the scope of this book to engage in discussion of spousal mistreatment, I urge great caution in marshalling statistics wrongly to present complementarian men as more likely to abuse their wives than non-complementarian (e.g., secular, egalitarian) men.[5] All responsible proponents of egalitarianism and complementarianism denounce all forms of spousal abuse.

Complementarity for Familial Flourishing

Complementarity insists on the propriety, joy, and sacredness of fatherhood and motherhood. Any deviation from this support and encouragement of

---

[3] Thomas R. Schreiner, "Another Complementarian Perspective," in *Two Views on Women in Ministry*, ed. James R. Beck, rev. ed. (Grand Rapids: Zondervan, 2005), 302–3.

[4] This statement is not about the division of labor between men/husbands and women/wives along the lines of traditional (e.g., 1950s) applications (e.g., a woman's/wife's place is in the home and a man's/husband's place is working outside the home). Thus, it disagrees with Belleville's non-nuanced discussion. Linda L. Belleville, "Women in Ministry: An Egalitarian Perspective," in *Two Views on Women in Ministry*, 25–26.

[5] For further discussion see Kylie Maddox Pidgeon, "Complementarianism and Domestic Abuse: A Social-Scientific Perspective on Whether 'Equal but Different' Is Really Equal at All," in *Discovering Biblical Equality: Biblical, Theological, Cultural, and Practical Perspectives*, ed. Ronald W. Pierce and Cynthia Long Westfall, 3rd ed. (Downers Grove: IVP Academic, 2021), 572–96; Nancy R. Pearcey, *The Toxic War on Masculinity: How Christianity Reconciles the Sexes* (Grand Rapids: Baker Books, 2023); Andreas J. Köstenberger and Marny Köstenberger, *God's Design for Man and Woman: A Biblical-Theological Survey* (Wheaton: Crossway, 2014); Melissa Kruger, "Is Complementarian Theology the Root of Domestic Abuse?" TGC blogs (April 5, 2016), https://www.thegospelcoalition.org/blogs/melissa-kruger/is-complementarian-theology-the-root-of-domestic-abuse/.

procreation is to be avoided and condemned, especially in light of our contemporary society and its disparagement of childbearing, child raising, and families.[6] At the same time, it should never come to the point of emphasizing multiplication of children over vocation (or vice versa), as Gen 1:28 commands men and women to contribute to both areas.

This point, as well as its recognition of the persistent mockery of the family in general and of motherhood in particular, specifically takes issue with Simone de Beauvoir and her demeaning of female identity: "Better that she identify herself as a human being who happens to be a woman. It's a certain situation which is not the same as men's situation, of course, but she shouldn't identify herself as a woman."[7] For Beauvoir, to so identify herself would mean that a woman concede passively to her nature and not act responsibly as an agent: "to give birth and to breastfeed are not *activities* but natural functions; they do not involve a project, which is why the woman finds no motive there [in childbearing] to claim a higher meaning for her existence; she passively submits to her biological destiny."[8] Contra Beauvoir, complementarity applauds a woman's choice (assuming she has chosen this path and not been coerced into accepting it) of marriage, pregnancy, childbirth, child raising (including breastfeeding), and dedication to family, and complementarity rejects the idea that such a choice is a passive surrender "to her biological destiny." On the contrary, it is a conscientious choice that will propel women as mothers to a more mature level, not of existence (because motherhood is not the essence of a woman) but of role (because motherhood is a role into which women, if that is their chosen path, mature).

Similarly, complementarity encourages married couples to have children if they can do so. The cultural mandate, for which both men and women bear responsibility, includes the aspect of procreation (and vocation,

---

[6] For further discussion see Brad Wilcox, *Get Married: Why Americans Must Defy the Elites, Forge Strong Families, and Save Civilization* (New York: HarperCollins, 2024).

[7] Margaret Simons, "Two Interviews with Simone de Beauvoir (1982)," *Hypatia* 3.3 (1989): 19.

[8] Simone de Beauvoir, *The Second Sex* (New York: Vintage, 2011), 73.

the topic of the next section). The expansion of the human race is a duty laid upon all able-bodied husband and wife teams. Some believers and churches will insist upon married couples having a large number of children, seeing this fruitfulness as contributing to the "redemption" (or at least resistance) of anti-Christian culture. Other believers and churches will insist on limiting the number of children due to economic and political realities. In both cases, such decisions are best left up to the couples as they seek divine wisdom, the leading of the Holy Spirit, and sage counsel of others. Again, to be repulsed is the general societal discouragement either to forego having children (for example, so as not to overpopulate the earth and waste its very limited resources) or to severely limit their number.

Complementarity for Vocational Flourishing

Complementarity champions the right, integrity, and honor of work for both able-bodied men and women. Any deviation from this support and encouragement of vocation is to be avoided and condemned, especially in light of our contemporary slothful society and its sense of entitlement, its lackadaisical work ethic, and its growing reliance on government handouts. Moreover, for married persons, it should never come to the point of emphasizing vocation over the multiplication of children (or vice versa), as Gen 1:28 commands men and women to contribute to both areas. This caution is particularly important to emphasize in our contemporary workaholic society that idolizes money, places its (misguided) hope in vast financial accumulation, and sacrifices (most) everything for the sake of vocational advancement.

Complementarity also cautions believers and churches to avoid so stereotyping the nature and types of jobs that are permitted to the two sexes that men and women who choose careers and work in professions that don't "fit the mold" become confused and doubt their maleness and femaleness and/or become discouraged about their contribution to the workforce. As just noted, such vocational decisions are best left up to the individual woman or man according to their God-given abilities while encouraging them to pray for divine wisdom, depend on the leading of the of the Holy Spirit, and consider the sage counsel of others.

Complementarity for Ecclesial Flourishing

While the complementarian-egalitarian debate about church leadership and ministry roles continues almost unabated, complementarity cautions believers on both sides to differentiate their interpretation of Scripture and their application of it, urging them not to identify the two such that even those who generally interpret Scripture as they do yet apply it differently in this arena become the target of criticism and dismissal.

Complementarity underscores that Pauline love mutualism must characterize men and women in the church. They are to love one another authentically and reciprocally. They are to outdo one another in showing honor. They are to favor one another in respect and care. They are to support and defer to and prioritize and sacrifice themselves for one another. Whatever be the church's decision about its roles and offices, there is a more foundational matter that should fill the church's vision, captivate its attention, and abound among its members: the complementarity of all women and all men.

Complementarity calls attention to the fact that the Great Commission was given to the church, to both men and women, and without the active participation of both sexes, the advancement of the gospel will suffer. If the church is called to make disciples of all the nations, then each local church should consider how to disciple all its members—both men and women—to be ministers of the gospel. While it is quite common to focus on what women cannot do in church, this negative approach should be transformed. Rather than churches discounting women, churches should help women as well as men identify their gifts, train them how to use their gifts, and direct and resource them in ministries in which they can use their gifts fruitfully.

On this point about spiritual gifts, while it is common to consider spiritual gifts and church offices as one and the same ecclesial phenomenon, the distinction should be retained (and this applies to churches on both sides of the debate). Specifically, spiritual gifts are endowments that are distributed to all church members by the Holy Spirit and that he empowers for the maturation and multiplication of the church.[9] Church officers in church offices are believers who are called by God and publicly (thus, officially) recognized by their church as its leaders, teachers, and shepherds for its maturation and multiplication. This point seems to be a key point of debate between complementarians, who tend to distinguish gifts and officers/offices, and egalitarians, who tend to minimize the distinction. But maintaining the difference is important for both positions. By so doing, complementarianism can insist that women to whom the Spirit has given the gifts of teaching, leading, and shepherding may exercise those gifts in certain ministries but not as pastors/elders. Similarly, egalitarianism can insist that women to whom the Spirit has given those gifts may exercise them in all ministries, including those at the highest level of church leadership, while still acknowledging that not every woman who has those gifts is a church officer serving in a church office.

[9] For further discussion see Gregg R. Allison, *Sojourners and Strangers: The Doctrine of the Church* (Wheaton: Crossway, 2012), 413–24. Gregg R. Allison and Andreas J. Köstenberger, *The Holy Spirit* (Nashville: B & H Academic, 2020), 426–34.

CONCLUSION

Complementarity: Dignity, Difference, and Interdependence explores complementarity, defined as God's design for his male and female image bearers to fill out and mutually support one another relationally, familially, vocationally, and ecclesially for their individual and corporate flourishing. First, this exploration presented definitions, proposals, and foundations of complementarity. Second, it offered a wide-ranging historical development of sex identity—sex unity, sex neutrality, traditional sex polarity, reverse sex polarity, and sex complementarity (both fractional and integral varieties) in five periods: the Greco-Roman world, the early church epoch, the early medieval period, the late medieval and Reformation era, and the early modern to postmodern age. Third, *Complementarity* focused on our contemporary context, tracing modern feminist movements, complementarianism, and egalitarianism. Fourth, the majority of this exploration was devoted to biblical considerations for complementarity, including matters of framework and setting (hermeneutics, the canonical and covenantal framework of Scripture, and Genesis 1–3), Old Testament considerations, and New Testament considerations. Fifth, it delved into theological considerations, defining what a man is and what a woman is, drawing implications for complementarity from biblical images/metaphors of the church, and presenting the offices of prophet, priest, and king as they intersect with complementarity. Finally, this book offered four arenas of application: complementarity for relational flourishing, familial flourishing, vocational flourishing, and ecclesial flourishing.

It is my hope that evangelicals, though beset by many divisions, may find in my writing a vision of and call to complementarity that can be actualized so as to arrive at some kind of consensus about male and female image bearers in relationship to one another, such that both women and men may flourish individually and their churches may flourish corporately.

GENERAL INDEX

A

Aaron, 232–33, 484–86. *See also* priesthood: Levitical
Abel of Beth-maacah, woman from, 244–46
Abigail, 182, 242–43, 439
abolitionism, 129
abortion, 130
Abraham, 225–26, 283, 421, 437, 440–41. *See also* covenant: Abrahamic; Sarah; seed of Abraham
Absalom, 243–45
abuse
 acceptance of, 412, 446
 of authority, 442
 and Bill Gothard, 153–54
 and complementarianism, 504
 and patriarchy, 156–57, 163
 prevention of, 163
 prohibition of, 357
 sexual, 141, 155, 221, 357
acquiescence, 446
Adam. *See also* covenant: Adamic; Eve; Hebrew words: *'adam*
 in Aquinas, 62–63
 in Christine de Pizan, 85–86
 creation of, 392
 and Eve's name, 220
 expulsion of, 473
 fall of, 98
 as federal head, 218
 as first, 47, 201, 205–7, 338, 340, 349, 351–52
 gullibility of, 350
 in Hildegard, 76
 in John Scotus Erigena, 57–58
 as leader, 199, 400
 in Maritain, 118
 pre-fall, 50, 178, 369
 as source, 372, 385–86, 391, 393
Aeneas, 321, 335
Aeterni Patris (1879), 75. *See also* Leo XIII
Agabus, 481
Agrippa, Henricus Cornelius, 105–6, 108, 207
Ahasuerus, 248–52. *See also* Esther; Haman; Mordecai
Ahaziah, 246
Albert the Great, 57, 59–60, 79, 88
alcohol, 255, 367, 431
Alighieri, Dante, 84
Allen, Prudence, 7, 10, 28–30, 34, 40, 43, 46, 53–54, 63, 75, 78, 81–82, 85, 90, 94, 101–3, 121–23, 139, 503

Alsup, Wendy, 216
Amnon, 243–45
Anderson, Hannah, 216
Andronicus, 446, 451–55. *See also* Junia
angels, 5, 58, 62, 64, 299–300, 302, 371, 382–83
anger, 68, 92, 233, 253, 277, 341
Anizor, Uche, 484, 486–87
Anna, 285, 482
Antioch, of Pisidia, 325
Apelles, 449–50
Apollos (Alexandrian), 331–33, 335
Apphia, 324. *See also* Philemon
Aquila, 324–25, 331–33, 335, 346, 449–50. *See also* Prisca
Aquinas, Thomas, 23–24, 29, 57, 59–75, 79, 88
archaeology, 53–56, 173, 180–82, 186
Arienti, Giovanni Sabadino degli, 90
Aristarchus, 325, 333, 449
Aristotelian Revolution, 82
Aristotle, 29–31, 33–35, 37–40, 52, 59–60, 64–69, 72, 74–75, 78, 81–84, 89–90, 108, 117
ark of God, the, 236
Arnold, Clinton, 406–7, 409, 411, 413
arson, 86
Artemis (god), 340–41, 351, 354
Astell, Mary, 112
Athaliah, 246
Augustine, 43, 53, 62, 65
    Confessions, 48–49
    on gender equality, 48
    on the Lord's Supper, 472
    on men as superiority, 45–46
    on resurrection bodies, 44
    on virtue, 49–50
    on women as incomplete, 47
    on women as inferior, 49, 51–52
    on women as temptation, 51
author, limitations of, 10–11

B

baptism
    and gender, 103, 330, 418, 423
    of the Holy Spirit, 314–15, 320, 323
    of John, 315, 332
    and priesthood, 96, 489
    as sign, 189
    superintendence of, 149, 164, 369, 490
    and unity, 2, 420, 426, 474, 489
    by water, 418
Barak, 237–42
Barbaro, Francesco, 88
Barnabas, 318, 324–28, 453, 481
Bartimaeus, 272
Bathsheba, 242, 244
beauty
    of Catholicism, 75
    of complementarity, 243, 255
    of love, 228
    of men, 114
    of women, 51, 84, 106–8, 261–62, 438
Beauvoir, Simone de, 131–32, 505
Belleville, Linda, 199, 206–7, 209, 216–17, 239, 339–40, 342–43, 346–48, 351–52, 354, 372–73, 397–401, 448, 504
bestiality, 38
Bethesda, pool of, 278, 305
Bilezikian, Gilbert, 161, 198, 208
Bilhah, 228
birth control, 130
Bisticci, Vespasiano de, 90
blamelessness, 363
blindness, 10, 273–74
Blomberg, Craig, 186, 210, 373–77, 379, 382–83, 386–87, 389, 399–400
Boaz, 247–48
Boccaccio, Giovanni, 84
body of Christ, 421, 423, 467, 477, 499
    diversity of, 9, 15
    and mutual submission, 404
    unity of, 2, 14, 420, 469–72
body politic, Greco-Roman concept of, 14

Book of Common Prayer (1549), 93
Bruce, F. F., 425
Bullinger, Heinrich, 93
Bullough, Vern L., 125
Bultmann, Rudolph, 184
Burer, Michael, 452
Burk, Denny, 145–46, 214. *See also* Council on Biblical Manhood and Womanhood
Burke, Tarana, 136. *See also* MeToo
Butler, Judith, 133–34. *See also* social construct, gender as; feminism: third wave

C

calmness, social, 439
Calvin, John, 9–10, 95–98, 218
Cana, wedding at, 270, 285
cannibalism, 38
capacities, human, 224, 462, 464–66, 499. *See also* properties, human
Castiglione, Baldassare, 103–5
CBE. *See* Christians for Biblical Equality
CBMW. *See* Council on Biblical Manhood and Womanhood
celibacy, 92–93
Celsus, 303
centurion, the, 154, 269–70, 294, 310
CEO, 5, 22
Cereta, Laura, 91–92
cessationism, 394–95
Chief Executive Officer. *See* CEO
childlessness, 226–27
Chloe, 324
Christian Feminism Today, 139
Christians for Biblical Equality (CBE), 139, 159, 161–64. *See also* Kroeger, Catherine
civic life, women in, 54
Clark, Steven, 416–17
classism, 137
cognition, 35, 464
Cohick, Lynn, 411–15, 469–70
compassion, 39, 280–81
  of Jesus, 268, 271, 273–77, 290, 292, 294–95, 304–6
  as virtue, 427
confessors, 49
conflict, 3, 125, 132, 242, 244, 315
consensus theologicum, 172
contentment, 92
Conway, Mary, 195–96, 198, 209–10, 218–20
Cornazzano, Antonio, 90
Cornelius, 322–23
Council of Paris (1225), 59
Council on Biblical Manhood and Womanhood (CBMW), 140, 145–47. *See also* Danvers Statement; Burk, Denny
courage
  in Aquinas, 60, 70–72
  in Augustine, 50
  in Baccaccio, 84
  in the Bible, 224, 231, 291
  in Hildegard, 76, 78
  as human property, 464–65
  of Jesus, 277, 305
  in Kant, 115
  in Plato, 37
  in Teresa of Ávila, 102
covenant
  Abrahamic, 188, 225–26, 232, 317, 440, 445
  Adamic, 188, 218
  Davidic, 188, 494–96
  definition of, 187
  of grace, 189–90
  old, 156, 188–90, 286, 293, 309, 323, 429, 468, 482, 486–87, 495–97
  Sarahonic, 445
covenant, new, 156
  and church leadership, 179
  and gender, 333, 429, 468, 476–77, 499
  and Gentiles, 323
  and kingship, 496–97
  Magna Carta of, 316, 482–83

and Mosaic law, 188–90
and priesthood, 486, 488
and submission, 403
covering, of the head, 370–71, 375–79, 381–83, 386–87
Cranfield, C. E. B., 447, 454
creation, manner of, 72, 205, 207–8, 371, 380–81, 385, 389–90
creation, order of, 106, 176, 205–6, 349, 351, 359, 372, 386, 424
creation, purpose of, 199, 205, 208–9, 371, 380–82, 385, 389
Crispus, 325, 331
cultural mandate, the, 194, 198–201, 205, 212–14, 216, 432, 498, 505
cunning, 51, 92
curse, divine, 187–88

D

Dante. *See* Alighieri, Dante
Danvers Statement, 145–48. *See also* Council on Biblical Manhood and Womanhood
d'Arezzo, Leonardo Bruni, 88
David (king), 242–46, 248, 272, 283, 293, 440, 479–80, 494–96. *See also* covenant: Davidic
Davids, Peter, 444–45
Day of Atonement, 479, 484
deacon, 9, 22, 96, 150–51, 164–65, 319, 341, 364–70, 430, 446–47, 502. *See also* diaconate
deaconess, 9, 22, 150–52, 164–65, 346, 366–70, 430, 448, 502. *See also* diaconate
Deborah, 23, 79, 237–42, 253, 481
Democritus, 35–36
depravity, total, 95
Descartes, René, 30, 102, 110–12, 118
desire, bodily, 35, 49, 121, 124
DeYoung, Kevin, 6, 156–57
diaconate, 96, 307, 365–69, 447. *See also* deacon; deaconess
dignity. *See* equal dignity
Dinah, 228
discord, 3, 152, 166
Discovering Biblical Equality (Pierce and Westfall), 164
dishonesty, 108
disorder, 395, 397–98, 400, 402, 439
dissonance, 3
division of labor, 189, 199, 201, 504
divisiveness, 3, 340
Drusilla, 334
dualism, 30, 38, 110–12
Dunn, James D. G., 446–48
Durgin, Celina, 6, 55, 185, 464

E

Eden, garden of, 214, 219, 473
edification, 2, 18, 395, 470, 483
education, access to, 112–13, 129, 163
elder
in complementarianism, 22, 144, 455
in complementarity, 24–25, 149–51
in egalitarianism, 23, 160, 164–65, 454, 466
in Judaism, 55
qualifications of, 327, 365–67
in Quiverfull, 156
Eli, 235–36
Elisabeth (prophetess), 482
Elizabeth of Bohemia, 111
Elymas Bar-Jesus, 481
Elyot, Thomas, 106
embodiment, 30, 38, 51, 90, 122, 193–94, 203, 394
endurance, 104, 259, 430
Ephraim, 206, 219
equal dignity
in Cereta, 91
in Christine de Pizan, 87
in complementarianism, 144, 146, 379, 390
in complementarity, 7, 27, 149, 200–201, 393–94, 426, 434, 465, 477, 499–500, 503–4
in Descartes, 111

in egalitarianism, 160
in Esther, 251
in Maritain, 118
in the new covenant, 497
in the Reformation, 97, 99
Er, 229
Erastus, 325
Erigena, John Scotus, 57–59
Esau, 206, 226–27
eschatology, 173, 177–80, 186, 383
essentialism, 76, 185, 463–64, 466
estate, spiritual, 96, 489
estate, temporal, 96, 489
Esther, 248–52. *See also* Ahasuerus; Haman; Mordecai
Eternal Functional Subordination (EFS), 141
eternal purpose, of God, 3
Eternal Relations of Authority and Submission (ERAS), 141
ethnoarchaeology, 182
ethnography, 181
Eucharist, the, 490, 492
eunuch, 131, 249, 320, 322–23, 335
Evangelical and Ecumenical Women's Caucus, 139, 160
Evangelicals for Social Action, 139, 161
Evangelical Theological Society, 145–46, 464
Evangelical Women's Caucus, 139, 160–62
Eve. *See also* Hebrew words: *'ezer*; Hebrew words: *ḥawwah*; Hebrew words: *ḥayah*; Hebrew words: *kenedgo*
in Aquinas, 62
and Artemis, 340
in Christine de Pizan, 86
expulsion of, 473
fall of, 98, 190, 349–50, 359
as first woman, 201
as helper, 210, 389
in Hildegard, 76
and interdependence, 370
in John Scotus Erigena, 57
in Maritain, 118
naming of, 199, 214, 219–20
pre-fall, 50, 178, 369, 400
as second, 47, 205–7, 338, 340, 349, 351
source of, 372, 380, 385–86, 393

F

factionalism, 3
fall, the. *See also* Adam: fall of; Eve: fall of
in Augustine, 50, 53
and authority, 178, 180, 217–18, 426
in Calvin, 98
consequences of, 190
and death, 214
and desire, 215–16
and hierarchy, 199–200, 220
in Hildegard, 77
in John Scotus Erigena, 57–58, 67
prior to, 369
responsibility for, 219
and Satan, 349
and submission, 176, 351
family of God, 423, 467, 475–77, 499
fear, 68, 71, 92, 213, 250–52, 256, 258, 262–64, 291, 295, 300, 303, 321, 323, 326, 403, 406, 410, 436, 441, 475
fearlessness, 231, 260, 305, 439, 445
Fee, Gordon, 354, 375–78, 380, 382–85, 387–88
Felix, 334
Feltre, Vittorino da, 88
feminism. *See also* individual feminists; Nineteenth Amendment
Christian, 139–41
evangelical, 146
first wave, 112
fourth wave, 136–38
second wave, 130–32, 161
third wave, 132–35
Foh, Susan, 145, 215

Fonte, Moderate, 106
forbearance, 427
forgiveness, 233, 306, 321, 323, 326, 427, 490–91
Forms, eternal, 30, 38. *See also* Plato
fortitude, 102, 257
Franc, Martin Le, 90
Freud, Sigmund, 117. *See also* psychology
friendship, 16, 25, 38, 41, 47–48, 75, 84, 155, 437
Fung, Ronald, 423

G

Gaius of Derbe, 325
Gasque, W. Ward, 161
genderedness, 426, 462, 464
gender identity, 7, 88, 101, 130, 134–35
generation. *See* procreation
generosity, 257, 318
gentleness, 427, 438–39, 443, 446, 464–65
Gentry, Peter, 193, 210, 214, 220
Glahn, Sandra, 341
godliness, 38–39, 341, 356, 363, 431, 439
Gogio, Bartolomeo, 90
Gothard, Bill, 153–55. *See also* abuse; Institute in Basic Youth Conflicts; patriarchalism; umbrella, of authority
grace. *See also* covenant: of grace; justification: by grace
  access to, 422
  in Aquinas, 68
  in Augustine, 44, 50
  in Calvin, 95
  of God, 288
  gospel of, 328
  in Hildegard, 76, 78
  of Jesus, 268, 277
  of life, 442–43
  in the nascent church, 318, 332
  in Ruth, 247
  and spiritual gifts, 15
gratitude, 271, 306, 427
Great Commission, the, 295, 492, 507
Greek words
  andres, 298, 314, 326
  authentein, 339, 344–48, 350, 353, 358–59
  diakoneō, 289, 299
  diakonos, 367–68, 447–48
  didaskalia, 347
  didaskein, 339, 344–45, 348, 350, 353
  episkopon, 365–66
  episkopos, 365
  exousia, 347
  gynē, 366, 377, 379, 382, 420
  hēsychia, 342, 344, 351
  huioi, 326, 417–18, 424
  hypotassō, 406–7, 410–11
  kephalē, 185, 370–75, 377–80, 382, 388, 407, 413
  koinōnia, 472
  mathētria, 321
  phobeō, 410
  prostatis, 447
  sōtēr, 414
  synergos, 449, 454
Groothuis, Rebecca, 209
Grosseteste, Robert, 83–84
Grudem, Wayne, 140, 145–47, 197, 199, 207–8, 210–11, 373, 443–44. *See also* Recovering Biblical Manhood and Womanhood
Guarino of Verona, 88
Gundry, Stanley, 161

H

Haddad, Mimi, 162. *See also* Christians for Biblical Equality
Haman, 249–52. *See also* Ahasuerus; Esther; Mordecai
Hannah, 235–36. *See also* Samuel
harassment, sexual, 132, 136
harmony, 1, 3, 16–17, 19, 37, 216, 411, 444

Haubegger, Christy, 136. *See also* Time's Up
haughtiness, 17
Hebrew words
  'adam, 191–92, 194–200, 203
  'el, 214
  'ezer, 209–10, 212, 389
  ḥawwah, 220
  ḥayah, 220
  ḥayil, 247, 258
  'ish, 205, 220
  'ishshah, 205
  kenegdo, 146, 209–10
  neqebah, 198
  zakar, 198
helper, woman as, 46, 203–5, 208–12
hemorrhaging woman, the, 290–92, 310
Hendrix, Scott, 94
hermeneutics, 169, 171–73, 221, 509
Herod Antipas, 325, 481
Hertwig, Oscar, 110
heteronormativity, 134
hierarchy
  in Aquinas, 73
  in Augustine, 53
  in Bible translations, 191–93, 195
  in Calvin, 97
  and Christ, 469
  and the church, 490
  in complementarianism, 196, 200, 220, 386, 389–90
  in egalitarianism, 198–99, 216–18, 352, 374, 386, 388
  Greco-Roman, 14
  in the *munus triplex*, 498
  and order of creation, 206
Hildebrand, Dietrich von, 117–18
Hildegard of Bingen, 57, 75–79, 81
Hippel, Theodor Gottlieb von, 116–17
holiness, 2–3, 358, 480
homophobia, 137
honor-shame culture, 15–16
hospitality, 14, 16, 18–19, 55, 182, 289, 306–8, 330, 455, 477
House, Wayne, 145–46, 173
Hove, Richard, 423
Hughes, Kent, 146
Huldah, 79, 239, 252–54, 481
Hull, Gretchen Gaebelein, 161
humanism, 84–85, 88, 100
humility, 14, 16–17, 186, 233, 253, 269–70, 405, 427, 465
Hylen, Susan, 55–56
hypocrisy, 15, 290, 489

I

image of God, 8
  in Aquinas, 60–61, 63, 74
  in Augustine, 45–47, 50
  in Calvin, 97
  in complementarianism, 144, 208, 390–92
  in egalitarianism, 160
  in Hildegard, 76
imitation of God, 220
inability, total, 95
industriousness, 183, 257, 259–60, 264, 432
inerrancy, 141, 172, 272
inferiority, of men, 138. *See also* superiority, of women
inferiority, of women, 11, 36, 40, 46, 50, 67, 207, 209–10, 379. *See also* superiority, of men
infighting, 3
injustice, 113, 163
Institute in Basic Life Principles, 153. *See also* Gothard, Bill
Institute in Basic Youth Conflicts, 153. *See also* Gothard, Bill
intelligence, 49, 84, 106, 110
interdependence
  and Adam and Eve, 370–71, 393–94
  in complementarianism, 386, 389–90
  in complementarity, 7, 24, 27, 143, 149, 159, 466, 503
  in egalitarianism, 384, 386, 388

in Esther, 251–52
and freedom, 382
and the image of God, 379
in the Reformation, 99
as synergy, 8, 32
intersectionality, 134–35
Isaac, 206, 226–27, 439
Ishmael, 206

J

Jacob, 206, 226–30, 248, 296, 439, 484, 496
Jael, 237–40, 242
Jairus, daughter of, 290–92, 322
Jehosheba, 246–47
Jesse, 248
jewelry, 255, 262, 438
Jewett, Paul, 416
Jew-Gentile divide, 19
Jezebel, 482
Joab, 244–46
Joanna, 288, 301, 314
Joash, 246
Jobes, Karen, 437–38, 441–42
Jochebed, 230–31
John the Baptist, 333, 386, 481
John of the Cross, 102
John Mark, 325
Johnson, Dru, 6, 55, 185, 464
Johnson, S. Lewis, 423
Jonadab, 243–44
Joseph (father of Jesus), 248, 283–84, 482
Joseph (son of Jacob), 206, 228, 230
Joseph of Arimathea, 299
Josephus, 303
Joshua son of Jehozadak, 485
Josiah, 239, 252–54, 494
joy, 1–2, 16, 84, 273–74, 300, 306, 320, 327–28, 504
Judah, 219, 227, 229
Judas (Barsabbas), 328, 481
Judas Iscariot, 314–15
Julia, 450–51, 454
Junia, 446, 450–55. *See also* Andronicus
justice, 37, 50, 60, 70–72, 76, 78, 86, 133, 186, 230, 242, 255, 495–96
justification
for both sexes, 326
by faith, 96
by grace, 225
as material principle, 99
and priesthood of all believers, 488–90
and resurrection, 301

K

Kant, Immanuel, 102, 113–16, 118
Keener, Craig, 335, 348, 352
kindness, 227, 231, 235, 247, 427
Knight, George, 199–200
Köstenberger, Andreas, 176, 341–45, 349, 351, 431
Kroeger, Catherine, 139, 161. *See also* Christians for Biblical Equality

L

language, descriptive, 39, 157, 173–76, 186, 216, 399, 467
language, prescriptive, 39, 173–75, 186, 216, 342, 426
Leah, 227–29, 439
Leave It to Beaver, 141
Lee, Dorothy, 176–77, 295, 299, 302, 313, 332, 371–73
Leeuwenhoek, Antoni van, 109
Leo XIII (pope), 75. *See also Aeterni Patris*
leprosy, 271
Levi, 228, 486
Lévine, Mark, 133
LGBTQIA2S+, 141
Long, Charles, 140
Lord's Supper, 2, 96, 149, 164, 369, 472, 474, 476, 490
love-mutualism. *See chapter 2, "An Initial Biblical Foundation of Complementarity"* (13–20)
Lucius of Cyrene, 325, 481
Luther, Martin, 96, 488–91

Lydia, 324, 329–31, 335
Lyon, Jo Anne, 161

M

Magdalene, Mary. *See* Mary Magdalene
Magnificat, the, 284. *See also* Mary, mother of Jesus
man, definition of, 148, 462, 464. *See also* woman, definition of
Manaen, 325, 481
Manasseh, 206
mandate, cultural, 199–201
Marinella, Lucrezia, 102, 106–8, 118, 207
Maritain, Jacques, 102, 118
Marquis de Condorcet, 112–13
martyrs, 49
Mary (associate of Paul), 325, 450, 454
Mary Magdalene, 288, 299–301, 314, 326
Mary, mother of James, 288, 299, 314
Mary, mother of Jesus, 248, 268, 282–88, 302, 314, 482, 496. *See also theotokos*
masculinity, toxic, 125
Mathews, Alice, 140–41, 221–22
Mathew, Susan, 13–14, 17–19, 53–54, 153, 368, 450–51. *See also* love-mutualism
Matthias, 315–16
maturity, 3, 429, 475
meaning, single, 173, 176–77, 186
meanings, multiple, 173, 176–77, 186
Melchizedek. *See* priesthood: of Melchizedek
MenEngage Alliance, 133, 137
Menius, Justus, 94
Meno, 36–37
menstruation, 32, 121
MeToo, 136. *See also* Burke, Tarana
Meyers, Carol, 180–82, 223. *See also* archaeology
Micah, mother of, 182
Mickelsen, Alvera, 162
miracle, 270, 273, 275, 285, 296, 302, 304–5, 317–19, 321–22, 327, 333
Mirandola, Giovanni Pico Della, 89–90
Miriam, 232–34, 239, 481
Moo, Douglas, 15, 346, 349–50, 417, 419–22, 424
Mordecai, 248–52. *See also* Ahasuerus; Esther; Haman
Moses, 98, 218, 239
  birth of, 230–31
  instruction of, 254–55
  and Israel's deliverance, 232–34
  law of, 189, 271, 326, 328, 334, 484–85
  prophet like, 480
  and Zipporah, 232
munus triplex. See chapter 23, "The Offices of Prophet, Priest, and King in the New Covenant" (479–98)
murder, 17, 86, 244, 495

N

Nabal, 242–43
Naomi, 247–48
Nebuchadnezzar, 248
Neo-Platonism, 84, 88, 106
Nereus, sister of, 450–51, 454
Nettesheim, Cornelius Agrippa von, 90
Nicholas de Condorcet. *See* Marquis de Condorcet
Nicholas of Cusa, 88–89, 100
Nicole, Roger, 161
Nineteenth Amendment (1920), 117, 129. *See also* suffrage, women's
normative principle, 173–74, 186. *See also* regulative principle
nuns, 50, 78
Nympha, 324

O

obedience
  and abuse, 446
  in Aquinas, 72
  in Aristotle, 39
  in Augustine, 52

in Calvin, 98
and the centurion, 270
of children and slaves, 411, 413
in Exodus, 231
in Gothard, 154
Greco-Roman, 444
in Greek literature, 257
of Hannah, 236
in Hildegard, 78
to Jesus, 274, 279, 306, 413
levels of, 475
in Luther, 94
of Mary, 283–84, 288
of Sarah and Abraham, 226
in Western tradition, 36–37, 41, 122, 124
of wives, 437, 439–41, 443
Onan, 229
opposites, metaphysical question of, 29–32, 40, 43–46, 61–65, 76, 89, 121. *See also* sex neutrality; sex unity
order of creation. *See* creation, order of
Origen, 369

P

papacy, the, 99
passivity, 30, 502
Passover, 254
pastor. *See* elder
paterfamilias, 95, 359
patience, 427, 464
patriarchalism, 185. *See also* abuse; DeYoung, Kevin; Gothard, Bill; Quiverfull
Christian, 155
Greco-Roman, 14
of Jesus, 335
in the Old Testament, 224
patriarchy
in ancient Israel, 182
Christian, 153
and complementarity, 157
and egalitarianism, 163
in the old covenant, 189–90
in the Reformation, 94
peace, 1–3, 18–19, 238, 246, 321, 340, 356, 395, 397, 400, 402, 427, 439, 485
penance, 76, 78
Pentecost, 287–88, 315–16, 323, 335
persecution, 49, 318–21, 323–24, 327, 333, 441
Persis, 325, 449–51, 454
Peter, mother-in-law of, 289, 299, 306
Petrarch, 84
Pharisees, 275
Philemon, 324, 449. *See also* Apphia
Philip, 320, 324, 333, 335, 482
Phinehas, wife of, 236–37
Phoebe, 368–69, 446–50, 454
Piper, John, 145–47. *See also Recovering Biblical Manhood and Womanhood*
Pizan, Christine de, 85–87, 100, 207
Plato, 29–31, 36–38, 40–41, 90. *See also* Forms, eternal; sex unity
Plotinus, 58. *See also* Neo-Platonism
politeia, 54
politics, women in, 54, 133
poor, the, 96, 201, 251, 257, 259, 262, 264, 305
pornography, 132
Potiphar, 230
Potter, Mary, 97
practical judgment, 92
preunderstanding, 173, 184–87
pride, 17, 234, 405
priesthood
of all believers, 93, 96, 99, 484, 488, 490–92
Levitical, 189, 483–84, 486–88
of Melchizedek, 480
royal, 468, 483, 487–88, 497
women in the, 78
priesthood-kingdom, 492, 495, 497
primogeniture, 205–7, 424
Prisca, 324–25, 331–33, 335, 346, 449–50, 454. *See also* Aquila
privation of male, female as, 30, 33, 89

procreation
  and Albert the Great, 59
  in ancient Israel, 182
  and Aquinas, 65–67
  and Augustine, 47
  and complementarity, 505
  and the cultural mandate, 194, 201, 505–6
  and interdependence, 386
  and Marinella, 107
  and science, 124
  in Western tradition, 34, 41, 109, 125
properties, human, 224, 462, 464–66, 499. *See also* capacities, human
prophecy
  evaluation of, 399–400
  of Huldah, 253
  of Jesus, 300
  and the new covenant, 482
  Paul's idea of, 151
  and the Spirit, 316
  as spiritual gift, 15, 394–96, 471
prophethood, of all believers, 483
prostitution, 132
protectiveness, 464–65
protoevangelium, 214
psychology, 117. *See also* Freud, Sigmund
Puah, 231
purgatory, 99
Purim, 251

Q

quietness, 175, 338–39, 342–43, 350–51, 353, 356–57, 438–39, 446. *See also* Greek words: *hēsychia*
Quiverfull, 153, 155

R

Rachel, 227–29, 439
racism, 137
rage, 92, 277
Rahab, 234–35
rape, 50–51, 136–37, 221, 228–29, 244
rationality, 29, 35, 59, 82, 114, 116, 121, 124, 257, 464–65
Rebekah, 226–27
Recovering Biblical Manhood and Womanhood (Piper and Grudem), 143, 146–49. *See also* Grudem, Wayne; Piper, John
regulative principle, 173–74, 186. *See also* normative principle
respectability, 363, 430
restraint, 92. *See also* self-restraint; unrestraint
resurrection
  in Aquinas, 61, 64, 73–74
  in Augustine, 43–44, 46, 50
  of Eutychus, 333
  in Hildegard, 77
  of Jairus's daughte, 291
  of Jesus, 172, 288, 298–304, 308, 315, 418, 453, 480
  in John Scotus Erigena, 57–58
Rhoda, 324
righteousness, 2–3, 441, 495–96
Roman Catholic theology, 29, 75, 489
Rousseau, Jean-Jacques, 113–14
Rufus, mother of, 450–51, 454
Ruth, 247–48, 258

S

Sabbath, 189, 275, 277–79, 289–90, 299–300, 305, 325, 329
sacraments, the, 99, 401, 491
Salome, 299–300, 326
Samaritans, 296–97, 320, 335
Samaritan woman, the, 296–98, 305, 480
Samuel, 154, 236, 493–94. *See also* Hannah
sanctification, 51, 93, 445
Sanguinetti, Michael, 137. *See also* SlutWalk
Sarah, 225–26, 374, 437, 440–41, 443, 445. *See also* covenant: Sarahonic

Saul (king), 154, 479, 494
Saul (Paul), 319–21, 324–25, 481
scandals, 369–70, 398
Scholer, David, 222, 416
Schreiner, Thomas R., 179, 206–7, 359, 374, 376, 399–401, 430, 446–48, 503–4
Scripture, perspicuity of, 172, 183
Secundus, 325, 333
security, 92, 113
seed of Abraham, 417, 421
self-control, 78, 343, 357, 363, 430–33
self-denial, 406, 501–2
self-restraint, 38–39. *See also* restraint; unrestraint
serpent, the, 86, 99, 212–14, 349, 359
Seth, 391
sex complementarity, 7, 31–32, 40, 43–44, 46–47, 49–50, 53, 57, 61, 64, 66–67, 70, 73–74, 76–77, 79, 82–85, 87, 90, 92, 96–97, 99, 102–3, 110–11, 114, 117–19, 122–23, 127, 138, 332, 503, 509
sexism, 130, 137, 335
sex neutrality, 99, 119, 127. *See also* opposites, metaphysical question of
  in complementarity, 200, 503
  definition of, 30, 40, 82, 122
  in Descartes, 110–12
  in Grosseteste, 84
  in logic, 83
  in Mirandola, 90
  in Platonism, 88
sex polarity, reverse, 99, 102, 119, 127, 509
  in Agrippa, 105–6
  in Castiglione, 103, 105
  and Cereta, 91
  in Christine de Pizan, 87
  and complementarianism, 148
  in complementarity, 200, 310
  definition of, 31, 40, 82, 122
  in egalitarianism, 503
  and feminism, 138
  in the 15th century, 90
  and intersectionality, 135
  in Marinella, 106, 108
  and Priscilla and Aquila, 332
sex polarity, traditional, 99, 127, 509
  and Agrippa, 106
  in Aquinas, 61
  and archaeology, 55–56
  in Aristotle, 34, 36, 40
  in Augustine, 44–45, 47, 53
  and Castiglione, 104–5
  in Cereta, 91
  in Christine de Pizan, 87
  and complementarianism, 148, 157, 185
  and complementarity, 200, 503
  in Cusanus, 89
  definition of, 30, 82, 122
  dominance of, 100
  and feminism, 131, 138–39
  in the 15th century, 88
  in Hildegard, 75, 78–79
  in John Scotus Erigena, 57
  in Leeuwenhoek, 109
  in Marinella, 108
  in modernity, 102–3, 117, 119
  in Plato, 41
  and Priscilla and Aquila, 332
  in the Reformation, 99
  as unscientific, 124
sex unity, 44, 58, 99. *See also* opposites, metaphysical question of
  and Aristotle, 82
  in Augustine, 43–44, 46, 48–50, 53, 57
  in Cereta, 91
  in complementarity, 200, 503
  definition of, 30, 40, 122
  dominance of, 200
  in John Scotus Erigena, 57–58, 77, 79
  in Mirandola, 90
  in Plato, 38, 41, 88
Shafer-Elliott, Cynthia, 182

Sheba son of Bichri, 245
Shechem, 228
Shelah, 229
Shunammite woman, 182
significant differentiation
in Christine de Pizan, 87
in complementarianism, 146
in complementarity, 7, 27, 149, 157, 200–201, 211, 427, 465–66, 503
in Descartes, 111–12
in Maritain, 118
in the new covenant, 497
Silas, 325, 328–31, 481
Simeon (Niger), 325, 481
Simeon (of Jerusalem), 481–82
Simeon (son of Jacob), 228
Simon Magus, 320
Sisera, 237–42
skillfulness, 257
slightness, 173, 180, 186
SlutWalk, 136–37. *See also* Sanguinetti, Michael
sober-mindedness, 14, 430, 434
social construct, gender as, 133–34, 185. *See also* Butler, Judith
social media, 136. *See also* feminism: fourth wave
Socrates, 36, 71
sola Scriptura, 97, 124, 187
solidarity, 16
sonship, 103, 417–18, 426, 476
Sopater, 325, 333
Sophists, the, 37
sorrow, 16, 99
Spencer, Aida Besançon, 173–74, 267
spiritual gifts, 15, 23, 99, 144, 160, 395, 425–26, 471, 482, 508. *See* grace: and spiritual gifts; prophecy: as spiritual gift
Stanton, Elizabeth Cady, 113
steadfastness, 2, 224
Stephanus, 405, 450
Stephen, martyrdom of, 319
Stjerna, Kirsi, 92–93
Stoicism, 84
strength, male, 38, 73, 76, 78, 92, 102, 147, 442
strife, 3
suffrage, women's, 113, 117, 129. *See also* Nineteenth Amendment
superiority, of men, 11, 46, 50, 219. *See also* inferiority, of women
superiority, of women, 90. *See also* inferiority, of men
suspiciousness, 92
Syrophoenician woman, the, 292–95, 305, 310

T

Tabitha, 321–22, 335
Tamar, 229, 243–44
teaching, false, 96, 175, 340, 345, 354–55, 358–59, 399, 431, 490–91
Tekoa, woman from, 244, 246
temperance, 37, 50, 60, 70, 72, 129
temptation, 51, 299
Teresa of Ávila, 102–3
thankfulness. *See* gratitude
theft, 17, 86, 348
theotokos. *See also* Mary, mother of Jesus
Thielman, Frank, 403, 405, 409–10, 412
Thiselton, Anthony, 373, 399
Thomas, 304
Time's Up, 136. *See also* Haubegger, Christy
Timothy, 325, 329, 332–33, 341, 355, 364, 449
Titius Justus, 325, 331
tongues, 316, 323, 395–98, 401, 471
toxic masculinity. *See* masculinity, toxic
trajectory hermeneutics, 187
transgenderism, 7, 135, 394
transphobia, 137
treason, 86
tree of life, the, 203, 214
Trophimus, 325, 333

Tryphaena, 325, 449–50, 454
Tryphosa, 325, 449–50
Tychicus, 325, 333

U

umbrella, of authority, 153–55. *See also* abuse; Gothard, Bill
unigenderism, 394
union with Christ, 416–18, 420, 426
United States Congress, women in, 133
unrestraint, 38. *See also* restraint; self-restraint
unworthiness, 269–70

V

Vashti, 248–49, 252
vice, 31, 38–39, 86–87, 106, 108
virtues
  Christian, 50, 464
  classical, 50, 60, 70–74
vocation, 47, 194, 212, 502, 505–6
Voice for Men, A, 137–38

W

Waegeman, Maryse, 257
Wallace, Daniel B., 452
Waltke, Bruce, 146, 256, 258
war, 86, 182
Ware, Bruce, 196–97, 208, 217, 390–93
weakness
  of Barak, 239–40, 242
  of wives, 442–43
  of women, 38, 85
Webb, William, 187
weightiness, 173, 180, 186
Westfall, Cynthia Long, 55–56, 172, 177–79, 338, 355–60, 423–25
White Ribbon, 132, 137
widowed woman, the, 295–96
Winter, Bruce, 54
wisdom, epistemological question of, 35–36, 48–49, 68–70, 77, 121–22
Wollstonecraft, Mary, 113
woman, definition of, 462. *See also* man, definition of
Woman Wisdom, 257–58
Woolf, Virginia, 10
worthiness, 69, 269–70

X

Xerxes I. *See* Ahasuerus

Z

Zipporah. *See* Moses: and Zipporah

SCRIPTURE INDEX

Genesis

1 *47, 199, 201–3, 206, 211–12, 220, 377, 420*
1–2 *118, 199, 217, 394, 400, 420*
1–3 *xvii, 146, 169, 188, 190, 509*
1–4 *196*
1:5 *219*
1:8 *219*
1:10 *219*
1:26 *191–92, 194, 198, 203*
1:26–27 *105, 196–97, 462*
1:26–28 *xvii, 5, 191, 193–94, 200, 377, 461, 467*
1:27 *6, 8, 47, 61, 192, 194, 198, 378, 381, 420*
1:28 *47, 92–93, 192, 198, 212, 432, 505–6*
1:30 *203*
2 *47, 199, 201–3, 205–8, 211–12, 349, 359, 370, 377, 380*
2–3 *202, 351*
2:7 *47, 62, 349, 352, 467*
2:7–8 *xvii, 202*
2:8 *473*
2:8–9 *213*
2:9–16 *203*
2:15 *473*
2:15–17 *219*
2:16–17 *203*
2:17 *212*
2:18 *46, 146, 209, 211, 263, 380*
2:18–24 *47*
2:18–25 *xvii, 62, 72, 202–3, 349, 352*
2:19–20 *219*
2:21–23 *373, 380*
2:22 *197, 473*
2:23 *197, 218–20*
2:24 *211, 409*
2:25 *197*
3 *199–202, 212, 217, 221, 349, 359*
3:1–7 *212*
3:6 *349*
3:8 *197*
3:8–13 *218*
3:8–19 *213*
3:9 *197, 218*
3:12 *197*
3:13 *349*
3:15 *214*
3:16 *xvii, 178, 213–15, 218, 352*
3:16b *215*
3:20 *197, 214, 219–20*

3:21 *202*
3:23–24 *473*
4:7 *215*
4:25 *202*
5:1 *202*
5:1–2 *197*
5:2 *196–97, 391*
5:15 *359*
6–9 *188*
6:17 *203*
7:15 *203*
7:22 *203*
8:20–22 *483*
12:1–3 *440*
12:3 *317*
12:5 *440*
12:10–20 *225, 440*
12–17 *188*
12–25 *225*
14:18 *486*
15:2–6 *225*
16:1–6 *225*
17:4–6 *225*
17:12–14 *232*
17:15–16 *225*
17:16 *440, 445*
17:17–22 *225*
18 *182*
18:9–15 *225*
18:11–14 *440*
18:18 *317*
20:1–18 *225*
21:1–6 *440*
22:1–18 *226*
22:18 *317*
24 *226*
25:21–22 *226*
25:27–28 *227*
27:1–45 *227*
28–35 *227*
29:31 *227*
29:32–24 *227*
29:35 *227*
30:6–8 *228*
30:9–21 *228*
30:23 *228*
32:24–30 *228*
34:1–2 *228*
34:25–27 *228*
35:9–15 *228*
35:16–18 *228*
38 *229*
39 *230*
39:6 *230*
39:19–20 *230*
49:25 *209*

Exodus

1:8–22 *231*
2:2–3 *231*
2:6 *231*
2:8 10 *231*
3:1–4:17 *232*
4:22 *418*
4:24–26 *232*
6:20 *231*
15:1–18 *233*
15:19–21 *233*
15:20 *481*
18:4 *209*
19:3–6 *468*
19:5–6 *492*
19:6 *483, 488, 497*
19–24 *188*
25–31 *473*
28:1 *484*
29:45–46 *473*
35:20–29 *255*
35–40 *473*

Leviticus

7:1–7 *484*
16 *479*
16:29–34 *485*
19:18 *408*
26:11–13 *473*

Numbers

3:6–9 *484*
3:12–13 *484*

6:22–27 *485*
12:1 *233*
12:1–2 *233*
12:3 *233*
12:14–15 *233*
12:15 *234*
15:19–21 *181*
26:59 *231*

Deuteronomy
7:6 *497*
7:6–8 *468*
14:1 *418*
17:14–15 *493*
17:15–17 *493*
17:18–19 *493*
17:20 *493*
18:15 *480, 485*
21:15–17 *206*
33:7 *209*
33:10 *484*

Joshua
2:1–6 *235*
2:8–13 *235*
2:14–21 *235*
6:25 *235*

Judges
3:9 *240*
3:15 *240*
4:4 *481*
4:4–24 *237*
4:5 *239*
4:6 *240*
4:6–7 *237–38*
4:8 *237, 240*
4:9 *237, 239, 241*
4:14 *238*
4:14–24 *237*
5 *238*
5:1 *241*
5:6–7 *241*
5:6–9 *238*
5:24–27 *238*
5:31 *238*
6:14 *240*
9:53–54 *181*
11:29 *240*
12:25 *240*
14:6 *240*
17 *182*

Ruth
2:1 *247*
2:8–9 *247*
2:11–12 *247*
2:20 *247*
3:10–11 *247*
3:11 *247, 258*
3:12–18 *248*
4:1–9 *248*
4:10 *248*
4:17 *248*

1 Samuel
1:5 *235*
1:11 *235*
1:17 *236*
1:19–20 *236*
1:28 *236*
2:1–10 *236*
2:35 *480, 485*
4:19–22 *236*
8:4–9 *493*
8:11–18 *493*
8:19–22 *494*
15:23 *154*
16:7 *438*
25 *182, 242*
25:3 *242*
25:4–17 *242*
25:18–31 *242*
25:32–35 *243*
25:38 *243*
25:39 *243*

2 Samuel
7 *188*
7:11–16 *494*

7:16 *480, 485*
11:21 *181*
13 *243*
13:2 *243*
13:3–7 *243*
13:8–10 *243*
13:12–14 *244*
13:15–18 *244*
13:18–19 *244*
13:20 *244*
13:21–33 *244*
14 *244*
14:11–14 *245*
20:14–22 *244–45*

1 Kings
5–7 *473*
11:29–39 *481*

2 Kings
4:8–37 *182*
8:1–6 *182*
8:25–27 *246*
11:1–3 *246, 495*
22:11–20 *252*
22:13 *253*
22:14 *253, 481*
22:15–17 *253*
22:20 *253*
23:1–27 *254*
23:24–25 *494*

2 Chronicles
15:1–8 *481*
20:14 *481*
34:22 *481*

Nehemiah
6:14 *481*

Esther
1:10–12 *248*
2:2–4 *248*
2:5 *249*
2:7 *249*
2:10 *249*
2:10–11 *249*
2:14 *249*
2:17 *249*
2:20 *249*
2:20–23 *249*
3:2 *249*
3:5–6 *249*
3:7 *251*
3:13 *250*
4:1 *250*
4:8 *250*
4:11 *250*
4:13–14 *250*
4:17 *250*
6:13 *250*
7:3–4 *250*
7:6 *251*
7:10 *251*
8:1–2 *251*
8:17 *251*
9:2 *252*
9:22 *251*
9:29 *251*
10:1–3 *251*

Job
1:5 *483*

Psalms
20:3 *209*
21:1–2 *209*
33:20 *210*
89 *188*
110:4 *480, 486*
115:9–11 *209*
121:2 *210*
146:5 *209*

Proverbs
1:1–7 *429*
1:4 *257*
1:7 *257*
1:20–33 *257–58*
1:26–7 *257*

1:28 *257*
3:1–6 *257*
3:10 *257*
3:13 *257*
3:13–18 *245*
3:27 *257*
4:5–9 *245*
4:6 *257*
4:8 *257*
4:9 *257*
4:12 *257*
4:22 *257*
6:6–11 *257*
7:4–5 *245*
8:1–36 *257*
8:14 *257*
8:17 *257*
8:32 *257*
8:35 *257*
9:1–6 *245, 257*
10:9 *257*
11:24–25 *257*
12:4 *247, 257*
13:9 *257*
13:24 *261*
14:1 *257*
14:21 *257*
16:16 *257*
18:19 *257*
21:15 *257*
22:6 *261*
24:5 *257*
24:30–34 *261*
26:13 *261*
26:13–16 *257*
30:25 *257*
31 *265*
31:1 *255*
31:10 *247, 256–58, 261*
31:10–12 *256*
31:10–31 *xvii, 182, 224–25, 247–48, 255, 432, 457*
31:10b *258*
31:11 *257–58, 263–64*
31:11–12 *256, 259*
31:11–31 *183*
31:13 *257, 264*
31:13–14 *259*
31:13–18 *256, 259*
31:13–27 *256, 259*
31:15 *259, 264*
31:16 *257, 259, 263–64*
31:17 *257, 259*
31:18 *257, 259*
31:19 *256, 259*
31:20 *257, 259–60*
31:20–27 *256, 259*
31:21 *257, 260, 264*
31:22 *260*
31:23 *260, 263*
31:24 *260, 263–64*
31:25 *260, 264*
31:26 *260, 263*
31:27 *263–64*
31:27b *257*
31:28–29 *256, 261, 263*
31:28–31 *256, 261*
31:29 *183*
31:30 *257, 262, 438*
31:30–31 *256, 261*
31:31 *260, 262–63*

Song of Songs
1:7 *262*
9:10 *262*

Isaiah
8:3 *481*
9:6–7 *496*
47:1–2 *181*
61:6 *483*

Jeremiah
31:9 *418*
31:31–34 *188*
33:14–18 *495*
37:7 *210*

Ezekiel
11:22–25 *237*

12:14 *210*
36:25–27 *315*
44:30 *181*

Hosea
1:10 *418*
6:7 *219*

Joel
2:28–29 *333*
2:28–32 *315, 482*

Micah
3:7 *479*

Zechariah
6:12–14 *485*
9:9 *439*

Matthew
1:1 *480*
1:16 *248, 283*
1:18 *282*
1:18–25 *282*
1:22–23 *283*
1:23 *282*
1:25 *282*
2:1–12 *285*
2:11 *285*
4:11 *299*
5:17–48 *189*
5:43 *408*
6:20 *348*
6:30 *294*
7:15 *490*
8:5–13 *154, 269, 310*
8:10 *294*
8:13 *270*
8:14–15 *289*
8:15 *299*
8:16–17 *298*
8:26 *294*
8:28–33 *279*
9:6 *383*
9:18–26 *290*
9:21 *291*
9:22 *291*
9:24 *291*
9:27 *480*
9:27–31 *271*
9:28–30 *272*
9:30 *272*
9:31 *272*
9:32–34 *279*
11:11 *386*
11:28–30 *439*
12:9–14 *277*
12:22–32 *279–80*
12:28 *496*
12:46–49 *475*
14:31 *294*
14:34–36 *298*
15:21–28 *292*
15:24 *293*
15:26–28 *293*
15:28 *294*
16:8 *294*
16:14 *480*
16:16 *480*
16:19 *490*
16:21–23 *303*
17:20 *280–81*
17:21 *280*
18:18 *490*
20:20–23 *302*
20:29–34 *271*
21:1–11 *439*
21:12–13 *439*
21:43 *496*
22:23 *318*
24:41 *181*
25:44 *299*
26:26–29 *188*
26:32 *300*
26:56b *302*
27:50 *298*
27:55–56 *299, 326*
27:57–60 *299*
27:61 *300, 314*
27:62–66 *300*

28:5–6 *300*
28:8–10 *300*
28:18–20 *295, 418*

Mark

1:1 *480*
1:15 *496*
1:21–27 *279*
1:29–31 *289*
1:32–34 *298*
1:38 *305*
1:40–45 *271*
2:1–12 *276*
2:10 *383*
2:13–18 *285*
2:27–28 *278*
3:1–6 *277*
3:5 *277*
3:20–21 *286*
3:20–35 *282, 285*
3:22 *286*
3:22–30 *286*
3:31–35 *475*
4:30 *496*
5:1–20 *279*
5:21–43 *290*
5:25–26 *291*
5:25–34 *310*
5:30 *291*
5:33–34 *291*
5:34 *292*
5:36 *291*
5:41–42 *291*
5:43 *291*
7:1–23 *190*
7:10 *189*
7:24–30 *292*
7:25–30 *310*
7:26 *293*
7:29 *293*
7:31–37 *273*
8:22–26 *274*
8:26 *274*
9:21–24 *280*
10:35 *302*
10:45 *502*
10:46 *272*
10:46–52 *271*
12:38–44 *310*
14:1–11 *310*
15:37 *298*
15:40–41 *299, 326*
15:42–46 *299*
15:47 *300, 314*
16:1–4 *300*
16:5 *300*
16:6–7 *300*
16:8 *300*

Luke

1:26 *282*
1:26–38 *282, 287*
1:31–33 *496*
1:35 *282*
1:38 *284*
1:41–42 *482*
1:45 *284*
1:46–49 *284*
1:67–79 *481*
2:1–20 *282*
2:19 *283*
2:21 *284*
2:25–26 *284*
2:25–35 *481*
2:29–32 *285*
2:33 *285*
2:34–35 *285*
2:36–38 *285, 482*
2:41–50 *285*
3:38 *480*
4:35 *289*
4:38–39 *289*
4:40–41 *298*
4:43 *496*
5:24 *321, 383*
6:6–11 *277*
7:1–10 *269, 310*
7:4–5 *269*
7:6–7 *269*
7:7–8 *269*

7:9 *269*
7:10 *269*
7:11–17 *295, 322*
8:1 *496*
8:1–3 *288, 324*
8:19–21 *282, 285–86, 288, 475*
8:26–39 *279*
8:38–39 *279*
8:40–42 *322*
8:40–56 *290*
8:49–56 *322*
9:23–24 *502*
9:37–43 *279*
9:42 *281*
9:44–45 *303*
11:27–28 *286*
13:10–17 *289*
13:18 *496*
13:20 *496*
14:1–6 *278*
17:20–21 *496*
17:35 *181*
18:31–34 *303*
18:35 *272*
18:35–43 *271*
18:43 *272*
19:6 *320*
19:9 *320*
19:17 *383*
22:4 *318*
22:52 *318*
23:44–46 *299*
23:49 *299*
23:50–53 *299*
23:54–56 *300*
24:3–5 *300*
24:5–8 *300*
24:9–10 *300*
24:9–11 *301*
24:10 *288, 314, 326*
24:12 *301*
24:21–24 *301*

John

1:14 *473*
1:33 *419*
2:1–12 *282, 285*
2:3–5 *285*
2:13–22 *473*
2:21 *286*
3:1–8 *496*
4:1–42 *296*
4:19 *480*
4:27 *297*
4:46–54 *270*
5:2–3 *278*
5:3b–4 *278*
5:5–16 *278*
5:19 *480*
5:36 *480*
7:5 *315*
7:9 *288*
7:16 *480*
7:42 *480*
9:1–7 *274*
9:14 *275*
9:16 *275*
9:17 *480*
9:22 *275*
9:24 *275*
9:25 *275*
9:35–38 *275*
9:39–41 *275*
10:37–38 *480*
12:49–50 *480*
13:16 *453*
14:8–9 *480*
14:10 *480*
14:16 *475*
14:17 *474*
14:23 *474*
14:24 *480*
14:26 *490*
17 *480*
17:21–23 *9*
19:25 *287*
19:25–27 *282, 287*
19:26–27 *287*
19:28–37 *299*
19:31–37 *299*

19:38 *299*
19:39–42 *299*
20:3–10 *301*
20:8–9 *301*
20:11–13 *301*
20:14–15 *301*
20:17 *301*
20:24–25 *304*
20:26–29 *304*

Acts

1:1–5 *314*
1:3 *496*
1:4–5 *419*
1:6–8 *314*
1:8 *323, 336*
1:9–11 *314*
1:12–14 *282, 287, 314*
1:12–15 *316*
1:13 *287*
1:14 *287, 314*
1:15 *315*
1:21–22 *315*
1:25 *315*
1:26 *315–16*
2:1 *315*
2:1–4 *419*
2:4 *316*
2:5 *316*
2:11 *316, 395*
2:14 *316*
2:16–18 *333*
2:16–21 *316*
2:17–18 *316, 335–36, 482*
2:17–28 *335*
2:33 *317, 419*
2:37 *317*
2:38 *317, 475*
2:41 *317*
2:42 *317*
2:43 *317*
2:44 *317*
2:44–45 *317*
2:46 *317*
2:47 *317*
3 *317*
3:1–3 *317*
3:6–8 *317*
3:9–11 *317*
3:11–23 *317*
3:22–24 *480*
3:24 *317*
3:25–26 *317*
4 *318*
4:4 *318*
4:12 *318*
4:18 *318*
4:23 *318*
4:29–31 *318*
4:32 *318*
4:33 *318*
4:34–35 *318*
4:36–37 *318*
5:1–11 *318*
5:14 *319*
5:15 *319*
5:16 *319*
5:17–41 *319*
5:42 *319*
6:1–4 *319*
6:1–6 *368*
6:5–7 *319*
6:8–7:60 *319*
8:1 *320*
8:1–4 *323*
8:3 *320*
8:4–13 *320*
8:4–25 *335*
8:5–8 *324*
8:7 *320*
8:8 *320*
8:9–13 *320*
8:12 *320*
8:14–17 *320*
8:18–24 *320*
8:26 *320*
8:26–40 *322, 335*
8:27 *320*
8:29 *320*
8:35 *320*

8:36–39 *323*
8:39 *320*
9:1–2 *320*
9:15 *321*
9:16 *321*
9:31 *321*
9:32–34 *321*
9:32–35 *321*
9:34 *322*
9:36 *321*
9:37 *321*
9:38 *321*
9:39 *321–22*
9:40–41 *322*
9:42 *322*
10 *336*
10:1–11:18 *322, 335*
10:2 *322*
10:9–16 *323*
10:24 *322*
10:34–35 *323*
10:43 *323*
10:44–46 *323*
10:47–48 *323*
11:19 *323–24*
11:19–24 *335*
11:19–26 *325*
11:21–22 *324*
11:23 *324*
11:24 *324*
11:25–26 *324*
11:27–30 *324*
12:1–2 *324*
12:3–5 *324*
12:12 *324*
12:13–16 *324*
13:1 *481*
13:1–4 *325*
13:2 *325*
13:5 *325*
13:6–12 *481*
13:13–41 *327*
13–14 *325*
13:26 *326*
13:30–31 *326*
13:38–39 *326*
13:44–47 *326*
13:44–49 *335*
13:48–49 *326*
13:49–50 *327*
13:52 *327*
14:1–7 *327*
14:4 *454*
14:8–10 *327*
14:8–19 *327*
14:14 *453–54*
14:20–21 *327*
14:21–23 *327*
14:23 *453*
15 *328, 453*
15:1 *328*
15:5 *328*
15:6–21 *496*
15:11 *328*
15:12–21 *453*
15:22 *328*
15:23 *328–29*
15:25 *328*
15:27 *481*
15:30–32 *481*
15:30–35 *329*
15:36–18:22 *325*
15:40 *325*
16:1–3 *325*
16:6–10 *329*
16:10 *325*
16:13–15 *329*
16:16–18 *330*
16:18 *330*
16:19–22 *330*
16:19–23 *330*
16:22–24 *330*
16:30 *330*
16:31 *330*
16:32 *330*
16:33 *330*
16:33–34 *330*
16:40 *324, 331*

17 *467*
17:4 *331*
17:5–9 *325*
17:11–12 *331*
17:24–28 *467*
17:30 *331*
17:34 *331*
18:1–2 *331*
18:1–4 *325, 450*
18:1–5 *335*
18:2 *450*
18:6–8 *331*
18:7–8 *325*
18:18 *450*
18:23–20:38 *325*
18:24–26 *332*
18:24–28 *325, 346, 450*
18:26 *332–33, 450*
18:27–28 *332*
19:1–7 *333*
19:9–10 *333*
19:21 *325*
19:29 *325*
20:3–4 *333*
20:4 *325*
20:7–12 *333*
20:17 *365*
20:17–35 *365*
20:17–38 *333*
20:28 *365*
21:5 *333*
21:8–9 *333, 482*
21:10–12 *481*
21:17–30 *334*
21–23 *333*
22:4–5 *334*
24:24–26 *334*
25:13 *334*
25:23 *334*
26:10–11 *334*
26:12–18 *453*
26:30–31 *334*
28:13–14 *334*
28:14–15 *334*
28:23–28 *335*

Romans

1:3–4 *480*
3:29 *226*
4:19–20 *226*
4:22–25 *225*
5:12–21 *219*
6:1–11 *418*
8:4–5 *475*
8:9 *475*
8:14 *476*
8:14–17 *476*
8:15 *476*
8:16–17 *476*
8:29–30 *475*
8:34 *480*
9:8 *441*
10:12 *468*
12:3 *14, 17, 405*
12:4–5 *14*
12:6–8 *15*
12:9 *15*
12:10 *15, 405*
12–13 *14, 17*
12:13 *16*
12:14–15 *16*
12–15 *13, 19*
12:16 *17, 405*
13:8–10 *17–18*
13:9 *189, 408*
13:14 *418*
14:5–9 *189*
14:13 *18*
14–15 *18*
14:17 *2*
14:19 *2, 18*
15:1–3 *18*
15:5 *19*
15:6 *2, 19*
15:7 *19*
15:8 *447*
15:8–12 *19*
15:16–17 *488*

16 *13, 325, 446, 455, 476*
16:1–2 *369, 450*
16:3 *324, 449–50*
16:3–16 *476*
16:4 *325, 450*
16:5 *324, 449–50*
16:6 *325, 449–50*
16:7 *451*
16:8 *449*
16:9 *449*
16:10 *450*
16:11 *449*
16:12 *325, 449–50*
16:21 *449*
16:25 *342*

1 Corinthians

1:7–8 *482*
1:10 *17*
1:11 *324*
3:9 *449*
3:16–17 *473*
4:1 *491*
4:9 *383*
4:17 *388*
6:3 *383*
6:17 *68*
6:19 *474*
7:17 *388*
7:17–24 *453*
7:37 *383*
9:6 *453*
9:19–22 *437*
10:16–17 *2, 472*
11:2–5 *397*
11:2–16 *146*
11:3 *370–71, 373–74, 377, 380*
11:3–7 *389*
11:3–10 *390*
11:3–12 *42*
11:3–16 *337, 370, 386, 393, 414, 434, 482*
11:4 *375, 377*
11:4–5 *151, 371, 375, 396*
11:4–6 *376, 378, 387*
11:5 *375, 379, 387, 390, 400*
11:7 *45, 208, 371, 377–81, 390*
11:7–8 *207*
11:7–9 *62*
11:8 *380–81*
11:8–9 *371, 378–80, 382, 384, 389*
11:9 *208, 211, 380, 389*
11:10 *371, 382*
11:11 *388, 390*
11:11–12 *371, 380, 384, 389, 393*
11:12 *386, 393*
11:13–16 *371, 386*
11:14–15 *375, 378*
11:15 *376*
11:23–26 *490*
11:33 *476*
12:12–13 *489*
12:12–14 *470*
12:13 *419–20, 468*
12–14 *395*
12:15–24 *470*
12:18 *470*
12:25 *470*
12:25–26 *477*
12:27 *469*
12:28 *454*
13:1 *383*
13:4–7 *2*
13:12 *186*
14:1–25 *395*
14:2 *395*
14:9 *395*
14:13–17 *395*
14:26 *395–97, 400, 402, 428*
14:26–40 *337, 395, 434, 482*
14:27 *395*
14:27–28 *395*
14:28 *342, 395*
14:29 *395, 397–98*
14:29–33 *400*
14:29–33a *395*
14:29–35 *453*
14:30 *342, 395*
14:31 *395, 402*

14:32 *395*
14:33 *388, 402, 439*
14:33–35 *152*
14:33a *395, 397*
14:33b *395*
14:33b–34 *400*
14:33b–40 *395*
14:34 *342, 396, 400–401, 455*
14:34–35 *69, 356, 397*
14:35 *396–98, 401–2*
14:36–38 *396*
14:37 *402*
14:39–40 *396*
14:40 *397, 402, 439*
15:6 *304*
15:6–7 *453*
15:10 *450*
15:58 *476*
16:15–16 *405*
16:16 *450*
16:16–17 *450*
16:17 *450*
16:19 *324, 450*

2 Corinthians

1:24 *449*
3 *188*
3:1 *446*
4:7 *442*
5:14–15 *502*
6:40 *447*
8:23 *449, 453*
11:3 *352*
13:11 *2*

Galatians

1:19 *453*
2:9 *453*
3:7 *417*
3:7–25 *417*
3:16 *421*
3:25–27 *103*
3:26 *418*
3:26–28 *337, 416–17, 425–26, 434, 476*
3:26–29 *423*
3:28 *45, 162, 222, 416–17, 419, 423, 425, 468*
3:29 *417, 421, 441*
4:1–7 *418*
4:11 *450*
4:28 *441*
5:13–14 *447*
5:14 *18, 408*
5:16–18 *475*
5:22–23 *464*
5:23 *439*
5:25 *475*
6:10 *476*
6:15 *421*

Ephesians

1:10 *3*
1:13 *475*
1:19–23 *480*
1:22–23 *469*
2:13–19 *468*
2:19 *476*
2:20 *453, 482*
2:21–22 *473, 476*
4:3–6 *2*
4:5 *467–68*
4:11 *428, 454*
4:11–16 *470, 483*
4:13 *3*
4:16 *372*
4:24 *418, 422*
5:18 *403–4, 407*
5:18–21 *475*
5:19–20 *412*
5:21 *402–3, 405–7, 410, 412*
5:22 *392, 406–7, 410–11*
5:22–23 *337, 372*
5:22–24 *374, 402, 406–7, 414*
5:22–33 *42, 402, 404, 432, 434*
5:23 *374, 408, 413*
5:23–24 *412*
5:24 *410, 412, 414, 470*
5:25 *408, 414, 416*
5:25–27 *402, 406, 408*

5:26 *408*
5:27 *408*
5:28 *407–8*
5:28–29 *52*
5:28–32 *402, 406, 408*
5:29 *372, 409*
5:30 *409*
5:31 *409*
5:32 *407, 409–10*
5:33 *402, 406, 410*
6:1 *411*
6:1–4 *404*
6:4 *346*
6:5 *411*
6:5–9 *404*
6:7 *413*

Philippians

1:1 *368*
1:2 *448*
2:3 *16, 404*
2:3–4 *405*
2:16 *450*
2:17 *488*
2:25 *449, 453*
4:3 *449*
4:18 *488*

Colossians

1:9–12 *429*
1:18 *372*
1:24 *469*
1:28–29 *429*
1:29 *450*
2:12 *418*
2:16–17 *189*
2:19 *372*
3:1–4 *427*
3:5–11 *427*
3:10 *422*
3:10–11 *418*
3:11 *419–20*
3:12–15 *427*
3:16 *337, 347, 427, 434, 487*
3:17 *429*
3:18 *407, 413, 432*
3:18–19 *42, 402*
4:11 *449*
4:15 *324*

1 Thessalonians

2:7 *454*
3:2 *449*
4:10–11 *439*
5:11 *450*
5:15 *432*
5:21 *490*

2 Thessalonians

2:15 *453*
3:11 *432*
3:12 *439*

1 Timothy

1:3 *345*
1:3–4 *356*
1:3–7 *339–40*
1:5 *430*
1:10 *347, 431*
1:18–20 *339–40*
1:20 *399*
2:1 *356*
2:1–3:16 *341*
2:1–4 *439*
2:1–8 *341*
2:2 *340–43, 356*
2:8 *339–41, 356*
2:8–10 *356*
2:9 *339*
2:9–10 *341*
2:9–15 *341*
2:10 *356*
2:11 *340, 342–43, 350*
2:11–4 *434*
2:11–12 *176, 339, 342, 351*
2:11–14 *172, 176, 179, 337–38, 340, 352, 354, 356, 359–60, 362–64, 426, 455*

2:11–15 *358, 455*
2:12 *146, 150–51, 207, 222, 263, 338, 340, 343, 347–48, 350–52, 355, 358–59, 454*
2:12–13 *205–6*
2:12–14 *97*
2:12–15 *42*
2:13 *176, 180, 206–7, 340, 349, 351–52, 359, 426*
2:13–14 *339–40, 349, 353, 359*
2:14 *176, 180, 213, 217, 340, 349, 352, 426*
2:15 *338, 340, 356, 358*
3 *368*
3:1 *363, 365*
3:1–2 *365*
3:1–3 *363*
3:1–7 *42, 151, 341, 343, 353, 363, 365–66, 448*
3:1–13 *364*
3:2 *345, 353, 363, 365–68, 428, 430*
3:2–7 *363, 365*
3:3 *9*
3:4 *353*
3:4–5 *363, 368*
3:5 *353*
3:8 *366–67, 430*
3:8–13 *341, 363, 365–66, 368*
3:9 *347, 367*
3:10 *352*
3:11 *337, 346, 364–68, 430, 434*
3:12 *346, 366, 368*
3:14–16 *341*
3:15 *341, 364*
4:1 *347*
4:1–8 *339*
4:3–4 *189*
4:6 *347*
4:10 *450*
4:11 *345*
4:13 *345*
4:16 *345*
5:1–2 *447, 476*
5:2 *370*
5:8 *347*
5:13 *339*
5:13–14 *432*
5:14 *42*
5:15 *339*
5:17 *345, 365, 428, 450*
5:20 *339*
5:20–22 *339*
6:1 *345*
6:2 *345*
6:3 *345, 431*
6:3–10 *339*
6:10 *347*
6:11 *430*
6:12 *347*
6:20–21 *339*
6:21 *347*

2 Timothy

1:5 *346*
1:13 *431*
2:18 *179*
3:14–15 *346*
4:3 *347*
4:6 *488*
4:19 *450*

Titus

1:1 *431*
1:5 *365*
1:5–9 *363*
1:7 *365*
1:7–8 *363*
1:8–9 *363*
1:9 *347, 428, 431*
1:10–16 *431*
1:12 *431–32*
1:16 *431*
2:1 *429–30*
2:1–6 *337, 429, 434*
2:2 *430, 433*
2:3 *430–31, 433*
2:3–5 *42, 346, 431*

2:4–5 *430–31, 433*
2:5 *263, 430, 432*
2:6 *430, 433*
2:7 *433*
2:10 *175, 433, 445*
2:10–15 *429*
2:12 *430–31*
2:14 *431*
2:16 *429*
3:1 *431*
3:8 *431*
3:14 *431*

Philemon
1 *449*
2 *324*
24 *449*

Hebrews
5:6 *480*
5:11 *486*
5:11–14 *429*
5:12 *347*
5:17 *486*
7:11–12 *189*
7:24–25 *480*
7:25 *486*
8:1–6 *486*
8:6 *486*
8:6–10:18 *188*
8–10 *189*
9:12 *486*
10:20 *488*
10:22 *488*
10:24 *488*
10:25 *488*
11:11 *226, 440, 445*
11:23 *231*
11:31 *234*
12:14 *3*
13:7 *353*
13:15 *487*
13:16 *488*
13:17 *353*

James
2:24–25 *234*
3:15 *70*

1 Peter
1:23–25 *445*
2:5 *486–87*
2:6–8 *437*
2:9 *468, 487, 497*
2:13 *436*
2:13–15 *436*
2:15 *436*
2:18–19 *436*
2:18–20 *436*
2:20–25 *436*
3:1 *432, 436*
3:1–6 *225*
3:1–7 *xviii, 435, 443–44, 457*
3:2 *432*
3:3 *438*
3:3–4 *262*
3:4 *438*
3:4–6 *439*
3:5 *437*
3:5–6 *374*
3:6 *437, 441*
3:7 *44, 442*
3:10–11 *3*
3:13–14 *441*
4:19 *441*
5:1–4 *365*
5:2 *365*
5:5 *365, 404*

2 Peter
1:16–21 *479*
3:13–14 *3*

1 John
2:27 *490*

3 John
8 *449*

Jude

3 *123*

Revelation

1:5–6 *497*
1:6 *486*
2:20 *482*
5:9–10 *468*, *486*
6:9 *488*
11:6 *383*
14:18 *383*
16:9 *383*
16:13 *481*
19:20 *481*
20:6 *383*
20:10 *481*